D079373

Farewell to the World

To Noemi and Matteo
that their lives may be free and happy

Farewell to the World

A History of Suicide

Marzio Barbagli

translated by
Lucinda Byatt

polity

First published in Italian as *Congedarsi dal mondo. Il suicidio in Occidente e in Oriente* ©
Società editrice Il Mulino, Bologna, 2009

This revised and updated English edition © Polity Press, 2015
Reprinted 2016

The translation of this work has been funded by SEPS
Segretariato Europeo per le Pubblicazioni Scientifiche

Via Val d'Aposa 7 - 40123 Bologna - Italy
seps@seps.it - www.seps.it

Polity Press
65 Bridge Street
Cambridge CB2 1UR, UK

S E P S

SEGRETARIATO EUROPEO PER LE PUBBLICAZIONI SCIENTIFICHE

Polity Press
350 Main Street
Malden, MA 02148, USA

ISBN-13: 978-0-7456-6244-2
ISBN-13: 978-0-7456-6245-9 (pb)

A catalogue record for this book is available from the British Library.

Library of Congress Cataloging-in-Publication Data

Barbagli, Marzio, 1938-
   [Congedarsi dal mondo. English]
   Farewell to the world : a history of suicide / Marzio Barbagli. -- English edition.
     pages cm
   "First published in Italian as Congedarsi dal mondo : il suicidio in Occidente e in Oriente,
Societa Editrice Il Mulino SPA, 2009"--Title page verso.
   Includes bibliographical references and index.
   ISBN 978-0-7456-6244-2 (hardback) -- ISBN 978-0-7456-6245-9 (paperback) 1. Suicide--
History. 2. Suicide--Sociological aspects. I. Title.
   HV6545.B24513 2015
   362.2809--dc23
                                            2014049462

Typeset in 10 on 11 pt Times New Roman MT by
Servis Filmsetting Ltd, Stockport, Cheshire
Printed and bound in the UK by CPI Group (UK) Ltd, Croydon

For further information on Polity, visit our website:
politybooks.com

3|17

Contents

Detailed Contents

Figures, Graphs and Tables

Figures

Graphs

Tables

Introduction

I have not thought about killing myself, yet. But five people whom I knew quite well have done so during the course of my life: a school friend, two male colleagues, the wife of a close friend and a distant relative. These five completely unexpected events left me amazed and profoundly shaken. I can still remember clearly how, many years ago on holiday in Tuscany, after receiving a phone call telling me that my friend's wife had taken her life, I sat motionless for some hours, thinking about her and her life, and wondering about the reasons underlying her choice.

However, what prompted me to study voluntary death were other, less painful surprises that occurred during the course of my teaching and research. On numerous occasions I have spoken to students about the most important theory we have on suicide, the one put forward in 1897 by the French academic Émile Durkheim, one of the founding fathers of sociology, and this usually generates great interest. I have always told them that this theory does not help us understand why my two colleagues killed themselves and why the idea has never occurred to me, yet it is very useful as a way to explain changes in the suicide rate over time and space, the differences between historical periods, countries and social groups. However, it gradually dawned on me that this theory had become increasingly inadequate, since it could not account for the unexpected new trends that had appeared in many countries. So I started (in 2001) to study the topic, following trails and using quite a wide range of sources, but from the outset choosing to approach the subject as comparative history. This book contains the most important results of that research.

0.1 Integration and social regulation

Durkheim's theory ascribes all variations in the frequency of voluntary deaths to just two major causes: social integration and regulation. Integration consists of the number and strength of the ties binding an individual to the various groups. The suicide rate is low when this integration is balanced, but it rises both when there is scarce integration and when it is excessive. In the first case we find 'egoistic' suicide, typical of modern society: 'if the individual isolates himself, it is because the ties uniting him with others are slackened or broken, because society is not sufficiently integrated at the points where he is in contact with it.'[1] As this occurs, 'the bond attaching man to life relaxes because that attaching him to society is itself slack'[2] and he risks giving way under the slightest pressure and killing himself. If, on the other hand, that integration is too strong it can lead to 'altruistic' suicide. This usually occurs in 'lower societies', among 'primitive peoples', where there is 'strict subordination of the individual to the group',[3] and 'the ego is not its own property, where it is blended with something not itself, where the goal of conduct is exterior to itself, that is, in one of the groups in which it participates.'[4] In these peoples, 'when a person kills himself [. . .] it is not because he assumes the right to do so but, on the contrary, because it is his duty.'[5]

The second cause is social regulation. 'Our capacity for feeling', writes Durkheim, 'is in itself an insatiable and bottomless abyss.' Our desires are 'unlimited' and 'cannot be quenched'. Yet, in every society, our 'inextinguishable thirst'[6] can only be curbed by regulations. Regulations define the rights and duties of those holding different social positions and establish the rewards owed to these people. If a society is too weakly regulated, there may be 'anomic' suicide, which is also typical of modern society. However, during a period of rapid change, whenever there is a period of crisis or strong economic expansion, these regulations weaken, blurring the limits 'between the possible and the impossible, what is just and what is unjust, legitimate claims and hopes and those which are immoderate. Consequently, there is no restraint upon aspirations.'[7] This lack of regulation causes suffering and provokes a rise in the number of anomic suicides. On the other hand, if a society is over-regulated, cases of 'fatalistic' suicide occur, committed by 'persons with futures pitilessly blocked and passions violently choked by oppressive discipline'. This is the suicide of very young husbands, of the married woman who is childless, of slaves. Durkheim regarded this fourth type of suicide as having 'little contemporary importance' and he dedicated only a few lines to it in a footnote of his book.[8]

0.2 Concepts and data

Having been virtually ignored for half a century after its publication,[9] Durkheim's book finally gained renown among sociologists from the 1950s onwards. Since then, everyone who reads it is captivated by the author's pleasing style, his stringent reasoning, his incomparable ability to explain the facts: in short, readers have the impression of having come upon a milestone in scientific literature. Yet the book has also been the target of extensive criticism. Given that they cannot be individually presented here,[10] I will highlight the two most important ones.

The first concerns the concepts used by the French sociologist, which many scholars have criticized for being poorly defined and used with insufficient clarity and rigour, on occasions even overlapping. Some critics, for example, have asserted that there is no significant difference between the two major causes of voluntary death identified by Durkheim: social integration and social regulation, and that there is therefore no need to draw a distinction between egoistic and anomic suicide.[11] Moreover, even those who maintain that there is a difference between these two concepts cannot agree on its exact nature.[12] All, however, are united in asserting that the concept of integration is not clearly defined and that it is used to refer to quite different things.[13]

The second criticism concerns the data used by Durkheim, namely the official statistics. Some scholars have argued that these underestimate the real number of suicides in a manner that is selective; in other words the degree of underestimation varies over space and time because it depends on the efficacy of the documenting mechanisms and the attitudes of particular societies to such events. According to these scholars, therefore, if the suicide rate increases from one decade to another, it is because registration methods have become more efficient and not because levels of social integration have diminished. Moreover, if the rates are lower in one country than another it is because suicides are less accepted in the former and there is a greater tendency to conceal them, rather than because of any other social or cultural difference.[14]

There are some grounds for these criticisms. It is true that Durkheim's concepts are not always strictly defined or applied. Likewise, statistics on suicide rates are the result of a complex process and variations can sometimes depend on changes made to the system of registration.[15] But none of these criticisms is really decisive. Social integration and regulation are phenomena that are probably interrelated but that can be kept distinct for analytical purposes and, as we will see, they can still help us to understand much more about what happened in Europe, even in the last century. As for official statistics, theoretical debates and empirical research have arrived at the conclusion that they do somewhat underestimate the real number of suicides but that this is not selective. Instead this shortfall largely depends on technical reasons (the difficulty, for example, of identifying the cause of some deaths) and very little on the moral attitude of the society or the officials completing the registration.[16] Therefore, they can (and must) be used, in those fortunate cases where they exist, while exercising the necessary caution that applies to any data or document.

0.3 Two unexpected changes

Based on Durkheim's theory, it was possible to foresee two broad underlying trends for the future. The first consisted of the disappearance of altruistic suicide, typical of 'primitive peoples', as the individual's subordination to the group gradually receded. By the end of the nineteenth century, only faint traces remained of this form of suicide in the army, but they too would vanish over the following decades. The second was the unstoppable growth of the egoistic and anomic forms of suicide produced by the growth of industrialized societies, accompanied by alternating periods of expansion and recession and by the loosening of those ties of social integration and regulation.

Instead, the last forty years of the twentieth century have witnessed two precisely opposite trends. Altruistic suicides have unexpectedly become extraordinarily important. Not only in the sense that they have increased rapidly in number as well spreading across a much larger geographical area. But in many countries they have also generated unprecedented political and social consequences. Yet, at the same time, in Western Europe the frequency of suicides (both egoistic and altruistic) has fallen steadily.

In the case of altruistic suicides the turning point came in Saigon, on 11 June 1963, when a Buddhist monk set himself on fire and died engulfed in flames as a protest against his country's government. Since then, his action has been repeated hundreds of times in India, Vietnam and Korea, as well as in the United States and Czechoslovakia where, on 16 January 1969, the university student Jan Palach immolated himself in protest against the Soviet Union's occupation of his country.[17] Another form of altruistic suicide began on 23 October 1983 in Beirut when a Hezbollah activist sacrificed his own life by driving a truck laden with explosives at full speed into a building in the US Marines Barracks, killing a large number of them. Suicide missions, as these acts are now called, have been repeatedly carried out since then, in many countries around the world, by men and women of different faiths taking their own lives in order to attack the enemies of their people.

On the other hand, suicide rates in the United Kingdom started to fall in 1964 and continued to do so for ten years. The downturn then continued in the mid 1980s in Denmark and, shortly afterwards, also in Germany, Sweden, Austria, Switzerland, France and many other areas of Western Europe. As we will see, this change started from the highest social groups in the large metropolitan centres and from the wealthiest and most advanced regions, and it is now spreading to the rest of the population.

What is highlighted by both these significant and unexpected trends moving in opposite directions, and what is backed up by the numerous facts and figures presented in the following pages, is the inadequacy of the theory that has dominated the social sciences, unchallenged for over a century, and which still today remains the guiding light for anyone approaching this difficult field of research. Neither the growing importance of altruistic suicides in much of the world nor the rapid decline of egoistic and anomic suicides in Western Europe can be explained by changes in social integration and regulation. The documentation gathered together in this book proves that altruistic suicides do not only occur when there is excessive integration, or in conditions of absolute individual subordination to a particular group. Certainly this does not explain why, over the past forty years, thousands of people (often highly educated, with a cosmopolitan outlook, a command of several languages and adepts of the internet) have sacrificed themselves for a collective cause, to help their own people and to fight their enemies. But, as we will see, even in the seventeenth and eighteenth centuries, the widows and the 'faithful maidens' who killed themselves for altruistic motives, in China, after the death of their husbands or fiancés were not passive women, subordinate to the higher demands of society at the time. Indeed, no one could think that, during the closing decades of the twentieth century, the declining numbers of individuals taking their own lives in Western Europe might be due to rising levels of integration. If this number has fallen during this period it is certainly not because the bonds uniting individuals with their families, their relatives, the parish, voluntary associations, trade unions and political parties grew ever stronger.

A theory of suicide that aims to explain the new trends that have appeared in many countries over the past forty years and the vast body of facts and knowledge revealed through studies undertaken by historians, anthropologists, sociologists, political scientists, psychologists and neurobiologists cannot limit itself to considering just two causes – social integration and regulation – nor can it continue to use a classification of suicides based on these two causes alone.

0.4   Types of suicide

The need to establish order among the infinite variety of forms of suicide, and to distinguish and classify them based on similarities and differences, pre-dates our modern scientific research by many centuries. The first typologies were put forward by specialists who analysed regulations and their infringement, namely by theologians and jurists. Henry de Bracton, an eminent thirteenth-century English jurist, identified three categories of people who took their life: suspected criminals, the depressed, and madmen and imbeciles. In 1637, another Englishman and ardent Anglican, John Sym, published the first treatise wholly dedicated to the question of voluntary death, in which he presented a carefully structured typology.

Many other classifications were put forward by anthropologists, psychologists, sociologists and demographers. Yet, the only one that became widely known, and has been reiterated and used countless times, is Durkheim's, which, as we have already seen, identifies four types of suicide: altruistic, egoistic, fatalistic and anomic. His classification is completely different from all the others and, as the French scholar himself wrote, it required him to 'reverse the order of study'.[18] All the other classifications always refer to the intentions of those committing suicide and attempt to identify similarities and differences. Durkheim's study, on the contrary, is an 'aetiological' classification of suicides and the 'causes which produce them'. Therefore, in 1892, for example, when the eminent

London-based 'alienist' George Henry Savage first proposed a distinction between egoistic and altruistic suicides, he was only referring to individual cases.[19] But when the French sociologist redefined these two categories five years later,[20] and added two others, he was referring to the broad social causes already mentioned (an excess or lack of integration or regulation).

As many authors have observed,[21] an 'aetiological' classification would be sustainable and usable only if the causes it identified were the sole ones in existence. But if this is not the case, it will be 'both restrictive and misleading'.[22] Moreover, given that social integration and regulation are, as will be seen, neither the only nor the most important causes of changing suicide rates over time and space, the classification outlined by the great French sociologist is no longer very useful.[23]

Over the course of the following pages I will use a different classification, based on individual motives and on the significance that individuals attribute to their action.[24] In the hope that it will be clearer by the end of this book, at this stage I will just say that the classification includes four different types of suicide and considers two aspects of the motives I mentioned earlier: the persons *for* and *against* whom an individual might take his or her own life. The first two types of suicide relate to the persons for whom this gesture is made. They keep the name of 'egoistic' and 'altruistic' and correspond to those categories proposed not by Durkheim, but by George Henry Savage; in other words they refer only to the intentions of the individuals carrying out suicide and not to the (social) causes that provoke them to act: it is possible to take leave of the world *only* for oneself or *also* for others.

The other two types relate to the second aspect, the people against whom suicides are committed, for example for revenge. Scholars have usually overlooked those acts motivated by these intentions,[25] probably because they have always been extraneous to the cultural repertoire of Christian Europe and seemed peculiar and incomprehensible. But, since at least 1602, the year when the Jesuit Matteo Ricci reported that, in China, men and above all women killed themselves 'to harm others',[26] European missionaries, merchants and explorers have noted this practice in many populations in Asia, Africa and both Americas. As we shall see, it also existed in pre-Christian Europe.

In the twentieth century this form of voluntary death aroused the interest of a number of researchers from different disciplinary backgrounds: they included historians of law, institutions and ethnologies at the end of the nineteenth century,[27] and more recently anthropologists and historians of Asia.[28] The suicide missions carried out in the past thirty or so years have not only confirmed the importance of this form of voluntary death, but they allow us to distinguish two different types. On the one hand are those who kill themselves 'to harm others' for private, individual reasons, like the Chinese men and women reported by Matteo Ricci or those belonging to some Indian castes, or again the examples cited in many tribes studied by anthropologists. On the other hand are those who kill themselves for a collective, allegedly noble reason (which may be political or religious), like the Kamikaze. I will call the first 'aggressive suicide', the second 'suicide as a weapon'.

0.5 A plurality of causes

Two crucial and quite different factors influenced the formation of Durkheim's theory: his concern that European society might be on the verge of breakdown, and his desire that sociology should achieve full recognition as an academic discipline.[29] The first led him to view suicide as a symptom of the ills of society, the second to explain it using only (some) sociological categories and to ignore the contribution of other human sciences.[30] These are two serious limitations that need to be addressed. What I will try to demonstrate in the first three chapters of this book, by analysing the changes that have occurred in the West over the past four centuries, is that the processes of social breakdown were not the only cause, let alone the main factor underlying the rise in suicide numbers up until the early twentieth century. Moreover, it is increasingly clear that an explanation of suicide cannot be fully posited without taking account of the results of studies carried out by historians and anthropologists, psychologists and political scientists.[31] More perhaps than any other human action, suicide depends on a vast number of psychosocial, cultural, political and even biological causes and must be analysed from different points of view.[32]

Durkheim's theory only uses a few sociological categories, the structural ones, while it overlooks the cultural ones.[33] So he regards egoistic suicide as the outcome of a single structural cause: the lack of integration. He explains anomic suicide through the absence of social regulations, not their content. Lastly, he attributes altruistic suicide to both a principal cause (excessive subordination) and a secondary one: the presence of regulations.[34] But in the latter instance, he sees individuals as passive beings, absolutely dependent on these regulations: an idea that is now difficult to accept.

As I have already said, some variations in the suicide rate over the course of the last century, both in the West and in the East, as well as the different incidences of suicide among certain social groups can be explained using the two Durkheimian variables: the extent of integration and the degree of regulation. However, my thesis here is that the factors that have most influenced the frequency of different types of suicide are cultural, or in other words they comprise the wealth of cognitive schemas and classification systems, beliefs and norms, meanings and symbols available to men and women.[35]

These components change over space and time. There are differences between countries and historical periods, as well as between social groups, in the cultural repertoires that define and limit the range of possible choices for individuals in terms of suicide. As I see it, there are four key aspects of this repertoire: the intentions of the person who carries out suicide, the way in which he or she does so, the significance that this person and others attribute to the act of suicide, and the rites celebrated before and after the act has been accomplished.

On the subject of intentions, although egoistic suicide is present in all repertoires (albeit with quite different interpretations), the other three types of suicide (altruistic, aggressive and suicide as a weapon) are only envisaged by some. Moreover, some cultures regard certain forms of voluntary death as more noble than others and reserve them (or at least consider them more suited) to certain individuals, defined by age, gender, civil status, class or caste.

As to the way of carrying out suicide, it is necessary to distinguish between the means and the setting. There are countless ways of taking one's life. 'Wherever you turn your eyes', wrote Seneca, 'you may see an end to your woes. Do you see that precipice? Down that lies the road to liberty; do you see that sea? that river? that well? Liberty sits at the bottom of them. Do you see that tree? Stunted, blighted, dried up though it be, yet liberty hangs from its branches. Do you see your own throat, your own neck, your own heart? They are so many ways of escape from slavery.'[36] But each country, historical period and social group has its own preferences. In terms of the setting, some cultures see suicide as a private act, carried out alone and in secret (see Plates 16–19), while in others it can also take place in public, in the presence of tens or hundreds of witnesses (Plate 2).

The significance attributed to the act may involve both causes and effects. Depending on the culture, voluntary death is explained by attributing it to supernatural or natural causes, to a dramatic event or to the state of mind of the individual committing suicide or the actions of the person who prompted him or her to do so. As for the consequences, suicide was seen as a source of disasters or mishaps in some places and during some periods, while in others it was deemed a felicitous event, capable of giving the person extraordinary powers, or even as an act not overly different from natural death.

Before accomplishing the act some cultures prescribe rituals, which, to different extents, may involve family members, friends and relatives of the person committing suicide, and even leading representatives of the community to which the individual belongs. More often, however, these rituals are celebrated after the act and differ extensively from one culture to another. In some, the body of the person who has taken his life is treated with deliberate brutality and subject to a process of dehumanization, while in others it is celebrated and glorified by hundreds, even thousands of people, and in yet others the body is buried by a few close family members, in secret and in silence, after nightfall.

One of the ways in which culture, in the presence of many other factors, can influence an individual's decision to commit suicide is through the emotions that she or he feels. Sadness, anger, fear, shame, disgust and joy are universal sentiments that all human beings have felt in every society and throughout history. Yet culture conditions both the expression and the production of emotions. With regard to expression, social norms exist to indicate who can show emotion, on what occasions and with whom (for example, in beauty contests, only the winner can cry, while the losers must smile).[37] As for producing emotions, cultural influence is again evident through social norms that dictate what we ought or ought not to feel in certain situations. But more often it is exerted through a simpler, subtler mechanism. Emotion stems from a cognitive and evaluative process. Sadness or joy are elicited in us not only by a situation or event but also through the meaning and value we attribute to that event. Faced with the same occurrence, two people from different cultures and with different goals, interests and desires experience different emotions (the sight of a viper arouses fear in most people, but satisfaction and delight in herpetologists).[38]

Political factors, too, are of great importance. Power relationships, and the interactions and conflicts between those giving orders and those executing them, between the power of action and the threat of it have repeatedly influenced the formation of repertoires of the methods of living and dying. In countries and historical periods when men and women's lives belonged to an overlord, suicide was often condemned. Yet people took their own lives not only for others, but also against them. As we shall see, this was sometimes done in personal conflicts in order to spite or punish someone or to take revenge on them. Moreover, sometimes this occurred and still occurs for collective causes, against one particular group and for another that the suicide belongs to or identifies with. Suicides of this kind mainly arise from particular political situations, often characterized by religious differences between two opposing groups and always by a strong asymmetry in the power relations between them, and they are used by the weakest groups as a means of narrowing their disadvantage.

To start with, these types of suicide were a genuine innovation, proposed by a small group of pioneers. In many cases an accompanying ideology legitimates the use of suicide in particular conditions, providing interpretative keys to understanding the social reality and explaining the sufferings of the people involved and the wrongs and offences to which they are subject. It also identifies those responsible and proposes a programme of action. Although new in part, this ideology draws inspiration from the cultural repertoire of the country where it has emerged.

When these innovations demonstrate an ability to achieve, at least in part, the desired ends, they gain support and are used increasingly often, thereby adding to the gamut of actions and deaths legitimated by tradition. Indeed, at times they prove so effective as to be adopted by people or by groups with different cultures. The most recent example of voluntary deaths to follow this pattern and be used as a weapon is suicide missions. But there have been many others during the course of the past two centuries.

The explanatory factors summarized thus far (cultural and political, as well as social integration and regulation) help to explain the differences between the different types of suicide over history, and in different countries and social groups, but they contribute little to understanding those among individuals living in the same country or belonging to the same social group. For this purpose psychological and psychiatric factors are much more useful, although until now they have been relatively ignored by social scientists.[39]

Numerous studies have shown that at least 90 per cent of those who take their own life suffer from mental illnesses.[40] Although, of course, this certainly does not mean that all, let alone the majority of persons affected by these disorders commit suicide. Reliable surveys have shown, for example, that 4.9 per cent of schizophrenics commit suicide.[41] However, it remains true that individuals with disorders of this kind have a much higher risk of taking their own lives than the rest of the population.

Yet there are major differences depending on the form of mental illness.[42] Obsessive-compulsive disorder, typically characterized by persistent and invasive thoughts and repetitive behaviour (regular hand washing, turning lights repeatedly on and off before leaving a room), is one of the few mental illnesses that does not carry an increased risk of suicide. On the contrary, persons with borderline personality disorder or schizophrenia are seven or eight times more likely to kill themselves than the rest of the population. The former is characterized by a marked inability to control the emotions and by an instable identity, manifested in plunging self-esteem and abrupt mood swings. The latter includes a class of disorders influencing the form and content of thought (such as faster or slower than average associative speed, delirium), affectivity (rapid oscillations from joy to rage), perception, instincts and action.

Individuals affected by major depression and bipolar disorder are exposed to an even greater risk of suicide (fifteen to twenty times higher than the rest of the population). The first group suffer from a pathological state of melancholy, which may last for long periods, a lack of interest in life and the world and a lack of desire, the tendency to regard their condition as ineluctable, and intense mental pain. The second group experience alternating episodes of mania (euphoria) and depression. Such individuals are classified as bipolar I when these episodes are of equal severity, or bipolar II when the latter are more serious than the former.

Some personality traits may increase the risk of suicide. The decision to take one's life is sometimes the result of a long planning process, lasting weeks or months. However, sometimes the decision is taken suddenly, just a few hours or even only one hour before its implementation. Based on the results of extensive research, it helps us to understand why there is a greater probability that a person might take this decision if she or he is impulsive,[43] in other words if there is 'a predisposition toward rapid, unplanned reactions to internal or external stimuli without regard to the negative consequences of these reactions to the impulsive individual or to others'.[44]

Relations between the psychological and psychiatric variables, on the one hand, and culture, political and social ones, on the other, are complex and have not been sufficiently studied for their relevance to suicide, but they are unquestionably numerous and highly important.

In the first place, the significance attributed to the symptoms of some disorders (both mental and physical), which, in combination with other circumstances, may lead a person to take their life, varies from culture to culture. Take the case of Virginia Woolf, the English author who, before drowning herself in the Ouse on 28 March 1941, had already attempted suicide on two previous occasions: in 1905, when she threw herself from a window after her father's death, and in 1913, during another crisis when she took an overdose of Veronal. She was bipolar and experienced bouts of mania and depression. During the former, she felt transported and became euphoric, talking continuously and suffering from visual and aural hallucinations. For example, during one of these episodes, she heard birds singing in Greek in the garden outside her window and she talked without a pause for three days and three nights before falling into a coma.[45] Then, after a while, she would succumb to the opposite phase, when she felt herself falling into a dark pit of depression and became unable to talk, as well as having no desire to eat or sleep. It was during one of these moments that she tried to commit suicide, when she felt the 'horror':

Oh it's beginning it's coming – the horror – physically like a painful wave swelling about the heart – tossing me up. I'm unhappy unhappy! Down – God, I wish I were dead. Pause. But why am I feeling this? Let me watch the wave rise. I watch. Vanessa. Children. Failure. Yes; I detect that. Failure failure. (The wave raises.) Oh they laughed at my taste in green paint! Wave crashes. I wish I were dead! I've only a few years to live I hope. I can't face this horror any more – (this is the wave spreading out over me).[46]

How would Virginia Woolf have acted had she lived in the Middle Ages? Of course, no one can say. However, she might well have interpreted her feelings very differently, attributing the 'horror' to Satan's influence.

In the second place, mental illnesses have quite different effects on the various types of suicide in different cultures. They certainly have a strong impact on voluntary death in contemporary Western societies. Yet they probably had less of an impact in the past on altruistic suicide in the East. Lastly, they have no effect at all on suicide as a weapon, at least on that of the kamikaze, for reasons that we will examine later.

In third place, impulsivity constitutes a risk factor only in those cultures where suicide is practised in solitude and in secrecy, not in those where the suicidal act is preceded by complex, lengthy rituals, solemn declarations of intent, processions and songs.

In fourth place, psychiatric factors may have considerable social consequences, to the extent of altering the suicide rate in human populations or in component groups. If, for whatever reason, the number of people affected by mental illnesses (or those not receiving treatment for such disorders) is higher in one population than in another, it is quite probable that, all things being equal, the suicide rate will be higher in the former than in the latter. The existence of links between the suicide rate and the spread of mental illnesses is almost impossible to verify for historical periods and countries for which we have no data. However, these links can be found in Western countries in the closing decades of the twentieth century.

Therefore, in all seven chapters of this book the reader will find suicide being traced to cultural, social, political and, more rarely, to psychological and psychiatric factors. For this reason, it is worth recalling that, contrary to Durkheim's assertions,[47] and those of many social scientists today, suicide also has a hereditary component. Those who have read twentieth-century literature know that the Nobel prize-winning author Ernest Hemingway, who committed suicide at the age of sixty-two, came from a family in which as many as five people killed themselves over a period of seventy years and four generations.[48] The results of studies carried out in the past thirty years suggest that the Hemingway family was not exceptional.

Some studies have compared identical or monozygotic twins with dizygotic twins, who are ordinary brothers and sisters. Born from a single maternal egg fertilized by one paternal sperm, the former have the same genetic heritage and the same physical characteristics (the same colour of hair and eyes). Instead the latter come from one or more maternal eggs, each fertilized by a different sperm. Comparative research has usually shown that, even with regard to suicidal behaviour, there is a much higher concordance among the former and this has been seen as evidence of the importance of genetic factors.[49]

Sceptics have also pointed out, however, that monozygotic twins are not only identical in genetic terms, but they also share a more uniform environment than dizygotic siblings, because they are usually treated in the same way by parents, relatives and all other people with whom they interact, and therefore the higher concordance found with regard to voluntary death might also simply be due to social factors.

In order to overcome these objections and gauge the differing contribution of genetic and environmental factors, studies have been carried out on adopted children, based on the simple idea that an adopted child who leaves his or her natural family at birth will keep the genetic heritage of the biological parents, but share the social and cultural heritage, as well as the experiences of childhood and adolescence, of the adopted family. By comparing a sample group of suicides who had been adopted with a control group of adopted individuals who were still alive, it was seen that there were many more suicides among the biological families than among the adoptive ones.

But mental illnesses that carry an increased risk of suicide (major depression, bipolar disorder, schizophrenia) are also partly hereditary in nature, so researchers have wondered if this is the reason why someone with a parent or relative who has committed suicide has a greater probability than others of taking his or her own life. However, studies have produced convincing results to show that the hereditary predisposition to suicide is independent from other psychiatric disorders.[50]

Although knowledge of this process is still limited, current research suggests that the genes responsible are those that regulate the serotoninergic system. Serotonin is a substance that acts as a neurotransmitter in the central nervous system, controlling interactions between the nerve cells, between the brain and the body, and between the various cerebral areas, and it plays a particularly important role in regulating mood, sleep and sexuality. Various studies have highlighted increased impulsivity and aggression when serotonin levels are too low and its transmission is impeded, possibly resulting in violence against others and also against oneself.[51]

0.6 Structure of the book

The book is divided into two parts: one on Europe and the West in general, and the other on Asia (or, more precisely, India and China) and the Middle East. In both parts I have tried to reconstruct and explain the geographical and historical changes in the frequency of suicides, as well as the differences between various social groups, between men and women, young and old, bachelors and spinsters, married or divorced men and women, between different social classes, between Catholics, Protestants, Jews, Muslims and Hindus, between believers and non-believers, immigrants and natives, black and white, homosexuals and heterosexuals.

In the first chapter I tackle the question of the trends of voluntary deaths in Europe over a very long arc from the Middle Ages to the early twentieth century, and I try to identify when, where and in which social groups the great rise in the number of suicides can be said to have started, which prompted such concern among European intellectuals in the second half of the nineteenth century. In Chapter 2 I trace this rise to a number of profound social and cultural changes, beginning in the closing decades of the sixteenth century and the opening decades of the seventeenth, that marked the crisis and decline of that complex of rules, beliefs, interpretative patterns, symbols and rituals linked to Christianity, which for centuries had guarded men and women against the temptation of taking their own lives. I continue this thesis in Chapter 3 by comparing the opposite trends of the suicide and murder rates during the period between the late fifteenth century and the early twentieth century, and by introducing a number of interpretative hypotheses. In Chapter 4 I outline and try to explain changes in the suicide rate caused by extraordinary events and changes in the twentieth century: two World Wars, the crisis of 1929 and the post-1945 economic boom, the birth and collapse of the Nazi and Soviet regimes, the Holocaust and the persecution of 'enemies of the people'.

In the second part of the book, which is dedicated to Asia and the Middle East, I analyse types of suicide that were unknown in Christian Europe but widespread, in certain historical periods, also on other continents. In the opening chapter on India, I cover the vast range of voluntary deaths (whether prohibited, allowed or rewarded) that were practised for centuries; I then focus on one of these, *sati*, by definition the most altruistic form of suicide in which, after her husband's death, the 'virtuous, chaste and faithful bride' joins her husband's corpse on the funeral pyre. I attempt to establish when, in what castes and for what reasons this practice came about, how it developed and when the custom began its downward parabola. Chapter 6 is devoted to China, which until recently had a relatively high suicide rate and reveals a number of unique aspects regarding the population categories most at risk. Here, too, in an attempt to understand whether these peculiarities are new to recent decades or whether they already existed in the past, I travel back in time to the period of the Ming and Qing dynasties, from the mid fourteenth century to the twentieth century, in order to reconstruct the vast cultural repertoire of voluntary death in this country. Lastly, in Chapter 7, I analyse the birth of the suicide mission phenomenon in the Middle East and its subsequent and extremely rapid development in many countries worldwide.

A reconstruction of changing suicide rates over decades and indeed many centuries might, at first, seem a hopeless enterprise. For most European countries we only have satisfactory statistics for the last 150 years. Quantitative data for the Middle East and Asia are even scarcer and refer only to the last two decades of the twentieth century or, in sporadic cases, to the early decades of that century.[52] As one moves away from Europe and the last 150 years the path becomes narrower, often impassable, and the researcher has to overcome huge difficulties in order to find documents of any sort on suicide, at the risk of making mistakes, even serious ones. Yet, over time, as I ventured along these paths and realized, on numerous occasions, that I was lost (in some cases, I did not even know the language of the populations I was studying), I became convinced that it is possible to make reasonable conjectures on the underlying trend of suicide rates. For Europe during the *ancien régime* this can be done using a variety of judicial, literary and iconographical documents, as well as two types of quantitative data: the statistics collected by the civil and religious authorities for particular areas, such as a parish or a city (sometimes published in long-forgotten works), and the results of quantitative research undertaken by historians over the last twenty years.[53] For Asia, there are various other sources that provide precious if fragmentary knowledge: the travel records left by European explorers, missionaries and merchants (which I have used extensively), the commemorative monuments to individuals (above all, women) who sacrificed themselves for a noble cause (in India), and the honours awarded by emperors over the course of the centuries to those who committed suicide for a noble reason (in China).

At all events, this reconstruction of the trend of suicide rates in Europe, India, China and the Middle East is only one of the goals that I set out to achieve. The other was no less important: it was to identify and describe the repertoires of cultural attitudes to voluntary death in the various countries and historical periods by analysing the four aspects that were outlined earlier: the intentions of the person committing suicide, the method used, the significance that they and others attribute to the act, and the rituals performed before and/or after suicide has been accomplished. Examined in this way, a historical and comparative analysis allows us to respond to major questions regarding the cultural differences between West and East, such as when they appeared, and if and when they may have increased or decreased.

My thanks go to the following persons for the information and advice they have given me: Evgeny Andreev, Giancarlo Angelozzi, James Benn, Barbara Bisetto, Beverly Bossler, Silvia Bruzzone, Cesarina Casanova, Martina Cvajner, Giovanni Dall'Orto, Francesca Decimo, Christoph Eggenberger, Christian Goeschel, Bryna Goodman, Christine Hartig, Martin Illi, Linda Ivanits, David Lederer, David Lester, Weijing Lu, Giovanni Lupinu, Elisa Martini, Gian Paolo Massetto, Ariel Merari, Erik Midelfort, Anna Oppo, Alessandro Pastore, Laura Piretti Santangelo, Gianfranco Poggi, Valentina Poggi, William Alex Pridemore, Colin Pritchard, Raffaella Sarti, Camille Schmoll, Vladimir Shkolnikov, Pieter Spierenburg, Kathy Stuart, Giulia Tabacco, Jeffrey Watt, Tahereh Ziaian, Andrea Zorzi.

I also thank those who took part in discussions at those venues where I presented some of the results of my research in 2005 and 2006: the Faculty of Sociology, Naples, the Department of Sociology, Turin, the Faculty of Sociology, Trento. I am particularly grateful for the comments I received on those occasions from Filippo Barbera, Giuseppe Bonazzi, Massimo Borlandi, Luca Ricolfi, Giuseppe Sciortino, Amalia Signorelli.

I have received valuable help from the staff of Green Library at Stanford University, Main Library at Berkeley University, Butler Library at Columbia University, and New York Public Library. The staff from my own departmental library, Biblioteca Mario Gattullo, have been even more helpful. For many years, with kindness, rapidity and professionalism, Viviana Fortunato and Alberto Scarinci have fulfilled all my requests and have miraculously traced the most obscure articles and books. Watching them at work has fully convinced me that the gap between the great American libraries and some of those in Italy, which once seemed unbridgeable, is now considerably narrower.

For their comments and criticism of an early version of this book, I am grateful to Federico Barbagli, Asher Colombo, Piergiorgio Corbetta, Francesca Decimo, Uberto Gatti, Rossella Ghigi, Mauro Mirri, Giovanna

Movia, Ottavia Niccoli, Anna Oppo, Donatella Pannacci, Maurizio Pisati, Gianfranco Poggi, Marco Santoro, Chiara Saraceno, Raffaella Sarti, Giuseppe Sciortino.

I would also like to thank three extraordinary editors at my publishers, Mulino, for all the assistance they have given me: Giovanna Movia, Laura Marra and Laura Xella.

The person to whom I am most indebted is without question my wife Donatella. For years she listened with interest and patience while I talked about other people's suicides. For years she has given me advice and her loving support.

Part I

In the West

1

The Worst Sin and the Gravest Crime

1.1 The rise in suicide, 'a most tragic fact'

Concern for the fate of the society in which they lived prompted many European scholars to study suicide in the second half of the nineteenth century. In their search for a response to these fears, they immersed themselves in the flood of statistics that the governments of some countries had begun to publish a few years earlier and they tried to verify the reliability of the data, and to process and interpret them. While coming from very different scientific backgrounds and with diverse religious and political convictions, they all arrived at the same conclusion. From the existing data, wrote Enrico Morselli in 1879, 'is demonstrated this most painful fact, that suicide has increased from the beginning of the century, and goes on continually increasing in almost all the civilized countries of Europe and of the New World'.[1] Some twenty years later, Durkheim would reiterate that 'the enormous increase in the number of voluntary deaths within a century' constituted 'a pathological phenomenon becóming daily a greater menace'.[2]

As will be seen, similar fears had already been expressed on countless occasions in the past, at least since the sixteenth century. However, the explanation furnished by the nineteenth-century scholars was different. The annual number of suicides, Karl Marx observed in 1846, has simply 'to be viewed as a symptom of the deficient organization of our society'.[3] 'For suicide', added Friedrich Engels, 'formerly the enviable privilege of the upper classes, has become fashionable among the English workers, and numbers of the poor kill themselves to avoid the misery from which they see no other means of escape.'[4] Suicides were unquestionably the 'fatal plague of our age',[5] commented Enrico Morselli. It was a sentiment that was reiterated by Émile Durkheim, who wrote: 'Our social organization, then, must have changed profoundly in the course of this century, to have been able to cause such a growth in the suicide rate.'

Four years earlier, in another work, the great French sociologist had explained how this change had come about: '[. . .] our societies are, or tend to be, essentially industrial. A form of activity which in this way has acquired such a position in the overall life of society can clearly not remain unregulated without very profound disturbances ensuing. Specifically, this is a source of general moral deterioration.'[6] The growing number of suicides was therefore due to a fall in the degree of social integration and regulation resulting from industrialization, rapid economic development, the cyclical alternation of expansion and recession, as well as increased social mobility. The clearest proof of this theory's validity lay in the chronological succession of the two processes, namely the fact that this 'enormous increase' had commenced in the early decades of the nineteenth century, immediately after the industrial revolution, which was regarded as the great watershed between traditional society and the modern world.

A comparison between the situations in the various countries during the nineteenth century raises some doubts as to the validity of this interpretation. First and foremost, in Britain, home of the industrial revolution, the number of voluntary deaths rose more slowly than in other less economically advanced countries in central and southern Europe. In the mid nineteenth century, the suicide rate in Britain was much lower than those in Belgium, France, Germany and Denmark. By the early twentieth century, the difference between the most industrialized country and other continental states was even more evident, in this respect.[7] Second, the United States retained a lower suicide rate than France, Switzerland, Austria, Germany, Belgium, Denmark and Sweden throughout the nineteenth century. Durkheim did not offer any explanation for these two anomalies. Morselli was surprised by the latter. 'Certainly it is to be wondered at', he observed, 'that the proportion of suicides is so small, considering the feverish business activities and the effects of the extremely rapid civilization of the Anglo-Americans.'[8] Third, in contrast to these nineteenth-century scholars, today we know of other unusual cases: in particular, two countries far removed from the Old World, namely minute Cuba and enormous China, where there was a much higher risk than in Europe, in the nineteenth century, that a person might take his or her own life. Moreover, between the closing years of last century and the start of the twenty-first, industrialization and urbanization in China led to a major fall in suicide rates, and not a rise.

But more serious doubts as to the validity of these nineteenth-century theories have been prompted by the results of historical research carried out in the last two decades, focusing on the exact moment when the number of suicides in Europe started to rise.

1.2   When did the figure start to rise?

Although insufficient documentation makes it quite difficult to reconstruct long-term and very long-term patterns of suicide frequencies in Europe, there are nonetheless figures and testimonials, albeit fragmentary and scattered, that allow us to trace a general picture of the great changes that took place. This picture is still uncertain and subject to numerous corrections, but it leaves no doubt on one point: the rise in the number of suicides started over a century prior to the point identified by Durkheim and the other scholars whose concerns prompted them to study this phenomenon in the second half of the nineteenth century.

In the Middle Ages suicide was sometimes seen as an act of heroism or martyrdom. At moments of crisis individuals belonging to religious groups persecuted by the Christians committed collective suicide. In the thirteenth and fourteenth century, there were occasional instances of this among the Cathars or Albigensians, when they threw themselves en masse into the flames, or among the Jews, who killed one another in order to escape their enemies.[9] However, for centuries, the number of people who took their own lives remained very low.[10] Yet by the sixteenth century, a number of leading figures had the impression that the frequency of voluntary deaths was rising rapidly. Luther, for example, claimed that Germany was affected by an epidemic of suicides in 1542, a thesis that was repeatedly advanced by protestant pastors in the decades that followed.[11] Erasmus and Montaigne also made similar claims.[12] In the absence of precise figures, we have no reason to think that this was the start of the steep increase. The results of one or two historical studies show that, in some areas of Germany, the suicide rate rose abruptly in the closing decades of the sixteenth century, before immediately returning to its starting level.[13] Therefore, these were probably short-lived changes rather than the start of the significant increase that came later.

In Russia, in the last fifteen years of the seventeenth century, there also were episodes of mass suicide. Between 1684 and 1691 at least twenty thousand men and women set themselves on fire. They formed part of the schismatic religious movement of the 'Old Believers', which began in response to changes to the rites and the liturgy imposed by the patriarch of the Orthodox church in Moscow. As well as seeing themselves as upholding the authentic values of their country's religious tradition, they were convinced that the end of the world was at hand and could be accelerated by their purifying sacrifice. Therefore, when they were attacked by the militia, many took their own lives.[14] These were dramatic but isolated explosions and they did not mark the start of the great wave of voluntary deaths given that even throughout the nineteenth century suicide rates remained quite low in Russia.

Instead, the striking increase started in Western Europe during the last decades of the seventeenth century. After 1680 there were numerous cases of voluntary deaths in England among the higher classes, and these events acquired a certain notoriety, at least among the reading public. Counts, barons, knights, rich merchants, successful professionals, book publishers, high-ranking prelates, civil servants and even a government minister killed themselves. Scholars and writers began to use the term 'the English malady' and to speculate on its causes. One of the first to do so was Henry Misson de Valbourg, who in 1698 was convinced that he had identified four 'destructive diseases' that were typically English: scurvy, consumption, rackets and hypochondriacal melancholy.[15] In that same year William Congreve questioned, 'Are there not more Self-murderers, and melancholick Lunaticks in England, heard of in one Year, than in a great part of Europe besides?'[16] In 1711, Defoe went further, commenting that, in London, he had the impression that the number of people who took their own lives in England exceeded those in the rest of Europe put together.[17] The French author Abbé Prévost was so convinced by this explanation that he called suicide 'le remède anglois' (the English remedy) and thought that his countrymen would not resort to it on account of their superior physical and mental resources.[18] The dramatist Destouches, the pseudonym used by Philippe Néricault who had lived in England between 1717 and 1723, observed that suicide was the type of death preferred by the inhabitants of that country and, in one of his comedies, he included this epitaph to describe the average Englishman: 'Here lies Sir John Plumpudding of the Grange, Who hanged himself one morning, for a change'.[19]

César de Saussurre visited England in 1727 and, in the letters he wrote to his family, he claimed that he had been struck both 'by the liberty granted by the government' and by 'the nonchalant way in which men kill themselves'. This made such a negative impression on him that he, too, began to feel ill: 'little by little, I lost my appetite and sleep. I was profoundly anxious and worried, for no good reason. In the end I fell into a deep and dark melancholy [. . .] Everything made me sad and anxious [. . .] If I had been an Englishman, I would have put an end to my sufferings.'[20] In 1733, in the best-selling book *The English Malady*, George Cheyne noted 'the late Frequency and daily Encrease of wanton and uncommon Self-murderers', which was greater in England than in other parts of Europe, and he attributed it to 'the Variableness of our Weather', to 'the Richness and Heaviness of our Food', to 'the Wealth and Abundance of the Inhabitants', to 'Inactivity and Sedentary Occupations', and to 'living in great, populous and consequently unhealthy Towns'.[21]

In 1749 Montesquieu wrote, 'The English are apt to commit suicide most unaccountably; they destroy themselves even in the bosom of happiness [. . .] among the English it is the consequence of a distemper [. . .] generated by the climate, which affects the soul to the point that it leads to disgust of all things, including that of life.'[22] It was above all French writers who observed that English suicide was often arbitrary and irrational. In 1745 Jean-Bernard Le Blanc described a gentleman acquaintance who had killed himself to avoid the boredom of getting dressed and undressed every day.[23] In 1759, Voltaire expressed this idea in *Candide* by giving these words to the 'old woman': 'I have seen a huge number of people who felt abhorrence for their own lives. But I've seen only a dozen voluntarily put an end to their wretchedness: three Negroes, four Englishmen, four Genevans, and a German professor called Robek.'[24] Madame de Staël, too, in 1813 asserted her conviction that suicides were

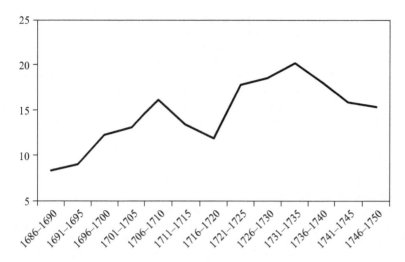

Graph 1.1   Number of suicides per 10,000 deaths in London, from 1686 to 1750.

Source: Elaborated using data from Süssmilch (1761).

frequent in England, although she denied that the climate was the cause, 'for the sky of liberty has always appeared to me particularly pure [. . .]'.[25]

This English fashion was also the butt of irony. Some said that it was highly advisable to delay a duel against an Englishman by a day or so because then it was likely that he would kill himself first. On the other hand, Jacob Zimmermann observed that, 'an Englishman suffering from melancholy would shoot himself in the head. A Frenchman suffering from the same disease would take monastic vows, which, as a matter of fact, is the same thing. The Englishman would not kill himself if there were monasteries he could go to.'[26]

The available statistical data point to the fact that the steep rise in the number of suicides (Graph 1.1) originated precisely in this period.[27] In London, the suicide rate (per ten thousand deaths) started to rise quite sharply after 1686, so much so that in the five years between 1706 and 1710 it doubled compared to the starting value. It then fell again slightly in the following decade before rising again and peaking in 1731–5 at three times its initial level. This figure fell back once again in the following decade, but then resumed its steady climb.

Close observers soon noted, however, that the 'English malady' had already spread or was spreading to other European countries. In a letter from Venice, dated 4 May 1759, Lady Montagu wrote: 'You see it is not in Britain alone that the spleen spreads his dominion.' 'Here is a fashion sprung up entirely new in this part of the world; I mean suicide.' In that week, a priest and a young monk took their own lives, apparently without reason. The former left a letter in his hat 'to signify his desire of imitating the indifference of Socrates and magnanimity of Cato'.[28]

The remarks made in the letters of Madame Palatine, wife of the Duke of Orleans and brother-in-law of King Louis XIV, are also interesting in this respect. In 1696 she reported the content of a conversation with the exiled Queen of England, who asserted that suicides had become very common among her subjects. But barely three years later, and taking her cue from a series of events ('last Monday, moreover, a lawyer shot himself in his bed'), Madame Palatine wrote that the phenomenon was spreading to France. Twenty years on, she returned to the subject when she noted in a letter that, 'The fashion in Paris is now to slough off one's life. Most drown themselves, many throw themselves out of windows and break their necks, others stab themselves.'[29]

Indeed, the subject of voluntary death had forced its way into the salons of Paris at the end of April 1671 and for days remained a burning topic for the witty, refined conversations so appreciated by the Frenchmen and, above all, by the high-ranking ladies who frequented these rooms. The suicide that had aroused such passionate interest did not concern a nobleman, rather his majordomo; the cause, however, was one that the aristocracy itself held in incommensurable regard: honour. The episode, which was described in endless accounts and became quite famous,[30] was made public in two letters, dated 24 and 26 April 1671, written shortly after the tragic event by Madame de Sévigné, who, with her unsurpassed ability to hold the rapt attention of those present, was an indefatigable source of conversation in these salons.

The Prince de Condé had organized a magnificent feast in the chateau at Chantilly. The king had arrived on Thursday evening and all the plans – to quote Madame de Sévigné – 'went off admirably well': the hunt, the lamps, the moonlight, 'the collation, which was served in a place set apart for the purpose, and strewed with jonquils'. But a disconcerting event suddenly occurred, unexpectedly undermining the magnificence of the court setting. The prince's majordomo, François Vatel, drew the attention of all those present and inadvertently became the key focus, upstaging even the sovereign himself. Owing to the excessive popularity of the feast and the fact that there were more guests than expected, there had not been enough meat on some tables. Although Vatel could not be blamed in any way, he could not forgive himself and continued to repeat: 'My honour is lost. I cannot bear this disgrace.'

To calm Vatel, various people had repeated the affectionate words of encouragement that the prince had spoken, reaffirming his esteem and disregarding the incident as being unimportant. But Vatel was deeply shaken, his confidence in his ability to plan undermined, and he now faced a night of anxiety as he prepared for the definitive test: his arrangements for lunch the following day, which in his view would provide a chance to redeem his professional honour. Since the meal was to be based on fish (an obligatory choice for a fast day), the majordomo had already ordered a huge quantity from the fishing ports along the Channel and now he waited nervously for it to arrive. At around four in the morning, he asked an ill-informed boy for news of the deliveries only to be told that just a handful of boxes had arrived. Overcome with despair and unable to face the prospect of another failure, Vatel shut himself in his room and, resting the hilt of his sword against the door, he thrust the blade into his heart. By a twist of fate, everything then started to proceed according to plan, as Madame de Sévigné writes: 'At that instant the carriers arrived with the fish. Vatel was inquired after to distribute it. They ran to his apartment, broke open the door and found him weltering in his blood.'[31]

From then on voluntary death became an increasingly common topic of conversation in France. For example, in his *Memoirs*, the Duke of Saint-Simon gives a detailed description of as many as twelve incidents in which individuals took their own lives, the first dating from 1693. In 1768, Grimm suggested that the subject should be banned from plays, but a year later there were 147 cases of suicide in Paris. In 1772 a Parisian commented in his diary that the city was witnessing a growing number of suicides and the 'peculiar character of the English' seemed to have taken hold of its inhabitants.[32] Some years later, Louis-Sébastien Mercier affirmed that there were 150 suicides a year in Paris, more than in London whose population was larger,[33] and the available data appear to back up his assertions. Between the English capital and the French one there was also, in Mercier's opinion, another major difference. In London, above all, it was the rich who committed suicide, because the 'affluent Englishman is the most capricious of men and consequently the most bored', while in Paris suicide cases were most frequently reported in 'attics and furnished lodgings'.[34] This distinction was shared by many other observers. In France – as Stendhal noted forty years later – one would never 'see a powerful minister like Lord Castelreagh, or a famous lawyer like Sir Samuel Romilly take their own lives'.[35]

A few years later, in 1781, in order to reassure the public, *Correspondence secrète* told its readers the story of a shoemaker in Saint-Germain who worked all day, because he found his family oppressive, and then spent every evening in the tavern, talking about literature with his friends. The only time he went home was to count his money. However, one night, he returned to the house to find that his wife had run off with another man, his daughter had been arrested and charged with obscene behaviour, his son had enlisted for the army, and that all his money had been stolen. In despair, he resolved to follow the fashion of the time and take his own life. He started to write his final letter of farewell, but then thought it would be elegant to finish with a few lines by Molière. But were they really by Molière, he wondered, or by Rousseau? As he could not remember, he decided to postpone his death and ask his friends the next day. One of the friends said that the quote came from Corneille, another attributed it to Marmontel. So the shoemaker gave himself another week in order to get to the bottom of the matter. As the days passed, and realizing that he had much to be thankful for, since he was now alone and had plenty of time left to save up some money, he put the idea of suicide completely out his mind.[36]

In 1797, the *Encyclopedia Britannica* stated that suicide was more commonplace in Paris than in London. This claim does indeed appear to be backed up by the few existing statistics which show that, during the eighteenth century (and for much of the nineteenth), the suicide rate in the English capital was 9 per 100,000 inhabitants, while the rate in Paris was two to three times higher.[37] The number of voluntary deaths in the French capital rose sharply, reaching 150 cases in 1782 – equivalent to a rate of 28 per 100,000 inhabitants,[38] which was similar to the overall rate in France at the end of the great increase, in the last decades of the nineteenth century. In 1793, the most dramatic year of the Terror, records reveal the most abrupt rise in the number of voluntary deaths documented until then, bringing the total to 1,300 (an estimated rate of 230 per 100,000 inhabitants).[39] The implications were even felt at the highest level of France's political institutions: in four years as many as twenty-seven members of the *Convention nationale* took their own lives or attempted to do so.[40] Two ministers, Étienne Clavière and Jean-Marie Roland de la Platière, and the mayor of Paris, Jérome Pétion de Villeneuve, also committed suicide.

Detailed information for other areas of Europe is still scant or inadequate. However, thanks to the steady accumulation of historical research data, it is becoming increasingly clear that the rise in voluntary deaths commenced much earlier than was previously thought. For example, we know for certain that in Sweden – both in Stockholm and in the agricultural region of Smaland – increased suicide rates were noted in the last decade of the seventeenth century,[41] and that here and in other localities they rose strongly in the second half of the eighteenth century.[42] In Finland, the rise occurred after 1790.[43] In the mid seventeenth century, pastors in Zurich remarked on the 'impressive number of suicide cases' in their city, and in 1691 Anton Klinger, leader of the church in Zurich, published a 500-page volume on the 'horrors' of the voluntary deaths that had become increasingly frequent. From the data in our possession (see Chapter 3, Graph 3.1), it is clear that these impressions were well founded because, having remained stable during the sixteenth century, the number of individuals taking their own lives rose rapidly throughout the seventeenth and eighteenth century.[44] The suicide rate in Geneva increased moderately during the first half of the eighteenth century, tripled in the next three decades and then doubled over the following twenty years.[45] This extraordinary rise was not preceded or accompanied by rapid changes in industrialization or urbanization. Although its population rose, Geneva remained a small centre for the whole of this period, and in the late eighteenth century it still only numbered 29,000 inhabitants.[46]

However, some geographical areas and certain social classes were a focus for the earliest and most striking increase in total suicide numbers. In the United States, newspapers started to publish alarming articles on

Table 1.1 Ratio between the number of male and female suicides in some European countries (1250–1850).

Country	Period	Male suicides/female suicides
Austria	1851–1854	4.59
Finland	1781–1790	6.00
France	1250–1400	1.50
	1836–1840	2.89
Germany	1350–1450	5.66
Geneva	1542–1700	1.48
	1701–1750	1.07
	1751–1798	2.69
England	1200–1500	1.83
	1485–1714	5.20
	1859–1860	2.55
Italy	1864–1866	4.09
Nuremberg	1400–1600	2.57
Paris	1766–1789	3.43
	1795–1801	3.35
	1834–1835	2.70
Prussia	1816–1820	4.11
Russia	1875	3.88
Schleswig-Holstein	1600–1800	2.25
Sweden	1781–1790	3.09
	1831–1840	4.06
Zurich	1500–1790	2.67

Source: Elaborated using data from Brierre de Boismont (1865); Morselli (1879); Verkko (1951); Cobb (1978, 6); Schär (1985); Merrick (1989); MacDonald and Murphy (1990); Midelfort (1995); Murray (1998); Lind (1999, 190); Watt (2001); Butler (2006b).

the growing number of voluntary deaths in the last two decades of the eighteenth century, and some commentators were convinced that the cause was the 'English malady'.[47] The rise first started in northwestern Europe – in Sweden, England, France, Germany – and here it grew faster in urban areas than elsewhere,[48] and among the higher social classes.[49] Indeed, until the mid nineteenth century, there was a growing difference between the suicide rates of Stockholm, Paris, London and Berlin and the rural populations and small towns in each of these countries respectively.[50]

It is harder to say whether this change started first in the male population or in the female one. The available statistical data (Table 1.1) show that, in Europe, from the mid thirteenth century to the mid nineteenth century, men killed themselves more frequently than women.[51] Yet the ratio between male and female suicides varied both geographically and over time. During the course of this book, I will repeatedly return to this point, to this difference and its causes. Here, it is worth noting that in Geneva, in the second half of the eighteenth century, the rise in the numbers of voluntary deaths was more rapid among men than among women, and therefore the gap between the two genders became more marked.[52] However, we cannot conclude that the great rise in the suicide rate started among men because exactly the opposite occurred in Paris, during the years from 1766 to 1835, and there the numerical ratio between male and female voluntary deaths reduced (Table 1.1).

No significant differences in age have emerged in those population groups in which the great rise started, and, broadly speaking, the young, the elderly and the middle-aged seem to have been affected alike.[53] Indeed, even in the seventeenth and eighteenth century, the same relationship probably existed between age and the frequency of suicide as was highlighted by the data collected in the nineteenth-century and which scholars of the time regarded as a 'law of statistics': namely that, in both males and females, suicide was extremely rare in childhood and adolescence, started to increase around the age of sixteen, then rose steadily until the age of eighty, before diminishing slightly among the few who lived beyond that age.[54]

1.3   The reasons for this growth

If we cannot attribute the apparently unstoppable rise in the number of voluntary deaths only (or mainly) to the social upheavals resulting from industrialization and urbanization, how can we explain the centuries-old growth in the suicide rate that started, depending on the country, at some point in the last decades of the seventeenth century and the first half of the eighteenth? Durkheim implicitly rules out that it could be attributed to cultural factors or to changes in 'moral evaluations' and norms, or the way men and women thought, their sensitivity, or their idea of life and death, happiness and the means of attaining it. Although he was convinced that these changes had taken place, he never once considered the hypothesis that they might have affected the frequency of suicide.

According to the illustrious French sociologist, social attitudes to suicide in Europe had gone through two main phases over the past two thousand years, gradually becoming more severe. In the first, which corresponds to the era of Greek and Latin civilization, individuals could not kill themselves acting on their own initiative, but it was permitted if they had the state's consent. In the second phase, however, condemnation was 'absolute and universal. The power to dispose of a human life, except when death is the punishment for a crime, is withheld not merely from the person concerned but from society itself. It is henceforth a right denied to collective as well as to private disposition. Suicide is thought immoral in and for itself, whoever they may be who participate in it. Thus, with the progress of history the prohibition, instead of being relaxed, only becomes more strict.'[55]

As a matter of fact, during the nineteenth century, there were growing signs that social attitudes towards those committing suicide were becoming increasingly tolerant, a fact that did not escape Durkheim's attention. But he was convinced that this was a brief interlude, not a trend inversion. 'If the public conscious seems less assured in its opinion of this matter today, therefore, this uncertainty may rise from fortuitous and passing causes; for it is wholly unlikely that moral evolution should so far reverse itself after having developed in a single direction for centuries.'[56] He was drawn to this conclusion by his firmly held belief that reprobation of suicide increases in parallel with the growth of individual as opposed to state rights, leading to the conception of human personality as being sacred, 'even most sacred [. . .], something which no one is to offend. [. . .] [The individual] has become tinged with religious value; man has become a god for men. Therefore, any attempt against his life suggests sacrilege. Suicide is such an attempt. [. . .] Hence, suicide is rebuked for derogating from this cult of human personality on which all our morality rests.'[57]

In reality, the history of the 'moral evaluations' of this act in Europe has been very diverse. As will be evident in the coming pages, for over a millennium it is true that European populations had a system of extraordinarily (and, in our eyes, unbelievably) severe rules for those who wished to take their own life. But this system started to change between the late sixteenth century and the early seventeenth century, and had in part vanished by the time Durkheim was writing.

The thesis that I propose in this and the next two chapters is that, while in existence, and still strong and well founded, this set of rules and beliefs, symbols and meanings, cognitive schemas and classification systems helped men and women to resist the idea of taking their own lives, but its crisis and decline fostered the great rise in the number of suicides.

1.4 Past reactions

'Suicide', wrote Cesare Beccaria in 1764, 'is a crime which seems not to allow of being punished strictly speaking, since such a thing can only be visited either on the innocent or on a cold and insensible corpse.'[58] This thesis, which found particular resonance among the cultured elite of many European countries in the closing decades of the eighteenth century and the early nineteenth, strikes us now as wholly incomprehensible because it refers to a social reality that has long disappeared. As we shall see, in Europe during the Middle Ages and early modern era, suicide provoked emotions, thoughts and actions that were radically different from those it evokes today. That distant world can be re-evoked through three cases with quite different historical and geographical settings.

Let us start from Rügen. In 1525, or shortly after that date, anyone passing through the streets of this small German town might have caught sight of a group of men equipped with picks, shovels, hammers and other tools, and working around a house. Sometimes they dug a tunnel under the front door, sometimes they made a large hole in one of the walls. If the passer-by was not German or French, but if he came from Italy, Spain or Portugal and was not familiar with local customs, he might have wondered what those men were really doing. He might have thought they were creating a hole in the wall for a new window. But what sense was there in digging a tunnel under the front door? No one would have thought that these men were installing a drainage system or sewers, because none of the houses at that time had sinks in the kitchens or bathrooms. But if the passer-by had had the patience to wait until the works were finished, he would have seen the purpose with his own eyes. Through the tunnel excavated under the front door, or through the opening made in the wall was passed the corpse of someone who had hanged themselves in the house. Although it was unheard of in Mediterranean countries, this ritual was practised for a long time in Germany and in some areas of France.[59]

Let us move now to northwest France, to Boulogne-sur-Mer.[60] On 27 March 1725, prompted by gossip he had heard, the head of the police and justice, Achille Mutinot, went in person to inspect the corpse of a man hanging from a tree in a marsh close to the town. Mutinot immediately opened an inquest into the cause of death and asked the clerk of court to prepare a precise report on the body, the position of the face and legs, the presence of blows and wounds, the thickness and length of the rope from which the dead man was hanging, his clothing. Moreover, having placed a wax seal bearing the municipal arms on its forehead, he gave orders for the corpse to be carried to the prisons. But before it was moved, another official arranged for two doctors to go to the place where the suicide had been found and draw up a detailed clinical description. Using all the information that had been gathered, the inquest concluded that the individual in the marsh was a disabled soldier, Jean Beacourt, and the cause of death was suicide.

At this point the public prosecutor asked the magistrate to appoint a receiver to 'put the corpse on trial'. Once the trial had commenced, five witnesses were called and, on being shown the person suspected of committing the crime (in this case, the lifeless Jean Beacourt), they were asked to reveal all that they knew about him. The trial, like every other, ended with a judgment, but in this case the soldier was pronounced guilty of 'murdering himself' and condemned to various punishments. In the first place he was condemned to *damnatio memoriae*, namely to the perpetual erasure of all trace or memory (his name and any likenesses or inscriptions). Then his body was tied to a cart and dragged, head down and face down, over the gritted streets of the city to a square where it was hanged upside-down from a gallow. Having been left for twenty-four hours in this position, the corpse was cast *à la voirie*, an expression that could be translated as being thrown to the dogs. Last of all, all the man's possessions were sequestered and confiscated.

We now move further south, to a village in the countryside around Bologna. On the morning of 8 May 1672, while her husband and relatives were at mass, Lucia Barbani took a sickle and killed her two grand-daughters: Domenica, known as Meneghina, aged six, and Susanna, known as Osanna, aged three. She then laid their bodies side-by-side on the floor of her bedroom, left the house and threw herself in the 'well', a water barrel that was not deep enough for her to drown in, as she had intended. When the family returned home and discovered this tragedy, they asked Lucia to explain what had happened. She said, using the same words that she would repeat in all subsequent judicial interrogations, that she had wanted to spare the little girls the sufferings they would have inevitably faced during the coming famine. For some time she had decided to kill herself and she did not want to leave the little girls uncared for given that she was their only guardian after their mother (her daughter) had died and their father had remarried. Lucia Barbani was imprisoned in Bologna where she was again interrogated. Having reiterated that she was responsible, she was found guilty of dual homicide and sentenced to be publicly hanged.

The woman was indeed hanged, but not while she was still alive: she committed suicide in the cell where she was held in the Torrone prison of Bologna by knotting together the few inches of string that held the straw in place around the flask-shaped water bottles. Yet justice was perpetrated on her corpse, as the law prescribed, and the events were recorded as follows in the judicial records: 'The aforesaid Lucia took her life while in prison by strangling herself with a piece of string; after her corpse had been recognized, by order of the Auditor, she was publicly hanged, dead as she was, as an example to others, in the place used [for executions].'[61]

1.5 Punishments for those who killed themselves or attempted to do so

For many centuries, theologians and jurists regarded suicide as a sin, a *delictum gravissimum*, the gravest that could be committed by a human being. Some ranked it at the same level as a theft of the worst kind, but many went further and judged it worse than homicide.[62] For them, taking one's own life was an act that was even more execrable and odious than killing another person, whether a stranger, an acquaintance, a friend or even a family member.[63] According to many jurists, the key justification for this difference was that 'whoever kills another can only kill the body, but absolutely not the soul. Instead, whoever kills himself certainly loses both his body and his soul.'[64] In other words, suicide was seen as a double murder, both physical and spiritual. According to theologians and the clergy, there was no remission for suicide because, by definition, it excluded any possibility of repentance.[65] Even in 1621, when this system of rules was starting to show the first cracks, Robert Burton, who described himself as a 'divine' who has 'meddled with physic', could write in his famous work, *The Anatomy of Melancholy*, 'if they dye so obstinately and suddenly, that they cannot so much as wish for mercy, the worst is to be suspected, because they dye impenitent'. Instead, 'divers have been recovered out of the very act of hanging and drowning themselves, and so brought *ad sanam mentem*, they have been very penitent, much abhorred their former act, confessed that they have repented in an instant, and cryed for mercy in their hearts.'[66]

Religious and civic authorities therefore inflicted severe punishments on those who took their own life or tried to do so. This happened all over the continent, although there were differences between countries (for example, between England, Germany and Russia) and changes over time in the procedures followed and the sentences imposed. Moreover, it also happened in the American colonies under Spanish, English and French rule, from the time when they first came into existence. An admonitory sermon of 1786, in England, pronounced: 'With us self-murderers are denied Christian burial, their goods are escheated, that respect to their families may deter people from it. In other places they have hung them up on gibbets; in others, they drag them through the open streets, in a way of ignominy and disgrace, in order to deter others from the shocking crime.'[67]

Just like today, it all started with the discovery of a body. The person who found the body was obliged to inform the judicial authorities which would then try to identify the cause of death. In England, for example, at the end of the twelfth century, it was the coroner's duty to establish whether suspicious deaths had been caused by accidents, homicide or suicide by examining the corpse and questioning witnesses.[68] In both the second and third case, irrespective of whether a person had been killed or had killed themselves, criminal proceedings were started against the person who had committed the crime. In the case of voluntary death, that person was clearly one and the same as the victim. The principle of *crimen estinguitur mortalitate*, namely that crime is extinguished by death, was applied throughout Europe during the Middle Ages. But an exception was made in the case of suicide,[69] and therefore anyone committing this crime was brought before the court.

From the moment that the death was deemed to be suicide, a process commenced that aimed at dehumanizing the mortal remains of the person who had dared to take his or her own life. With inordinate force, this process expressed the horror, repugnance and aversion felt not only by the civic and religious authorities but by the entire population. Regarded as despicable and bestial, the lifeless body of the guilty party provoked contempt, fear and disdain, and was treated with deliberate brutality.

The suicide was often condemned by the court to be hanged, or as Montesquieu wrote in 1715, 'Suicides are, so to speak, put to death a second time.'[70] In medieval France, if a man had committed suicide than his corpse was hanged, as if he were a live murderer. Often, however, merely hanging the corpse on a rope from a gallows was not sufficient and it would be suspended from a forked pole with two pointed ends. Sometimes even more degrading forms of execution were used: corpses would be tied up and left hanging, head down, from the top of a tree, like roosting bats. As a sixteenth-century observer wrote, 'nowadays, to make the matter more ignominious, we hang them head down'.[71] On other occasions, the corpse would be 'strangled', as if the man 'were still alive'.[72] If it was a woman who had taken her own life, then her body would be burnt.[73] In Spain, too, in the sixteenth century, the bodies of those who had committed suicide were hanged upside down from a gibbet, whereas in Germany they were more frequently burnt.[74] In the constitutions of Modena, dating from 1671, 'proceedings are started against the memory of whoever, being of sound mind, kills himself, by appointing a relative to defend him, and if nothing can be proved in his defence, the corpse or effigy is hanged from the gibbet'.[75] Again, in the constitutions of Piedmont of 1770, 'if an individual of sound mind should cruelly attack his own body and commit self-murder, criminal proceedings must be taken against his memory, and his body must be condemned to be hanged from the gallows, and where there is no body then his effigy shall be hanged'.[76]

So much for those who succeeded in taking their own lives, but civic and at times also the religious authorities also acted against those who attempted to do so but failed. However, there was no real consensus, wrote De Damhouder, a leading sixteenth-century European jurist, on the punishment to be meted out. In Florence, in the mid fourteenth century, a failed suicide was sentenced to pay a fine.[77] In Geneva, from the mid sixteenth to the mid seventeenth century, the sanctions imposed were whippings and banishment.[78] In Sweden, anyone attempting to commit suicide was condemned for centuries, and faced scourging, torture, forced labour, detention on a diet of bread and water, as well as various forms of public humiliation (such as standing on the 'stool of shame' during church services),[79] and occasionally even the death penalty. In Massachusetts, in the last decades of the seventeenth century, the sanction for this crime amounted to 'twenty lashes and payment of a fine'.[80] In Russia, according to the penal code approved by Peter the Great in 1716, premeditated suicide attempts would be punished with the death penalty.[81] In Austria, the penal code introduced by Joseph II (1787) stated that whoever attempted suicide would be sentenced to detention until the individual became convinced that the preservation of his own life was a duty to God, the state and himself, and until he had fully repented.[82] Even in 1838, when regulations on this aspect had been repealed in many European countries, the 'penal code for the states of His Majesty King of Sardinia', as promulgated by Carlo Alberto of Savoia, stated that 'the person guilty of attempted suicide' would be taken to a safe place of custody and held under strict surveillance for between one and three years'.[83]

Throughout Europe, the body of the suicide was subject to a variety of ritualized violations and deconsecrations.[84] If found inside a house, the corpse was sometimes thrown from the window or the roof into the street.[85] While awaiting trial in prison, it was preserved using salt or embalming. After the sentence, it was tied to a horse with a strong rope and dragged through the streets, squares and fields of the village. At other times it was placed on a hurdle, or sometimes fastened by the feet or neck. This ritual was performed even if the corpse had reached an advanced state of putrefaction when it was placed in a sack or replaced with a puppet. The ritual had at least two ends. The first was to dirty the corpse because it was believed that a mud-coated corpse was a fitting container for a soul perverted by the devil.[86] The second was to expose the body to the scorn and mockery of the entire population. As the law of Beaumont (enacted in 1182) affirmed: 'a man who has taken his own life shall be dragged through the fields as cruelly as possible, in order to show the experience to others'.[87] Similar customs existed in England,[88] Germany and Geneva[89] in the sixteenth and seventeenth centuries. In sixteenth-century Venice, the Senate decreed that the body of a young man who had killed himself in gaol should be carried on an uncovered boat down the Grand Canal and then pulled to pieces by the hangman with red-hot pincers.[90] Instead, in southwest Germany and in some parts of Switzerland (Zurich, Lucerne, Basle), it was customary from at least the thirteenth to the sixteenth century to seal the body inside a barrel, which was then cast into the river.[91] Lastly, in some instances, the suicide's corpse was decapitated, mutilated or quartered with extraordinary ferocity.[92]

The process of dehumanizing and degrading the culprit did not end with hanging. After the execution, the body was left on the gallows or gibbet, at times for six or even twenty-four hours, at times for several days. As De Damhouder wrote, the purpose of this was 'for the sake of the spectacle, for the eyes of the people, so that the people might thereby see that he has murdered himself and has taken away his own life'.[93]

As well as punishing the body, the sentence also encompassed the suicide's property. In the thirteenth and fourteenth centuries, in some areas of France, suicides – like murderers and rapists – were not exempt from *ravage*, a ritual devastation and sacking of the goods and property they had owned in life. Their houses were pulled down (or seriously damaged), their fields burned, their vines cut and uprooted.[94] Similar customs existed in Germany, England and other European countries. It was a form of revenge on property, one that substituted or emphasized the ravaging of the physical person of whoever had committed the crime. But it was also intended to 'abolish ownership', debasing the malefactor, reducing him 'from the status of a free man, a member of the tribe, to the status of savage, *quasi lupus*, like a wolf'.[95] However, at a certain point, this custom was replaced by the simple confiscation of the suicide's property, which had been introduced at least a century earlier. Indeed, in a French document of 1205 we read, for the first time, that 'the movable goods of those who voluntarily take their own lives shall be allocated to the king or the baron'.[96] On the other hand, the *Coutumes de Beauvaisis* of 1283 categorically state:

> Whoever is killed accidentally – for instance, should he fall into a pit or into a river and be drowned, or fall down from a tree or from the

roof of a house, or be killed accidentally in any other way – shall not forfeit his property, but it must be delivered to his heirs. But, when it is clearly known that his death was intended, for instance, should they find him hanged or should he have said 'I will drown myself – for what they have done to me – or on account of what has overcome me', then justice must be administered, and his property shall be forfeit and accrue to the seigneur on whose estate the property is situated.[97]

During the same period, in England, legislation was passed, stating that whosoever took their own life, whether man or woman, of sound or unsound mind, would forfeit all their property by confiscation.[98] This sanction was subsequently incorporated in the law codes of many European countries.[99] The following procedure was normally used. While the corpse was being tried, the court asked for an inventory to be drawn up of all the accused's possessions, and these were then sequestered and handed over to the collector of the lord or sovereign. The subsequent confiscation could be the main punishment for the crime or the accessory penalty, and it could relate to movables, immovables, or both. Similarly, the sentence might refer to the individual property of the guilty party, or to family property, which therefore also included the spouse's goods. At all events, it nullified any testamentary dispositions and often had disastrous effects on the economic conditions of the surviving relatives.

The existing documentation also suggests that this practice was also used in southern Europe. In Sardinia, for example, the *Carta de logu*, a charter enacted by Eleonora d'Arborea in an unknown year, but certainly before 1392, stated:

Furthermore, we order that whosoever should kill himself with pre-meditated design in any way whatsoever, his body must be dragged and hanged on a gibbet, which must be done in the village where he killed himself; and then the bailiff of that village must list all his possessions, on our orders; and he shall investigate and question the witnesses and goodmen of that village for details of why that man killed himself, and the bailiff shall write a report and shall bring that report to Us so that We may show it to our Councillors who will advise us what should be done with the said possessions.[100]

However, there were major differences between the customs of the various European countries and regions.[101] In some cases confiscation included both movables and immovables, in others only the former, and in still others only part of a suicide's possessions. For example, according to a law of 1568, in Geneva not all a suicide's property was confiscated if the latter had children, because in this case they were entitled to part of the inheritance (the children's share).[102] In some instances, too, the wife was at least partly protected by the right of usufruct, which meant that neither *ravage* nor the confiscation of her husband's property could occur during her own lifetime. Moreover, practice varied depending on the gender of the suicide. Therefore, in some parts of Germany the overlord was entitled to half of the possessions if a man committed suicide, but only a third if instead it was a woman.[103]

Disputes also arose between civic and ecclesiastical authorities over who could claim the confiscated assets. This is what happened in Lodi, for example, after the commander of the ducal guards, Danino del'Acqua, took his own life on 9 June 1468, having been 'prompted by great despair'. The vicar of the Bishop of Lodi, the magistrate and other officials all rushed to his house where it was ascertained that 'the man had hanged himself'. The fiscal authorities of the church and the Ducal Chamber disputed possession of the poor commander's goods, which were worth between 300 and 800 Imperial lire. At one point the Bishop of Lodi asked Duke Galeazzo Maria Sforza to give him the property as a donation, 'to make a *balduchino* [sic]', given that the previous canopy had been 'broken and torn' during the Duke's entrance into Lodi.[104]

Legislation in the kingdom of Castille was a little less severe than in other countries in central and northern Europe. An article on *desesperados* in the *Libro de las leyes* (later more commonly known as *Siete partidas*), which was written between 1256 and 1265 by a commission of illustrious jurists at the behest of King Alfonso X, identified four principal motivations for suicide: to avoid sanctions after committing a crime, to avoid the unsupportable pain of certain illnesses, on grounds of madness or after having suddenly lost power, wealth or honour. The confiscation of property was only stipulated in the first case.[105] But two centuries later, the *Ordenanzas reales*, drawn up in 1484 by the jurist Alfonso Diaz of Montalvo for the Cortes of Toledo, prescribed that all the property of a person committing suicide, for whatever reason, should be confiscated by the crown, but only if the suicide had no descendants.[106]

1.6   Dishonourable burial

The punishment most frequently imposed on suicides concerned the place and manner of burial. For a long period, and in widely diverse cultures, the decision about where and how a corpse should be interred represented a powerful and effective symbol of inclusion into a community or exclusion from it. Even Plato had affirmed that 'one who kills the person that is most of all his own, and is said to be dearest to him', therefore the suicide, from 'lack of effort and unmanly cowardice', should, 'off by themselves without a single companion tomb . . . be buried without any fame, in uncultivated and nameless boundary regions' without 'tablets or name markers indicating the tombs'.[107] In Christian Europe, the first document highlighting this practice dates from 570, when the body of a Frankish count who had taken his own life was buried in a monastery, but 'the corpse was not put among the Christian dead, and no Mass was sung for him'.[108]

It is precisely from this period that a profound change occurred in attitudes towards death and funeral customs throughout the Christian world (first in Africa, then in Europe).[109] Up until this time the dead had always been regarded with suspicion and fear, and kept as far as possible from the living. The Roman law of the Twelve Tables laid down that 'no corpse be buried or burned within the city limits'. Indeed, in antiquity cemeteries had always been sited at a distance from the city centres. The early Christians never changed these customs because many of them, still influenced by pagan superstitions, attributed scant importance to the place of burial.

However, these attitudes altered drastically following the birth and spread of the cult of the saints and their tombs. The saints, it was believed, were particularly close to God, and indeed held 'the sole key to Paradise'; moreover, they assured protection of the deceased's body and transmitted part of their own virtue to it. As a result, the Christian dead started to be buried *ad santos, apud ecclesiam*, in the vicinity of the church and around the tombs of the saints. Given that the latter were gradually moved within the city walls, cemeteries too came nearer the city centre. From the ninth century, cemeteries were officially consecrated and burial rites were revised and now only performed by the clergy. When the bells proclaimed to the community that a member of the congregation had died, the corpse was followed by a solemn ecclesiastical procession, first into church where Mass was celebrated, often with chants, and then to the cemetery where it was interred, close to others, in hallowed ground.[110]

The bodies of suicides, on the other hand, were buried outside the city, far from the living and from the churches and the tombs of the saints. During the Middle Ages, the Catholic church always banned anyone who had taken their own life – and likewise heretics, murderers and other serious criminals – from receiving funeral rites, namely the usual funeral liturgy and burial in the cemetery, in consecrated ground close to the other Christian dead. Orthodox Christians, Anglicans and Lutherans behaved very similarly.[111] Nonetheless, this punishment took different forms depending on the country and the historical period in which it was practised.

The most severe penalty was to leave the corpse unburied. In Sardinia, for example, during the Middle Ages, 'the suicide's body was hung from a gibbet on the exact spot where he had died, and it was left dangling in the wind to be eaten by carrion crows'.[112] In Middleburg, Holland, at the beginning of the seventeenth century, the suicide's body was left hanging from the gallows until it had rotted away and been eaten by animals. After a certain period of time, the gallows was removed and the skeleton was left lying on the ground.[113] In some cases in England, the corpse was abandoned at a crossroads, with a stake driven into it, so that it would be trodden on by passers-by.[114] In Scotland, suicides were buried immediately outside the cemetery, in a grave marked by a small mound of earth, and passers-by were obliged to throw a stone at it.[115] In many more cases, however, in various areas of Europe, the body was buried in a pit, without a coffin.[116]

No less harsh was the so-called *sepultura asini*, also known as *asinara*, *asinaria* or *canina*,[117] in which the corpse was treated as if it were that of an animal (indeed, the expression has a long history since it also appears in the Bible, in the book of the prophet Jeremiah: 'He shall be buried with the burial of an ass, drawn and cast forth beyond the gates of Jerusalem').[118] In Germany, the body was buried by the hangman under the gallows, immediately after hanging.[119] In Sweden, it was also buried by the hangman, but in the woods, far from any settlements.[120] In still other cases the body was thrown into a 'receptum stercorum'.[121] In Paris, in the seventeenth century, the bodies of those who had cut their own throats were cast into carrion pits, where dead animals were left.[122] In other regions, they were buried in isolated spots, without any stones or inscriptions that might have marked the presence of a tomb.[123] In Massachusetts, in the closing decades of the seventeenth century, the body of a suicide was buried at a crossroads under a 'cart-load of stones', as 'a brand of infamy and a warning to others to beware of the like damnable practices'.[124] Sometimes the place and manner of the burial depended on the way in which the suicide had occurred. In Zurich, for example, if a person had jumped from a height, he was buried under a mountain, with three stones on his head. If he had drowned, he was buried in sand, not far from the water's edge. If he had killed himself with a knife, a wooden wedge was driven into his head.[125]

Another form of punishment consisted of putting the suicide's body in a barrel and then throwing it into a fast-flowing river (see Plate 3, for Basle in the early sixteenth century). This custom (known as *rinnen*, floating away, in German) was in use as early as the ninth century and continued to be widespread in central and western Germany, and in parts of Switzerland, for many centuries.[126] A public memorandum from Strasburg, dated 1497, reads: 'If anyone puts himself to death, whether man or woman, young or old, the council shall pay five shillings and no more to drag the body out of the house, shut it in a barrel and get rid of it.'[127]

During the course of the seventeenth century, this practice was gradually replaced by others. The bodies of those who had taken their own lives were sometimes sunk in swamps or buried under the gallows. Others were cremated, and yet others were interred in remote, isolated places, rarely visited by men or beasts.[128]

There were also less harsh punishments than these. In Saxony, the body of a suicide was sometimes buried in the part of the cemetery reserved for children, or in a part close to the wall.[129] In France, from the seventeenth century onwards, an area started to be reserved in cemeteries to bury suicides who could not be interred in consecrated ground. In Franche-Compté, for example, this area was enclosed by a continuous, low wall, so that the body had to be passed over it in order to get inside.[130] In Sweden, Germany and other countries, suicides were sometimes buried in consecrated ground, but without any religious ceremonies; occasionally, this happened in the presence of a priest, in private, without any bells tolling, or late in the evening.[131] Even by the early decades of the nineteenth century, in Bologna, the bodies of those who had taken their own life were buried in an area outside the Certosa cemetery, close to that reserved for non-Catholics and Jews.[132] In Russia, the bodies of some suicides were thrown into a swamp or left unburied in deserted areas, while others were carried to an *ubogii dom*, a 'wretched house', namely large pits sometimes covered by wooden shacks, known as 'chapels for prayer'.[133]

In some cases, three different types of burial were used depending on the motives for the suicide: *honesta, inhonesta tamen umana, canina sive asinina*.[134] In Nuremberg, for instance, during the sixteenth century, if the person who had taken his own life was deemed to have been mad or demented, the first method was chosen and the body was allowed to be buried in the cemetery, but 'in silence', namely without ceremony, sacred chants or tolling of the bells. If, on the other hand, he had acted because he was poor or desperate, or out of shame or cowardice, the second method was chosen and the body was carried outside the city, on a hangman's cart, without a coffin, attracting the attention of layabouts and busybodies. Lastly, if the suicide had killed himself after being charged or convicted with an office, then the only option was the last most degrading form of burial, literally dog-burial or ass-burial in unhallowed ground.[135]

In some cases the family members or relatives of those who killed themselves succeeded in obtaining a more clement verdict, or at worst they could avoid the shame of a *sepultura asini*, by offering money to the bailiff.[136]

Complete absolution was only possible if a person had attempted suicide and had then repented. Bouteiller reported the case of a man who had tried to drown himself, close to Tournai, in the late fourteenth century. Having survived, he then returned home and confessed to a priest. However, when he died shortly afterwards from his injuries, the resulting trial absolved him because he was repentant.[137]

In Vienna, in order to obtain a Christian burial in consecrated ground, the suicide had to have invoked the names of Jesus and Mary, even while in the act of taking his own life.[138] In other cases, burial without ceremony was conceded. This is what happened, for example, in the eighteenth century, in the small evangelical community of Brusio, in Val Poschiavo, in the Italian-speaking canton of Grisons, Switzerland.

On 20 January 1770, the local notary wrote a report on the death of Malgaritta Galezia, who, 'having taken poison to intoxicate herself [. . .] took her own life'. A few hours before dying, the woman had been visited by the pastor of the community who described the episode as follows:

I found her in great pain, but still conscious and talkative [. . .] I asked the woman if it was true that she had used a remedy of this kind and had given in to such horrible excess, which is prohibited by nature, and by human and divine law? She answered that, unfortunately, it was true; I asked whether she was persuaded and convinced that she was guilty of a terrible transgression and horrendous sin? She answered: Unfortunately, I am persuaded and convinced of my horrendous sin and if it had not happened, I would not do it, but I hope and pray that divine mercy will have pity on me and pardon all my multiple sins.

A year later, Giovanni Galezia, Malgaritta's husband, tried to kill himself with a knife. Before dying, he managed to make a will in which he commended 'his Soul to the Omnipotent God his Creator, praying that His Divine Majesty would pardon all his sins and especially the atrocious sin he had committed against himself'. Giovanni went on to ask also for pardon 'for all our evangelical church of Brusio, and for the scandal caused for the latter'.

In both cases the relatives of the dead asked the church assembly ('the men who voted in our Sacred Temple') to authorize the Christian burial of the bodies. To this end they paid the sum of 55 lire by way of compensation, while Giovanni left 200 lire to the church in his will. After 'various reflections and considerations, and diverse opinions', the assembly accepted the requests but subject to conditions. With regard to Malgaritta's body, it was decided that 'it would be laid to rest in an isolated corner of the cemetery, above the church, in the new cemetery', and 'the church's funeral pall would not be laid over the box, which would be carried into the cemetery through the upper gateway', without further ceremony. In Giovanni's case, the assembly decided that the burial would be held 'at the northern end of the cemetery, in the evening at dusk, without bells or funeral pall, nor the usual followers'.[139]

1.7   On the formation of Christian ethics regarding voluntary death

In order to understand how the cultural universe described in the previous sections came about, with all its norms and interpretative schemas, those symbols and rites that were used to justify the choices taken by ordinary men and women, we need to take a step back in time.

In ancient Rome, voluntary death had a completely different significance and value. All free men[140] had the right (provided they did not do so through hanging) to take their own life for a variety of reasons:[141] illness, physical pain, fear, the desire for revenge, loss of a dear one, *furor*, namely a fit of rage, *insania* or inability to control their actions, or the experience of rape or military defeat.[142] However, suicide was not just tolerated. Among the intellectual elite, with its vogue for stoicism, it was regarded as the highest expression of liberty, the only form that allowed humans to be equal to and even to exceed the gods, who were destined to be immortal.[143] This explains why the act of suicide was public, almost theatrical, and it was carried out calmly, without betraying anger, desperation or fear in front of numerous witnesses.[144]

During the Roman Empire, this cultural climate started to change. Some neoplatonic philosophers, like Porphyrus or Macrobius, condemned suicide on moral grounds, because – as the latter wrote – 'the man who violently expels [his soul] from his body does not permit it to be free. Anyone who, weary of indigence, or because of fear or hatred – all these are considered passions – takes his life into his own hands, defiles his soul by the very act of forcibly expelling it, even if it was free from these taints before.'[145]

An important change also occurred in law. During the republican period, some Romans, having been accused of a crime punishable by death and the confiscation of their property, had killed themselves before the sentence in order to avoid this second sanction (based on the legal principle that 'crime is extinguished by death'), thereby defrauding the state. In Imperial Rome (presumably between the first and second century CE), a law was emanated to prevent this detriment to the fisc by confiscating the property of anyone who committed suicide while standing trial for a crime that carried the death penalty.[146]

The break with the cultural universe of Rome, however, began in fifth century CE, when Augustine laid the foundations of the Christian ethics on suicide.[147] Before then, the church fathers had rarely made any pronunciations on the subject or, if they had, they had done so with hesitation and ambiguity. While their judgement on infanticide and abortion had been clear and unequivocal, that on voluntary death, albeit negative, as a whole, allowed numerous important exceptions.[148]

Augustine was forced to arrive at a clear, articulate position because of the need to respond to two pressing issues of his time: the twin problems of martyrs and virgins. In previous centuries, some Christians had escaped pagan persecution by killing themselves. But in the fourth century, after Constantine's conversion to Christianity, the church's position was radically altered and the faithful were no longer oppressed. It was at exactly this moment, however, that a schismatic movement, known as Donatism, developed within Christianity. In the name of purity and martyrdom, the Donatists affirmed the legitimacy of individual and collective suicides. At the same time, after two failed attempts, the Visigoths overran Rome in 410, sacking houses and raping women, many of whom took their own lives through shame and dishonour.

In commenting on these events, Augustine strongly condemned the suicides of both the Donatists and the women who had been violated. But he also formulated a more general proposition in which he defined voluntary death as 'a detestable crime and a damnable wickedness'. His assertion was based on the fifth commandment ('Thou shalt not kill') and he argued that this prohibition not only referred to others, but also to the person on whom the command is laid. He supports this interpretation by citing the fact that when a commandment referred solely to relations with others,

God had explicitly indicated this ('Thou shalt not bear false witness against thy neighbour').[149] Therefore, suicide was no different from homicide. Both were extremely grave sins against God's Holy Law.[150] 'How shall that man be judged innocent', Augustine questioned, 'to whom is said, "You shall love your neighbour as yourself", if he commit murder upon himself which he is forbidden to commit upon his neighbour?'[151]

As a matter of principal, taking one's own life was not allowed on whatever occasion and for whatever reason. In concluding a series of remarks and arguments, Augustine made the following, firm, solemn and irrefutable statement:

> But this we say; this we assert; this we in all ways approve: that no man ought voluntarily to inflict death upon himself, for this is to flee from temporal ills by falling into eternal ones. No one ought to do this because of the sins of another, lest, by doing so, he who would not have been defiled by another's sin incur the gravest guilt of his own. Again, no one ought to do so because of his own past sins, for he has all the more need of this life so that these sins may be healed by repentance. Finally, no one ought to do so out of desire for the better life which is hoped for after death, for that better life which comes after death does not receive those who are guilty of their own death.[152]

Yet, even Augustine had to admit, with some embarrassment, that Christian ethics allowed exceptions. In the first place, those 'holy women' (like the young women, Berenice and Prosdoce), who threw themselves into a river to preserve their chastity and who continued to be venerated as martyrs by the Catholic church. 'Of these women I do not venture any casual judgement', Augustine wrote, well knowing that his position was very different from the official line held by the Church. No less discomfiting was the case of Samson, the Israelite hero whose great deeds are told in the Old Testament. The most extraordinary of these took the form of a private vendetta, provoked by his erotic involvement with a woman and resulting in him killing a large number of his enemies. Having fallen in love with Delilah, the third Philistine woman with whom he had an affair, he was betrayed by her and seized by the Philistines, who shaved and blinded him. Samson was forced to perform feats of strength before three thousand of them who crowded into a temple and onto its roof. Samson braced his hands against the two columns supporting the temple and pushed them down, with the words: 'Let me die with the Philistines!' It was an aggressive suicide (suicide used as a weapon), committed in a desperate situation with the aim of killing the greatest possible number of enemies ('So the dead that he killed at his death were more than he had killed in his life'),[153] not unlike the actions of modern suicide bombers (as we will see in Chapter 7). Samson's actions were therefore even more extreme than those of the Donatists and further from the principles asserted by Augustine. Yet, Augustine had no choice but to describe the behaviour of Samson and the 'holy women' as exceptions, justified by the 'divine command' which they had certainly received. 'For when God gives a command and shows without any ambiguity that it is His command, who will call obedience a crime? Who will reproach the submission of godliness?'[154]

Augustine did not stop at outlining a coherent and comprehensive picture of prohibitions. He made a critical re-examination and redefinition of the concepts and beliefs formed since time immemorial, which continued to inspire the thoughts and actions of people in his time. Perhaps those who kill themselves, he observed, 'though not to be praised for the soundness of their wisdom, are nonetheless to be admired for their greatness of soul? If you consider the nature of the case more carefully, you will hardly call it greatness of soul which leads someone to do away with himself because he cannot manage to bear hardships of some kind, or the sins of others.'[155] This was because, in his moral universe, greatness of soul, wisdom, reason, sufferings, honour had now taken on a completely different meaning.

Until then suffering had been regarded as an absurd negation of man, a limit and an obstacle that, above a certain threshold, made life impossible. Instead, Augustine gave meaning to pain, by considering it a means to an end, because it allows man to 'assert himself in his essence, as a creature that suffers for the glory of his creator'.[156] He therefore thought 'we might more properly call a soul great if it can bear a life full of calamity and not flee from it'.[157]

Likewise, when discussing the question of female chastity, Augustine questioned the predominant concept of honour. The pagans had celebrated Lucretia's virtues. Her story had been told by Titus Livius (Livy), Rome's most authoritative historian. Sextus Tarquinius 'drew his sword and made his way to Lucretia's room. She was asleep.' He threatened to kill her if she uttered a word. 'But all in vain; not even the fear of death could bend her will. 'If death will not move you', Sextus cried, 'dishonour shall. I will kill you first, then cut the throat of a slave and lay his naked body by your side. Will they not believe that you have been caught in adultery with a servant – and paid the price?' Then Lucretia yielded and Sextus enjoyed her. After having sent a messenger to her father and to her husband Collatinus, Lucretia told them what had happened. 'What can be well with a woman who has lost her honour? In your bed, Collatinus, is the impress of another man. My body only has been violated. My heart is innocent, and death will be my witness. Give me your solemn promise that the adulterer shall be punished.' 'What is due to *him*', she added, 'is for you to decide. As for me, I am innocent of fault, but I will take my punishment. Never shall provide a precedent for unchaste women to escape what they deserve.' With these words she killed herself with a knife, which she had concealed beneath her robe (Plate 14).[158]

It was not only the pagans but also the early Christians who venerated those women who had taken their own life after being raped or to avoid such dishonour. Before Augustine, some of the Church Fathers, like Eusebius of Cesarea, Ambrose and Jerome, had deemed it lawful for women to commit suicide in order to protect their chastity.[159] In about 320, for example, Eusebius had spoken about the Roman women who, 'dragged away to seduction, surrendered their spirits to death rather than their bodies to dishonour'. He told the story of the 'most wonderful of all', who to avoid rape, asked to be excused for a moment, then 'alone in her room, she impaled herself on a sword and died quickly. Her corpse she left to her procurers, but by deeds more eloquent than any words she announced to all that the only invincible and indestructible possession is a Christian's virtue.'[160]

On the contrary, Augustine rejected the view that rape could make a woman lose her honour and as a result drown her in shame. He maintained that, unlike strength, beauty and health, chastity was not a personal physical attribute, but rather 'a spiritual virtue assisted by fortitude'. Therefore, if a woman was violated, she might lose the integrity of her body, her virginity, but not her chastity. Rape was nothing but a 'shameful lust' committed against the woman not with her. 'When a woman's body is overpowered, but the intention to remain chaste persists nonetheless, and is unaltered by any consent to evil, the crime belongs only to the man who violated her by force.'[161] One saying more than any other captured the essence of rape: 'Marvellous to relate, there were two people, but only one of them committed adultery.' This enabled the deed to be separated from the intention, considering 'not the union of their members, but the separateness of their minds', and contemplating 'an entirely shameful lust on the one side, and an entirely chaste will on the other'.[162] Therefore, if she did not lose her chastity or her honour, a violated woman had done nothing for which she ought to take her own life. If, in spite of this, she did kill herself, she was committing a most grave sin: the crime of self-murder, namely the murder of a chaste and innocent person. Therefore, unlike Lucretia, Christian women, victims of rape and violation, should ensure 'they did not avenge another's crime upon themselves; and it was because they feared adding to the crime of others a crime of their own that they did not do so'.[163]

Likewise, Augustine unreservedly condemned those who took their own lives in order not to fall into the hands of their enemies or because they were persecuted, and he held up the example of the prophets, the patriarchs and the Apostles, who never even took this possibility into consideration. He also recalled that when Christ urged them to escape, in order to save themselves from persecution, he never encouraged them to kill themselves. Given then, 'that He did not command or admonish them to depart this life in such a fashion, even though He had promised that He would prepare eternal mansions for them against departure, it is obvious that, whatever examples are proposed by "the nations that forget God", this is not lawful for those who worship the one true God'.[164]

Augustine's arguments – and his condemnation of voluntary death (almost) without exception – had an enormous influence on the doctrine of the Catholic Church and its official stance. In 452 the Council of Arles did not condemn all suicide (as Durkheim wrongly asserted)[165] but only that of *famuli*, namely slaves and servants who killed themselves 'in prey to a diabolical fury', to the detriment of their masters' interests.[166] In 533 the Council of Orleans, too, only dealt with the voluntary death of those accused of other crimes, ruling that priests should not accept the offerings of the suicide's family for mass and prayers to be said for the dead person. Instead, the councils of Braga (563) and Auxerre (578) were the first at which all forms of suicide were condemned.[167] These principles were mirrored by the civil laws of temporal rulers. The prohibition against funeral rites for those taking their own lives, as iterated by the Council of Auxerre, became enshrined in the *capitularia* of Charlemagne and the Carolingian kings.[168]

At the end of the thirteenth century, canon law was further enriched and articulated by Thomas Aquinas. In his *Summa theologiae*, Aquinas appropriated and set out Augustine's ideas: based on the fifth commandment, he stated that suicide was a sin, a grave sin, one that was even 'more dangerous' than murder since it left no time for expiation. At the same time, taking his cue from Aristotle, Thomas Aquinas outlined three further reasons why suicide should be deemed unlawful. First because it is contrary to charity, according to which every individual ought to love themselves, and to natural law, which promotes self-preservation. Second, since all individuals form part of a society, by killing themselves they wrong society. Here we find Aristotle's thesis which states that anyone who cuts his throat commits an injustice not to himself but to the *polis* to which he belongs, and this is why the polis punishes him with some form of public infamy. Third, because life is a God-given gift and whoever takes their own life sins against him, in the same way that 'anyone who kills a slave sins against its owner'. Man is endowed with free will, and may dispose of himself and is free to choose his own actions, but only in matters pertaining to this world. God alone can decide on the passage from this to another existence.

Similar arguments to those set out above were propounded by all Christian denominations. The Lutherans and Calvinists in central and northern Europe, as well as the Anglicans and Puritans in England all severely condemned suicide, often seconding the arguments put forward by Augustine and Aquinas. Luther also declared his support for the 'strict observance' of those 'political ceremonies' used to remove a suicide's corpse from a house.[169] Orthodox Christians in Russia, from the fourth century on, followed the eighteen canons of Timothy I of Alexandria (which were officially ratified by the sixth ecumenical council in 691), one of which stated that, unless the suicide had been 'out of his mind', the priest ought not to accept offerings for prayers made by his next-of-kin. This rule was reaffirmed many times over the course of the centuries and in 1417 the head of the Christian Orthodox Church issued a general pronouncement to the clergy stating that the corpse of a suicide must not be buried in consecrated ground nor must priests officiate in any way or pray for his soul.[170]

1.8   Chastity, rape and adultery

Many centuries would pass before Augustine's more innovative ideas fully gained support among the Christian population, creating a new culture, a new set of norms and interpretative models, shared symbols and rites. His ideas on virgins and rape probably faced greater opposition than the others. By criticizing not only pagan customs but also the accepted views of authoritative Church Fathers, Augustine started two major conceptual revolutions. In the first place he questioned afresh the dominant view of sexual relations between a married woman and a man who was not her husband. In ancient Rome no distinction was made between adultery and rape because the event was thought to have a contaminating effect on a married woman, irrespective of whether the act was consensual or the result of assault.[171] Instead Augustine drew a distinction using the simple and highly effective phrase already cited earlier: 'Marvellous to relate, there were two people, but only one of them committed adultery.' Secondly, he countered the ethics of shame with the ethics of blame. Lucretia had killed herself not because she felt guilty but to avoid the shame, because she knew that others would see her rape as a form of adultery that had sullied and dishonoured her. Instead, Augustine was convinced that what mattered most was not the act but the intention, the 'entirely chaste will' of the woman who had been raped, her conscience.

No one better perhaps than the Catholic theologian Jean-François Senault has understood and described this contrast:

> This Roman Lady, and consequently haughty, was more carefull of preserving her glory, than her Innocencie, she feared least she might be thought guilty of some fault, if she should out-live the out-rage that was done her; and thought she might be judged to be confederate with Tarquin, should she not take vengeance on herself: Christian Women, who have had the like misfortune, have not imitated her despaire, they have not punisht the faults of others in themselves; nor committed Homicide, to revenge a Rape: The witnesse of their Conscience, was the glory of the Chastity; and it sufficed them that God who is the searcher of hearts, knew their Intentions.[172]

In practice, even long after Augustine's change of heart some Christian women did take their own lives after rape or in order to avoid it.[173] Of course, no statistics exist on the subject and we do not know when their number began to diminish. However, it is clear that for centuries many leading Christian spokesmen did not take up the proposals advanced by the Bishop of Hippo. Even at the end of the seventh century, Aldhelm,

Abbot of Malmesbury and Bishop of Sherborne, in a treatise in praise of 'pure', 'intact', 'incorrupt', 'inviolable', 'uncontaminated' virgins, when discussing the question of sexual violence refers to Eusebius rather than Augustine and affirms that suicide was the best way that a woman had to defend her own chastity.[174] The situation did not change for many centuries if it is true that, until the mid twelfth century, canon lawyers took a very lenient view of Lucretia and did not disapprove of her on moral grounds for having taken her own life.[175] The first medieval canonist who took up Augustine's ideas was Huguccio of Pisa. In an authoritative tract written in about 1190, he severely condemned the suicide of the Roman woman: 'In doing so she did wrong and sinned mortally [. . .]. No one may lay hands on themselves, in whatever circumstances and for whatever reason.'[176] Furthermore, unlike Augustine, he asserted that Lucretia was also guilty of adultery: 'Note that although St Augustine speaks of Lucretia as if she had been forced by "absolute coercion" and – as a consequence – not sinned, according to the true story she was not forced "absolutely", but "conditionally". Whence I say that she sinned mortally in this intercourse and committed adultery.'[177]

The canonists discussed at length whether the Roman woman had been subjected to absolute or conditional violence or whether, as others maintained, her case was an example of 'direct' or 'indirect will', but, after Huguccio, all agreed in condemning her suicide.[178]

1.9   Arabs, Christians and martyrs

Social and political conditions were certainly more congenial to the acceptance of Augustine's ideas on martyrs rather than those on virgins, not only because the persecutions ended while rapes certainly did not, but also because Theodosius I made Christianity the official religion of the Roman Empire (in the edict of 380 CE). Yet four and half centuries after Augustine's statements, other Christians took their own lives in testimony to their faith. It happened in Cordoba, between 850 and 859 CE.

In 711 the Arab-Berber army had crossed the Straits of Gibraltar and within a few years it had conquered much of the Iberian Peninsula and created the al-Andalus Emirate (whose capital was initially at Seville and then Cordoba) based on the teachings of the Koran. The defeated Christian population found themselves subject to a people whose language, religion and culture were very different from their own. Yet the victors allowed them to continue praying in their churches. Over time, some Christians converted to Islam, others began to talk Arabic instead of Latin, to form part of the Islamic army, to work in administrative positions in the Emirate, to circumcize their sons and, if they could afford it, to keep a harem. They became mozarabs, persons who, to use the definition proposed by al-Azharī, a tenth-century lexicographer, were 'not of pure Arabian descent, who have introduced themselves among the Arabs, and speak their language, and imitate their manner of appearance'.[179] Other Christians, in order to protect their own faith from the harmful influence of Islam, withdrew from economic life, inspired by monastic and ascetic ideals[180] and severely criticized those who had forgotten the Holy Scriptures, no longer used the Latin tongue, and had set aside their traditional clothing.[181] This was the group from which the new martyrs emerged.

It all started on one day in the year 850 when Perfectus, a priest of the Basilica of St Aciscius, was accosted by a group of Muslims on his way to the market. He was asked to explain his religion and in particular what he thought of Jesus and Muhammad. Well aware of the danger of his position, he only vouchsafed his opinion after his questioners swore not to harm him. Then speaking in perfect Arabic, the priest denounced the false prophets 'who come to you in sheep's clothing, but inwardly are ravenous wolves' (taking the words from the book of Matthew), and added that Muhammad was the worst of all of these false prophets because he was an emissary of the devil and had sown a diabolical doctrine in the hearts of his followers. On this occasion the Muslims kept their word and let Perfectus go. However, a few days later, on meeting him again, some of the men brought him before a judge who, having heard him repeat the same insults against Muhammad, condemned him to death for blasphemy.

A year and a half later another Christian, called Isaac, deliberately sought out martyrdom. Born into a wealthy, noble Cordoban family, Isaac was fully bilingual, was well versed in Islamic literature and held a high-ranking position in the city government. However, he suddenly gave this all up and retired into the mountains, to the monastery at Tabanos where he lived for three years studying Christian theology. At the end of this period he returned to Cordoba with a precise aim in mind. Having reached the amir's palace, where he used to work, he went to visit the judge and asked him to explain some principles of Islamic doctrine. When the latter started to reply, Isaac brusquely interrupted him, speaking in Arabic and accusing him of lying. He proceeded to vilify Muhammad by saying he was a disciple of the devil. He then invited the judge to convert to the Christian faith. The judge lost his temper and accused Isaac of being drunk, which the latter denied, citing the well-known passage from the Beatitudes: 'Blessed are those that are persecuted for the sake of righteousness, for theirs is the kingdom of heaven.' Isaac was promptly arrested and condemned to death for blasphemy in public.[182]

Four days later, Isaac's example was followed by a further six monks (one of whom was his uncle, Jeremiah, and two were close friends of Perfectus) who also insulted the Prophet and swore against Islam before a judge. They too were sentenced to death. Similar cases were repeated in the months and years that followed. The most clamorous case was that of the monk Rogelius and the Syrian pilgrim Servus Dei who entered the Cordoban mosque and started to preach to the worshippers present that truth could only be found in the gospel, whereas Islam was nothing but falsehoods. Saved by the authorities from being lynched by the irate crowd, they were sentenced to particularly severe punishments for having desecrated a place of worship.[183] Eulogius, the most authoritative of all the martyrs and author of *Martyriale Sanctorum*, an account of all the Christian martyrs who preceded him, died in the same way, and for the same reasons, on 11 March 859. This brought the total number of martyrs to forty-nine in just nine years. For all that we know, there may well have been others in the decades that followed. However, the number of cases of intentional martyrdom gradually diminished.[184]

The Christians who lived in the emirate of al-Andalus enjoyed freedom of worship and were not persecuted for their religion by the Muslims. However, they knew that to insult and offend Muhammad was strictly forbidden. Therefore, the death they deliberately sought was a form of 'indirect suicide'.[185] What was it that prompted them to make such public, vituperative declarations against Islam? Historians have tried on numerous occasions to find an answer to this question. Some have attributed this deliberate search for martyrdom to an extreme attempt to defend their own religious and cultural in an environment where, through conversions, mixed marriages and the formation of intermediate groups (the *mozarabs*), the boundaries between the Christian and Islam populations were becoming increasingly shifting and uncertain.[186] Others have instead explained the indirect suicide of some Christians using psychological categories, namely depression and the desire for death.[187] It is hard to say whether these interpretations are sufficient. One thing is certain, however, that Augustine's condemnation, four and half centuries earlier, of those who intentionally sought martyrdom had not yet become a shared heritage of the Christians of al-Andalus.

1.10   Christian beliefs regarding the causes of suicide

As well as an ethics, Christianity also elaborated a system of beliefs concerning the causes of voluntary death. This started to take shape in the fourth century among some of the church fathers, Anchorite monks who lived in alone in the desert, dedicated to their work, to meditation on the Scriptures, to prayer and ascetic practices. These beliefs developed and spread across Europe in the centuries that followed.

Not unlike the Greek and Roman intellectuals who preceded them (from Aristotle to the Epicureans or Stoics), the church fathers gave great importance to the emotions, which they saw as being responsible for most human actions. However, they examined them in a completely different light, and from the outset regarded them as sins.[188] The foundations of this system of beliefs were laid by the monk Evagrius Ponticus, who lived from 383 onwards in the Nitrian desert, close to Alexandria. He maintained that there were eight 'evil thoughts' that troubled the human mind and would, if not dispelled, become sins: gluttony, lust, avarice, sadness, anger, sloth, vainglory and pride. These thoughts were inspired, insinuated and suggested by demons, who crowded the air and inhabited the celestial atmosphere. In order to succeed, these demons resorted to various tricks and stratagems. By listening to men's words and observing their actions, they could guage the tenor of their thoughts and whether it was appropriate to tempt them. If the demons were unable to overcome a man's resistance, they would withdraw in order to try to understand what virtue was being neglected at that moment. Then they would unexpectedly renew their attack through that weakness and tear the 'unhappy soul' to pieces. Sometimes these demons would enlist the help of other demons who were even more impure. To undermine the resistance of the sick, they would maliciously exhort them to practise abstinence and to recite the psalms while standing.[189]

Another monk, John Cassian (Cassianus), who lived in the Egyptian desert from 385 to 399, moving from one hermitage to another, adopted this list of eight 'capital vices'. A century later, Gregory the Great changed this list, removing sadness (which was combined with sloth) and vainglory, and adding envy. Since then there have always been seven deadly sins, like the seven days of the week, the seven sacraments and the seven works of mercy, and lastly the seven requests in the Pater Noster, and they have played an enormously important role in European culture and everyday life. Stemming originally from monastic life and from the monks' needs, these seven sins, the septenary, soon affirmed themselves as a moral code and belief system for the entire Christian community and for more than one thousand years this was presented, defined and discussed in theological treatises, in confession manuals and in sermons, providing the faithful with a model of behaviour to follow and formulae that could be used to explain human thoughts and actions.

Being capital and therefore fundamental, the seven vices were intimately linked to one another; one sin often gave rise to another or produced a multitude of secondary vices, in an unbroken concatenation.[190] Pride was at the root of all the sins, since it fostered vainglory which in turn gave rise to envy. From this stemmed envy, which produced sadness and avarice, which in turn engendered gluttony and then lust. In the war waged every day against the human soul, these ruthless enemies headed an army of lieutenants and soldiers. Accompanying them was their queen, pride, ready to occupy the hearts of men and women and to consign them to other vices; here was vainglory accompanied by vanity, arrogance, insolence; here was envy followed by hate, slander, detraction, defamation, pleasure in the misfortune of others, ingratitude; here was anger, which ushered in indignation, haughtiness, violence; here was sloth and sadness, ahead of indolence, bitterness, anxiety, rancour, desperation; and lastly here was avarice, with gluttony and lust, each bringing their own retinue of vices.

Suicide was explained by attributing it to three of these negative emotions: anger, sloth and sadness.[191] Unlike gluttony, lust and avarice, which were physical vices, these spiritual vices originated from social relations.

According to Evagrius, anger might stem from injustice or from an injury received, from an undeserved calumny, an unjustified reproach or unfulfilled wishes which 'provide fuel for anger'.[192] Like the 'wine of dragons', it makes one irrational, turning a man into a serpent or into a wild sow.[193] To quote St John Cassian: 'For any reason whatsoever the movement of wrath may boil over and blind the eyes of the heart, obstructing the vision with the deadly beam of a more vehement illness and not allowing the sun of righteousness to be seen. It is irrelevant whether a layer of gold or one of lead or of some other metal is placed over the eyes; the preciousness of the metal does not change the fact of blindness.'[194]

Anyone blinded by fury or who cannot clearly distinguish good from evil may turn his aggression on others and kill, or may even take vengeance on himself and take his own life. In the fifth century, the Christian poet Prudentius, in his poem *Psychomachia*, showed Wrath attacking Patience and, being unable to overcome her, killing himself with his own hands. From the ninth century or earlier, this image can be found in countless illuminated manuscripts, frescoes, stained glass windows and in sculpture. Both vice and virtue are usually personified as two women, one brandishing a sword in her right hand and holding a shield in her left, while the other, unarmed, raises both hands as a sign of peace. The sword splinters, and the splinters are transformed into arrows. Wrath grasps one of her own arrows and pierces herself in the chest. Patience says: 'Fury is its own enemy and destroys itself.'[195] In these representations, Fury's example is sometimes followed by other vices, and Pride, Lust and Avarice take their own lives, one after the other.[196]

The term *akēdia* literally means not caring, but it also was used to signify indolence in doing good, indulgence, negligence and other forms of spiritual listlessness. It was to this vice that monks attributed the repetition of sensations and reactions, which they had frequently observed in day-to-day life. Often, between the fourth and the eighth hours (namely between ten o'clock in the morning and two o'clock in the afternoon), when the sun was high in the sky and the heat unbearable, the hermits were overcome by this disagreeable feeling of listlessness. They felt that time had slowed to a standstill, and they became increasingly indolent and restless; they constantly went to the window to look out, wanting to leave their cells, and pacing to and fro to see if anyone were approaching. They scorned their fellow brothers and bore an indescribable hatred for the place and their lives there. According to St John Chrysostom, these restless monks were overcome by sloth, like 'clouds without water vapour, carried along by winds'.[197]

Occasionally, the situation deteriorated and the monk fell into a state of atony, anxiety, disgust, discouragement and deep depression: he fretted and behaved 'like a child, with impassioned tears and shaking', wrote Evagrius Ponticus.[198] St John Chrysostom added that this was a condition of athymia, despondency, debasement, dejection, which might even include horrific manifestations: 'wringing of the hands, squinting of the eyes, foaming at the mouth, strange inarticulate cries, shiverings, and frightful visions'.[199] Finally, if this demoralized state continued, the monk, in a desperate attempt to escape his sense of inner vacuum, was driven to 'delirious folly and forgetfulness of his original, human state',[200] or in other words he would try to kill himself. The church fathers were in no doubt as to why this happened: the monk was prey to a particular emotion, the 'noonday demon', sloth.

Lastly, there was sadness, which – as Cassian observed – renders the soul useless, having been 'eaten away and devoured'; it prevents us living in peace with others, it makes us impatient and 'strange in all divine offices' and 'ultimately it makes us appear mad, inebriated and desperate in every way'.[201] However, as St Paul the Apostle had already said,[202] there are two quite different forms of sadness. The first, a 'godly grief', works repentance unto a lasting salvation. It is 'obedient, courteous, humble, mild, gracious, and patient'.[203] Christians, Paul had recommended, should take care not to be too severe on a sinner who found himself in this state: 'For such a one this punishment by the majority is enough; so you should rather turn to forgive and comfort him, or he may be overwhelmed by excessive sorrow.'[204] The second form of sadness, 'worldly grief', 'produces death'. 'Sadness is the maw of a lion and readily devours one afflicted by it', said Evagrius Ponticus. 'Sadness is a worm in the heart, and consumes the mother who gives it birth. A mother experiences pain in giving birth to a child; when she gives birth, she is freed from the pain. But when sadness is begotten, it provokes much toil, and since it stays on even after the birth pains, it causes not a little suffering.'[205] It is often provoked by the impossibility of fulfilling selfish needs and is preceded by a feeling of disappointment and emptiness. But in some cases it is subtly instigated by the devil and is so profound that 'we are unable to welcome with our usual courtesy the arrival even of those who are dear to us and our kinfolk'.[206]

In some ways sadness and sloth are different. The former may sometimes be positive, while the latter is always negative. The first often stems from an unfulfilled wish, whereas the second is generated by both hate and desire, and anyone who suffers from it 'detests the things that are present and desires those that are not'.[207] However, they have sometimes been used as synonyms and are often regarded as being closely related.[208] They have always had a shared offspring: despair. It is only by provoking this strong emotion and generating this vice, that sadness and sloth can goad a person in to taking his own life.

This was the link in the long and complex chain of primary and secondary vices that above all attracted the attention of the church fathers when they sought to explain suicide. However, it would be wrong to think that the categories of interpretation used in the Middle Ages to explain voluntary death were similar to those used today. The term despair had two profoundly different meanings. The first is the one used today: a failure of hope in doing, achieving or accomplishing something, a failure to resolve problems or to find a way out. In this sense, desperation is felt by an unemployed person who cannot find work, a mother as she watches her child die, a patient who is terminally ill. The other meaning of despair, which is now quite rare, meant that it was the opposite not of hope but of faith. In this sense, as Augustine observed, it was not only about things future, but also things past and present.[209] According to this definition, despair stemmed from the conviction of not being able to dispose of God's grace and mercy, of no longer obtaining his forgiveness for sins committed and his help in solving serious and overwhelming problems.[210] While despair was only a state of mind in the first definition, in the second it was a deeply negative emotion, a grave sin, into which one fell when one failed to resist the devil's temptations (Plate 8). It presupposed, to use Augustine's words: *desperatio Deo est contumeliosa*, an underlying mistrust in God's ability to absolve sins through his mercy. Therefore, in English, French and other languages, despair, *désespoir, desesperación, desesperance* were used as euphemisms of suicide.[211]

The septenary, the system of beliefs that slowly spread through Christian Europe after the fourth century and that remained in place for over one thousand years, did not offer psychological explanations. Yet it did not stop at attributing an individual's voluntary death to a series of emotions and events, namely to despair, depression, sadness, sloth, anger, unfulfilled desires, the inopportune meetings or misfortunes. At every stage of reasoning, at every link of the chain of explanations, it introduced supernatural factors. These were the demons that prompted Evagrius' eight evil thoughts. It was the Devil that caused sadness. It was Satan, condemned to despair for eternity, who filled humans with desperation by distancing them from divine grace.

The emblematic figure in this triumph of the forces of evil has always been Judas. In the fifth century, Augustine had affirmed that, by hanging himself with a rope, Judas 'increased rather than expiated the guilt of that accursed betrayal. For though he was penitent at death, he left himself no room for wholesome penitence when he despaired of the mercy of God.'[212] In the following centuries, the figure of *Judas desperatus*, depicted with the noose around his neck (Plate 6), was always regarded as the sinner par excellence, not merely because he had betrayed Christ, but rather because he had lost his faith in God and, doubting his forgiveness, took his own life. This was the opposite of Mary Magdalen, a woman who had been a great sinner but had repented and had had faith.[213]

According to the church's teaching, a Christian should never succumb to despair, nor doubt Christ's power and mercy. Primarily, he should continue to hope for a miracle, or for a saint or the Virgin Mary to intervene, enabling him to escape from the situation in which he found himself. In the second place, he could resort to a variety of resources to protect himself. For example, to guard against demonic possession he could resort to the rite of exorcism, based on the sign of the Cross and the use of holy water, through which the priest ordered Satan to depart. But to save himself from despair and suicide the simplest and most powerful means was confession, the sacrament that the Fourth Lateran Council (11–30 November 1215) made obligatory at least once a year. By going to a priest, rehearsing one's sins and doing penitence, the believer would receive absolution and imme- diate reconciliation with God.

This system of beliefs remained dominant and unchallenged in Europe for over a millennium. We find it constantly evoked in the weighty volumes written by theologians. For example, in his *Dialogus miracolurum*, dating from the early thirteenth century, the monk Cesarius of Heisterbach told of many episodes of suicide because of despair. An elderly nun, known for being devout and charitable, was suddenly overcome by a profound sense of sadness and started to lose her faith, becoming irreverent, even blasphemous, and refusing the sacraments. Fearing that after death her body might not be buried in consecrated ground, she tried to take her life by throwing herself into the Moselle. Similarly, a lay brother from a monastic community, who was highly esteemed for his moral rigour and religiosity, had an attack of profound melancholia. Unlike the nun, he did not become disrespectful and blasphemous. Instead, he lost all hope in his own salvation because he thought God would be unable to pardon him because he had committed many grave sins. He therefore jumped into a water reservoir and drowned.[214]

The same belief system can also be found in the iconography. From the fifth to the fourteenth century, the death of Judas was one of the most frequent themes to appear in Christian art.[215] Yet rather than the figure of Judas as the betrayer of Christ, it is Judas the suicide who appears in the sculptures, the miniatures, the carved wooden panels and the frescoes. An ivory panel, dating from the year 420, shows Judas hanging from a rope attached to a branch, which curves under his weight, with his eyes shut and his arms immobile. Beside him, in higher relief, is the crucified Christ, who symbolizes the good death, contrary to that of the suicide. From the scene that appears here, Christ is flanked by St John and the Virgin, but all those present turn their back on Judas.[216] With minor changes, this model was reiterated countless times, throughout the Middle Ages.

In the eyes of the faithful another model, which was adopted by numer- ous artists, must have appeared even more threatening and convincing. In the fresco painted in 1492 by the Piedmontese artist, Giovanni Canavesio, for the sanctuary of Notre-Dame-des-Fontaines at La Brigue (Plate 9)[217] (and also in a stained glass window by an anonymous artist from Alsace, Plate 10), the figure of Judas hangs from a tree by a large, twisted rope, but his tunic is open and a gaping slash runs from his chest to his abdomen. In Canavesio's fresco, the stomach, parts of the smaller intestine and the two lobes of the liver are revealed, as well as a small, naked creature with male genitals, who looks very similar to Judas himself. This creature is being torn out of the hanged man's entrails by a horrendous beast, standing at his left, which is covered in coarse, black hair and has a long tail, bat's wings, two long, twisting horns, and fierce, rapacious eyes. Clearly, this foul, imaginary animal represents the devil who has taken possession of the hanged man's soul, which could only pass through his burst abdomen given that his mouth had been sanctified by kissing Christ in the garden of Gethsemane.[218]

This belief system also found other forms of iconographical expression. On the façade of Notre-Dame, Paris, despair is shown as a figure stabbing himself below the personification of hope. In the Scrovegni Chapel, Padua, Giotto painted a woman who had hanged herself because she could not resist the devil's temptations (Plate 7). But numerous similar images can be found, throughout Europe, in illuminated manuscripts, as well as in the doorways, stained glass windows and candelabras in churches or public buildings.[219]

The various Protestant denominations that emerged after the Reformation also reaffirmed this same belief system, with even greater conviction. Luther attributed great importance to despair and even claimed that suicide was nothing less than homicide committed by Satan himself.[220] Calvin was convinced that voluntary death was provoked by 'demonic possession' and that only Satan was capable of suppressing an individual's instinct for self-preservation. Similar ideas were voiced in England, by both Anglicans and Puritans. 'Satan', wrote the Puritan minister, Richard Gilpin, 'seeks the ruin of our Bodies, as well as of our Souls, and tempts Men often to self-murther.'[221] In 1618, Thomas Beard affirmed that the most convincing proof of the devil's intervention and presence was provided by the circumstances in which suicide sometimes occurred. Otherwise, what could explain the fact that many succeeded in taking their own lives in situations in which it was very difficult to perish? Among other cases, he cites, those who 'have beene hanged with their knees almost touching the ground; others upon a weake twigge, not strong enough to beare the weight of one tenth part of their bodie; others [have] beene drowned in a puddle of water'.[222] In 1637, John Sym, a militant puritan born and raised in Scotland, wrote the first treatise wholly dedicated to this subject, in which he stated that, behind every suicide are 'the strong impulse, powerfull motions, and command of the Devill'.[223]

However, we owe the most telling literary expression of this system of beliefs to another devout protestant, the English poet Edmund Spenser.

1.11 Despair and the Redcrosse Knight

In his great unfinished poem of 1590, *The Faerie Queene*, Spenser specifically describes attempted suicide by attributing it to a powerful allegorical figure, justly named Despaire. Preceded by a description of the terrible effects provoked in those he meets (as in the case of Trevisan, a terrorized young knight, who flees, galloping away 'halfe dead with dying feare'), Despaire, the direct emanation of Satan, simultaneously presents the repellent and persuasive traits of the great deceiver. Before Despaire even appears, we are told of the power of his words and the fascination he exerts on anyone who listens: his language is an instrument 'That like would not for all this worldes wealth: His subtile tong, like dropping honny, mealt'th Into the heart, and searcheth every vaine', robbing all strength and capacity to resist.[224]

Whoever listens to Despaire is lost, not unlike those who were seduced by other great mythical figures of temptation, like the Serpent and the sirens. Trevisan's friend, suffering from unrequited love, promptly killed himself, urged on by the persuasive words of this dangerous character, and having witnessed this event Sir Trevisan flees, having struggled to tear himself away from the insidious fascination of Despaire. Such is Trevisan's incomparable fear that it is only after repeated questioning by the poem's hero (Redcrosse, an evident allegory of holiness) that he agrees to guide Redcrosse close to the enemy's 'cabin', before riding off for good.

The scene that presents itself shortly to the hero's eyes is grim in the extreme: shrouded in eternal night, Despaire's abode evokes images of death, ruin, destruction, like an enormous tautological representation of the forces that pervade the creature who dwells there. His dwelling is a low, dark cave, at the foot of a craggy cliff: it resembles an old tomb, regularly visited by death, rather than a house in our sense of the word, but at the same time it is animated, as if by magic, by a constant, voracious search for other corpses. An owl nests on the walls outside and its baleful cries ward away the cheerful presence of other birds; only the wailing ghosts, who flit about the cave, echo the bird's shrieking call and accentuate the melancholy sound.

From Despaire's abode, as if from the very hub, the deathly atmosphere of filth spreads across the surrounding countryside, turning it into a single manifesto of death: desolate cliffs, gnarled old trees, bare for eternity, whose branches have only borne, hanging like deathly fruit, the bodies of the hanged whose bones, now scattered over fields and rocks, represent an unnatural vegetation, intentionally reminiscent of the similar trophies that surround sirens and reveal their real, deadly effects.

Everything is desolate in this cursed place, yet a feeble thread of life runs underground either fuelling those very destructive mechanisms that dominate the environment or assuming a stagnated existence: in this way the house-cum-tomb of Despaire acquires the ferocious vitality of an eternally voracious being, 'like a greedy grave, That still for carrion carcases doth crave'. Whereas the rocks to which the trees hung with suicides cling have 'ragged rocky knees', as if the limbs of a vast hidden body might start to rise out of the cliffs, animated by a secret, imprisoned life.

The inhabitant, the owner and lord of all this, is a perfect emblem of the place; unlike other tempters who work under false and attractive guise, he appears as the epitome of all the evils within him: he is a horrible old man, with long grey, dishevelled and overgrown locks partially covering an emaciated face, 'through which his hollow eyne Lookt deadly dull'; uncaring and unkempt, he lies half-naked, his sides barely covered by 'many ragged clouts, With thornes together pind and patched'.

Beside this creature, who resembles nothing more than a living corpse, lies the body of the young knight (Trevisan's friend) who had just taken his own life: he has a knife in his chest, and from the wound fresh, lukewarm blood continues to well up in a 'gushing flood' of life-giving liquid. Once again, the creature that is still part of life (the horrible old man) is seen as being already dead; while the individual who is no longer present in life (the young suicide) acquires the mendacious appearance of a body whose functions are still working. Life is disguised as death; death takes on the deceptive appearance of continuing life.

What is it then that attracts those who come across this repulsive being, this monstrous procurer of destruction? Nothing, until he starts to talk, because, as we already knew but had forgotten, overcome by this meeting, his strength, his almost irresistible fascination lies in his persuasive tongue, in the power of his arguments. To the young hero Redcrosse, who in his horror announces his desire to avenge the suicide of the miserable young lover, the tempting rhetorician replies: 'What justice ever other judgement taught, But he should dye, who merites not to live? None els to death this man despayring drive, But his owne guiltie mind deserving death. Is then unjust to each his dew to give? Or let him dye, that loatheth living breath? Or let him die at ease, that liveth here uneath?'

Redcrosse listens with perfect self-control. But after these general questions, Despaire makes a lucid, melancholic and calm speech, expressing the existential need for peace present in every human being, and here his voice suddenly acquires a tone of concise, solemn eloquence, couched in poetic terms. It is difficult to remain unaffected by the fascination of such words:

What if some little payne the passage have,
That makes frayle flesh to feare the bitter wave?
Is not short payne well borne, that bringes long ease,
And layes the soule to sleepe in quiet grave?
Sleepe after toyle, port after stormie seas,
Ease after warre, death after life does greatly please.[225]

However, this marks the start of a dangerous duel of words that raises considerable problems even for the champion of faith: at the start, he easily counters Despaire's arguments with the most classic of arguments against suicide ('The terme of life is limited, Ne may a man prolong, nor shorten it; The souldier may not move from watchfull sted, Nor leave his stand, until his Captaine bed'). But Redcrosse's words become increasingly unsure as he tries to respond to the flow of questions from Despaire: has God not decreed that all forms of life must end with death? Who can escape this absolute imperative? And what is life if not a gradual and unstoppable accumulation of sin? Therefore why not shorten this sinful path whose obligatory end is death? Why not bring an end to pain, illness and misadventure? If as individuals we are responsible for our errors, for which we must pay in person, why not act before the process becomes irreversible, consigning us to eternal damnation? Only death is the end of all evil.

As he listens to Despaire's words, Redcrosse weakens, because he knows them to be true and, subjected by the power of their persuasion, he is unable to see that the truth is only partial; instead, his antagonist, noting how he wavers, drives home the point and is about to win over his last resistance. To the power of words, Despaire adds visual means and suddenly shows Redcrosse a painting of the damned ghosts, eternally in torment. Irremediable human guilt is answered with irremediable and burning divine wrath, which becomes more terrible than the human death, because it is eternal.

Shaking and dismayed, Redcrosse sees before him a destiny of punishment, and he is about to accept the escape proffered by his tempter, who makes a variety of suicide instruments available (sword, ropes, poison, fire); the bewildered hero even accepts 'a dagger sharpe and keene' which Despaire gives him, and which he lifts up to stab into his chest. He is only saved by Una (namely Truth), his companion of adventure: she snatches the cursed knife and reproaches him for his sudden faint-heartedness. How could the tempter's devilish words make him forget that despair has no claim on those protected by heaven? Where there is justice, she says, 'there grows eke greater grace', and no condemnation is final. Returned to his sense, the hero rises and leaves that cursed place.

Despaire is overcome by anger and disappointment at the failure of his plans, which had been about to succeed. His violence turns on himself. He seizes a rope and hangs himself, alone, 'unbid unblest', without a single tear to accompany his final act: but he cannot die. We then learn that this horrible being has already tried to kill himself on countless occasions, but without success. In this grandiose demonstration of divine retaliation, he who lives to instigate the death of others will be destined to relive, in eternity, the same spiral of despair that he induces in others, attempting a thousand times to commit suicide, until divine justice finally breaks this cycle and condemns him to his true end: eternal damnation.

1.12   Pre-Christian beliefs on the consequences of suicide

Throughout the Middle Ages, and in some countries and sections of the population even in early modern Europe, another system of beliefs survived (one that regarded not the causes but the effects of suicide). This had developed before the advent of Christianity, which had nonetheless been incorporated, with some adjustments, or with which it had co-existed without too many clashes. According to these pre-Christian beliefs, voluntary death was not only immoral but first and foremost a pernicious act because of its disastrous consequences for the individual's family, relatives, friends, acquaintances and the entire community in which she or he lived.

Suicide was thought to be contagious, contaminating, a source of misfortune and disgrace. The suicide's corpse, house, fields and flocks, as well as the place and means of death were all regarded as contaminated and it was thought dangerous to touch or enter them. In some areas of Europe, no one would approach the body of a person who had hanged themselves or drowned themselves in a river because of the fear of contagion. In Germany, in the seventeenth century and until the start of the eighteenth century, a suicide's corpse was only handled by special officials employed by the civil authorities (like the executioner or gravedigger), who for this reason were regarded as being impure and untouchable.[226] The custom of throwing a suicide's body into a river, which continued for many years in some parts of Germany and France, can be readily interpreted as a rite of purification.[227] On the other hand, in Scotland, it was believed that if a pregnant woman passed over a suicide's grave, then the newborn would be also destined to take his or her own life.[228] In Russia the corpses of suicides, as well as those of wizards, witches, drunkards, murder victims and those who drowned were categorized as 'dirty' or 'impure dead'. Even the ground was believed not to accept their bodies, an aversion manifested by the fact that their bodies would not rot or rise from their tombs.[229]

The spirit of a suicide was a harbinger of disasters. It was believed that these troubled souls were forced to wander between the world of the living and that of the dead because they had left the former without having been accepted into the latter. For this reason, in some regions of France the sound of water flowing over pebbles was believed to be the groans of those who had drowned themselves since they were condemned for eternity to roll the stones over and over in the riverbed.[230] Thus, by remaining forever or for long periods in this transitional or liminal state, suicides retained a desire to return among the living and came to be regarded as a threat or danger. They were blamed for frosts or periods of drought, hurricanes and floods, earthquakes and landslides, poor harvests and famines.

Local chronicles record that in Augsburg, on 25 April 1300 (the feast of St Mark's), after a poor wretch had hanged himself, there was a violent storm that wreaked terrible damage to inhabitants and their possessions. After that it was decided that every year on St Mark's day, Christians would fast in order to obtain divine protection against suicide. It was also related that in 1342, in Venice, 'the water rose so high that ships were floated on to the land and the bridges were under water'. This was said to have been caused by 'a schoolmaster, who through poverty or despair gave himself, body and soul, to the Enemy, in that he was found to have hanged himself by the throat'. The Doge then ordained a procession and a mass at St Mark's to make amends for the suicide.[231] In France, for many centuries, it was believed that a tempest was a sign that someone had hanged or drowned themselves, and that the devil had come to look for them.[232]

It seems likely that these beliefs also had an empirical foundation, namely that they were confirmed by repeated observations of a coincidence or association between waves of suicides and natural disasters. However, also on account of the prevalent approach to natural death at the time, these observations led to a reversal of cause and effect and therefore the possibility that natural disasters might actually lead to suicide, rather than vice versa, was not taken into account.[233]

Christian and pre-Christian customs stem from these fears and beliefs. The community protected themselves from contamination by mutilating a suicide's corpse and destroying his house, in the ritual known as *ravaire* (or ravage). They defended themselves against the spirit of the person who had taken their life by passing the corpse under the threshold or through a window, at times also changing the bolts, keys, doors and windows to prevent their spirit returning.[234] It was for the same reason that suicides were buried far away from cemeteries, in the forests or at crossroads, with a stake through their bodies. These beliefs were so deeply rooted in popular culture that any subsequent natural calamity was attributed to a failure to confirm or apply one of these customs.

In his masterpiece, Jacob Burckhardt describes how, with reference to another sort of crime, when Piacenza was struck by violent and prolonged rainfall, 'it was said that there would be no dry weather till a certain usurer, who had been lately buried in San Francesco, had ceased to rest in consecrated earth. As the bishop was not obliging enough to have the corpse dug up, the young fellows of the town took it by force, dragged it round the streets amid frightful confusion, and at last threw it into the Po.'[235]

Similar events also occurred for suicides (Plate 4). In Augsburg, in 1593, the city council had given permission for the body of Hans Wagner, a wealthy merchant who threw himself out of a window on Easter Monday, to be buried in consecrated ground. But the advent of a violent storm on the day after his death prompted the city's inhabitants to protest. In 1682, the population of Brackenheim petitioned Duke Friedrich Karol to object to the burial of a suicide inside the churchyard.[236] In Russia, peasants attributed a period of drought to the burial of a suicide using the Christian ritual. If it did not rain for many days, they would then pour water onto the grave, praying that God would send them a few drops. If this method failed, the deceased was exhumed and buried in a wood or some other unconsecrated place, or thrown into a nearby river.[237]

1.13   Suicide as theft and desertion

This system of fears, prohibitions, condemnations and extremely severe penalties was probably fostered by some aspects of feudal society, particularly its strong bonds of personal dependency and the existence of '"men" of other men'.

In *Phaedo*, Plato wrote that 'we human beings are in some sort of prison, and that one ought not to release oneself from it or run away'. He added: 'if one of your belongings were to kill itself, without your signifying that you wanted it to die, wouldn't you be vexed with it, and punish it, if you had any punishment at hand?'[238]

Cicero returned to this thesis (in the first century BCE), but introduced a military metaphor. Citing Pythagorus (and perhaps referring to Epictetus),[239] he asserted that we should 'stand like faithful sentries and not quit our post until god, our Captain, gives the word'.[240] Five hundred years later, Macrobius, one of the greatest pagan neoplatonic philosophers writing in Latin, put forward a similar argument, that:

> the gods are our masters, who govern us with care and forethought, and that it is wrong, moreover, to remove, against their will, any of their possessions from the place in which they have set them. Just as the man who takes the life of another man's slave will be liable to punishment, so he who seeks to end his own life without the consent of his master will gain not freedom but condemnation.[241]

It was these ideas that inspired the norms underlying some societies in which men belonged to other men. For example, in ancient Rome, there was considerable tolerance of suicide in general, provided that it was not committed by persons belonging to two sectors of the population: soldiers and slaves. When soldiers took the oath or *sacramentum* promising to dedicate themselves wholly to the fatherland, their lives became the property of the state and therefore, if they committed suicide, they were charged with robbing the state and deserting the army. This explains why if a soldier attempted suicide he was punished with the death sentence.[242] In the case of slaves, anyone selling a slave who had attempted to commit suicide was obliged to inform the buyer, so that he was aware of the risk he was incurring.[243]

The suicide of subordinates was strongly discouraged in feudal societies, which also had 'men' of other men. A count was the king's man. A vassal was sometimes referred to as the lord's 'man of mouth and hands' because the former's oath of fealty in exchange for the latter's protection was sealed by a ceremony in which the vassal placed his joined hands between the hands of his lord, and the two kissed on the mouth. Lastly, serfs were also the lord's men and were obliged to work for free on his lands for a number of days a week, in exchange for a grant of land and his protection.

In a society of this type, for a man who belonged to another man to kill himself was equivalent to committing a crime of theft from the *dominus*. A serf who committed suicide damaged his lord by stealing his labour; for a vassal, a 'man of mouth and hands', the consequences were worse because as well as depriving the lord of his person, he also broke his oath. It comes as no surprise, therefore, that feudal lords severely punished suicides and their families. As well as having substantial interests to defend, these seigneurs were also ideally placed to mete out punishment since the administration of justice was in their hands and the courts under their strict control. They chaired the courts in person, or delegated the task to a trustworthy person. What was more they also appointed their own family members, relatives, friends and dependants to sit on the jury.

Some scholars have hypothesized that in Europe the severity of punishments imposed on those who committed suicide increased until the tenth century, in parallel to the growing strength of feudal institutions.[244] The existing documentation neither confirms nor denies the truth of this thesis. However, if a serf or a vassal killed themselves, the lord undoubtedly did everything in his power to secure some form of compensation for the damage incurred, without this being regarded as an arbitrary act either by himself or others. Even when the custom of *ravage* existed, namely when the suicide's house was destroyed and his fields burnt, the feudal seigneur still demanded 'one year's fruits from the wrongdoer's property',[245] as is recorded in the *Coutumes d'Anjou et du Maine*. The custom of *ravage* disappeared by the end of the thirteenth century, not because the punishment inflicted on suicides became any less severe, but because the seigneur preferred to confiscate the assets instead of destroying them.[246]

We have already seen that the *Coutumes de Beauvaisis* of 1283 stated that the property of the suicide would be forfeit and 'accrue to the seigneur on whose estate the property is situated'. On the other hand, the *Etablissements de Saint-Louis* of 1270 asserted that 'should it so happen that someone hang himself, or drown himself or die in no other manner than by suicide, his and also his wife's entire movable property shall pass on to the baron'.[247] However, it is worth remembering that in the Middle Ages the concept of property was quite different from our own understanding of the term. A vassal could hold feudal lands, which were assigned to him in usufruct by the seigneur. If he took his own life, then his family lost these properties not because they were confiscated but because the period of concession was automatically terminated. However, a vassal might also own allodial lands, namely lands that were entirely his own and not subject to feudal dues or burdens, and these would be eligible for confiscation in the event of voluntary death.

The concept of suicide as theft to the detriment of a seigneur or master has also been dominant in other societies and during other historical periods. In the seventeenth and eighteenth centuries, Portuguese, Dutch or French merchants who transported African slaves to America, held in chains under the decks, or the colonials who bought them, regarded those who committed suicide as thieves, and they tried to discourage these acts in countless ways. In the mid seventeenth century, in Barbados, after losing three of his strongest slaves, Colonel Walrond took a radical step to pre-empt further economic losses: he planted a three-and-half-metre-high pole in the ground and impaled one of the three heads on it. Other merchants and slave-owners decapitated the corpses of those who committed suicide or burned them. But the choice of such ferocious responses was inspired less by models of punishment used in medieval Europe and more by the beliefs of the slaves themselves. Many of the Africans who were forcibly transported to America believed that by committing suicide they could escape slavery and return to their own country, where they would rejoin their companions and friends, in some happy region, in which they would be provided with plenty of food and beautiful women. They thought they would return home by flying across the ocean, as if they were huge seabirds, fast and strong.[248] This belief was so widespread and deep-rooted that slaves used to lay their own bandannas on the suicide's body so that it would fly with him to the distant motherland and reach the people who were left there.[249] But this return journey was only possible if the suicide's body remained intact. Therefore, by decapitating the corpses of slaves who had killed themselves, Colonel Walrond hoped to convince others not to follow their example.

Starting from this belief and from the saying, common to many African peoples, that 'the king on earth forever remains a king, while the slave shall always remain a slave', other slave-owners resorted to a second stratagem, namely they threatened to commit suicide themselves and follow the slaves to Africa, whip in hand, where they would treat them far more severely than they had until then.[250] On the other hand, in Brazil, and on the islands of Martinique, Guadalupe and Reunion, slaves of African origin sometimes killed themselves as a way of taking revenge, knowing that this would damage their owner economically.[251]

The idea that voluntary death was a theft that damaged a seigneur also appeared during the twentieth century in some non-Western populations. Among the Ewe-speaking people of the Gold Coast, for example, suicide was regarded as a crime and punished with monetary fines, because all people in the land belonged to the king. For the same reason, in the French Cameroons, the village head was obliged to compensate the king if any of his men took their own lives.[252]

In addition to being seen as theft, for many centuries suicide was regarded as a form of desertion from the army. The military metaphor made famous by Cicero was repeated by numerous writers during the Middle Ages. In the twelfth century, for example, John of Salisbury used it as an argument in his condemnation of voluntary death.[253] So did Petrarch in the fourteenth century, when, to the archdeacon of Genoa, he wrote: 'If a soldier remains at his post at the behest of a mortal commander and does not abandon it unless ordered, or if he does so and loses his commander's goodwill, he is at risk of ignominy, prison, beatings and death, what shall we say of a man who scorns a divine order.'[254]

In the case of soldiers, suicide continued to be seen as an act of desertion even after the laws that imposed punishment for this crime were repealed. For example, in order to put a stop to the numerous cases of voluntary death occurring among his forces during the Italian campaign, Napoleon – who is said to have attempted suicide himself on the night of

13 April 1814 – solemnly proclaimed that any soldier showing evidence of this 'shameful weakness' would be 'condemned as ignoble and as a deserter'.[255]

1.14 A 'new crime, that would hardly be believable'

On arriving in Stockholm in 1652, twenty-two-year-old Pierre-Daniel Huet, future bishop of Avranches, Normandy, and tutor to Louis XIV's son, the Grand Dauphin, announced that he had discovered a 'new crime that would hardly be believable'.[256] What convinced him to draw this conclusion was not the fact that a respectable Swedish citizen had stabbed a four-year-old boy, but rather the confession that was made before the court. 'I know very well', stated the accused, 'that there is no surer way to achieve eternal salvation than if the fully conscious soul exits a strong body . . ., and is carried upward to God by the pious prayers of people of faith . . . I realized it would be impossible to die this way unless I committed a capital crime, so I thought it would be easiest . . . if I killed a boy not yet corrupted by this life.'[257] These words may seem obscure today, but Pierre-Daniel Huet immediately understood the motives behind the act of that reputable Swede after hearing that he went to his death 'joyfully, loudly singing sacred hymns'.

A similar case had occurred the year before.[258] Paul Wulff, a German goldsmith who had settled in Stockholm, had killed the infant son of a woman who undertook various domestic services for him. He immediately reported himself to the magistrates, who refused to believe him at first, thus causing him to despair; he had explained to them that 'he did not want to live any longer' and hoped for a rapid death sentence, before which he would repent in full thus redeeming his soul and assuring his eternal salvation.

Born in Nuremberg, the son of a sculptor who abandoned his wife shortly afterwards, Paul had tried to kill himself several times while he was still young. After emigrating to Stockholm and having lived there for some years, working as an artisan, he again decided to shoot himself, but the fear of eternal damnation stopped him just as he was about to pull the trigger. At that point he decided to change strategy and chose a solution that enabled him to save his soul: by killing a child, who thanks to his innocence was untainted by sin and would therefore be welcomed to paradise, Wulff would then have enough time to repent in full before his execution, thereby also assuring himself a place in paradise.

These were not the only cases. In the past few years historians have discovered that, between the early seventeenth century and the end of the eighteenth century, there were many other persons in Germany, England and Austria who acted like Paul Wulff, and for the same reasons.[259] (Plates 11 and 12) All of them have one thing in common. After killing someone or committing some other serious crime, they made no attempt to run away or hide, or to evade justice or, if arrested, deny what they had done; instead, they confessed everything to some civil or religious authority, or to the first person they met on the road, and they asked to be condemned and sentenced to death.

In 1740 in Stockholm, after murdering a neighbour's daughter, a young woman called Christina described how six months earlier she had decided to put an end to her life, but that she had immediately realized that 'if she had died for some misdeed against herself, she would be lost; but if she died for someone else, she, as many others, would be assured of salvation'.[260] In 1746 Johanna Martauschin, a prisoner in Spandau who had killed the son of a fellow inmate, said that 'she had committed murder because she was tired of living; that she had killed the child and not herself because she believed the child would now be saved, whereas as a suicide she would have gone to the devil. But now there was still time for her to convert.'[261] In 1768, in London, Mary Hindes, who drowned a seventeen-month-old infant in a lake in Hyde Park, confessed that 'she was wearied of life, and had had a great many disquietudes with her husband [. . .] which had given her a great deal of anxiety; she concluded with saying, she was desirous of dying, and that led her to do that sort of an act, for which she said she knew she should receive no mercy of the jury.'[262] When the justice of the peace asked Hindes, 'If you was determined to die, why did you not drown yourself?', she answered, 'I know the difference betwixt that and self-murder.'[263]

During the eighteenth century the ballads that were printed and sold on the streets to mark the executions of the most atrocious offenders in Denmark, Sweden and Germany give us an insight into popular opinion. They usually tell the story of individuals who were tormented by the devil until they finally gave in and committed homicide. However, in prison, while waiting to be executed, these same individuals then repented, trusting in divine mercy.[264]

That a new crime had emerged in Europe was clear to the experts in both God's law and worldly law. In 1766 an authoritative German jurist, Karl Ferdinand Hommel, called it 'indirect suicide' and set the blame squarely on religious preaching. 'Persons who are not in the best spirits', he wrote, 'but who fear Hell [. . .] and have often heard from the pulpit that no self-murderer can be saved, then become tired of life and often murder the innocent children of other people or adults. [They] then turn themselves into the authorities as if they had done a righteous Christian deed, with the burning desire to be publicly executed, in order to be more sure of getting to Heaven.'[265] It is true that indirect suicide was a perverse result,[266] an unwanted and unforeseen consequence of Christian morality, which led the faithful to believe that there was no other way out for anyone wanting to end their life but at the same time wanting to be assured of their soul's salvation. All men and women living in Europe at the time were well aware that anyone committing homicide would be entrusted to the care of a priest before being executed and would therefore have time to repent.

Between those who took their own lives and those who resorted to other ways of achieving this aim there were significant differences. Most of the former were men (as we have seen), whereas most of the latter were women.[267] Direct suicides were also less bloody than indirect ones. In the seventeenth and eighteenth centuries, the male population most frequently killed themselves by hanging, the female population by drowning.[268] Anyone, whether male or female, who committed indirect suicide, murdering another in order to receive a death sentence, did so with a weapon, usually a knife with which they cut their victim's throat.[269]

There were, however, other forms of indirect suicide. In order to be sentenced and hanged, some confessed to being guilty of bestialism or zoophilia, namely having had sexual relations with animals. Others claimed to have killed someone and if the judge, in the absence of a corpse, failed to believe them, then they went and did so. For example, in 1696, in Stockholm, Brita Andersdotter pretended to have committed infanticide, but the court did not believe her. Impatient to take leave of the world, the woman then cut a neighbour's son's throat, while thanking God for allowing her to die soon.[270]

The increase in the number of suicides committed through homicide during the seventeenth century, which in Stockholm came close to the number of direct voluntary deaths (Table 1.2), prompted the magistrates and the political authorities to adopt measures to discourage them. In 1668, in the sentence condemning Barbro Persdotter for having killed a three-year-old boy, the city court of Stockholm admitted, with some embarrassment, to having considered the possibility of not imposing the death sentence on her before then discarding it because it was not permitted by the laws of man and God.[271]

Table 1.2 Suicides and indirect suicides (preceded by a homicide) in Stockholm from 1600 to 1719.

	Suicides	Indirect suicides	Rate per 100,000 inhabitants
1600–1609	2	0	2.2–3.2
1610–1619	2	0	2.2–2.5
1620–1627	2	1	2.8–4.7
1636–1649	1	1	0.3–0.8
1650–1659	1	1	0.5–0.6
1660–1669	1	2	0.6–0.9
1670–1679	7	3	1.9–2.4
1680–1689	17	5	4.0–4.4
1690–1700	21	8	4.8–5.3
1701–1709	18	13	5.6–6.3
1710–1719	21	13	7.8–8.6

Note: The estimated rate is based on the sum of suicides and indirect suicides.

Source: Jansson (2004).

In 1702, the government of the imperial city of Nuremberg issued an edict to increase the severity of the penalties inflicted on anyone killing a child or an adult, 'out of an imagined weariness with life and in the Godless opinion, that if only they do [not] rob themselves of life, but instead forfeit life and limb for killing other innocent persons and are executed, then [. . .] after righteous contrition and penitence, Heaven's gate must stand open to them'.[272] On 27 March 1706 an edict was published in Austria to the same purport. Anyone committing this crime would be condemned to death after a period of extreme physical suffering, either by drowning or impaling (two methods that had fallen into disuse for some time).

Many decades would pass before it was realized that harsher punishments would have no effect on those who wished to die at all costs. In the middle of the eighteenth century, the Danish jurist Henrik Stampe affirmed with conviction that capital punishment would not act as a deterrent in cases of homicide committed by would-be suicides. A few years later, Gothif Samuel Steinbart, a German theologian, criticized German pastors who helped such individuals and encouraged them to believe that they would be pardoned through repentance. Instead, he proposed banning these clerics from accompanying offenders to the place of execution.[273] Indeed, between 1767 and 1794, Denmark, Sweden,[274] Schleswig-Holstein[275] and Prussia emanated laws decreeing that 'if someone who is otherwise of sound mind commits a murder . . . with the intent of being executed, he should not achieve his goal'.[276] Instead such offenders would be condemned to harsh and degrading punishments: they were publicly whipped, branded on the forehead, chained and forced to undertake hard and shameful labour all day long; 'once a year on market day such criminals will be led from the penitentiary in a hideous outfit, with uncovered head, flying hair, and with a rope around their necks, with hands bound and their feet in chains, with a board attached to their chest with this inscription: "Murderer of an innocent child." But they would not be put to death.

1.15   Internal and external controls

If the number of suicides in Europe remained quite contained, albeit with some fluctuations, until the closing decades of the seventeenth century, it was principally because men and women were prevented in many different ways from taking their own lives. In the first place by using internal forms of control, namely through the norms and beliefs that they had absorbed.[1] Nothing more than 'indirect suicide' can help us to understand

---

[1]   As Ruys has noted (2014, 230): 'In the Middle Ages, suicide was not necessarily a concept that was unthinkable, but it was one that remained largely unspoken and sometimes – even for the most articulate of writers – ultimately unspeakable.'

the extraordinary influence that Christianity's outright condemnation of voluntary death had on European men and women, together with the threat of eternal damnation for those who, by taking their own lives, could not then repent. But, at a more general level, the culture that had slowly taken shape after Augustine's historic turning point, provided a highly effective and powerful system for the social regulation of emotions. It did so by attributing to some events and situations a different meaning to that given to them by men and women in other cultures, in other parts of the world and at other times.

For example, let us consider rape. The women who shared the Christian ethics that were formed after Augustine certainly continued to feel anger, scorn, hate and resentment against those who assaulted them or attempted to do so, and in some exceptional cases they took their own lives.[277] But compared to other cultures, it was more difficult for them to see rape as a threat to their honour, it was rarer for them to feel shame and guilt, and it was less commonplace for them to kill themselves for this reason (as we shall see in the second part of this book).

The same conclusion is apparent if we consider the social and psycho-logical consequences of military defeats. The warriors of Christian Europe certainly always attributed great importance to courage, honour and glory. But, unlike their distant Roman forebears or their contemporary Chinese, Indian or Japanese counterparts,[278] they rarely took their own lives, or exhorted their soldiers to do so in order to avoid the ignominy of defeat and the humiliation of imprisonment. Miguel de Cervantes wrote the tragedy *The Siege of Numancia* in 1580, in which he remembered how, seventeen centuries earlier, part of the population of this Spanish town preferred to commit suicide rather than surrender to the Romans. But episodes of this kind never happened in Christian Europe, at least until 1945 (as we shall see). For many centuries, there were no cases like those of Gaius Gracchus, Publius Quinctilius Varus or Gaius Vulteius Capito in this part of the world.

On the other hand, the women and men who had interiorized the values and norms of Christianity attributed a different meaning to physical and mental suffering compared to people from other cultures and they prob-ably managed to curb it better. Generally speaking, Christian norms and beliefs blamed suicide on particular emotions, such as anger (Plate 5), sloth, sadness and despair, but they regarded these as sins and therefore forbade believers from succumbing to such sentiments and urged them to make every effort to keep them at bay. The countless images of Judas with a noose around his neck served to frighten the faithful by showing them the consequences of giving rein to such emotions. As the Dominican friar, Giordano da Pisa, said in a sermon in 1305, 'Above all things of this life, the remembrance of the Judgement and of punishment is most useful, for this reason: it seems that sinners will never refrain from evil if not through fear: they almost never keep away from it, if not for fear of punishment.'[279]

These emotions were also partly inhibited by the belief that by giving way to them one might fall under the influence of the devil. This conviction was common not only to theologians and priests. All the documents we have (letters, autobiographies, court proceedings, chronicles and records of events) lead us believe that, during the Middle Ages and often long afterwards, men and women in Europe explained voluntary death using a plurality of categories. They attributed it to economic disaster, dishonour, the death of a loved one, ill fortune in love. In this, too, they thought that there were differences between women and men, and that the former killed themselves as a result of infidelity or their husband's violent abuse, whereas the latter did so for gambling losses or financial ruin. But they were convinced that voluntary death was also due to supernatural causes and they believed that the devil was responsible for urging individuals to kill themselves. Satan was regarded as God's great cosmic antagonist, an omnipresent, irresistible force; moreover, leading a horde of demons and evil spirits, as he could assume a variety of guises in order to tempt and seduce human beings. In England, in the early seventeenth century, at least 139 of the patients being treated by the physician and astrologist Richard Napier said that Satan had tempted them to kill themselves. In the same period, the Puritan Nehemiah Wallington described how the devil had appeared to him eleven times, always in different forms: pretending to be his sister, or a raven, or a church minister, or even a pure, disembodied voice, and on each occasion had exhorted him to take his own life. On the third time, Nehemiah Wallington had been on the verge of succumbing, and had drawn his knife and put it to his throat, ready to cut it. But the thought of God and his goodness had persuaded him to resist and therefore save himself.[280]

Even the French poet, François Villon, that incorrigible pleasure-seeker and madcap, a deviant imprisoned for having committed various offences, confessed that if it had not been for religion, he too would have ended his life. In 1461 he wrote in his *Testament*:

Now he's got to go begging
Necessity obliges it
Day after day he longs to die
Sadness so works on his heart
Often but for the fear of God
He'd commit a horrible act
And it may yet happen he breaks God's law
And does away with himself.[281]

[Or luy convient-il mendier:
Car à ce, force le contrainct.
Requiert huy sa mort, et hyer;
Tristesse son cueur si estrainct,
Souvent, si n'estoit Dieu qu'il crainct,
Il feroit un horrible faict.

Si advient qu'en ce Dieu enfrainct,
Et que luy mesmes se deffaict.]

On the other hand, in 1539 when Benvenuto Cellini was imprisoned in
Castel Sant'Angelo by Pope Paul III, he found the experience so distress-
ing that he tried to kill himself with a 'wooden pole'. But he was 'seized by
an invisible power', he wrote in his autobiography, certainly by the hand
of God, and 'flung four cubits from the spot, in such terror that I lay half
dead'. After falling into a deep slumber, 'a marvellous being in the form
of a most lovely youth' appeared to Cellini in his dreams, and scolded
him fiercely, saying: 'Knowest thou who lent thee that body, which thou
wouldst have spoiled before its time? [. . .] So then hast thou contempt for
His handiwork, through this thy will to spoil it? Commit thyself unto His
guidance, and lose not hope in His great goodness!'[282]

In the second place, the women and men who lived in Europe until the
closing decades of the seventeenth century were restrained and discouraged from taking their own lives by external forms of control. The French
jurist, De Pastoret, was probably right when he wrote in 1790 that, albeit
railing against those surviving rites of profanation and desecration: 'it
remains to be understood whether, in view of the human heart, it is not
established that the fear of this infamy is the strongest reason in favour of
existence. Is not the image of the hangman despoiling his corpse perhaps
enough to stay the sword, pistol or dagger which the unfortunate man
holds in his hands?'[283]

The women and men who lived in Europe during this historical period
knew full well that suicide was a heinous sin and the gravest crime that
could be committed, and the sight of the periodical retributions in the
streets and squares served to remind them that it was punished by the civil
and religious authorities with extraordinary severity. They were also well
aware that if they did take their own lives, they would be judged by a court
and sentenced to be hanged, after which their corpse would be treated like
that of an animal, and would be buried together with beasts and not with
other Christians. It was also common knowledge that their possessions
might be confiscated by the feudal lord or by the sovereign. But the worst
threat was the catastrophic consequences that their choice would have for
their loved ones, for their spouse, children, parents and other relatives. As
well as the pain of loss, the latter would experience shame, dejection and
despair owing to the reactions of the community and the humiliations they
would undergo. They would also be questioned by magistrates, would
watch as the corpse was dragged through the streets, would lose at least
part of their possessions, and would be treated with suspicion, malice,
scorn. Never again would they be free from the burden of being related to
someone who had committed the worst sin and the gravest crime.

2

The Key to our Prison

If we think about what used to happen, in Europe and in the American colonies, when a person committed suicide, and about the scenes that were repeated inside houses and in the streets, in courtrooms and prisons, in the churches and cemeteries, and we compare these with what happens nowadays, it is readily apparent that the two theses proposed by Durkheim (and adopted by social scientists) have no foundation. To start with there are no grounds for the idea that 'as history progressed' the prohibition against taking one's own life became 'ever more strict'. As we will see in the following pages, the great edifice of values, rules, sanctions, beliefs, symbols and categories of interpretation condemning or discouraging suicide, which had been formed in Europe from the fifth century onwards, and which had dominated, unwavering and imposing, for centuries, at some point started to crack and shake, before finally collapsing much later, in spite of all the efforts made to shore it up and keep it standing. Equally unfounded is Durkheim's other thesis that censure of suicide grew in parallel with the development of the rights of the individual against the state, and the more the human person was regarded as a sacred entity. Indeed, everything points to the fact that exactly the opposite occurred. It goes without saying that the crisis of this moral approach to voluntary death was provoked by numerous factors. But among these, a particularly important role was played by the affirmation of each and every individual's right to life, liberty and property, but also to the right to choose when to bid farewell to the world.

Whatever the causes, this long and profound change has had enormous consequences. The weakening and subsequent collapse of the beliefs, laws, sanctions, symbols and interpretative models that, for centuries, had, in countless ways, discouraged European men and women from succumbing to the temptation of taking their own lives caused a rapid and seemingly unstoppable rise in the number of suicides.

2.1   The lawfulness of suicide

Christian ethics on suicide showed the first signs of crisis, in cultural elites, at least, between the mid sixteenth and seventeenth centuries. Of course, we do not know how many nobles, intellectuals and more educated members of the bourgeoisie started to confess in private, to family members, friends and acquaintances, that they were becoming less convinced by the tenets of Augustine, Thomas Aquinas, Luther and Calvin, and increasingly uncomfortable with the rites of desecration to which the corpses of suicides were subjected or with the punishments to which they were condemned. Nor do we know precisely how many of them felt strongly enough to put pen to paper and write an essay on the lawfulness of voluntary death. However, it is probable that this happened more often than we are inclined to believe nowadays based on the writings that have survived to our day.

In view of the risks run by those who publicly expressed their ideas on such a delicate argument, it comes as no surprise to find that almost all of them proceeded with the utmost caution, not signing their works, consigning them to the flames soon after they were finished, refusing to publish them, or, if they decided to do so in the end, resorting to various stratagems to conceal or soften their positions, or to divert the attention of the authorities. For example, a manuscript of 1578 in favour of voluntary death, entitled *Whether It Be Damnation for a Man to Kill Himself*, was found, unsigned, among the papers of Sir John Harrington, now conserved in the British Museum.[1] In the late sixteenth century, Justus Lipsius destroyed the essay he had written on the lawfulness of suicide.[2] A few years later, the theologian and poet, John Donne, circulated among his friends the book he had finished writing in 1610 in favour of voluntary death, without ever publishing it. To one of them, he sent this message: 'It is a book written by Jack Donne and not by Dr Donne.'[3] Before his death, in the copy left to his son, and in those he had given to two friends, he wrote: 'Publish it not, but yet burn it not.'[4] But the book was eventually printed in 1647, under the title *Biathanatos*, literally 'violent death' (from *biaios* and *thanatos*). Likewise, David Hume decided at the last moment, when it was already in proofs, to destroy his essay, *On Suicide*, which he finished in 1755.[5] According to some, he had been prompted to write it by a friend (perhaps Adam Smith) in response to the protests of William Warburton, the future Anglican bishop. A few copies were circulated clandestinely and one ended up in France where it was translated and published anonymously in 1770. Even more dramatic was the case of Johann Robeck, a Jesuit of Swedish origin who lived for a long time in Germany, and in 1735 finished *De morte voluntaria*, a Latin treatise in favour of suicide. But instead of offering it to a publisher, he went out alone in a boat on the Weser and killed himself, letting his body drift downriver. His work was published posthumously by a colleague, who confuted his arguments page by page.[6]

Three great figures of European culture had also, with considerable caution, made their ideas public at different moments. Thomas More dared to defend some forms of suicide in 1516, setting them apart in a society that was radically different from the one in which he lived: a rational, happy and perfect society, an island that was distant in both time and space, a Utopia. In 1580 Michel Montaigne prefaced his comments on this theme with a cautionary proem:[7] 'If as they say, to philosophize is to doubt, then, a fortiori, to fool about and to weave fantasies as I do must also be to doubt. For it is the role of apprentices to ask questions and to debate: the professor provides the solutions from his chair. My professor is the authority of God's Will, which undeniably governs us and which ranks way about human controversies.'[8] Lastly, Montesquieu set the heroine of his *Persian Letters*, Roxana, in Persia, where she committed suicide, and in the second edition of the book, published in 1754, thirty years after the first, he added a brief letter aimed to soften his thesis. Likewise, Madame de Staël and Chateaubriand also chose distant settings for their heroines, Zulma and Atala, who would come to the same end.

But to return to Thomas More, the inhabitants of Utopia owed their happiness to the 'large and magnificent' cities in which they lived, to their common ownership of property, their strong sense of social solidarity, their good government, and the affectionate care they lavished on the sick. Moreover, if any had an incurable disease, causing excruciating and unremitting suffering, the priests and public officials would remind the sick person 'not to let the pestilence prey on him any longer', given that he was by then 'unequal to any of life's duties, a burden to himself and others'.[9] Those who were persuaded by these arguments would either starve themselves to death or were put to sleep.

Thomas More's ideas were, however, less radical than those put forward by Montaigne, Donne and, later, Montesquieu, Radicati di Passerano, Hume, Voltaire and other Enlightenment philosophers.[10] Firstly because not even in Utopia were the gravely sick free to take their own lives if they did not have the permission of the civic and religious authorities. Secondly because the only form of suicide regarded as 'honourable', and therefore permitted, on this island was euthanasia, occasioned by the pain of an incurable illness. If a person took his or her life for other reasons not deemed correct by the priests and magistrates, the suicide would not be deemed worthy of burial or cremation and the corpse would be thrown 'unburied and disgraced, into a bog'.[11] However, even More's proposals questioned Augustine's idea that pain was not a limit and obstacle for humans, but a means to 'affirm their essence'.

Montaigne also described the customs of people living on a remote island, Keos (or Cea) in the Aegean, in the Cyclades archipelago. Here, elderly people used to take their own lives, without asking for anyone's permission, not when they were seriously ill but rather still in good health, not as a means of escaping suffering but rather of preventing it. He describes the case of a woman of over ninety, of high rank, 'blessed in mind and body', who justified her decision to commit suicide, saying: 'For my part, I have assayed only the kindlier face of Fortune; fearing that the desire to go on living might make me see an adverse one, I am happy with this happy death giving leave of absence to the remnant of my soul and leaving behind me two daughters and a legion of grandchildren.'[12] With these words she exhorted her family to live in peace, divided her possessions among them and took the cup containing the poison and swallowed it at once. Montaigne also compared this act to the customs of another 'Hyperborean' nation, with a gentle climate, whose inhabitants often lived to an advanced age. When they were 'weary, having had their fill of life', it was their custom to 'hold a joyful celebration and then leap into the sea from a high cliff set aside for this purpose'.

John Donne also reflected and wrote frequently on death and he was always struck by the fact that there were 'too many examples of men that have been their own executioners', who have always 'had poison about them, in a hollow ring upon their finger, and some in their pen that they used to write with', while others 'beat out their brains at the wall of their prison'.[13] However, he also wrote a highly erudite book supporting the lawfulness of suicide, a real treatise of theology or Christian morals that was certainly the first of its kind to be published in Europe, and he returned to this theme in other writings.[14] Having studied theology at Cambridge and at Lincoln's Inn, London, Donne felt confident to attack the dominant doctrine using complex arguments and citing a large number of authors and works. Following the scheme used by St Thomas, he divided *Biathanatos* into three parts, each of which aimed to confute one of the alleged grounds for the unlawfulness of suicide.

In the first part, he questioned the belief that self-homicide, as he called it, was contrary to natural law. He asserted that it was practised by some animals (such as pelicans and bees), that it had been deemed legitimate in many other non-Christian societies that differed greatly from one another (like those of ancient Rome or India), and that even among the early Christians there were martyrs, in the fourth century, who had taken their own lives. He therefore concluded that 'in all Ages, in all places, upon all occasions, men of all conditions have affected it, and inclin'd to do it'.[15] By reporting facts and citing the positions of illustrious authors, Donne repeatedly affirmed that, far from being contrary to nature, the desire for death was innate in human nature. In the second part, Donne criticized the idea that homicide itself was contrary to rational law. By questioning St Thomas' idea that suicide was unlawful because it removed a creature from the universe and a subject from the body of the state, he observed that the same thing happened when a mercenary leader of great valour retired to a monastery or a person emigrated to another country. In the final part, Donne then argued against the idea that homicide itself was a violation of God's law. He was convinced that the only pivotal commandment of Christian doctrine was 'Thou shalt not kill'. But yet there were countless exceptions to this rule. The magistrates could sentence a person to death (even if he had already taken his own life) and, in a just war, a private man could kill another who was his enemy, even if that person were his own father. In this case, what grounds were there, he wondered, for not regarding self-homicide as another exception? Had Samson not killed himself, even though he is celebrated by the Church as a martyr? And what of Christ's death? It was with this point, this most delicate of questions, that the Anglican poet and theologian delivered his winning thrust.

Contrary to what was generally believed, Christ had not surrendered to death. Donne was in no doubt that his crucifixion was not simply an act of obedience, humiliation or love. Instead, Christ was in full control, and fully conscious of the process that had led him to death. However, Christ 'did as much as any could be willing to do. And therefore, as himselfe sayd, "No man can take away my soule" and 'I have power to lay it down. So without doubt, no man did [take it away], nor was there any other than his owne Will, the cause of his dying at that tyme.'[16]

Donne not only expounded his thesis in print – although he knew that the book would not be published during his lifetime – he also presented it in public, in a sermon he gave on Easter Day 1619. Christ's soul, he announced on that occasion, 'did not leave his body by force, but because he would, and when he would, and how he would; Thus far then first, this is an answer to the question, *Quis homo*? Christ did not die naturally, nor violently, as all others doe, but only voluntarily.'[17]

Therefore, one of the two great events that Christians considered central to the history of the world, Christ's death, was the result, according to the Anglican poet and theologian, of sin and of the most serious crime that a human being could commit. It was an extraordinarily daring, impious and sacrilegious idea, one that impressed a great twentieth-century poet, Jorge Luis Borges. Indeed, the latter was so impressed by Donne's writings,[18] that he claimed that *Biathanatos* contained 'a baroque idea': 'the idea of a god who fabricates the universe in order to fabricate his scaffold'. Borges continued: 'Christ died a voluntary death, Donne suggests, implying that the elements and the world and the generations of men and Egypt and Rome and Babylon, and the Kingdom of Judah were drawn from nothingness to destroy him. Perhaps iron was created for the nails, thorns for the crown of mockery, and blood and water for the wound.'[19]

If Donne had suggested that suicide was not a sin, a century later Montesquieu, one of Europe's leading intellectuals, endeavoured to ensure that it was no longer regarded as a crime. In 1721, in his epistolary novel *Persian Letters*, he used Usbek as a mouthpiece, a cruel Persian despot accustomed to living in a harem, with many wives and eunuchs, who then travelled to France with a young countryman. As the two travellers encounter this entirely new cultural universe, seeing it through foreign eyes, so Montesquieu invites readers to reassess, with a critical eye, the customs they have always known, and which seemed to them the best, including those on suicide. 'It seems to me', wrote Usbek in a letter, 'that these laws are most unjust. When I am crushed by physical pain, by poverty, by scorn, why should anyone wish to prevent me from ending my suffering, and cruelly deprive me of a remedy which lies in my own hands?'[20]

Montesquieu renewed a debate on the lawfulness of suicide that was joined, as the century wore on, by the most brilliant European intellectuals. In 1732, in London, the translation was published of a book written by a Piedmontese nobleman in exile, Count Alberto Radicati di Passerano. It ended with these words: 'Let us conclude; That a Man, weary or satiated with living, may die when he pleases, without offending Nature: Since in dying, he makes Use of the Remedy which She has kindly put into his Hands, wherewithal he may cure himself of the Evils of this life.'[21] Cesare Beccaria and Voltaire supported the reform of criminal codes and the depenalization of suicide. 'It is no crime with regard to man', wrote the former, 'because the punishment, instead of falling on the offender, falls on an innocent family', whereas 'political liberty supposes all punishments entirely personal'.[22] The latter decried the main effect of European legislation on the matter, which was to dishonour the suicide's family and reduce them to poverty, punishing a son for having lost a father and a widow because she is deprived of a husband.[23]

The new ethic of voluntary death was an expression of the profound cultural changes in European society. In the closing decades of the seventeenth century and throughout the eighteenth, a number of important economic, social and political factors led to the emergence of a new understanding of life and the world, the family and the individual, the state and the law. In the light of these changes, all human beings were unique and each possessed an inalienable right to life, freedom and property in order to fulfil, in perfect autonomy, their personal goals and happiness.

From the mid sixteenth century onwards, suicide was seen – by those who argued for its lawfulness – as an expression of the individual's autonomy and freedom. According to this new ethic, the lives of men and women no longer belonged to God or to their feudal overlord or sovereign, not even to the head of the household, but solely to themselves, and therefore the decision to renounce that life was theirs alone. Montaigne was a strong supporter of this, and in doing so was ahead of his time. '[. . .] the greatest favour that Nature has bestowed on us', he wrote, 'and the one which removes all grounds for lamenting over our human condition, is the one which gives us the key to the garden-gate; Nature has ordained only one entrance to life but a hundred thousand exits. [. . .] The fairest death is one that is most willed. Our lives depend on the will of others: our death depends on our own. [. . .] Living is slavery if the freedom to die is wanting.'[24] This explained why, 'Just as I break no laws against theft when I make off with my own property or cut my own purse, nor the laws against arson if I burn my own woods, so too I am not bound to the laws against murder if I take my own life.'[25] Life, like movable and immovable property, belonged to the individual. Two centuries later, David Hume was even more firmly convinced of this truth, declaring in the opening lines of his book: 'Let us here endeavour to restore men to their native liberty, by examining all the common arguments against Suicide.'[26]

Even John Donne had seen suicide as an expression of individual freedom. In the work he never dared to publish, he had written: 'whensoever any affliction assails me, methinks I have the keys of my prison in mine own hand, and no remedy presents itself so soon to my heart as mine own sword'.[27] He was well aware that others would have regarded this proposal as heretical. But he was convinced that the first to possess the keys of his prison, the first to assert the freedom to leave the world when he wanted to was Christ, who said: 'No man can take away my soul [. . .] I have power to lay it down.'[28]

This conviction was so strong that Donne expressed it on many other occasions, not only in abstract discussions of theological principles but also speaking of his own life.[29] In a letter to Sir Henry Goodyer in September 1608, he wrote:

I would not that death should take me asleep. I would not have him merely seize me, and only declare me to be dead, but win me and overcome me. When I must shipwreck, I would do it in a sea where mine impotency might have some excuse; not in a sullen weedy lake, where I could not have so much as exercise for my swimming. Therefore I would fain do something, but that I cannot tell what is no wonder. For to choose is to do; but to be no part of any body is to be nothing.[30]

Montesquieu ended *Persian Letters* with a surprise suicide, a bid for freedom committed through rebellion against Usbek himself, who had affirmed an individual's right to end his or her sufferings. In the last letter in the book, Roxana, the favourite wife of the Persian tyrant, regarded as the most faithful of all, makes a terrible revelation: 'How could you suppose me so credulous as to believe that the sole purpose for my existence was to adore your caprices [. . .]. No: I may have lived in servitude, but I have always been free: I have rewritten your laws to conform to those of nature, and my spirit has always remained independent.' Moreover, 'You were amazed at not seeing me in the ecstasies of love: if you had truly known me, you would have seen in me all the violence of loathing [. . .] we were both happy; you believed me deceived, and I was deceiving you.'[31] Shortly before writing the letter, Roxana had taken poison and now she felt her strength fading, 'the pen falls from my hand; I feel that even my hatred is fading away: I am dying'.

According to Alberto Radicati di Passerano, the goal that the 'Goddess Nature' proposed to fulfil through the creation of animals was their 'felicity'. She gave them life on the condition that they find it 'sweet and agreeable', on the understanding that they could 'restore it to her immediately when it becomes loathsome'. 'To this Effect, she has given to Men an intire Liberty to quit life when it is become troublesome to them.' To prove this, he repeated an old metaphor: 'there are a Thousand Doors open whereat to issue out of this vital Prison, which could not have been, had not Nature left them so.'[32]

These arguments in favour of the lawfulness of suicide were also triggered by other far-reaching cultural transformations taking place in Europe at the time, such as the establishment of utilitarianism and contractualism, and the tendency to give growing importance to the search for personal earthly pleasure, in the here-and-now not in the world to come. Moreover, this search was increasingly regarded as an essential impetus to virtue and public wellbeing. These transformations further undermined the idea that those who took their own lives committed a crime against the *polis* to which they belonged. Cesare Beccaria observed that 'He who kills himself does a less injury to society than he who quits his country for ever; for the former leaves his property behind him, but the latter carries with him at least a part of his substance.'[33]

But before him, others argued from the standpoint of society seen as a contract with the individual, from which each could withdraw when it was no longer profitable to him. 'Society', Montesquieu wrote, 'is based on mutual advantage; but when it becomes a burden to me, why should I not renounce it? Life was accorded me as a favour; I can then therefore give it back when it is no longer such; the cause ceases to be and consequently the effect ceases also.' But was it really true, wondered the French philosopher, that others, all the others, prevented him from making this renunciation? 'Is it the prince's will that I be his subject when I do not receive the advantages of that condition? Can my fellow-citizens demand such an iniquitous distribution – their benefit and my despair? Does God, unlike all other benefactors, want to condemn me to receive blessings which oppress me?'[34] Hume was thinking along the same lines when he wrote: 'All our obligations to do good to society seem to imply something reciprocal. [. . .] I am not obliged to do a small good to society at the expense of a great harm to myself; why then should I prolong a miserable existence, because of some frivolous advantage which the public may perhaps receive from me? If upon account of age and infirmities, I may lawfully resign any office [. . .] alleviating, as much as possible, the miseries of my future life: Why may I not cut short these miseries at once by an action which is no more prejudicial to society?'[35] Lastly, the idea that voluntary death disturbed the order and harmony of the universe was questioned by differing conceptions of the world that began to acquire increasing importance during this period. These ranged from the epicurean or neo-epicurean view of a perennially alive and active nature, in a state of continual transformation and regeneration, to the deist view of a completely rational deity, lacking any supernatural and dogmatic components. For example, Montesquieu affirmed that Providence would not be changed if humans altered the qualities of matter, or if they squared a sphere that the laws of movement decreed should be round, or even if they killed themselves, because the new arrangement that was formed would be no less perfect than the previous one. 'Do you believe that when my body', he asked, 'has become an ear of corn, a worm, or a sod of turf, it will have become any less worthy to be called a work of nature? And that my soul, freed from everything about it that was earthly, will have become less sublime?'[36] Indeed, it was clear that the idea that suicide might alter the harmony of the world stemmed from man's pride. Humans 'wish to count for something in the universe', and refused to acknowledge their 'insignificance', or admit that 'one man less or more in the world – what am I saying? – that all men taken together [. . .] are nothing but a delicate, tiny atom that God sees only because of the immensity of his knowledge'.[37] In those same years, Alberto Radicati di Passerano wrote that the world was governed by general laws of matter and movement and he attributed all the divine qualities to the natural architect, to the 'Goddess Nature': power, wisdom, and perfection. From this point of view, voluntary death was only a transition of matter from one form of existence to another: 'we cease to exist in one sort, in order to begin to exist in another'.[38]

Hume also asserted that suicide could not alter, in any way, the order and harmony of the universe. The lives of men and other living beings did not depend on the Almighty but were subject to the 'general laws of matter and motion', created by the latter. 'For my part', the philosopher observed, 'I find that I owe my birth to a long chain of causes, of which many depended upon voluntary actions of men.' Therefore, given that the universe was governed by general, unchanging laws, fixed since the beginning of time, nothing could disturb it: neither the diversion of the Nile or the Danube, nor the voluntary death of a human being. Moreover, matter was eternal. 'When I shall be dead, the principles of which I am composed will still perform their part in the universe, and will be equally useful in the grand fabric, as when they composed this individual creature. The difference to the whole will be no greater than betwixt my being in a chamber and in the open air. The one change is of more importance to me than the other; but not more so to the universe.'[39] For this reason, 'The life of man is of no greater importance to the universe than that of an oyster.'[40] In 1770, Baron d'Holbach presented an even more radical thesis. Given that life is the supreme asset in our disposal, he affirmed, it is clear that if a man commits suicide, he does so because he is compelled by an irresistible force, or by Nature's orders. When the latter prevents him from being happy, he ceases to be useful to himself and others, and there is no other course of action for him than to obey her request and quit.[41]

2.2 A changed sensitivity in the literature

It is in literature that we find the first signs, in many European countries, of a change in attitude towards suicide. To tell the truth, even in the Middle Ages, voluntary death was not represented and judged in the same way by all literary genres. In French religious plays of the fourteenth and

fifteenth centuries, showing scenes from the Bible and from the lives of the
saints, suicide was always viewed with horror and condemned irrespective
of the reasons for which it was committed. Equally severe during this same
period were the *chansons de geste*, those long epic poems in hendecasyl-
lable verse, celebrating religious faith and loyalty to the king.[42] But in
other genres and in other works we find a view of suicide that differs, in
part at least, from that of the Christian theologians. Dante placed 'the
violent against themselves' in the seventh circle of *Inferno*: having torn
themselves violently away from their own bodies, they were now imprisoned in giant thorn bushes, and these plants, although inferior in nature
to human beings, continued to inflict cuts and wounds, just as the suicides
had done to themselves in life. But in Canto XIII, which is dedicated to
those who have committed violent acts, there is no trace of either sloth,
despair or even the evil tempter himself. Morever, Dante placed Cato
Uticensis (a pagan suicide, morally condemned by Augustine) at the
start of *Purgatory*. Indeed, Virgil introduces Dante to Cato with the well-
known words: 'Tis liberty he seeks – how dear a thing That is, they know
who give their lives for it.'

The image of voluntary death offered by the courtly romance also differed from that of the Christian theologians. Born in northern France, the
roman usually narrated legendary tales and fables of knights, their deeds
and their loves. At a formal level, the authors of these romances always
paid homage to the principle of Christian morality, declaring that suicide
was a sin, a great folly, an affront. But when recounting the deeds of their
heroes, of Lancelot and Guinevere, Parsifal or Tristan, they justified and
approved of suicide committed under special circumstances. Therefore,
unlike treatises on theology, manuals for confessors, church frescoes or
other literary forms, these courtly romances showed understanding or
even admiration for anyone ready to sacrifice their own life for love, for
the death of a friend or to save another's life, to preserve their honour by
not submitting to the victor, or to express repentance after committing an
ignoble deed. The most famous was undoubtedly suicide for love, which
was regarded as the only or indeed the noblest and most elegant way for
knights, and sometimes ladies, to protect the purity of their sentiments.
Anyone who killed themselves in order to remain faithful to their loved
one, or because they had done wrong, or had been refused by them, far
from deserving condemnation should be praised and even exalted.[43]

Suicide for love was also regarded as being heroic in other countries
and in other literary genres. In Italy, in the fourteenth century, Giovanni
Boccaccio, commenting on Canto XIII of the *Divine Comedy*, had recalled
that taking one's own life was a sin and he decisively disapproved of this
act.[44] Moreover, in a novella in the *Decameron*, Boccaccio told the sad
story of Guido degli Anastagi, who was 'condemned to eternal torments'[45]
for having committed suicide. Yet in other works Boccaccio did not
conceal his admiration for those who killed themselves for love, given that
he was convinced of the irresistible power of love, capable of triumphing

over reason and overcoming any social barrier. Ghismonda, daughter of Tancredi, Prince of Salerno, is the central figure of one of Boccaccio's most touching and famous novellas. After being widowed she falls in love with Guiscardo, her father's valet. Having discovered their affair and blinded by his jealousy for the young lovers, Tancredi gives orders for Guiscardo to be killed and for his heart to be placed in a golden chalice and sent to his daughter. Although Ghismonda is aware of committing a grave sin, she drinks a draught of poison and then addresses her father with these last words: 'Remain here with God, for I am going.'[46] In the fifteenth and sixteenth centuries, many authors of pastoral literature in Italy and Spain[47] sang the praises of bucolic suicide, like Torquato Tasso, who in *Aminta* told the story of a shepherd who had fallen madly in love with the nymph Silvia, and was twice on the point of killing himself for her.

However, the closing decades of the sixteenth century and the early seventeenth century marked the start of a radical change as other literary genres adopted an increasingly open-minded attitude to voluntary death. In France, this was true of the novel and of the nascent genre of tragedy. Authors put forward the Church's official positions on the subject, but these came to be seen as a sort of moral façade, incapable of hiding the growing tide of sympathy for those who committed suicide for love, remorse or to save their honour. Moreover, novels often presented the pros and cons of suicide, and the arguments in favour started to win the day. When Compte de Melisse, the central character in a novel by Jean d'Intras, dating from 1609, wonders whether he might kill himself after being rejected by the woman he loves, he is faced with the negative arguments repeated again and again by philosophers, theologians, moralists and priests over the centuries: namely that suicide was contrary to the laws of heaven, of nature and love itself. Yet the count succeeds in turning these arguments on their head and reaches the conclusion that heaven, nature and love 'have given us the weapons of freedom only to combat unhappiness', and he 'let his spirit breathe the sweet air of the heavens'.[48]

The changes that took place in England were even more radical, in both novels and plays, including comedies and tragedies. Elizabethan theatre (starting in 1576) heralded enormous stylistic, technical and thematic innovations. It freed dialogue from rhyme by adopting blank verse, in flowing iambic pentameter. The action on stage became much dynamic (and more similar to what we think of as film), thanks to a rapid and frequent series of scenes, which allowed the actors to move rapidly in space and time, passing from one location to another and jumping days, months and even years. It broke social taboos by tackling banned subjects, such as sex, madness, natural and also voluntary death. Interest in suicide, as well as in the human events that led to self-murder, and in the different suicide methods used grew enormously in plays from this period. The number of works in which characters killed themselves on stage, or tried to do so, rose exponentially: from eight in the first sixty years of the sixteenth century to fourteen in the next twenty years, forty-one in the period from

1580 to 1600, and a record ninety-nine from 1600 to 1625.[49] There was also an increase in the average number of characters who committed suicide. While there were never more than two in each play before 1580, after that date it is common to find three, four or even five. This reflected a change in the moral judgement of playwrights, who began to regard suicide not as a diabolical deed but rather as a human choice, not a symbol but rather a possible cause of death, and they therefore presented it in a light that gradually became less unfavourable.

The playwright who showed the greatest interest in suicide and devoted the greatest space to it in his works was William Shakespeare. He tackled it in thirty-two of his plays, resulting in the suicide of as many as twenty-four characters.[50] By not following a theological argument or even a strictly ethical one, the great English playwright broke away from the contemporary intellectual custom of making voluntary death the abstract object of a philosophical debate. Instead he did not classify it as either a sin or an offence. Like Montaigne, Shakespeare showed an open mind to those who killed themselves with their own hands. He stopped short of condemning them, nor did he exalt them. Instead he tried to regard them as individuals capable of meaningful actions, and he tried to reconstruct their human experience and understand the reasons for their choice. With extraordinary effectiveness, he again posed the question, in the most famous lines of world literature (Hamlet's soliloquy), as to whether it is better 'to die, to sleep' rather than 'bear the whips and scorns of time, Th' oppressor's wrong, the proud man's contumely, The pangs of disprized love, the law's delay, The insolence of office, and the spurns that patient merit of th' unworthy takes'? To this he replies, in layman fashion, that men and women usually opt not to 'quietus make with a bare bodkin', and the reason is not because they fear God's anger or the punishment of the authorities but because they do not know what might happen after death, in 'The undiscovered country from whose bourn No traveller returns.'

In England, these shifts of attitude among literary circles towards voluntary death became even more striking because they reached a wider and socially more heterogeneous public than elsewhere. Across Europe, poetry and romances were only read by a small, cultured elite, or even simply a literate one. Instead, the open-air theatres of Elizabethan London were attended by people from all walks of life: men and women, young and old, aristocrats, merchants, artisans, apprentices, servants and unemployed vagabonds.

Therefore, during the closing decades of the sixteenth century and the early years of the seventeenth, poets, authors of romance but above all playwrights signalled the arrival of a new wave of sensibility towards suicide. They removed it from the shadow of taboo, where it had lain for centuries, and they placed it at the centre of their reflections and their stories. They told the passionate stories of men and women who, in ancient Rome or contemporary Europe, had killed themselves for noble motives, and they presented them to the public in a different light. Unlike in the past, they focused their attention not on moral doctrines, values and concepts but rather on the real individuals, in flesh and blood, on their emotions and ideas, and on the actual situations in which they found themselves, probably knowing that at least some of the public no longer shared the theses on suicide put forward by Augustine and Aquinas, Luther and Calvin.[51]

If these authors preceded other groups of intellectuals in offering a new answer to the old question concerning the lawfulness of voluntary death, it was primarily for two reasons. The first was for aesthetic and practical reasons. The act of suicide was a powerful dramatic resource, and one that was extraordinarily spectacular. By putting on stage a character who then killed himself, the author of the play was certain to arouse strong emotions in the public who would cry out, weep and then debate the question. The second was to ensure that the theatre (in particular, under Elizabeth) was a free space, a place where all is permitted and where the viewer could forget the thousand prohibitions of everyday life and for a few hours give full rein to his or her ideas and sentiments.

2.3 A new name for an old deed

One indicator of this profound cultural change was the linguistic shift that took place in around the mid seventeenth century, namely the appearance of a neologism to describe the act of someone taking his or her life, a word that spread rapidly throughout the most educated sections of Europe's population. Contrary to what one might think, the term suicide is relatively recent in origin. Despite the fact that it is comprised of two Latin words, *sui* and *cudere*, *suicidium* did not exist in ancient Latin, although words like *parricidium*, *matricidium*, *fratricidium*, and *tyrannicidium* did.[52] On the other hand, a distinctive, specific noun for the act of ending one's own life had long been missing, even from the main European modern languages. The tendency to regard suicide as a crime no less grave than homicide had been so strong that the latter was also used, also in linguistic terms, to indicate the former. Augustine called the act *crimen homicidi* and the person committing it *homicida*. In English, people spoke of self-homicide, or self-slaughter. Shakespeare used the expression *self-slaughter*, Spenser *self-murdring*, Donne *self-homicide*, Burton *to be their own butchers*. Montaigne, in his essay on the 'Custom of the Isle of Cea', spoke of *homicide de soy-mesme*, although the expressions *meurtre de soi-meme, homicide de son corps, homicide de lui mesme par desespoir* were also used in French.[53] In Italy, theologists and jurists had for many years used the terms *homicida* and *sui ipsius homicidium* in their writings, before introducing the expression *omicidio di sé medesimo*.

The changing attitudes to voluntary death ushered in the need to introduce a different term to describe it, one created a clear distinction between this and killing another person, which was now deemed much more serious. It was Sir Thomas Browne, in a work published in 1642, who introduced the neologism 'suicide' with reference to that of the pagan Cato, in order to distinguish it from the 'self-killing' condemned by the Christian religion. This new term was then used ever more frequently in the following decades, in books and in dictionaries. It was introduced in France in 1734 by Abbé Prévost, who had spent many years in England,[54] and was later repeated by Voltaire, Helvétius, d'Holbach and many others.[55] But its progress was slow. Even in 1773, Jean Dumas published a book whose title included both the old and new terms, as if they were synonyms: *Traité du suicide, ou du meurtre volontaire de soi-même*.[56]

It probably reached Italy thanks to Giuseppe Baretti and his *Dictionary of the English and Italian Languages*. Published in London in 1760 and in Venice in 1787, the English–Italian volume of the work contained the term 'suicide', defined as '*suicidio, l'orrido delitto di distruggere se stesso*' [suicide, the horrible crime of destroying oneself]. In 1761 the neologism was reiterated by Agatopisto Cromaziano, in his *Istoria del suicidio*, and three years later by Cesare Beccaria.

It appeared in Spain in 1770, again thanks to Giuseppe Baretti's English–Spanish dictionary, and in Portugal in 1844.[57] In Germany, the term *Selbstentleibung* was introduced in the eighteenth century, and *Suizid* in the late nineteenth.[58]

2.4 Natural and supernatural causes

On an unnamed day in 1480, Father Thomas Vassen (or Wyssem), prior of a monastery near Brussels, had an unusual visit: a few of his monks, who had set off for Cologne some time previously, came to ask him to help with a serious problem that had arisen among the group on their return journey. One of their companions, by all accounts the most illustrious, had suffered a violent crisis one night, when he had suddenly started shouting that he was doomed and condemned to eternal damnation. He would not stop crying out, repeating these desperate words and, if the others in the group had not forcibly restrained him, he would certainly have injured or killed himself. Unable to calm their fellow monk, or to find any solution for his difficulties, the brethren had continued to travel slowly back to Brussels, where they had arrived much later than anticipated but had promptly come to the prior for advice.

Father Thomas left immediately and met the sick monk; he also listened to the companions' versions of what had happened, which had by now certainly been embellished with extra detail, and then he prescribed a cure reminiscent of biblical tradition. In the same way that David had calmed Saul by playing his harp when the latter fell prey to bouts of fury, so the prior recommended that music, if played frequently to the sufferer, might also succeed in soothing such profound anguish and might placate the effects of that 'melancholic affliction' for which other contemporaries also recommended sound therapy. Yet, despite the repeated sound of instruments playing, and the pleasant entertainment offered to the sick man, anguish continued to dominate his mind and he went on shouting and talking excitedly as before, clearly obsessed and referring to himself again and again as a 'child of perdition'.

Only after returning to the monastic community, as the chronicles of the monastery record, where he was cared for assiduously, day and night, did the brother recover or, at least, his crisis receded. Although demoted to the rank of *conversus* (an intermediate rank between the lay brethren and the regular monks),[59] but allowed to return to his work, which he had continued to exercise even after taking his vows, he lived for another year. During that time, he constantly professed the humility that, according to the chronicler, had been lacking from his earlier religious experience, and he completed his moving last work of art.

Following the onset of this *crise de nerfs*, the monk had been helped by his half-brother, who had also taken vows in the monastery and had formed part of the group journeying to Cologne. The half-brother, Nicolaas, had reported the details of the spectacular outburst of delirium not only to his companions and to the prior but also to Brother Gaspar Ofhuys, who shortly afterwards become *infirmarius*, or physician, to the monastery, as well as its new prior. Many years later, as the representative of the monastery, Ofhuys wrote a chronicle of the community, which included a report on this unusual case; it was thanks to this that his work would be later saved from oblivion by attracting the attention and analysis of experts from a wide range of disciplines.[60]

The reason was that the patient in question, if he can be defined as such, was far from being an obscure monk, overcome by *pusillanimitas*, or excessive scrupulosity in devotion, which, in the late Middle Ages and other historical periods, almost became a pathological phenomenon and was relatively widely reported. Instead, the monk in question was none other than Hugo van der Goes, one of the greatest Flemish artists of the late fifteenth century. At the pinnacle of his career, when he was a widely admired artist in great demand, this extraordinary painter had decided to enter the Roode Clooster, a monastery near Brussels, in around 1475. Like many other Catholic communities of the period, the monastery was renowned for its reformatory zeal. Prompted by a genuine religious piety, and by an equally authentic artistic fervour, Hugo had enjoyed special privileges within the monastery from the outset. The prior (that same Father Thomas who, five years later, would try to relieve the artist's explosive symptoms) had allowed him to continue painting and to remain in contact with persons outside the monastery walls, including some high-ranking patrons (like Archduke Maximilian, the future German emperor), with the result that, in practice, parts of the monastery became a sort of artist's workshop.

Torn between such different worlds and callings, even in the years of his novitiate, which should have been characterized by the search for and practice of constant humility, Hugo retained secular interests and habits: he continued reading non-devotional texts (with excessive interest, one might say, given that the chronicler noted that 'he devoted himself too often to the reading of a Flemish book'; he regularly drank wine while acting as a representative and when meeting titled guests; he was absorbed, entirely at a worldly level, by this excessive burden of work (it would have taken him nine years, at least, just to complete the works he had started).

Hugo was certainly different from the other monks, and he too was aware of this distinction: the physician-cum-prior chronicler noted that he refused to comply with the day-to-day rules of the monastery and ate his meals in the refectory reserved for the regular friars, instead of in the less prestigious refectory for the lay brothers, where as a *conversus* he belonged. Indeed, Hugo's nervous breakdown most probably stemmed from the unbridgeable gulf between two equally demanding vocations, namely between the practice of his art and the tension of his religion convictions. Yet the breakdown was sudden and unexpected, and it occurred after he had lived and worked quietly for five years inside the monastery.

Writing thirty years after these events had occurred, with the aim of including them as a particularly interesting episode in the life of the monastic community, Father Gaspar Ofhuys gave his account the vividness of a first-hand experience, in spite of the fact that he had pieced together the events from eye witnesses. Yet he also detached himself by moving onto a discussion of the possible aetiologies of the case, taking advantage of his position as prior, a man of culture and a physician. He came up with three different explanations.

The first was the traditional Christian aetiology of demonic possession. The second moved away from this schema, but nonetheless made reference to another supernatural power: divine intervention. Hugo had sinned through pride by transforming the religious experience into a social advantage that was even more emphatic than the one he might have achieved as a member of the lay community; his acknowledged artistic excellence, and the homage and admiration that this entailed, had swollen his pride to abnormal levels, resulting in a condition of spiritual damnation. But 'God's all-loving providence' had decreed otherwise by sending him a 'chastening affliction', one that had recalled him to his unfulfilled duties of humility and repentance, and opening a path to salvation through suffering. Once restored to an awareness of his own miserable condition, Brother Hugo, 'having been restored to health, dedicated himself to a life of the utmost humility'.

Father Ofhuys wrote passionately and at length about this providentialist interpretation, which seemed the most convincing in his eyes. However, as a doctor, he did mention another, a natural explanation to which he gave scarce credence. The crisis, he wrote, might have been provoked by the ingestion of 'melancholic food', or 'strong wines' that alter the humoral balance of the body, 'heating the body juices and burning them

to ashes', or by an excess of black bile, which is congenital in anyone predisposed to the disease.

Father Ofhuys could certainly not have imagined that, a century later,
it would be precisely this third explanation, which attributed suicide and
mental disorders in general to natural causes, that would start to gain
ground among the cultured elites across Europe.

2.5   Melancholy, hypochondria and hysteria

From the mid sixteenth to the mid seventeenth century, many European
intellectuals (doctors, philosophers, theologists) thought that they were
facing a new form of epidemic, unlike any that had decimated the population until then: melancholy spread very rapidly through many parts of the
continent. 'This disease is most frequent in these days', wrote Girolamo
Mercuriale, one of the most renowned Italian physicians of the time, in a
treatise of 1601. 'In our times scarcely anyone can be found who is immune
from its contamination', asserted another doctor, Giulio Cesare Chiodini,
six years later, who was also convinced that it was 'the fountain of almost
all other diseases' and had spread through all levels of the population.
Robert Burton considered his 'chief motives' for writing *The Anatomy of
Melancholy* in 1621 to be the 'generalitie of the Disease, the necessitie of
the Cure, and the commodity or common good that will arise to all men by
the knowledge of it'. Burton's work runs to two thousand pages, in three
volumes, and is dedicated to the study of this disease, its causes, and the
ways to prevent it or treat it. This same idea was the subject of countless
treatises, written in Latin or in the vernacular, and published during this
period in England, France, Germany and Italy, as well as the vast repertoire of popular pamphlets containing stories, songs, jokes and dialogues
offering remedies for the disease.[61]

The term melancholy (or as it was used then, in the various European
languages, *melancholia, mélancholie, Melancholie*) covered a wide range of
meanings, including the full range of what we now call anxiety, mood and
personality disorders, numerous phobias, hallucinations and delirium.
Among the huge army of melancholiacs spread all over Europe at this
time, there were those who did not want to expose themselves to the sun
in the conviction that they were made of butter and would melt, those
who thought their relatives and friends were plotting to kill them, and
those who believed that their stomach was home to an entire colony of
frogs. According to Aegidius Albertinus, secretary at the Bavarian court
in the early seventeenth century, this army included Urbin, a stable boy
who believed he was emperor. Wearing a paper crown, he used to hang a
painted sheet on the stable walls depicting the pope, cardinals, kings and
princes, as well as the imperial knights in council, while he issued decrees
against the Turks.[62]

According to Burton, the symptoms of this disease could affect the mind or the body. The most important symptoms for the mind were fear and sadness. Sufferers were always frightened and trembling, prey to a profound sadness that sometimes turned to despair. They did not stop worrying, sighing, falling into despondency, complaining, pitying themselves and crying. There were also countless secondary symptoms. Melancholiacs were extremely cautious, wary, circumspect. They were timid and retiring, and reluctant to trust anything and anyone. Frightened of being constantly watched and overheard, they were concerned that everyone was talking about them, laughing at them, deriding and mal-treating them. They preferred to be alone, unobserved. They spoke little and thought a lot. Absorbed in their own thoughts and fantasies, they could remain pensive for long periods. They suffered from chimeras and visions. As the doctor and theologian Timothie Bright observed in 1586, in his work *A Treatise of Melancholy*: 'These most seeke to avoyde the society of men, and betake them to wildernesses, and deserts, finding matter of feare in every thing they behold, and best at ease, when alone they may digest these fancies without new provocations, which they appre-hende in humane societie.'[63] The bodily symptoms identified by Burton were thick lips and swollen veins, diarrhoea and constipation, flatulence and heavy breathing, vertigo and palpitations, tremors and stuttering, stomach aches and insomnia.

Melancholy was also an underlying cause of other non-fatal diseases, like epilepsy, blindness and madness. But in some cases it could also result in death, because it made life painful and unbearable, and even led to suicide. According to Burton this occurred above all when the victim was overcome by sadness, fear and anxiety. Those who fell prey to these ter-rible emotions were unable to sleep at night, because 'if they do slumber, fearful dreams astonish them', and during the day they 'are affrighted still by some terrible object', and 'as so many wild horses' they could not be quiet for a moment but were obsessed by its presence: 'they cannot forget it, it grinds their souls day and night, they are perpetually tormented.'[64] So, 'deprived of reason, judgement, all, as a ship that is void of a pilot must needs impinge upon the next rock or sands, and suffer shipwreck',[65] they end by taking their own lives.

What were the causes of this disease? The oldest and most authorita-tive response to this question was provided, in the fourth century BCE, by the Greek physician Hippocrates of Kos with the theory of the 'four humours'.[66] Following this theory, everything under the heavens is made up of four fundamental elements (earth, water, air and fire), each of which possesses two of the principal qualities of the body: hot, cold, dry and moist. The human organism contains four different humours, which reside in the four main organs: blood in the heart, choler or yellow bile in the liver, melancholy or black bile in the spleen, phlegm in the head. Each of these humours corresponds, according to Hippocrates, to one of the fundamental elements and therefore possesses its qualities. The blood, like air, is hot and moist; choler, like fire, is hot and dry; melancholy, like the earth, is cold and dry; phlegm, like water, is cold and moist. It is normal, therefore, that melancholy is present in all humans because it is merely one of the four humours that are physiologically present in the body. However, it may become a pathological condition, a disease that is both psychic and somatic, when the quantity and quality of black bile becomes abnormal.

Therefore, according to Hippocrates' theory, the causes of melancholy, like all other pathologies of the body and mind, were natural. A human being was healthy when the four humours within the body were balanced, and ill when this perfect proportion between the parts was lost and a single humour became dominant. The changes in melancholy, or indeed any of the other humours, were attributed to natural factors. They increased during the course of the day, and over the course of the seasons, and during life itself. 'Blood', wrote a philosopher in the High Middle Ages,[67] 'resembles air, increases in spring and dominates in childhood. Red [yellow] gall resembles fire, increases in summer and dominates in adolescence. Black gall resembles earth, increases in autumn, dominates in maturity. Phlegm resembles water, increases in winter, dominates in old age.'[68] The predominance of one humour in the general make-up of the body was also linked to the predominance of a planet: the sanguine temperament was governed by Jupiter, the choleric by Mars, the melancholic by Saturn, and the phlegmatic by the moon. The pathologies associated with black bile were also attributed to living conditions, to the climate and to diet. For example, the foods that provoked melancholy were cold and dry.

As the Christian doctrine of emotions (discussed in the previous chapter) gradually gained ground, so the theory of the four humours slowly faded. The concept of melancholy changed radically or was replaced by idleness, sadness, despair.[69] Suicide, like many sentiments felt by men and women and their actions, as well as their physical and mental disorders, was no longer seen as a natural phenomenon but rather one attributed to supernatural causes.

In the second half of the sixteenth century, the situation changed again. The concept of melancholy reappeared with a vengeance in the writings of European intellectuals and acquired semantic extensions and a relevance it had never had previously. Robert Burton affirmed that the pathology applied not only to humans but also to animals and plants ('vegetals and sensibles'), not 'to men only' but to the body politic. Melancholy was not just an affliction that made individuals sad and frightened, and caused them to lament and cry, nor was it limited to 'wild horses' who took their own lives. 'Kingdoms, provinces, and politick bodies, are likewise sensible and subject to this disease', and there 'the land lye untilled, waste, full of bogs, fens, deserts', and injustice, poverty, plagues, rebellions and wars abounded.[70]

Theologians tried to incorporate these explanatory models into Christian teachings on the emotions. In their writings, the category of melancholy often took the place of sloth and despair, and they made increasingly frequent reference to the relationship between the four humours. But they continued to attribute everything to supernatural causes. So, for example, at the start of the seventeenth century, the Milanese friar, Francesco Maria Guaccio, in his *Compendium maleficarum*, wrote, 'the demon is the external cause of sickness when he comes from without to inhabit a body and bring diseases to it'. Moreover, 'he induces the melancholy sickness by first disturbing the black bile in the body and so dispersing a black humour throughout the brain and the inner cells of the body'.[71] A few years earlier, the English Calvinist theologian, William Perkins, recalling the Hippocratic tradition, had affirmed that melancholy was 'a kinde of earthly and blacke bloud, especially in the spleene, corrupted and distempered', which emitted 'noysome fumes', resembling 'clouds or mists', that corrupted the imagination and made 'the instrument of reason unfit for understanding and sense'.[72] These physical causes were secondary, however. The primary ones were metaphysical and naturally concerned demonic intervention whereby the devil possessed the individual's imagination.[73]

It was widely believed that the devil attacked persons who suffered from melancholy and religious despair, urging them to blaspheme against God and to kill themselves. Hamlet, too, in the second act of the play, wonders whether the ghost he has seen 'may be the devil', and 'perhaps, out of my weakness and my melancholy – as he is very potent with such spirits– abuses me to damn me'.[74] During the course of the sixteenth century, many scholars had repeated that black bile was none other than the *Balneum diaboli*, and that the Devil delighted in bathing in the humour and taking advantage of the emotions it aroused. It was thought that Satan's predilection for this humour depended on the fact that there were several common features: both were dark, cold and were vaguely reminiscent of excrement.[75]

To tell the truth, Timothie Bright had already taken a few steps forward in his 1586 treatise, in an attempt to reconcile the Hippocratic and Christian traditions, when he distinguished between two different kinds of melancholy, one physiological, caused by the humours of the body and treated by the physician, and the other spiritual, caused by Satan's provocations and the sole competence of the theologian.

> Much lesse can a body overcharged with melancholy, & drowned in that darke dungeon see the comfortable beames of his daystar, & brightnesse of the cheerfull Sunne of God aboundant mercie, and a mind whose actions are hindered by meanes thereof, whereby it neither conceiveth nor judgeth sincerely and uprightly as the case requireth: and neither so only affected, but blinde folded by the humour, and brought into this darknesse of feare, is buffited also and beaten with Sathan on all sides.[76]

In the hands of the evil one, melancholy became a powerful and terrible weapon, used 'to all advantages of our hurt and destruction'. It is 'the very seate of the devill being an apt instrument for him, both to weaken our bodies with, and to terrifie our minds with vaine and fantasticall feares, and to disturbe the whole tranquillity of our nature'.[77]

Forty years later Robert Burton took another step forward. Like Bright he attributed melancholy to both supernatural and natural causes of black bile – namely diabolical intervention and the working of the liver and gall bladder – and to the relationship between this and the other three humours. But contrary to the earlier philosopher, Burton affirmed the importance of another group of factors, those of a social order. Melancholy was caused, he wrote, by the influence of the environment, education during childhood, the moral qualities of the child's wet nurse, relations with other adults, and traumatic events, like the deaths of dear ones or professional failures.

These two different understandings of the causes of melancholy and hysteria clashed publicly in London, in 1602, during the trial for witchcraft of Elisabeth Jackson. Catholics and Puritans both argued the supernatural origin of the woman's disturbances, while the Anglicans and some doctors attributed them to natural causes. One of these physicians, Edward Jorden, wrote a pamphlet in which he defended medicine's autonomy from religion, affirming that some physicians, 'not knowing what to prescribe, would flie unto divine causes, and neglecting naturall meanes for their reliefe, would wholy relie upon expiations, incantations, sacrifices, etc. cloaking their ignorance under these shadows'.[78] From then on, a growing number of doctors and members of the cultured elite of Western Europe abandoned spiritual and religious explanations of melancholy and mental disorders in favour of scientific causes.

After the second half of the seventeenth century the term melancholy began to be used less in medical texts and to be replaced by hypochondria, hysteria, spleen and vapours, all of which were understood as synonyms of the same type of disorders in men and women. Indeed, in addition to being caused by black bile, it was thought that melancholy was produced by the malfunction of the hypochondriac organs, sited in the upper and side parts of the abdominal cavity, and also in the spleen (a homonym for the pathology), liver, bladder and womb.[79] For example, when a man's spleen failed to absorb the black bile from the blood or the liver, dangerous vapours were formed that rose to the head, causing hypochondria. The female equivalent of this disease was hysteria, which instead was caused by disorders of the womb. If humours were accumulated in its vessels or in its veins, they rapidly became malignant and generated vapours that reached the brain and other parts of the body.

Therefore, in the last twenty years of the seventeenth century, many doctors started to think that Europe had been overtaken by a new epidemic, not of melancholy but of hypochondria or hysteria. In 1681, Sir William Temple wrote that these two affections (known in popular terms as 'the vapours' and 'the spleen') already 'employ our Physicians, perhaps more than other Diseases'.[80] In 1733, in *The English Malady*,

George Cheyne even claimed that almost one-third of the population was affected by these illnesses, but they were even more frequent in London and in the other large cities.[81]

In the closing decades of the seventeenth century, Thomas Willis, professor of medicine at the University of Oxford, who is now regarded by many as the father of modern neuroanatomy and neurophysiology, presented a completely new explanation of the origin of melancholy, hypochondria and hysteria. By denying the very existence of black bile, Willis threw the Hippocratic theory of the four humours into crisis. He revealed that men too suffered from attacks of hysteria, therefore demonstrating that the cause of this affliction should not be sought in the workings of the womb, but that its symptoms were broadly the same as those of hypochondria. At the end of a long period of observation and study, he reached the conclusion that hysteria and hypochondria were not caused by vapours rising from the womb and the spleen to the head, but instead originated in the brain and the nervous system.[82]

2.6   Depenalization de facto

Durkheim stated that the punishment of suicide in France continued throughout the eighteenth century, and even during the decades immediately prior to the Revolution. 'The property was confiscated', he wrote in 1897. 'Nobles incurred the loss of nobility and were declared commoners; their woods were cut, their castles demolished, their escutcheons broken.'[83] Yet later historical research has demonstrated that the Revolution of 1789 swept away laws against suicide that were already a dead letter, and had not been followed or imposed for some time.[84] Even Voltaire, in 1777, showed that he had perfectly grasped these changes when he commented that the old customs in this sphere 'have now been forgotten, even if they have not been legally abolished'.[85] It is true that the surviving documentation indicates that during the first half of the eighteenth century trials against those who had killed themselves became much rarer and then disappeared almost completely by the second half of the century. By 1712, a decree issued by the French king stated that 'suicides are often unpunished', because it was rare for Christian burial to be denied to those who took their own lives.[86] A study based on a series of 218 suicides occurring in Paris between 1764 and 1789 highlights that only three were sentenced by the courts to be hanged in effigy, probably because all three had committed other crimes (attempted murder, theft and burglaries).[87]

This was the result of far-reaching changes that had started much earlier at the various levels of society. Moreover, they also affected the magistrates and police. The French novelist and journalist, Louis-Sebastien Mercier noted in 1782 that 'the police try to remove suicide victims from public view. When someone kills himself, a police officer out of uniform comes to draw up a report without making a fuss, and then he compels the parish priest to bury the corpse without causing a scandal. Suicide victims, who were pursued after death by worthless laws, are no longer dragged on a cart.'[88] Changes were also underway among the religious community. Although the Catholic church remained unmoving in its outlook, parish priests stopped short of proposing the abolition of the old laws but quietly did whatever they could not to apply them.[89] The 1712 Declaration made by the crown noted that, if suicides often went unpunished, it was because their families reported 'untruthful' events to the priests, who believed them and pretended that they were true. What was even more surprising was that in some cases even the people expressed their distrust of the traditional customs by protesting violently against a sentence on a suicide victim. In 1753, in Puylaurens, when the corpse of a cobbler who had taken his own life was put in prison, as usually happened, prior to the trial, a group of armed individuals forced their way into the cell and 'freed' him. Two years later, in the administrative district of Castres, a furious crowd gathered to attack the court that had sentenced the lifeless body of a comb-maker.[90]

The information we have about the situation in England speaks even more clearly. In 967, King Edgar decreed that the goods of those who killed themselves would be forfeited to their overlord, 'unless [the suicide] was urged [to carry out this act] by madness or by illness'.[91] In the thirteenth century Henry de Bracton, one of the first great English jurists, distinguished three types of persons who killed themselves: suspected criminals, the depressed, and those who were mad or imbeciles (*furius qui rationem non habet, de mente capto, freneticus, infantulus*).[92] All movables and immovables were confiscated from the first group, while only movable goods were confiscated from the second group, and neither from the third. However, recent historical research has revealed that, contrary to Bracton's recommendations, the majority of suicide victims in the thirteenth and fourteenth centuries were sentenced, irrespective of whether they were men or women, rich or poor, in their right minds or otherwise. Suicides were rarely absolved if they were thought to be suffering from a mental disorder. Only the so-called frenetics were granted a little more indulgence, but confiscation was not imposed on depressed victims, lunatics, the furious and the demented (although there was no sign yet of melancholiacs in the sentences).[93]

Between 1487 and 1510 the judicial system underwent a series of reforms. Trials against those who took their own lives were conducted by the coroner's jury. Comprised of men who mainly came from the lower middle classes (tradesmen and farmers) living in the village or local area, this jury had the dual task of carrying out any investigations and passing the final sentence. Those who formed part of the jury were bound to visit the site where the corpse had been found, look for and listen to witnesses and then pronounce a verdict of guilty or innocent.[94] In the first case, anyone accused of having taken his own life was declared *felo de se*, namely self-homicide, and his goods were confiscated and he was denied Christian burial. In the second case, he was considered *non compos mentis*, not master of himself, suffering from folly, a madman or lunatic, and no punishment was imposed. The new laws introduced between 1487 and 1510 decreed that the coroner should be responsible for making inquiries into every violent or suspicious death that occurred within his district, after which he would send the results to the royal court and be paid for each sentence passed.

The relatives and defenders of the victim often made every possible effort, producing witnesses and various types of evidence, to show that while alive he or she had suffered from one or other form of mental disorder, including depression and acting strangely. But for a long period, the English juries almost never took these elements into consideration in their verdicts. During the first decade of the sixteenth century only two per cent of those accused were declared *non compos mentis*. This percentage remained stable for the rest of the century and only rose slightly in the first half of the seventeenth century, although it always remained less than ten per cent.[95] The situation only started to change in the closing decades of that century.

First of all, juries started to deliberately underestimate the value of the property owned by the self-homicide. Between 1485 and 1660, fewer than 40 per cent of suicides were recorded to possess assets that could be confiscated because many of them were destitute, or women. But during the following half century, this percentage shrank abruptly, reaching ten per cent in 1710. Moreover, the value of these possessions were increasingly often underestimated by the courts, falling from approximately one third of suicides who owned assets worth over one sterling to just seven per cent fifty years later.

In the second place, the number of acquittals, which had remained modest in the first half of the seventeenth century, rose rapidly in the second half of the century. The number of those accused who were declared *non compos mentis* doubled from 1660 to 1680, and tripled in the subsequent two decades to reach 40 per cent. This increase continued apace and, by 1760, 90 per cent of those committing self-murder were acquitted because they were judged to be mentally deranged. It was the aristocratic and bourgeois families who benefited most from greater clemency on the part of the courts, primarily because they were more influential and faced greater economic risks in the event of a sentence. Gradually, however, the advantages of this new development spread to all the social classes. During the course of the eighteenth century, the small, and declining, number of sentences that imposed penalties on those deemed to be of sound mind were for other crimes that would otherwise have escaped punishment if those accused committed suicide in prison. During the century, therefore, the idea gradually gained ground, among the juries, as well as in the highest ranks of English society, that anyone who killed themselves was *non compos mentis* and this radically changed the cultural significance of suicide.

The changing attitude of the intellectual elites – and of judges and doctors, in particular – to suicides probably started in the great urban centres of northern Europe. Undoubtedly this was true of London, where in 1601 the lifeless body of Richard Allen was judged *felo de se* by the coroner. But a few days later, Allen's friend visited Dr Edward Standhope, chancellor and vicar-general of the diocese of London, to request permission to bury the suicide's corpse in consecrated ground. He explained that Allen had cut his throat because of a terrible illness, but that before dying he had seen the local parson and had fully repented. The friend presented the case in such a convincing manner that he immediately obtained leave to do as he wished.[96]

At that time, the chancellor and vicar-general was a layman with legal training, who presided over the bishop's court, granted various licences (to marry, to practise midwifery), granted probate for wills and bequests, and undertook a variety of other duties. In the first half of the seventeenth century, the person holding this office was also responsible for approving requests for the interment in consecrated ground, alongside other Christians, of suicides' bodies condemned under civil law. Naturally, the petitions he received from the relatives or friends of offenders contained justifications for the unjustifiable act they had committed. In similar terms to the petition received from Richard Allen's friend, they often stated that the suicide had repented with his or her last breaths. But in many cases they also attributed the inconsiderate act committed by their dear ones to a state of profound melancholy, unsatisfaction, depression or mental confusion.[97] By accepting many of these petitions, in spite of the fact that they concerned condemned persons, the chancellor and vicar-general of the diocese of London has left us an unequivocal sign of the great transformations that had taken place in the city since the early seventeenth century concerning the meaning and moral judgement of suicide.

In Amsterdam attitudes to voluntary death changed radically after the first half of the seventeenth century. The works of the leading Dutch jurist, De Damhouder, point to the fact that, already by the mid sixteenth century, there were major differences between the written law and customary practice. Suicide through madness and despair were justified by the former and condemned by the latter. But a century later the situation had changed. On 26 June 1668 the corpse of a person condemned for suicide was hanged on the gibbet. He was a man who was in the habit of asking his wife for money to buy brandy, and when his request for two pennies was declined, he had threatened, 'I will hang myself, or let the devil take me'. 'Do want you will', his wife had replied, adding, 'you always say that.' She turned away to get on with her work. Shortly thereafter she found that her husband had hanged himself in their house.[98]

This was the last sentence executed in Amsterdam against someone committing suicide but not guilty of other crimes. From that time on, in this city and in other parts of Holland, suicide was only regarded as a crime if it occurred *ob conscientiam criminis*, namely to escape a sentence received for having committed another offence. Instead, anyone who killed themselves for any other reason, whether despair, melancholy, illness, financial or family difficulties, was not brought to trial and, in the worst cases, risked being buried in a cemetery with others, but in silence, without music and the customary ritual.[99]

In the Spanish Netherlands, the percentage of suicides attributed to madness and mental disorders in trial records rose from 13 per cent in the early half of the sixteenth century to 25 per cent in the latter half, before reaching 29 per cent in the first half of the seventeenth century. Over this same period, a diminishing number of suicides received severe court sentences while the number of those interred in consecrated ground rose.[100]

'Forgetting all fear of God', reads a sentence emanated by the court of Geneva in 1657, 'she abandoned herself, with malignant and unfortunate effect, and threw herself voluntarily into the Rhone, where she drowned, a case and crime deserving of severe punishment': the punishment decreed that the 'dead body of the said woman should be dragged by the executor of high justice on a hurdle around the city and then to the gallows where it would be buried'.[101] However, over the following years, the attitude of the magistrates and other social classes altered and punishment of those taking their own lives became increasingly less severe.[102] After 1680, the judges and pastors viewed voluntary death not as a 'revolt against God' but more often as a 'disease of the soul', and they made frequent reference to 'melancholy', 'frenzy', 'furor' and 'dementia' as circumstances that diminished the responsibility of the suicide.[103] After 1732, there were no further condemnations to execution by hanging for anyone who had committed suicide. During the closing decades of the seventeenth century and throughout the eighteenth, it became increasingly rare for the body of a person who had killed himself to be dragged through the city streets. The practice of confiscating their property was almost completely abandoned, inasmuch as only one per cent of those committing suicide after the second half of the seventeenth century were sanctioned in this way. Even the last remnant of the old system of punishment, the denial of Christian burial, lost most of its significance. From a staggering 98 per cent during the period 1550–1650, the percentage of suicides not buried in consecrated ground fell to 46 per cent during the following century and a half.[104]

Similar changes probably occurred during the course of the seventeenth and eighteenth centuries in many other parts of Western Europe. Certainly, the results of studies carried out in some regions of Germany seem to point in this direction, although their political, religious and social history differs extensively from that of the English.[105] From 1532, the Caroline constitution (*Constitutio criminalis carolina*), introduced by Emperor Charles V, was in force in Bavaria, and Article 135 defined suicide as a grave offence (on a par with homicide and infanticide), but the sanction of confiscation of property was only prescribed for those cases where a person took his or her own life to avoid punishment for another crime.[106]

In Bavaria, it was up to the district judges and parish priests to carry out the required investigative activities to determine whether a death had been voluntary, while it was the role of the Aulic Council to judge those who took their own lives. Owing to the constraints of the Caroline constitution, between 1611 and 1670, the Aulic Council of Munich requested inventories of the movables and assets of offenders in only ten per cent of approximately three hundred suicide cases brought before it, in order to decide whether to proceed to confiscation or not.[107]

Most of the activities of this council were focused on establishing whether the suicide deserved a church burial. One of the criterion used to reach this decision was the suicide's reputation. The more it could be established that, during his or her lifetime, the suicide had been a pious, devoted, God-fearing and observant Christian, and the greater esteem enjoyed by the victim's family and friends, the more likely it was that the council would recommend burial in consecrated ground. But an even more important criterion of evaluation concerned the motive behind the act, the mental state of the defunct prior to committing suicide. Suicide, it was thought, was above all provoked by religious despair, a serious form of apostasy, namely the rejection of one's belief in the resurrection and eternal life, which could only be instigated by the devil. For this reason, it was held that voluntary death could also be prompted by a completely different mental state, melancholy, madness, mental infirmity, pusillanimity or physical illness, plague, headaches, Hungarian fever. The Aulic council usually decreed dishonourable burial in the first case, and ecclesiastical rites in the second. However, there was a radical shift in the rulings issued by this body between 1611 and 1670, since the number of cases of religious despair fell, while the others increased, leading to a rising number of suicides who were given liturgical burial rites in cemeteries.[108]

Not dissimilar changes also occurred in Schleswig-Holstein during the course of the seventeenth and eighteenth centuries. From 1630 onwards, there was a growing separation in this state between legal norms and the praxis of the civil and religious authorities. While the former continued to condemn suicides to dishonourable burial, the latter became increasingly clement, and their judgements took account of numerous other criteria touching on the social conditions and mental state of the victim. This led to a steady rise in the percentage of suicides buried alongside the other faithful, in consecrated ground, and the number even reached 85 per cent by the second half of the eighteenth century.[109]

Having started in the cities, these changes only began to affect rural areas much later. In Paris the practice of bringing the body of the suicide victim to court was abandoned in the opening decades of the eighteenth century, but in small towns and villages it continued for much longer.[110] In many European countries, groups of peasants or artisans living in small farming communities opposed, sometimes vociferously, the ending of these traditional rites during the course of the nineteenth century. In late summer of 1817, in Poznan, one of the largest cities Prussia had seized from Poland, a minor government official called Wildenheim took his own life. The Lutheran church elders granted him the honour of a religious burial and his body was taken to the cemetery on the congregation's hearse, while the church bells tolled. But this decision deeply disturbed some of the faithful and three of them, a tailor, a carpenter and a glover, orchestrated a protest. They publicly attacked the elders and, having accused them of allowing the congregation's hearse to be desecrated, they demanded their resignation. Two assemblies of the entire Lutheran community were held and tensions ran so high that the elders were felt obliged to seek the protection of the head of police.[111]

In 1842, Abbé Duret, parish priest of Champtoceaux, a small French village, wrote a concerned letter to the bishop of Angers about a case that had deeply troubled him and for which he had been unable to find a satisfactory solution. One of his congregation had committed suicide a few days earlier. The victim was a woman who went to mass every Sunday and who suffered from leprosy. When told of this event, Abbé Duret had tried to persuade the woman's relatives into saying that the deceased had certainly acted in a moment of madness. But they persisted in believing and telling everyone that she was sane, although by doing so they knew she would be denied burial in consecrated ground. Even the other parishioners had urged the parish priest not to allow the woman who had taken her life to receive religious rites.[112]

In a small rural community in Russia, on the night of 24 April 1893, a peasant's wife left her home, passing quietly through five doors without anyone hearing her, and drowned herself. Her husband stubbornly insisted that she should be buried in the village graveyard, but he was strongly opposed by a large group of peasants who did not hesitate to submit a petition to the police, in which they reported that the woman had been 'of sound mind and purposely brought herself such a death without confession and without receiving holy communion'. Believing this protest to be the result of 'ignorance' and 'superstition', the police allowed her to be buried in consecrated ground. Throughout the summer, however, a series of natural calamities affected the village (fires and accidental deaths), and this provoked the peasants to take action by desecrating the poor woman's corpse.[113]

2.7   Depenalization de jure

The gradual abrogation of laws imposing a condemnation for suicide started in the English colonies of North America. In 1701, Pennsylvania and Delaware did away with the laws detailing the confiscation of property for those taking their own lives. In 1777, Virginia too followed their example, institutionalizing Thomas Jefferson's belief that 'Suicide is not to incur Forfeiture, but considered as a Disease'.[114] A few years later, the same decision was adopted in Maryland and New Jersey. In Europe, the first sovereign to reflect this new sentiment was the young ruler Frederick II of Prussia. In 1731, his father, Frederick Wilhelm I, had tightened the strictures against those who killed themselves, even if motivated by melancholy.[115] Instead, Frederick passed two edicts, in 1747 and 1751, abolishing the crime. In a radical reversal of an attitude that had been dominant for centuries, he identified the sole causes of suicide as 'madness', 'dementia', 'melancholy' and other mental disorders, and declared that treating this act as a criminal offence was not only pointless but also damaging, since it forced the suicide's relatives to 'prostitute themselves' and to resort to other unlawful means of surviving.[116] Moreover, Frederick II was convinced that individuals should not only have the right to take their own life, but that in special situations this was unavoidable if they wished to save their own moral dignity.[117]

This process of revising the criminal codes was a Europe-wide phenomenon, but it was implemented at relatively different times, so much so that two and a half centuries were to pass before it was wholly complete. Frederick II's example was followed in 1786 by Grand Duke Pietro Leopoldo of Tuscany who decided to exclude suicide from the list of offences. This also happened in Geneva in 1792, and in France during the years of the Revolution. On 21 January 1790 the constituent National Assembly passed a decree that, in the first place, defined offences as 'personal', thereby ruling out the possibility of confiscating the offender's property and damaging innocent heirs, and in the second place, established that the crime was extinguished with the offender's death, thereby reintroducing the principle of the non-imputability of suicide.

However, the next four years witnessed an increase in the number of persons committing suicide to escape the guillotine and this prompted the authorities to reverse their decisions. On 19 November 1793, the Convention passed a decree reintroducing forfeiture for those accused by the revolutionary court who subsequently took their own lives. Robespierre, Bourbotte, Babeuf and Darthé, all of whom had attempted to commit suicide, were dragged to the guillotine while still half-alive. On 16 March 1794 the revolutionary court of Marseille abruptly reinstated a practice that had been used for centuries by executing the already lifeless bodies of Étienne Goutte and Jean Guérin, 'dressed in red shirts'.[118] But this sudden return to past practice only lasted a short time. On 2 May 1795, the National Convention decreed that all property forfeited by suicides after 1793 should be returned to their families.

In Baden the decriminalization of suicide occurred in 1803, and in Bavaria in 1813.[119] In Amsterdam the law prohibiting convicted criminals from taking their own lives was abrogated in 1793.[120] In Austria, Joseph II's 1784 code introduced a less stringent law for those who committed suicide, ruling that they could be buried in cemeteries with others, provided that they repented before dying. However, it was only in 1850 that suicide was no longer regarded as a crime.[121] In Sweden suicide was decriminalized in 1865, and in Ireland this never formally occurred until 1993. The English parliament abolished the obligation to bury suicides outside the cemetery in 1823, and to confiscate their property in 1870,[122] but the criminal charge of voluntary death was only abrogated in 1961. By then, however, these laws were virtually a dead letter. It was rare for suicide cases to appear in court, and even rarer for cases to end with a sentence of *felo de se*. For the few that did, the sentence acquired a radically new meaning compared to the one it had had for centuries. It was no longer the clergy and beliefs in diabolical temptations that shaped these outcomes, but the concrete and solid interests of insurance companies and the growing number of life insurance policies they succeeded in selling throughout the nineteenth century. These companies refused to make any payment to the families of those who committed suicide when the court passed a sentence of *felo de se*, and this gave rise to widespread debate, polemic and further proceedings.[123]

In Italy, Article 585 of the 'Criminal Code of the States of His Majesty King of Sardinia', enacted in 1839 by Carlo Alberto of Savoia, stated that 'any person who kills himself voluntarily shall be regarded by the law as vile, and, having been deprived of civil rights, as a consequence of which any dispositions and last wishes that may have been made shall be deemed null and void, shall also be deprived of funeral honours of any kind'.[124]

In Russia, as late as 1835, the law regarded suicide as being on a par with homicide, denying religious burial to those who took their lives, while they punished with exile to Siberia and forced labour anyone who attempted to kill themselves, on condition that they were of sound mind. The criminal code introduced in 1845 no longer placed suicide and homicide on the same plane, and punishment was only inflicted on the former if it was intentional and had not been committed in a state of madness or temporary insanity brought on by illness. Moreover, these sanctions were much less severe than they once had been and were limited to invalidating the last will and testament and denying the suicide a Christian burial. The courts of Imperial Russia applied these norms to the trials of thousands of people. Yet, between 1830 and 1860, the percentage of those sentenced dropped from 46 per cent to 20 per cent.[125]

Last of all, in the Catholic world, although a number of priests had adopted a more open and lenient stance towards those who took their own life, the Church stuck, in appearance at least, to its traditional position. As late as 1917, the code of canon law promulgated by Pope Benedict XV reiterated the ban on ending one's own life. Yet, this was an affirmation of principle that lacked major practical repercussions. In reality, all that was needed was a medical certificate attesting to some kind of psychic disorder for the suicide to be entitled to all the religious ceremonies. The need for such a certificate was not dropped until 1965 at the Second Vatican Council. The 1917 code also stated that anyone who had attempted to commit suicide could not act as godfather at a baptism. In 1983 the bishop of Paris announced that suicide was no longer a sin but rather a disgrace, and he promised mercy towards those who took their own lives. Nine years later, this position was ratified by the official catechism, whose Article 2280 reads: 'Everyone is responsible for his life before God who has given it to him. It is God who remains the sovereign Master of life. We are obliged to accept life gratefully and preserve it for his honour and the salvation of our souls. We are stewards, not owners, of the life God has entrusted to us. It is not ours to dispose of.' The next article states that suicide 'contradicts the natural inclination of the human being to preserve and perpetuate his life. It is gravely contrary to the just love of self', and to 'love for the living God'. However, Article 2282 acknowledges that 'Grave psychological disturbances, anguish, or grave fear of hardship, suffering, or torture can diminish the responsibility of the one committing suicide.' Moreover, Article 2283 solemnly states that, 'We should not despair of the eternal salvation of persons who have taken their own lives. By ways known to him alone, God can provide the opportunity for salutary repentance. The Church prays for persons who have taken their own lives.'[126]

This ended a historical period that had begun one thousand five hundred years earlier with Augustine's pivotal condemnation.

2.8 Saving endangered lives

The radical nature of the cultural changes described in the preceding pages is also borne out by the establishment and diffusion, during the course of the eighteenth century, both in Western Europe and the United States, of programmes to save endangered lives and to prevent suicides, a trend that would have been unthinkable while that great edifice of beliefs, symbols and interpretations of voluntary death, which had been formed from the fifth century onwards, still held sway.

As early as 1620, Sebastian Albinus, a Protestant pastor in Saxony, argued that Christians had a moral duty to do everything possible to save anyone whose life was in danger because of some accident or disaster, irrespective of its nature.[127] In 1734, the Swedish Imperial Code obliged all subjects to intervene if they happened to witness an attempted suicide, establishing severe penalties for those who failed to act.[128] Over the following years, the political authorities in Britain, France, Denmark, Saxony, Prussia and the United States devised and published new life-saving programmes.[129] In Amsterdam, in 1767, the first private life-saving society was founded to aid those falling into water. The following year in Venice, the Provveditori alla Sanità approved a programme to save these victims. It was based on a report by Doctor Francesco Vicentini, which highlighted the need 'to instruct our People who are still ignorant of the possibility, now well known to all civilized Nations, of reviving some of the Drowned, even if apparently dead'.[130] This example was followed in Florence in 1773, and in Bologna and Lucca in 1774.[131] All these initiatives promised 'generous rewards' to those who saved a person's life: a medal and a sum of money. For example, in 1768, the Provveditori alla Sanità of Venice established that 'Anyone playing a part in the recovery and complete revival of submerged persons, whether by rescuing them or calling a medical practitioner to revive them, and also any doctor or physician involved in the recovery, shall receive from this Magistrature, subject to faithful assurance of revival, a cash reward corresponding to the part played.' On the contrary 'corporal punishments' would be imposed on those who 'neglected to rescue the said submerged persons'.[132]

These programmes also encountered incomprehension and resistance. Throughout Europe instant, unexpected and violent death had aroused suspicion and fear for so long because it was seen as a divine punishment. For centuries, on the part of many, there had been an engrained resistance or hesitation to approach the bodies of those dying in this way. These fears and taboos were still present in some sectors of the population in the eighteenth century, albeit much less strong and widespread than in earlier times. As Doctor Pietro Manni wrote in 1826, in Germany it had long been held, and some still thought that 'it would offend a gentleman's honour to rescue a drowned man'.[133] On the other hand, in some European countries, for a long time it had been unlawful 'to touch a drowned man or drag him from the water before calling an officer of the law who would record the event, and it was only after all the details had been noted regarding the situation and the circumstances of the corpse that any such attempt could be made'.[134]

2.9 The freedom to take one's own life

The huge increase in the number of suicides that aroused such concern among European commentators and scholars in the second half of the nineteenth century had started at least a century earlier than they thought. Far from being attributable only (or even mainly) to a breakdown in social integration and regulation, as they supposed, it was caused by the crisis and decline of that body of norms, sanctions, beliefs, symbols and rituals, interpretative categories and repertoires of ways of thinking and acting that for centuries had discouraged European men and women from taking their own lives.

The repeal of the laws condemning suicide was merely the last stage in a process of change that, moving at different paces, had affected the whole of Europe, both west and east. It would be wrong to think that this abrogation was the product of the Enlightenment alone, or of the declarations and requests of a group of leading intellectuals of the calibre of Montesquieu, Beccaria and Voltaire. Undoubtedly, their writings were immensely influential both for the cultured elite and for enlightened rulers. For example, it is unquestionable that Frederick II was inspired by Voltaire, with whom he corresponded, when he decided to repeal the laws banning suicide. But the thoughts of these and other intellectuals were in essence only the reflection of a change of mentality that had occurred much earlier.

This change started in the late decades of the sixteenth century and during the early years of the seventeenth, when a number of prominent figures in European culture – philosophers, playwrights, writers of comedies, even theologians – started to question the lawfulness of voluntary death and severely criticized the Christian view of it as the worst sin. This transformation became wider and more far-reaching when the old interpretative schemas collapsed and suicide was explained, not by supernatural causes, such as demonic possession and a lack of faith in God, but by natural ones. The first of these natural causes was melancholy and the malfunction of the hypochondriac organs – the spleen, liver, bladder and womb – and secondly it was attributed to problems of the brain and the nervous system. It was owing to this cultural change, and this process of secularization and medicalization,[135] that an individual committing suicide was no longer regarded as a criminal, but rather as a victim of cerebral physiology and life's misfortunes, a person 'deserving of compassion', as Frederick II wrote in his decree of 1747, because he was prey to 'folly', dementia, and melancholy.[136]

Little by little, a growing number of people in the most educated groups of urban society stopped believing that suicide was a heinous sin against the creator. While being held in the Tower of London, the poet and explorer Walter Ralegh (or Raleigh) tried to commit suicide on 19 July 1603, but did not succeed. However, he did so in the conviction that his action would not offend God, as he wrote in a letter to his wife: 'Be not dismaide that I dyed in dispaire of God's mercies. Strive not to dispute it. But assure thy selfe that God hath not left me, nor Sathan tempted me. Hope and dispaire live not together. I knowe it is forbidden to destroye our selves, but I trust it is forbidden in this sorte, that we destroye not our selves dispairinge of God's mercie.'[137] A few years later, John Donne made a similar argument: 'none may iustly Say, that all which kill themselves have done it out of a despaire of God's mercy'.[138]

Again in London, on 18 April 1732, a few days after the publication of Count Alberto Radicati di Passerano's book, a bookbinder charged with debt named Richard Smith and his wife Bridget shot their toddler in the head and hanged themselves in their rooms. On a table they left behind three suicide notes. In the first they asked their landlord to find a home for their dog and elderly cat, and they left him some money for this purpose. In the second, addressed to a relative, they accused a creditor for being responsible for their disastrous financial circumstances. While in the third, they justified their actions. Resorting to a sort of scientistic deism, they affirmed their belief in God, not purely on grounds of faith but for rational reasons, 'deduced from Nature and from the Reason of Things'. By looking through the microscope at this world of infinitely tiny things, they were convinced that not only did God exist, but that he was benevolent and merciful, and they therefore felt confident to resign their souls to him. Challenging the doctrine of the extraordinary deterrent of ritual profanation and deconsecration, they asserted their view by claiming 'the Thing being indifferent to us, where our Bodies are laid'. 'It is the Opinion of Naturalists', they added, with some satisfaction, 'that the bodies of men are constantly changing. New matter replaces the old, and a great many poor men have new Bodies oftener than new Cloathes.'[139]

The way in which individuals with suicidal ideas perceived and interpreted their physical and mental conditions also changed. In 1682, a bookseller in northern Germany attempted to kill himself but remained alive for several days. During that time he spoke to both the pastor and his physician. To the first he expressed his bewilderment at what had happened. When he felt the self-destructive urges sent by the devil, he had requested God's intervention and he now wondered, with bitterness, why his prayers had not been answered. For the pastor it was easy to answer that this was a clear sign of God's grace: he was still alive and had the chance to do penance for his deed. Instead, to the physician the bookseller listed the symptoms of all the ills that beset him and had prompted him to attempt suicide: sleeplessness, headaches, visions of small flames, buzzing in his ears, stomach pains, and anxiety.[140] Therefore, when describing and explaining what had happened, the bookseller resorted to the prevailing cultural code, which differed from that used eighty years earlier by the patients of the English physician and astrologer Richard Napier, and to demonic temptations he added melancholy, because the symptoms listed were indicative of this illness.

This code continued to change over the course of the following decades. In 1759, in Germany, a gardener's apprentice, who had unsuccessfully tried to kill himself with a knife, gave a different explanation of what had happened to him. He told his doctor that he had been overcome by melancholy, to which he was 'predisposed' by 'hidden haemorrhoids' that would violently break out from time to time, and which he was convinced he had inherited. He made no reference to the devil or other supernatural causes. A few years later, after she attempted to commit suicide, a German woman did not list melancholy as the cause of her action. Instead, she said, she usually ate, drank and slept well, like any other healthy person. Yet she complained that occasionally her head would become 'heavy and foolish' and that everything would begin to spin around her and she had strange, twisted, compulsive ideas. It was apparently during one of these moments of mental disorientation that she had tried to kill herself.[141]

Contributing to this crisis in the body of norms, beliefs and interpretative categories that had held Europeans back from killing themselves were other factors that signalled the onset of profound social and cultural changes. In 1611 John Donne painted a picture of the type of society that demanded the ability to dispose of the 'keys of my prison':

And new philosophy calls all in doubt,
The element of fire is quite put out,
The sun is lost, and th'earth, and no man's wit
Can well direct him where to look for it.
And freely men confess that this world's spent,
When in the planets and the firmament
They seek so many new; they see that this
Is crumbled out again to his atomies.
'Tisall in pieces, all coherence gone,
All just supply, and all relation;
Prince, subject, father, son, are things forgot,
For every man alone thinks he hath got
To be a phoenix, and that then can be
None of that kind, of which he is, but he.[142]

It was a world in which the Scientific Revolution was already underway and the doctrine of mechanism was gaining ground in philosophy. The astronomical discoveries of new planets obliged men to set aside the cosmological framework of the past. The idea that the universe was subject to unchanging natural laws raised questions regarding many magical and religious beliefs, beliefs in supernatural powers, spirits, Satan, demonic possession and temptations, and the efficacy of prayer.[143] The principle that knowledge was not certain until it had been demonstrated, that every scientific proposition had to undergo factual scrutiny and analysis of the experience and experiment, discredited such dogmas and revealed truths, as well as magical and religious explanations of events.

The decline of feudal society had been underway for some time, yet at its height, it had encouraged the view of suicide as theft. The breakdown of this fabric of strongly dependent personal relations, characterized by the presence of men of other men, heralded a crisis that laid the foundations for Montaigne's assertion that 'I am not bound to the laws against murder if I take my own life', because that life that does not belong to others, but is personal, in the same way that 'I break no laws against theft when I make off with my own property or cut my own purse'.

It was a world in which profound changes were taking place in the understanding that each individual had of themselves and of others. Each individual was regarded increasingly as unique, a Phoenix without peer, a single atom free to seek its own self-fulfilment, earthly pleasure, happiness, and to regard the latter as an asset that was greater than life itself, and therefore to decide not only how to live, but also how long.

There are good grounds, therefore, for thinking that the rising wave of suicides, which began between the late seventeenth and early eighteenth century and continued throughout the nineteenth century, was not so much a pathological social symptom but rather a consequence of the growth of individual autonomy, the affirmation of a new right to decide 'one's own life and death', as laid down in Article 6 of the *Declaration of the Rights of Man and of the Citizen* which was proposed and debated in 1793,[144] as part of the work on the new French constitution. It was a right that aimed to stand alongside those of property, liberty, and freedom of speech, expression and worship. Initially a bourgeois right, it started to be asserted, as we shall see, by those belonging to the highest social classes, but over time it would spread through all walks of life.

3

Killing God, Oneself and Others

On 1 November 1786, after having journeyed through numerous Italian cities, Goethe arrived in Rome. For some years his diary entries had recorded how his desire to see 'this capital of the world' had become 'my ambition and my torment', for which the cure lay only in 'my real living contact with the things themselves'. The city lived up to his expectations. 'Everything is just as I imagined it, yet everything is new', he wrote shortly after his arrival. With a feeling of calm and serenity, such that he had not experienced for years, he abandoned himself to the magnificent sights of old Rome and the modern city, he visited piazzas and gardens, triumphal arches and columns, palaces and ruins. But he also met a large number of people, whom he observed and listened to, and he was surprised by a few local customs, namely how frequent murder was yet how unusual it was to hear of self-murder. 'What strikes any foreigner, and what is still the subject of every conversation today throughout the city', he wrote on 24 November, 'are the murders, which happen almost every day. In our quarter alone there have been four in the last three weeks.'[1] Only a few hours earlier, a Swiss artist had been assaulted by a Roman who had stabbed him twenty times. Suicide, on the other hand, seemed 'utterly outside the range of their comprehension. One killed other people. Yes. That one heard of almost every day. But to take one's own precious life, or even contemplate doing so, that I had never heard of in Rome.'[2] Goethe thought that the rarity of suicides and the high frequency of murders was a peculiarity of the Italians and this prompted a number of bitter remarks. 'All I can say about the Italians is this: they are children of Nature who, for all the pomp and circumstance of their religion and art, are not a whit different from what they would be if they were still living in forests and caves.'[3]

The great German poet's impressions were well founded because Italy, in the closing decades of the eighteenth century, had a murder rate that was four or even five times higher than that of suicide.[4] But if Goethe had lived two or three centuries earlier, he would have seen that also in the cities of his country and elsewhere in Western Europe, the murder of others was much more frequent than self-murder. Although the data we have are fragmentary, they are quite clear in this respect. From the thirteenth to the fifteenth century, in England and in France, the number of homicides was ten to fifty times greater than the number of suicides.[5] In Zurich, in the first half of the sixteenth century, the former were forty times more numerous than the latter, in Amsterdam, during the same period, ten times higher, in Geneva, in the second half of that century, five times higher, and in Stockholm, in the first half of the seventeenth century, twenty times higher.[6]

3.1   Two opposite trends

Today, in all Western countries, the numerical ratio between suicides and homicides is reversed compared to what Goethe found in late eighteenth-century Rome or what had existed in central northern Europe in the previous centuries. Between 2001 and 2005, the former outstripped the latter in all of these countries. Just to cite a few examples, in Italy the frequency of suicide was seven times higher than that of homicide; in the United Kingdom it was eight times higher, in Belgium ten times higher, and in Austria a massive twenty times higher. This reversal is the result of the two opposite trends followed by suicides and homicides over the centuries. Far from being progressive or linear, these two trends reveal pauses, apparent breaks, and even short-term inversions. Yet, in the long term, the number of suicides rose significantly, while the number of homicides diminished.

The available statistics appear to show that the frequency of suicide in central-northern Europe overtook that of homicide much sooner than in southern Europe. For example, this occurred in London in about 1680,[7] in Zurich shortly afterwards (Graph 3.1), in Stockholm in the early decades of the eighteenth century, in Geneva after 1750,[8] in the rest of England and in Germany between the late eighteenth and early nineteenth century,[9] and in Italy a century later (Graph 3.2). This explains why, throughout the eighteenth century, to French and German visitors London seemed to have the highest suicide rate in the whole of Europe, while in the closing two decades of that century, some visitors regarded it as the city where murder was least frequent.[10]

In Italy, towards the mid nineteenth century, the number of homicides was three or four times higher than the suicide rate. Yet the next thirty years saw a brusque drop in the former, and slow rise in the latter. The two lines crossed in 1890 and remained quite close for about a decade, then drew apart once again. Since then, there have been various fluctuations, above all during the post-war periods. After the First World War there was a steep rise in the number of murders, reaching the same level as suicides, and the murder rate again soared after the Second World War. However, except for these two brief, abnormal periods, the number of those taking their own lives over the past century in Italy has always exceeded that of those taking the lives of others (Graph 3.2).

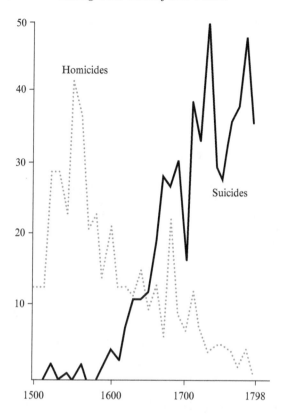

Graph 3.1   Homicides and suicides committed in Zurich from 1500 to 1798.

Source: Elaborated using data from Schär (1985).

This shift happened at different times in different regions of the country. It occurred in urban centres before rural areas, and in northern regions ahead of southern ones. Suicides outstripped homicides in 1870 in the northwest and in Emilia, in 1880 in Tuscany, in 1900 in Umbria and Lazio, and in 1930 in almost all southern regions except for Calabria where this inversion only occurred in 1995.[11] In Western Europe the two processes began at different times and progressed at different speeds. Estimated as between 30 and 50 per 100,000 inhabitants per year in medieval times, the murder rate dropped in the sixteenth century (10 to 20 homicides per 100,000 inhabitants) and continued to fall steadily, with the occasional fluctuation, up until the 1950s. It fluctuated again during the decades that followed but has now reached the lowest level for the past five hundred years (fewer than one per 100,000). This trend started in England, between the late fifteenth and early

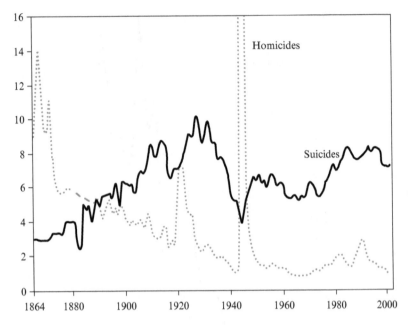

Graph 3.2   Suicide and homicide rates in Italy from 1864 to 2006.

Source: See Appendix.

sixteenth century, and a little later in some cities in Belgium and Holland. In Brussels, for example, the rate fell from 20 to 10 murders per 100,000 inhabitants between the fifteenth and sixteenth centuries.[12] In Amsterdam, from the late fifteenth till the end of the sixteenth century, it dropped from 43 to 28 murders per 100,000 inhabitants.[13] In Scandinavian countries the change happened towards the middle of the seventeenth century, and the same can be said of Germany and Switzerland.[14] Instead, in Italy and other Mediterranean countries it happened much later.[15] As well as starting at different times, the murder rate also declined at different speeds. This explains why, in the first half of the seventeenth century, there were such widely varying murder rates in different countries, ranging from a minimum of 2 per 100,000 inhabitants in England to a maximum of 12 per 100,000 in Italy.[16] On the other hand, as we have already seen, the rise in suicides occurred much later, from the closing decades of the seventeenth century. Yet this, too, started in the central northern countries of Europe before spreading to southern countries like Italy, Spain, Portugal and Greece much later.[17]

3.2   Two channels of a single stream

The relationship between homicides and suicides has long been a focus of interest for scholars, and it continues to be debated today.[18] The first historian to question it was André-Michel Guerry, in 1833, and after presenting some statistics for France, he remarked that there was an inverse geographical relationship between the two phenomena, because the 'departments where homicide was most frequent were precisely those where suicide was least common'.[19]

Other statistics and other studies were published in the decades that followed until, in 1886, Enrico Morselli,[20] summing up the key results to date, affirmed that there was a sort of antagonism between these two phenomena, in the sense that where one was present in a social body the other was lacking. This was apparent, in the first place, from the geographical variations. From an analysis of the numerous maps of Western Europe elaborated in painstaking detail by contemporary statisticians and demographers, it was immediately obvious that suicides were more frequent in the north and homicides in the south. Furthermore, similar differences could be identified within individual countries. In Italy, for example, the Piedmontese, Lombards and Ligurians were more likely to commit suicide, while the Sicilians and the inhabitants of Calabria and Puglia had a greater propensity to kill others.

Secondly, this antagonism was also apparent from comparisons between the component groups of European society, identified by religion, education and wealth. Protestants were more likely to resort to suicide, Catholics to murder. Suicide was also prevalent among university graduates and those who had completed secondary school, while murder was characteristic of the uneducated or those who had only spent a few years at school. Similarly, professionals, industrialists, those involved in large-scale commerce or in possession of considerable family wealth tended to commit suicide, while the unemployed, farm labourers and those who worked in factories and the service industries were more likely to murder others.

Lastly, this antagonism also emerged from the study of historical data series. The few figures that were available at the time revealed two opposite tendencies: the unstoppable decline in murder, and the equally unstoppable growth in suicide.

Starting with these findings, Morselli and other scholars saw suicide and homicide as two opposing phenomena within the social body, one vying against the other, whereas in the individual they were produced by the same causes. As the Italian criminologist, Enrico Ferri, wrote, 'since both suicide and homicide are forms of personal violence, it is natural that they are determined, broadly speaking, by the same causes and are manifested with similar frequency; on the contrary, the direction of this violence, whether against the self or against others, is manifested inversely'.[21]

According to these scholars, an appropriate analysis of these two phenomena had to start from the idea that they stemmed from two distinct processes, one concerning the production of personal violence, the other its direction. Suicide and homicide were therefore, in their opinion, 'two different channels of a single stream, fed by a single source, which consequently cannot move in one direction without receding to an equal extent in the other [. . .] two manifestations of the same state, two effects of the same cause' (as Durkheim wrote, cogently summarizing their positions).[22] The breadth and force of the current depended purely on individual factors (such as age), while its direction was the result of social variables. For example, the two opposite trends that had begun to be identified (the diminution of homicide and the growth of suicide) were attributed to changes in values and mentalities. The reason, wrote Enrico Ferri, was that 'while barbaric and violent men, being confronted with obstacles, prefer to sacrifice the life of others, civilized and gentle men, owing to their greater moral sense founded on respect of others, prefer self-sacrifice'.[23]

More recently, scholars have repeatedly returned to the metaphor of the stream and its two channels to explain the relationship between suicide and homicide. Both appear to be produced by severe frustration, or by the failure to attain a goal, to satisfy a need or to fulfil a desire. If the aggression arising from this frustration is directed against others, the result is homicide; or if directed against the self, the result is suicide. Here, too, the choice of one of these two expressions of personal violence appears to depend on social factors.[24]

Yet, when all is said and done, the theory of the stream and its channels cannot help us to explain the extraordinary, centuries-long process whereby homicides decreased and suicides increased. This was heavily influenced by the system of values peculiar to the historical period in which it was proposed, one in which there were still traces of the ethics that set suicide on the same level as homicide. Moreover, it reveals a theory of human action based on hydraulic principles that is hard for us to understand now. Instead, everything points to the fact that taking one's own life and killing others are two actions that are neither antagonistic nor complementary, since they have absolutely nothing in common and are completely independent, and on the contrary they depend on a number of totally different factors.

Furthermore, this theory is not confirmed by any of the statistics or facts that we now know. Although both processes continued over several centuries, they were initially separated by a gap of nearly two hundred years and therefore there is no reason to believe that they are 'two channels of a single stream, fed by a single source'.

3.3   Public and private crimes

The reason why homicide used to be committed much more frequently than suicide is that social relations and the system of beliefs and values discouraged the former much less than the latter. For centuries, the highest

Christian moral authorities had judged suicide much more severely than homicide because, as we have seen, it did not allow the sinner to repent or, as Augustine affirmed, the act of killing a human being became more execrable the closer the proximity between the person committing the act and the victim. 'For if a parricide be on that account more wicked than any homicide, because he kills not merely a man but a near relative [. . .] without doubt worse still is he who kills himself, because there is none nearer to a man than himself.'[25]

A similar hierarchy was used in the criminal codes of the past, albeit for partly different reasons. In the late nineteenth century, a renowned French anthropologist and sociologist, Marcel Mauss, stated that homicide was a crime introduced relatively late into public legislation,[26] and every study carried out since then has demonstrated the validity of his thesis. For the earliest European criminal codes the most heinous crimes were those against God, religious offences that would provoke divine anger and injure society: heresy, blasphemy, suicide and, later, witchcraft.[27] Witches and heretics were severely punished, and as is well known accusations often led to death at the stake. It is less widely known that harsh penalties were also imposed on those 'who took God's name in vain'.

Absent from the sevenfold capital sins, blasphemy came to be regarded as a mortal sin by the late twelfth century because it was an offence against the person of God, either directly or indirectly through the saints. Theologians at the time affirmed that, if blasphemy stemmed from a 'blasphemous spirit' and was repeated, it was a worse sin than homicide.[28] Until then canon law had only imposed a fine, as well as penitence, on those who violated the third commandment. But from the twelfth century onwards, even civil laws started to regard blasphemy as a crime. The statutes of Arles, for example, punished blasphemers with a fine and whipping. Increasingly harsh punishments were gradually introduced in all European countries against those committing this crime. These ranged from being muzzled like a dog to imprisonment or exile, piercing the tongue or removing it altogether, and even death.[29]

Suicide, heresy, witchcraft and blasphemy were regarded as crimes of lèse majesté, both divine and human, since they offended both the Lord and the sovereign. According to some medieval theories, the king was a 'mixed person', partly natural and partly supernatural, while others held that he was endowed with two bodies, one natural, which was subject to the passions and to death, and the other 'a Body politic, and the Members thereof are his Subjects': 'and he incorporated with them, and they with him, and he is the Head, and they are the Members, and he has the sole Government of them'.[30]

The idea that offences against the sacred were particularly severe persisted for centuries as an underlying principle of European penal codes during the *ancien régime*. In 1562, in England, when reading the sentence against a man who had committed suicide, the court emphasized that suicide was a threefold crime: an offence against Nature, against God and against the King, 'in that hereby he has lost a Subject, and he being the Head has lost one of his mystic Members'.[31] A century later in France, the criminal ordinance of 1670, sanctioned by Louis XIV, decreed that the principle whereby criminal liability was extinguished by the death of the offender did not apply to the four most grievous crimes: lèse majesté, both divine and human, suicide, armed rebellion against justice, and duelling. In all of these cases the corpse would appear on trial, 'to serve as an example to others'.[32] But even in 1776, by which time the situation had changed dramatically, an authoritative French jurist, François Serpillon, affirmed that suicide was 'a crime of divine lèse majesté' and was deemed much graver than assassination.[33] A few years earlier, another French criminal lawyer, Muyart de Vouglans, had opined that this act violated not only the religious order but also 'the political, under which every citizen is responsible, from birth, for his own life before his prince, his fatherland and his parents'.[34]

Precisely because they betrayed both God and the king, and threatened both religious and political order, suicide, heresy, witchcraft and blasphemy were among the first crimes to be regarded as public, and as such to be punished with public retribution, in a procedure known as inquisitorial, officially started by a magistrate in the name of the public interest, without waiting for the victim, witness or other person to press charges.

Homicide, on the other hand, even when committed outside the family (as it was in 90 per cent of cases),[35] was for a long time not regarded as a religious violation or an act that was injurious to the community, a public offence; instead, it was considered a personal injury, committed by one individual to the detriment of another. For this reason, it was not punished publicly, but privately, with an act of revenge or vendetta, namely another homicide carried out by the victim's family or friends, or with negotiations and settlements, reconciliation and agreements, sometimes reached by the parties themselves or through the intervention of the court, through a prosecution process initiated by the relatives of the victim.

Revenge homicide was therefore a (private) form of justice. This concept was clearly set out in *Il libro de' vizî e delle virtudi*, by Bono Giamboni, judge of the civil court of the *podestà* from 1261 to 1291. Justice, he wrote, was a virtue that was found in nine forms: religion, piety, safety, revenge, innocence, grace, reverence, mercy and concord. Safety is a 'virtue by which revenge is taken on evil deeds, and no one is allowed to go unpunished'; revenge is a 'virtue by which everyone is allowed to vanquish his enemy, ensuring he does no evil or injury and protecting himself from him'.[36]

Therefore, while suicide and blasphemy, heresy and witchcraft were punished quite severely by the civil authorities, homicide outside the family area was tolerated, justified or approved in some situations. In France, in the second half of the thirteenth century, the leading jurist, Philippe de Beaumanoir defined it a 'fine event' when it was committed as revenge for an offence. In Italy, from the twelfth to fourteenth centuries, the city statutes not only did not ban it, but they protected private vendetta, restricting themselves to specifying who could carry out a vendetta and how. The twelfth-century statutes of Pistoia, for example, stated that if a person were killed, it was legitimate for his closest relatives to take revenge or they could delegate the vendetta to armed men who would act *pro domo sua*. A statute of Bologna dating from 1252 and a Florentine one of 1325 acknowledged that the injured party had the right to take revenge, or if he had been murdered then this could be done by his close family. Furthermore, the Florentine statute also stated that the vendetta had to be proportionate to the offence, on the basis of like for like: death for death, severe injury or mutilation for corresponding injury or mutilation.[37] In England, at first sight the laws seem to be more stringent, since there were three distinct categories of homicide between the thirteenth and fourteenth century: culpable homicide when the offender was sentenced to death, excusable homicide, which could be pardoned by the crown, and justifiable homicide which was liable to be acquitted by the jury. Yet in practice, the laws were reasonably merciful towards those committing such crimes. Of 2,667 individuals accused of homicide between 1300 and 1348, as many as 88 per cent were acquitted, compared to 31 per cent of those charged with larceny or burglary.[38] In Zurich by the end of the fourteenth century, the butcher Welti Oechen, who had killed another butcher in a fight, was sentenced to pay a sum of money to the victim's family, because the court had learned that he had been insulted by the victim.[39]

Revenge and violence against others stemmed from the enormous importance attributed to honour. Honour was deemed equivalent to life itself, and therefore it had to be constantly and insistently defended from any act that might endanger its preservation or result in its loss, an event that was seen as irreparable, like the loss of life itself. Physical aggression, insults and non-verbal gestures all constituted a lack of respect. Indeed, it was often these acts and gestures, as Philippe de Beaumanoir noted, that led to murder. 'Homicide', he wrote in 1284, 'is when one kills another in the heat of a fight, in which tension turns to insult and insult to fighting, by which one of those involved often dies'.[40] Precisely because they were necessary to defend a person's honour, these homicides had to be committed in public, and seen by the largest possible number of witnesses, during daylight, in the marketplace or in other crowded places, so that everyone would know what it meant to insult the perpetrator.[41]

A man's honour not only depended on his birthright and lifestyle, on what he did and the people he frequented, on his virility and on the respectability of his womenfolk, it also depended on his ability to take revenge swiftly and effectively in the event of an insult. As the Florentine thirteenth-century saying went, 'Injury is done to those who do not avenge injury', or 'Whoever is fearful of revenge will make many wicked', or even 'An enemy's blood stain brings joy'.[42] Whoever failed to live up to the social obligation of retaliation and let insults pass unheeded lost his honour and became an object of derision and scorn. The sort of expressions used in fourteenth-century Tuscany were: 'Fie, fie, have you no shame? Avenge the death of your son who was killed', 'You're lying through your teeth since you know your father was killed. Avenge yourself or be ashamed of appearing among the people', 'Whoring bitch you are, take revenge for your nephews who were killed and thrown across your doorstep', 'And if you're as brazen as you pretend, go and take your revenge! Go and avenge the son of Puccino Vannucci!'[43] Anyone who was insulted had to take revenge, even if they knew they had been insulted with good reason.

This certainly does not mean that medieval society was overrun by anarchy or dominated by destructive, murderous impulses. Historical research over the past thirty years has shown that, far from being an expression of uncontrolled violence, vendetta served as a means of settling conflicts. In addition to written statutes (like the statutes of those Italian city states mentioned earlier), the unwritten laws of custom dictated precisely who had the right to take revenge for a wrong incurred, how this could be done and against whom. This system of conflict resolution was flanked by another private system: the agreements and compromises reached through the intervention of a moral authority.

This system, which is now known by medieval historians as 'negotiated justice',[44] was widely practised throughout Western Europe. By way of example, Gualtieri (Walter) of Brienne, the Angevin overlord of Florence between 1342 and 1343, convinced 400 families (therefore a few thousand individuals) to sign peace agreements in the communal palace or the church of San Piero Scheraggio within the first six months of his rule. These individuals agreed to pay compensation for their insults, or declared that a conflict was finally over after vendetta had equalized the insult.[45] They sealed the 'peace' with ritual gestures, touching hands, embracing or kissing on the mouth.[46] The purpose was not to punish the author of the crime, but to make up for and satisfy the insult. This satisfaction could take various forms: it might be monetary, namely paying the relatives of the dead man in cash or other goods; or symbolic, in the form of public displays of repentance and the humiliation of the guilty. For example, in Rome between the fourteenth and fifteenth centuries, the injured party slapped the guilty person on the face, and then the two would kiss forty times on the mouth.[47]

From the fifth to eighth century, anyone who killed another person was obliged to pay money to the victim's relatives, as compensation for the damage caused. This was known as *guidrigildo* in Italian, from *wergeld*, a man's price. The sum varied from one region to another, and also depended on the victim's gender and social status, as well as how he or she had been killed. The price was higher if the victim had belonged to a noble family, or if he or she had been drowned, or killed in an inhabited house or by an armed band.[48]

Over time the custom of paying *guidrigildo* gradually faded, until it almost disappeared in the fourteenth century. Yet homicide was long after still regarded as a private crime, which called for some form of

compensation payable to the victim's family. The principle of the inesti-
mable value of human life discouraged any monetary arrangement. Yet
this was still possible in private transactions between the parties. But if
legal process was chosen involving the courts then recourse was made to
other forms of reparation to the victim's relatives, such as masses to be
said or pilgrimages to be undertaken. For example, in 1453, in the town
of Nivelles, Brabant, having killed Antoine Jackelart, Jehan Germain and
his family and friends negotiated a peace pact with the victim's father
through the intermediation of a group of 'arbiters'. This pact was recorded
before a magistrate and stated that the murderer should undertake four
pilgrimages 'by way of reparation': one to the Holy Land and the others to
Santiago de Compostela, Notre-Dame de Rocamadour and Sainte-Larme
in Vendôme. It was also stated that Jehan Germain might avoid the first
by paying the victim's father an agreed sum of money, but that the other
three should be accomplished within four months.[49]
   In Holland the authorities used to proclaim a certain period of peace
immediately after a murder. This served two purposes: first it made it
illegal to carry out acts of vendetta, and second it encouraged the parties
to come to terms with the help of intermediaries. If reached, the agreement imposed a series of obligations on the two parties and called for
certain ritual acts. The relatives of the murderer would give the victim's
family a sum of money that varied depending on the circumstances of
the murder, the victim's social standing and the financial wherewithal
of the murderer's relatives. Then, they would undertake to carry out a
number of good deeds, including a pilgrimage, for example. Lastly, all
the men in the murderer's extended family, occasionally numbering up to
two hundred-strong, would humiliate themselves in public, barefoot and
humbly clothed, prostrating themselves before the victim's relatives and
begging for their pardon. At this stage the latter had to swear solemnly
that the vendetta was over, and that the two extended families would now
be reconciled. On occasions some men who were related to the murderer
would then pay homage to the victim, thereby acknowledging the existence of firm new bonds of friendship between the two families.[50]
   In all these cases, the civil authorities expressed no moral judgement on
the murder nor did they punish the murderer. Instead, their efforts were
focused on reaching an agreement between the parties and calculating,
with the utmost precision, the compensation owed to the victim's family,
in cash, masses, and pilgrimages. The function of the civil authorities was
therefore not to sanction the offender, but to establish a new equilibrium
based on the delicate parity between offences incurred and given, one that
would above all break the chain of vendetta murders.
   The code of values was shared by the political authorities of the time,
since in the late medieval period they had no monopoly on either justice
or legitimate violence. This code regarded crimes against God as being
much more serious, while homicide was only a private offence that did
not threaten public order.[51] In France, in the early fourteenth century,

subjects who had committed a crime could petition the king for pardon, either in writing or orally. If the sovereign decided to accept it, his pardon ended and concluded the normal course of the law and reinstated both reputation and possessions to the accused. In a series of judicial processes reminiscent of the sacraments (supplication, repentance, penitence, confession, absolution), this procedure applied to all crimes of the period: suicide, blasphemy, lèse majesté, rape, theft, homicide and many others. Yet during the course of the fourteenth and fifteenth centuries, French kings showed quite different attitudes to these offences.[52]

One of the most easily pardoned crimes was homicide, above all if carried out to avenge an injury incurred.[53] Crimes against religion, such as blasphemy, were punished far more seriously. In 1286 Luigi IX passed an edict against those who committed this unlawful act. Since then, all successive kings, up to the start of the seventeenth century, continued to introduce new and increasingly severe measures to punish blasphemers.[54] For example, in an ordinance of 7 March 1397, Charles VI made it obligatory for witnesses to report this crime. And even when granting pardons, French sovereigns took sterner measures against those who assaulted God by blaspheming against him, compared to those who had killed another individual.[55]

3.4   What brought about these changes?

The fall in homicides and the increase in suicides can be attributed to numerous changes taking place in Europe, most of which were entirely unconnected. Primarily, there was a radical change in the moral evaluation of these two actions and the act of killing others began to be regarded much more severely than the act of taking one's own life.

At the end of the Middle Ages jurists embarked on a lengthy and critical reassessment of homicide and pronounced it to be a public crime. They also considerably reduced the grounds for justifying it as an act of self-defence by reversing the burden of proof. Previously, this had fallen on the accused who had had to demonstrate the voluntary nature of the crime. Thereafter, the legal presumption of guilt was introduced, unless the defence could prove that the act had been accidental and involuntary.[56] The gradual acquisition by the state of a monopoly of justice also dates from the same period. Negotiations, reconciliations, agreements and private pacts between parties became irrelevant as the inquisitorial procedure replaced the accusatory one and the state became responsible for formally initiating the process, rather than waiting for the injured party to denounce a crime. The numbers of murderers who stood trial and were sentenced rose steadily. In short, this period marked the start and continual development of the system of justice typical of the modern state, whose key aim is not to compensate the injured party and re-establish peace, but rather to punish the guilty and enforce law and order.

By the mid seventeenth century, the same countries saw the start of the depenalization of the 'gravissimum' crime of 'self-murder'. As we have already seen, judges in England showed growing clemency to those who had committed suicide and the number of absolutions grew. In central and northern Europe, the practice of subjecting suicides' corpses to degrading and deconsecrating rituals was gradually abandoned, as were the customs of putting suicides on trial, confiscating their property and burying them far from cemeteries.

The depenalization of suicides benefited from the crisis of feudal society and of the absolute subordination that characterized it, which had led to the view that voluntary death was equivalent to theft and perjury. Moreover, it was also hastened by the decline in traditional belief systems concerning the causes and consequences of suicide and the slow affirmation of scientific categories of interpretation.

The criminalization of homicide was made possible by the birth and rise of the modern state and its monopoly of legitimate violence. In order to acquire this monopoly it had to strip citizens of all the arms that had long been used to fight and enforce justice on their own grounds. In Europe, the aristocracy had maintained bands of heavily armed men for the everyday purposes of defence and attack. For example, in Bologna, even in the seventeenth century, noble families still kept 'an armed guard at the entrance, consisting of many men armed with guns who would march to and fro, without a break, under the loggias and below the portico in full sight'.[57] The military strength of the grandest families was frequently much greater. In sixteenth-century England, Robert Dudley, Count of Leicester, had sufficient arms for 200 knights and 500 infantry. During the same period in Spain, the Duke of Gandia possessed an arsenal large enough to arm 600 musketeers. Others owned numerous canons. Weapons were also commonly owned by families from other classes: in addition to knives for fighting, these might include swords, lances, clubs, halberds, helmets, full suits of armour, and even rudimentary firearms, like culverins.[58]

In order to acquire a monopoly of power, rulers and lords throughout Europe tried, on numerous occasions, to limit the ownership and use of these weapons. In 1287 and 1487, the King of France banned the carrying of 'bows, crossbows, halberds, lances, swords and daggers'. In the mid sixteenth century, the Duke of Florence, Cosimo I de'Medici, introduced a licensing system to authorize the use of weapons. From the fifteenth century onwards the English crown similarly decreed limits and prohibitions. Yet everywhere these attempts met with lively resistance. In Florence, for example, weapons continued to be so widespread in the sixteenth century that if a man was not armed then it was presumed he was a priest.[59]

In order to establish a monopoly of legal violence, states had to institute a variety of bureaucratic structures, armies and forces of public order. France was the first country to introduce a police force in both Paris and rural centres, while England and other European countries only followed its example much later.

The modern state succeeded in reducing the number of homicides, not only by acquiring a monopoly of legal violence but also by establishing broader legitimacy.[60] In those areas where the state struggled to win the trust first of its subjects, and later its citizens, as was the case in Italy and other Mediterranean countries, the murder rate declined later. In the mid nineteenth century, a French author, Edmond About, noted that if the inhabitants of Rome relied on their blades to settle private disputes, it was because they had little faith in the state and the courts. What was more, he added, in the Papal States, the clergy only viewed 'crimes against God' as unpardonable. 'Rome punishes sins and the ecclesiastical court condemns blasphemers to the galleys', yet the Church was indifferent to the fact that 'workers and peasants would slit each other's throats after vespers on Sundays'. Indeed, if an assassin took refuge inside a church, a monastery or a hospital, he would be safe because the clergy refused to hand him over to the lay authorities.[61]

The criminalization of homicide and the drop in numbers were also accelerated by a gradual shift away from the obligations of vendetta, something that was in turn provoked by two factors. Firstly by the gradual decline in the role of the family honour, and secondly by the fact that insults traded in public, before as many people as possible, threatening honour and prompting the need to defend it, started to become less frequent, at least in London by the closing decades of the seventeenth century.[62]

An important impetus was also given by the Protestant church.[63] In Holland, after 1580, the leading church authorities repeatedly expressed extremely severe judgements against murder in moral tracts and condemned those who committed murder. If they were ministers, they were deprived of their office in provincial and regional synods. They questioned and subsequently rejected in full the traditional rites of mediation and settlement between the murderer's family and that of the victim, which were still widely practised. In the strong conviction that they should do everything possible to punish the assassins, the authorities decided at the Synod of Gouda in 1586 that, while continuing to advocate peace and forgiveness among the faithful, ministers could not be involved, in any way, in the 'reconciliation that follows a murder'.[64] Furthermore, they forbade any activity aimed at securing a royal pardon for anyone who committing such a crime. The churchmen repeatedly invited the lay authorities to take a firm stance against anyone who killed another person and they solemnly requested the secular courts to bring them to trial and, wherever possible, to condemn them to death. In the latter half of the seventeenth century duelling and the honour code that regulated it were also strenuously condemned.

The Catholic church exerted a different influence. For centuries its clergy had, to a great extent, shared the moral principles of the society in which they lived. For example, in the thirteenth century, Fra Salimbene had praised a man who only killed one other man in a vendetta, instead of two. Likewise Franciscan preachers attacked the Jews in many Italian cities in the fifteenth century, inciting the population to ransack their houses not only because they were seen to be constantly guilty of the sin of usury but also as a way of avenging Christ's crucifixion.[65] In the 1490s, an anonymous treatise on penitence continued to affirm that fornication was a sin 'more detestable than murder or theft, which are not substantially evil'. For, in certain case, one is authorized to kill or to steal; but 'no one can deliberately fornicate without committing a deadly sin'.[66]

The situation certainly altered in the sixteenth century. The Jesuits made huge efforts to settle disputes between individuals and among families. In those cities where factional struggles were most marked, they got in touch with the leaders of the groups involved and did everything possible to convince them to forgive each other. In 1545, Padre Pascasio Broët wrote a letter describing the measures he had taken in Faenza:

I spoke with some of the leaders, prudent and suitable men who would know how to bring peace to these disagreements; and in this way the Lord brought peace, through his goodness and mercy, and with great solemnity over one hundred man gathered in the main church, and they all forgave one another, for the love of Christ, Our Lord, for the homicides committed in the past, for wounds, insults, and other ills that resulted from such hatred.[67]

In order to achieve this end the Jesuits also introduced some very spectacular ceremonies. For example, in 1668, in a place in Puglia, they persuaded the leaders of two opposing bands to be tied together with a rope around both of their necks, symbolizing the 'servitude that bound them both to the Virgin' and the 'indissoluble bonds that linked them'.[68]

These measures certainly contributed to the decline of the code of vendetta. But at the same time, by continuing to treat the family that had been insulted as the injured party instead of the entire community, the Jesuits delayed the institution of the modern penal system.[69]

3.5 At the forefront of change

Even if they are separated by a gap of almost two centuries, the two long-term trends under investigation here, the falling homicide rate and the growing number of suicides, both began in the same middle-to-upper sections of central-northern European society that had also seen other major changes, such as the rise of the nuclear family, voluntary birth control and declining fertility rates.

Already by the mid nineteenth century and using the earliest available statistical data, scholars had shown that suicide was more frequent in the upper levels of society.[70] Half a century later and statistics revealed that members of the intellectual bourgeoisie were most likely to take their own lives. In Prussia – as Durkheim noted – there was a particularly high suicide rate among the corps of public officials.[71] While in Italy, according to Morselli's figures, suicide was most frequent among those belonging to the 'managerial classes', especially the intellectual professions: academics, scientists, journalists, engineers, 'all those, in short, who make the greatest use of their brain power'.[72] Studies carried out over the following years, on the situation at the end of the nineteenth century and during the opening decade of the twentieth, reached the conclusion that, 'the higher the position of a group in the social hierarchy, the greater the frequency with which its members killed themselves'.[73] According to Morselli, the spread of suicide among the upper classes was due to 'the direct ratio it has with the increased overuse of brain power'.[74] On the other hand, Durkheim attributed it to the extent of social disaggregation, because the spread of education and the growth of the intellectual classes were effects of this disaggregation, and this in turn contributed to the increased frequency of suicide.[75]

Today even the most plausible of these explanations, that put forward by the great French sociologist, no longer appears convincing. There is nothing to indicate that members of the intellectual classes were less integrated in society, or less cared for and supported by others, than those on the lower rungs of the social ladder who had more limited financial resources. Moreover, there was a greater likelihood that the latter would suffer from physical and mental illnesses that might push them towards suicide.

The reason why members of the upper classes of society committed suicide more frequently than others during the nineteenth and early twentieth centuries was therefore not a lack of integration and social support but because they were pioneers of a major cultural shift. They were the first to move away from that set of values, laws, beliefs and interpretative categories that had dominated Europe for centuries, the first to realize that men and women did not kill themselves because of supernatural causes or because they were unable to resist demonic temptations, the first to accept that their lives belonged not to God or their sovereign but to themselves alone, and that only they could decide whether or not to end them.

It seems likely that, during the Middle Ages, the frequency of suicide was similar across all social classes. However, it is clear that the great growth in suicide numbers started, in Western Europe, and much later also in Eastern Europe (as we shall see), among the upper classes. It is among the English aristocracy and the affluent middle classes that, based on a range of documents, the 'new way' of ending one's life first began in the last twenty years of the seventeenth century. On the other hand, unequivocal statistical data reveal that when the number of voluntary deaths started to rise in Geneva, in the first half of the eighteenth century, merchants were the most frequently reported victims, although this group remained the city's wealthiest and most powerful class throughout this period. By the second half of the century, this behaviour spread to the intermediate social classes.[76] This interpretation is also confirmed by the far-reaching changes in the relationship between social class and suicide risk that took place in Western Europe during the twentieth century, and by the fact that this relationship is now the opposite to what it once was. For several decades in all Western countries, it is now not the most educated, nor the wealthiest or those with higher social standing who most frequently take their own lives, but rather the most socially disadvantaged. By the middle of the twentieth century, in France, the frequency of suicide grew in reverse proportion to social origin. Labourers were five or even seven times more likely to commit suicide than members of the upper classes. Contrary to the situation in the closing decades of the nineteenth century, teachers and other professionals (doctors, lawyers, architects, engineers) had a very low rate of suicide.[77] This was also the case in Finland, in the United States and in Hungary. Today, in all the countries for which we have data, the risk of someone committing suicide grows in relation to the lack of schooling and income.[78]

Homicide rates also started to fall among the highest echelons of society. During the Middle Ages, the culture of vendetta and blood feud affected families at all levels of society, yet it was the nobility that most frequently reacted violently to the slightest insult or affront. Four reasons can be put forward. In the first place, the nobility had a keener sense of family honour, while secondly, embarking on vendettas called for significant physical, social and financial resources. As the Florentine merchant, Paolo da Certaldo, claimed, 'vendetta drains the soul, the body and all your belongings'.[79] Indeed, vendettas were so expensive that, like banquets and dowries, they ended by being seen as a demonstration of wealth and power, an instrument of conspicuous consumption and a sign of extensive networks of friends and family.[80] Thirdly, the nobility could call on bands of armed retainers at particular stages of these conflicts. Lastly, the nobility enjoyed many privileges and continued to see themselves as being above the law for many years to come.

Various documents indicate that this happened in most of Western Europe. In Bologna, for example, in the thirteenth century, the nobles were so violent that they were widely known as 'ravaging wolves'.[81] But more specific figures refer to Venice during the course of the fourteenth century. At the time the city's population was divided into five distinct groups. At the top were the patricians, representing about four per cent of the population, closely followed by the clergy (three per cent) and the merchants and wealthy professionals (11 per cent). The vast majority of Venetians (77 per cent) formed part of the *popolani* or workers, while the remaining five per cent were vagrants or vagabonds.[82] The most violent of these groups, and the most prone to excess, was without doubt the nobility. Moreover, although the system of criminal law was under its control, the nobility committed more verbal and physical acts of aggression than other groups, including assault, rape and homicide.[83]

In England and Holland, however, it was the nobility that during the sixteenth and early seventeenth centuries was at the forefront of changes that would bring about a fall in the acts of violence.[84] In some countries, this change resulted from the spread of duelling, a form of formalized combat between two men for the purpose of defending honour, which gradually replaced the much more violent practice of vendetta. As Count Annibale Romei wrote in 1586, it too was a 'fight between two equals, over a cause of honour, at the end of which the vanquished falls in infamy and the winner retains his honour'.[85]

Also in central and southern Europe it was among the families in the higher echelons that changes were first seen, but considerably later. In France this occurred during the eighteenth century.[86] In Bologna, in the mid seventeenth century, the canon lawyer Ghiselli noted his opinion of the nobility in his chronicle: 'they are quick to take insult, and are wounded by the least pinprick, all too willing to start a vendetta; as hasty in their resentment as they are unforgiving in their enmity, they stop at nothing to crush their adversary. They are impetuous in their indignity and do not disdain to violate and defile the holy institution of Christian life with inhuman actions. They have no respect whatsoever, whether for the loss of property or life, because they are exempt from taxation and do not fear justice, certain of avoiding its consequences through flight, and impeding its enforcement by removing evidence, so that they are many crimes of which the nobility can never be proved guilty.'[87] After the mid seventeenth century, noble violence changed slightly in that the majority of homicides were committed by assassins. But in the last two decades of the century, it found an outlet in carefully regulated duels, leading to a diminution.[88] This change occurred even later in Sardinia, where in 1767–99 the minor rural nobility committed violent crimes much more regularly than other social groups.[89]

Although the change was first noticeable among the upper classes, the differences between them and the rest of the population in terms of aggression and levels of violence were such that, even by the mid seventeenth century, the nobility committed more homicides in London than other groups.[90] Yet, by the nineteenth and twentieth century, this record was overtaken by the lower classes right across Europe, even though the tendency to kill others continued to fall in all social groups.

Among the lowest social strata right across Europe a culture of violence for the purpose of defending honour persisted for many years, leading to armed fights between young men, which in some ways resembled the duels that were commonplace among the aristocracy and bourgeoisie. These fights were usually also triggered by a verbal exchange of insults; they too were consensual, took place between two youths armed with equal weapons and followed agreed rules. However, these popular duels stemmed for the most part from affronts to male identity and they were fought without seconds, not with a pistol or sword, but with a knife. Moreover, the rivals aimed above all to gash their adversary's face, because a scar was a symbol of insult.

In Amsterdam these popular duels became less common from the second half of the eighteenth century, and then almost disappeared altogether.[91] Yet in other parts of Holland, as in many other countries (including Italy and Greece, for example),[92] they survived until the early twentieth century. In 1861 the French author Edmond About noted that the Roman populace had the same attitude to those fighting with knives as the Parisians had towards duels between gentlemen, concluding that the assassin was right and the victim wrong. Using words reminiscent of those used six centuries earlier by his fellow countryman Philippe de Beaumanoir, he wrote: 'when in the heat of argument two men exchange certain words, they know that blood must flow between them. War is implicitly declared. The acknowledged battlefield is the entire city. Both accept that the crowd will act as the witness and that they must be on guard at every moment, day and night.'[93]

Today, in all Western countries, even though gender and age are the most influential factors affecting the probability that an individual might commit murder, those who actually kill others are most frequently characterized by a low level of schooling and income.

Therefore, the relationship between social class and the risk of committing suicide or homicide has changed drastically throughout Europe, albeit for different reasons and over different periods. While in this past it was the upper classes who were most exposed to this risk, today it most frequently affects those from the more disadvantaged social groups.

3.6 Despair, anger, hatred

It will be easier to explain the two opposite and multi-secular trends in the suicide and homicide rates if we succeed in adequately reconstructing the changes that have occurred, in Europe, over the past seven or eight centuries, in the ways in which men and women feel and express their emotions. Anger, hatred, shame, disgust, sadness, despair, fear or joy are universal sentiments, experienced by all. But the motives that cause them, their intensity, and the way they are expressed have varied over time and space.

A number of well-respected studies have tried to trace their history, comparing the changes in that way that we feel and express sentiments to human emotional development from infancy to adulthood and maturity. 'To the world when it was half a thousand years younger', wrote Johan Huizinga in 1919, 'the outlines of all things seemed more clearly marked than to us. The contrast between suffering and joy, between adversity and happiness, appeared more striking. All experience had yet to the minds of men the directness and absoluteness of the pleasure and pain of child-life.'[94] It was a world marked by a 'general facility of emotions, of tears and spiritual upheavals', 'cruel excitement and coarse compassion'.[95] The daily life of that period was coloured by a 'vehement pathos' that was profoundly different from our own.[96]

Twenty years later Norbert Elias developed this idea in greater depth and elaborated it as his theory of the civilizing process. He too saw the Middle Ages as having an 'affective structure' that was radically different from the modern one. 'The instincts, the emotions were vented more freely, more directly, more openly than later.'[97] Elias describes the peoples of Europe as being 'wild, cruel, prone to violent outbreaks and abandoned to the joy of the moment'.[98] They shifted rapidly from one profoundly different mood to another, from incredible explosions of joy to irresistible outbursts of anger, hatred and aggressiveness against others. Precisely because in medieval society emotions are 'expressed in a manner that in our own world is generally observed only in children, we call these expressions and forms of behavior "childish"'.[99]

The situation changed profoundly in the following centuries and individuals gradually abandoned spontaneity and impetuousness and learned to control themselves, to curb their drives, passions and aggressiveness. Elias has shown 'how the regulation of the whole instinctual and affective life by steady self-control becomes more and more stable, more even and more all-embracing'.[100] This happened when a stronger territorial power triumphed over weaker ones and established a monopoly of legitimate state power. Warriors were transformed into courtiers and military skills were replaced by the verbal skills of debate and persuasion. The 'battlefield' had 'in a sense, moved within'. Part of the drives and passions that had, until then, been expressed as aggression towards others, started to be 'worked out within the human being'. This formed a sort of 'specific "super-ego"' that constantly endeavoured 'to control, transform or suppress his affects in keeping with the social structure'.[101] Medieval men and women, therefore, had a child-like emotive life. They were simple, natural, coarse, violent, uninhibited and shameless. Modernity brought with it maturity, wisdom, equilibrium and self-control.

It is certainly no surprise that Elias' theory of the civilizing process had an enormous influence on the study of social sciences. By providing a neat link between the multi-secular decline of homicidal violence and the affirmation of the state, through the transformation of the affective structure and growth of self-restraint, it seemed to offer a convincing explanation of a crucial aspect of the passage from the medieval era to the modern age. Yet, in the past few years, it has been subject to a growing body of criticism.[102]

In the first place, the thesis that the history of the last five centuries in Europe may have been characterized by growing individual control of emotions is not confirmed by the results of countless studies on various aspects of social life. France, for example, witnessed the burgeoning of 'sentimentalism' in the eighteenth century, which was accompanied by a marked tendency to express piety, love and gratitude far more than ever before.[103] Throughout Western Europe, between the seventeenth and eighteenth century, there was a profound change in domestic life, and fathers and mothers, who had previously kept their children at a distance, began to express their sentiments much more openly, spending more time with them, and caressing, kissing and hugging them.

In the second place, the civilizing process theory has been criticized because it is based on a hydraulic understanding of human actions, even if it partly differs in meaning from the concept of the two channels of a single stream. Not unlike those who believed in the medieval system of humours, Huizinga, Elias and the other scholars who followed their approach regarded the emotions as fluids, present in every individual, which could overflow, expand and flood delicate spaces, causing damage, or as instinctive tendencies that could be controlled, repressed, channelled, sublimated.[104] On the contrary, a growing number of psychologists and historians do not view the emotions as natural impulses, nor do they think that any is irrational or infantile. Instead, according to these scholars, emotions are eminently mouldable in nature. They depend, above all, on beliefs and social norms, on language and schemas of classification. Second to that, emotions are the product of a cognitive and evaluative process, as well as of our expectations and aspirations, of how we perceive an event, or the meaning we give to it.

Reconstructing the long-term changes affecting the way that men and women in Europe felt and expressed their emotions is a very difficult task that will only attain satisfactory results after many years, even though a growing band of historians have dedicated themselves to this field with enthusiasm, basing their research on surviving documents (letters, trial records, autobiographies, chronicles, literary works).[105] At the current state of our knowledge we can nonetheless hypothesize that European history over the last five centuries has been characterized not only by the widespread growth of individual emotional self-restraint but also by profound cultural changes. These range from shifts in customs and beliefs, cognitive and classification schemas, symbols and meanings, as well as in aspirations and expectations, which have made it more difficult to feel and express some of these emotions but easier to experience and manifest others.

Feudal culture fostered anger and hatred. For the men and women who lived in that society, a number of incidents, which we might regard as trivial today – such as not standing back to let a person of higher rank pass, or not bowing or removing a hat in their presence – assumed such importance that they aroused explosive rage. Moreover, upper-class men, above all, were urged by the expectations of the time to be angry and behave in a tough, scornful manner towards others, since this was believed to be the only way to preserve honour. On the other hand, Christian ethics tried to alleviate and relieve suffering and despair. It encouraged the belief that particular dramatic events, such as military defeat and rape, were not shameful, and it persuaded individuals not to fall into the sin of despair, convinced that they would not benefit from God's grace and mercy.

We can therefore hypothesize that the cultural changes that occurred in Europe over the past five centuries (which were produced or aided by the birth and development of the modern state, by the fading importance of honour, by the scientific revolution, secularization, and by the medicalization of suffering and mental disorders) influenced emotions in various ways, making it more difficult to experience and show anger and hatred, and easier to feel and express pain and despair. Yet only the results of future historical research will reveal whether this hypothesis has any basis.

4

When Poverty Does not Protect

In 1930, when analysing the changes of the previous decades, the French sociologist Maurice Halbwachs found that the concerns expressed by scholars in the latter half of the nineteenth century, namely that suicide rates would rise 'steadily and without limits' in the future, were unfounded.[1] Instead, the long historical series of data he had examined showed that in Europe for some years the rate had tended towards stabilization[2] and 'convergence' between countries and population brackets.[3] The numbers of those taking their own lives had continued to grow where the figures were lowest (in Italy and Spain, for example, or in rural France or Sweden), but they had remained unchanged or had even fallen where rates had previously been highest. Owing to this spread, this meant that the differences between northern and southern Europe were narrowing, as were those between urban and rural centres, and between Protestants, Catholics and Jews.

In this chapter we will see how, during the course of the twentieth century, suicide rates underwent further unexpected changes: during the two World Wars and in the aftermath of both wars, in the years of economic crisis or rapid growth, during the periods of the persecution of the Jews or the 'enemies of the people', or after the collapse of the Nazi and Soviet regimes. During this century the distinctions between the various population brackets (defined by gender, age, size of the town of residence, or religion) changed a number of times with revolutionary effects on the geography of voluntary deaths. The convergence trend between the various Western European countries continued in the closing decades of the century. But, during the same period, the suicide rate in these countries fell, while that in Eastern European countries increased dramatically.

Some of these changes, as well as some of the differences between individual sections of the population, can be attributed to different degrees of integration and social regulation. For example, when examining the situation in Russia and other former communist countries after the collapse of the Soviet Union it is impossible to ignore the concept of anomie (which is present, as Durkheim explained,[4] when man's activity lacks regulation and people suffer accordingly). Other changes, however, can only be attributed to cultural factors. If men and women, whether black or white, believers or non-believers, or immigrants from various countries, committed suicide in Europe during the last century, albeit to diverse extents and with various means, it was because they had different ways of looking at the world, different beliefs, and different cognitive schemas and meanings.

But the two important trends of the twentieth century, first the rise in the number of suicides (which was higher in 'backward' areas) and then its fall, can be interpreted as the effects of major cultural changes. The century was marked by a continuation of the process of the secularization and medicalization of suicide,[5] which had started among the higher classes in northern and central Europe during the seventeenth century. The idea that suicide was not due to supernatural causes also spread through those populations with strong religious beliefs in the remotest regions. At the same time, the proportion of the population that regarded voluntary death as morally acceptable grew slowly but steadily.[6] These changes were accompanied by the approval of new laws permitting the practice of active euthanasia (as happened in 2002 in Holland and Belgium) or passive euthanasia or assisted suicide (as in other countries).[7] These changes prompted a growing number of suicides and a convergence between countries and different sectors of the population.

But the process of secularization and medicalization also introduced another facet that has produced diametrically opposite consequences: the falling suicide rates witnessed in most Western countries over the past twenty years. Throughout the twentieth century but above all in the closing decades a growing number of individuals started to view some of their disorders (such as depression, for example) not as an unpleasant and unavoidable trait of their character but as a disease requiring specialist treatment. Therefore, doctors have not only become experts in helping others to bid farewell to the world, but they also play an increasingly important role in treating the physical and mental disorders that can prompt individuals to commit suicide.

4.1   Sociology's 'one law' and what remains

In the last decades of the sixteenth century a few Catholic polemicists claimed that Lutherans took their own lives more frequently, and 'lapsed into despair and despondency more often' because 'their new faith was a dry well: they had neither the true nectar of God's pure faith nor the great sustenance of the seven sacraments'.[8] No one could then have imagined that this violent accusation, made in a period of profound religious conflict, would become a dispassionate scientific proposition two and a half centuries later. Adolph Wagner, a Protestant economist, was the first to realize that his fellow churchmen killed themselves more frequently than Catholics.[9] 'In Europe', he wrote in 1864, 'suicide is most frequent among the Protestants. It is rarer among Catholics, and even more so among the

Greek Orthodox. It is even more unusual among the Jews compared to the Catholics, and perhaps has the same frequency, or slightly less, as among the Greek Orthodox.'[10] A few years later, when analysing collected data, Enrico Morselli wrote that 'the purely Catholic nations, Italy, Spain, and Portugal, stand on the last step of the scale of suicide, whilst those exclusively or mostly Protestant, take the first grade'.[11] He also added that Jews and Muslims committed suicide less frequently than Catholics.[12]

Durkheim incorporated this empirical rule into a theory which claimed that the different frequency of suicide among Protestants and Catholics was not to be attributed to cultural and regulatory factors (because both of these religions strictly forbade voluntary death) but rather to structural ones, namely to social cohesion. Protestants had a marked tendency to commit suicide because their social integration was weaker, and consequently they had less psychological support on which to rely. For the same reason, namely because they enjoyed particularly strong bonds of solidarity, Jews killed themselves less frequently than all the rest.

A more recent version of this theory underlined the importance of some forms of support available to Catholics, thanks to confession, one of the seven sacraments, which provides a cathartic function, comparable to modern psychotherapy. By opening one's heart to a priest and confiding to him one's private sins, a believer freed him or herself from traumatic experiences, situations of conflict, and guilty feelings, thus warding off the idea of suicide.[13]

Sociologists, who have always been fascinated by scientific laws, perhaps because they have never found any themselves, became convinced over time that Durkheim's theory had at least some of the requisites in order to become such a law,[14] and, not without a touch of irony, they called it 'sociology's "one law"'.[15]

For some time now the results of historical and sociological studies have raised numerous doubts regarding the validity of this theory. In the first place, some have affirmed that the difference between suicide rates among Protestants and Catholics does not depend on integration and social support, but on belief in the next world, therefore on cultural factors. While it is true that these two religions share the idea that sinners will be punished and go to hell, it is also true – as researchers have pointed out – that they present quite a different picture of this place of torment. For Protestants, hell is an abstract concept that only causes moral torment. For the Catholics, on the other hand, it is an actual physical place, an abyss into which the damned will be cast after the Last Judgement, to remain for all eternity surrounded by fire that will burn every part of their bodies while preserving them in perpetuity, in everlasting torment. Those researchers who support this thesis therefore affirm that if Catholics do commit suicide less frequently than Protestants it is not because they are more integrated socially, but because they are terrified of the flames of hell.[16]

Secondly, some researchers have asked themselves whether the difference in suicide rates between Protestants and Catholics might be spurious, resulting not from integration or eschatological beliefs but from other social and economic factors. Indeed, still in the early twentieth century, compared to their Catholic counterparts, Protestant populations showed some traits that were at the time more clearly predisposed towards suicide: they lived in more industrialized and urbanized areas, they were better educated, and they were more likely to belong to the middle and upper classes.

The profound changes in Europe and other Western countries during the last one hundred and fifty years have shifted the emphasis away from this debate. In the second half of the nineteenth and early twentieth century, the difference in the suicide rate between Protestants and Catholics everywhere narrowed considerably.[17] Many data sets suggest that this process has continued since then, although not always in a linear fashion. It is particularly instructive to look at the trend of the suicide rate over the past century in East Germany (traditionally Protestant) and in West Germany (predominantly Catholic).[18] In 1901, the rate in the former was almost double the latter (31 versus 17 per 100,000 inhabitants). In the last two decades, the frequency of suicide in Germany has fallen across the entire country, but most of all in Eastern areas (where the rate plummeted to 12.6 per 100,000 in 2007) compared to Western ones (11 per 100,000) and the difference between the two has disappeared almost entirely (Graph 4.1).

There are other significant aspects. Between 1913 and 1939 Austria, which has a prevalently Catholic population, had the highest suicide rate of all Eastern and Western European countries, and this rate remained higher than many traditionally Protestant countries in the following decades. In Italy and Spain today suicide is more frequent than in England and Wales. The suicide rate in Portugal and Ireland is much higher than in England and marginally lower than in Sweden, Denmark and Germany.[19]

For decades now, in Western countries, the key difference is not between Protestants and Catholics but between religious and non-religious societies,[20] therefore a cultural factor. This is because, although the situation has changed radically (as was seen in the first two chapters), Christian ethics still takes a negative view of voluntary death.

4.2 When the Jews lost their 'ancient immunity'

In January 1943, Hannah Arendt noted, as she looked back in an attempt to reconstruct and explain such important changes, that 'Jews had the lowest suicide rate among all civilized nations' in the past, yet now, in major cities across Europe and the United States, they were taking their own lives much more frequently. 'We are the first non-religious Jews persecuted', she concluded, 'and we are the first ones who, not only *in extremis*, answer with suicide.'[21]

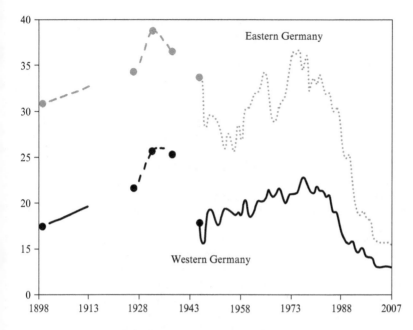

Graph 4.1   Suicide rates per 100,000 inhabitants in western and eastern
Germany from 1898 to 2007.

Source: Elaborated from data of Werner Felber (http://www.suizidprophydaxe.de).

In his work of 1897, Émile Durkheim had identified 1870 as the starting
point for this change, the year in which Jews 'begin to lose their ancient
immunity', because the figures showed that, in many regions of Germany,
they were killing themselves with the same frequency as Catholics.[22]
Returning to this question twelve years later, the great French sociologist came to the conclusion that in Bavaria, on the basis of new statistics,
suicide among Jews had reached the same levels as among Protestants.[23]
No one, at this stage, could have foreseen that this trend would continue
throughout Germany until the Second World War and that, after 1933, it
would also spread to other countries.

During the Second Reich, the number of voluntary deaths rose in
all sectors of the population, irrespective of their faith, but it was most
noticeable among Jews. Indeed, suicides among Jews outstripped first
Catholics then Protestants in many regions in the first decade of the twen-
tieth century. The same happened during the Weimar Republic. In 1925 in
Prussia, where this process was more rapid than elsewhere, suicides among
Jews were double those of Protestants, and four times those of Catholics.
This change was also noted in Amsterdam,[24] while in Lodz and Budapest,

Warsaw, Vienna and New York, Jews preserved their 'ancient immunity' for the first twenty years of the century, with fewer suicides than among other Christian communities.[25]

The newspapers dedicated increasing column space to what they began to call 'the suicide epidemic among German Jews'. Concerned about this turn of events, Jewish associations discussed the motives for this 'epidemic' and organized conferences and debates. Fritz Kahn, one of their leaders, saw the extraordinary rise in voluntary deaths among his co-religionists as the sign of a process of disintegration. 'We must indict ourselves', he said in one of his speeches, 'because we connived at the development, in our German fatherland, of a Jewishness without Judaism, which can offer no moral support to the losers, to those in the grip of despair.'[26]

In 1909, Durkheim attributed the rise in suicide among Jews to their growing assimilation in German society. After 1930, other scholars[27] provided a more articulate and convincing interpretation of what had happened prior to the advent of Nazism. This can be summarized as follows. The period of the Weimar Republic marked the culmination of a process that had started some decades earlier. A growing number of Jews became employed in the professions and in business, thereby joining the middle classes, a step that had various important consequences. They began to marry both less and later, more frequently choosing a partner of a different religious faith and then having fewer children. They emigrated en masse to the large towns and cities. Their religion began to be regarded as a private affair and they became 'German citizens of Jewish faith'. This weakened the bonds that had united them for so long and, as a result, many of the social conditions that had protected them until then from the risk of voluntary death gradually became less effective.

4.3 The effects of Nazism and Fascism

The rising suicide rates among Jews continued after Hitler and the Nazis came to power on 30 January 1933, but for quite different reasons. The process of integrating Jewish communities into German society was abruptly halted by the new government, which immediately implemented the first steps of its anti-Semitic programme. From 1 April that year, boycotts were held against Jewish professionals, teachers, shopkeepers and businessmen and some of those persecuted took their own lives. On 24 April, having recently visited a Jewish cemetery in Berlin, the journalist Max Reiner learned from a friend that many of the new double graves he had seen there belonged to couples who had killed themselves together.[28] In that year, the suicide rate among Jews (who then numbered 525,000 people) reached a high point of 70 per 100,000 inhabitants,[29] almost double that reached eight years earlier in Prussia. Frightened and saddened by what was happening, some rabbis made public appeals to the faithful. 'Under the shattering impact of the events of recent weeks during which suicide claimed victim upon victim within our community, we turn to you, men and women of the Jewish community, with the appeal: Maintain your courage and will to live, preserve your confidence in God and in yourself! [. . .] Let us bear it together and help one another fraternally!'[30]

These appeals by the rabbis and the moral support of the community were not sufficient to stop this growing trend. The curve of voluntary deaths continued its crescendo, rising most sharply in 1938 when the Nazis' anti-Semitic policy reached a climax in the pogrom organized by the SS on the night of 9–10 November (*Kristallnacht*). Some one hundred Jews were killed, synagogues were set on fire, cemeteries profaned and thousands of shops were ransacked. In Berlin, for example, the number of Jews who committed suicide rose from 65 to 113 a year during the period from 1933 to 1938.[31] For the most part it was civil servants who killed themselves after being sacked because of their Jewish blood, but the suicides included doctors, lawyers, magistrates, university professors, artists and businessmen.

The situation deteriorated still further in the autumn of 1941 when mass deportations to the concentration and death camps began. On 22 October of that year, Tobias Ingenhoven, a lawyer from Hamburg who had sent his daughter to England for protection, addressed these words to her in a letter:

Today the first deportation of Jews from Hamburg has begun . . . . I am not on the list, but it is widely known that more deportations are to follow and I am forced to believe that all Jews from Hamburg and most probably from the whole of Germany are going to be deported . . . . No one knows where we are going to be deported to, but it is certain that only a fraction of the deportees are able to survive this ordeal. Many commit suicide in order to escape the horrific humiliations and degradations, the hunger and cold, the dirt and the illnesses that await us. I don't know what I will do when it is my turn but I thank the almighty that I have the strength to save you, my beloved child, from such a fate.[32]

These 'waves' of deportations left literally hundreds of voluntary deaths in their wake. Based on the best estimates available, the suicide rate among the Jewish population (now reduced to 134,000 people) reached 200 per 100,000 inhabitants in Germany during the period 1941–2, with a maximum of 400 per 100,000 in Berlin.[33] In the German capital, the percentage of Jews among the total number of suicides rose from 18 per cent in 1941 to 40 per cent in 1942, with a peak of 75 per cent in the third quarter of that year.[34] In total, 1,279 Jews took their own lives in Berlin between 1941 and 1943, a number so great that to be buried in the Jewish cemetery at Weissensee (the largest in Europe) there was an average waiting time of two weeks.[35] For the first time ever a special ward was set up in the Jewish hospital for those who had botched their attempt to commit suicide.[36] But in some instances, the number of voluntary deaths was even higher. When in August 1942, the last 450 elderly Jews who had remained in Wiesbaden were told that they would be deported to Theresienstadt, forty-seven of them decided to commit suicide.[37]

A few suicides made public denouncements of the countless injustices they had suffered. Hedwig Jastrow, for example, an elderly retired teacher, wrote a letter on 29 November 1938, just before taking her own life:

> This is not an accident or an attack of depression. I am leaving life as someone whose family has had German citizenship for over 100 years and has always remained loyal to Germany. I have taught German children for 43 years and have helped them through all their trials and tribulations. I have done charity work for the German Volk for even longer, both in times of war and times of peace. I don't want to live without a Fatherland, without a homeland, without an apartment, without citizenship rights, ostracized and reviled. And I want to be buried with the name my parents both gave me and passed on to me, which is untainted. I do not want to wait until it gets defamed. Every convict, every murderer keeps his name. It cries to heaven![38]

For the most part, however, German Jews left life on tiptoe. As Hannah Arendt wrote in early 1943, 'our friends leave no explanation of their deed, no indictment, no charge against a world that had forced a desperate man to talk and to behave cheerfully to his very last day. Letters left by them are conventional, meaningless documents. Thus, funeral orations we make at their open graves are brief, embarrassed and very hopeful. Nobody cares about motives, they seem to be clear to all of us.'[39]

As well as becoming more frequent, suicides by Jews under the Nazis took on new characteristics. Firstly, there was a change in the gender composition of suicides. In the early years of the twentieth century (as in earlier periods) it was prevalently men who took their own lives, but after 1933 this decision was taken with increasing frequency by women too. For example, many Jewish wives of 'Aryan' husbands killed themselves in the hope of saving their family from persecution.[40]

Secondly, from the autumn of 1941, when the mass deportations began, suicide increasingly became an act that was carefully prepared and planned, often for many months. Well aware of the fate of those who were deported, many German Jews habitually carried barbiturates or cyanide pills with them, or hid two razor blades in a shoe, so they would always have the option to 'put an end to it'.[41] This allowed them to keep a strong sense of control over their own fate, and to hope that they themselves could decide whether to live or die.

Thirdly, there was a profound shift in the attitude of Jewish doctors towards the suicide of their fellow Jews. To begin with many tried to discourage this choice. 'I resolved to end my life', wrote Camilla Neumann, who had been conscripted for forced labour. 'I went to our good Dr. Lissner and asked him to prescribe Veronal. He refused. Yet, eight days later he himself took poison. Sixteen tablets I had already, but that quantity was no use, especially as I was determined not to leave Ludwig [her husband] behind on his own. At that time Veronal was very much in demand, the Jews paid 1,000 Marks for 30 tablets.'[42] Yet during the period of deportations, an increased number of doctors were willing to provide their patients with cyanide or morphine in order to end their lives. Moreover, in 1942, a gathering of Jew ish doctors was convened in Berlin at which it was unanimously resolved to respect the last wish of those who had attempted to take their own lives.

Lastly, the position of the political authorities also changed. In the thirties, the Nazis (like the Fascists in Italy) welcomed any news of Jewish suicides with celebrations, scorn or irony. In the summer of 1933, when the Stockholm-based businessman Fritz Rosenfelder committed suicide, a Nazi paper commented that it was an important contribution to the solution of the Jewish question.[43] In Italy, in 1939, when the publisher Angelo Fortunato Formiggini threw himself from the Ghirlandina Tower in Modena, Achille Starace commented: 'he jumped off a tower in order to save a bullet; how like a Jew!'[44] Yet, by the autumn of 1941, when plans for the final solution were underway, the Nazis began to discourage Jewish suicide in any way they could, convinced that it was only the 'Aryans' who should decide when and how Jews should die. In Berlin, they stopped sending out deportation notices with a week's advance warning, and the pharmacy at the Jewish Hospital was subject to increasingly strict checks to stop drugs being dispensed to those wishing to commit suicide.

The growing number of suicides among Jews was also reported in other countries. In Austria, for certain, after it was invaded by German troops in March 1938 and the Nazis humiliated Jews by making them kneel in the streets and clean them.[45] It was then that Anna Freud asked her father whether it would not be a good idea to commit suicide? Sigmund Freud, who shortly afterwards to England, is said to have responded: 'Why? Because they would like us to?' In an article on Austria, an English paper reported that 'doctors and chemists are pestered by people asking for poisons or drugs to end their existence'.[46] Indeed, it is estimated that in Vienna, on *Kristallnacht*, the suicide rate among Jews reached 367 per 100,000 inhabitants.[47] However, it rose higher still in 1941 when the deportations began.[48]

The same happened, after 1939, in western Poland when it was invaded by Germany and the Nazis set up ghettos in some cities. They entered Lodz, the richest and most modern (and, as described by Levi, 'the ugliest') city, on 9 September and immediately began to persecute the 230,000 Jews who lived there. The SS set fire to the synagogue. They hauled a hundred Jews out of Café Astoria and shot them. Others were hounded from their homes, their property confiscated, and some were forced to leave the city and move elsewhere. However, the Nazis soon decided to use the rest for labour and they enclosed them in a ghetto, created in an area measuring four square kilometres, north of Lodz, surrounded by barbed wire. As if this community were a small state, the Nazi authorities made one man, Chaim Rumkowski, into a virtual king.[49] Formerly a failed small industrialist, he enjoyed the esteem of his 'subjects'. A new currency was minted with which to pay the workers employed in the textile industries for the German army, and a police force was set up to keep order.

The Jews of Lodz suffered all forms of tribulations and abuse, as well as starvation, destitution and many other hardships. The number of those who decided to take their own lives rose sharply, although it remained below the level reached in Berlin or in Germany as a whole. During the four years between 1941 and 1944, the suicide rate inside the ghetto averaged 44 per 100,000 inhabitants.[50]

In Italy, in a letter to his mother, dated 18 December 1938 from prison, the anti-Fascist Ernesto Rossi wrote that there appeared to be a 'real suicide epidemic'.[51] It was an exaggeration, yet there was probably an increase in voluntary deaths also in Italy between 1936 and 1943, coinciding with the period of Jewish persecution.[52] It is estimated that just over ten per cent of a population of 51,000 Jews emigrated, but around one per thousand took their own lives.[53] Giuseppe Jona did so on 16 September 1943 in order not to be forced to give the Germans the names of members of the local Venetian community, of which he was president. The suicide of Angelo Fortunato Formiggini was another act of protest, which was meticulously prepared for several months. The Modena-based publisher first considered this possibility on 27 June 1938 when the Office for the Study of the Problem of Race introduced a clear-cut distinction between 'Aryans' and Jews. He realized that a period of tremendous hardship lay ahead for his firm and, that evening, he wrote an epigram in the third person, which clearly set out his intentions: 'but when despicable pens/ launched a racist campaign, / indignant / he condemned himself to death for high treason, / putting himself in the place of the actual guilty party/ to avert damage and shame from his Fatherland, / the subject of his loving delight.' For months Formiggini must have hoped that the situation would change. But on 17 November, when the Fascist government approved the 'Provisions for the Defence of the Italian Race' he realized that there was no other choice and he decided to commit suicide on 29 November. That day he turned down a friend's invitation to lunch, saying that he 'had to go very high up'. To another friend, whom he bumped into close to the Ghirlandina bell-tower, he jokingly said: 'I'll go up using the stairs, but come down the fast way, it's easier.'[54]

Others bid farewell, silently and discreetly. On 14 March 1939 Giuseppe Sacerdoti killed himself, five months after he had lost his job teaching violin and viola at a secondary school in Venice.[55] A few days before Christmas 1940, a Jewish woman who had been left alone took her life at Riva. In a letter to her two sons, both far away – one in Bombay and the other in Ecuador – she wrote:

It is impossible for me to join you from here, and I cannot go on living like this. Once you left, your father died of a broken heart after a few months; perhaps you'll have heard by now. What was left to me was the house, his things, your things. They destroyed those too. I had to flee Germany and take shelter here: I've tried to make a life here, but I cannot. I have no strength, I have no roots. I realize that I might have continued to live there, because even when you don't belong to anyone any more, you still belong to things; and I belonged to his books, to the bed where you were born, to the little statue from Nanjing which Harry gave me, to the teapot bought in Venice on our honeymoon [. . .] Think of me with gentleness, without too much pain. In spite of everything I am one of the lucky mothers. I can join him since I have nothing left to do in the world and I know you two are safe abroad. Just think how many mothers have survived while their sons have been massacred![56]

4.4   Concentration camps and prisons

During the twentieth century, millions of people spent part of their lives in prison or in concentration camps, two institutions with much in common. For those condemned to enter, both result in the loss of freedom. Both isolate their inmates from the rest of the world, both are encompassing or total; they subject those interned to continual control and place them in a position of complete subordination. In both, day-to-day activities are rigidly defined by a system of formal rules, imposed from above, and everything happens in one place, under one authority, in close contact with others who are doing the same things at the same times. Both can have devastating effects on the life and personality of those incarcerated. On entering, they are subject to a process of humiliation and degradation aimed at stripping them of their identity.[57] Prisoners are detached from family and friends, their routines eliminated, their image of the world shattered; the goal is to make them distrust others and themselves, to create fear, a sense of helplessness, uselessness, inadequacy, depression. Therefore both the concentration camp and the prison may prompt those who spend time in them to take their own lives.

That is not to say that there are not differences. There are within each of the categories. There were, and still are, differences between prisons. For example, some prisons copied the Philadelphia model, founded on the principle of continuous isolation, day and night, obliging detainees to spend their time alone in a cell; others referred to the Auburn model, which only required night-time isolation; and still others imposed a system of communal life for all prisoners. There were similar differences between concentration camps. The Soviet gulag system was not completely identical to the Nazi lagers, and within the latter there were distinctions between the concentration camps, which doubled as places of detention, labour and physical degradation, and the death camps (like Belzec, Sobibor, Treblinka) where all deportees were killed on arrival.

The differences that most interest us here are those between the two categories of total institution, prison and concentration camp. The former detains people for what they have done, the latter for who they are. The first contains those who have committed fraud or have robbed, kidnapped, killed or raped others, the latter held the Jews, gypsies, homosexuals or (in the Soviet Union) 'enemies of the people', or simply the wives of enemies of the people. Those who are imprisoned in the former know exactly the term of the sentence they will serve, those who were sent to the latter had no idea when they would be released and were condemned to a 'provisional existence of unknown limit'.[58]

The conditions of life in the best concentration camp were crueller and more inhumane than any in the worst prisons. In the German lagers and Soviet gulags,[59] prisoners were subject to ferocious and degrading experiences, to an unending series of physical and mental violence and they found themselves in a state of helplessness and complete uncertainty, prey to hunger, thirst, cold, tiredness, disease and the risk of death. It is not surprising that the psychiatrist Viktor Frankl, a Holocaust survivor, described how the detainees in his camp envied the prisoners serving life sentences, whom they would sometimes see walking past, 'for their relatively ordered, relatively safe, relatively hygienic life'. 'These people were allowed baths on pre-established days, we used to think with great nostalgia. They certainly had toothbrushes, clothes brushes, camp beds (one each, just for them), and they received post once a month and knew where their families were, and whether they were still alive. For a long time, we had had none of this.'[60]

We might therefore think that both prison and the concentration camp encourage suicide, but that the latter does so more than the former. But is this really the case? Unfortunately, there is a disparity in the available documentation. On the one hand, we have a vast number of accurate and reliable data on voluntary deaths in prison, while on the other, for the concentration camps, we have few statistics and many survivor testimonies. Overall, however, the existing information does allow us to compare the effects of these different institutions and to put forward some explanations for their differences.

The idea that detainees kill themselves more frequently than others probably appeared soon after the birth of the modern prison. We know that already in the late seventeenth century, the alarm raised by repeat suicides in the Bastille prompted Louis XIV's confessor to appoint a Jesuit to investigate what was happening.[61] It was not until the last three decades of the nineteenth century that the first systematic surveys were carried out that unequivocally proved that prisoners took their own lives more often than others.[62] All the studies carried out since then have reached the same conclusions, enormously enriching our knowledge of the subject. In all Western countries, prison has always been the place where suicide rates are highest. But in the last fifteen years, it has risen still further in some countries.[63] We also know that prisoners take their lives more frequently than the ordinary population but that the difference varies in time and space. In Italy and Britain, the suicide rate inside prison is fifteen times higher than outside, while in other countries, such as France and Austria, it is not quite as high (eleven times), and in others still, such as Denmark, Sweden and Portugal, it is even higher (between seventeen and twenty-five times higher).

The suicide risk varies depending on the various sectors to which the prison population belong. It is greatest in the first few days because the shock of finding oneself in this environment can lead to major depression. It is also high in prisoners on remand probably because the uncertainty of sentencing and their future fate becomes an acute source of anxiety that some cannot tolerate. It is also high in lifers and those serving long jail sentences because their existence ceases to have any meaning.[64] The risk is also great for prisoners held in solitary confinement.

For concentration camps, on the other hand, there are very few statistics. Those collected by Doctor Otto Walden for a section in Auschwitz show that there were no suicides among 1,902 internees who died between 20 September 1943 and 1 November 1944.[65] Other figures from Buchenwald indicate that no more than 0.5 per cent of deaths were voluntary.[66] Moreover, all the survivors concord that voluntary deaths were not very frequent in Nazi lagers and Soviet gulags. 'The thought of suicide was entertained by nearly everyone', wrote Viktor Frankl, 'even if only for a brief time.'[67] Yet all or almost all rejected this solution immediately and decided not to throw themselves onto the barbed wire. In the lagers, as Hannah Arendt wrote, there was 'an astonishing rarity of suicides'.[68] Aleksandr Solzhenitsyn remarked that, in the Soviet gulag, 'for some reason there were no suicides! Condemned to a misshapen existence, to waste away from starvation, to exhaustion from labour – they did not put an end to themselves!'[69] Similar affirmations were made by Primo Levi, Bruno Bettelheim, Jean Améry, Elie Cohen, Nadežda Mandelstam and many others.[70]

It is true that in the concentration camps there were 'Muselmanns', a word used to describe a sort of 'living dead', the 'walking corpses' who vegetated on the edges of the lager. Enfeebled by lack of food, with partially atrophied muscles, they could no longer control their own bodies and could barely stagger along. Mentally drained, lacking memory, they were unable to concentrate and sometimes did not remember their own name. Overcome by their surroundings, with a passive and fatalistic outlook, they were shunned and chased away by all, scorned, insulted and beaten more often than others, by both the guards and their own companions, yet they did not react and remained isolated. When they died, while at work or in the latrines, or in the huts set aside for the ill and the sick, or while asleep in the night, almost no one noticed their passing.[71] However, the behaviour of these prisoners has been seen by all the survivors and by other scholars not as a conscious renunciation of life, an occult suicide, but rather as a consequence of starvation.[72]

Not all concentration camps, nor all their sectors, had the same suicide rates. Suicides seem to have happened relatively often among the so-called special squads of prisoners,[73] namely those in charge of the crematoria. In exchange for meagre 'privileges' (a little more food), these men had to perform the most terrible tasks: to accompany groups of new arrivals to the gas chambers, where they would die within a quarter of an hour, to spray the corpses with water jets, to extract the corpses and pull gold teeth from jaws, cut the women's hair, transport the bodies to the crematoria, then extract and dispose of the ashes. Some of them took their own lives before they too were sent to the gas chambers.

There was also a higher suicide rate at the camps that were used as death factories, and where the people arriving were left alive only for a few days or few hours. One survivor[74] described how, among the Jews arrested in Amsterdam and deported to Mauthausen, there was a genuine suicide epidemic in February 1941, because they realized immediately that there was no hope. As soon as they arrived, fifty of them were pushed naked against the electrically charged barbed wire. On the second day, the remainder were taken to work in a quarry and made to run up 148 steps carrying a crushing burden of huge stones. In despair, some threw themselves over the edge. On the third day, others were rounded up and shot by the SS. Lastly, on the fourth day, many prisoners took their own lives by jumping off a height, holding hands in groups of ten or twelve. But these were extreme cases, exceptions. The general rule, according to all survivors, was that internees did not take their own lives.

The thesis that suicides were relatively rare in concentration camps raises two questions. The first concerns the parameters of comparison on which the affirmation is based. What population is being used as the comparison in the statement that suicides were rare? Solzhenitsyn was the only one to clearly indicate what he was referring to: 'I even imagine that, statistically speaking, there were fewer suicides per thousand of the population in camp that in freedom. I have no way of verifying this, of course.'[75] But other witnesses may have been comparing what they saw with what they expected to see and they defined suicide as 'rare' because they thought the inhuman living conditions in the camp would have prompted more people to take their own lives.

The second question concerns the likelihood of whether a prisoner would have been able to estimate (even very roughly) the numbers of voluntary deaths occurring in the camp. How could a detainee in Auschwitz, Buchenwald or Dachau know whether those fellow sufferers who took their own lives were few or many? Even today, anyone living in a small or middle-sized town would find it impossible to say whether the suicide rate was high or low, or greater or smaller than in another city or another period? For a prisoner in a concentration camp it would have been even more so. As Primo Levi wrote, 'the prisoners could barely acquire an overall vision of their universe. [. . .] Surrounded by death, the deportee was often in no position to evaluate the extent of the slaughter that unfolded before his eyes. The companion that worked beside him today was no longer there on the morrow: he might be in the hut next door, or erased from the world; there was no way to know.'[76]

We will never know precisely how many people killed themselves in the Nazi lagers and Soviet gulags. It is possible that contrary to what many well-respected authors have affirmed, the suicide rate in concentration camps was not lower than that in the rest of the population. However, the limited figures we have, coupled with many testimonies, suggest that it was less frequent than in prisons, where suicide was and continues to be between ten and twenty-five times higher than in the ordinary population, depending on the country.

Comparisons between the various effects produced by these institutions were made by some of the survivors who had been in both. Evgeny Gnedin, for example, a Soviet diplomat, son of a revolutionary, wrote that he had thought of taking his own life in prison and also later when he was in exile, but not once during the eight years spent in concentration camps. 'Every day was a fight for life: how, in such a battle, was it possible to think about leaving life? There was a goal – to get out of that suffering – and hope: to meet with the people one loved.'[77] How can we explain this difference?

According to Hannah Arendt, the 'astonishing rarity' of suicides in lagers was partly due to the fact that a spontaneous act of this nature was inadmissible, and hence hindered and prevented in every way, in an institution that aspired to absolute dominion over men.[78] Indeed, the SS prohibited and tried to prevent the suicide of camp prisoners in many ways. At Dachau, in 1933,[79] it was decreed that anyone attempting to commit suicide (and failing) would receive twenty-five lashes and then be confined to the punishment cell.[80] When someone hanged themselves, the German officers rushed to the scene, took countless photographs of the corpse and opened an inquest. As one survivor sarcastically commented, 'they played at detectives. Why? Why did they do this at Auschwitz, this valley of death where tens of thousands ended up in the gas chambers every day? Simply because a poor Jew took his own life quietly, against the wishes of the SS, without waiting to be condemned to death.'[81] In other words, the SS strictly banned suicide because they regarded it as a challenge to their absolute power. This is what a Gestapo officer shouted at a member of the special squads who was stopped as he tried to join a group of blind Jews being led into the gas chambers: 'You asshole, get it into your stupid head: we decide how long you stay alive and when you die, and not you.'[82]

All this does not help to explain why the suicide rate was lower in concentration camps than in penitentiary institutions. For different reasons, both in Nazi Germany and in Soviet Russia, the police have always done everything possible to prevent those accused, whether criminals or political prisoners, from taking their own lives. In the Soviet isolation cells, if a warder saw that a prisoner's hands were hidden under the cover while sleeping, he would enter the cell and wake the prisoner to check whether he was concealing a rope to hang himself with.[83]

Another hypothesis that seems rather unconvincing, although proposed by a number of historians,[84] is that the lower suicide rate in the camps can be attributed to a strong sense of integration among the prisoners. Integration, as has been seen, probably protected the Jewish community from voluntary death in the second half of the nineteenth century. But this did not happen in the lagers. Some sense of cohesion was formed among those prisoners who shared an ideology (the military communists, for example) or a strong religious faith (Jehovah's Witnesses). Yet, the situation of the vast majority of prisoners was altogether different. Hunger, thirst, disease and the danger of death did not foster union, solidarity or mutual support, but instead bred distrust and a constant struggle among prisoners, which was unending and stopped at nothing. As Primo Levi wrote, in the camp everyone was 'desperately and ferociously alone'[85] and, according to one woman survivor, everyone quickly learned the principle that 'I come first, second and third. Then nothing, then again I; and then all the others.'[86]

For many of the survivors the reason for this was the proximity of death, and the degree of familiarity that one learned to have with it. 'One struggled against him, but one was no longer afraid of him. And to anyone who has ceased to fear death, life belonged truly, completely, and without any restriction.'[87] For Elie Cohen, a Dutch doctor who spent three years in Auschwitz, life in the concentration camps taught one to regard death as normal, in the way that outside the camps, life was normal. And while one can escape from the realm of life by killing oneself, from death the only escape is through life.[88] According to another survivor, Jean Amery, the prime reason why there were few suicides in the camps was because, in their moral order, the difference between voluntary and involuntary death disappeared and therefore suicide lost all its meaning. The prisoner was concerned 'not with death, but with dying'. '[O]ne was hardly concerned with whether, or the fact that, one had to die, but only with how it would happen. Inmates carried on conversations about how long it probably takes for the gas in the gas chamber to do its job. One speculated on the painfulness of death by phenol injections. Were you to wish yourself a blow to the skull or a slow death through exhaustion in the infirmary? It was characteristic for the situation of the prisoner in regard to death that only a few decided to "run to the wire", as one said, that is, to commit suicide through contact with the highly electrified barbed wire. [. . .] Dying was omnipresent, death vanished from sight.'[89]

Primo Levi, who died on 11 April 1987, having committed suicide some say,[90] put forward two hypotheses (Plate 21). The first is that, in the lagers, the 'aims of life' multiply and these are 'the best defence against death'. While he was at Auschwitz, Levi wrote that, 'I almost never had the time to devote to death; I had many other things to keep me busy – find a bit of bread, avoid exhausting work, patch my shoes, steal a broom, or interpret the signs and faces around me':[91] 'precisely because of the constant imminence of death, there was no time to concentrate on the idea of death'.[92]

The second is based on the assumption that suicide 'is born from a feeling of guilt that no punishment has attenuated'. Now, for the detainees in the lagers 'the harshness of imprisonment was perceived as punishment, and the feeling of guilt (if there is punishment there must have been guilt) is relegated to the background only to re-emerge after liberation'.[93]

Aleksandr Solzhenitsyn also returned to the question of guilt to explain why there were fewer suicides in the gulag than in prison. 'It was in this nearly unanimous consciousness of our innocence that the main distinction arose between us and the hard-labor prisoners of Dostoyevsky', he wrote. The vast majority of these prisoners had an 'unconditional consciousness of personal guilt', while the camp detainees knew 'that barbed wire was only a nominal dividing line between us', and they had 'the consciousness of disaster on a mammoth scale'. 'Just not to perish from the disaster!' was the key: 'It had to be survived.'[94]

Wladyslaw Fejkiel attributed the rarity of suicide in the concentration camps to 'the systematic starvation. A starving person is indifferent to the problem of death and incapable of committing suicide. The few suicides in Auschwitz that are known to me were committed by inmates who were hardly emaciated.'[95] Referring to the experience of the more politicized prisoners, as well as his own, Benedikt Kautzsky affirmed that, in the concentration camps, the instinct for self-preservation appeared in the guise of defiance and detainees ended up asking themselves why they should 'do those pigs the favour of killing themselves?'[96]

The higher suicide rate in prisons compared to concentration camps was probably also due to the way in which the populations of these two worlds were formed. Inmates in both institutions were not only different in terms of the level of privation and suffering to which they were subjected, but also in many other ways, owing primarily to the method of their selection. The prison population is absolutely not representative of the general population in the country concerned. There is an over-representation of drug addicts, alcoholics, those suffering from major forms of depression, bipolar disorders and schizophrenia, all of which carry a high suicide risk.[97] This explains, or largely explains why such a high proportion of offenders take their own lives. It is confirmed by the results of studies carried out in England and Wales, and in Switzerland, which show how offenders who serve their sentence in the community rather than in a penitentiary institution have the same probability of committing suicide as those in prison.[98]

The population of concentration camps is also selected, but in the opposite way. It did not just include Jews, gypsies, homosexuals or 'enemies of the people', but also people who were less vulnerable than average, with a greater capacity to deal with extreme situations. This is also borne out by the fact that, as has been noted, the more fragile and defenceless took their lives before arriving at the camps, when they feared arrest or during transit.

4.5   The Great Wars

Over the past century and a half, wars have usually influenced the frequency with which people have taken their own lives in the West. In
the second half of the nineteenth century, there were only local conflicts
between neighbouring countries in Western Europe, of short duration and
limited scope: one took place in 1866 between Austria and Italy, another
in 1870–1 between France and Germany. Yet, in both cases the suicide
rates in the countries involved fell slightly.[99]

The effects of conflict in the twentieth century were much greater, particularly since warfare reached unprecedented levels in the two World
Wars. The first, which started on 28 July 1914 with Austria's declaration of war on Serbia and ended on 11 November 1918, involved the six
great European powers (Great Britain, France, Austria, Germany, Italy
and Russia), Japan and the United States, but not the Nordic countries,
Holland, Spain and Switzerland. A few months after the start of hostili-
ties, the suicide rate started to fall, reaching the lowest point in 1917 or
1918, before rising again after the Armistice. It fell particularly sharply in
France, Great Britain and Germany, and a little less clearly in Italy. Yet,
the frequency of voluntary deaths tailed off not only in the warring countries but also in the neutral ones, for example in Switzerland and Sweden,
where the drop was steeper than everywhere else.[100]

The Second World War lasted even longer (from September 1939 to
8 May 1945 in Europe, and 15 August in Japan) and its spread was even
greater, involving several countries on every continent (in Europe, the only
ones to remain neutral were Spain, Sweden, Switzerland and Portugal).
However, unfortunately we have no data for some of the major countries,
including Germany, the Soviet Union, Poland and Hungary. Yet, in those
countries for which reliable statistics exist, the number of voluntary deaths
certainly diminished during this period. In Italy and Japan by 40 per cent,
in Britain, Australia and the United States by 25 per cent, in Sweden by
only five per cent.[101] However, in Switzerland the frequency of suicide
remained broadly unchanged.[102]

The fall in voluntary deaths during wartime has been attributed to the
increased social integration that forces people 'to close ranks and face
the common danger'.[103] A more precise formulation of this explanatory
schema has been provided by other scholars,[104] according to whom wars
have no influence whatsoever, from this point of view, either on the entire
population or on the large majority, but only on the small sector at risk
for whatever reason (those affected by mood or personality disorders, for
example). By allowing some of these individuals to attribute the cause of
their own ills to an external enemy, indeed to the national enemy, wars help
to ward off the very idea of suicide, either temporarily or definitively.[105]

However, this schema still does not suffice to explain what happened
during the World Wars. First of all, because the falling suicide rate of
some countries during this period can be traced back to completely

different factors. For example, in Denmark, it was mainly the forced reduction in alcohol consumption, which plummeted from ten to two litres per capita between 1915 and 1918 (owing to the scarcity of commodities and increased taxes), that resulted in a significant fall in the suicide rate in that period. Yet this fall did not occur in all sectors of the Danish population, but only among alcoholics.[106]

Secondly, in some years of the Second World War and in some countries, the number of voluntary deaths stayed the same or even rose. This was the case, for example, in those countries invaded by Germany in April and May 1940. In France the suicide rate did not drop significantly in that terrible year. In Denmark, it remained constant between 1940 and 1942, with a marked rise in the three years that followed. In Norway and Belgium there was no variation in 1940, while it shrank between 1941 and 1944, and then rose in 1945. In Holland there was a sharp increase in 1940 from 8.5 to 12.2 per 100,000 inhabitants, before it returned to previous levels between 1941 and 1944, and then rose again in 1945.[107]

In Austria the suicide rate increased in 1938, the year of annexation, after which it fell until 1943–4 and then rose steeply in 1945, reaching 69 per 100,000 inhabitants.[108] There are no statistics for Germany at all for the entire period of the war. However, we know that in Berlin, the suicide rate dropped in 1940 and 1941, before returning, during the three-year period 1942–4, to the relatively high values it had reached by the mid 1930s.[109] However, the situation deteriorated even further in the opening months of 1945 during which the city experienced a wave of suicides without precedent in European history. At the start of that year, in a confidential report about popular morale, the security service of the SS claimed that 'many are getting used to the idea of making an end of it all. Everywhere there is great demand for poison, for a pistol and other means for ending one's life.'[110] The extent to which these concerns proved grounded became all too clear a few weeks later. In April, 3,881 people killed themselves in Berlin, and in May approximately 1,000, compared to previous years when voluntary deaths had averaged 200 a month.[111] At Demmin, a small town with some 20,000 inhabitants, 900 people hanged or drowned themselves in May (an absolutely exceptional rate of 4.5 per cent). There were also countless suicides at Teterow.[112]

To explain these dramatic exceptions other factors and elements need to be taken into consideration. In the first place, the war does not just provoke a new closeness between members of the same nation. As well as fighting a common enemy, people may sometimes still be in conflict with one another, as members of groups with profoundly different economic, political and religious identities and interests. Secondly, these groups may feel more or less threatened by the enemy's triumph. Thirdly, the events of the war, including bombings, loss of one's home, hunger, forced separation from friends and family, a feeling of helplessness at witnessing the suffering and death of others, defeat, along with the accompanying violence and abuse to which the vanquished were subjected, all this and more may be experienced differently depending on the prevalent attitudes towards life and death in a particular country.

The Jews, for example, continued to feel threatened by the Nazis even if they succeeded in fleeing Germany and settling in distant countries. After hearing that some of his books were among those burned in Berlin in 1933, the Viennese author Stefan Zweig emigrated in 1934 to London, and six years later to the United States. But even there, he wrote in his diary on 15 June 1940: 'Hitler's soldiers are taking up their posts in front of the Arc de Triomphe. Life is no longer worth living. I am almost 59 years old, and the coming years will be horrifying – why then still go through with all these humiliations?'[113] Two years later he and his second wife took their own lives.

In her country house outside London, Virginia Woolf recorded in her diary the emotions that the war roused in her, her husband and her friends. 'What would war mean?' she wrote on 5 September 1938. 'Darkness, strain: I suppose conceivably death.'[114] Some months later she commented: 'everything becomes meaningless: can't plan: then there comes too the community feeling: all England thinking the same thing: this horror of war.'[115]

Her mood worsened on 13 May 1940 when the radio announced, at eight o'clock in the morning, that the German army had invaded Holland and Belgium. That day, her husband Leonard told her that he had 'petrol in the garage for suicide should Hitler win'.[116] Two days later, Virginia wrote: 'this morning we discussed suicide if Hitler lands. Jews beaten up. What point in waiting? Better shut the garage doors.'[117] Anxiety continued to grow and conversation returned to the possibility of suicide when the BBC announced that German tanks and parachutists had occupied Amiens and were closing in on Boulogne, while the French government had abandoned Paris. 'Rodmell burns with rumours. Are we to be bombed, evacuated? Guns that shake the windows. Hospital ships sunk. So it comes our way.'[118] And ten days later she added: 'capitulation will mean all Jews to be given up. Concentration camps. So to our garage.'[119]

The Germans launched a strategic bombing campaign on Great Britain, but they never marched into London and Leonard Woolf never took his life in the garage at his country house. Instead, Germany occupied the whole of France and Belgium, two countries with large Jewish populations, and one might suggest that this prompted a growing number of them to commit suicide. Available data show that this certainly happened in Holland, where the suicide rate of this persecuted group soared from 20 per 100,000 at the end of the 1930s to 234 per 100,000 in 1940.[120] But that year was also marked by the suicide of non-Jews, including the author Menno Ter Braak. Writing about him, a friend commented: 'he did not commit suicide, he killed Hitler in his body. He did not want to see the man and the only way not to do so was to close his eyes.'[121]

Therefore why did voluntary deaths rise in the last months of 1944 and in 1945 in those countries that had been invaded by Germany? The answer to this question lies in the phenomenon of collaborationism, namely in the formation in these countries of groups that supported the occupiers. Collaborationist governments were established in France and Norway, while the National Socialist movement gained support in Holland. When it started to look increasingly likely that the Third Reich would collapse, those who had collaborated began to fear the outcome and many of them escaped or abandoned their activities, and a small number took their own lives. Studies carried out to date have shown that this was certainly the case in Holland from September 1944 onwards, when the southern region was freed from German occupation. Members of the National Socialist movement fled to Germany in their thousands, and some committed suicide.[122]

The growing number of people who took their own lives in Berlin (and presumably elsewhere in Germany) in the second half of the war can be explained by the start of a new phase of terror. As well as targeting the Jews, the Nazi regime persecuted a large number of people who were regarded as dangerous, or simply seen as deviants or undesirables. The Gestapo arrested, interrogated and sometimes imprisoned ordinary citizens suspected of not wholly backing the regime and the Führer's ideas. These included travellers, the homeless, and the 'asocials'. The Gestapo also carried out a ferocious campaign against homosexuals and tortured some of them. The campaign asserted the view that the Nazi regime could stamp out homosexuality through castration, an idea that was adopted in a draft bill by the Minister of Justice. The Gestapo also arrested 200 members of the Rote Kapelle (or Red Orchestra), a name used to refer to a network of resisters. Some were assassinated immediately and many others condemned to death.

There was also a huge increase in the number of suicides in the German army itself. During the first two and half years of the war there were 1,190 suicides, but over two quarters of 1943 (the second and the third) the number soared to 6,898.[123] The regime was outraged by this conduct, which was regarded as a serious sign of weakness and cowardice, tantamount to surrender or desertion, and the product of bourgeois individualism. Harking back to an idea from the past, the regime asserted that no soldier could freely dispose of his own life, no one could abandon the *Volk*.

As in the past, violation of this rule led to sanctions. Any soldier who attempted suicide and failed had to face a firing squad. The corpses of suicides were denied military honours and burial with others. In response to the rising numbers of suicides among officers and soldiers, Heinrich Himmler went even further: he ordered that the dead should be arrested and buried with their hands tied.[124] But these traditional measures were accompanied by a modern retaliation, only possible in a welfare state. The Wehrmacht authorities had the faculty to deny a pension to the families of soldiers who had committed suicide if the act was deemed a form of cowardice.[125]

This unprecedented rise in the number of voluntary deaths in the closing months of the war was foreseen, with extraordinary clarity, by Hannah Arendt. In an article dated January 1945, after noting the various waves of suicides that had affected Germany, she claimed that another even larger wave was about to break and she pinpointed the cause. When the shock of the catastrophe makes the Germans realize that they were not just 'cogs in the mass-murder machine' but also 'murderers', their 'way out will not be that of rebellion, but suicide'.[126] Her prediction proved correct and there was also some truth to her explanation. However difficult it is to demonstrate, it can be surmised that the deep sense of collective guilt shared by many Germans contributed, at least in part, to the horrific wave of voluntary deaths that affected eastern Germany in the spring of that year. It is also possible to conjecture that all those who took their own lives then shared a huge sense of insecurity and an immense fear of the future. Yet, underlying their decision were two different motives. The first is related to the events of those terrible months, while the second concerns the way those events were experienced, in the light of the conception of honour, heroism and suicide that had formed under Nazi Germany.

Turning to the first of these motives, the approach of the Red Army and its arrival in eastern Germany provoked a huge sense of panic in the population. In order to incite resistance, Nazi propaganda had stressed the terrible consequences of the invasion by the 'Mongol-Bolshevik hordes', describing all that the 'Red Beast' might do in garish tones. In cinemas, incredulous audiences watched newsreels filled with the images of women and children, assaulted and slaughtered by Russian troops on their march westwards. In February 1945, the Red Army was a little over fifty kilometres from Berlin and a few weeks later it made a triumphal entry into the capital. 'I shudder', wrote Ruth Andreas-Friedrich, a journalist, in her diary on 6 May 1945. 'For four years Goebbels told us that the Russians would rape us. That they would rape and plunder, murder and pillage.'[127] Was this all about to happen now?

On the approach march, Russian soldiers had raped many women in Romania and Hungary,[128] in Vienna and in Lower Austria.[129] But when it reached East Prussia and then Berlin the numbers rose even higher, prompted perhaps by the desire to take revenge for the countless atrocities and unspeakable humiliations that they, and moreover Russian civilians, had received at the hands of the German army.[130] Sometimes the Russians tried to win over the women by offering them food. More often, though, they took them forcibly, without even a word. Or again, a soldier would approach, holding a pistol and uttering just a single phrase: 'Frau, komm', 'Woman, come'.[131] All women were vulnerable, aged from sixteen to seventy. But the Russians preferred the youngest, the well rounded, the ones that corresponded best to their aesthetic ideals. They raped them everywhere, in the cellars, on the stairs, in their apartments, on the streets, in the squares and even in the corners of churches, sometimes in front of others, neighbours, relatives, children, husband. This wave of violence reached a peak between 26 April and 5 May 1945, in what became known as 'the week of mass rapes'. No one knows exactly how many German women were raped then. But according to estimates from the two largest Berlin hospitals, there were 95–135,000 in the German capital alone.

The victims of rape were humiliated and disgusted, and they felt angry and helpless. Their feelings towards their body changed profoundly. Having been raped on several occasions at that time, a German journalist, Marta Hillers, wrote that 'I am constantly repulsed by my own skin' in her diary (which was published anonymously).[132] 'I don't want to touch myself, can barely look at my body.'[133] Jewish women also felt betrayed, leaving their hiding places to welcome their liberators only to be seized by their clothing as they heard the usual phrase: 'Komm, Frau, komm.' According to some, they felt no guilt because for them sexual violence was just one of countless misfortunes to affect them in that dramatic period and even the rapes became routine in the end. As Marta Hillers wrote in her diary on 8 May 1945: 'Here we're dealing with a collective experience, something foreseen and feared many times in advance that happened to women right and left, all somehow part of the bargain. And this mass rape is something we are overcoming collectively as well.'[134] A few days earlier, Hillers had asked herself: 'What does it mean – rape? When I said the word for the first time aloud, Friday evening in the basement, it sent shivers down my spine. Now I can think it and write it with an untrembling hand, say it out loud to get used to hearing it said. It sounds like the absolute worst, the end of everything – but it's not.'[135]

A week later, Margaret Boveri described in her diary how she had bicycled, 'a short stretch with a nice bedraggled girl . . . imprisoned by Russians for 14 days, had been raped but well fed'. Then on 8 May 1945, she wrote: 'The usual rapes – a neighbour who resisted was shot . . . Mrs Krauss was not raped. She insists that Russians don't touch women who wear glasses. Like to know if that is true . . . the troops were pretty drunk but did distinguish between old and young which is already progress.'[136]

This exceptional wave of violence prompted many women to kill themselves, as the occupiers also recognized. On 12 March 1945, the head of the secret police service in northern East Prussia reported to Beria that 'suicides of Germans, particularly women, are becoming more and more widespread'.[137] Some took their own lives to escape this violence. Marta Hillers described how 'a woman across the street jumped out a fourth-storey window when some Ivans [Russians] were after her'.[138] 'Professor Schiller of the Rutberg-Krankenhaus', wrote Monsignor Giovanni Battista Montini, the Vatican's representative in Berlin, in October 1945, 'killed his wife and daughters and then himself not to have to bear the anguish of their rape'.[139] A Swiss journalist instead reported how, in some cases, in their eagerness the Russian soldiers did not 'even notice that they [the women] are dying because they swallowed poison'.[140] Others took their lives after being raped. Sometimes they did so because they were regarded as abject, filthy, repellent and were rejected by their husband or fiancé, or they were scorned by fellow Germans, by relatives and neighbours, for having given in too quickly to the invaders. It was repeatedly claimed that 'German soldiers had fought for six years, German women only for five minutes'.[141] More simply, they committed suicide because they could not bear the shame. On 6 May 1945, the journalist Ruth Andreas-Friedrich wrote in her diary:

> Suicide is in the air. They conceal girls in attics, under piles of coal and they bundle them up like old women. Almost none of them sleeps where she belongs. 'Honor lost, all lost', a bewildered father says and hands a rope to his daughter who has been raped twelve times. Docilely, she walks to the nearest window and hangs herself. [. . .]. 'If you have been raped, you have nothing to expect but death', a teacher declares to a class of girls two days before the final collapse. More than half the students came to the anticipated conclusion, as expected of them, and drowned themselves and their lost honour in the nearest body of water. Honor lost, all lost. Poison or bullet, rope or knife. They are killing themselves by the hundreds.[142]

It is estimated that out of approximately 100,000 women raped in Berlin, some 10,000 died, 'mostly from suicide'.[143] This is undoubtedly an exaggerated figure because records exist that document the suicide of 3,996 women in Berlin in 1945, and some of these were for other reasons. However, this does nothing to undermine the fact that the number of women who took their own lives because they were raped was exceptionally high.

As mentioned earlier, the Red Army troops also raped many Austrian women, some of whom also committed suicide.[144] In England, France and western Germany, thousands of women were raped by American soldiers,[145] and by Moroccan troops in Italy.[146] In all of these countries, the victims of sexual violence were subject to enormous humiliation and suffered indescribable hardship. Although few studies exist on this aspect, we can surmise that some of these women may have killed themselves. However, the figures that are available suggest that suicide as a result of rape was much more frequent in eastern Germany and in Lower Austria than it was in Italy or France. In 1945 the number of female suicides as a percentage of total voluntary deaths (a figure that had always been very low in Europe) reached 43 per cent in Austria and as much as 56 per cent in Berlin, while it varied less in France, Italy and other European countries.[147]

The wave of voluntary deaths in the closing months of the war was also due to a second motive, this time of a cultural nature: the conception of honour, heroism and suicide that grew up in Nazi Germany. The leaders of the regime severely condemned the suicide of serving soldiers, especially while there were still hopes of success. However, they regarded as heroic the suicide of vanquished soldiers or those taken prisoner. Hitler supported these ideas wholeheartedly. On 1 September 1939, the day Germany attacked Poland, he pronounced these words in a speech to the Reichstag: 'I now wish to be nothing other than the first soldier of the German Reich. Therefore I have put on that tunic which has always been the most holy and dear to me. I shall not take it off again until after victory is ours, or – I shall not live to see the day!'[148] Four years later, on 30 January 1943, despairing that his army could defeat the Red Army, Hitler promoted General Friedrich Paulus, who was charged with the operation, to the rank of Feldmarschall. He reminded him that no German with that honour had ever been taken prisoner and he suggested that he should take his own life rather than capitulate. Paulus took care not to follow these instructions and surrendered, and shortly afterwards he accepted the request of the Soviet authorities to make radio appeals against Hitler.

The importance of heroic suicide was also seconded by the minister for propaganda, Paul Joseph Goebbels, in February 1945 in a radio speech and at a press conference. Citing Cato the Younger, who had preferred to take his own life rather than surrender to Caesar, and taking as his model Frederick the Great, who had fought the Seven Years' War on the principle of 'victory or death', Goebbels had taken a solemn oath that in the event of German defeat he would 'serenely take leave of life'. It was this attitude that made the concept of suicide missions possible. The missions were launched in April 1943 by the minister for armaments and war production, Albert Speer, against the hydroelectric dam north of Moscow, therefore anticipating the Japanese by one year, a fact that ensured Goebbels' enthusiastic support and secured Hitler's approval.[149]

This conception of suicide was broadly shared by the intermediate ranks of the Nazi regime, which exalted military virtues, strength of will and courage, and regarded self-sacrifice as necessary, in special circumstances, in order to protect one's own honour. Therefore, not wishing to be taken by surprise on the day of catastrophe, Nazi politicians and many ordinary citizens started to carry capsules of potassium cyanide or razor blades with them, in pockets and bags, precisely as the Jews had when they found themselves persecuted and derided years earlier. Hitler allegedly gave cyanide pills to his secretaries before his final farewell, and members of the Hitler Youth are said to have distributed poison to the audience during the last concert of the Berliner Philarmoniker on 12 April 1945.[150]

For certain, before the capitulation, a huge number of leaders and middle-ranking Nazi officials took their lives. On 30 April 1945 Hitler and Eva Braun killed themselves, having been married the day before. Their example was followed by Goebbels, Bormann, Himmler, the minister of justice, the minister of culture, many regional leaders of the National Socialist party, the SS, generals and commanding officers of the armed forces and Luftwaffe, admirals and countless lower-ranking officers. This probably also influenced the decision taken by thousands of men and women who also took their leave of life in those days.

4.6   Emigrations

Every migratory process is by definition highly selective. Those who decide to go and live, for a varying length of time, in another country tend to be younger, more educated and better qualified (and perhaps also more dynamic, enterprising and creative) than those who stay where they were born.

Emigrations (at least those in the last fifty years or so) are also selective in terms of the conditions of health. Studies in many European countries and in the United States show that, in cohorts of the same age, immigrants fall sick less often and have lower mortality rates than natives, even if they come from disadvantaged backgrounds and have fewer economic resources.[151] These differences can be explained by cultural factors, such as eating habits and lifestyle. For example, North African immigrants to France have a diet that protects them from many diseases: they eat vegetables, fruit and cereals more often, and make more use of vegetable fats rather than animal fats. However, these differences also depend on the selective nature of emigration processes, namely the fact that those who decide to travel to another country are healthier than those who remain in the place where they were born.

If it were to emerge that emigrations were also selective in terms of mental health too, namely that those leaving their native country suffer less frequently than those who remain from mood disorders, depression and schizophrenia, then we might expect to find a lower suicide rate among immigrants. Unfortunately, our knowledge of the mental health of those leaving their own country is still quite slight. One study in the early thirties highlighted for the first time that Norwegian immigrants to the United States were hospitalized more frequently for schizophrenia than those who remained at home.[152] Research carried out in the last twenty years, using various methods, has shown that African Caribbean immigrants to the United Kingdom and Holland suffer from schizophrenia much more often (2–14 times more frequently) than natives. However, it is not yet clear whether this is also true of immigrants from other countries, nor have any causes been suggested.[153] Equally little is known about the differences between immigrants and natives with regard to depression.

Nonetheless, emigration was so important in the twentieth century that we cannot avoid asking whether it influenced the frequency of suicide and if so what effects it produced. It is a question that was first asked in the United States a century and a half ago. In 1861 a journalist in the *New York Times* reported that, 'The last decade shows an extraordinary increase of the suicidal mania among us. This increase may be attributable, in part at least, to the great German and Irish emigration of the decade.'[154] The paper reported that of those who had taken their own lives in recent years, a quarter were Germans, another quarter Irish, and a quarter had been born in the United States, while the remainder came from various other European countries.

Early studies on the immigrants who settled in New York, Chicago, Boston and San Francisco in the 1920s and 1930s showed that the concerns formulated years earlier by the *New York Times* were broadly true.[155] There were two key findings. Firstly, it was found that immigrants committed suicide more frequently than natives. This was attributed to the stress and maladjustment sometimes caused by emigration rather than to the fact that Europeans who moved to the United States suffered from more severe mental disorders than those who stayed in their own country. Secondly, considerable differences were found between the immigrants, depending on the suicide rate of their country of origin.

In the first fifteen years of the twentieth century the frequency of suicide in Europe varied significantly from one country to another. In this respect, it is possible to divide the countries (for which data exist) into three groups. In the first (with an annual suicide rate of over 20 per 100,000 inhabitants) were Germany, Austria, Denmark and Hungary. The second (with a rate of between 10 and 19) included Sweden, Belgium, England and Wales. The third (with a rate under 10) comprised Italy, Holland, Scotland, Norway, Spain, Portugal, Ireland and Greece. These differences were due to various factors, not least to cultural reasons, namely the repertoire of meanings, symbols and beliefs existing in each country.

When they left, migrants took this cultural heritage with them and continued to conform to it even after arriving in the United States. Therefore, those who came from countries with a higher suicide rate (like Germany, Austria and Denmark) had a very high rate of voluntary deaths, while those from countries where suicide was less frequent (like Italy, Spain and Ireland) had a lower rate.[156]

Research using more sophisticated methodologies carried out recently on immigrants resident in the United States, Canada, United Kingdom, Australia and France shows an even more complex picture of what happens, in this respect, to those who leave their own country.[157] These studies show that immigrants aged over sixty, who find it more difficult to adapt and are often exposed to considerable stress, take their own lives more than natives. But the factors that have the greatest influence on the frequency with which migrants kill themselves are cultural in nature and concern the norms and beliefs about voluntary death that they learn during infancy and adolescence. The suicide rate among immigrants varies little depending on the country of destination, but considerably according to the country of origin. By way of example, the Greeks and Italians rarely take their own lives whether they emigrate to Canada, Australia, the United Kingdom or the United States, while Austrians and Hungarians take their own lives more often, irrespective of the country they go to live in.

The enormous importance of cultural factors is also borne out by the effects of living for long periods in the country of destination and the assimilation process itself. The longer immigrants stay in the host country and learn its rules, the more they tend to behave like the natives, also with regard to suicide. Mexicans who emigrate to the United States are just one example. Suicide rates in Mexico are three times lower than in the United States. Immigrants have therefore learnt beliefs and norms that protect them from suicide, and for some time after arrival they continue to follow the national model and take their own life less frequently than native Americans. But the longer they stay in the United States and the more integrated they become, the more they tend to kill themselves with the same frequency.[158]

That cultural factors have an extraordinary influence is also evident from the information we have regarding the chosen method of ending life. This choice has for a long time differed between countries, and continues to do so today. For example, in Italy the most frequently used method is hanging, in Sweden poisoning, in the United States a pistol or other firearm. If immigrants decide to take their own lives then they usually continue to behave as if they were in their own country and choose accordingly. Already in the closing decades of the nineteenth century, the figures for New York showed that 'even away from their own country, the English and Irish preserve their predilection for poison and the pistol, whilst the German always retains his pre-eminence in hanging'.[159] The same continued to be true throughout the twentieth century. If they had only recently arrived in the new country, immigrants killed themselves by the preferred methods used by their home countries, but as time passed then they abandoned these ideas and adopted those of the host country.[160]

Therefore, also in relation to voluntary death, emigration reduces the differences between populations, because the suicide rate of individuals from different countries gradually converges with the country of destination: either increasing, as happened not only to Mexicans but also to Italians, Greeks and Spaniards who went to live in the United States, or diminishing, as in the case of Austrians, Germans or Hungarians who emigrated to the United Kingdom or Australia. The same process of gradual absorption can also be seen in relation to the means of suicide used.

4.7   Suicide is a 'White thing'

On 14 July 1699, while in Damma, in the Congo, the Capuchin missionary Luca da Caltanissetta witnessed a scene that he had no hesitation in describing as 'horrendous'. A woman with a small infant at her breast heard her master talking to a slave trader who wanted to buy her. Convinced that the request would not be refused, 'she took her child and threw him angrily against a rock, and then grabbed a number of arrows or darts from the hands of an onlooker and furiously thrust them into her chest, dying thus in despair and without baptism'.[161] Three years later, another Italian missionary, Padre Antonio Zucchelli from Gradisca, observed that many Kongolese slaves were so disgusted by the prospect of being 'shipped to Brazil' that they chose to die 'voluntarily', 'turning both eyes and tongue inwards, of their own accord, they were suffocated by the devil for the past relations they'd had with him'. The merchants used fire to prevent these deaths: 'when they [the slaves] started to die by swallowing their tongues, if the Whites were at hand to touch them with a fiery brand, the devil would desist from this activity and they were preserved from death.'[162]

The only statistics available, which relate to crossings between 1792 and 1796, show that between one and two per thousand Africans forcibly transported to the Americas took their lives on the journey.[163] Taking into account those who, according to many witnesses, killed themselves in the first two or three months after arriving, it is clear that, in this phase, suicide among slaves was not rare.[164] However, it was not solely due to the appalling conditions in which they were forced to live after being taken captive or being purchased by the European traders: the inhuman effort required to walk in chains to the port of embarkation, the ocean crossing in dark, confined spaces after being branded with the mark of each owner, and the hard labour in the American plantations or mines, deprived of all rights and even their own names, all took their toll.

Above all, it was factors of a cultural nature, namely the systems of belief and meaning then held by African populations, that fostered suicide among the slaves who were forced to abandon their native country. In 1765, when Olaudah Equiano, an eleven-year-old Ibo boy, was loaded onto a slave ship, he fainted at the sight of some Africans chained beside a large bronze kettle-like object that looked like a cooking pot, because he thought that his companions were going to be eaten by their new masters. When he came round, he asked whether the slaves on board 'were not to be eaten by these white men with horrible looks, red faces, and loose hair'. Although he was reassured that this would not happen, he was unconvinced, and wrote that 'still I feared I should be put to death'.[165]

The question in his mind and that of other Africans was why did these strange men have such an insatiable need for slaves? Why would they take them captive or buy them and carry them off? The obvious response was that they wanted to eat them, for lunch or supper. This conviction was firmly rooted in the minds of their victims: white slavers were cannibals and therefore the slaves would be used to feed their masters either during the voyage or on reaching their destination. In 1848, referring to the practice of force-feeding slaves through funnels if they refused to eat, an African called Augustino told the Select Committee of the House of Lords in London how, during the crossing 'the young ones had the right of coming on deck, but several of those jumped overboard for fear they were being fattened to be eaten'.[166]

Belief in white cannibalism continued for a long time to influence the meaning given by African slaves to the white men's words and deeds. In many African languages, men from the West were called 'red' rather than 'white', because it was believed that they ate human flesh. When slaves first saw their master drinking red wine they were terrorized, because they thought it was the blood of erstwhile companions, and if they met their master beside an oven they tried to run away.[167] Moreover, the African slaves believed the traders or plantation owners would crush and press their bodies to make oil, grind their bones into gunpowder or even use their brains to make cheese and their blood to dye flags.[168] It is also worth recalling, as was mentioned earlier,[169] that these slaves were convinced that, after death, they would fly back to Africa as large birds, and this may explain why some took their own lives.

Over time, the traders and plantation owners noticed striking cultural differences between the African tribes and populations, and how these affected their capacity to adapt to the new way of life and their propensity to suicide. For example, the Macau were seen as 'generally quiet, docile and lazy', while the Mandinga were esteemed as 'calm, obedient and honest', but the Lucumí were regarded as 'very proud and haughty; they are brave, and are often known to commit suicide under the irritation of punishment or disgrace'.[170] 'Constitutional timidity' and 'despondency of mind' frequently led the Ibo to 'seek, in voluntary death, a refuge from their melancholy reflections'.[171]

These differences affected the economic value of particular slaves. One eyewitness described the slave market in Pernambuco, Brazil, in his diary for 1828, and he remarked how newly disembarked African slaves were sold at prices ranging from twenty to one hundred pounds depending on their origin. The most expensive, 'a race called Minas' were the 'highest in repute being the best tempered, strongest and healthiest men'. Next came the Angolans, while the least appreciated were those from Mozambique, 'being weak and sickly and more apt to give way to despondency and commit suicide'.[172]

The situation has changed in the last two centuries but, in terms of the frequency of suicide, not in the way we might have expected. In the United States, until 1865 at least, the descendants of these black Africans continued to live in slavery. After that, for another one hundred years or more, they were the victims of discrimination and segregation. Lacking the most basic rights, they were barred from eating in restaurants reserved for whites, or sleeping in their hotels; they could not send their children to white schools, let alone intermarry. For generations, they were scorned and hated, dominated and at the same time feared.

All the observers, and even the most informed experts, expected to find a high suicide rate among black Americans because of the hard conditions in which they lived and because it was not unreasonable to suppose that they might turn the scorn and hatred expressed by others on themselves.[173] But this is not what happened. The earliest statistical data refer to 1850, when just over three million blacks lived in the United States (88 per cent in slavery and 12 per cent as freedmen), yet these figures show that the suicide rate of African-Americans was very low and certainly lower than that recorded the previous century during the forced trans-Atlantic crossings or shortly after landing. This drop in the frequency of voluntary death can certainly be attributed to the ending of the most brutal period of the slave trade, and also to the fact that beliefs had changed: slaves no longer believed in white cannibalism, nor that they would fly back to their motherland after death. Yet, these data revealed two further, very surprising findings: whites took their own lives more frequently than blacks, and blacks were more likely to commit suicide if they were free.[174] If the end of slavery produced an increase in suicide rather than a fall, then it was clear that it was not the way of life and living conditions that prompted suicide.

Equally surprising are the figures for the most recent half-century. Throughout this period African-Americans have experienced economic conditions and lifestyles that entailed considerable risk factors in terms of health and suicide. They have always been less educated, poorer, and more frequently unemployed than whites, and more of them resorted to alcohol or more dangerous drugs. There is no doubt that anyone finding themselves in these conditions, taking drugs, and with fewer economic and cultural resources, will have poorer health, a shorter life and a higher rate of suicide. Indeed, African-Americans do suffer from poor health and do also die younger than whites from heart disease, apoplexy, lung and breast cancer, Aids or as murder victims. They also suffer from depression to the same extent as whites.[175] Yet, in spite of all this, they kill themselves more rarely.

In 1950, white Americans had a much higher suicide rate than African-Americans. The differences between the two groups were more marked in the female population than in the male, and among the elderly than among the young. It was extremely rare for an African-American woman to take her own life. Moreover, the probability that she might did not increase with age, as instead was the case among white women. The sector of the population in which the differences between whites and blacks were most striking was the frequency of suicide in under thirty-five-year-old males.[176]

For forty years or so, almost until the end of the 1980s, there was a rising suicide rate among young people, but this growth was steepest among African-Americans. As a result, the latter group now has a suicide rate that is almost the same as that for whites (indeed, in New York it is higher).[177] Then in 1994 there was another trend inversion and today, among this particular sector of the population, young white men take their own lives much more frequently than their black counterparts. In terms of the entire population, it is worth noting that differences between the two groups have widened over the last thirty-five years. While in 1970 the white suicide rate was double (2.03 times) that of blacks, in 2010 it was 2.6 times higher.[178]

Both then and now this surprising difference is not peculiar to the United States. It is not just in the world's richest country that voluntary death is still relatively rare in the most disadvantaged social group. The same was true in South Africa, a country where in the last half-century the black population were segregated from and discriminated against by the small white minority. Here, too, the latter have always committed suicide more frequently than the former.[179]

The low suicide rate among African-Americans can be traced to socio-cultural factors; in the first place, to their extensive relational networks. Although it is true that conjugal relations are often very weak and unstable, and that they often live in truncated nuclear families, made up of a mother and her children, yet it is equally true that bonds between blood relatives are extremely strong, with three generations frequently living under the same roof. The family is therefore enormously important. There is a constant exchange of information, phone calls, visits and financial assistance between grandmothers and grandchildren, between sisters who are married or have children, and between aunts and cousins. Women play a central role. They have learned to cope with poverty, discrimination, illness and death by forming strong social networks and sharing available resources.

As well as this rock-solid family system, bonds among African-Americans are also assured by the churches that have always tried to provide for their community's economic, social and political needs, supporting their members through countless battles and backing them in many different ways. Seen as an 'extension of the family', African-Americans have described black churches as 'our mother, our protection, our only hope'.[180]

In the second place, the low suicide rate of African-Americans is due to cultural factors. Over time, they have developed numerous strategies for coping with adversity and many of these stem from the Methodist and Baptist religious traditions. It is thanks to these traditional beliefs regarding the world, the cause of events and death, that they succeed in attributing meaning to tragedy and accepting reality. Moreover, they are able to overcome the most difficult situations through prayer and an unshakeable faith in God and his power to create new purposes.[181] This also explains why, after being diagnosed with cancer, they are able to cope with anxiety and depression better than whites, and they take their own lives much less frequently than them, irrespective of the fact that they may receive less medical care.[182]

But even when they do not succeed, and when they are overwhelmed by pain and despair, their traditional customs and beliefs prevent them from turning to suicide. The religious aspect is particularly important because many African-Americans follow the teaching of Methodist and Baptist pastors and believe that suicide is a very grave sin and those who commit it lose their soul and are condemned to hell for eternity. Yet even those educated outside the church view suicide as 'a White thing',[183] a way suited to a people with a different history, one without slavery, discrimination and unfair treatment, and a course of action suited to a people who did not learn to put a brave face on disaster, who did not learn to be strong, patient, tenacious and persevering, nurturing an ability to bounce back.

In African-American culture, voluntary death is still such a taboo today that when someone commits suicide, it is difficult for the relatives and family to receive comfort and support from the community. Not only from friends and acquaintances, but also from their church pastors who often prefer to ignore what has happened and even avoid those in mourning when, on the contrary, these people desperately need their help.[184]

4.8 Has suicide become a little less male?

'The death, then, of a beautiful woman', wrote the American poet, Edgar Allan Poe in 1846, 'is, unquestionably, the most poetical topic in the world.' Indeed, a woman's suicide is at the heart of some of the world's greatest literary masterpieces: from Sophocles' *Antigone* to Tolstoy's *Anna Karenina*. In tragedies, romances and operas, women take their own lives for the most varied reasons: to affirm their independence, to protest, to defend their honour ('Death with honour is better than life with dishonour' are the words read by Madame Butterfly shortly before she commits suicide) or because they succumb to a severe, incurable disease: *le mal d'amour*. In the nineteenth century, female suicide became a sort of 'cultural obsession' and found a place in some of the great novels by Flaubert, Tolstoy, Ibsen and Strindberg, which have moved many subsequent generations of Western readers.[185] But what happened and what happens in reality?

Book lovers are usually not great fans of statistics. But if they happened to look at them, they would be struck to discover that women take their lives much less often than men in the West. It is a fact that people always find surprising, not only those who cannot forget Emma Bovary, but also those familiar with the scientific literature on mental disorders. About one hundred and seventy years ago, the French psychiatrist, Jean-Etienne Dominique Esquirol wrote, 'Although women may be more exposed to mental diseases than men, suicide is, nevertheless, less frequent among them.'[186] This scholar's views have been repeatedly criticized and scientific research in this field is far more extensive than it was then. But his affirmation is still correct.

Schizophrenia and bipolar disorders are distributed equally in the male and female populations, but depression affects twice more women than men, and major depression four times more.[187] It is an enormous difference whose causes are not yet entirely clear. This is the case not only in Europe, North America and Australia, but also in Asia and Africa, even though the greatest differences between the numbers of women and men suffering from depression are found in those countries with the fewest gender inequalities (like Denmark and Holland).[188] Since depression, as we know, carries a high risk of suicide, we would expect to find that women take their own lives much more frequently than men. Yet, in Western countries this is not the case and never has been, for the past seven hundred years at least.

As was seen in Chapter 1, the available figures show that in Europe, from the mid thirteenth to the mid nineteenth century, men killed themselves more frequently than women. Much fuller and more accurate records show that between the late nineteenth and the early twentieth century gender differences continued to be huge. In all Western countries, the suicide rate among men was almost three times that of women, and in many cases four times. However, in Sweden, the rate was five times higher and in Norway, a record six. (Table 4.1) Although the past century has seen this difference narrow in almost all countries, men still commit suicide more frequently than women.

The fact that the gap has narrowed most in Sweden and that the difference between men and women (in voluntary death rates) is lower here than in other countries might point to a correlation with gender inequalities, namely that the difference is least when there is a greater probability that members of either sex will be educated, find employment, earn the same wage, etc. Yet this hypothesis is not confirmed by the figures. Having examined the eighteen Western countries shown in Table 4.1, one reaches the conclusion that there is no statistical correlation between social in equalities between genders and differences in the frequency with which men and women commit suicide.[189]

The most important reason for this difference is cultural.[190] This is clear from a comparison between West and East (as we shall see in the second part of this book). But it also emerges from the information we have on Europe. If women have always taken their own lives much less than men on this continent, in spite of having suffered more from severe depression, it is because they have been protected by culture, by their outlook on the world, by the importance given to their own bodies, to their health and to their relations with others. Even today, women learn different modes of conduct in families and schools, which teach them the importance of caring for themselves and others rather than focusing on risk, aggressive behaviour, and violence. It is still true today that women resort less to alcohol and drugs. Moreover, for many centuries, compared to men, women were more deeply influenced by religion, both Christianity and Judaism, both of which had a very negative view of suicide.

The importance of cultural factors is clear if we also take parasuicides into account. It is estimated that in the West for every successful suicide there are at least ten attempted suicides.[191] Significant differences can be pinpointed between those who succeed in taking their own lives and those who fail. The former predominantly include men and the elderly, whereas women and the young are among the latter. Successful suicides are usually carefully planned, while the latter are frequently impulsive acts.[192]

However, the outcome of attempted suicide also depends on the method used, a choice that is undoubtedly influenced by cultural factors. In Europe, over the past one and a half centuries, some changes have taken place in the methods individuals use to take their own lives. Yet there continues to be a difference between the female and male populations (Table 4.2), with the former still choosing the less lethal means of poisoning and, in the past,

Table 4.1 Ratio between male and female suicide rates in some Western countries, from 1901 to 2001.

	1901	1911	1921	1931	1941	1951	1961	1971	1981	1991	2001
Holland	3.0	2.8	2.7	2.2	1.5	1.9	1.6	1.6	1.5	1.8	2.2
Sweden	5.4	4.5	3.9	3.9	3.5	3.3	3.1	2.4	2.4	2.4	2.3
Denmark			2.6	2.3	1.8	2.1	2.0	1.7	1.8	2.0	2.4
Switzerland	4.8	4.1	3.9	3.4	3.1	2.6	2.6	2.7	2.4	2.5	2.6
Austria			2.3	2.2		2.3	2.2	2.5	2.7	3.0	2.8
Germany	4.1	3.2	2.3	2.5		2.3	1.8	1.9	2.0	2.4	2.9
France				3.3	2.8	3.2	2.9	2.7	2.6	2.6	2.9
Norway	6.4	4.4	3.9	4.4	4.3	3.6	4.2	2.4	2.8	2.9	3.1
Spain	4.7	3.3	3.6	3.6	3.0	3.1	2.8	2.9	3.0	2.9	3.3
Italy	3.8	2.5	2.8	3.3	2.8	2.9	2.3	2.3	2.5	2.7	3.4
Canada			3.5	3.5	2.8	3.1	4.0	2.5	3.1	4.1	3.5
Portugal			2.5	3.3	2.9	2.9	3.7	3.5	2.4	3.2	3.6
Finland	4.1	4.7	4.2	5.5	5.7	4.5	3.7	3.7	4.0	4.2	3.6
England and Wales	3.1	3.0	3.1	2.6	2.2	1.9			1.8	3.5	3.7
Australia		4.2	4.5	4.8	2.8	3.0	2.4	2.2	3.1	3.8	3.8
United States	2.9	3.2	3.3	3.7	3.1	3.4	3.3	2.6	3.2	4.3	4.3
Ireland	3.8	3.3	3.7	3.2	5.0	3.6	2.3	6.0	2.4	4.5	4.3
Belgium	5.0	3.9	2.9	3.8	2.4	2.7	2.7	1.9	2.0	2.5	5.2

Source: Elaborated using data from World Health Organization (WHO).

Table 4.2 Suicide methods used by men and women in five European countries, in 1863–76 and in 2000–04.

	Italy		Switzerland		Belgium		Germany		England	
	M	F	M	F	M	F	M	F	M	F
1863–1876										
Hanging	17	18	46	23	56	45	65	45	45	30
Poisoning	5	8	2	9	2	7	2	6	7	18
Drowning	25	49	23	55	20	40	14	41	13	27
Firearm	31	3	19	4	14	–	13	–	6	–
Knife	6	3	7	5	4	3	4	5	20	17
Jumping	11	15	1	3	1	2	1	2	2	3
Other	5	4	2	1	3	3	1	1	7	5
Total	100	100	100	100	100	100	100	100	100	100
2000–2004										
Hanging	55	29	27	19	57	37	55	38	55	36
Poisoning	12	15	17	40	11	21	12	26	26	45
Drowning	5	12	3	10	7	19	2	7	2	5
Firearm	7	2	34	4	12	4	10	1	4	1
Jumping	14	33	9	15	3	7	8	14	3	4
Other	7	9	10	12	10	12	13	14	10	9
Total	100	100	100	100	100	100	100	100	100	100

Source: Elaborated using data from Marselli (1879) and Värnik et al. (2008).

drowning, rather than firearms, knives or hanging, the preferred male choices. This is because women are less accustomed to the use of violence and also more concerned that their bodies and in particular their features should not be disfigured.

The choice of method also depends on the social class of the individual. In Italy there is a correlation between a lower level of schooling and the choice of hanging as a means of voluntary death by both men and women. On the other hand, suicide through jumping becomes more frequent the higher the level of education (Table A.6, Appendix).

4.9   Sexual orientation

On 13 January 1998, in Rome, a militant gay Catholic, Alfredo Ormando, set himself alight in St Peter's square. He had meticulously planned the success of his action, choosing the means and the place of his farewell and informing a few of his friends. In one of his last letters, he wrote:

My preparations for suicide move forward inexorably; I feel that this is my fate, that I've always known it and never accepted it, but that this tragic destiny is there waiting for me with a saintly patience that's barely credible. I haven't managed to get this idea of dying out of my head, and I feel I can't escape it, let alone pretend to get on with life and plan for a future that I won't have: my future will never be anything but the continuation of the present. I live with the awareness of someone about to abandon earthly life, but this doesn't horrify me. In fact, quite the opposite! I can't wait to end my days; they'll think I'm mad to have decided on Piazza San Pietro as the place, when I could equally well have done it here in Palermo. I hope they'll understand the message I want to send: it's a form of protest against the Church which demonizes homosexuality, thereby demonizing nature, because homosexuality is the product of nature.[193]

His dramatic and spectacular end divided the Italian gay community. Some regarded him as a martyr who had sacrificed himself for a worthy cause, thereby deserving an annual commemoration in a public and entirely secular ceremony. Others argued that he should have remained alive in order to fight on behalf of the gay movement.[194]

It was an exceptional event, and one that provoked an unusual level of controversy. During the past thirty years or so, other militant homosexuals, many of them renowned in their own societies, have committed suicide. In March 1983, Mario Mieli decided to do so, at the age of thirty-one (Plate 23). In September that year, he was followed by another militant gay (a fervent Catholic), Ferruccio Castellano. But both left this world without a scene, and above all without transforming their gesture into an act of protest. As a result their deaths did not cause dissent and

debate in the gay movement. Lesser-known gays and lesbians have taken
their own lives, under an even greater pall of silence, in both Italy and
other Western countries, and some did all they could to prevent their
families from hearing of their sexual orientation and the reason for their
deaths.

All this helps us to understand how very difficult it is to ascertain,
using a rigorously scientific approach, whether a person's sexual orientation has a bearing on the risk of suicide. It is unheard of for any country
to collect information on the sexual orientation of suicides. But even if
such an attempt were to be made, considerable obstacles would have to
be overcome. Not least because information of this nature is often only
known to a small group of people, but also because sexual experience can
be divided into three distinctly different dimensions: emotions (the attrac-
tion and love experienced towards a person of the same or different sex),
behaviour (the erotic activity experienced with this person) and identity
(whether the individual regards herself or himself as heterosexual, homosexual or bisexual). Moreover, in practice, these three dimensions often do
not coincide since an individual can be attracted by another of the same
sex or enjoy an erotic same-sex relationship without identifying himself or
herself as homosexual.

In the last twenty years, these methodological issues have, at least in
part, been overcome. Studies carried out in various Western countries on
representative population samples have shown that all those who have
homoerotic feelings, same-sex partners or regard themselves as homo- or
bisexual frequently entertain suicidal thoughts and make more attempts
than others to take their own lives. The risk that this actually happens
increases exponentially precisely in the last phase of coming to terms with
this identity, namely at the moment of 'coming out' or externalizing one's
own sexual orientation.[195]

This is because, even today, in all Western countries, a significant proportion of the population are hostile to anyone who has a homosexual
experience. Therefore, an individual who is attracted by a person of the
same sex or makes love with them soon realizes the risk of seriously com-
promising his or her social image and of losing the esteem and affection of
close friends and family. They may feel shame and even scorn or hatred for
themselves. Moreover, they may see themselves as victims of a serious and
undeserved injustice. Alfredo Ormando indeed asked himself:

> Why must I live? I can't find a single reason why I must continue this
> torture [. . .] In the afterlife the fact that I'm gay won't make any-
> one's hair stand on end or make them wrinkle their noses [. . .] I can't
> understand why I am set on in this way. I don't tempt anyone away
> from the straight path of heterosexuality, anyone who comes to bed
> with me is grown-up, a consenting adult and either homosexual or
> bisexual [. . .] I've lived with this prejudice and have been marginal-
> ized since I was ten. I can't accept it any longer. My cup is full.[196]

Surviving documentation leads us to suppose that in the past, gays and lesbians ran even greater risks of committing suicide. In the early decades of the twentieth century, first novels and then films featured numerous homosexual characters who killed themselves or were killed.[197] But this trend was probably an expression of the belief, widely held at the time, that homosexuality could not by definition bring happiness.

The data reported in 1914 by one of the most authoritative sexologists in Europe, the German doctor, Magnus Hirschfeld, are much more convincing. He wrote that, when examining homosexual men, he had often found signs of suicide attempts on their bodies: scars of cuts made close to arteries or firearm wounds on the chest or head. He also added that many of them carried with them a cyanide pill. Moreover, based on the results of some of his studies (whose scientific rigour can hardly be doubted) Hirschfeld estimated that some three per cent of homosexuals took their own lives (a rate that was even higher than that among Jews during the Nazi persecutions), that 25 per cent had attempted to commit suicide and 75 per cent were thinking of suicide or had thought about it.[198]

As well as being more frequent than among heterosexuals, the suicide of homosexuals was marked by a further two key traits in the opening decades of the twentieth century. Firstly, they were rarely acts of sudden impulse, but, on the contrary, deliberate and premeditated. From this point of view, 'it is less of a tragedy and more of an end to a tragic life'.[199] Secondly, the suicides were often 'doubles', in other words they were most frequently committed by two gay men or two lesbians who passionately loved one another and preferred to die together, in an embrace, holding hands or with their wrists bound tightly together.[200]

There were numerous factors that prompted individuals with homoerotic

Fig. 4.1 Suicides of 'mollies', from *The Women-Hater's Lamentation*, 1707.

Source: Bray (1995, 91).

desires to commit suicide. In the first half of the twentieth century, the English criminal code proscribed the offence among the unnatural crimes, while German law punished 'an unnatural act committed between males' with imprisonment, and the men who were charged, arrested and sentenced for having committed this offence killed themselves more frequently than others. Those who were the victims of blackmail or the targets of scandal also ran a greater risk of suicide.[201]

For example, Alfred Krupp, the richest man in Germany at the time, took his own life in 1902 after a number of newspapers, including the Marxist *Vorwärts*, had accused him of indulging in 'homosexual practices with youths from the island of Capri'. 'This corruption', the newspaper article continued, 'had become so indecent that photos of some episodes could even be seen in a photographer's studio on the island. And after Krupp's money had made the island famous, Capri became a hotbed of homosexuality.'[202] In England, in 1922, a Liberal member of parliament, Viscount Lewis Hartcourt, took his own life for fear that his homosexuality might be made public and cause a scandal.[203]

The highest risk of suicide at the time was among those who were expelled from the army or sacked from public office or from private companies solely on account of their homosexuality. After moving from one job to another and falling into poverty, some convinced themselves that they belonged to the most despised and hated group of humanity and so took their own lives.

It seems likely that the frequency with which homosexuals committed suicide rose from then on. Even in the absence of precise figures, it is reasonable to suppose that following Hitler's rise to power in 1933, the situation of homosexuals deteriorated still further in Germany and Austria and the number of those taking their own lives rose yet higher.[204]

4.10   Economic depressions and crises of prosperity

'Poverty protects against suicide',[205] wrote Durkheim in his analysis of the relations between the economy and suicide. Indeed, it was in the poorest regions of Europe, such as Calabria, that Durkheim noted the lowest suicide rates in the closing decades of the nineteenth century. However, he alleged that the same conclusion could be reached by analysing the effects of the economic cycle. The suicide rate stayed low in periods of stability (even if it was stability of poverty), and rose in both phases of recession and expansion, namely during periods of sudden change. If such crises caused an increase in voluntary deaths, it was not because of reduced wealth or because people fell on hard times. This was borne out by the fact that also the so-called 'fortunate crises', namely the phases of rapid economic growth leading to sudden improvements in individual circumstances, had the same effect. The most important aspect was that both recession and expansion were crises, namely 'disturbances of the collective order' that generated anomie and acted as 'an impulse to voluntary death'.[206]

Thirty years later, analysing the historical series of economic trends and voluntary deaths in his own country and in Germany, another French sociologist, Maurice Halbwachs, came to a different conclusion. The data showed that suicide rates rose only in years of economic depression, not in those of expansion.[207] In his view, this meant that the impact of the economic cycle was unrelated to a growth in anomie.

The economic history of twentieth-century Europe appears to prove Halbwachs' thesis. The crash of the New York stock market in October 1929 marked the start of the worst crisis experienced by Western countries. Having exploded in the United States, the repercussions spread to Europe causing major economic, social and political difficulties in 1930 or the following year in some countries, like France. Banks, insurance companies and private firms went bankrupt. Unemployment rates soared, while household wealth diminished. Suicide rates also rose, but at times and with intensities that differed in individual countries.[208] The steepest rises occurred in Austria, the United States and Spain, while Germany and Britain experienced less dramatic increases, and Italy none at all.[209]

'Crises of prosperity', on the other hand, have not had the consequences that Durkheim predicted. For almost thirty years, between 1945 and 1975, all Western countries underwent the fastest economic growth ever experienced, but the suicide rate did not rise as sharply as might have been expected.[210] Only three countries – Holland, Sweden and the United States – saw rising rates, although even these were quite contained. Suicide rates remained stable in Austria, Belgium, Denmark, Ireland, France and Switzerland. They fell in Italy, and from 1964, dropped consistently for about a decade in Britain, an event that, as we shall see, had nothing to do with economic trends.[211]

The oil crisis from 1973 onwards was accompanied by a sharp upturn in suicide rates, above all among the young.[212] But from 1986 the richest countries of Western Europe started to see a fall that is still in progress.

4.11   The unforeseen consequences of the shift to methane

It is impossible to know for certain whether the large increase in suicide rates during the seventeenth and eighteenth centuries really started in England, as the author of *The English Malady* and many other contemporaries believed. However, we can be sure that the fall in suicide rates over most of Europe, which began in the last two decades of the twentieth century and is still continuing, had its starting point in the United Kingdom, but for completely different reasons compared to those that prompted a similar trend twenty years later in Austria, Germany, France, Switzerland, Denmark and Sweden.

To start with no one thought to comment on the falling numbers of suicides in Britain in 1964 and 1965. Even to experts, accustomed to short-term fluctuations in this and other social indicators, it did not appear to be particularly important. But numbers continued to drop steadily until 1975, with growing significance given that over twelve years voluntary deaths fell from 5,714 to 3,693. At this point, it was inevitable that researchers began to look into the reasons for this unexpected change. Since at least 1880 Britain had always had the lowest suicide rate of all central and northern European countries. How could this dramatic change in the rate between 1964 and 1975 be explained?

Classic explanations proved unable to provide an answer. It was clearly untenable to suggest that the level of social integration in Britain could have increased over such a short period. Instead, precisely from 1965, there had been a strong rise in crime rates and in the numbers of marriages ending in divorce. Nor could economic trends be used as an explanation given that unemployment rates rose sharply over these years. In the end a cause was identified but it was a fact that, until then, no one had imagined as being even remotely related to suicide.

At the end of the 1950s, coal gas, which had a high concentration of carbon monoxide, was gradually replaced by the much less toxic natural gas, methane. The reasons for this change were purely economic, but it had other consequences. Until then, in half of British homes, individuals had killed themselves by turning the gas on in appliances. It is not hard to understand why this method was so popular. It was widely available, everyone knew how to use it, it required less courage than other methods, and it was painless, non-violent and left no disfiguring marks. The transition to methane made it increasingly difficult to use this means as a way of taking one's own life, so the number of suicides committed using carbon monoxide plummeted from 2,368 in 1963 to 23 in 1975. One might expect that an individual living in Britain who wished to commit suicide would have used other means: poisoning, hanging, drowning, firearms. But instead, once gas was no longer available, many gave up the idea of killing themselves and the total number of voluntary deaths fell sharply.[213] Most probably it was the more impulsive individuals who had acted in this way, those who tended to react suddenly to external events and to the feelings they were experiencing, but also those who were most likely to rethink their decision if they were hindered in implementing it or once the immediate shock had faded.[214]

This sequence of events highlights, more clearly than any study, the plethora of factors involved in the decision to commit suicide. Even the strongest and apparently most irreversible urge to self-destruction, provoked or fostered by a varying range of causes, does not necessarily lead to suicide if the means of accomplishing it are not available or are too difficult or too repugnant to use. The idea that there is nothing easier than finding a way to end one's life, once the decision has been taken, is simply not true. In practice, the choice of method often influences the outcome. This is also borne out by similar events that have happened in other countries.

In Switzerland, too, there was a steady drop in suicide numbers between 1958 and 1968, for exactly the same reason, namely that coal gas was replaced by methane during precisely that period. Here again, most of those individuals who might have used coal gas as a means of committing suicide found it impossible to choose other methods and therefore renounced the idea of killing themselves.[215] If the fall in voluntary deaths was much less striking here compared to Britain, it was only because until then the Swiss had resorted less frequently than the British to domestic gas.

A similar case was reported in a country with a very different cultural background: Japan. In January 1933, a young woman, Meiko Ukei, leapt into the crater of Mount Mihara, an active volcano. The legend soon spread that her body had been cremated instantaneously and her soul had risen to heaven in a cloud of smoke. The crater acquired iconic status and a growing number of people threw themselves into it. The phenomenon lasted for years, in spite of police controls and a barbed wire enclosure. Finally in 1955 a young couple who threw themselves into the crater were saved and this destroyed the myth of instant cremation, which had attracted so many people.[216]

4.12   The trend inversion in central and northern Europe

In the last twenty years suicide rates have fallen in most central and northern European countries, a trend that is still in progress and is likely to continue for some time. It started in Denmark in the first half of the 1980s, but soon spread to both Germanys (which were still divided at the time), Sweden, Austria, Switzerland, France, the United Kingdom, Norway and Finland. It also affected some parts of Italy and, perhaps, other Mediterranean countries, although the frequency of voluntary death in these areas has not fallen overall, and in some cases has even risen slightly.

There are three good grounds for supposing that this process, whose importance has not been fully recognized even by the international scientific community, represents a trend inversion compared to the centuries-long pattern of rising suicide rates which was analysed in previous chapters. The first is that within a short period (generally not more than fifteen years) suicide rates fells sharply, by 30 per cent in some countries (Sweden, Switzerland and Austria), but by 44 per cent in others (such as Germany) or even 55 per cent (in Denmark). The second is that today in many of these countries suicide rates are much lower than at the end of the nineteenth century. Although in at least one country, Denmark, we have to go much further back to find such a low suicide rate (13.6 per 100,000 inhabitants in 2001 compared to 24.8 in 1881 and 21.1 in 1821). The third is that in each of the countries in question the change started in the places and among the social groups that first saw the strong rise in suicide rates,

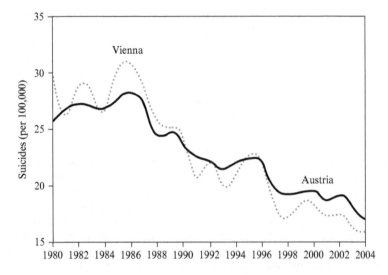

Graph 4.2   Suicide rates in Austria and Vienna from 1980 to 2004.

Source: Elaborated using data from Nestor D. Kapusta.

thus highlighting the likelihood that, within a few years, the change will spread to the rest of the population.

In the vanguard of the new trend were undoubtedly the large urban centres and, probably, individuals from the upper tiers of society. Consider, for example, what happened in Austria. At the end of the nineteenth century, Vienna had a suicide rate that was double that in the rest of the country.[217] By 1980, this difference had shrunk significantly. But since then the suicide rate has fallen more steeply in the capital than in the rest of the country (Graph 4.2). Since 1981 Austria has seen falling suicide rates in both urban and rural areas, but the fall has been sharpest in the former.[218]

The same happened in France,[219] the United Kingdom, Australia and the United States.[220] In the latter, the suicide rate in major cities between 1970 and 2002 decreased by ten per cent for men, while it more than halved for women. In rural areas, on the other hand, it grew considerably for men and remained unchanged for women.

Similar trends have been reported for years also in Italy. Here, the suicide rate over the past twenty years has remained relatively stable, at seven or eight per 100,000 inhabitants. But provincial capitals have seen quite a different trend compared to peripheral towns. In 1881 the number of voluntary deaths in the former was fifteen times higher than in the latter. But after peaking in 1914, the suicide rate in provincial capitals oscillated between phases of falling numbers and stability, with the result that it is now significantly lower than in the late nineteenth century, while

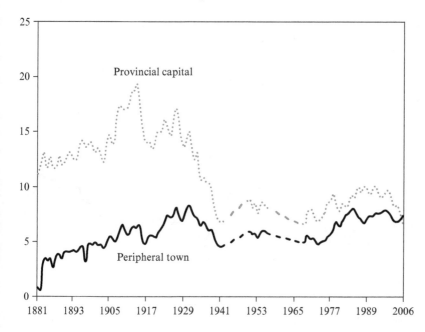

Graph 4.3   Suicide rates in Italian provincial capitals and peripheral towns from 1881 to 2006.

Source: See Appendix.

that in peripheral towns has continued to rise, therefore causing the two curves to meet (Graph 4.3).

These changes revolutionized the geography of suicide in Western Europe. The tendency of the various countries to converge, which had already been noted, as we saw, in the early 1930s, re-emerged strongly in the closing two decades of the century. The marked differences that used to exist between northern and southern Europe, in the frequency with which people took their own lives, have gradually narrowed.

The internal geography of each country has also been transformed. We have already seen that Germans living in what was East Germany now have the same suicide rates as those in Western areas, whereas the former had much higher rates in the late nineteenth century (Graph 4.1). Similar changes happened in other countries. Here, too, Italy's central and northern regions were always more similar to other European countries than the southern regions and the islands. But the differences between the former and the latter have become less noticeable over time (Graph 4.4). The convergence between the major cities in the north and those in the south is even more striking. In 1881 the numbers of suicides in Turin, Rome and Milan were much higher than in Naples, Palermo, Catania and Bari.

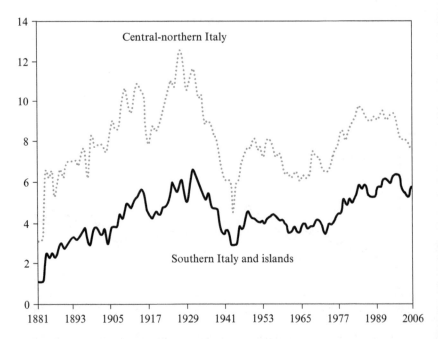

Graph 4.4 Suicide rates in central-northern Italy and in southern Italy and the islands from 1881 to 2006.

Source: See Appendix.

Suicide rates in these cities fluctuated over time. Yet, since the early 1930s, rates in the northern cities have fallen and they are much lower today than in late nineteenth century, while those in the south are still at the same level as they were 120 years ago. As a result, the two curves have drawn so close that they almost touch (Graph 4.5).

Throughout Italy, but above all in the central and northern urban centres, these changes were led by the upper middle classes (Table A.5, Appendix). If we view the Italian population as a whole, we see that from 1981 to 2001 the suicide rate fell sharply among graduates and those with school-leaving qualifications, while it increased or remained the same in those with lower levels of schooling. The decrease was particularly striking among graduates aged over forty-five in central and northern regions and among the same age cohort with school-leaving qualifications living in southern regions of Italy and on the islands.

In France, in 1880, the Île-de-France *département* had the highest number of suicides, while fewer people took their own lives in rural regions to the east and west of the country. Today, on the contrary, it is the most urbanized and wealthy *départments*, with the highest rates of female employment, the largest numbers of graduates, managers and

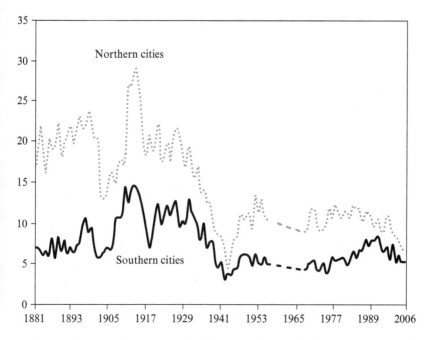

Graph 4.5   Suicide rates in major cities in northern Italy (Turin, Milan and
Genoa) and in southern Italy (Naples, Bari, Catania and Palermo) from 1881 to
2006.

Source: See Appendix.

the self-employed (Île-de-France, Eure-et-Loire, Eure et l'Oise) that have
the lowest suicide rates, with the fewest suicides in the centre of this area
(Paris, Val-de-Marne, Seine-Saint-Denis), while numbers are higher in the
less economically and socially developed areas of the country.[221]

Radical changes have also taken place in the breakdown by age of
people taking their own lives. As we have already seen, in the nineteenth
century and prior to the 1970s, there was a strong positive correlation in
Western countries between age and the risk of voluntary death. Yet, this
correlation weakened in the last thirty years of the twentieth century.
The fall in suicide rates started, and was most evident, among the over-
sixties. In some countries (Austria, Germany, Switzerland, Denmark)
numbers also started to drop among younger people aged between fifteen
and twenty-four. But in others (the United Kingdom, France, Sweden,
Norway and Finland, as well as in the United States) the frequency of
suicide among young males in this age group increased in the 1980s and
early 1990s, before dropping back and returning, in some cases (such as
the United States),[221] to the level of the 1970s.[223]

4.13 The medicalization of suicide and its effects

Clearly we cannot explain this massive trend inversion using classical models or by attributing it to an increasing degree of social integration. Experts researching this field debate over whether, and to what extent, the past few decades have experienced reduced integration in Western countries, but none of them has ever proposed the opposite, namely that social integration increased. Furthermore, the inadequacy of classical models as explanations for this major change is confirmed, if more proof were indeed required, by the fact that it started in the large urban centres, which in many Western countries now have lower suicide rates than small provincial towns. In order to understand what has happened, we need to turn our attention to some important cultural and social shifts that have taken place in the West.

The secularization and medicalization of voluntary death made considerable progress in the twentieth century. Even after people stopped using supernatural causes to explain suicide, many men and women suffering from mental disorders continued to regard their sufferings not as the symptoms of a disease but as the effects of a difficult moment in their lives.[224] However, the situation slowly changed and, above all in the last thirty years of the century, a growing number of people in all Western countries started to view mental suffering differently. This brought about the realization that anxiety, fear, panic, phobias, paralysing melancholy, mania, delirium and hallucinations are neither normal nor unavoidable and that specialists could provide the appropriate treatment.[225] Therefore, the number of individuals with mental disorders undergoing various forms of psychotherapy or receiving medication steadily increased. But the effects of these treatments varied depending on the type of disorder.

In some countries, at least, patients with schizophrenia take their own lives much less frequently today than they did twenty or thirty years ago. In Denmark, the country where, as was seen earlier, the trend reversal first started and, to date, has been most pronounced, the suicide rate for schizophrenics fell at the same rate as the rest of the population.[226] It seems likely that this was probably due to improved psychotherapeutic treatments or increased supervision after the first attempted suicide. Instead the effects of drugs have been limited. Antidepressants and mood stabilizers, which a good number of patients now use, appear to have had no effect from this point of view. Clozapine, an antipsychotic whose use was approved by the US Food and Drug Administration in 1989, has been moderately effective but is not thought to have saved many lives to date.[227]

As for patients with bipolar disorders, antidepressants and antipsychotic drugs do not reduce the risk of suicide and might even increase it. But according to the results of the most stringent studies in this field, treatment with lithium salts, on a continuous basis, significantly diminishes the probability that patients might try to kill themselves or that their actions might prove fatal. This probability is six times lower during treatment and rises again two or three weeks after treatment is stopped. Furthermore, attempted suicide by patients treated with lithium is much less lethal than that in patients not using these drugs.[228] Given that this therapy has been used in Western countries since the early 1970s in a growing percentage of patients, it is not unreasonable to suggest that it has contributed to reducing voluntary deaths.

Medication has played a major role in cases of depression. An increasing number of patients suffering from this disorder have been treated with serotoninergic drugs, also known as selective serotonin re-uptake inhibitors (SSRIs). These substances are used to regulate synaptic transmission disorders that may occur during depression, thereby increasing the cerebral availability of serotonin, the neurotransmitter to which most symptoms appear to be linked. SSRIs were first introduced in Germany in 1984 and shortly afterwards in other Western European countries, and they became widely used in the 1990s. Lively debates have taken place in recent years, both in the media and in scientific journals, on the effects produced by these drugs, with some experts asserting that far from reducing they actually increase the tendency of depressed patients to kill themselves. This has indeed happened occasionally, probably because – the experts assure us – the medication was taken by patients instead suffering from undiagnosed bipolar disorders or who were not yet adults. Nevertheless, meticulous research carried out in twenty-six countries concluded that the use of SSRIs to treat depression has significantly contributed to lowering suicide numbers. It also highlighted that this reduction has been greatest in the countries that first allowed the use of these new drugs and where the number of patients treated has grown fastest. It is estimated that one suicide is avoided for every additional 200,000 pills sold. And given that ten pills cost about one dollar, it has been calculated that in this case it costs about 20,000 dollars to save a life.[229]

4.14   The treatment of pain and other illnesses

Those suffering from AIDS, multiple sclerosis, Huntington's disease, kidney failure (undergoing dialysis), spinal cord injuries and cancer have a greater risk of taking their own lives than the general population.[230] Over the two-year period 2005–6, oncologists were particularly surprised by the results of two major studies which showed how, age being equal, American, Swedish, Danish, Finnish and Norwegian women with breast tumours are 37 per cent more likely to kill themselves than unaffected women[231] and, secondly, American men with prostate cancer have a much higher risk of suicide – all of 4.24 times higher – than the general population.[232] However, many studies show that all forms of cancer increase the probability of suicide, although to different degrees.[233] The probability is particularly high for cancers of the head or neck, which according to experts have a negative impact on the nervous system and cause mood disorders,[234] but also pancreatic cancer and all those which have a poor prognosis.[235] The risks are also high in the first six months after diagnosis and in metastases, namely when cancer causes psychological stress and physical pain that is extremely hard to bear.

However, in the last four decades of the twentieth century cancer became a much less important risk factor for suicide in many Western countries. Today cancer patients still commit suicide more frequently than the rest of the population, but the gap has narrowed over the past forty years.[236] There are several reasons for this important change. Above all, tumours are discovered earlier than in the past. Treatments have also improved significantly, with innovations that have reduced the negative psychological impact (using conservative instead of radical breast surgery, for example) and increased the chances of survival. Furthermore, pain management and palliative care have also developed in all Western countries, even if to different degrees.

For centuries it was thought that physical suffering might prompt suicide when pain became insupportable. Even Pliny the Elder, in the first century CE, concluded that 'the disease causing the sharpest agony is strangury from stone in the bladder; next comes disease of the stomach, and after that pains produced by diseases of the head; these being about the only diseases that are responsible for suicides'.[237] But this hypothesis was only recently confirmed by research. In the 1990s, a follow-up study was carried out on a sample population of Finnish farmers suffering from back pain in order to establish the relationship between back pain and heart attack, but instead the study discovered that these farmers had a greater probability of killing themselves.[238] Other studies have shown that chronic pain provoked by migraine headache, central nervous system lesions or metastases can increase the risk of suicide, crucially because these pathologies lead to major episodes of depression.[239]

Considerable advances have been made in controlling and reducing suffering. The traditional concept of pain as a sort of punishment, to be accepted with resignation, has been replaced by the view that it represents an alarm signal to be silenced as soon as its function has been accomplished. Therapeutic medicine, focused on healing, is now flanked by palliative medicine aimed at minimizing the patient's pain and psychophysical discomfort using drugs or admission to special units (similar to the hospice model set up in London in the 1960s) that combine the characteristics of the hospital and the home.

4.15   The steep rise in Eastern Europe

Fears of an epidemic of suicides, which circulated on several occasions, from the second half of the sixteenth century onwards, in some Western European countries, finally arrived in Russia nearly three centuries later. In 1872 the leading national newspapers started to report that suicide had become a sort of 'cholera that has gotten into a rotten place expressly created for its maintenance'.[240] Ten years later the papers talked of the 'seasonal epidemic' of suicides, now regarded as almost routine, like influenza. At the same period, the theme of voluntary death appeared in novels by two of Russia's leading writers, Tolstoy and Dostoevsky, prompting interest and excitement in the most affluent sectors of society.

The upper and middle urban classes then started to undergo the same process that had occurred much earlier in northwestern Europe. Suicide rates rose so steeply that in St Petersburg, in 1910, they reached 25 per 100,000 inhabitants,[241] a level higher than in Switzerland, France or Germany. No major changes were noted, however, in the countryside, which accounted for huge areas of Russia. In 1903, suicide rates here were 4.6 per 100,000 inhabitants, very similar to those in Mediterranean countries and between two and six times lower than those in northwestern Europe.

However, the culture of suicide changed in 1917 with the advent of the Soviet regime, affecting the significance of the act, the cognitive schemas used to interpret it, and the moral judgement of it and those who committed it. The founding fathers of this working-class movement did not attribute any importance at all to voluntary death, although they attributed its causes to the contradictions of capitalist society, but their early twentieth-century successors were divided on the subject. In 1911, at the age of seventy-one, the French socialist, Paul Lafargue, took his own life, accompanied by his wife Laura, almost as if they were following the customs of the Isle of Cea described by Montaigne (Plate 20). 'Healthy in body and mind', he wrote, in a brief suicide note, 'I end my life before pitiless old age, which is taking from me my pleasures and joys, one after another, and stripping me of my physical and mental powers, shall paralyse my energy and break my will, making me a burden to myself and to others.' Laura was Karl Marx's daughter. Yet many Marxists disapproved of their decision. One of them, Franz Mehring, writing on that occasion, echoed the military metaphor made famous by Cicero: 'In the struggle for proletarian emancipation, it is truer than ever before that service rendered to liberty is hard service, and it does not permit a veteran, even if richly decorated with a laurel wreath, to leave his post while he has a single breath of strength left in his body.'[242]

When they came to power, the Bolshevik leaders encouraged the formation of a new culture. In the first place, they started to explain suicide using categories that were quite different from those their forefathers had used for centuries, and also to those gaining ground in Western Europe. Voluntary death was seen as the outcome of the contrast between external reality and individual identity, which in turn depended on biological, political and class factors. Class played an all-important role. Those at greatest risk of suicide were individuals from the privileged classes under the Tsarist regime. Petit bourgeois women, for example, could contaminate their husbands with their limited outlook, thereby prompting them to take their own lives.[243]

Secondly, the Bolshevik leaders followed in the lead of Mehring, rather than that of Lafargue and Laura Marx, by condemning suicide as a form of bourgeois individualism. In the new society, good communists and good workers, they maintained, ought not to take their own lives because they belonged not to them, but to the Party and the class. As one doctor, Vladimir Ivanovich Velichkin, wrote in 1930: 'No one has a right to die according to his desire . . . Reproduced by society, a person belongs to it, and only society, in the interests of the majority, can deprive him of life.'[244] Suicide was a form of desertion, the product of weakness, pessimism, egoism, a mistaken tendency to place individual needs and wishes above those of the collectivity.[245] After Sergei Esenin took his life in December 1925, this idea was expressed in the newly coined word 'eseninism', indicating a moral–psychological and pathological condition.[246]

In spite of superficial similarities, the Bolshevik attitude to suicide was profoundly different from that of Nazism. The former was reminiscent of the concept that had dominated medieval Europe, even if God and the monarch had been replaced by the working class and the state. Instead the latter was closer to the classical attitude to suicide, which prevailed prior to Augustine's volte-face. The Bolsheviks condemned anyone who committed suicide, while the Nazis only punished soldiers, unless they were defeated or taken prisoner. It followed that only the Bolsheviks imposed sanctions on those who took their own lives, whatever the grounds.

If a party member committed suicide, the leader would call a meeting of the cell or committee in question in order to form a 'collective opinion' (as it was called) of the matter and to identify those responsible for the incident. During the discussion, those present distanced themselves from the suicide and stopped referring to him or her as 'comrade'. A resolution was then approved (unanimously, of course), which usually decreed the suicide's posthumous expulsion from the Party and banned members from attending the funeral.

Not even the great leaders were spared these proceedings. In 1925 the leading revolutionary and civil war hero, Evgenia Bogdanovna Bosch, who had held important government positions but was by then gravely ill, took her own life. This caused a lively debate among the top ranks of the Party about whether a funeral should be held, and if so, in what form. Some maintained that, even in the light of an incurable illness, suicide remained an act of disobedience that revealed a spirit of opposition. In the end, it was decided not to hold an official funeral for Bosch nor to permit her ashes to be placed close to other heroes of the Revolution.[247]

In 1924–5 there was a sharp rise in suicides among Party members, leading to many more discussions in cells and committees. Then in the early 1930s, silence fell. Yet, in December 1936, at a plenary meeting of the central committee, Stalin condemned the action of Furer, an official who had taken his life in protest against the unjust arrest of his friend. It was one of the 'easiest means', he declared in forthright terms, 'that before death, before leaving this world, one can for the last time spit on the party, betray the party'.[248]

In any case, the government stopped publishing statistics and studies on the subject.[249] It was not until the collapse of the Soviet regime that precise data once again became available. Later, scholars were fortunately able to find a breakdown of statistics by causes of death from 1956 onwards.[250] But of the trend of suicide rates during those terrible years in Soviet history between 1930 and 1955 we know nothing.

It is possible that, as happened in Germany, there were waves of suicide during the years of terror in the Soviet Union, when everyone lived in constant fear of hearing the police knock at the door at four o'clock in the morning, when millions of people were arrested, imprisoned, interrogated, tortured, tried, interned in labour camps, and killed. This is borne out by some of the surviving testimonials. For example, Zosia Zaleska, a Polish aristocrat who had dedicated her entire life to Communism, had attempted to kill herself three times during her trial. 'She tried to hang herself – they pulled her down; she cut her veins – but they stopped her; she jumped onto the window sill on the seventh floor – but the drowsy interrogator managed to grab hold of her by her dress. They saved her life three times – so they could shoot her.'[251]

'Many other people thought about it, too', wrote Nadezhda Yakovlevna Chazin, remembering that time and adding, 'not for nothing was the best play in the Soviet repertory entitled *The Suicide*'.[252] At the most difficult moments, she was 'consoled and soothed' by the thought of this last resort. In 1934, after her husband, the great poet Osip Mandelstam, had been arrested and imprisoned for having written some satirical verses about Stalin, she had proposed that they should commit suicide together, but he had 'always sharply rejected the idea'. 'Why do you think you ought to be happy?' Osip responded, who was full of the joy of life, although he did not appreciate talk about happiness and unhappiness.

However, Mandelstam started to think about suicide when he was sent to the political prison camp at Cherdyn and he persuaded himself that this was the only way to escape the firing squad. 'Very well, if they shoot us, we shan't have to commit suicide',[253] joked Nadezhda, and Osip laughed heartily. But shortly after he returned to this obsession. He was ill on arrival at Cherdyn and spent five days in hospital with his wife, who stayed awake in order to watch over him. On the last night, having fallen into a troubled sleep, she heard a slight noise and found him sitting on the window-sill, putting his legs outside. She heard the sound of his fall. He threw himself from the second floor, a very high second floor, but survived it. He died some years later in a prison camp.

The lack of statistical data prevents us knowing whether there were waves of suicide during the period of the Terror or, for that matter, what happened during the Second World War. All we know for certain is that in 1929, twelve years after the Revolution, the Soviet Union, along with

Greece, Spain, Portugal and Ireland, was still one of the countries in Europe with the lowest rate of suicide (6.4 per 100,000).

Yet by 1956 the situation had changed. With a suicide rate of over 15 per 100,000 inhabitants, Russia was by then halfway between the Mediterranean countries and those in central and northern Europe. Since then, the rate has continued to rise, reaching 22 per 100,000 in 1965 and 38 in 1984.[254] In 1985–86 it dropped sharply, but then rose again over the three years between 1988 and 1990. Suicides were therefore at quite a high level when the Soviet Union disintegrated. However, the process of political collapse prompted a fresh and unprecedentedly sharp rise in the suicide rate, taking it to 43 per 100,000 inhabitants in 1994,[255] a European record reached only by Austria in the 1930s. Although it fell back in later years, in 2004 the suicide rate in Russia (34 per 100,000) was still two or three times higher than that in the United States, and more particularly those in Western Europe (Graph 4.6).[256]

Throughout this period, these changes have been strongest in the male population (Graph 4.7). In 1956, men killed themselves 4.1 times more frequently than women, rising to 5.2 times more frequently in 1970. In 1985 and 1986 the male suicide rate fell more steeply than that for women, consequently narrowing the ratio between the two sexes to 3.5 times. But the rise in the 1990s was also more pronounced for men than for women, pushing the ratio to record levels. In 1996 Russian men killed themselves 5.7 times more frequently than women and, as was seen above, between two and three times more frequently than in most Western countries.[257]

The suicide rate showed a similar trend in other Soviet Union countries, like Belarus, Ukraine and the Baltic states (Estonia, Latvia and Lithuania). It had already been high in the latter in the 1970s (higher than in Russia), but it continued to rise until 1985 when it fell sharply over the next four years, before increasing again and breaking all records after the collapse of the Soviet Union. Since the mid 1990s Lithuania, for example, has had the highest suicide rate worldwide, an unenviable record it continues to hold today.[258]

The media and Western experts (above all in the German Federal Republic)[259] repeatedly asserted that the rising number of people taking their own lives in communist countries was also a form of protest against the regime. Certainly, in the USSR and later in its satellite states, some suicides of this nature were committed not only in the thirties,[260] but also in the 1960s and 1970s. Three of these cases caused international repercussions. In many ways, they moved away from the European tradition and harked back to the self-immolation of the Buddhist monk, Thich Quang Duc, in Saigon on 11 June 1963 (Plate 47).[261] All three suicides were carried out by dousing their clothing and bodies with petrol and then setting themselves alight as a public protest, for a collective cause, in front of the largest possible crowd.

The first suicide took place in Czechoslovakia on 16 January 1969 when Jan Palach (Plate 22), a university student and leader of a group of young

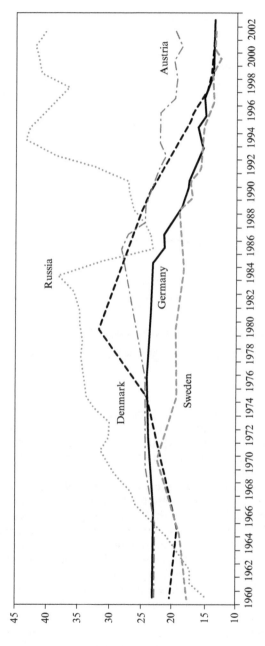

Graph 4.6   Suicide rates per 100,000 inhabitants in Sweden, Denmark, Germany, Austria and Russia from 1960 to 2003.

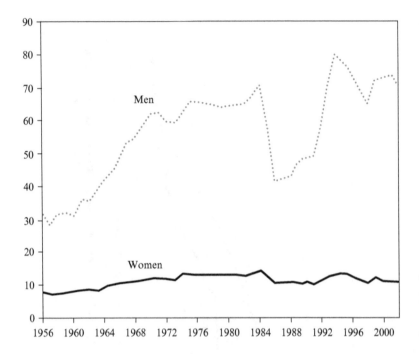

Graph 4.7   Gender differences in suicide rates in Russia from 1956 to 2002.

Source: Elaborated using data kindly provided by Evgeny Andreeva, Vladimir Shkolnikov and William Alex Pridemore.

militants against the Soviet invasion, burned himself alive in Wenceslas Square, in the heart of Prague, leaving some notes and declarations of protest in his backpack. His funeral was attended by several hundred thousand mourners and shortly afterwards a further seven students took their own lives in protest.

The second suicide was in Lithuania on 14 May 1972. Romas Kalanta, a nineteen-year-old student, set himself on fire in Kaunas, in front of the municipal theatre, leaving a note that read: 'Only the political system is guilty of my death.' The police forced Romas' parents to sign a declaration stating that their son had committed suicide not for political reasons but because he suffered from mental disorders. They authorized the funeral on condition that there were no flowers and that the youth's body was buried far from others. In the following days, thousands of young people marched in protest through the city, shouting anti-Russian and pro-independence slogans.

The third suicide took place in the German Democratic Republic on 18 April 1976. Oskar Brüsewitz was a forty-seven-year-old Protestant pastor, who had long accused the communist government for repressing young-sters at school. The final trigger for his decision came when even his own church sided with the state rather than with him. He immediately decided to carry out an appalling gesture and to set himself on fire in the central square in Leitz. In the following months, four more people immolated themselves for political reasons. Moreover, many other fellow country-men threatened to do the same unless they were given permits to leave the country.[262]

The number of these extreme acts of protest was relatively small and certainly it is not to them that we should look in order to understand what happened. The extraordinary growth in the number of suicides during the last few years of the Soviet Union and after its dissolution can be attributed to a number of causes. First and foremost among these is the increased alcohol consumption, a factor whose importance has long been underestimated by social scientists.[263] Although present in other coun-tries, the relationship between alcohol consumption and voluntary deaths has been particularly strong for the last thirty years or so in what is now the former Soviet Union, and excess drinking, drunkenness and vodka intoxication are quite frequent.[264] Reductions in the suicide rate between the 1980s and 1990s, and again in the 2000s, were caused or at least sup-ported by similar falls in the levels of vodka consumption. For instance, the sudden, sharp fall in voluntary deaths between 1985 and 1986 was certainly an effect of the anti-alcohol campaign launched by Gorbachev in May 1985, which led to falling production and higher prices – producing a collapse in vodka sales through state shops – the growing use of *samogon* (illegally distilled at home), as well as a lesser but nonetheless significant drop (about 25 per cent) in real consumption. The effects of this campaign were particularly noticeable in the male population, causing the suicide rate to plummet (Graph 4.7). Yet they were short-lived and the number of Russian citizens who were tempted to drown their worries in vodka started to climb once again. Alcohol consumption increased even more rapidly after the collapse of the Soviet regime, reaching record levels by the closing years of last century, so much so that Russia had one of the highest rates worldwide. It is estimated that the per capita annual consumption of alcohol reached fifteen litres, compared to ten in the European Union and seven in the United States.[265] And, as we have seen, the more vodka that was drunk, the higher the number of citizens of the former Soviet Union who took their own lives. On the other hand, the statutory restrictions on the production and use of alcoholic substances, which came into force on 1 January 2006, have helped to reduce the number of voluntary deaths.[266]

In the second place, the abrupt rise in suicide that began after the col-lapse of the Soviet regime was probably triggered by the severe crisis in the health system, which until then had provided a vast range of medical services to citizens of all social classes and from all regions. When finan-cial resources became scarce, the system started to deteriorate and it was in part this breakdown (as well as the increased vodka consumption and worsening living conditions) that led to increased mortality rates owing to a broad range of diseases (cardiocirculatory disorders and infectious pathologies) accompanied by an unprecedented drop in life expectancy from 63.8 to 57.6 years for men, and from 74.4 to 71 for women.[267] As a result, in all the former Soviet Bloc countries, the period 1991–2 marked the start of a trend that was precisely the opposite of that in Western Europe given that a diminishing number of patients received medical treatment for those physical and mental illnesses that carried a high risk of suicide.

But the third and most significant reason for the abrupt rise in suicide after 1991–2 was the state of social anomie triggered by the collapse of the Soviet regime. 'In the case of economic disasters, indeed, something like a declassification occurs which suddenly casts certain individuals into a lower state than their previous one. [. . .] Time is required for the public conscience to reclassify men and things. So long as the social forces thus freed have not regained equilibrium, their respective values are unknown and so all regulation is lacking for a time. The limits are unknown between the possible and the impossible, what is just and what is unjust, legitimate claims and hopes and those which are immoderate.'[268]

This passage, written by Émile Durkheim in 1897 to define situations of anomie, can still shed light on the events in the Soviet Union after 1991. The collapse of the regime prompted enormous changes within a very short period of time, the transition from a totalitarian state to a democratic system, and from a centrally planned economy to one that was market based. The network of state services, which, since 1920, had provided full employment, controlled prices, basic education and free health care, disintegrated leading to a doubling of the unemployment rate and massive poverty. After having been isolated for centuries from the rest of the world, Russia was invaded by mass media from the West and values that, until then, had been condemned, like individualism, economic success and an entrepreneurial spirit, spread rapidly. This meant that many citizens of the former Soviet Union countries not only felt poor and insecure but also disoriented, confused and homeless.

Early studies have shown that for many Russians the decision to commit suicide was not only prompted by calamities and tragic events (illness, loss of a relative) but also by disorientation, an inability to continue in the absence of any security, the inability to make sense of a new life or to understand the rules of the society that was being formed. Marshal Akhromeyev, for example, killed himself in his office in the Kremlin on 24 August 1991, leaving farewell notes and cards for his family on his desk. In one of these was written: 'at least in this way let it be recorded in history that one man, albeit just one alone, protested against the break-up of so great a state. But history will judge who is right and who is wrong.'[269] A few weeks later Timeryan Zinatov, a war veteran and defender of Brest fortress, took his own life. 'If I had died from my wounds during the war', he wrote in the letter that was found in his pocket, 'at least I'd have known what I was dying for: the Fatherland. Instead now, I am dying because of this wretched dog's life. They can even write it on my tomb if they want . . . But don't think that I'm mad.'[270] Margarita Pagrebichaya, a fifty-two-year-old doctor, attempted to take her own life when she heard that her beloved ten-year-old grandson had been killed in Baku, in the conflict between Armenia and Azerbaijan. What prevented her from coming to terms with the news was her utter exhaustion, and her refusal, fostered by her heroic view of Stalin, to accept that Soviet military uniforms and medals could be sold on market stalls in Moscow, and even red flags marked with Lenin's silhouette. In short, she found it impossible to live without a new faith.[271]

1. Ajax prepares to impale himself on a sword in order to avenge himself on his enemies and regain his honour (amphora, 6th cent. BCE).

2. Julius Schnorr von Carolsfeld, *The Death of Saul* (1851–60). Saul, first king of the Kingdom of Israel, fell on his sword in front of his soldiers following his defeat by the Philistines.

3. The ritual of the barrel and *Rinnen*. The corpse of a monk who had committed suicide is placed in a barrel and cast into the Rhine (Basle, early 16th cent.). *Die Schweizer Bilderchronik des Luzerners Diebold Schilling.*

4. Beliefs regarding the consequences of suicide. A man whose marriage failed committed suicide in Rossau, near Zurich, and was buried in the cemetery. Fearing that this would provoke disasters, the villagers disinterred the body and burned it (1581). Zentralbibliothek Zürich, Ms. F 29a, f. 178r.

5. *Ira se occidit* (Anger commits suicide, 12th cent.), a capital in Notre-Dame du Port, Clermont-Ferrand.

6. The suicide of Judas depicted on a capital in Saint-Lazare Cathedral, Autun
(12th cent.).

7. Giotto, *Despair* (c. 1302), Scrovegni Chapel, Padua.

8. Master E. S., *Consolation against Despair*. St Peter, St Mary Magdalene, the good thief and St Paul gathered around the dying man's bed to ward off the temptation of despair.

9. Giovanni Canavesio, *The Suicide of Judas* (1492), fresco, Chapel of Notre-Dame-des-Fontaines, La Brigue.

10. Anonymous Alsatian artist, *The Suicide of Judas* (1520), polychrome stained glass, The Art Institute of Chicago.

11. In 1742 Maria Elisabetta Beckensteinerin strangled her six-month-old son in order to die and at the same time save her own soul through repentance. Left: the infant's soul rises to heaven where it is greeted by an angel with open arms.

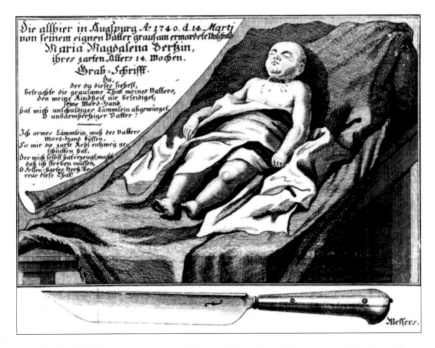

12. In 1740 fourteen-week-old Maria Magdalena Bertzin was killed by her father, who wanted to die but also desired eternal salvation. Both engravings are taken from Stuart, 2008.

13. Benezur Gyula, *Cleopatra* (1911), Déri Museum, Debrecen.

14. Paolo Veronese, *Lucretia* (c.1580), KHM-Museumsverband, Vienna.

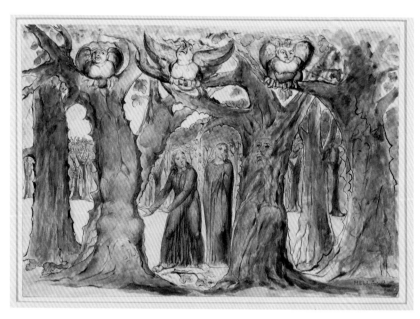

15. William Blake, *The Wood of the Self-Murderers: the Harpies and the Suicides* (1824–7), Tate, London.

16. George Cruikshank, *The Poor Girl Homeless, Friendless, Deserted, Destitute, and Gin-Mad Commits Self-Murder* (1848), Victoria and Albert Museum, London.

17. George Grosz, *The End of the Road* (1913), Museum of Modern Art, New York, (c)Photo SCALA, Florence.

18. Édouard Manet, *The Suicide* (1877–81), Foundation E. G. Bührle Collection, Zürich.

19. Frida Kahlo, *The Suicide of Dorothy Hale* (1939), Phoenix Art Museum.

20. Paul Lafargue and Laura Marx.

21. Primo Levi.

22. Prague: Monument to Jan Palach who killed himself by setting himself on fire on 16 January 1969 to protest against the Soviet occupation of his country.

23. Mario Mieli, militant of the gay movement, who committed suicide in 1983 at the age of thirty-one. Portrait by David Hill.

Part II

In the East

5

Before Becoming a Widow

Roop Kanwar killed herself on 4 September 1987 at Deorala, a village two hours' drive from Jaipur, the capital of Rajasthan.[1] She was eighteen and had been married for eight months. Her husband had died of gastroenteritis and the young woman, having shut herself into her room to reflect for a few hours, had decided to take her own life. Wearing her red and gold bridal gown, she processed at the head of a funeral cortège, accompanied by music and religious chants. On reaching the village square, she climbed onto a pyre, which had been prepared for her dead spouse, and she immolated herself beside him, burning alive in front of a crowd of four thousand onlookers. Roop Kanwar was not an illiterate peasant; she had grown up in the city, was educated, elegant and married to a young graduate from a well-to-do family. Moreover, Deorala is one of the most modern and affluent villages in Rajasthan.

As the news of her decision spread, thousands flocked to the village to receive the blessing of the woman who, through her act, would become a *sati mata*, a pure mother, endowed with supernatural powers that could heal every ill. On 16 September, for the *chunari*, the ceremony of glorification, although the government had banned the use of public transport, 300,000 people travelled to Deorala, on foot, in carts pulled by camels, or in taxis and private buses. Having thronged to the place of martyrdom, they made offerings of incense and coconut, and purchased souvenirs showing the widow's cremation alongside her husband. That same day, in order to deify Roop, her mother-in-law organized a feast for one thousand and one Brahmins and erected an altar in honour of her daughter-in-law in a ground-floor room in her house.

The authorities were slow to react. For many days, the state and national governments, the judiciary and the police force did and said nothing. Only on 19 September were warrants issued for the arrest of Roop's mother-in-law, her two brothers-in-law (one of whom was accused of having lit the pyre), a few uncles, and a priest who had officiated over the ceremony. Then on 29 September, the Prime Minister, Rajiv Gandhi, declared that '*sati* is a national shame'. But none of those arrested or any other individual was charged for what had happened.

During the same period, in various parts of India, other women also took their own lives after their husbands' deaths. In 1984, this had happened in a village twenty kilometres from Deorala. In 1988 in Uttar Pradesh, a twenty-eight-year-old woman burnt to death on the pyre of a husband who had abandoned her many years earlier. Other cases have been reported in the last ten years,[2] but they are undoubtedly the last of a custom that held sway for centuries: *sati*.

5.1   *Sati*

Sati is a word that over time, and even today, has acquired different meanings in India and the West.[3] At times it was used to describe the action, at others the person accomplishing it. In Sanskrit, the word is the feminine present participle of *sat*, which means both 'being' and 'having to be', and therefore refers to what is real, true and good. In India, the term *sati* has always meant the 'virtuous, chaste and faithful bride' who, precisely for this reason, immolates herself on the pyre immediately after her husband's death. The British introduced the noun 'suttee' (translated in French as *sutty*) to indicate not the woman taking her own life but the ceremony of widow burning itself. Today, in languages other than English, the term *sati* is sometimes used in the feminine to indicate the person and in the masculine to indicate the ritual event. But there are also those who call the latter *suttee*.[4] But this terminological difference corresponds to one of meaning. When speaking of *sati*, Hindus were referring to a woman who was so devoted and faithful to her husband that she decided, freely and with full knowledge, to follow him to death. Instead the Western travellers, who left many written descriptions and images (engravings and miniatures)[5] of this custom, continued to use the word with reference to the act, namely to the cremation of the widow, whom they regarded as a passive victim of religious fanaticism and of a distant and incomprehensible culture.[6]

The rite took two main forms. In the first, the widow was burnt together with her spouse. This was called *sahagamana* (going with) or *sahamarana* (dying with) (Plates 30–1). In the second, the woman immolated herself a short while after her husband's death, holding some object that had belonged to him, like his shoes, a turban or his bridal vestments. Or, as Father Vincenzo Maria of St Catherine of Siena wrote in 1678, 'when the deceased's corpse is not present, the same ceremony is carried out using a figure that represents it'.[7] This usually happened when the man died far from home, perhaps on the battlefield, or when the widow was pregnant and waited to give birth before killing herself. The terms used in this case were *anugamana* (going after) or *anumarana* (dying after) (Plate 32).

These were the two most commonplace forms and they were practised when – as was usually the case – the husband's corpse was cremated. In those areas where the corpse was interred, on the other hand, then the widow was buried alive with her husband. In Bengal, for example, members of the weavers' caste, the *jugi*,[8] followed this usage (Plate 33). Instead, in Bali widows sometimes preferred to kill themselves using a *kris*, a dagger with an undulating blade.[9]

5.2 The rite

The ritual sequence of *sati* began formally with a solemn declaration of the widow's intent. In the same way as all Indians who decide to make a sacrificial act, she too publicly announced her intention to end her own life. She expressed this wish without showing any fear, in a clear and unwavering voice. Her relatives were expected to console her and beg her to reconsider her decision on behalf of her children. But the expectation was that she would not be swayed.

After reaffirming her wish to become a *sati*, the woman started to prepare.[10] She put on her bridal gown, and her bracelets and wedding jewellery, and covered her head with bridal flowers. She then prostrated herself before her elders and asked for their blessing, and they in turn asked for hers. Lastly, before leaving for the place of cremation, she coated her right-hand palm (which is pure, unlike the left, contrary to many other cultures) in a vermillion or saffron-coloured paste and then covered the doors and walls of her home with handprints, sealing her decision to immolate herself (Plate 24). In Nepal, the irreversibility of a woman's choice was made even more visible by a gate in the city wall that was always used by *satis* and which, once crossed, could not be re-entered (Plate 25).[11]

The ceremony that culminated in the widow's self-immolation was public and involved processions, feasting, banquets and the participation of hundreds, sometimes thousands of people. Although many features remained constant, there were variations. The French abbot, Jean Antoine Dubois, who had spent some years in India as a missionary, described how, when the ruler of Tanjore died in 1801, he left four legitimate wives and the Brahmins convinced two of them to immolate themselves. After a day of preparations, an enormous cortège left the Royal Palace. It was led by a number of armed guards, followed by musicians. Then, on a litter, came the body of the king, accompanied by his closest collaborators and relatives who, as a sign of mourning, were not wearing turbans. Immediately after came the two wives, on two resplendent sedans, 'laden rather than ornamented with gems'[12] and surrounded by relatives with whom they often spoke. Bringing up the rear of the procession was a multitude of people belonging to every caste.[13] Instead the procession witnessed by the English surgeon Richard Hartley Kennedy, on 29 November 1825, was led by the widow's son, a twelve-year-old boy, who carried a vase containing the sacred fire, taken from the domestic hearth, with which he would light the pyre to cremate his father's corpse and his mother's living body.[14]

In many cases, the husband's body did not form part of the cortège but instead awaited the wife and all those attending the ceremony in the place where the cremation would be held.[15] The Moroccan chronicler, Ibn Battuta, who visited India in 1333, described how, having spent three days 'in concerts of music and singing, and festivals of eating and drinking as though they were bidding farewell to the world', the widows of three men killed in battle had processed on horseback, 'richly dressed and perfumed', to the place where they would die. 'In her right hand she held a coconut, with which she played, and in her left a mirror, in which she could see her own face.'[16] The Venetian jeweller, Cesare de' Fedrici, who travelled to southeastern Asia to buy gemstones, described how in Bezeneger [Vijaya-nagar], in 1587, a widow who was going 'to burne herself', 'appareled like to a Bride, was carried round the Citie, with her haire downe about her shoulders, garnished with Jewels and Flowers, according to the estate of the partie [. . .] she carrieth in her left hand a looking-glasse, and in her right an arrow [*frezza*]'.[17] Gasparo Balbi, a merchant who travelled in India for many years, described 'a pit filled with burning charcoals' that he had witnessed on 30 October 1580, in Negapatan [Nagapattinam], at which 'a beautiful, young woman arrived in a sedan chair carried by her relatives, in the company of many other women friends, with great cel-ebrations, holding in her left hand a mirror, and in her right a lemon, with which the young woman played all sorts of games. And having arrived at the flaming pit she was helped down to the ground.'[18]

Forty years later Pietro della Valle was present at a similar scene. On 22 December 1623, in the city of Ikkeri [Karnataka], he encountered a widow who made a deep impression on him because, as soon as her husband died, she had decided 'to burn herself'. The woman, he wrote in his diary, 'rode on horse-back about the city with face uncovered, holding a looking-glass in one hand and a lemon in the other, I know not for what purpose; and beholding herself in the Glass, with a lamentable tone sufficiently pitiful to hear, went alone I know not whither, speaking or singing certain words, which I understood not; but they told me they were a kind of Farewell to the World and herself.'[19] 'They carried a great Umbrella over her, as all persons of quality in India are wont to have.'[20]

Sometimes, instead of on horseback, the widow processed on an ele-phant or in a sedan chair, carried by eight men, or she walked if she was of humble birth. Surrounded by family, the crowds parted either side of her as she went. The women in the crowd called out to her, praising her virtues, eulogizing her and stretching their hands out towards her, trying to get closer. Convinced that she had acquired supernatural powers, they begged for her blessing and asked for prophecies. Then the *sati*, with gentle grace, tried to answer all of them, promising many sons to one, a long and happy life to another, and great honours to a third.[21]

At last the procession (Plate 26) reached the place where, as Cesare de' Fedrici wrote, 'they use to make this burning of women, being wid-dowes'.[22] It was usually close to a river or a small lake, because anywhere beside water was regarded as propitious. Everything for the pyre was ready, but its form varied according to the region. In the northern areas of India wood was piled up to a height of three metres. Not far away were banqueting tables, set out with plenty of food, to which the widow and all those accompanying her then went and started to eat. De Fedrici noted how 'she that shall be burned eateth with as great joy and gladnesse, as though it were her Wedding day; and the feast being ended, then they goe to dancing and singing a certain time, according as she will.'[23]

Once the songs and dances were over, the widow took off her gowns, removed her jewels and flowers, and gave them to her relatives and closest women friends. She then entered the river to be purified, before being covered with a long, yellow cloth (a colour that, like red or black, was believed to keep wicked spirits at bay),[24] or in some areas she wore white. She sometimes held kusha grass or sesame seeds in her hand, or in some cases a coconut that she held silently up to the sky as a divine offering. She often chewed betel leaves, which were handed to her by other women. She then made three or seven rounds of the pyre, from left to right, or clockwise. Meanwhile, as another traveller, Niccolo Manucci (or Mannuzi) wrote in 1717, the husband's corpse, lying supine on the wood pyre, 'its head to the south and feet to the north', was anointed with butter and all the closest relatives 'threw five or six grains of uncooked rice into his mouth'.[25] The family members then offered the widow seven coconuts and started to cry. But she comforted them, telling them – as a traveller from Vicenza, Antonio Pigafetta, described – 'not to cry because she would be dining with her husband and would sleep with him that night'.[26] Then she turned to all those who had accompanied her and asked them to care for her children and relatives. Turning to the men, she said, 'Behold, gentlemen, how indebted you are to your wives, who being in liberty, burn themselves alive with their husbands.' Looking back to the women, she added: 'Look, ladies, at what you are obliged to do for your husbands, and how you must accompany them as far as death.'[27] Then she climbed onto the pyre and sitting beside her husband, gently held his head in her lap, kissing and caressing it. Then she lay down on his right-hand side. In some cases, the relatives 'called out to the woman by name', asking her if she wished 'to go to glory', and only after she responded with an affirmation was the pyre lit.[28] This task was normally performed by the eldest son or, in his absence, by another family member.

In the south, the rite took a slightly different form. Sometimes, instead of a wooden pyre, a ditch was used, measuring ten metres square and three metres deep, which was filled with wood. As soon as the fire was lit, Jean-Baptiste Tavernier wrote in 1676, the husband's corpse was carried to the edge of the ditch and then the widow arrived, 'dancing and chewing her betel'. The woman walked three times around the ditch, kissing relatives and friends each time. At the end of the third round, the Brahmins threw the corpse into the fire and pushed his wife towards the ditch, her face looking away from it, so that she would fall in backwards.[29]

5.3 The effects of polygamy

In the nineteenth volume of his *Bibliotheca historica*, Diodorus Siculus gives an extraordinarily realistic account of an event that happened at the death of Ceteus, commander of the Indian soldiers who had fought, alongside Eumenes, in the first war of the Diadochi, between 319 and 315 BCE.[30]

Diodorus recounts how Ceteus had two wives, both of whom had followed him onto the battlefield: a young woman, whom he had only recently married, and an older one, to whom he had been married some years, 'both of them loving him deeply'. When the time came for his funeral, they argued passionately over 'the right of dying with him', 'as if it were a prize of valour'. Both women appealed to the same law, which allowed the spouse to follow her husband onto the funeral pyre. But in this case, there were two wives, and each presented claims with different merits: the senior wife claimed greater prestige and entitlement owing to her age, while the younger wife argued that the other was pregnant and therefore obliged to protect the life of the child she was carrying, as the law specifically stated.

The decision was put to the generals who, having confirmed that the elder wife was indeed pregnant, exonerated her from fulfilling her rightful duty. This announcement provoked an outburst of violent despair: on hearing the sentence, the one who had lost threw her wreath to the ground and tore her hair, sobbing violently, 'just as if some great disaster had been announced to her'. The other wife, 'rejoicing in her victory', made her way to the ceremonial place, surrounded by her family, who bound fillets around her head and sang hymns in honour of her virtue. Dressed in magnificent clothes, she was followed by her household, as if processing to a wedding. Once she reached the pyre, on which Ceteus' corpse lay, she took off her resplendent jewels and distributed them among friends and servants, as keepsakes; then she embraced them and was helped by her brother to mount the pyre and lie down beside her husband. The entire army then marched three times about the pyre before it was lighted. As the flames quickly leapt up, the young woman remained silent and never cried out once.

Other sources provide information that differs from Diodorus Siculus regarding the rights and duties of widows in polygamous marriages. Some travellers state that only the first wife was given the privilege of being burned alive. While, according to others, no wife could escape this duty. The king of the noble city of Bisinigar [Vijayanagar], wrote Nicolò di Conti in the late fifteenth century, 'is more powerful than all the other kings of India. He takes to himself twelve thousand wives, of whom four thousand follow him on foot wherever he may go, and are solely employed in the service of the kitchen. A like number, more handsomely equipped, ride on horseback. The remainder are carried in ornate litters', and two thousand of these were said to be his wives, 'on condition that at his death they should voluntarily burn themselves with him, which is considered to be a great honour for them'.[31]

Although customs varied throughout India in this respect, and also changed over time, there are grounds for supposing that the above and other reports concerned extreme cases or were exaggerated to varying degrees. According to Hindu beliefs, the principle of polygamy also applied to the next world and every other life, and therefore it seems unlikely that the right of mounting the husband's funeral pyre would have been granted to only one widow. At most, she could enjoy certain privileges solely with regard to how the rite was performed. For example, according to Nicolò di Conti, if a husband had several wives, 'the one who was dearest to him, the favourite, would place her arm under his neck and would burn together with him. The other wives would then throw themselves into the fire once it was alight.'[32] But the decision of whether to climb onto the pyre or not was taken individually by each of the widows in polygamous marriages, subject to the same constraints as for monogamous couples: permission was not granted to wives who were too young, to those who were pregnant or had a young child, and to those who were menstruating.[33]

The fact that many women took their own lives in this way is documented extensively.[34] In 1724, when Raja Aijtsingh of Marwar died, sixty-four women threw themselves into the flames. In 1799, following the death of a Brahmin with over one hundred wives, the funeral pyre burned for three days, consuming thirty-seven of them. We do not know the frequency of such events. However, from the data collected by the British administration for the period 1815–28, only one woman took her life in 98.4 per cent of rites. It is impossible at present to say whether this percentage fell or increased over time. What is certain, however, is that at the beginning of the nineteenth century, and also earlier, polygamous households were not commonplace given that only a small minority of men could afford more than one wife.

5.4 Funeral and wedding ceremonies

To the many European travellers who, from the closing years of the fifteenth to the mid nineteenth century, were able to observe these rites with their own eyes, *sati* always appeared as a dark, indecipherable custom, as well as a barbarous one. Coming from countries where suicide was condemned as the worst crime, one committed in silence and solitude, these men clearly struggled to understand how *sati* could be encouraged, praised and celebrated with feasting, songs and dances in India. The barriers to their understanding were made even more insurmountable by the large number of symbols with which they were not familiar. Why, for example, wondered Pietro della Valle, did the widow go to her death holding a mirror and a lemon? Or why, asked Gasparo Balbi, did she play many 'tricks' with this lemon? Why, too, did the woman and her accompanying cortège go to the place of cremation with a smile on their lips or, as Cesare de Fedrici observed, 'they goe with as great joy as Brides doe in Venice in their Nuptials'?[35]

The rites that these Europeans described with such dismay were undoubtedly funeral ceremonies. What they saw was a complex series of rites of passage, divided into various phases of separation, transition or liminality and aggregation, which imposed constraints and prohibitions (because, according to Hindu beliefs, all contact with death was ritually impure).[36] For example, it was in funeral rites that coconuts were used. A coconut was placed at the feet of the deceased by his daughter-in-law. Coconuts were offered by relatives before the corpse was placed on the pyre. A coconut was also used to 'break the skull' so that the soul could escape.[37] A lemon, on the other hand, was a good luck omen that served to protect the widow from evil spirits during the transition phase.[38]

But the Europeans who witnessed *sati* rituals were usually not aware that they were also attending a wedding ceremony. The woman who was about to immolate herself would be dressed in her wedding clothes and adorned with jewels and flowers, because she was celebrating her marriage once again. It was this that made her joyful and enabled her to process with grace, serenity, even 'cheerfulness', a fact that was particularly astonishing to European observers. Likewise, it was to this wedding that the strange objects she carried referred. The mirror she held in her left hand recalled the one given to her by her husband at the moment of marriage as a good omen, so that she could look at the image of herself which was traditionally deemed to be part of the soul.[39] The bamboo arrow she carried, in her right hand, was none other than the one that, in some castes or regions, was carried during the marriage ceremony.[40] Even the coconuts, as well as being used in funerals, were also present at weddings because in Rajasthan their exchange sealed the marriage vows. Lastly, many of the gestures the woman made prior to the cremation were a replica of those made at the wedding. Now, too, she gifted ornaments and jewels to family and women friends, as she had done at her wedding. Here, too, she circled the pyre seven times, as at her first wedding she had taken seven steps with her husband, in a clockwise direction (although at the funeral the opposite direction was sometimes prescribed).[41] Now, too, she joined her husband in a new bed that had been prepared: the pyre, where they lay, facing one another, their bodies touching. The pyre would not burn a corpse and a living body, but rather a single body, composed of two inseparable halves.[42] The ashes of the two spouses would be mixed in symbolic reaffirmation of the unity formed through the sacred nuptial fire.

5.5   For love or through coercion?

For centuries, foreigners who came into contact with India asked themselves whether the burning of widows on their husbands' pyres was the outcome of a free choice or of constriction. This question was often answered when they attended the ceremony and were able to observe closely the expressions and gestures of the principal players. Ibn Battuta described how, in Amjari, in 1333, when a woman who wanted to immolate herself realized that some men were holding a cloth in front of the pyre, as if they wanted to hide it, she tore it from their hands, saying, 'with a smile': 'Do you think I will be frightened by the fire? I am quite aware that it's a fire!' Then, 'joining her hands above her head as a sign of respect for the fire', she threw herself into it.[43]

In the early sixteenth century, Duarte Barbosa gave a minute description of the ceremony and noted that the widow accomplished every act 'with gestures and an expression that were so joyful and willing that she did not seem about to die'.[44] 'Do not think', wrote Ludovico de Varthema in 1535, addressing the astounded readers of his own country, 'that she is unwilling, indeed she believes that she will soon be carried to heaven'.[45] In the mid seventeenth century, François Bernier, a French doctor who lived for twelve years at the court of Aurangzeb, the sixth Moghul emperor of India (1658–1707), was struck by the conduct of the widow and the 'brutish boldness, or ferocious gaiety depicted on this woman's countenance; her undaunted step; the freedom from all perturbation with which she conversed, and permitted herself to be washed; the look of confidence or rather of insensibility which she cast upon us'.[46] In 1770 the Dutch traveller, Stavorinus, similarly remarked: 'What most surprised me, at this horrid and barbarous rite, was the tranquillity of the woman and the joy expressed by her relations [. . .] The wretched victim, who beheld these preparations making for her cruel death, seemed to be much less affected by it than we Europeans who were present.'[47] Ten years later, William Hodges, after carefully observing the celebration of one these rites, wrote that the widow demonstrated 'perfect composure of countenance' and even a few instants before sacrificing herself, she spoke some words to those present, without 'the least trepidation of voice'.[48] In 1810, a correspondent of *The Times* of London, who had also witnessed one of these ceremonies, was surprised by 'the most entire fortitude and composure' with which the widow climbed onto her husband's pyre.[49]

On other occasions, it was a chance meeting with a widow, several hours before the ceremony began, and her conversations with others that satisfied the curiosity of European travellers. At Patna, in the mid seventeenth century, Jean-Baptiste Tavernier found himself, along with some other Dutchmen, at the house of the city governor (a Muslim who was trying to discourage *sati*) when an attractive twenty-two-year-old woman arrived. In a resolute and firm voice she asked him for permission to burn herself with the body of her dead husband. The governor tried to dissuade her and, in view of her stubborn insistence, he asked her whether she realized how agonizing the flames would be and whether she had ever accidently burned her hand. 'No, no', the woman replied, with more courage than before, 'I do not fear fire in any way, and to make you see that it is so, you have only to order a well-lighted torch to be brought here.' At length a torch was brought and the woman ran in front of it and held her hand firmly in the flame without the least grimace; then she pushed in her arm up to the elbow, till it was immediately scorched.[50] In 1823 a correspondent of *The Times* who had tried to persuade an Indian widow not to immolate herself, recounted how she listened to him with immense calmness and thanked him before repeating her intention to burn on her dead husband's pyre. However, he added, 'I felt her pulse, and it was far calmer than my own at the moment I am writing.'[51]

On still other occasions, some European travellers gained a greater understanding of these Hindu customs when they were told how particular widows took the decision to immolate themselves. They heard how some had dreamed that their husbands had died while far away, either in battle or on a dangerous journey, and when they woke up, even in the absence of further confirmation, they had chosen to immolate themselves by *anumarana* ('dying after'). They were prompted to do so by certain Hindu beliefs whereby, firstly, oneiric visions were said to correspond to reality, and secondly, such dreams indicated the guilt of the living towards the dead. The Europeans also heard how some women, immediately after their husbands' deaths, felt themselves falling under the sway of a dark and insatiable supernatural power; they felt as if consumed by an inner fire, and they started to tremble. A stream of words tumbled out of their mouth: 'I am going to eat the fire', 'I am going to follow my husband', '*sat, sat, sat*'.[52]

When attending a *sati*, Pietro della Valle had also noted how the widow climbed onto the pyre 'with a calm and constant countenance, without tears, evidencing more grief for her husband's death than her own, and more desire to go to him in the other world than regret for her own departure out of this'.[53] But, as if distrustful of his own impressions, he had decided to gather more information. So, having learnt that a woman whose husband had died a few days earlier wanted to commit *sati*, he made every effort to meet her, accompanied by an interpreter. He arranged to visit her on 16 November 1623 and, like a modern anthropologist, he made careful notes about the place where she lived and the way those around her moved and interacted, before carrying out a lengthy interview with the widow.

He found her in a courtyard, seated with others with whom she was 'talking and laughing in conversation'. She was about thirty years old, 'of a complexion very brown for an Indian and almost black', of attractive appearance, tall and well proportioned. She was dressed in white, her hair covered with flowers, 'and she also wore a garland of flowers, spreading forth like the rayes of the sun; in brief, she was wholly in nuptial dress and held a lemon in her hand, which is the usual ceremony'. She stood up and came towards the Italian traveller and his companion and stayed to talk with them for a long time. She told me that her name was Giaccamà, that her husband was a drummer and that he had died eighteen days ago, leaving her and two other wives. The latter had immediately declared that they were unwilling to die because they had many children. Having discovered that Giaccamà herself had a seven-year-old son and a daughter who was a little older, Pietro della Valle asked why she had come to this decision. 'She answer'd me that she left them well recommended to the care of an Uncle of hers there present, who also talk'd with us very cheerfully, as if rejoicing that his Kins-woman should do such an action; and that her Husband's other two remaining wives would also take care of them.' Appealing to the young age of her children and to the situation in which she would leave them, the Italian traveller tried to persuade the widow to reconsider her decision, but to no avail. 'She still answer'd me to all my Reasons, with a Countenance not onely undismay'd and constant, but even cheerful, and spoke in such a manner as shew'd that she had not the least fear of death. She told me also, upon my asking her, that she did this of her own accord, was at her own liberty and not forc'd nor perswaded by any one.'[54] Pietro della Valle was resigned, but he 'promis'd her that, so far as my weak pen could contribute, her Name should remain immortal in the World'. He then wrote three sonnets in memory of Giaccamà, with the title 'On a woman who burned herself alive at the death of her husband' (which have only recently been rediscovered).[55] One of them reads:

As was their custom, herself she burned,
After her dead spouse on a pyre was consumed;
A life without him was not her desire.
At least in this earthly world
Let such praiseworthy love be told.[56]

That the immolation of Indian widows on their husbands' pyres often appeared to be an act of free will is also clear from other first-hand accounts[57] written in different historical periods and by persons with a detailed knowledge of Hindu customs. In 1978 an Indian scholar, a committed supporter of the women's liberation movement for many years, warned her Western colleagues against an ideological interpretation of *sati* by telling them that her great-great-grandmother burned herself alive, holding her husband's corpse in her arms, even though the rite had been prohibited by the British authorities. This woman not only had decided of her own free will but also had to overcome the objections of her children and grandchildren who did everything they could to dissuade her because of concerns over the legal consequences of her act.[58]

Nonetheless, there were cases where *sati* was a result of constraint. Even Giaccamà herself, when asked by Pietro della Valle whether Indian widows were forced to undergo self-immolation, replied that 'ordinarily' this did not occur. However, she admitted that even among 'persons of quality' this was sometimes the case: 'when some widow was left young, handsome, and so in danger of marrying again (which amongst them is very ignominious), or committing a worse fault; in such cases the friends of the deceas'd Husband were very strict, and would constrain her to burn her self even against her own will, for preventing the disorders possible to happen in case she should live'.[59] In these situations the women were drugged or tied to the pyre or enclosed by stout bamboo canes.[60] No one knows exactly how frequent these cases were. However, it is possible the number of coerced *sati* may have increased in the early decades of the nineteenth century, when the practice was gradually starting to become illegal.

Even when a widow chose immolation of her own accord, there was always the danger that she might be overcome by fear and flee when she saw the pyre. Precautions were therefore taken to prevent this, since it would have brought dishonour to her and her family. The Brahmins played a key role in this respect. It was they who comforted the widow at crucial moments in the ceremony, talking to her with 'good words, and persuading her' not to be afraid of death, indeed encouraging her 'to despise the present life' because it was 'brief and vain', and promising her that, after death, she would enjoy 'many pleasures with her husband, and infinite riches and precious garments, as well as countless other things'.[61] They also ensured that they never lost sight of the woman when she went to the river to be purified, in case she might prefer drowning to death in the flames.

Other measures were taken to reduce suffering or to prevent flight at the last minute. The widow often anointed her head and body with oil. After she had thrown herself into the flames, Ludovico de Varthema wrote, 'her relatives hit her with sticks and some with pitch balls. They do so to ensure that she dies quickly'.[62] Sometimes, it was the circle of relatives, friends and acquaintances who surrounded her, cutting off any escape. 'If a widow is terrified of taking this step', wrote Nicolò di Conti, 'as sometimes happens, or if the sight of the strange movements and the cries of other widows already on the pyre frighten her, because they appear to wish to escape, causing her to faint from fear, then the bystanders around her will help her to throw herself into the flames, or they may even throw her in by force.'[63]

5.6 Suicides: condemned and admired

The idea, put forward by Durkheim and many other authors, that altruistic suicide is allegedly predominant in 'primitive societies' is not confirmed by Indian history for two different reasons.[64] Firstly, because in the past this country had an extensive cultural repertoire of voluntary death, which differed in terms of the meaning attributed to the different forms, how they were judged morally, and the type of rites celebrated before or immediately after they were accomplished. Secondly, because the further back one goes in time (towards a more 'primitive' society in which the individual shows a greater degree of subordination to the group) the less important *sati* appears to have been. Let us start with the first point.

In India some forms of voluntary death were morally condemned for centuries, while others were admired and encouraged, depending on the reason for taking one's own life, the place where this happened, and the gender, status and caste of the individual concerned.[65] Therefore, it was approved and honourable for a woman to immolate herself on her dead husband's pyre, but censured if she was unmarried or married but compelled by strong emotion. Different terms were used to distinguish between these forms of voluntary death. *Atmahatya* and *atmatyaga* were used if the suicide was condemned, or *tanutyaga* and *dehatyaga* if it was approved.[66]

Kautilya, an influential Indian statesman and political philosopher who lived between the second and first century BCE, left a collection of the main moral teachings of his time in which he severely condemned:

those men and women who under the infatuation of love, anger, or other sinful passions, commit or cause to commit suicide by means of rope, arms or poison. They should, according to him, be dragged by means of a rope along the public road by the hands of a *candela* [untouchable]. For such murderers neither cremation rites nor any obsequies, usually performed by relatives, shall be observed. Any relative who performs funeral rites for such wretches shall either himself be deprived of his funeral or be abandoned by his kith and kin.[67]

Some fifth-century texts stated that the act of those committing suicide by poison, fire, hanging, drowning or throwing themselves off a cliff should be regarded as a very grave sin.[68] Two centuries later, other authoritative voices affirmed that if a man or a woman took their life through pride, anger, pain or fear, they would be 'consigned to the darkness of a hell for sixty thousand years'.[69]

If an individual took his or her life for these reasons, the community reacted in a very different way to when a widow immolated herself on her husband's pyre. The corpse was sometimes removed from the house through a hole specially made in the wall. It was maltreated and defiled, and, as Kautilya wrote, it could not be cremated or buried. Mourners walked around the corpse not in clockwise direction (as they normally would in the event of natural death) but anticlockwise.[70]

Yet many kinds of suicide, in addition to *sati*, were allowed and indeed praised. The oldest, which is mentioned by two of the last *Upanishads* (the sacred texts of Hinduism), was the 'great journey' undertaken by the *sannyasin*, a person who had entered the final phase of life and renounced all material goods in order to devote himself to his own spiritual path. The expectation was not that he would commit an act of self-violence, but rather that either he would set out on a journey north, towards the Himalayas, without drinking or eating, or that he would jump off a high rock.[71] Suicide was also allowed at the end of a pilgrimage, in ancient Prayag (Allahabad), which lies at the confluence of two of the most sacred rivers, the Ganges and the Yamuna, and also of a third river, the invisible and mysterious Sarasvati.[72] Suicide was also permissible if committed by persons who were so ill they could no longer perform any of the main purification rites, by those who had committed such a terrible sin that it could not be expiated in any way,[73] or by those who had been condemned to death. Marco Polo had already described how, in India 'when a man is doomed to die for any crime, he may declare that he will put himself to death in honour of such or such an idol, and the king then grants him permission to do so'.[74] Many other sources indicate that the expiatory suicide of a criminal was consented.[75] After abdicating, it was also permitted for kings to take their life by throwing themselves into the water (sometimes at Prayag) or into the fire.[76] Lastly, there was the custom of *jauhar* whereby, faced with military defeat, men would fight to the death, while their wives and sometimes even their children would kill themselves with swords or throw themselves into the flames to avoid capture and dishonour.[77]

All these permissible and admired forms of suicide have two distinctive features in common: they occurred when life had reached its end and for reasons that were not solely personal.[78] *Sati* too was viewed positively because the woman's life (seen as being incorporated in her husband's) came to an end when he died, and because the wife's death would allow her to remain close to him. Likewise, the *jauhar* of the entire population of a vanquished city or the suicide of a *sannyasin*, a pilgrim who had reached Prayag, or a king after his abdication, took place when their lives came to an end and for motives that were not just personal.

The choice of one of these approved forms of suicide was irreversible. Having announced an intention to proceed, anyone who failed to act or changed his mind was guilty of an extremely grave sin, one that would incur divine wrath and bring family dishonour and public scorn.[79] This explains why the Brahmins would push a recalcitrant widow towards the pyre to ensure that she kept faith with her decision. But the rule of irreversibility also affected the decision of a *sannyasin* or that of a pilgrim journeying to Prayag. For them too, every step backwards would be equivalent to killing a Brahmin, namely committing the worst possible sin.

There was, however, an exception to this rule of taking one's life when it had reached its end and not for purely individual motives. Brahmins, who embody and defend ritual purity, were entitled to kill themselves as a way of taking revenge against someone whom they felt had treated them unjustly.[80] For example, it was said that some Brahmins killed themselves in revenge against the Raja of Rajput, 'pouring maledictions on his head with their last breath' because he had levied an unfair tax on them, and that the daughter of a Brahmin family, having been seduced by a certain raja, burned herself to death.[81] Over time, this practice was adopted also by castes. In southern India, some stone slabs carved with figures of a man cutting his own throat have for centuries commemorated the revenge suicide of a number of workers against a king of Warangal because he did not keep his promise to pay a sum of gold for digging a large tank.[82]

This probably led to the practice of 'sitting in *dharna*', namely when a creditor, or more usually the victim of an injustice, started to fast at the door of the debtor's house or the house of the man who had offended him, and threatened to abstain from all food until his requests had been met.[83] Sometimes the victim placed a stone on his head, or sometimes he brought with him arms and poison. It was also possible to recruit the services of a Brahmin to exert this kind of moral pressure, because to cause the death (through starvation) of a priest was a serious crime. Therefore, for example, if the parents of a girl who was engaged to be married thought that her fiancé might leave her, they would engage the services of a Brahmin who would start to fast in the girl's defence.[84]

There were other forms of revenge suicide in Indian society. Some eighteenth-century travellers observed how, in the kingdom of Marava, if one of the parties took his own life during a quarrel, then the other would be obliged to do the same. If a woman who had been insulted killed herself by hitting her head against the door of the man who had offended her, the man would be forced to do likewise. Also in the event that someone was driven to poisoning themselves, the individual who had been the cause would then have to do the same. If this did not happen, then the individual would be severely punished and maltreated in countless ways, his house would be burned and his livestock slaughtered.[85]

Therefore, in ancient India, at a time when there was a greater degree of subordination between the individual and the group, there were various forms of suicide, but many of them were far from being altruistic.

5.7 The origin and spread of *sati* as a custom

Moving to the second point, it is not known for certain when *sati* was first introduced. We do, however, know that it is never mentioned in either the *Brahmanas*, the priestly texts written between 1500 and 700 BCE, or in the *Grihya-sutras*, which give an accurate description of domestic ceremonies and were written between 600 and 300 BCE.[86] Indeed, when detailing the funeral rites, the *Grihya-sutras* emphasize that after her husband's cremation, the widow had to be accompanied back to the house by either her brother-in-law or a trusted servant. Moreover, the sutras continue by wishing her a long and prosperous life. It is not until after the third century CE that the first evidence regarding the existence of *sati* is found, precisely in coincidence with the period that some experts have identified as the start of a decline in women's social status.[87] For example, for the first time the laws mention the practice of *sahagamana*, indicating that after her husband's death, a woman should either live without remarrying or should burn herself on his funeral pyre. Yet, these rules stated that *sahagamana* should be optional not obligatory.[88]

However, the earliest evidence of the origins of this custom appears in the accounts of those historians who wrote about Alexander the Great and his conquest of India: Onesicritus, Aristobulus, Strabo and then Diodorus Siculus.[89] It is to the latter that we owe the first and strangest explanation for the origin of this practice. According to Diodorus Siculus, *sati* was introduced in order to protect men from their wives since the latter had started to poison their husbands when they wanted to change partners. Therefore, 'when this evil became fashionable, and many were murdered in this way, the Indians, although they punished those guilty of the crime, since they were not able to deter the others from wrongdoing, established a law that wives, except such as were pregnant or had children, should be cremated along with their deceased husbands'.[90]

In various guises this explanation was reiterated on countless occasions by those Europeans who took an interest in India.[91] For example, Cesare de' Fedrici was told that

> this lawe was of an ancient time, to make provision against the slaughters which women made of their husbands. For in those daies before this lawe was made, the women for every little displeasure that their husbands had doone unto them, they would presentlye poyson their husbands, and take other men, and now by reason of this lawe they are more faithfull to their husbands, and count their lives as deare as their owne, bicause that after his death, hir owne followeth presently.[92]

A further two (not necessarily rival) hypotheses put forward by some scholars on the origins and development of *sati* appear more convincing. The first is that it grew out of the ancient custom of rulers and lords to carry with them into the afterworld all their most precious and useful chattels and possessions: clothing, arms, horses, and therefore also wives. The second asserts that *sati* developed among the families of warriors, who attributed enormous importance to heroism. This meant that if the husband were killed in battle, his wife would immolate herself courageously so as not to fall into the hands of his enemies. In order to assess the validity of these and other hypotheses, and in order to gain a clearer understanding of the significance that *sati* retained for centuries, we should examine the renown it enjoyed among the various groups in the complex hierarchy of Indian society, the period when it first appeared in these groups, and the varying degree to which it later spread.

Indian society was divided in the past into four *varnas* or castes. At the top were the Brahmins, originally sorcerers and witchdoctors but later priests and men of learning, although their training was predominantly literary and focused on memorizing the sacred Vedic texts. Then came the *Kshatriya* caste of nobles and warriors whose role was to provide military protection for the population. They were followed by the *Vaishya* caste who spanned the various professions and producers, from merchants to farmers and herdsmen. At the bottom of this pyramid was the *Shudra* caste, made up of unskilled workers, domestic servants, potters and other artisans, perfume and oil sellers.

Sati seems to have first been documented among the Kshatriyas, namely in the second highest caste.[93] It was from this group that Ceteus came, the military commander referred to by Diodorus Siculus, and also the other warriors killed in battle whose funerals were described by Ibn Battuta some 1,600 years later. This is the caste to which many of the men depicted on funerary stones belonged, since they are shown on horseback, with spear and armour; his wife or wives are usually ranged below him, their arms crossed over their bosom.[94] For many centuries, the practice of *sati* remained confined to this caste. The self-immolation of the widows was regarded as a heroic act, comparable to their husbands' feats on the battlefield. Still today, there is a saying among the women of Rajasthan that although the lion, unlike other animals, will circle a fire, a lioness will jump right into it.[95] The meaning of this old proverb is clear: Rajput men and women are both lions, in the sense of having extraordinary courage, but the latter have more than the former. While the men risk their lives on the battlefield, the women embrace certain death as they ascend the pyre.

The ritual suicide of widows was for centuries prohibited to Brahmin women.[96] Indeed some laws decreed that any person who encouraged a Brahmana widow to immolate herself on her husband's pyre would be 'guilty of the dreadful and unatonable sin of the murder of a Brahmin's wife'.[97] In around 1000 CE, namely more than thirteen centuries since it had first appeared among the Kshatriya caste, *sati* began to be practised by some priestly families. The ancient ban was reinterpreted and applied only to *anumarana*, namely 'dying after', while *sahagamana* ('going with') began to be regarded as legitimate.[98] Some centuries later *sati* also spread to the middle and lower castes, even reaching quite humble families, like oil pressers, shepherds, weavers, tanners and drummers (as in the case of husband of Giaccamà who was discussed earlier).[99] According to the data collected by the British authorities in India, almost 40 per cent of widows who self-immolated between 1815 and 1826 were Brahmins, six per cent *Kshatriyas*, four per cent *Vaishyas* and 50 per cent *Shudras*.[100]

Here too there is evidence of that process often referred to as 'Sanskritization' by which members of lower castes emulated the customs, rituals, ideology and way of life of higher castes that became a model for their aspirations. Yet, in spite of this, it was at the top of the social hierarchy that *sati* was always most widely practised. Taking account of the different sizes of the four castes, it is easy to draw the conclusion that Brahmins (who represented between five and ten per cent of the population) carried out *sati* more frequently than *Vaishyas* or *Shudras*. Moreover, in these higher caste families, the roots of *sati* were so deeply felt that they continued to practise it even when they emigrated to another country. For example, in 1722, when a rich Indian merchant died in Astrakhan, Russia, the local authorities forbade his wife from burning herself with him. Only when the other Indian merchants living in the region threatened to remove their factories and commerce was permission given and the *sati* took place with 'due pomp and publicity'.[101]

As it spread, *sati* took on a different nature. When only practised by

Kshatriyas, its significance had been exclusively heroic, but as it was gradually adopted by other castes, it acquired an increasingly religious character and became a Brahminic rite, a cult for the entire Hindu population.[102] This change is confirmed by the multiplication of commemorative monuments after 1300 CE. These sometimes took the form of walls or simply doors on which (as we have seen) the widow left the imprint of her right hand before she left for the place of sacrifice. On other occasions they were funerary stele or stone slabs set vertically in the ground, with inscriptions or decorations. The stones were often carved with the right hand and forearm of the immolated *sati*, and were marked with the sun and moon, symbols of eternity,[103] or the swastika, a good luck omen (Plates 27 and 28).[104]

As well as socially, *sati* spread geographically over time. There appears to be no question that it first started in northern India, and in particular Kashmir, perhaps because – as some experts have noted – it was closest to central Asia where the Scythian tribes lived (nomads of Siberian origin whose civilization developed between the eighth and fourth century BCE across the entire Eurasian region). Yet the poet Bāna (c. 625 CE) expressed his vehement opposition when he wrote: 'To die after one's beloved is most fruitless. It is a custom followed by the foolish. It is a reckless course followed only on account of hot haste. It is a mistake of stupendous magnitude.'[105] Even Medhātithi, the much respected commentator of Manu between the eighth and ninth century CE, condemned *sati*.[106] Yet, very slowly, this custom spread from the northern regions to the central and southern parts of India. Its geographical distribution remained patchy even during the period of its greatest expansion. For example, it never became established in Malabar (what is now known as Kerala), where there was a partially matriarchal society.[107] By the early nineteenth century, it was still more widespread in the north, in the northwestern regions of Punjab and Rajasthan, as well as in Bengal in the northeast. According to the statistics gathered by the British authorities for all three provinces that were completely under British control – Bombay, Madras and Bengal – of over six thousand widows who immolated themselves with their husbands between 1815 and 1825, only ten per cent lived in the first two regions, while 90 per cent resided in the third. But even here, in Bengal, there were considerable regional differences, since the majority lived in Calcutta.[108]

Precise figures are lacking which would have enabled us to say with certainty whether, and to what extent, there was a change over time in the number of women who burned on their husbands' pyres. However, information from the funerary steles and other commemorative monuments, as well as from other sources, point to the likelihood that *sati* was relatively rare in antiquity, grew during the medieval period and reached a zenith in the modern age, from the mid seventeenth century to 1829, the year when it was banned by law.[109]

The statistics for the last historical period of this custom are few and far between, as well as fragmentary. In 1803 an English missionary carried out a census in an area extending thirty miles around Calcutta and concluded that in one year a total of 438 widows had self-immolated.[110] Reported data from the Bengal Presidency under British rule show 8,134 cases of *sati* between 1815 and 1828.[111] Some scholars have claimed that, throughout India, at least 100,000 widows were burned every year. Even according to the most accurate estimates, this number was certainly no fewer than 33,000.[112] This means that, in the nineteenth century alone, before *sati* was made illegal under British rule, almost a million women took their own lives after their husbands died. It is certainly an incredible number. However, we should not forget that the total number of widows was huge. In the light of these figures, it has been estimated that, in the general population, about one widow per thousand burned herself, while this rose to two cases per hundred in those areas where the custom was most widely practised.[113] The figures amassed by British officials contradict the thesis, supported by many travellers, whereby very young women were often among those who immolated themselves. Only three per cent of the widows who killed themselves were under nineteen, while almost half of them were fifty and over (and two thirds were older than forty).[114]

The earliest statistical data[115] on the frequency of voluntary death (in all its forms, including those that were morally condemned) refer to the situation in British India in 1907, when the use of *sati* was already in decline. In that year, when the population was just short of 203 million, there was a suicide rate of 4.8 per 100,000 inhabitants, not that different from the rate in Spain or Portugal, Italy or Ireland.[116] The most striking factor was that in 1907 in India, unlike Europe, women took their own lives much more frequently than men, and in some provinces the gender gap was huge (Table 5.1). This ratio was reversed during the course of the twentieth century and, for the past forty years or more, the male suicide rate has been slightly higher than that of women.[117]

Table 5.1 Ratio between male and female suicide rates in British India (1907), by province, and in India (1967–97).

British India	*0.58*
Assam and eastern Bengal	0.67
Bengal	0.56
Bombay	0.92
Burma	1.17
Madras	0.74
Central provinces	1.01
Northwest frontier provinces	0.54
United provinces of Agra and Ondh	0.34
Punjab	0.79
India	
1967	1.32
1977	1.34
1997	1.32

Source: Elaborated using data from Von Mayr (1917); Steen and Mayer (2004).

5.8   *Sati* or widow

Why did hundreds of thousands of Indian women ritually kill themselves after losing their husbands? What prompted them to climb onto the funeral pyre or throw themselves into the pit and die in the flames? The response formulated more than a century ago by Émile Durkheim, namely that this depended principally on the particular social structure and, in particular, on 'the strict subordination of the individual to the group', now seems completely inadequate in the light of today's findings. Firstly, because in India *sati* did not exist before the third century BCE and was only practised very occasionally in the following millennium, yet throughout this lengthy period individuals were no less subordinate to the communities to which they belonged. Secondly, because analogous forms of 'altruistic' suicide did not exist, in the same period, in extremely 'primitive' societies in which individual needs were held in scant regard.

If we wish to explain *sati* solely with reference to the type of social structure, we can certainly not limit ourselves to considering the relations between the individual and the group but instead must use a gendered viewpoint, namely an analysis of the relations between men and women. Already by the early fifteenth century, the Spanish traveller Pero Tafur had clearly identified the logic of *sati* in terms of social relations, expectations and role behaviour. 'If the man dies first the woman has to burn herself [. . .] But if the women dies first the man does not have to burn himself, for they say woman was made for the service of man, but not man for the woman.'[118] Indeed, we know well that while hundreds of thousands of widows were immolated on their husbands' pyres, not a single widower ever did the same for his wife.

But in order to really explain *sati*, its slow rise and subsequent spread, we need to start, not from the social structure, but from Indian culture, namely the complex set of meanings and symbols, mindsets and beliefs, as well as the classification systems shared by almost all the population of that country, which controlled the emotions by prescribing what should and should not be felt in a particular situation or following an event, and by suggesting how such feelings should be expressed. It is to this system of governing the emotions, so different from that in the West, that we can not only trace the practice of *sati*, but also other important but otherwise incomprehensible aspects of the rite. And among these, first and foremost, the fact, recorded on countless occasions by European travellers, that Indian widows appeared to go to their own deaths with a serene countenance and a smile on their lips.

There are two categories of motives why, for centuries, hundreds of thousands of Indian women sacrificed themselves on their husbands' pyres: first, they were, in some way, attracted by the idea of becoming *sati* and/or, second, they wished to escape the only alternative path that awaited them, life as a widow. In 1030 when Alberuni, the astronomer and historian of modern-day Khiva (then known as Khwarizm), Uzbekistan, visited India, he wrote that a woman, after her husband's death, 'has only to choose between two things – either to remain a widow as long as she lives or to burn herself, and the latter eventuality is considered the preferable, because as a widow she is ill-treated as long as she lives'.[119] 'When a man is dead and his body is being cremated', noted Marco Polo two centuries later, 'his wife flings herself into the same fire and lets herself be burnt with her husband. The ladies who do this are highly praised by all. And I assure you that there are many who do as I have told you.'[120] If they refused, as Duarte Barbosa commented in the early sixteenth century, 'their kindred shave their heads and treat them as disgraced and a shame to their families. And as for some who have not done it, to whom they wish to show favour, if they are young they send them to a temple there to earn money for the said temple with their bodies.'[121]

Becoming a *sati* was regarded as the model to which a virtuous, chaste and faithful wife should aspire. Underlying this was the belief that, by following this path, a wife could redeem herself and her husband from all misdeeds they had committed while alive. Moreover, she would become a supernatural being, endowed with enormous powers, and she would bring prestige for many years to their descendants on both sides of the family. This model was handed down from generation to generation,[122] because, as François Bernier wrote, 'the Mothers, from their youth besotted with this superstition, as of a most virtuous and most laudable action, such as was unavoidable to a Woman of honour, did also infatuate the spirit of their Daughters from their very infancy.'[123] The custom was also constantly revived by the celebration of women who had immolated themselves and by the creation of funeral stele and temples in their honour.

If Hindu women ritually took their lives after losing their husbands, it was also (or above all) because they did not wish to become widows. For many centuries in India, even after a husband's death, it was the wife who could decide whether or not to become a widow. This proposition, which was completely incomprehensible to Westerners, was coherent with the Hindu belief system,[124] based on a totally different concept of widowhood to ours. It stated that a woman's married status did not change following her husband's physical death, but only after his cremation, when his soul acquired a form without substance that would then continue on its spiritual path. Therefore, a woman who climbed onto the pyre and was cremated with her husband never became a widow but instead remained married (for all eternity). This idea was expressed through numerous symbolic acts. For example, a woman who had decided to sacrifice herself wore the bracelets that demonstrated her married status, whereas she had to break them if she chose to become a widow (Plate 35). This is clearly shown in depictions on the funeral stele of *satis*, where together with the widow's right hand and forearm, these bracelets were always present as a sign that these women had preferred to remain married (Plates 27 and 29).[125]

The significance of the chants sung by Indian women after a husband's death should be seen in the light of these beliefs:

Buy me a forehead ornament – do it quickly little brother-in-law
I will follow my husband [as a *sati*]
Dear younger brother-in-law – yes, O dear little brother-in-law
Cool the *sati* under a shady banyan tree
Bring me a nose ring – do it quickly . . .
Buy a necklace – do it quickly . . .
Buy a saffron-coloured sari . . . [and] a blouse piece – do it quickly
. . .
Buy toe-rings – do it quickly . . .[126]

If in these requests, which were addressed to their husband's younger brother, the relative they felt closest to, these women seem anxious, impatient, incapable of waiting another moment before they immolate themselves with their husband, it is because they believe that spouses must die together in order to remain united forever.

The decision to sacrifice themselves with their husbands therefore implies a choice between two radically opposed conditions. If a *sati* is happy, a widow is unhappy. While the former is loved, venerated and celebrated, the latter is hated, despised, avoided and abandoned. If one is remembered after death, the other is forgotten, even while still alive. Widowhood represents a violation of the Hindu moral code. One of the principles of this code is that 'the husband is to be followed always: like the body by its shadow, like the moon by moonlight, like a thundercloud by lightning'.[127] This means that it is expected that a wife should die before her husband or together with him, never after. Indeed, at a wedding the Brahmin priest turns to the woman and says, 'May you be one who accompanies her husband (always), when he is alive and even when he is dead!'[128] Therefore, a woman who chose not to climb onto the pyre and instead became a widow was contravening these rules.

What was more, a woman who decided to outlive her husband stained herself, according to Hindu beliefs, with even worse guilt because she was held responsible for his death. The ideal Hindu wife was a *pativrata*, literally a woman who took a vow (*vrat*) to her husband (*pati*). At the marriage she undertook to protect him in three different ways, in order to guarantee him a long life: firstly, by serving him, preparing his food and caring for him; secondly by performing rites, fasting or wearing a necklace that would be replaced each year as a sign of her renewed commitment; and lastly, by remaining devout and faithful. By conducting herself in this way, a *pativrata* acquired extraordinary, almost supernatural power, and indeed it was believed she could 'set the world on fire and stop the movements of the sun and moon'.[129] Therefore, if suitably 'protected and controlled', this woman became a symbol of society's capacity to 'maintain moral order'.[130] Yet if her husband died, she was blamed because she had failed to care for and protect him.

But even if the wife did keep her vow, the death of her husband could be attributed to a sin she had committed in an earlier life (according to the doctrine of *karma* every disgrace was brought about by a guilty act). In the same way that individuals were born into the caste they deserved, depending on their conduct in a previous life, so a husband's death could be caused by a wife's guilty action committed in another life. What was certain was that the only way for a woman to resolve that terrible suspicion was to climb onto her husband's pyre, and therefore choose not to become a widow.

More generally, according to Hindu custom a widow was impure: she lacked any social identity, and was a constant source of disorder. A woman existed only if she was married and could bear children. If her husband died, she would continue to live in the house that had belonged to her spouse and his family, but as an outsider, in a situation of complete precariousness. She had neither role nor identity. She was unprotected and uncontrolled.[131] She was solely a living temptation to violate other norms. 'Just as birds flock to a piece of flesh left on the ground, so all men try to seduce a woman whose husband is dead.'[132]

In the light of this system of Hindu beliefs and customs, it can be understood why, as the French abbé Jean Antoine Dubois wrote, a woman drew close to her husband's corpse and, punctuated by sobs and shrieks, asked a long series of questions:

Why hast thou forsaken me? What wrong have I done thee, that thou shouldst thus leave me in the prime of my life? Had I not for thee all the fondness of a faithful wife? Have I not always been virtuous and pure? Have I not borne thee handsome children? Who will bring them up? Who will take care of them hereafter? Was I not diligent in all the duties of the household? Did I not sweep the house every day, and did I not make the floor smooth and clean? Did I not ornament the floor with white tracery? Did I not cook good food for thee? Didst thou find grit in the rice that I prepared for thee? Did I not serve up to thee food such as thou lovedst, well seasoned with garlic, mustard, pepper, cinnamon, and other spices?[133]

Shortly after this, the widow was subject to a ceremony of social degradation (Plate 35). Female relatives and friends would visit her at her house and eat the food prepared for them, then they would embrace her and exhort her to show fortitude, before lastly pushing her violently to the ground. One of the closest female relatives would cut the gold cord suspending the *tali*, an ornament only worn by married women.[134] After this she could no longer wear colours, either on her face or clothing. She had to abandon the *kumkum*, the bright red mark on her forehead, the *sindooram*, the vermillion line in front of the hair parting, and only use white ash. For the rest of her life she would only wear a white or ochre sari. Therefore, the symbols of sexuality and fertility gave way to those of sacrifice, purity and death.

The widow's head was shaved. Indeed, at the end of the funeral, the son also had to shave off his hair. This was seen as one of the ways (together with the ritual bath) of regaining the state of purity lost through contact with the dead body, one of the most powerful sources of temporary impurity. It was thought that hair was a particular conduit of contamination and that every drop of water which fell upon the widow's head polluted her husband's soul as many times as there were hairs on her head.[135] But while the son only performed this ritual after the funeral, the widow had to continue to shave for the rest of her life, at least once a month. According to an old saying, 'just as the body, bereft of life, in that moment becomes impure, so the woman bereft of her husband is always impure, even if she has bathed properly'.[136] This was why, as Father Dubois observed, the term *mounda*, 'shorn-head', was one of the most insulting names a woman could be called in a quarrel.[137]

The symbolic shaving of a widow's head also had another meaning. In India, as in many other cultures, a luxuriant head of hair is a symbol of vitality and sexual energy. On the contrary, a head that is partly or entirely shaved indicates loss of power and freedom, as well as a detachment, limitation or renunciation of sexuality. Buddhist monks, who fully shave their heads and beards, are an eloquent example of this, as are Brahmin priests, who instead retain a single tuft of hair. The regular shaving of a widow's hair therefore represented a sort of symbolic castration, the forcible elimination of all erotic desire; it indicated her future chastity, her renunciation of any form of sexuality and fertility.[138] Not only could she never remarry, but she could not even see another man, let alone name him.[139]

These ceremonies of degradation marked the woman's transition to a radically new and different status, a condition of sacrifice, mortification, penitence and social death. For the remainder of her life, she would have to sleep on the ground, eat once a day, never chew betel or be seen by others.[140] Excluded from all feasts and family celebrations, she could not even attend the weddings of her sons. Despised by all, she was often insulted and sometimes beaten.

Therefore, if Indian women chose to ascend their husbands' pyres following their death, it was (above all) to escape the shame and humiliation of widowhood, as well as the hatred of others, including close family and her intimate women friends. It was such an intolerable condition that some women who had initially preferred it to self-immolation subsequently changed their minds, even years later. From the records collected by the British government between 1815 and 1820, in some cases widows chose self-immolation (using the rite of *anumarana*) five, ten or even fifteen years after their husband's death.[141]

This system of customs, values, beliefs, symbols and meanings had not always been present in India. In the distant Vedic era, gender relations were quite different from those outlined here, as were the concept of widowhood and the rules governing first and second marriages. Women were not subordinated to the same degree as in later centuries. With regard to religion, wives enjoyed the same rights and privileges as their husbands.

They could celebrate rituals and ceremonies alone or with their spouse.[142] Divorce was permitted and could even be requested by the woman.[143] Widows were not despised and humiliated, but could remarry or follow the custom of *niyoga*, a form of levirate whereby women who had lost their husbands could have one or more children with their husband's brother, marrying him or going to live with him.[144] Since it was deemed a terrible disgrace to die childless, it was regarded as being the duty of the dead man's brother to have sexual relations with his sister-in-law in order to conceive one, two or three children, so that they would have as much family blood in their veins as possible.[145] The brother of the deceased could also keep more than one wife since polygamy was allowed in India. Thanks to the custom of *niyoga*, the same term (*devara*) was used to refer to both a widow's second marriage and a brother-in-law (specifically a woman's husband's brother).[146]

This situation changed gradually but radically over the centuries. The degree of subordination to which women were subjected increased massively. They lost all the rights they had enjoyed in religious practice. After the fifth century BCE, the opportunities for divorce became increasingly limited, above all in the highest castes. The custom of *niyoga* became the target of fierce criticism, followed by restrictions (concerning the length of time that had to pass after the husband's death before *niyoga* could start, and how many children a widow could conceive with her brother-in-law). It slowly dropped out of use, disappearing completely in the sixth century CE. Opposition to the remarriage of widows grew after the third century CE and it was finally banned in around 1000. The perception of widows also changed and women who had lost their husbands were increasingly regarded as an ill omen, leading to the custom of shaving their heads and subjecting them to other ritual and social degradations.[147]

The current state of historical knowledge makes it likely that the start of *sati* and its gradual affirmation were preceded and encouraged by the changes taking place in gender relations, in the customs regarding second marriage and the concept of widowhood.

5.9 A clash of cultures

The history of *sati*, its rise and decline, allows us to understand more fully what can happen when cultures with profoundly different customs, beliefs, symbols and interpretations of suicide come into contact and co-exist for long periods. While travelling for lengthy periods in India, a number of European visitors, from the mid sixteenth to the mid nineteenth century, tried to counter the practice of *sati* and attempted to convince widows not to burn themselves on their husband's funeral pyre. Pietro della Valle, for example, promised to help Giaccamà in many ways if she would agree not to kill herself, but he could not persuade her.

The efforts made by other travellers were also usually in vain, although there were exceptions. François Bernier recounted a dramatic meeting with a widow, 'seated at the feet of her dead husband; her hair was dishevelled and her visage pale, but her eyes were tearless and sparkling with animation while she cried and screamed aloud like the rest of the company, and beat time with her hands to this horrible concert'. In order to persuade her to change her mind, he appealed to her, reminding her of the children she would abandon, the relatives who implored her not to do it, and he put forward many other arguments. But the woman answered, with a determined look, 'If I am prevented from burning myself, I will dash out my brains against a wall.'[148] Then the French traveller played his last card by making a terrible threat: 'Let it be so then, but first take your children, wretched and unnatural mother! Cut their throats, and consume them on the same pile; otherwise you will leave them to die of famine, for I shall return immediately to Danechmend-kan and annul their pensions.'[149] At these words the widow relented and promised not to die by her own hands.

In 1789, while he was in India, the Count of Grandpré was informed by his servant that a 'young and handsome' widow had already twice put off the funeral ceremony and would not be able to do so a third time. Convinced, like many Westerners, that if they could choose, these women 'would never consent to so cruel a sacrifice', he decided 'to save her' and organized an expedition. In the sloop he took with him two officers, two servants and twenty 'good European sailors', 'a dozen musquets, eight pistols, and a score of sabres'. He promised the sailors 'the sixth part of the value of whatever jewels the woman should have about her', stating that the others would be left to her if she did not choose to stay with her rescuer. In fact, he intended to give the widow the freedom to choose, whether to go with him or to settle in Calcutta with her jewels. Once the preparations were complete, he set off and soon arrived at the place of the ceremony only to find that 'the dreadful sacrifice had been completed the preceding evening. I had been misinformed of the day.'[150]

On 29 November 1825, when an English surgeon, Richard Hartley Kennedy, went to observe one of these ceremonies, he also timidly tried to make the widow change her mind. He already knew her because some years earlier he had done a courtesy to her husband and, when the procession reached the place where the rite would take place, he remarked how 'Her manner was wonderfully collected, and even graceful.' He took the opportunity 'to whisper in her eye, that if she felt any misgiving, my presence would prevent it from being too late, even at the supposed last moment'. But her 'look of reply was quite sufficient; she had not come without counting the cost'.[151]

The reactions of groups from the other cultures that governed tracts of this huge country for long periods were of course quite different in scope.[152] The Portuguese banned *sati* as soon as they took control of Goa, which remained their colony from 1510 to 1961. Likewise, the Dutch, French and Danish did the same in those cities under their control in the early nineteenth century. However, as far as we know, the outcome of these measures was that Hindus continued to celebrate the rite in those areas where it was allowed. The influence of the Muslims was probably more efficacious: they controlled various parts of India for differing lengths of time from the thirteenth century onwards and they made no secret of their disapproval of *sati*. It is said that Akbar, the Moghul emperor of India in the second half of the sixteenth century, rode in haste to Bengal to prevent a young widow being immolated against her will. His successors also tried to discourage the practice in different ways. 'The Mahometans, by whom the country is governed', wrote François Bernier in the mid seventeenth century, are 'doing all in their power to suppress the barbarous custom.' The practice 'is checked by indirect means. No woman can sacrifice herself without permission from the governor of the province in which she resides, and he never grants it until he shall have ascertained that she is not to be turned aside from her purpose … Notwithstanding these obstacles, the number of self-immolations is still very considerable.'[153] However, many European observers affirmed that this system was undermined by corruption and that permissions for self-immolation were often granted in exchange for money.[154]

After 1765, when the English East India Company took control of Bengal, also the English had to deal with the question of *sati*. The dilemma they faced had been summarized thirty years earlier by Voltaire in the dialogue between two characters in one of his philosophical novels, *Zadig*. Zadig tried to convince Setoc that 'such a barbaric practice should, if at all possible, be abolished'. To which Setoc countered:

Women have been free to burn themselves for more than a thousand years. Which of us shall dare to change a law which has been hallowed by the passage of time? Is there anything more respectable than a time-honoured abuse?

'Reason is more time-honoured still', Zadig retorted. 'Speak to the tribal chiefs, and I shall go and find the young widow.'[155]

From the outset the East India Company chose to follow Setoc's approach, and repeatedly declared that it did not wish to interfere in the 'customs and institutions' of the Hindu population. But its provincial representatives increasingly often found themselves in difficult situations. Many of them called on the supreme court and government for precise instructions on how to behave, but many years lapsed before they received a reply. Some intervened by prohibiting the rite in extreme cases, such as when the widow to be immolated was under fourteen. In 1813, some British officials consulted the Pundits, namely the scholars studying sacred Sanskrit texts, on their reading of the *Dharma Sastra* and whether it allowed a woman from the Jugi caste to be buried with her husband's corpse and they received an affirmative response.[156]

From 1813, the year when they were admitted to India, missionaries began to request that *sati* be abolished, stating that it was foreign to the religious tradition of the country.[157] At this point the British authorities were forced to break their silence. In 1813 the supreme government of Bengal approved a regulation that appealed to the principle of religious tolerance and banned *sati* in those cases not specified by Hindu religious tradition, namely when the widow was under sixteen or pregnant, or if she was obliged to self-immolate by her relatives using either force or drugs. A second regulation, approved in 1817, extended the ban to cases in which the woman was menstruating or had children under the age of four, or under seven if there was no one who would take care of them. It also made it compulsory to inform the police prior to celebrating the rite.

The British government wanted to affirm its complete respect for local customs and institutions. But, by threatening to punish those who did not conform with these customs, it also aimed to reduce the frequency of suicide among widows. Yet this all produced exactly the opposite effect. The number of *satis* soared. In Bengal, between 1815 and 1818, the number rose from 378 to 839 a year.[158] It was not difficult to understand why: by presenting itself as a more authentic interpreter and strict defender of Hindu tradition, the British government had legalized *sati* in all but name (Plate 34). In previous years, the idea that the dominant power might regard the practice as barbarous had raised doubts among families from a number of social backgrounds. But when it became obligatory to ask the police force of the ruling power for permission to perform *sati* and it was then celebrated in the presence of its officials, these doubts were dispelled. This change is clearly illustrated by James Peggs, the English missionary who, more than any other, fought against this custom, when he reported that a widow's relative had said: 'Now she must burn, for the *boro Sahab* (the great Gentleman) has sent her permission to burn!'[159]

This failure provoked indignation and reopened debate, both in India and Britain. New petitions were sent to the British authorities urging them to end the practice of widow burning. The missionaries of the Baptist Missionary Society of Bengal tried to mobilize public opinion back at home. At the same time, a movement gathered force in India, led by the Bengali scholar, Rammohan Roy, which aimed to gradually abolish *sati* by persuading people that it was contrary to the teaching of the Hindu sacred texts. Lord William Bentinck, who was appointed Governor General of India in 1827, took all of this into account.[160] He was immediately convinced of the need to approve laws to prohibit this custom, but before doing so he wished to ensure that there would be no negative repercussions. In the first place, fearing protests by the sepoys, Indian troops who served in the armies of the East India Company, he consulted with forty-nine of the most well-regarded British officers. The overwhelming majority reassured him that the prevalent attitude among the sepoys on this question was one of indifference. Just four officers advocated greater caution, fearing that the Brahmin priests, who gained both prestige and money from the cremation of widows, would object and try to convince the general public that the British authorities wanted to convert them to Christianity. After this, Lord William Bentinck consulted a number of Hindu theological scholars on the origins of the rite that he was proposing to abolish. He reached the conclusion, which he publicly announced with considerable satisfaction, that this rite 'is nowhere enjoined by the religion of the Hindus as an Imperative duty'.[161] On 5 December 1829, therefore, the Governor General of India signed a regulation that prohibited *sati*, which from that moment was classed as culpable homicide and punished with a fine or confinement. It could also become a capital offence if the widow had been obliged to burn herself through the use of force.

These regulations were also approved in the other provinces under British control, namely Madras and Bombay, giving rise to resistance and opposition. In Calcutta, a committee was formed for their abrogation. Moreover, numerous Hindu families travelled to celebrate *sati* where it was permitted, given that many northern and mid western states, which had not been conquered by the British, continued to allow these old customs. For example, the ceremony celebrated in Idar in 1833 generated an outpouring of emotion when seven queens, two concubines, four female slaves and a male servant burned themselves alive on the raja's funeral pyre surrounded by an enormous crowd of onlookers. It was at this time that Baron Thomas Babington Macaulay, while drawing up the India criminal code, listened to the requests of the two extreme groups – liberal Englishmen who, like Voltaire's Setoc, were opposed to any interference in local customs, and Indian conservatives in favour of *sati*. He therefore proposed a reintroduction of the 1813 distinction between legal and illegal *sati*, but in the end this amendment was not approved.

Even after it became illegal throughout India, widow burning continued to be reported, often in forms that differed from tradition. These events became increasingly private and were performed at home, by setting a pile of wood or paraffin-soaked clothing on fire. However, over time, their number diminished, but only very slowly. Indeed, even now, one hundred and eighty years after Lord William Bentinck's reform, the occasional Hindu widow will undergo the ancient rite of immolation.

The religious cult of these *satis* has proved even longer-lived than the act. Throughout the nineteenth century and for most of the twentieth, millions of people in India have continued to venerate the widows who ascended their husbands' pyres, with ceremonies, processions, prayers, and in sacred places where temples have been built in their honour. It was only on 1 October 1987, less than a month after Roop Kanwar's death at Deorala, that the Indian government approved a decree prohibiting these rites of glorification and banning the creation of foundations or the raising of funds in memory of past *satis*.[162]

6

Making the Strong and Powerful Tremble

The official statistics on suicide published for the first time by the Chinese government during the 1990s elicited considerable surprise in European and American research centres and academic circles. Until then the widely held public opinion in the West had been that suicides in that country were rare, certainly much rarer than elsewhere. In part, this idea had been generated by the image presented to the outside world by the Chinese government, whereby suicide, like criminality, unemployment, depression and unhappiness, was unthinkable in a socialist country. However, in part, it had also come from other sources. Those who adhered to Èmile Durkheim's theories might well think that voluntary deaths would be infrequent in a population that in the main lived in the countryside, in huge families held together by very strong bonds, and in a society that was periodically subject to waves of collective enthusiasm. Instead quite a different picture was painted by the Chinese government's statistics. In actual fact these data only related to a sample ten per cent of the population and they led the experts and research institutes that analysed them to widely varying estimates, ranging from a maximum annual suicide rate of 30 per 100,000 inhabitants (some 340,000 people) to a minimum of 22 (250,000).[1] Clearly, however, even the most prudent estimate reveals that, in China in the 1990s, voluntary deaths were more frequent than anywhere else in the world: more than in Australia or the United States, or in most Asian or European countries (with the exception of Russia, Hungary and Finland).

This aside, it is difficult to resist the temptation to explain this high suicide rate using Durkheimian categories, namely diminished social integration and regulation. There is no question that the changes taking place in China over the last twenty years recall, on the one hand, those in Western Europe during the nineteenth century and early decades of the twentieth century, when it seemed that the growing number of suicides was unstoppable. China's economy has indeed experienced exceptional growth, so much so that it has become the world's leading producer of steel, cement, coal and fertilizers, and the second largest producer and consumer of those pesticides often used by its peasant farmers to take their own lives. However, all this has been accompanied by rapid urbanization, growing social inequality, weaker ties between relatives and within families themselves, as well as a breakdown in other forms of social integration. On the other hand, however, China's other great transformations resemble those that happened in the last two decades of the Eastern European communist block (which also saw a rapid increase in suicide numbers). A sudden turnaround in the governing elite was accompanied by change on an enormous scale, heralding the transition from state socialism to a market economy. State and collective ownership of the means of production was replaced by private ownership, while centralized planning gave way to the two-way flow of supply and demand. Values and attitudes that had only recently been condemned spread rapidly: a desire for economic and social success, an entrepreneurial spirit and individualism. This transformation certainly gave rise to situations of anomie.

Instead, as will be seen in the coming pages, these two great historical experiences, and Durkheim's categories, do not help us to understand what happened and is still happening in China with regard to suicide. In practice, in order to explain why its suicide rate was so high at the end of the twentieth century, and why it presents particular features unknown in Europe, both now and in the past, it is necessary to look back into the history of this great country and rebuild the system of customs, values, beliefs and concepts about the meaning of life and death that for centuries governed the emotions of those who lived there.

6.1 The past

Official statistics are only available from 1989 and they show that throughout the 1990s the suicide rate remained unchanged. But what happened before then? However scant, fragmentary and heterogeneous the information available (including some of a statistical kind), it tells us that in the second half of the twentieth century the frequency of suicide was as high as it is today and indeed in some years it was even higher. An increase in the number of voluntary deaths in 1950 can presumably be attributed to the approval of new legislation on marriage which, echoing the liberal Western tradition, aimed to abolish the 'feudal system' of arranged marriages and introduced the possibility of divorce. This law led to resistance and opposition across broad swathes of the population, resulting in an explosion of family tensions that had until then been kept under control and prompting many couples (above all wives) to take their own lives.[2] There was also a wave of suicides after Mao launched a campaign against corruption, tax evasion and fraudulent actions against state property in 1951 and 1952. It is estimated that between 200,000 and 300,000 persons took their own lives at this time.[3] So many people committed suicide in Shanghai by jumping from the top floors of buildings that a new metaphor was coined and they became known as 'parachutes'. Moreover, if you asked why these people did not choose another way of ending their lives, you were told that, 'If you jumped into the Huangpu River and were swept away so the Communists didn't have a corpse, they would accuse you of having escaped to Hong Kong and your family would suffer. So the best way was to leap down to the street.'[4] Throughout the 1950s, numerous Red Army veterans also took their own lives (sometimes with their wives) because they felt betrayed or at least unfairly treated by their companions who had made their way into positions of power.[5] Lastly, the number of suicides also rose between 1966 and 1976, the decade when hundreds of thousands of teachers, magistrates, party members and intellectuals were arrested, interrogated, beaten and tortured in the name of the Cultural Revolution.[6]

But even if we leave aside this period of the Communist regime and move further back in time, we still find signs of high suicide rates. Western readers have often been struck by the large number of voluntary deaths present in the pages of the great literary works of Imperial China.[7] Moreover, this is borne out by the memoirs of Europeans and Americans who travelled to this country or lived there. As far as we know the first to report the frequency of voluntary death was Matteo Ricci, in 1602.[8] 'Suicide is very common', wrote Evariste Huc two centuries later, a French missionary who had arrived in China in 1839 and remained for more than ten years. 'The extreme readiness with which the Chinese are induced to kill themselves is almost inconceivable; some mere trifle, a word almost, is sufficient to cause them to hang themselves, or throw themselves to the bottom of a well.'[9] Similar observations were made by missionaries, doctors, diplomats or educated travellers from other European countries, from the United States or Australia. 'The Chinese are perhaps more prone to commit suicide than the people of any other country in the world', noted John Henry Gray in 1878, who had been archdeacon of Hong Kong.[10] In 1863, while visiting Peking and Shanghai, the American geologist Raphael Pumpelly discovered that Western insurance companies refused to sell life insurance policies to the Chinese because they often committed suicide to save their families from poverty by claiming the sum assured at the death.[11] Others were even more blunt in their judgements. 'China has the unenviable notoriety of having more suicides than any other country', wrote an American, Dyer Ball, in 1893.[12] Or, four years later, the French doctor, Matignon, noted: 'There is no other country in which suicide is so frequent as in the Middle Empire.'[13] Even the Australian journalist, George Ernest Morrison, was absolutely clear: 'China is the land of suicides. I suppose more people die from suicide in China in proportion to the population than in any other country.'[14]

Similar conclusions were also reached by those who had been able to compare the behaviour of immigrants of different nationalities. Thousands of workers were recruited from countries across Europe, Asia and Africa to build the railway along the Panama Canal between 1850 and 1855. All were put to hard labour under difficult conditions. But not all reacted in the same way. The Chinese, as Commander Bedford Pim reported, were notable for their 'strong suicidal tendency': 'it was not uncommon in the morning to find half-a-dozen bodies suspended from the trees in close proximity to the [rail]road.'[15] Within a short period of time, 125 of them had hanged themselves, while a further 300 killed themselves by drowning or machete blows, or by starving themselves to death.[16] In the same period, a similarly high number of suicides was reported among the Chinese who went to work in Peru. The phenomenon became so significant that, on the Peruvian islands of Chica and Guanape, employers used guards to prevent the Chinese labourers from throwing themselves into the sea to drown.[17] The same happened in Cuba where, from 1847 onwards, coffee and sugar plantation owners started to hire Chinese labourers. They soon realized that the new workers had a major defect, even though they were diligent, hardworking, gentle and remissive: they had a strong tendency to kill themselves. 'They have enormous difficulty learning our language', wrote one of these owners. 'They bond to no one and nothing, including their very own lives, for they kill themselves with extraordinary ease and with the most horrific indifference.'[18] That this was no exaggeration is proved by some statistics for 1862 which show that the Chinese population living on the island had a suicide rate of 500 per 100,000,[19] one of the highest found in a human community.

Struck by this 'tendency', some Westerners also attempted to estimate its frequency. By the late nineteenth century, a missionary who had spent many years in China calculated that in this country the suicide rate might range between 30 and 50 per 100,000 inhabitants.[20] However, we luckily have precise and reliable figures, at least for some areas, as well as rough estimates. In 1917, in Peking, a city with more than 800,000 inhabitants, the suicide rate was 16 per 100,000 residents.[21] From the statistics gathered by the Japanese government during its forty-year rule of Taiwan, the large Chinese island it had conquered by military victory in 1895 – and incidentally the best that are available – it appears that this area had a suicide rate of about 19 per 100,000 inhabitants in the first two decades of the twentieth century,[22] higher than that reached in the same period by many European countries after the steep rise during the eighteenth and nineteenth centuries.

It is possible that the frequency of suicide in China underwent short-term fluctuations in the last century and a half and that it fell before rising once again. But what information there is reveals that, in this country, unlike Europe, the suicide rate did not rise strongly and steadily over several centuries, and that there may be no real difference between the rate until the 1990s and that in the mid nineteenth century. What is clear instead is that from 1991 to 2011, during the period of extraordinary economic growth, the frequency with which the Chinese took their own lives fell drastically, from thirty to just over eight cases per 100,000 inhabitants.[23]

6.2   Chinese peculiarities

On closer examination, it is immediately clear how profoundly different, also in this respect, the situation in China is from that in other countries. The available figures show that, in the 1990s, suicide in China was characterized by a number of peculiarities. The first concerns its different frequency in the male population compared to the female one.

As we have seen, in Europe men have always killed themselves more than women, at least from the thirteenth century onwards, and today the suicide rate among the former is between two and five times higher than among the latter. This is also the case in many other countries, in Australia, South Africa, and North and South America. Indeed, in some countries in this last continent (like Puerto Rico and Chile), the difference is even more marked (Table 6.1).

Yet, in the last two decades of the twentieth century, the opposite happened in China. Voluntary deaths were more frequent in the female population, and this trend was particularly evident in rural areas (Table 6.1).[24] As well as in China, this skewed situation is also a feature of Iran,[25] some areas of Turkey,[26] and, as we have already seen, of early twentieth-century India. In the second half of the century, this also happened in some tribes or small populations of farmers or hunter-gatherers in Peru or New Guinea.[27]

In other Asiatic countries, like Japan, Singapore or the Philippines, it is men not women who commit suicide more frequently. The difference between the sexes has increased over time, but is still less than in other continents.[28]

The second peculiarity concerns the frequency of suicide at different stages of life. In European countries, the suicide rate gradually rises with age. This occurs in both the male and female populations, but the tendency is more evident in the former. In China in the 1990s old people killed themselves more often than the young. But the age curve for voluntary deaths differs from the European model. The suicide rate rises sharply from ten to twenty years old, then falls until forty before increasing steeply again to peak at eighty. The correlation with age is slightly different in the male population: after the age of seventy, suicide is more frequent in men, while on the contrary suicide is more frequent in women between the ages of fifteen and forty.

The third peculiarity relates to the distribution of voluntary deaths between the country and the city. In Europe, throughout the nineteenth century and the early decades of the twentieth, suicide rates were higher in large urban centres than in small provincial towns. Today, in some Asiatic countries (India, Sri Lanka, Taiwan), the rural areas have slightly higher suicide rates compared to the cities.[29] However, China is again different from all the other countries because it has a far higher suicide rate in the countryside (at least three times higher) than in urban centres. These differences become more marked in the over-seventy age group. Old people

Table 6.1 Ratio between male and female suicide rates in some countries of Asia and Latin America (1905–2011).

Country	Period	Male/Female suicide rate
China		
Canton	1929	0.58
Hangzhou	1929	0.57
Peking	1929	0.62
Shanghai	1929	0.63
Rural areas	1995–9	0.80
	2011	1.16
Urban areas	1995–9	1.00
	2011	1.21
Total	1995–9	0.80
	2011	1.19
Philippines	1975	1.25
	2003	1.47
Japan	1910	1.68
	1990	1.69
	2004	2.78
Hong Kong	1990	1.24
	2004	2.78
Iran	1999	0.87
Singapore	1990	1.27
	2003	1.64
Taiwan	1905	0.70
Thailand	1985	1.86
	2003	3.40
Chile	2000	6.10
Costa Rica	2000	7.10
Mexico	2000	5.46
Puerto Rico	2000	10.80

Source: Elaborated from data taken from WHO; Wolf (1975); Aliverdinia and Pridemore (2008); Phillips et al. (2002a); Steen and Mayer (2004); Lotrakul (2006); Liu and Yip (2008); Zhang et al. (2014).

in rural areas are exposed to a fourfold risk of killing themselves compared to their peers in the city. But even among the young (aged 18–25) the differences between the countryside and the city are striking. Young peasant women (and men too, but to a lesser extent) have a suicide rate that is four or five times higher than city workers or office staff. Generally speaking, in the Chinese countryside the risk of suicide among people aged between eighteen and twenty-five and those over seventy is higher than anywhere else in the world, even Hungary or Russia.

These Chinese peculiarities lessened or even disappeared altogether in the first decade of this century. Suicides have remained much more commonplace in rural than in urban areas. But after 2005, both in the country and in cities, men have taken their lives slightly more often than women. The correlation between age and voluntary death has also changed, becoming more similar to that in Europe.[30]

6.3   Continuity and change

These findings quite clearly show that suicide in China today presents quite different characteristics compared to what it was in Europe during the nineteenth century and most of the twentieth. How can these differences be explained? Why should Chinese peasant women take their lives far more frequently than other social groups, whether rural or urban, in other countries? Some scholars[31] have looked for the answer to this question in the demographic policies of the People's Republic of China. Since 1979 the government has implemented a one-child policy through the use of incentives and disincentives, rewards and sanctions. Those couples that contented themselves with an only child received top-up payments to their salaries and pensions, larger houses and free medical care. Instead, those that had two or even three children were penalized through pay cuts. These coercive measures undoubtedly provoked resistance and protests among the public. Moreover, according to some historians, they also led to an increase in the number of young mothers who took their own lives. A number of studies have shown that abortion causes an increased risk of suicide, due to unresolved grief and depression, both of which are likely to be greater the more the interrupted pregnancy is caused by external pressures and the more the mother wishes to have another child (as may be the case in the countryside). But this suggested interpretation is not confirmed by existing figures.[32]

In practice, in order to answer the above question, we need to establish whether and to what extent the peculiarities of the Chinese suicide model are limited to the past few decades or whether they also existed in the past. From the mid nineteenth century onwards, many Western travellers noted that as well as being more widespread in China, suicide also presented some specific traits.

Firstly, it was more frequent in the female population than in males. Herbert Allen Giles, a British diplomat who worked in China for almost thirty years, wrote in 1876 that the 'Candidates [for suicide] are for the most part women'.[33] Twenty years later, in her travel journal, an American missionary, Adele Fielde, confessed her surprise at the frequency with which unhappy daughters-in-law killed themselves.[34] In the early twentieth century, the American sociologist Edward Alsworth Ross remarked that, unlike the situation in Western countries, female suicides in China were five to ten times more common than in males.[35] In the same period, Reginald Fleming Johnston, a Scottish sinologist who was tutor to Puyi, the last Chinese emperor, wrote that 'Over ninety per cent of the persons who make away with themselves belong to the female sex, and the great majority of them are young married women or young widows.'[36] The surviving statistical data show that these comments were well founded and that the difference between women and men used to be even greater than it is today. Up until 1930, in Chinese cities, the female population presented a much higher suicide rate than that for men, whereas today this is no longer the case in urban centres but only in the countryside (Table 6.1).[37]

Secondly, the age distribution of Chinese voluntary deaths often appears unusual to Western observers. In the mid twentieth century, an American sociologist, the author of an important study, reported that although they lacked the backing of reliable statistics, all observers agreed that in China suicide occurred very rarely among the elderly – indeed it was rare after the age of thirty-five – yet it was widespread among the young, above all among young women.[38] Also in this case, the most interesting data were those collected by the Japanese, in the first forty years of the twentieth century, in Taiwan.[39] These show that, in 1905, the suicide profile was radically different from that in Europe. In the female population, the frequency of suicide diminished with age. It was very high under the age of twenty-four and then fell rapidly in subsequent phases of life, reaching its lowest point in old age.[40] The women on this large Chinese island killed themselves more often than those in Switzerland, Denmark and France when they were between twenty and twenty-four, but much less after the age of sixty. Taiwanese men, on the other hand, took their own lives as often as in those three countries, both when they were young and in old age.[41]

Lastly, again in Taiwan, for the first half of the twentieth century at least, suicide rates were higher in rural areas than in the cities.

6.4 Old people and filial devotion

Compared to the past there has been a striking change precisely in the opposite direction to that recorded in other parts of the world. In the second half of the twentieth century, the suicide rate among the elderly diminished in many Western countries (as we have seen), while it increased in China. Therefore, in China today, and also in Hong Kong, Taiwan, Singapore, Korea and Japan, the over-sixties take their lives two to three times more frequently than in Europe, the United States, Canada or Australia.[42] This enormous change can be traced without doubt back to the radical changes that have taken place in the country's structure and family relations. If elderly Chinese people rarely killed themselves in the past (certainly less frequently, as far as we can tell, than in northern and central Europe) it was because they lived in strongly integrated domestic environments and they enjoyed the material and emotional support of many relatives. For a number of centuries, men and women married early and therefore formed large families in which the elderly couple lived with their sons, wives and grandchildren.

These households were characterized by very strong bonds between elderly parents and adult children.[43] As in many farming societies, their relations were based on reciprocity, on the idea that the father and mother would be repaid in the future by their children for all the efforts and sacrifices they had made to bring them up. Children had a strong sense of gratitude towards their parents which was expressed, not only in the material and affective support they gave them, but also in the sumptuous funeral rites that were celebrated following a father's or mother's death, and the three years of mourning that followed (the three years corresponded to the time spent as infants in their parents' arms).

Filial devotion was more important in China than elsewhere. As we shall see, this Confucian virtue was promoted by the state throughout the imperial age. Exemplary offspring were rewarded with symbolic tributes, while those who did not fulfil their moral duty to respect and help their parents incurred a variety of risks. Above all, they could be disinherited. Even when old people lacked the strength to continue working, they still retained control of the land and of their inheritance and to this extent they could decide to exclude a son if he had not behaved well. Secondly, the parents could ask the authorities to prosecute a son and he could be sentenced to strangulation even if the parents could find no evidence to bring against him (on the principle that 'no parent in the world is wrong'). Furthermore, the community was also involved in ensuring that the duty of filial devotion was respected. Indeed if a son committed parricide, not only would the murderer be beheaded, but his neighbours would be severely punished, his teacher would be sentenced to death, the local magistrate would be disgraced and lose his job, and the provincial prefect and governor would also be downgraded: in short, all would be held jointly responsible for this disgrace.[44]

The reason why elderly Chinese people now take their own lives more often is because this domestic world has in part disappeared. The method of family formation has slowly changed. It is more common for spouses to establish their own household, setting up their own home in a new place, and elderly parents are increasingly frequently left alone. Furthermore, land has lost much of its value and therefore the threat of disinheriting a son is now no longer that effective. A law of 1996 solemnly reiterated that 'Support of the elderly depends mainly upon family members who should show concern for and take care of their elders.'[45] But the bonds between the elderly and their adult children have been weakened by economic development, the emigration of the young from the countryside into the cities, and the reform of family law in 1949, which was also intended to combat filial devotion. The decline of the role of family members in the care of the elderly has not been compensated for by the growing intervention of the state and a large number of over-sixty-five-year-olds living in the rural areas of China do not have any form of pension.[46]

6.5 Suicide among Chinese women

In other respects the current Chinese model of suicide reveals striking resemblances to the past. As we saw earlier, women have had a higher suicide rate not only in the last decade of the twentieth century but at least since the second half of the nineteenth century. Several historical studies have shown that this Chinese peculiarity has even older origins and dates back to at least the seventeenth and eighteenth century.[47] The suggestion has also been put forward that three centuries ago the difference between female and male suicide rates was even greater than it is today. However, in the absence of precise and reliable statistics, we do not know whether, and to what extent, this hypothesis corresponds to reality. What is certain is that many women in China took their own lives in the seventeenth and eighteenth century and consequently female suicide became a thorny issue. The subject caused heated debate, it forced the emperor to enact decrees in an attempt to exercise some sort of control over these acts, and it prompted a large number of scholars (those expert in writing) to compose poems and novels on the events and passions that led daughters, wives, widows and concubines to take their own lives. Evocatively named women like Gold Ring, Mandarin Duck, Blue-Black Jade and Bright Cloud, who enliven the palaces, pavilions and gardens in *Dream of the Red Chamber*, the greatest eighteenth-century Chinese novel, filling these spaces with their conversations, their quarrels and their subtle perfumes, threaten to kill themselves and do kill themselves with great ease, as if the transition to the realm of the Great Void was just a straightforward step.

Perhaps the first Western testimony of this peculiar feature dates back to 1779, the year that saw the publication of a volume of texts by a large group of French Jesuits who had spent many years in China as missionaries. 'With regard to suicide', write these acute observers, 'the weaker sex have a courage and temerity that make one tremble with horror. Women and girls hang themselves merely for a word. Matters have reached a stage when the wellheads have had to be barred in order to save them.'[48]

All this leads us to suppose that the exceptionally high suicide rate among Chinese peasant women today can not only be ascribed to changes during the last thirty years in this country's economy and society, but that rather it may also depend on long-term factors. But what factors, one might ask? When he was still very young, and he had just joined the students' revolutionary associations, Mao Zedong put forward an explanation for the frequent suicides of Chinese women. Although his main intention was to seed political dissent, his theses have since enjoyed considerable support among scientific circles and, for some years, they guided the research undertaken by many scholars.

6.6 Mao Zedong and the May Fourth paradigm

Chao Wu-chieh's wedding was due to take place on 14 November 1919 when she was twenty-three. Her marriage to Wu Feng-lin had been arranged by her parents with the help of a matchmaker, but Chao refused to even countenance the idea because she had taken an intense dislike to her future husband, even though she had only met him once, for a few minutes. Yet her parents were adamant and refused either to break off the engagement or to postpone the wedding. Therefore, as was the custom, on 14 November Chao was taken in a procession to the groom's house in a sedan enclosed by red silk hangings. But when the procession arrived and the curtains were opened, her family and friends discovered that the girl had cut her throat with a razor she had managed to conceal in her garments. Although her parents feared that something like this might happen, they were amazed because before leaving home the girl had been carefully searched, precisely to avoid leaving her alone with a knife or some other dangerous weapon.[49]

Although this might sound like an ordinary story, one of many, Chao Wu-chieh's suicide immediately assumed a special importance. It struck the young Mao and inspired him to write nine impassioned articles, in quick succession, on the case of 'Miss Chao', which were read by an enormous number of people, causing heated arguments in the universities, in families and in the most well-to-do circles. In the weeks that followed, these accounts were followed by hundreds of other articles on the same topic, which appeared in the new magazines that were burgeoning at the time.[50] That this story, which ordinarily might have passed unnoticed, aroused such interest can be attributed to the fact that it took place at a moment of tremendous collective effervescence. On 4 May that year, a movement had been founded in Peking and spread rapidly to every city in the country. Today this date is regarded as a turning point in China's history and as the start of the modern period. The spark that ignited the movement was the decision taken at the Versailles conference to assign Germany's territorial possessions in Shantung to Japan. This prompted a wave of student demonstrations which were soon joined by some groups of intellectuals and sectors of the urban bourgeoisie, triggering a revolt that attacked Confucianism (which was regarded as the quintessence of Chinese tradition) and other key aspects of society, including the family and the status of women. But, over and above this new cultural environment, Mao's interest in Chao's story was also prompted by events that had affected him personally. When he was thirteen, his father had arranged for him to marry a nineteen-year-old woman. Mao made every effort to oppose this decision and, in order to convince his father, he left home, saying that he would only return when he was free to decide whom to marry and when. Mao succeeded in winning this battle of wills and some years later he married a woman with whom he had fallen in love. But the experience had convinced him of the need to abolish the old-fashioned custom of arranged marriages.

What had provoked Miss Chao's suicide? This was the question posed by Mao in his first article, published on 16 November 1919, but written just a day after the event. He had no doubts at all in pinpointing the cause: it was the environment in which this young woman lived that had prompted her to commit suicide. There were three main components that made up the environment: Chinese society, Miss Chao's own family and the family of the husband she did not want. These three factors constituted 'three iron nets', forming a kind of 'triangular cage'. If her parents had not compelled her to act against her wishes, if her future in-laws had not ignored her refusal, and if all the others, her relatives, friends and acquaintances, had not explicitly or implicitly supported these two families, Miss Chao would certainly not have died.

According to Mao, even though her parents knew that their daughter did not like the husband they had chosen for her, they wanted to compel her to marry him, to share his bed and even to love him. By doing so they committed a terrible sin, that of 'indirect rape', and therefore they were morally condemnable. But the root of this crime was society itself. In Western society there were no matchmakers and arranged marriages and such forms of parental violence were unthinkable. 'If this had been in Western society', Mao wrote, 'and Miss Chao's father had slapped her in the face when she refused to get into the sedan chair, she could have taken him to court and sued him, or she would have resisted in some way to protect herself.'[51]

Therefore Mao too, like Durkheim twenty years earlier, thought that in order to understand suicide one had to start with society. 'The reason why in society there are people who want to commit suicide is because society seizes their "hopes" and utterly destroys them, with the result that they are left "completely without hope".'[52] But in China, according to Mao, the deep-rooted causes of the impressive number of female voluntary deaths were the oppression of women by the rigid patriarchal family system, inspired and supported by neo-Confucian teaching, the custom of arranged marriages, and the superstitious belief in the doctrine of predestined marriages. If Durkheim had been able to read or hear Mao, he might have recognized in Mao's description the kind of suicide he defined as 'fatalistic' ('It is the suicide deriving from excessive regulation, that of persons with futures pitilessly blocked and passions violently choked by oppressive discipline')[53] to which he dedicated a few lines, written in a brief footnote to his magnum opus.

Following Mao's reasoning, others who joined in the debate affirmed that Chao had had the great merit of fighting against the traditional Chinese family system using the only weapon at her disposal: taking her own life. Even those who did not approve of her action were forced to recognize her as 'one who sacrificed herself to reform the marriage system'. This was why she had 'declared war on the demon of despotism', and why she did not commit suicide at home while she was still a 'regular daughter', but instead did so sitting in her bridal sedan with its red hangings that was carrying her to her fiancé.[54]

The 'May Fourth paradigm' (the term often given to Mao's proposed interpretation) has for years guided the studies of the many scholars who have attributed the high number of female voluntary deaths to the patriarchal system that, through arranged marriages and other ways, oppressed young women to the point of desperation and even suicide. This system, according to these scholars, was fostered and legitimized by the so-called neo-Confucian schools of thought that flourished in the eleventh and twelfth century, simultaneously giving rise to a host of other significant changes: the declining social status of women, the spread of foot binding – a practice that aimed to attain the aesthetic ideal of the 'golden lotus' (a tiny foot, no more than eight centimetres long) – the cult of chastity among widows, and the high number of daughters-in-law who committed suicide.[55] One of the leading theorists of Confucian doctrines, the philosopher Cheng Yi, used to say: 'To starve to death is a very small matter, but to lose one's integrity is extremely grave.'

Historical research in the last twenty years has highlighted that the May Fourth paradigm alone cannot explain why so many women killed themselves in the past in China.[56] Above all, these studies have shown that there is no correlation between the birth and development of neo-Confucianism and the suicide rate. The number of female voluntary deaths started to rise slowly in the fourteenth century, accelerated in the sixteenth – many centuries, therefore, after the establishment of these ways of thinking – and reached a peak in the seventeenth and eighteenth centuries. Secondly, historical studies have revealed that the patriarchal system and custom of arranged marriage were not the only motives for suicide among Chinese women. As we will see, they killed themselves for many other reasons, including sometimes, on the contrary, to remain faithful to the man their parents had selected for them. Therefore, they were not merely victims of an oppressive system, rather they had the ability to choose. Their voluntary death was not only or not necessarily an expression of weakness, passivity, defeat or despair. On occasions it was a passionate act of independence and self-affirmation, even a challenge.[57]

6.7 The cultural repertoire of suicides

For many centuries suicide played an extremely important role in Chinese history and culture. Buddhist catechism condemned to hell those who took their own lives for purely egoistical reasons, but acknowledged that it could be justified by 'fidelity to the sovereign, filial piety, chastity, justice, war'.[58] On the other hand, Confucius, while not approving of suicide in general, held that in some circumstances individuals should renounce life. One of his maxims states that, 'Our physical bodies, hair and skin are all gifts from our parents and cannot be shamed.' But another affirms that 'The determined scholar and the man of virtue will not seek to live at the expense of injuring their virtue. They will even sacrifice their lives to preserve their virtue complete.'[59] Liu Hsiang, author of the first Chinese collection of female biographies, praised voluntary death in women,[60] if its purpose was to save a woman's husband or as a result of his death. The historian Sima Qian, in explaining why after falling into disgrace he had preferred castration to suicide, wrote that 'even the lowest slave and scullery maid can bear to commit suicide'. Mencius, the philosopher, a great systematizer and divulger of Confucian teachings, wrote: 'I like fish and I also like bear's paw. If I cannot have both of them, I shall give up the fish and choose the bear's paw. I like life and I also like righteousness. If I cannot have both of them, I shall give up life and choose righteousness. I love life, but there is something I love more than life [. . .] I also hate death, but there is something I hate more than death.'[61] The choice of suicide is therefore justified by attainment of a higher value. This was based on the idea that not only should you make good use of life but also of death. As Sima Qian wrote, 'A man has only one death. That death may be as weighty as Mount Tai, or it may be as light as a goose feather. It all depends upon the way he uses it.'[62] If a person took his or her own life for other reasons, he or she risked being buried without regular funeral rites.[63]

Numerous forms of voluntary death were condoned, although some were regarded as nobler than others and more suited to certain roles (to fiancées, widows, debtors or generals, for instance). Suicide as a means of avoiding the indignity of public execution was reserved to, although possibly not appreciated by, high-ranking imperial officials found guilty of treason, so that they could join their ancestors with their body intact. It was usually ordered by the emperor himself who would send the official in question a sheet of gold leaf (swallowing gold was a metaphor for poisoning oneself) or a yellow silken cord so that they could take their own life.[64] Instead, a voluntary death committed for the sake of honour after a political or military failure by a man who had held a top-ranking state position was praised and honoured. This category included civil servants, generals, princes, and even the ruler himself. Indeed, as many as five of the 259 emperors who reigned between 221 BCE and 1911 took their own lives.[65] Self-immolation, which in China was reserved for Buddhist monks, began to be practised from the late fifth century in various ways and for different reasons.[66] It was usually accomplished by self-cremation, namely setting oneself on fire in public, before state officials and even the emperor. But monks sometimes used other methods, 'making a gift of themselves' by drowning, throwing themselves off a high cliff, starving themselves to death or abandoning their bodies to the birds, worms or other animals. They did so for the benefit of others, to defend their own communities or countries from invasion, war, famine, drought, floods, hunger, and sometimes also in protest.

However, suicides committed for many other reasons were also permitted and respected: as an act of loyalty to the emperor, one's parents or one's spouse; as a form of reaction to oppressive social conditions, as a means of protest or to attain justice or revenge. For a long period of time those who killed themselves for these reasons were praised and honoured by the supreme state authorities.

6.8   The state and honouring the virtuous

For almost nineteen centuries the Chinese state made every effort to promote and inculcate the 'Confucian virtues' of filial piety or devotion, righteousness, loyalty and fidelity in the population. They did so by employing large numbers of men at great expense and following the guidelines set out in a document from the third century: 'Award insignia to the virtuous, and set apart the vicious. Give honorific emblems to their houses and villages, so making illustrious the good and imposing affliction upon the evil.'[67] The virtuous were therefore rewarded in various ways: they were exempt from servile work or they were given honorific tablets to hang over their doors, noble titles, letters of commendation written by the emperor himself in his elegant calligraphy, gifts of grain and silk, and financial help to build celebratory stone arches (Plates 36–7).[68] These gifts not only came from the emperor and his court, but also from local authorities, governors, magistrates and other officials.[69]

Over this extremely long period the key features of this huge programme of honours enacted by the Chinese state changed various times, as did the definitions of the virtues themselves, the criteria used to identify and reward the virtuous, their numbers, the honours granted, and the type of behaviour deemed praiseworthy in individuals and families.[70] Only the concept of Confucian male virtue remained relatively stable: the devotion shown by sons to their parents, the loyalty of officials to their emperor, the righteousness of men within a community. For centuries, honorific tablets and commendations continued to be awarded to young people who refused to leave their father's or grandfather's tomb, or to brothers who managed to live in peace, without breaking up the family inheritance, forming huge *frèrèches* in which all the sons lived with their wives and children in the family home.[71]

As for the female virtues, Table 6.2 sets out the moral choices that faced a Chinese woman during the Ming and Qing dynasties after certain significant events: after the death of her fiancé or her husband, if she became a victim of sexual harassment or violence, or in the event of a military defeat or the collapse of a regime. The second column gives the most commonplace reaction, while the other two columns list the behaviours deemed to be virtuous and those that were rewarded by the authorities. Therefore, if her husband died, for example, the vast majority of Chinese women would remarry. But tribute was paid to those who chose to remain widows or who took their own lives in opposition to family pressure to remarry.[72] These continued to be the key female forms of behaviour that were honoured. Yet, as we have seen, the attitudes of local and national

Table 6.2 Principal moral choices of a Chinese woman following certain events
during the Ming and Qing dynasties (1368–1911).

Event	Most common choice	Virtuous actions	
		In life	Through death
Death of fiancé	Becomes engaged to another man	Remains unmarried	Takes own life
Death of husband	Remarries	Remains widow	Takes own life
Assault or sexual violence	Remains alive		Takes own life
Military defeat or fall of regime	Remains alive		Takes own life

Source: Elvin (1984); Wakeman (1985); Davis (1996); T'ien Ju-K'ang (1988); Theiss
(2004b); Lu (2008).

authorities towards these actions changed several times over the course of
this long period.

The procedures used to choose and reward the virtuous also changed
radically. To start with, imperial officials would identify those who
deserved to be honoured by gathering information in villages, and such
honours were awarded on special occasions, when a revolt was put down
or a new sovereign came to the throne. But over time the process of awarding honours became increasingly complex. Requests had to make their
way through an ever-growing web of bureaucracy, which sometimes took
many years. They also had to pass through an endless series of assemblies,
bodies, councils, committees and boards inside the vast imperial machine,
which batted petitions back and forth after carefully sifting, weigh-
ing, checking, analysing and discussing every particular. A petition was
usually submitted by the relatives of the virtuous person who requested
the assembly of village elders to bring the case to the attention of the local
magistrate, who in turn solicited the opinion of the neighbours of the
person involved. From there the petition slowly made its way through the
various levels, from prefecture up to the regional officials, and from there
to the Ministry of Rituals, which then, having examined it, sent it back
for further verification. The court of the censors was eventually informed
of the petition and it requested the opinion of other authorities. Only if
all these bodies expressed a positive judgement did the minister of ritual
finally accept the petition and even then, the process was not over. Having
reached this stage, all the petitions were passed to the emperor who examined them on a solemn occasion once a year, and some were rejected.

After this, at long last the pace of honorific recognition quickened,
becoming increasingly rapid. The number of awards and commendations
increased over the centuries, throughout the Ming (1368–1644) and Qing
(1644–1911) dynasties. In two centuries, from the mid sixteenth century

to the mid eighteenth, the emperors assigned more than 217,336 honours, 98 per cent of which were to women, in many cases widows who had refused to remarry or who had taken their lives in order to remain faithful to their husbands.[73] But many other rewards were presented to virtuous individuals by local authorities.

Therefore, for centuries, some forms of suicide were approved and encouraged through this elaborate process of assigning honours that was unparalleled in any other country or in any other period of history. Firstly, because unlike other countries that awarded medals for military and civil valour, the Chinese government recognized behaviours that were considered virtuous in private and everyday life. Secondly, because unlike the Catholic church which, for an equally long period of time, had beatified and sanctified individuals with exceptional qualities who had performed miracles or 'prodigies', the Chinese state rewarded behaviours that were regarded as normal.[74]

As we will see, although approved and encouraged socially, these forms of suicide were not committed by passive individuals who were submitting to the supreme demands of their group. Undoubtedly some were acts of deference to superiors, but others were the result of violent conflicts with the individual's family or that of her husband or fiancé, and still others were expressions of dissent, disobedience, protest and a desire for revenge.

6.9   After a husband's death

In 1498 a shrine was built in the province of Jiangsu in honour of the widow Qian who killed herself there in 1435 after her husband's death. The woman's heroic fidelity was celebrated in prose and poetry, and her name was exalted in local history. A peasant's daughter, she was given in marriage to Lu Mao and immediately began living an exemplary life as a virtuous wife, and her biographers describe her 'filially serving her parents-in-law and settling disputes between the wives of her husband's brothers'. After a while, Lu Mao became ill and when he understood that he would not live, he called his wife and said to her: 'I am ill and unlikely to leave my bed again. You are young, and we have no children. Moreover, you will be poor, with no one to depend upon. It would be permissible for you to remarry. Do not take me into account in making your decision.' Weeping, Qian answered him, saying: 'I have heard that nowhere is there a woman who can serve two husbands.' Qian's parents also started to look for another husband for her. However, when Mao died, the widow wept bitterly and prepared his funeral, then after the rituals were over, she hanged herself by the side of the corpse.[75]

The story of the widow Qian was not an isolated case. Much earlier, in the Han era (206 BCE – 220 CE), there had already been women who preferred to die rather than remarry because, as one of them wrote in verse, 'My heart is not a stone / it cannot roll / my heart is not a mat / it cannot be rolled up.'[76] But Durkheim's idea that altruistic suicide dominated primitive societies, and therefore that its importance grew the further one goes back in time, is not confirmed even in the history of China. In this country, the number of women who took their own lives after their husbands died started to rise under the Yuan dynasty (1279–1368) and rose even more rapidly during the long period of the Ming (1368–1644) and Qing (1644–1911) dynasties, to the point that in 1688, the Kangxi emperor banned the practice having expressed the concern that 'If we continue to give them honourable recognition, it is to be feared that an increasing number of lives will be cut off'. However, the decree still made it possible for a widow who wished to take her own life to request for special permission from the Ministry of Rituals.[77] Yet this ban cannot have been very effective because in 1728 the Yongzheng emperor was obliged to pass another edict to curb what he defined as acts 'outside the norms of everyday morality'. 'The heroic widow', the document continued, 'follows her husband [. . .] below the earth with a generous resolution. [. . .] It is difficult to be a heroic widow, but harder yet to be a faithful one. This is because to follow a husband in death requires only the resolve of a moment. To preserve chastity requires a perpetual regard for the husband.'[78] Choosing the latter path, the edict concluded, meant that the widow would take 'the place of a son in serving her father and mother-in-law', and take 'the place of a father in teaching and rearing her descendants', facing with courage an infinite number of everyday difficulties. But the situation was reversed again in 1851 when the Xianfeng emperor reinstated the custom of honouring widow suicides.[79]

The surviving documents have led some historians to believe that, throughout this long period, not only did the number of widow suicides increase but their nature also changed. In the Yuan period the suicide of a widow was provoked above all by strong external pressure. In 1367 when the Ming army was besieging his city, Bo Tie'mu'er led his wife and concubines onto the balcony of his house and told them: 'Now the city has fallen and I will surely die here. Can you follow me?' All the women answered in the affirmative and then hanged themselves. During the long Ming and Qing eras, a woman's decision to kill herself stemmed increasingly often from her free choice and from a strong bond of affection to her husband. Take the example of Mrs Zhang, for example, who had married a scholar at the age of eighteen. Four years later, knowing that he was close to death, her husband tried to free her from the moral obligation of following him to the tomb. But she objected, weeping: 'Do you think I have two hearts? If we had a son, I would preserve my chastity and rear him as your heir, which is the duty of any wife. Having no son, a wife's purity can only be preserved by following her husband in death.'[80]

The women who killed themselves after their husbands' death did so for two different reasons. Firstly, they wished to 'follow him in death', just as they had always followed their husbands in life, and to serve them 'below the ground' without abandoning them. Indeed, the women were convinced that they would find their spouses in the life hereafter and that they would then remain together for ever after.[81] Such women were celebrated in literature as being heroic martyrs of chastity, the personification of passion. Theirs was a 'good' death because, in addition to showing their own self-control, it also showed their absolute faithfulness and a great capacity for control over the arbitrary nature of biological events.[82] But it was also seen as a 'grand' death, one that would perpetuate the name of the woman who took her own life.[83] Indeed, it is this, in a sense, that is the meaning of the words addressed by the scholar Wang Yuhui to his wife when he heard that their daughter had killed herself as soon as she became a widow: 'Our third daughter has already become an immortal. What are you crying for? She died well, and I only wish I could die for such a good cause myself!' Thus, throwing back his head in laughter, he said: 'She died well, she died well!' Then, laughing out loud, he left the room.[84]

Some Chinese women committed suicide for their husbands even when the latter had maltreated them all their lives or was guilty of some terrible crime against others. The man that Kao married, for example, was found guilty of murder and imprisoned. He fell gravely ill and his wife went to visit him. But as soon as she was alone with him in his cell, she tried to hang herself using her foot bandages. The guards discovered her and then she took refuge in the temple of the city where, before hanging herself, she prayed: 'I wish to die as my husband is dying. His misery is my misery. How can I live on alone? My will is fixed: rather than die with him at the end, I shall be the one to go first. Only the God understands my situation.'[85]

Secondly, some widows took their own lives as a means of escaping family pressures to remarry, which came either from their parents or their in-laws for financial reasons. Second marriages were harshly judged (so much so that some scholars described them as 'a crime that deserves more than death')[86] and a widow who remarried was thought to have lost her moral integrity. For this reason, some women were willing to do anything in order not to accept another husband after their first had died. They were in full agreement with the statement of a Chinese peasant woman: 'If I remarry, how will I have the face to meet my buried husband?'[87] They therefore defended themselves using that powerfully symbolic weapon, their body. Attractive young widows would mutilate or slash their faces, cutting off nose and ears.[88] While others recalled the words of the Neo-Confucian philosopher Ch'eng Yi, 'To starve to death is a very small matter, but to lose one's integrity is extremely grave', and preferred to end their lives rather than remarry.[89]

6.10   Differences compared to *sati*

While strikingly similar, the suicide of Chinese widows was different from *sati* (although it resembled it more closely than the other forms of female voluntary death encouraged by the Chinese state). In the first place this was because of the different concepts of widowhood in India and China, its causes and consequences, and the duties incumbent on women who found themselves in this situation. In China, the mother of Wang Daomei gave her newly widowed daughter the following advice: 'Do not mourn excessively. There are three courses open to you. The first is martyrdom: to follow your husband in death. The second is fidelity: to keep yourself as pure as frost and ice, in order to serve your parents-in-law. The third is to do what ordinary people do [i. e. remarry].'[90] In exactly the same period an Indian mother might have said the same words, but she and her Chinese counterpart would not have agreed on the ideal course. In China it was certainly the second: to live as a faithful widow, not to remarry but to care for the children and her parents-in-law. In India, on the other hand, it was the first: to climb onto her husband's pyre, remaining with him forever and thus evading the terrible suspicion of being responsible for his death.

An eloquent illustration of this difference is provided by the women who killed themselves some years after their husbands' death instead of straight away. In India, as we have seen, this happened when a woman had initially chosen to live as a widow rather than commit *sati*, but when this became intolerable she eventually chose the latter. Instead in China the postponement of suicide usually occurred because women put their duty as mothers and daughters-in-law first and that of joining their husbands second. This is shown by the story of Li, for example. In some parts of China a 'minor' form of marriage was practised for a long time in which the future wife was adopted years earlier by the husband-to-be's parents. The latter took in a very young girl from another family and they raised her as their daughter until she was sixteen or seventeen when she was married to their son, with whom until then she had lived as a sister.[91] Li, too, had been adopted when she was eleven and raised by the Wu family as the future wife of their son Du. But seven years later when her fiancé was drowned in a well, Li decided to remain in the house with her intended in-laws, and she started to serve and care for them as if she were a daughter-in-law. Later she succeeded in adopting a son to whom she was a loving mother. She sent him to school and arranged his marriage. At this point she told Du's older brother, 'Your parents are now dead and in our family there are enough people to carry on the rites for them in our ancestral hall. The person in the well has waited for me a long time. I should follow him.' Then, twenty-one years after her fiancé's death, indeed on his birthday, Li drowned after throwing herself into the very same well.[92]

In the second place, Indian and Chinese widows used different methods to end their own lives. The ceremony of *sati*, with the procession, the festivities and the banquet, as well as the throngs of relatives, women friends and onlookers, and, above all, the presence of Brahmin priests, underlined the absolute dependency of these women on the community. On the contrary, Chinese women usually killed themselves in complete solitude and out of sight,[93] throwing themselves into wells or rivers, or into the sea, cutting their throat or swallowing gold leaf to cause asphyxia, or poisoning themselves with raw opium.[94] The use of opium was so widespread that the number of women committing suicide varied, during the course of the year and from one year to the next, depending on the supply of this substance. 'When the opium is harvested', wrote Edward Alsworth Ross in 1912, 'there is a crop of female suicides'.[95] And when the opium price rose, then fewer women took their lives. 'When suicide costs as much as ten cents, it is a luxury that few can afford. In a province where a servant gets eighty cents a month [. . .], this is not to be wondered at.'[96]

It was only in some parts of the country that women committed suicide in public, in the presence of others and following two profoundly different rituals. The first was called *tat'ai* ('to put up a platform') and was celebrated almost exclusively in Fujian, on the southeastern coast of China, by fewer than a fifth of those women who took their own lives. The second, which was even less frequent, was instead used in Huichou and a few other areas and involved abstaining from food and drink.[97] The first method most closely resembled *sati*, while the latter had a greater affinity with other forms of suicide.

The rite of *tat'ai* was celebrated in Fujian from the mid sixteenth to the mid eighteenth century.[98] It took place on a large wooden platform, which was built for the purpose not far from the woman's house. According to descriptions left by some Western missionaries[99] in the second half of the nineteenth century, when a widow decided to follow her husband or fiancé into the tomb, she chose the date of the ceremony in agreement with her family and then announced her intentions to others, either orally or in writing, and invited all those who were interested in witnessing the act to attend. On the morning of the appointed day, wearing a dress suited to a great ceremonial occasion, she was carried in a sedan by four men to a temple built to commemorate virtuous widows and there she burnt incense before votive tablets.

A few hours later she was accompanied to the place where the platform had been built, and after mounting onto it, she and some female relatives enjoyed a repast prepared for her at a table. Then a child in arms was set on the table and she proceeded to caress and adorn the infant with a necklace taken from around her own neck. After this she gave a short address thanking those who had accepted her invitation and were gathered around the platform, and she threw rice, herbs and flowers among the crowd. Then she walked towards a wooden beam over which a red rope was suspended. With complete self-possession and devoid of emotion, she placed the noose around her neck, covered her head with a handkerchief, and stepped off the stool onto which she had climbed.

Sometimes, however, the rite of *tat'ai* was transformed from a form of submission to the community into an act that challenged its rules, a way to influence the decisions taken by its leaders. For example, in 1854 widow Chang was asked for the sum of twenty thousand bronze coins in order to house the honorary tablets dedicated to her parents-in-law in the ancestral hall. For her this was an enormously important honour, but because she was poor and did not have a sum of this nature, she had fixed the date for her voluntary death on the platform. Having heard the news, the provincial magistrate succeeded in raising the necessary funds and convincing widow Chang to go back on her decision.[100]

The second ritual was radically different from *sati* and *tat'ai*, and was only practised in some areas of China. It took the form of suicide by starvation, a long and agonizing death. Those women who chose this method refused to eat and drink, and often took between five and seventeen days to die. A few remained alive for more than forty days, probably because they continued to drink water. The agony of starving to death was horrendous. The prospect of such suffering also explained why some women who had started to fast subsequently gave it up and took their lives either with opium or by throwing themselves into a well.

Unlike hanging, drowning or poisoning, the effects of fasting were not immediate and this enabled those who had embarked on this course of action to interact with others, asking favours and negotiating and obtaining concessions. The key lever exercised by the woman who was gradually fading, hour by hour, consisted in confronting others with the dilemma of either negotiating and accepting some of her requests or resigning themselves to being responsible for her death. It is often thought that hunger strike is a form of political struggle, undertaken in order to attain improved circumstances (e.g. a better cell) or as an act of protest in favour of a worthy cause. Instead it is clear that the Chinese women (and others as well) who used this form of suicide inside the domestic sphere, following their husband's or their fiancé's death, did so to attain private goals, such as being granted an adopted child, if they had not had any of their own, or better living and working conditions in their parents-in-law's home where they would continue to reside.

6.11   Following the death of a fiancé

Thirteenth-century China saw the start of a new phenomenon: it took the form of young women who remained faithful to their fiancé in the event of their death before the day of the appointed marriage by refusing to take another partner. Initially described as 'faithful maidens' (*Zhennü*),[101] they also became known as 'betrothed wives' or 'betrothed widows', even 'wives who are not yet married'. They grew rapidly in number over the next few centuries, particularly in the seventeenth and eighteenth centuries, reaching a peak in the first half of the nineteenth century. This custom was found all over China, but it was more widespread in southern regions where a developed economy was accompanied by a higher level of education among the population.

A woman who decided to become a 'faithful maiden' under the Ming and Qing dynasties could take one of three courses of action: remain in her parents' home and care for them, move to the family home of her ex-fiancé, or take her own life.

Her entrance into the dead man's family sometimes happened without ceremony, but more frequently it was celebrated with a marriage 'in spirit' with the deceased. The rites for this new type of union were gradually introduced after the sixteenth century. As far as possible, these imitated the traditional marriage rite. For example, the faithful fiancée was carried to the house of the new family in a sedan chair. But in other aspects, these rites were created *ex novo*. The participants began to dress in mourning and the use of music and brightly coloured decorations was abandoned. Such was the atmosphere, half funeral half wedding, in which the young woman took her marriage vows with the effigy of the man to whom she had been betrothed (Plate 42).

As she performed these rites, the young woman changed status radically in the space of a few hours. After years of betrothal, she at last attained the ardently desired position of wife, only to lose it immediately by becoming a widow for the remainder of her life. In spite of this, as part of her new family, she sometimes managed to achieve another longed-for ambition: having a child. Without a husband, she could become a 'chaste mother' and adopt a son of her late husband's brother or cousin or even a child of another relative.

If she decided then to take her own life, the faithful maiden, in Fujian above all, would follow the rite of *tat'ai* (as a widow) or, more frequently, that of *benxun*, by announcing her suicide in public but executing it in private. Having decided to take her own life, the young woman would usually bid farewell to her parents and her family, gathered together for the occasion, and would then go to her late fiancé's house to hang herself in his bedroom after celebrating a number of rites. In the rest of China, on the other hand, these women killed themselves in private, escaping the watchful eyes of family and friends to throw themselves in a well or river, or to swallow poison (Plates 40–1). They frequently wore a bridal dress, as well as the white garments worn at funerals or while mourning a family member. Before killing themselves, they would decide what to do with their dowry, their clothing, shoes, household linen and the embroideries sewn with such care for many years. Some left these to relatives or women friends, while others ripped them to pieces and burned them as a token of their conviction. Occasionally, the actual suicide weapon was a betrothal gift received from their fiancé. In addition, if the woman was from an educated background, she often composed a poem. Yuan Shuxiu, for example, had been given a gold ring and a jade mirror, and she took her own life by ingesting the former (probably a metaphor for poison) and recalling the latter with sorrow in the verses she left to her parents:

[I die] in order to keep the promise of the golden ring,
How sad is my feeling toward the jade mirror!
Not ashamed, facing the ring and the mirror,
I only feel my body is light.[102]

This practice, too, also began among the more educated families, or even at the imperial court. For example, in 1426, a young woman called Kuo hanged herself at the age of nineteen following the death of her betrothed, one of the nephews of the thirty-third son of the emperor. Seven years later, another of the emperor's nephews wrote a play that was inspired by this event, which for centuries has continued to move Chinese audiences, men and women alike.[103] Over time, this practice spread to the middle and lower strata of society.[104]

These faithful maidens soon became the focus of a cult. The court started by awarding official recognition to young women who remained with their natal families or entered those of their betrothed. But from 1430 awards were also conferred on those who took their own lives. It was established that, in order to attain this recognition, the women had to remain chaste until they were fifty and that their fiancé had to have died before they were thirty. The cult became firmly established from the mid sixteenth century and acquired growing importance in the following two centuries.

Scholars wrote biographies and poetry to commemorate these faithful maidens, recounting their deeds and virtues. Moreover, arches, tombs and shrines were also erected so that their heroic actions could set an example for the rest of the population,[105] and members of the public would meet there to celebrate these women. The shrines were often very large, and contained a statue of the faithful maiden; a pine tree was planted at each of the four corners to symbolize nobility and strength of character, and to embody the heroic spirit of these women.[106]

The conferment of honours to these faithful maidens certainly helped to spread this custom. However, it does not follow that these young women were merely passive beings, victims of Confucian ideology, and wholly subordinate to the demands and requirements of the groups to which they belonged. Instead, in practice, in order to affirm their status as faithful maidens they went against the wishes of their families, sometimes even the entire extended family, and they were obliged to defend their views with considerable stubbornness. Unlike our modern expectations, they did not fight against marriages arranged by relatives and matchmakers, but instead they wished to respect the choice that others had made for them by remaining loyal to the man whom they would have married.

The request to remain unmarried stemmed from the young women themselves and almost always was met with fierce opposition from both their own family and that of their former fiancé. Like all Chinese at the time, parents believed that a woman was predestined for marriage and that, without a husband, their daughter's life would be incomplete and she would be eternally unhappy. Moreover, they found the new custom unacceptable because they were accustomed to the idea that a woman could become a widow, and remain loyal to her husband's memory, only if she had married. On the other hand, the parents and brothers of the deceased fiancé usually believed that the arrival of a faithful maiden among their family would give rise to a series of problems. Without a husband, who traditionally played the role of intermediary, the newcomer might easily come into conflict with other women in the household. This conflict would only become more accentuated if she then adopted a son because this would give her the right to inherit part of her new family's property and wealth.

For all these reasons, a young woman's decision to remain unmarried marked the start of a period of disagreement, resulting in tussles, negotiations and clashes between her and her relatives. Even though filial devotion was one of the more widely respected and practised moral obligations at the time, and even though parents would use every possible means to arrange a new betrothal for their daughter, the latter defended her intentions with a strength and obstinacy that are hard to imagine today. If she realized that arguments were useless, then she would resort to expressing her volition through her body. This gave rise to those acts of disfigurement which, in Confucian tradition, were used to reinforce an oath or a solemn promise: she cut off her ears, her fingers, or her hair (Plates 38–9). Or she might have used a completely new form of pressure, one that was indeed introduced into the cultural repertoire by these faithful maidens, namely tattooing. One faithful maiden, for example, tattooed four characters on her face in order to offer a clamorous message to outsiders: 'My heart will not change.'[107] Finally, if all this did not suffice, the young woman would escape the clutches of her relatives by taking her own life.

A major motive for this decisive wish to remain faithful after the death of a fiancé and loyal to the betrothal promise was the Chinese custom of arranging marriages while the couple were still very young, often when both were still children, sometimes as young as three or four years old. Many years therefore passed between betrothal and marriage and during this time the young couple gradually came to see themselves as husband and wife. In many cases, even though these arrangements were decided by others, they were also attracted by and felt affection for one another.

This custom can be traced back as early as the Song dynasty (960–1279). At that time finding a marriage partner for one's children was regarded as such an immensely important and complex duty that parents started looking for potential spouses very early on, sometimes even before their son or daughter was born. Moreover, arranging an early engagement was seen as a sign of the strength of the ties between two families.[108] Throughout the lengthy Ming and Qing dynasties, this custom spread even more widely among Chinese families.[109]

6.12 A way of not submitting to enemies

Violent social and political upheavals, like wars, revolts, revolutions, collective movements and the fall of dynasties often produced a spike in the number of suicides in China. This happened not only, as we have seen, in the transition to the Communist regime in 1949 and in subsequent years,[110] or during the Cultural Revolution of 1966–76, but also well before. An early example, during the years 1275–9, was when the Mongols led by Genghis Khan invaded China and overthrew the Song dynasty. According to some contemporary sources, as many as one hundred thousand people died defending the fatherland, many of them (between one third and half) as suicides.[111] The final assault on the city of Tanzhou (now Changsha) resulted in mass suicides: 'No wells in the city were empty of human corpses, while strangled bodies hung in dense clusters from the trees.'[112] It is possible that these accounts were exaggerated.[113] Yet, it is clear that the arrival of the Mongols prompted many Chinese to take their own lives. Analogous events occurred in 1644, when the Manchu, a semi-nomadic people, occupied Peking and China.

In April that year, when the Chongzhen emperor realized that defeat was inevitable, he ordered that his heir and his younger brother be removed to a place of safety and, when bidding them farewell, he said to them: 'If your lives should be spared, remember in time to come to avenge the wrongs which your parents have suffered.'[114] Then he commanded wine to be brought and drank a considerable quantity before summoning the empress and the concubines. He addressed them, saying: 'All is over. It is time for you to die.' The senior concubine tried to escape but he killed her with his sword. The empress fled to her Palace of Feminine Tranquillity and hanged herself. Then the emperor proceeded to slaughter his daughters.

At five in the morning, as dawn was breaking, he changed his clothing and donned a short dragon-embroidered tunic and a robe of purple and yellow. With his left foot bare as a sign of humility, he left the palace and climbed the hill. After gazing sorrowfully at his city, he wrote on the lapel of his robe:[115] 'I, feeble and of small virtue, have offended against Heaven; the rebels have seized my capital because my ministers deceived me. Ashamed to face my ancestors, I die. Removing my imperial cap and with my hair dishevelled about my face, I leave to the rebels the dismemberment of my body. Let them not harm my people!'[116] Then he hanged himself, but not before some two hundred women of the imperial palace had committed suicide.

There are numerous reasons for the rise in voluntary deaths during times of violent social and political unrest. In the first place, officials thought it their duty to remain loyal to the emperor and suicide provided a heroic demonstration of this moral obligation as well as a refusal to serve the new ruler. In 1275, while the Mongols were conquering China, an official, Jiang Wanli, affirmed: 'I must still live or die with the empire.' Then he threw himself into a pond, followed by his son, other relatives and numerous other associates; their corpses were so numerous as to appear 'like a pile of stones'.[117] In 1644, on hearing that the Manchu were approaching, another official, Han Mo, said: 'I have read the writings of the sages and I should die to preserve righteousness. One cannot live one's life in carelessness, seeking only for the self';[118] after which he threw himself into a well, followed by his wife and eldest son.

In the second place, it was thought that, in the event of a war, invasion or rebellion, women were obliged to take their own lives in order not to submit to their captors or to marauders, and in order to defend their chastity.[119] In 1275, just before the Mongols reached Kaifeng, hundreds of the emperor's courtesans drowned themselves, together with their maidservants, for fear of being raped or ending up in the harem of some foreign ruler.[120] During the Ming dynasty (1368–1644), many women took their own lives, sometimes alone, sometimes in groups, as a way of resisting invaders. Before doing so, some of those who came from the educated elite wrote poems, on paper, cloth, walls, even cliff faces, preceded by short autobiographical introductions providing details concerning the circumstances; these writings set out the reasons for their action, thereby demonstrating to the writers themselves and to others an ability to confront the situation and make a choice (Plate 43).[121] 'Chastity', said the wife of You Quan, addressing her daughter, 'is the most important part of being a good wife. Faced with calamity, a good wife has two choices: water or metal. Remember this!' Or, as Lady Zhao observed: 'If bandits come and I do not die, I am not faithful; if I do not die at the appropriate time, I lack righteousness.'[122] Likewise in the 1640s, the rebellion of Li Tzu-ch'eng, who for years rampaged through the countryside leading an army of bandits, caused a great number of women to commit suicide,[123] before forcing the last Ming emperor to hang himself.

The overriding fear that prompted many women to make this choice was that they would lose their honour. As Lady Ye put it, 'Even if I were to survive, the judgements that would be made about me make death better.'[124] It was a concern shared by men, because the marital fidelity of a woman to her husband and the political loyalty of a man to his ruler were closely intertwined virtues.[125] The old saying that 'loyal ministers do not serve two sovereigns and faithful wives do not serve two husbands' neatly summed up the idea of this profound connection. Both Chen and Zhu drew inspiration from this, when they took their own lives as the Mongols entered Kaifeng in 1275, leaving behind a short note in which they wrote:

We did not disgrace the empire
And fortunately have been spared personal disgrace [. . .]
We humble women die
To preserve a solitary chastity.[126]

6.13   After assault and sexual violence

On the evening of 26 February 1736 Mrs Lin was alone in the house. Her brother-in-law and his wife had gone to see the 'lantern festival' and her husband had been absent for months, because he had found a job in a distant city. She was busy with a number of chores at home when Han Zhifu, a thirty-one-year-old wine merchant whom she had known for some time, visited her on a pretext and made her an indecent proposal. Lin started screaming and immediately chased him out of the house. An hour later, still in a state of agitation, she told her brother-in-law all that had happened and begged him to ask Zhifu for an explanation. But, in addition to denying the facts, the wine merchant added that, after the woman's husband had left, she had given daily proof that she did not know how to behave correctly. Two days later, Mrs Lin hanged herself from the front door of her home.[127]

Thousands of young Chinese women reacted in the same way to similar situations during this period. Mrs Chen took her own life because a neighbour, finding her alone, had touched her leg. Mrs Yu killed herself because a Taoist priest from her village had placed his hand on her breast. Another woman known as Chen, a widow of ten years with two daughters, followed the same course of action because a neighbour had offered to pay her a monthly sum if she became his lover.[128] Such acts appear inexplicable to a Western reader today. Even an analysis of the events that preceded them, the story of these women's lives, does not reveal much more. Take the case of Mrs Lin, for example. Although she was only twenty-four, she was already on her second marriage, and moreover her husband was fifteen years her senior and certainly not well off. It is probable therefore that she was weak and insecure, and that she would fear being gossiped about more than other women. But is this really enough to explain her suicide?

According to a moral custom dating back to the Yuan dynasty, if a woman was touched, on any part of her body, by a man who was not her husband, she was regarded as dishonoured and obliged to take her own life.[129] Given that this was the case, the results of one of the most rigorous and wide-ranging studies yet carried out may seem surprising. These results show that, in the eighteenth century, the probability that a Chinese woman might kill herself if she became the victim of sexual assault was higher in those cases where the aggression was less serious.[130] Based on these results, women who were raped took their own lives in 15 per cent of cases where their assailant was condemned. Moreover, those women who did take this course of action had usually been raped in illegal circumstances or embarrassing situations (when they were stealing, for example). Yet the quota of women committing suicide rose to 44 per cent if they had undergone attempted (but unsuccessful) rape, and approached 60 per cent in the event of sexual harassment. In the latter two groups, many of those who did not choose suicide were revenged by their husband or brother killing their attacker.

When sexually attacked or harassed, a woman immediately turned to her closest relatives, her husband, her brothers-in-law and her mother-in-law, and in between copious tears and outbursts of anger, she told them exactly what had happened. The family members listened to her very carefully, they minimized and set the events in context, and consoled her. But, often, this was not enough:

> I came home in the evening and my mother and wife told me that [the neighbor] had come over and caressed my wife's shoulder to flirt with her. My wife screamed and he ran off. Because this was a matter concerning face, I comforted my wife and did not speak about it. My wife said she had been humiliated by [him] and could no longer be human. My mother and I repeatedly consoled her, but my wife only wept and wailed. My mother was afraid she would kill herself and kept watch over her at home. [A few days later] I thought my wife's fury had subsided and went out to plow . . . . In the afternoon I came home . . . and to my surprise my wife had hanged herself from a beam.[131]

A group of gifted female historians[132] have luckily put forward a number of interpretative schemas to clarify and explain such initially obscure data and facts, like those mentioned above. It is clear that, also in the eighteenth century, there were women in China who were willing to have pre-marital and extramarital sexual relations under particular conditions. But many others had absorbed the values of chastity and fidelity so profoundly that they regarded any form of aggression or sexual harassment as a terrible threat to their honour. For them, the most important thing was to demonstrate that they had been unwilling victims of such attacks. Paradoxically, this was most easily achieved when a woman was raped or injured. Instead, it became more complicated in the case of attempted rape, or if she was touched, caressed or received an indecent proposal. In the absence of witnesses, her word was equal to that of her assailant and it was not always simple to establish whether the latter's actions were truly unlawful. As one observer wrote at the time, 'the expression "proposition" refers to many things: sometimes verbal hints, sometimes eye signals, sometimes jokes, sometimes obscene comments'.[133]

The victims of sexual assault therefore immediately sought out their relatives not just to vent their outrage or seek emotional support but instead, and above all, because they wished to dispel any doubt regarding their honesty. They besought their husband, or another man in the family, to do everything possible to achieve this aim by reporting the assailant to the magistrate or obtaining from him an informal promise of public apology. But in many cases, these women were unable to obtain the sort of help they needed from their family. Fearing loss of face in the event that rumours might start to circulate, the woman's husband, her brothers-in-law and father-in-law would try to convince the poor woman that nothing serious had happened and that the best thing would be to calm down and forget it. It was this that prompted some women to take their own lives.

Take the case of Mrs Liu, for example.[134] One of her husband's workmates came to visit her one evening, knowing that she was alone.

Once inside the house, there was the usual scene. He paid Mrs Liu a few compliments and then tried to embrace her. She started to scream and wriggled out of his clasp. On hearing her husband's footsteps, the man fled, leaving his hat. A few hours later, another work companion dropped by to visit the couple, and having heard what had happened, persuaded the husband to ignore the episode on the grounds that, if the news spread, then everyone would lose face. However, the following day, when she was at the well, where all the village women went to draw water and to gossip about local affairs, passing judgement on all the villagers' comings and goings, Mrs Liu met Mrs Wang, the wife of the man who had pestered her. They started to talk and Mrs Wang joked in an easy manner about what had happened the previous evening. But Mrs Liu concluded that her honour and chastity were in doubt and she went home and hanged herself.

The decision taken by Mrs Liu and thousands of other Chinese women like her was not impulsive or irrational, but rather the product of despair and also the certainty of having forever lost her honour. Indeed, it was a premeditated act, the last and only possible option that would preserve or even increase and add lustre to that honour. 'He humiliated me like this, but you are not willing to express outrage on my behalf. I can only take the path of seeking death',[135] said these sexually harassed women to their reluctant husbands, fully aware that this was the only way of resisting and, at the same time, passing to the counterattack in order to defend themselves and torment their attacker. These women knew well that the decision to take their own lives would have four enormously important consequences.

Above all it would banish any doubts concerning the woman's honesty and faithfulness to her husband. Anyone who had questioned her moral conduct, even if only fleetingly, would be forced to reconsider. The woman's lifeless body would finally provide the judge, and all the villagers, with definitive proof of her innocence.

Secondly, it would set in train a lengthy court process, usually resulting in the punishment of the aggressor. A decree issued in 1773 by the Yongzheng emperor stated that if a woman took her own life because she had been the victim of rape or even sexual harassment, the man responsible would be sentenced to strangulation immediately after the assizes. On the other hand, statutes that were approved seven years later established that if a woman had committed suicide because she was insulted by the obscene utterances of some 'ignorant peasant' (even if he had had no intention of sexually assaulting her), the latter would be sentenced to receive one hundred strokes of the heavy bamboo, life exile and payment of a fine of three thousand *li*.[136] Moreover, according to the criminal code that remained in force until the early twentieth century, a rapist would be condemned to death even if the person committing suicide was the husband, father, mother or some other relative of the woman who had been attacked. The sentence was less severe in the event that the woman was not 'chaste', in other words if she was found guilty of adultery.[137]

As a way of explicitly indicating and accusing the person responsible for their suicide, Chinese women often killed themselves in an individual's presence or inside or in front of his house. Mrs Chen cut her throat before Ning Si, the neighbour who had stroked her leg. Mrs Yuan hanged herself by night in the doorway of Zhao Cui, an acquaintance who had attempted to have sex with her.[138] Mrs Gao Wang Shi threw herself into her nephew's well after he had spoken disrespectfully to her. Su Li Shi killed herself by violently hitting her head against a beam in the house of the man who had touched her hand and made her an indecent proposal.[139]

Thirdly, by turning herself into a phantom presence, the woman who had committed suicide could continue for years, indeed for the rest of his life, to torment the man who had forced her to take this step, as well as all those who had cast doubts on her chastity. According to a popular Chinese saying, the soul of a person who had been killed unjustly could return to earth as a vengeful ghost.[140] The phantom was thought to be particularly powerful if it appeared dressed in red and therefore some women would dress in clothing of this colour before hanging themselves.[141] Originally, these beliefs concerned above all those who had been assassinated, but over time they included suicides. In particular, these beliefs were spread and reinforced by theatrical plays which repeatedly staged the stories of women who had taken their own lives and then returned in spirit form to avenge themselves against the man or persons who had forced them into taking this action.[142]

Fourthly, in 1733, the Yongzheng emperor enacted a series of laws that announced the possibility of attributing honours, or canonization, to women who killed themselves as a result of rape or attempted rape, or because they had been harassed with obscene propositions, dirty jokes or vulgar gestures. Therefore, the daughters, wives or widows who committed suicide for these reasons were all deemed eligible and their families and descendants derived great prestige, while the assailant's family were discredited.

6.14   Against arranged marriages

In some parts of China, women committed suicide as a way of rejecting an arranged marriage over a century before the start of the May Fourth movement. This was particularly true in the province of Kwantung, where for many years families were formed using the custom known as delayed transfer marriage.[143] According to this custom, the bride was separated from her husband on the third day after the wedding and would remain with her parents for at least three years (often longer). During this period, she was expected to visit her husband and his family three or four times a year, on feast days and for celebrations. At the end of this period, she then transferred to her husband's house and became his resident spouse.

During this period of transition, the woman remained a sort of bride–daughter, still under her own parents' authority. She lived with them, ate with them, obeyed and worked for them, as well as giving them most of what she earned. She only saw the man she had married a few times each year, and she was only permitted to have sexual relations with him on those occasions. She was expected to take care not to become pregnant. On her visits to see her husband and her parents-in-law, she would only eat the food she brought from home, refusing anything that had been made by her mother-in-law. She cooked for herself and ate alone. If she accepted to eat at the same table as her husband and his relatives, the separation period would end, making her a resident spouse and wife, subject to the authority of her husband and his mother.

This transition often took place when the woman became pregnant, preferably during the last month of her pregnancy. But other factors, usually of an economic kind, could influence the length of separation. Sometimes, the husband's parents asked for the period to be shortened, while the wife's parents, or even the wife herself, would try to extend it. In some cases, when a bride–daughter was forced to join her husband's family earlier than expected, she might take revenge by killing herself and her parents would then ask the in-laws for compensation.[144] On other occasions, the bride–daughter herself raised objections to the custom and refused to move, threatening to commit suicide if she was forced to do so. Because the marriage had been arranged, the husband she was obliged to visit three or four times a year was therefore a stranger, one whom she found in her bed for a few hours and whom she often despised and disliked.

Emotional bonds were often formed among girls who had to undergo this experience as young women. They would all spend time at a 'girls' house', a large building belonging to one of the families, which was only found in Kwantung, the province where this custom prevailed. The girls would meet there in the evening, after dinner, in groups of six or seven, and for a few hours they would play, sing, tell stories and talk. They would talk about everything, and in particular they swapped tales about the countless attempts at matchmaking undertaken by parents on behalf of their elder siblings or acquaintances. A few years later, when they too found themselves the focus of such plans, some of them would band together forming anti-marital alliances or planning to resist settling with their husbands' families. Given that there was often no way out, these bonds might even lead to group suicides. The young women would wear their finest clothes, whether marriage or ceremonial gowns, and then throw themselves into the nearest river, in groups of eight, ten or twelve, holding hands or binding themselves closely together.[145]

6.15 The origin of the changes

The pattern of female suicide in China's long history, its slow rise during the fourteenth century followed by the steeper increase that began in the sixteenth century and peaked in the next two centuries, can be attributed to a plethora of factors. These include the frequency of wars, rebellions and invasions, not to mention widespread banditry and raids; and also the growing social and geographical mobility of the male population, which in the seventeenth and eighteenth century meant that many husbands spent long periods away from home, leaving their wives alone and unprotected. None of these factors, however, would have caused an increase in voluntary deaths in a different cultural context (such as Europe, for example). Instead the most important factor affecting this pattern can be identified as the changes to values and norms regarding women, the roles they played at different stages of life, as daughters, fiancées, wives, concubines, mothers and widows, and the significance attributed to their actions.

Up until the thirteenth century, the most prized female virtue, and the one most frequently rewarded in the honorific system devised by the Chinese state, was filial devotion to one's parents. Chastity (which for a widow meant taking her own life or at least not remarrying) was less important, especially in comparison to the much greater status it would assume in later centuries. This depended on the method of family formation, the system of family ties and the laws of inheritance that had been dominant until then, which allowed a woman to maintain strong bonds with her own parents even after marriage. After marrying, the two spouses would often follow the practice of neolocal residence by setting up their own home. The wife would remain the lifelong owner of any goods that formed part of her dowry, even after her husband's death or in the event of divorce, and also if she remarried. There was no law forbidding remarriage and therefore widows would frequently return to their parental home where efforts would be made to arrange another marriage.[146]

Profound changes occurred in the following centuries. The first can be dated to between 1260 and 1320, during the period following the Mongol conquest. Still heavily dependent on nomadism and a pastoral economy, the conquerors had a system of family formation and inheritance that was quite different from that in the society they had vanquished. According to Mongol tradition, marriage marked the definitive transition of a woman from her natal family to that of her husband, in exchange for a compensatory payment made by the latter to the former. The bride owned no goods, and if her husband died, she was obliged to remain within her husband's family and marry one of her brothers-in-law (according to the custom of levirate marriage).

As soon as they took power, the Mongols started to alter the customs and institutions of the peoples they now ruled over and in 1271 they introduced the obligation of levirate marriage for all widows. This met with strong resistance among the Chinese who were accustomed to regarding the marriage of a widow and her brother-in-law as a form of incest. A statute that was passed five years later tried to overcome this resistance by permitting a woman to avoid the obligation of levirate if she remained 'chaste', namely if she did not remarry and continued to live with her in-laws. Other laws enacted in the early fourteenth century introduced even more radical changes by stating that widows had no further rights to their dowry and that they would lose all their possessions if they remarried.

Together with many other social transformations and new ideals, the laws promulgated during the Mongol domination encouraged the development, at first slowly and then with increasing rapidity, of the cult of female chastity that would culminate some three or four centuries later, in the seventeenth and eighteenth centuries. A sign of this change can be found in the criteria established to identify and reward, using the methods described earlier, chaste widows who refused to remarry and continued to live with the parents of their late husband. To start with, in order to be considered for honorificence, these women had to have been widowed prior to the age of thirty and could not remarry, at least until they were fifty. After 1723, it was only necessary to have remained faithful to their husband's memory for fifteen years, and in later years the limit was further reduced to ten.[147]

The cult of chastity that burgeoned in China under the Ming and Qing dynasties focused on two female virtues, which should be kept quite separate in any analysis.[148] The first virtue (purity, termed *jie*) referred to absolute fidelity to one husband. A woman was pure if she followed the maxim, 'loyal ministers do not serve two sovereigns and faithful wives do not serve two husbands',[149] and if she refused to remarry and continued to show great devotion to her in-laws even after her husband had died. The second was heroism or the willingness to face martyrdom (*lie*), namely a commitment to fidelity and sexual purity that was ready to contemplate self-sacrifice ending in death.

Clashes sometimes emerged between these two aspects of the cult of chastity, due to the differing importance assumed, on the one hand, by the married couple and the bride's 'romantic devotion' to her husband; and on the other hand, by the patrilineal family, comprised of the husband's parents and brothers, and their interest in benefiting from the widow's work. The prevalence of the first of these alternatives corresponded with the triumph of heroism, while the latter coincided with the refusal of a second marriage and devotion to her parents-in-law and brothers-in-law.[150]

The nature of this conflict is well illustrated by the story of Zeng Rulan, a woman who, in the early eighteenth century, was widowed after twelve years of marriage. Because she had no children and had promised her husband that she would follow him to the grave, she tried, unsuccessfully, to hang herself twice. At this point, her father-in-law, a widower, bade her to desist, but instead of obeying him Zeng Rulan turned to the county magistrate for information on how to behave. The magistrate replied that she should take her husband's place in fulfilling the obligations of filial devotion by caring for her father-in-law and adopting a son. The widow complied with his instructions and chose an heir, taking him into her home and working day and night for the family. But some years later she again submitted a petition to the county magistrate: 'Though my husband is dead, his brothers are able to care for [their father]. An heir has been adopted, so he also has a son. I previously vowed to follow my husband by committing suicide, and I shall go smilingly into the darkness. Were I to be unfaithful to my earlier words, how could I look my husband in the face when I go below the ground? I beseech you [to grant me permission] as an especial kindness.' Once again, however, the magistrate replied that her overriding duty was to dedicate herself to the family that she had joined through marriage, and to care for her father-in-law and his adopted son. Zeng Rulan again complied with the wishes of the authorities. Yet, three years later, after her father-in-law had died, she at last carried out her promise and killed herself after writing a poem on white paper.[151]

As the cult of chastity spread, violence became 'integral to notions of femininity and female virtue for the first time in Chinese history'.[152] The outstanding importance of the ideal of chastity was accompanied by a tendency to attribute growing emphasis to the 'bodily nature' of women's social responsibilities and to the physical suffering these entailed. From early childhood, at the age of six or seven, a Chinese girl became accustomed to this pain and suffering when, in the first major rite of passage, her feet would be tightly bound by her mother, drawing her toes as close as possible to her heel in order to achieve the aesthetic ideal of the 'golden lotus'. The girl would therefore be subjected to constant torment which would have to be endured for a long time. But Chinese women also had to deal with pain and violence on many other occasions: at work, or in childbirth. Or, as we have seen, if she lost her fiancé or her husband, if she was threatened by bandits or by rebels, or if she was shamed by sexual harassment, insult or violence. And in these last cases, in order to retain her virtue, she was constrained to use violence on herself and take her own life.

6.16   Against oneself and others

It is only by starting from the idea that the significance of suicide varies over space and time, from country to country and from period to period, that we can understand why, for many centuries, women took their own lives more often than men in China. Over thirty years ago, in a work that is now regarded as a classic, an American sinologist, Margery Wolf, observed that when suddenly faced with a case of suicide, Westerners and Chinese people react by asking completely different questions of themselves and of others. In the West, we tend to ask 'Why?' and look for a cause in some dramatic event and in the victim's state of mind; in China the question is more commonly 'Who? Who drove her to this? Who is responsible?',[153] thereby prompting the search for a guilty party.

For centuries in China, suicide was not only a desperate act but a choice made for or against someone. For centuries, women killed themselves not only to remain chaste and loyal to their husband, if the latter was still alive, or if he died or was defeated in war, or to follow their parents to the tomb, but also to protest or take revenge. For centuries, ending one's own life was the most 'damning public accusation'[154] a woman could make against her mother-in-law, her husband, her sons or some other relative. It was an accusation that others would always take seriously and which had extremely high moral and economic costs for the person singled out as being responsible. In extreme cases, these costs were so high that they could provoke another suicide. 'There was one woman in our village', wrote a person living in southern China at the end of the nineteenth century, 'whose daughter-in-law hanged herself and when the mother-in-law came in and found her thus, fearing the demands that could be made upon her by the girl's parents, she got another rope and hanged herself beside her daughter-in-law. There could then be no exactions by the friends of either party, for each had harmed the other to the same degree.'[155]

During the nineteenth and twentieth centuries, Western travellers and observers constantly stressed the exceptional importance that revenge had always had in China. Some scholars have recently attributed this peculiarity to the differences between Confucian ethics, which regarded vendetta as a duty to which the offended individuals and families were beholden, and Christian morality, which instead demanded forgiveness of the offenders.[156] These studies have also highlighted how, in China, some acts of revenge were allowed or even encouraged by laws enacted during the Ming and Qing dynasties (between 1368 and 1911), whereas in Europe they were prohibited by various law codes. Yet, insofar as concerns us, the most important difference between China and Europe is not so much the role of vendetta but the way it took place. In Europe vendetta exclusively took the form of aggressive acts against others, and in the worst cases led to feuds or private wars between groups of families that produced an endless chain of murders and violence. In China, on the other hand, it was expressed as acts of aggression against oneself.

One of the first Europeans to note this peculiarity of Chinese vendetta was probably the Jesuit Matteo Ricci, who in 1602 commented that 'in order to harm others', every year 'many thousands of men and women hang themselves in the fields, or at the doors of their enemies, or throw themselves into wells or rivers, or take poison, for quite trifling matters. As their numbers increase, so the law takes action against those who are charged with having caused their death; and being accused by the dead person's relatives, these individuals are fined and punished by the courts. Therefore, if a law were to be passed stating that such persons would not be punished, as is done in edicts issued by many prudent magistrates during their term of office, not so many people would take their own lives because they would realize that by doing so they would not harm their enemies.'[157]

Others also made use of this form of aggression, namely those in a hierarchically inferior position could use it against their superiors. In medieval China, suicide was used by both the vassal against his lord, and by a son against his father. If a vassal came into conflict with an overlord, the former could threaten to take his own life, a gesture that was regarded as having 'horrible potency', sufficient 'to put constraint upon his will'.[158] The same sometimes happened in noble families. When the honourable Chu entrusted a more able but younger son with a very delicate and important mission, the firstborn son turned to him with these words: 'if Your Excellency does not send me and sends my younger brother, I shall kill myself.'[159]

In the second half of the nineteenth century and the early decades of the twentieth, many other Westerners who lived for some time in China noted the importance of this form of voluntary death. For the Australian journalist, George Morrison, most of the suicides in this country were provoked by an urge for revenge. 'In China', he wrote in 1902, 'to ruin your adversary you injure or kill yourself. To vow to commit suicide is the most awful threat with which you can drive terror into the heart of your adversary. If your enemy does you wrong, there is no way in which you can cause him more bitterly to repent his misdeed, than by slaying yourself at his doorstep.'[160] 'It is revenge', wrote the British diplomat Herbert Allen Giles in 1911, 'which prompts the unhappy daughter-in-law to throw herself down a well, consoled by the thought of the trouble, if not ruin, she is bringing on her persecutors. Revenge, too, leads a man to commit suicide on the doorstep of some one who has done him an injury, for he well knows what it means to be entangled in the net which the law throws over any one on whose premises a dead body may thus be found.'[161] Therefore, if you wished to take revenge on a person who had done you serious harm, in Europe you killed them, but in China you killed yourself.

According to Western observers there were many factors that made this Chinese 'anomaly' possible: in the first place, the presence of a well-founded belief system concerning the supernatural powers that would enact the vendetta. Giles told the story of 'a Chinese woman who deliberately walked into a pond until the water reached up to her knees, and remained there, alternately putting her lips below the surface, and threatening in a loud voice to drown herself on the spot, as life had been made unbearable by the presence of foreign barbarians. In this instance, had the suicide been carried out, vengeance would have been wreaked in some way on the foreigners by the injured ghost of the dead woman.'[162]

Secondly, it can be explained by the existence of special laws. As we have seen this was already noted by Matteo Ricci in 1602. But other Westerners made similar observations. 'Chinese law', wrote the French missionary Evariste Huc, 'throws the responsibility of a suicide on those who may be supposed to be the cause or occasion of it. It follows, therefore, that if you wish to be revenged on an enemy, you have only to kill yourself to be sure of getting him into horrible trouble; for he falls immediately into the hands of justice, and will certainly be tortured and ruined, if not deprived of life. The family of the suicide usually obtains, in these cases, considerable damages; so it is by no means a rare case for an unfortunate man to commit suicide in the house of a rich one, from a morbid idea of family affection.'[163]

Thirdly, it can be explained by the advantages of suicide compared to murder, because – as emphasized by Huc – in killing an enemy 'the murderer exposes his own relatives and friends to injury, disgraces them, reduces them to poverty, and deprives himself of funeral honors, a great point for a Chinese and concerning which he is extremely anxious.'

Fourthly, in the late eighteenth century, the French Jesuits, who had spent many years in China, commented that 'public opinion, so far from disapproving of suicide, honours and glorifies it. The conduct of a man who destroys his own life to avenge himself on an enemy whom he has no other way of reaching, is regarded as heroic and magnanimous.'[164]

Therefore, according to the French Jesuits, unlike in Europe, in China 'it is often the weakest who make the strong and powerful tremble, by holding suspended over their heads the threat of suicide, and forcing them by that means to do them justice, spare them, and help them'.[165] 'The poor', wrote Evariste Huc some eighty years later, 'have recourse sometimes to this terrible extremity, to avenge themselves for the hardheartedness of the rich.'[166] It was not only women who used suicide (or attempted suicide) as a means of revenge, but also others in the weakest sectors of Chinese society. In the late 1930s, George Danton, who witnessed the event, described how some foreigners living in a Chinese city sacked a local Chinese maidservant for very good reasons. The next day the woman's husband tried to kill himself in front of the gate to their house, a scene that was repeated for the next few days. In order to stop him, the foreigners turned to the police, who were extremely polite but instead of intervening, beseeched them to go and live somewhere else. Surprised and bewildered, these foreigners later learnt from friends that the attempted suicides of their former maid's husband had made them lose face and in such conditions it was impossible for the police to help them.[167] Likewise, for centuries, peasants or workers would take revenge on a pitiless creditor by killing themselves before his door.[168] On the other hand, retailers who owed a lot of money would procure all the necessary implements to hang themselves, in order to demonstrate that they were ready to do away with themselves, but at the same time they would send a son to their creditors so that on hearing of the situation they would be able to negotiate a large discount on whatever sum was outstanding.[169] Even the victims of theft could sometimes use the threat of suicide to regain possession of their goods. Eugène Simon, who was French consul in China for many years, tells the story of a man who succeeded in reacquiring his stolen money when he told the thief that he would drown himself if the money was not returned.[170]

Of course, anyone taking their own life for revenge had to take all possible precautions to ensure that the act would have the desired effect. A person could kill themselves at the gate or front door of the person they wanted to ruin, or leave some handwritten notes in a pocket explaining why they had taken this step, or even leave the name of the person responsible written on their skin, safe in the knowledge that no one would have dared to erase it from their corpse.[171] Other relatives, friends and acquaintances would immediately show their support through rites and symbols. Two French scholars wrote in the early twentieth century that, when a person killed themselves for this reason, 'society takes on the cause and wreaks vengeance on those who are to blame. Neighbours run to help and place a broom in the dead person's hand, brandishing it left and right. In this powerfully symbolic act, the hand brushes away the fortune, prosperity and family from the guilty party's house. With a subtle change of meaning, people say that "the dead seizes the living".'[172]

The possibility that the suicide could seriously damage a person deemed liable for causing their death was supported by the law in numerous cases. If a father or mother killed themselves in a moment of anger because of a son's behaviour, the latter would be sentenced to execution for having caused the death of his parents.[173] As for adultery, Chinese law, like that of many European countries, for centuries adhered to Cato's principle: 'If you caught your wife in adultery, you could kill her with impunity without bringing her to court; but if you have committed adultery or were about to do so, she dare not lay a finger on you, since it is not lawful.' But unlike Europe, in China if a husband who had not succeeded in killing his wife's lover then took his own life, whether in anger or in shame, the adulteress would be sentenced to strangulation.[174] Similarly, if a person killed themselves because they had been threatened, insulted or offended by another with words or gestures, the latter would be severely punished. For example, Hsaio Wen-han thought that he had discovered the man who had robbed him and so he followed the suspect back to his house. However, when the man left by a back door, Hsaio instead threatened the man's wife, scaring her terribly. As a result the woman first hanged her children and then herself, and for this Hsaio was sentenced to decapitation.[175] The same might happen if a person was subject to threats, pressure and constant harassment in order to obtain something. A younger brother sent his wife to his older brother to extract some money. On entering her brother-in-law's house the woman had first burst into tears, then she had proceeded to knock her head against the wall, and lastly she twisted the necks of the man's children. Not content with this, the younger man then sent some friends to his brother's house and they took his food, which they cooked and ate, and drank his wine. Stung by all these insults the man hanged himself, for which the younger brother, being held responsible, was sentenced to strangulation.[176]

But over and above the law, punishment for those responsible for another person's suicide was demanded by social custom. For example, the vice-prefect of Na Chan had for many months had awful relations with

Father L. of the Lazarite order, who in the end had won a case against him. One Sunday morning in March 1911, accompanied by his retinue, the vice-prefect went to visit the missionary. After the two men had greeted each other, exchanging ritual courtesies, Father L. left his guest alone for a minute or two while he went to fetch a pen and paper. When he came back he found him half dead, lying in a pool of blood having cut his throat with a knife. The members of the official's retinue immediately ran all over the city shouting that their lord had been killed by the missionary. A great outcry ensued and a mob rushed into the Lazarite mission and killed Father L.[177]

Clearly there were also cases where these rules were abused. In special circumstances, someone who was well acquainted with a person wishing to commit suicide and knowing their intentions could redirect their aggression towards another individual. In the early nineteenth century, for example, a widow tried repeatedly to escape her mother-in-law's tyranny both by running away and by attempted suicide, without succeeding at either because her brother-in-law always managed to capture or save her. After many years, frustrated in spite of his success, the man realized that he could benefit much more from the widow's desire for revenge and so he agreed to give her a rope and a stool if she would hang herself from the tree of a neighbour he hated.[178] In 1829 another man called Wang tried to persuade a servant, who was gravely ill, to kill himself in the field of his enemy Li. He succeeded in the end, but the court charged him with premeditated homicide and sentenced him to be beheaded.[179]

These values and beliefs had such profound roots that the behaviour of the Chinese did not change even when they emigrated to a country with a completely different culture.[180] As we have seen, by the mid nineteenth century, when the supply of African slaves had started to run short and their cost rose, Cuban sugar plantation owners began to recruit Chinese workers on eight-year contracts which prescribed a twelve-hour working day in exchange for board and lodging, the cost of a return journey to China and a very modest wage. Over a twenty-year period some 114,000 Chinese workers arrived in Cuba, but over half of them died: some from malnutrition and overwork, others from tropical diseases, and still others because they committed suicide. 'Everything they did was in silence', an observer wrote, including taking their own lives, sometimes alone or at other times in small or larger groups. For example, in 1879 fourteen workers on the Dos Marias sugar estate killed themselves on the same evening. They jumped into a well or, following the example of African slaves, hanged themselves from a branch of a guásima tree. 'They are docile', wrote an American visitor to Cuba in 1860, 'but many of them become discontented. And if so, or if whipped, they often commit suicide, having no regard for life [. . .] The number who commit suicide is very large.'[181]

Not unlike their predecessors in China, some of them killed themselves for vendetta, often as a way of taking revenge against those who exploited them, in the conviction that this was the only way 'the weak man could make the strong and powerful tremble'. Certainly, many of the Chinese workers who committed suicide to avenge the wrongs they had endured knew that in Cuba, unlike in their own country, the law would impose no punishment on those who had prompted them to end their lives. They also knew that their family and relatives lived too far away to be able to take action in order to obtain some form of compensation, whether financial or moral, for such wrongs. Yet, they continued to believe that, after death, their spirits would return to earth to torment those who had made them suffer. But given that their belief was not shared by the native population, it could not make the plantation owners tremble, and indeed far from feeling threatened in any way, the latter found it all too easy to replace those who had thrown themselves into a well or hanged themselves from the branches of a guásima tree.

6.17   Female suicide in the last two decades

Writing in the late nineteenth century, Arthur Smith claimed that 'every year thousands upon thousands of Chinese wives commit suicide', tens of thousands of other persons (husbands, sons, relatives) are therefore involved in serious trouble, millions of dollars are expended in 'extravagant funerals and ruinous law suits'. All this is the outcome of the 'Confucian theory that a wife has no rights which a husband is bound to respect. The law affords her no protection while she lives and such justice as she is able with difficulty to exact is strictly a *post mortem* concession.'[182] Over the course of the last century, China's economy, society and political system have changed enormously. The rules of family formation have changed, and the distribution of power within it and the relations between husband and wife, parents and children, mothers-in-law and daughters-in-law are less asymmetric than they once were. The grandiose custom of rewarding the virtuous has not existed for some time nor has that of honouring those women who took their own lives for reasons regarded as noble. Yet female suicides were very frequent and, unlike in the West, the rate remained much higher than among men until 2005.[183] Why has this Chinese anomaly persisted and why has it resisted such radical changes? In an attempt to answer this difficult question we need to turn to the results of ethnographical studies that have painstakingly reconstructed, in a certain number of cases, the seemingly insignificant and major factors that precede and foster female suicide, the significance attributed to the event by close family members, the broader family, friends and acquaintances, and the way in which all those involved react. We will focus on two of these cases, one of which occurred in northern rural China, and the other in the southern provinces.[184]

Ling killed herself in 1997 at the age of thirty-two. The daughter of peasant farmers, she had married another peasant twelve years earlier.

Theirs was a love match that had not been approved nor blessed by the groom's parents. Until then Ling had lived in a hillside village, where her family grew tea and bamboo, while her future in-laws were rice-farmers who, fearing that she would not help with the farm work, had hoped that their son would choose another woman. The couple had decided to live independently in a house that was quite close to Qiu's parents and also to Qiu's younger brother who was already married. Ling grew increasingly aware that to her husband's family she remained an outsider. Her in-laws referred to her as the 'mountain girl' and when they had guests they preferred to invite the younger son and his wife rather than Qiu and Ling. Tensions with her mother-in-law rose over time, exploding into the open on several occasions, when Ling twice insulted her by calling her a whore. In both cases her husband intervened in support of his mother by slapping his wife. On the second occasion, Ling was so hurt that after crying alone in the kitchen for some time, she threw herself into a nearby river.

When they heard the news of her death her in-laws spent many hours removing all the most valuable objects from their home and taking them to relatives and friends because they knew that, according to local custom, Ling's parents would be entitled to destroy their house and their property in order to avenge their daughter. Indeed, it was not long before Ling's parents arrived, accompanied by twenty-eight relatives, but they were persuaded not to carry out their plans because, it was pointed out, that by attacking and destroying everything in their anger they would hurt, above all, Ling's two children. Yet Ling's parents could not resign themselves to leaving their daughter's in-laws unpunished. In partial compensation for their loss they asked that a large and extremely costly funeral should be celebrated. As a result Qiu's family was obliged to pay for the funeral and for the costs incurred by thirty of Ling's relatives for the journey, their board and lodging, the clothes they bought for the occasion, and also the costs of other rites which were performed for seven weeks after the funeral in order to placate the spirit of the young suicide. This amounted to a vast sum, more than their entire earnings for one year. Many saw this as one of the three key objectives that Ling had achieved by killing herself. The second was that of destroying her mother-in-law's reputation forever, while the third was to be regarded, for the first time, as the most important daughter-in-law.[185]

Xiv'er Zhang poisoned herself by swallowing pesticide in 1995, at the age of twenty-six. She was beautiful, intelligent and married with a son. Her husband, Xiaobao Qie, who had one blind eye, had fallen head-over-heels in love with her a few years earlier and had asked her to marry him. She accepted because she thought she would improve her economic status. After the wedding, Xiv'er would have preferred to set up her own home with her husband, but local custom obliged Xiaobao Qie, an only child, to follow the rule of patrilocal residence and bring his wife to his parents' house. After a while the parents were convinced by other relatives and friends to allow the young couple to 'cook and eat' separately: a compromise that gave them greater autonomy while keeping up appearances. But quarrels between mother-in-law and daughter-in-law became increasingly frequent, ending with the former insulting the latter.

Xiv'er went back to her parents' home for six months. She wondered about the possibility of divorce and finally understood the significance of an expression she had heard repeated countless times: married daughters are like water thrown away. Had she decided to follow this path she would have found herself without any possessions, completely dependent on her parents and forced to pay her husband a considerable sum by way of compensation (a requirement imposed by law on the spouse who initiated a divorce). So instead she decided to return to the Qie household, to Xiaobao's parents. But her in-laws stipulated that she should be the first to speak (implying that she was the one making an apology) and she refused. Xiv'er then gave her husband an ultimatum: either they should go and live independently or she would kill herself. When Xiaobao rejected the first solution, she chose the second.

On hearing of their daughter's suicide Xiv'er's parents were not only distraught but overwhelmed with indignation and anger. They told the relatives who tried to console them that they held the mother-in-law responsible for their daughter's death and they made plans for revenge. Xiv'er's father threatened to draw his knife and her brothers wanted 'a massacre'. As an alternative the Zhang family considered reporting the case to the police and the courts. For some days many feared that open conflict would break out between the two extended families. But mediators set to work and family councils met on various occasions in an attempt to find an amicable settlement. The Qie offered to give the Zhang a modest sum of 200 yuan. The Zhang family regarded this as offensive and let it be known that they would only accept twenty or thirty thousand. A series of long and complex negotiations then ensued regarding the amount of money to be paid and its significance. Too small and it could only be deemed a courteous token of sympathy; a larger sum would instead have been seen as a form of compensation and therefore as admission of liability by the Qie. A written agreement was at last reached, which was stipulated in five copies, stating that the Zhang would receive payment of 7,500 yuan. In spite of this, the Zhang still threatened not to attend the funeral, a clear sign that they held their in-laws responsible. In order to overcome this last hurdle, two women from the Qie family accompanied Xiv'er's son to visit his grandparents and kneeling in front of them, they said: 'Prostrate yourself before your grandmother. Tomorrow is your mother's funeral and we will all be present.'

How can the suicides of Ling and Xiv'er be explained, along with those of thousands of Chinese peasant women who, finding themselves in similar situations, took the same decision in the past decades? Certainly not by attributing them to the oppression of the patriarchal family system inspired by Confucianism. It was not to refute their arranged marriages, their parents' demands or the despotism of their mothers-in-law that these women killed themselves. Instead, the source of their anxieties and sufferings must be sought in the contrast between the old and the new, between their aspirations as women and the resistance they encountered in the society in which they lived, in short in the modernization process that for years has been underway in China. But not even this is enough to explain why such a high number of Chinese peasant women took their own lives. Similar processes have generated unease and suffering in other parts of the world, but not these high suicide rates. If this is the case in China it is because suicide here continues to be seen in a different light.

The cases of Ling and Xiv'er show that voluntary death is still interpreted along traditional lines. When a woman kills herself, the question that is asked is not 'Why?' but 'Who? Who drove her to this? Who is responsible?' Still today, after a suicide even trivial events, let alone major disasters, are said to be caused by the dead person's spirit: illnesses, economic losses and misfortunes suffered by the family thought to be responsible for the death or strange noises heard in the dead person's house, doors that creak, windows that open unexpectedly, or the sound of the wind moaning in the eaves.[186] Yet these beliefs are becoming less and less commonplace today, and those who commit suicide increasingly often rely for revenge, not on a spirit, but on a close friend or relative, a parent or a sister, or they do it themselves. For example, a seventeen-year-old girl, who worked for a marketing agency, finally took her own life after being raped and then continually tormented by her boss. But before committing suicide, she wrote a letter to her parents in which, after asking for their forgiveness, she set out the facts. 'Mum', she wrote, 'after I am gone, please redress the injustice and seek revenge for me and have him punished [. . .] This is the only way I can reduce my mental pain.'[187]

In China today, there are still some, both men and women, who continue to think that, in certain situations, suicide is the only means of making a person who has made them suffer tremble. But this happens much less frequently than it used to. Between the close of the twentieth century and first fifteen years of the new millennium, as a growing proportion of the rural population migrated into the city, the number of those taking their own lives has fallen sharply. Therefore, industrialization and urbanization, which were blamed by those late nineteenth-century European scholars as the principal causes of the 'enormous increase in the number of voluntary deaths', have instead encouraged a steep drop in such deaths in China over a century later.

7

The Body as a Bomb

Dhanu killed herself on 21 May 1991 in Sriperumbudur, a small town some fifty kilometres from Madras. She wore a ceremonial dress and flowers in her hair, had a black *bindi* on her forehead to protect herself from evil spirits, and carried a sandalwood garland in her left hand. Like Roop Kanwar, who had committed suicide four years earlier, she was young, attractive, of Hindu religion and she had grown up in a village that held altruistic suicide in high regard. Like her, too, she had been encouraged to make this sacrifice by others and had walked to her death with a smile on her lips, becoming a martyr for tens of thousands of others. Yet unlike Roop, she did not sacrifice herself for a man but against one, not for love but for hate, and she carried out this act not having reflected, alone, for a few hours but as the culmination of a long process of training and preparation in the company of others.

Dhanu came to Sriperumbudur, accompanied by five others, to attend a political rally held by the Indian Prime Minister, Rajiv Gandhi. On the morning of 21 May, she arrived at the rally quite early together with her companions, and when the Indian leader finally started to make his way along the red carpet, thronged on both sides, she tried to make her way towards him. For a moment she was stopped by a policewoman. But Gandhi himself intervened in her favour, saying: 'Don't worry, relax.' These were his last words. Dhanu knelt before him and, with a simple, rapid gesture, exploded the grenade-packed belt she was wearing under her dress, killing herself, the Indian leader and sixteen other people (Plate 48).

It may have been personal reasons that prompted Dhanu to perform this act: the desire to revenge the insults and assaults of Indian soldiers who, according to unverified rumours, had raped her or her mother, killed one of her brothers and wrecked her home. Yet she also acted out of a sense of duty, for a greater, collective cause, to aid her own people, the Hindu Tamils, to found an independent state in the northeastern part of Sri Lanka. She was entrusted with this mission by the Tamil Tigers, the organization that, from the mid 1970s, had fought to free their people from Sinhalese rule, the island's Buddhist ethnic majority.

The idea had come to this group's charismatic leader, Velupillai Prabhakaran, after watching a *Death Wish*-like film, released for the South Asian market. The movie tells the story of a beautiful girl who, as she pretends to present a bouquet to the President of the United States, sets off a bomb concealed beneath her clothing, killing herself and the world's most powerful man.[1] Once the decision had been taken, in November the previous year, the organizational machine of the Tamil Tigers went into action, studying the timing and plans of action, and recruiting and training the individuals who would carry it out. Dhanu was flanked by three women and two men. The former had the task of helping her to get close to the Indian leader, and one of them acted as a reserve and would have taken over if for any reason she had not managed to set off her explosives. One of the two men would take photographs of the scene, while the other pretended to be a journalist. In order to be quite certain of accomplishing their delicate mission successfully, these six individuals made trial runs of the attack on 21 April and 6 May.

All this information is useful to understand how Rajiv Gandhi died. Yet, as the following pages will show, in order to explain the sudden appearance of suicide missions and their extremely rapid spread worldwide, we should start, not with the psychological and social traits of the individuals who carry them out, but with the political and military demands of the organizations that decide and prepare them, with the desperate efforts they make to achieve ambitious aims with limited means, and also, of course, with the cultural traditions of the countries in which they operate.

7.1 Suicide attacks and terrorism

Acts like that of Dhanu and her group are called by quite different names in everyday speech and in the scientific literature.[2] In the following pages those who carry them out and the acts themselves will be referred to using the expressions 'suicide bombers' and 'suicide attacks (or missions)'. These are violent actions undertaken, for political reasons, by one or more individuals who voluntarily use their bodies to carry the bombs or explosive materials in order to attack, kill or gravely maim others, in full knowledge that their own death is a necessary condition to the success of the operation and that they and those around them will die simultaneously.[3] On the part of those committing them, these actions presuppose a desire both to kill and to die. An attack cannot be defined as a suicide attack unless there is a high probability, although not the certainty, that the person carrying it out will die or will kill themselves after having killed others. Of course (as in the case of both suicides and homicides) these missions can be either completed, namely successfully accomplished, or attempted, as is the case if they are discovered before being accomplished or if the person carrying them out makes a mistake (see Plate 49, for example). In 2004, for instance, Israel foiled 74 per cent of the planned attacks and arrested 365 militants.[4] Obtaining precise and reliable information on failed missions is quite difficult (as it is for attempted suicides in Western countries) and therefore the statistical data used by all experts are those for completed attacks.

The expression 'suicide terrorism' is often used to describe these attacks, but it is imprecise and inadequate. Strangely, there is no consensus among experts on a common definition of the term 'terrorism'. However, it is usually used to indicate the strategic use of violence by a political group in opposition, targeted indiscriminately at civilians and non-combatants. By using this definition, it will become clear that some suicide missions are not terrorist by nature. Those famous missions carried out by Japanese pilots, the kamikaze, at the end of the Second World War against US aircraft were not terrorist attacks, for example, because they were none other than forms of combat by one state against another. Nor can attacks made on the army or police force of a particular country be described as terrorist. Therefore, we can only talk of terrorist suicide attacks when they are used to target civilians and guerrilla suicide missions when targeting the military.

Consider, for example, some dramatic events that happened in Spain in the early months of 2004.[5] On 11 March that year, ten bombs planted in four crowded commuter trains exploded between 7:37 and 7:40 killing 191 persons and injuring hundreds. The execution of the attack did not lead to the death of either the organizers or those who carried it out: seven young North Africans (five Moroccans, a Tunisian and an Algerian) who had emigrated to Spain a few years earlier. Within a few days the police had identified those responsible for the attack and discovered where they lived: on 3 April they surrounded their house. The seven young militants then decided to commit suicide by killing as many policemen as possible, and many of them informed their parents of this decision by phone. They died soon after by exploding a bomb and a policeman died with them. If we are to strictly apply the definitions outlined earlier then the former was a terrorist attack (because it indiscriminately targeted the general public) but not a suicide one (because those carrying it out did not use their own bodies as bombs), and the latter was a suicide attack but not a terrorist one (because it targeted the forces of order, not civilians).

Neither the terms used in this chapter nor the numerous others present in the international scientific literature are accepted by the groups that organize these attacks. Referring specifically to Palestine, an authoritative Muslim theologian argued that 'to call these operations suicide attacks would be a mistake and misleading. These are examples of heroic sacrifice [. . .] A suicide takes his life [. . .] But what we are talking about is killing yourself for your religion and your people. A suicide is someone tired of himself and Allah, but a mujahadin is imbued with faith in Allah's grace and generosity.'[6] Similarly, in Sri Lanka, the Black Tiger units of the Tamil Tigers explicitly decline to use the term *thatkolai* to describe these attacks, meaning simply to kill oneself; instead they use a term that may seem similar to us but which has a profoundly different meaning: *thatko-dai*, namely to make a gift of the self, a donation. As one of the leaders of this organization said, 'When one enrols, there is no remuneration. The only promise is I am prepared to give everything I have, including my life. It is an oath to the nation.'[7]

7.2 The modern phenomenon of suicide missions

The guard could not remember the driver's age or even his skin colour or features, but only that he was at the wheel of a large yellow truck and that suddenly 'he looked right at me . . . and smiled'. It was 6:20 on 23 October 1983 and Corporal Eddie di Franco was standing guard outside the US Marines GHQ at Beirut International Airport. The yellow truck made its way slowly forward as breakfast was being prepared for the soldiers who would get up in ten minutes' time, as they did every Sunday morning. Then the truck driver suddenly accelerated, hurtling through barriers and driving straight into the large four-floor building where the Marines were sleeping. Laden with bombs, the truck exploded violently, making the building collapse and leaving a crater that was almost ten metres deep and forty wide. Two hundred and forty-one Marines were crushed in their sleep by the falling blocks of iron and masonry, and a further one hundred were injured. Forty seconds after this explosion, another truck-bomb crashed at full speed into a six-floor building, some three kilometres away, where the French paratroopers were sleeping. The building was destroyed, killing fifty-eight soldiers and wounding five others. On 3 November a third truck-bomb exploded close to the Israeli headquarters in Sidon, massacring twenty-eight soldiers and thirty Lebanese citizens.

There had been similar attacks a few months earlier, in November 1982, against the Israeli occupying forces in Tyre, and in April 1983 against the US embassy in Beirut. But it was those on 23 October 1983 that left the world dumbfounded. As the headlines appeared in countries across the globe, it became clear that a new form of guerrilla warfare or terrorism had been born, one even more powerful and lethal than those already in existence, given that it had taken just two people willing to sacrifice their own lives and two truck-loads of explosives to kill nearly 300 soldiers from enemy forces.

Organized by Hezbollah militants (which in Arabic means 'God's party'), a movement formed by young Shiite Muslims with the aim of forcing US and French troops, as well as the Israeli army, to withdraw from Lebanon (which Israel had invaded in June 1982), these attacks had an enormous impact. The suicide mission of April 1983 had already humiliated the world's greatest military power by forcing it to move its embassy from the capital to Aukar, a less important city in the north of the country. Having again been targeted on 23 October, the United States did indeed withdraw its forces from Lebanon because, as Ronald Reagan would write sometime later, 'The price we had to pay in Beirut was so great, the tragedy at the barracks was so enormous . . . We had to pull out . . . We couldn't stay there and run the risk of another suicide attack on the Marines.'[8] In 1985 the Israeli army withdrew from most of southern Lebanon.

Until 1987 suicide attacks remained confined to Lebanon and continued to be carried out only by Hezbollah which, thanks to the success it achieved, grew in size and strength, passing from a small group of militants in 1982 to an organization with nearly seven thousand members by 1986. But after 1987, suicide attacks were also adopted by the Tamil Tigers, or LTTE, in Sri Lanka. After Britain had relinquished control of the country (until then known as Ceylon), the ruling Sinhalese majority had done everything to exclude the Tamil minority from public life. From 1983 the LTTE started to carry out guerrilla operations against the government. Not long afterwards, its leaders, who had been favourably impressed by the suicide attack launched by Hezbollah against the Marines on 23 October 1983, tried to imitate it. On 5 July 1987 a twenty-one-year-old, Vallipuram Vasanthan (whose *nom de guerre* was Captain Miller) drove a truck loaded with explosives into a military base of the Sri Lankan armed forces on the Jaffna peninsula, killing himself and seventy soldiers. From then on, as well as continuing its other guerrilla activities, the LTTE made extensive use of suicide missions, which it adapted to suit its needs. In most cases (about a quarter of the total) they were used to assassinate political leaders who could not have been killed by any other means. Two years after the assassination of India's Prime Minister Rajiv Gandhi, another suicide mission caused the death of the President of Sri Lanka, and the following year an even more spectacular mission killed a large number of parliamentarians and prominent members of the Sinhalese party.

In 1993 suicide missions reappeared in the Middle East. On 16 April that year Shahar al-Nabulsi, a militant in the Sunni organization, Hamas (an acronym for 'Islamic Resistance Movement') which had been set up in 1987 at the start of the first Intifada by Sheik Ahmed Yassin, drove a car full of explosives into a service area on the Jordan Valley motorway where Israeli soldiers often stopped, and he exploded it, killing himself, a Palestinian worker and a number of civilians and military personnel.[9] Over the next four years, Hamas and the Islamic *jihad* carried out many other suicide attacks against Israel with the aim of liberating the Palestinian territories, namely the Gaza Strip and the West Bank, occupied by Israeli armed forces during the Six Day War in 1967.

In 1996 suicide missions were used in Turkey by the PKK, the Kurdistan Workers' Party. The Kurds are Sunni Muslims who form the majority population of Kurdistan, an area that occupies large parts of Turkey, Iraq, Iran and Syria. The PKK was founded in 1978 by the Marxist leader Abdullah Ocalan, and it fought for Kurd independence and social revolution. After setting up two military organizations, for years it also carried out numerous guerrilla operations against the Turkish government, without ever winning the consensus of the Kurd population it sought to represent and defend. In 1996 this led to the first wave of suicide attacks. A year later, these were suspended only to be resumed between 1998 and 2000.

In 2000 a number of separatist groups in Kashmir carried out suicide attacks against the Indian army. In the same year, similar attacks started to be used in Eastern Europe. Chechnya, an autonomous republic within the Russian Federation, declared its independence in 1991 and launched a war against Russia. After significant losses, the Chechen separatists chose the tactic of suicide missions, following the model first used by Hezbollah seven years earlier. On 7 June 2000, a young Islamic woman and a man drove a truck laden with explosives into a Russian military base where they exploded it, killing themselves and two soldiers, as well as injuring many others. Chechens undertook further suicide attacks in the four years that followed, also affecting civilians, mainly within their territory but occasionally in Russia as well.

On 11 September 2001, nineteen young men belonging to al-Qaeda – fifteen Saudis, an Egyptian, a Lebanese and two from UAE – seized control of four scheduled aircraft flying over the United States and used them to carry out the most daring suicide mission ever accomplished. Two planes were used to strike the Twin Towers in New York, causing them to collapse, a third was flown into the Pentagon, Washington, and the fourth crashed close to Pittsburgh. These four attacks caused the death of nearly three thousand people and shook the world.

Since then the use of suicide operations has spread to many other countries worldwide, including Spain, the United Kingdom, Morocco, Tunisia, Egypt, Kenya, Jordan, Pakistan, Indonesia, Afghanistan and Iraq. In Afghanistan, for example, the first suicide attack was carried out on 9 September 2001, two days before the attack on the Twin Towers. Two Arabs, both al-Qaeda militants pretending to be journalists, succeeded in gaining an appointment to interview Ahmad Shah Massoud, the military leader of the United Islamic Front for the Salvation of Afghanistan. As soon as they were close enough, they blew themselves up and killed him and two collaborators. There were no suicide attacks the following year, but 2003 and 2004 saw two and three attacks respectively. Then suddenly, although no one was expecting it, the numbers rose sevenfold, from 17 attacks in 2005 to 123 the following year.[10]

In Iraq suicide attacks began immediately after March 2003, when the country was occupied by the armed forces of the United States and United Kingdom and their many allies. They have not ceased since then. As well as being targeted at American soldiers, attacks have also taken place on the army and police forces of the new regime, against some Kurdish and Shiite politicians, and above all against the Shiite population who have been taken by surprise in markets, mosques or funeral processions.

From 1983 to the present the number of suicide attacks carried out

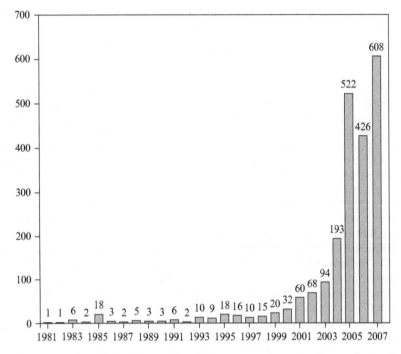

Graph 7.1   Number of completed suicide missions in the world between 1981
and 2007.

Source: Merari (2010).

across the world has risen continually, first slowly and then at a staggering rate of increase. The overall number remained quite low during the
1980s (around 4.7 attacks a year); it then tripled in the following decade
(16 attacks a year) and has risen sharply since 2000. From 60 in 2001 it
grew to 94 in 2003, 193 in 2004, and over 500 the following year.[11] After
falling back slightly in 2006, the total again rose to a peak the following
year (Graph 7.1).

7.3   The rationality of weak players

Those who have made an attentive study of the hundreds of suicide attacks
committed in the world during the past twenty-five years have been struck
by their heterogeneity.[12] Yet there are some things that a large majority
of these attacks have in common. The most important and the one that
serves as our starting point is that almost all are decided and prepared
by an organization and executed with its backing. Often, as in the case of

Dhanu and the five individuals who acted with her, attacks are undertaken as a team.[13] Moreover, suicide attacks are not chance or isolated events, but form part of organized campaigns involving a succession of attacks aimed at achieving political concessions from a national government.[14] So, for example, from 1983 to 2002, there were eighteen organized campaigns worldwide, some of which lasted a few months, others up to four or five years, producing between two and a maximum of ninety attacks.[15]

We have already seen that the rites of both *sati* in India and *tat'ai* in southeastern China were celebrated in the presence of a large number of people, who supported the widow emotionally, controlling her and helping her fulfil her decision to follow her husband in death. But in the case of suicide missions, the role played by the organizations is vastly greater. Two scholars have used a phrase written by the English novelist, Eric Ambler, in a completely different context, in order to show much greater it is: 'The important thing to know about an assassination or an attempted assassination is not who fired the shot, but who paid for the bullet.'[16]

Bearing in mind their aims and the constraints under which they act, it can be said that the organizations act in a rational manner. Their use of suicide missions as a new weapon of struggle is a strategic choice that stems predominantly from calculations of the cost–benefit ratio. It is a choice that is always made by weak organizations, with limited financial and military resources, that are obliged or want to fight against strong states and therefore find themselves in evidently asymmetric circumstances. For many organizations suicide missions become the last means to which they can resort after having failed to achieve their aims using conventional arms or even guerrilla techniques. Suicide missions often therefore start quite some time after the conflict has started: not in the first but in the second war between Chechnya and Russia, not in the first but in the second Palestinian Intifada, and not in the first but in the second Kurdish revolt.

Compared to other terrorist or guerrilla operations, suicide attacks present a number of tactical advantages.

In the first place they produce a higher number of victims. The average number of victims in a terrorist or guerrilla operation is 3.3 for a shooting attack or 6.9 if a bomb is exploded remotely, but suicide attacks result in an average of 82 victims, both casualties and the dead, if committed using explosive belts or jackets, and 92 if carried out using an explosive-laden car or truck.[17] Their destructive power derives from the fact that suicide bombers can change both the timing of the explosion and the target up to the very last minute, and for this reason these attacks are sometimes called 'intelligent bombs' or 'guided missiles'. In this way the organizations that use suicide attacks make up, at least in part, for the technological handicaps they have compared to the super powers, because – as has been already observed – the latter invest 'huge amounts of time and money to create weapon systems that can mimic certain aspects of human intelligence', while 'terrorist groups have decided to apply human intelligence directly to the delivery and detonation of the weapon'.[18] Ramadan Shalah, the secretary general of Islamic *jihad*, summed up the logic of the new form of terrorism as follows: 'Our enemy possesses the most sophisticated weapons in the world and its army is trained to a very high standard . . . We have nothing with which to repel killing and thuggery against us except the weapon of martyrdom. It is easy and costs us only our lives . . . human bombs cannot be defeated, not even by nuclear bombs.'[19]

Second, the economic cost of suicide attacks is relatively low in relation to the effects they produce. In many cases (45 per cent) they have been carried out to date using the simplest technique: namely an explosive belt concealed under outer garments. Use of a car or truck, as in the case of Iraq in 2003, or even an ambulance laden with bombs is also frequent. Other methods are less common, such as using bags or similarly boats packed with explosives.[20] It has been calculated that the cost of preparing a suicide attack using an explosive belt is not much more than 150 dollars. But even the largest and most lethal attack realized to date, that of 9/11 on the Twin Towers in New York City, cost the al-Qaeda group that organized it about 500,000 dollars but generated damages of over 500 billion dollars.[21]

Third, suicide operations can penetrate heavily guarded areas and hit targets that would otherwise be extremely difficult to reach. This is because the attack needs no escape route or complex rescue operations given that the perpetrators never come back.

Fourth, for the same reason there is no danger that the attackers will be taken prisoner and forced to reveal precious information to the enemy.

Lastly, compared to other forms of attack, suicide missions have an incomparably greater public resonance and generate huge levels of fear in the general population. If it is true, as many experts have affirmed, that terrorists aim to gain public attention and to spread terror in order to achieve maximum potential leverage, and if 'Terrorism is theatre' in the sense that attacks are often carefully choreographed to attract the attention of the mass media,[22] then there can be no question that suicide attacks are far and away the most effective means of achieving these aims. They are also so violent, so bloody, so overwhelming and all-encompassing that no broadcaster or newspaper can avoid reporting them to the public. These attacks are committed by individuals ready to sacrifice their lives to attain their ends and as such they represent threats against which there is no possible defence.

In their use of human resources and in their division of labour, terrorist organizations usually act with the rationality of a business structure. For example, knowing full well that suicide attacks are complex operations, requiring considerable skills and expertise, these organizations assign their most delicate and difficult missions to their most educated and expert members. Studies carried out on the Palestinians who undertook suicide attacks on Israel between 2000 and 2005 showed that the higher the level of education and expertise the more likely it was that they were used to attack key targets and the higher their 'productivity': they were rarely caught before completing their missions and succeeded in killing a greater number of people.[23] The assignment of tasks by gender was also done in a way that would not raise suspicion. For example, only male Black Tigers (the elite Tamil Tiger suicide unit) conducted suicide missions using cars or trucks, because women do not generally drive in Sri Lanka.[24]

Considering the tactical advantages offered by suicide missions, the leaders of these organizations became convinced of their efficacy compared to other forms of terrorism or guerrilla attacks as a means to achieve the organization's ends. 'This weapon', wrote a member of Hamas' political bureau, 'is our winning card, which turned our weakness and feebleness into strength, and created parity never before witnessed in the history of struggle with the Zionist enemy.'[25] This conviction is not the product of unrealistic hopes but instead, as some studies have shown, based on a careful breakdown of costs and benefits.

Of course, it is not easy to assess whether, and to what extent, the weak players that have resorted to suicide attacks in their struggle against the powerful have achieved any degree of concessions or success. First of all because each organization has a variety of different aims, both short- and long-term, transient and definitive. Secondly, because among the aims made public by these organizations, it is not always clear which are merely propagandistic, aimed at terrorizing and persuading peoples and governments, and which are deemed realistic by those who express them. This may explain why a number of studies have reached different conclusions. After analysing the campaigns carried out in the last two decades of the twentieth century, some researchers concluded that the parent organizations attained their political goals (those that were not overly ambitious at least) in 55 per cent of cases, namely they succeeded in making a target government change policy.[26] For others, on the other hand, this occurred much less often, in 24 per cent of cases,[27] or even less frequently.[28] However, it is undoubtedly true that in some cases the organizations carrying out campaigns of suicide attacks managed to achieve some notable concessions.

The first suicide attack campaign in modern history, which was carried out by Hezbollah, led to the complete withdrawal of US and French armed forces from Lebanon, and this was followed by the Israeli army's withdrawal from most of the country. Today, this goal might be regarded as being limited, because US and French forces were in Lebanon on humanitarian grounds and Israel retained control of the southern part of the country for a further ten years. Yet at the time it was seen by other organizations as an important victory, one that could not have been achieved using conventional weapons or other forms of terrorism or guerrilla warfare. Many years later, the Islamic *jihadi* leader Ramadan Shallah stressed that 'the shameful defeat that Israel suffered in southern Lebanon and which caused its army to flee it in terror was not made on the negotiations table but on the battlefield and through *jihad* and martyrdom'.[29]

Other groups also decided, at a certain point in their history, to use suicide missions because their leaders realized that in their particular situation it was the only path that would allow them to achieve their ambitions given the limited means at their disposal. 'With perseverance and sacrifice', Prabakaran argued in 1984, 'Tamil Eelam can be achieved in 100 years. But if we conduct Black Tiger [suicide] operations, we can shorten the suffering of the people and achieve Tamil Eelam in a shorter period of time.'[30]

Suicide attack campaigns were used by the organizations that launched them for other political ends: to acquire visibility, to win legitimacy and prestige, to expand their following and to gain financial support by seeing off rival groups operating on the same stage.[31] For example, it was by using this tactic that during the 1980s the LTTE achieved pre-eminence among all the other groups vying to represent the Tamil population. The same can be said of Hamas which, when it was set up in December 1987, had to compete with a much stronger and more expert rival: the Palestine Liberation Organization.

7.4   Nationalism and religious differences

The idea that suicide attacks should be blamed entirely on Islamic fundamentalism is not borne out by the results of the major studies carried out to date. Going back to the start of the brief history of these attacks, only eight of the forty-one Hezbollah followers who acted as suicide bombers between 1982 and 1986, in order to force Israeli and Western armed forces to leave the country, were Islamic fundamentalists, while three were Christian and all the others were socialist or communist party members.[32]

A breakdown of the suicide missions carried out worldwide between 1983 and 2003 revealed that half or over half were organized and launched by secular organizations. The greatest number of attacks was organized by a secular or at least a non-Islamic organization: the Tamil Tigers.[33]

Secular and religious organizations launched their attacks against varying targets. In the last two decades of the twentieth century approximately 43 per cent of suicide operations were aimed against civilians, and 44 per cent against the army or police.[34] Yet suicide attacks launched by Islamic organizations were more frequently terrorist than those launched by secular organizations. The percentage of operations targeted at civilians reached 74 per cent for Hamas and fluctuated between 60 and 70 per cent for Fatah (the main lay nationalist Palestinian organization set up in 1959 by Yasser Arafat) and for the Islamic *jihad*, while it was below 30 per cent for the LTTE and even below 12 per cent for Hezbollah.[35] Therefore, the organization which carried out the highest number of suicide missions against civilians in the last two decades of the twentieth century was not the LTTE but Hamas.[36]

One factor that has prompted the spread of suicide missions in the last two decades of the twentieth century at least, has been nationalism.

Namely, the belief among members of a community in a particular geographical area 'that they share a distinct set of ethnic, linguistic and historical characteristics and are entitled to govern their national homeland without interference from foreigners'.[37] During this period suicide attacks were often used in national liberation campaigns, against the military occupation of an area, with the secular and strategic goal of compelling modern democracies to withdraw their troops from the territories they claim. It was to achieve these goals that Hezbollah organized suicide missions in the 1980s against the US, French and Israeli armed forces present in Lebanon for various reasons, and why in the 1990s Fatah, Hamas and the Islamic *jihad* launched them to liberate Palestine from Israeli occupation. These missions were also used in campaigns that are usually described as separatist, like the Tamil Tigers against the Sri Lankan government, the Chechens against Russia, the PKK against Turkey and Kashmiri groups against India.[38]

Another factor that fostered the use of suicide missions was religious differences between the occupying and occupied countries. This difference accentuates conflict by making the boundaries between two conflicting peoples seem more clear-cut and unbridgeable. Indeed, we know that in 87 per cent of suicide attacks, the victims' religion is different from that of the suicide bombers.[39] This is true not only between Muslims and Christians, and Muslims and Jews, but also between Hindus and Buddhists, Muslims and Hindus, and Muslims and Orthodox Christians. Of course, there is no shortage of exceptions. On the one hand, civil wars have taken place between different religious groups without any recourse to suicide attacks. And on the other, the Kurds have used these attacks on those who share the same religion, the Turks, who are Muslims like themselves.[40]

7.5 The globalization of suicide missions

The modern phenomenon of suicide missions has altered radically since 11 September 2001. In the period of time that has lapsed since then not only have the aims of the organizations that plan and realize such attacks changed but so has their ideological stance, their structure, and even some traits of the suicide bombers themselves.

The growth, dating from 1999,[41] in the number of suicide attacks carried out by Islamic organizations has increased even more rapidly since 9/11 and after the invasion of Iraq by the armed forces of various nations. As many as 98 per cent of attacks carried out from 1 September 2001 to the end of 2006 were claimed by Islamic groups.[42] Such attacks are increasingly often seen as the first option rather than a second stage after having attempted conventional tactics.[43] Moreover, they are less frequently used as weapons of national liberation in ethnic conflicts or as a means of compelling an occupying army to withdraw.[44]

During the 1990s and at the start of the new millennium, many Islamic movements shared an approach that favoured *jihad* (or armed struggle), even when carried on outside their own countries. Although often in disagreement, they ended up by fighting both their 'close enemies' (the Egyptian, Saudi Arabian and Algerian governments) whom they accused of having abandoned traditional religion, and their 'distant enemies' (the United States and the West in general).[45] According to al-Qaeda, the movement that was led by Bin Laden, the final objective of this armed struggle against 'distant enemies' was to create a worldwide Islamic state, capable of defending Muslim interests against the 'assault' of the 'Zionist–crusader alliance'.[46]

This explains why, from the late 1990s, suicide attacks were often undertaken in countries where there were no occupying forces, such as Bangladesh, Indonesia, Jordan, Morocco, Saudi Arabia, Turkey, Uzbekistan, with the aim of overthrowing moderate or pro-Western Islamic governments and replacing them with more radical ones. This is what happened, for example, in Algeria in 1995–8, in Morocco in May 2003, and in Saudi Arabia in the first five years of the new century. But it also happened in countries that were occupied by Western forces, like Afghanistan or Iraq. The organizations that launched such an extraordinary number of suicide attacks in Iraq after March 2003 aimed not only to force the withdrawal of allied troops but also to topple the new regime (by destroying its police force and encouraging civil war between Shiites and Sunnis) in order to bring about a new Islamic state. For this reason, from 2003 the attacks were focused not on US and allied military bases and non-Muslim civilians, as had been the case in the 1980s and 1990s, but rather on the police force of the new Iraqi state and against the Shiite community.

Since 2001 there has been a growing trend for suicide missions to be decided and organized in countries other than those in which they have been launched. This is true not only of the 9/11 attacks, which were meticulously planned in Afghanistan, Hamburg and London, but also the Djerba attack of April 2002, which was planned in Pakistan, and the Bali attack of October 2005 prepared in the Philippines.

Moreover, there has been a complete change in the relationship between the place of birth and the place of death of those individuals prepared to sacrifice their lives in order to kill their enemies. While the Lebanese, Chechen, Kurdish or Tamil suicide bombers were born and grew up in the countries or regions for whose liberation they were fighting, those who self-immolated in the first decade of this century came from different countries, even different continents. As was seen earlier, the young men who crashed into the Twin Towers came from Saudi Arabia or other Arab countries (Plate 53). Some of those who exploded themselves in Afghanistan had been born and had lived for most of their lives in Pakistan.[47] The attack on the hotel in Amman, Jordan, was carried out by suicide bomber from Iraq.

At the same time, a significant number of those carrying out suicide attacks in Iraq came from other parts of the world: Jordan, Kuwait,

Saudi Arabia, Syria or Lebanon. Or sometimes even from Europe, from France, Belgium, Spain and even Italy. They had often been born in North Africa, in Algeria, Morocco or Tunisia, and they left their native countries on political grounds and sought refuge on the other side of the Mediterranean. In the end, some of them decided, of their own accord, to die in Iraq and they travelled there, with little money and a passport, often passing through Syria. On arrival, they were assigned to a group and would live for a while in a house, awaiting their turn, after having added their names to a list kept in the 'martyrs' room', as it was widely known.[48]

From the mid 1990s onwards, some groups began to play an increasingly prominent role in what was called the 'netwar',[49] moving from a pyramidal and hierarchical organizational structure to one that was decentralized and flexible. After 9/11, al-Qaeda moved much more decisively in this direction in order to protect itself from attacks by American and European intelligence and their military forces. Leaving behind its monolithic and bureaucratic organizational model, it turned itself into a lightweight, fluid movement, made up of small units spread throughout different countries, some quite far away, and all very independent, with weak ties with one another and the centre. Experts say that al-Qaeda today consists of a central group and several satellite ones, which used to collaborate in various ways with Bin Laden in the past, as well as various informal local cells, only tenuously linked to the centre, and other smaller groups (sometimes made up of second-generation immigrants living in Western countries) who have no links at all but are inspired by the ideological announcements made publicly by al-Qaeda.[50] Each of these small cells decides, often on an individual basis, how and against whom a suicide attack will be launched. Indeed, it is sometimes the case that a cell is only recognized and accepted by the movement after having successfully carried out the attack.[51]

Many experts believe that al-Qaeda is increasingly becoming a transnational political grouping, without a leadership: a heterogeneous set of cells that take on an appearance of unity thanks to ideological manifestos from the centre and the existence of the internet. Although the claim made by an American paper that al-Qaeda is 'the first guerrilla movement in history to migrate from physical space to cyberspace'[52] is exaggerated, there is no doubt that that the shift to a new, lightweight and horizontal structure has been made possible by the new communication technologies.

7.6 Cyberspace

In the spring of 2004 a number of papers informed their readers in a few lines that the Saudi police in Riyadh had discovered not only guns, explosives, hand grenades, rocket-propelled bombs and many thousands of rounds of ammunition in an al-Qaeda cell, but they had also found an array of electronic devices, including faxes, video cameras, laptop computers,

CD burners and a high-speed internet connection.[53] These meagre details tell us all we need to know about the means of communication, recruitment and mobilization used by the groups that organize suicide attacks and how these means have fostered their changing structure.

One of the first groups to use the new media were the Tamil Tigers, which set up a website called TamilNet.com in 1995, followed by many others, using servers in India, Australia, the United Kingdom, Norway and Canada, all countries with communities of immigrants from the northeastern region of Sri Lanka. From the outset, the websites aimed to garner support for the Tamil freedom fighters by spreading information on the history of the Tamil people and their charismatic leader, Velupillai Prabhakaran, and all those who had died for this cause.[54] The same path was then followed by all the groups who used suicide bombers. Hezbollah was among the early ones, setting up twenty websites in English, French and Arabic, with different aims and audiences. Hamas too followed suit, launching sites in six languages,[55] as did al-Qaeda. For the latter the web became, as has been pointed out, a sort of 'virtual sanctuary', a means for those in the front line to communicate, with extraordinary rapidity and efficiency, with followers, sympathizers and supporters of the movement around the world.[56] This has led to a few thousand websites being set up, all of which are linked in some way to Islamic groups, addressing and encouraging a vast audience and inviting them to engage in *jihad* and fight for Islam, as well as to fulfil many other functions.[57]

These websites, which now form the large majority, are used above all to spread ideology and propaganda concerning the political aims of the organizations, thus escaping all forms of government control and censure. Complete virtual libraries of pro-*jihadi* texts offer visitors a range of theological, ideological and political works by leaders and key personalities from the Islamic world. They also give first-hand information regarding their activities and successes, providing quite a different image of their organizations to that given by the mainstream media.

Secondly, the websites are used to provide distance training for militants. Detailed manuals can be found online, with long and often very precise descriptions illustrated with photos and occasionally short videos, showing militants how to fight the enemy, use weapons and take hostages. They also give details on how to prepare a suicide mission, build the necessary home-made bombs, conceal them on your person and approach the chosen target without causing suspicion. In some cases, these websites provide even more specific information. To give an example, a request submitted by a person signing himself Abu Jendal appeared on the website for Hamas' Ezzedeen al-Qassam brigades: 'My dear brothers in Jihad, I have a kilo of acetone peroxide. I want to know how to make a bomb from it in order to blow up an army jeep. I await your quick response.' The answer appeared on the same website an hour later explaining in detail how to use the homemade explosive as a roadside bomb.[58]

The leaders and militants in these groups use the internet to prepare suicide missions and other attacks, researching and analysing photos, maps, diagrams and all sorts of other information on the potential target. Even the 'Manchester manual', a guide written by al-Qaeda and found by the English police in a raid on a cell in that city, affirms that 'it is now possible to gather at least eighty per cent of information on the enemy openly without recourse to illegal methods'.[59]

Lastly, the internet serves to put people and units who have never seen one another before in contact, creating new relationships and reinforcing existing bonds. Forums and emails offer sympathizers and militants from various countries a chance to discuss topics of shared interest and to swap texts, photos, videos and audio recordings. Under the cloak of anonymity, these communications encourage people to share intimate and confidential information. Moreover, by creating a sense of equality and shared ideological beliefs, they foster a sense of belonging to a large community, that of Islam itself.[60]

7.7 Becoming a suicide bomber

The peculiar feature of suicide missions is that they can only take place when there is an organization that decides, plans and prepares them. This reinforces the view that in order to explain why they occur, it is more important to find out 'who paid for the bullet' and not 'who fired the shot' (to repeat Eric Ambler's expression). But it is also true that no suicide mission could take place unless there were individuals willing to blow themselves up by pulling the lever on a belt of grenades or driving a car, truck or ambulance laden with explosives (Plates 54–55). What is it that drives these people to sacrifice their lives?

When confronted by the news and television images of these missions, most Westerners reacted with the same shock and amazement that European travellers had expressed for centuries on the subject of *sati*, but with far greater concern. Suicide attacks were seen as dark, incomprehensible, irrational acts, the product of economic poverty and religious fanaticism. Moreover, the suicide bombers themselves were depicted as socially alienated youngsters, lacking any future prospects. These young men were semi-illiterate and mentally disturbed, chronically unemployed, and filled with resentment and hatred, making them easy targets for Islamic fundamentalism. Yet these ideas have not been substantiated by the results of research work undertaken to date.

Suicide bombers differ in many ways from the individuals who commit suicide in Western countries, and above all they differ in age, social background and mental health. Suicides in Europe, the United States, Canada and Australia have a higher mean age than the rest of the population but lower schooling and income levels. On the contrary, the suicide bombers who blew themselves up between 1983 and 2002 were relatively young, although their age varies from group to group: it was approximately twenty-one for the Lebanese, twenty-two for the Tamil Tigers, 23.6 for PKK members, almost twenty-seven for al-Qaeda suicide bombers, and nearly thirty for Chechens.[61] They had a higher level of education and income than the rest of the population, and were rarely unemployed. Most had middle-class jobs or were workers.[62] Among the suicide bombers, and the militants in general, there is a higher percentage of graduates and, in particular, among these a majority of graduates from key university faculties. Mohamed Atta, the leader of the group of nineteen men who carried out the attack on the Twin Towers on 11 September 2001, was the son of a lawyer, had two sisters who were university lecturers, and had graduated in architecture from the engineering faculty of Cairo University. This might be an exception, yet in practice the available data show that engineers are strongly over-represented among radical Islamists of all nationalities, both East and West.[63] However, those who have become suicide bombers in Afghanistan since 2001 form an interesting exception because they are generally poor and less educated (Plate 50).[64]

Turning to the question of mental illness, there are no systematic studies, comparable to those mentioned in the introduction to this book, on the personality and psychological profiles of suicide bombers.[65] But the scant biographical information available, taken mainly from descriptions in the media or from inquiries undertaken by the police or magistrates, has led many experts to conclude that they do not usually suffer from personality or mood disorders.[66] It is a plausible hypothesis, even if one not based on firm evidence, and the explanation put forward is similarly plausible.

It is possible that among aspiring suicide bombers there is an over-representation of those with antisocial, paranoid and borderline traits, who tend to be violent, impulsive and unstable, not to respect rules, and to view the behaviour of others as malevolent and aggressive. But the organizations who recruit them follow a highly selective process that discards individuals who are not normal or who could not be depended on to carry out the assigned mission, both because they might arouse suspicion and therefore be monitored and detained, and because they would be unable to work in a group or might be more likely to change their mind at the last moment and botch an operation.[67]

Therefore, the information we have undermines the views, widely circulated among Western public opinion, that those who decide to become martyrs are driven by poverty or by social marginalization, or that they are 'abnormal' and suffer from mental illnesses and personality disorders. So what are the factors underlying their behaviour?

Some experts (above all economists) use the same categories to explain the organizations' decision to resort to suicide attacks and that of individuals to undertake them, and they regard both as the product of instrumental rationality. They state that both the organizations and the individuals behave in the same way because, given their aims and the information available to them, they choose the most appropriate means of attaining those aims. Seen in this light, the willingness of some individuals to die in order to kill others (their enemies) stems from a sort of contract with God, one that they believe will lead to enormous rewards not in this world (which they agree to renounce) but in the hereafter.[68]

This proposition appears inadequate on several counts.[69] First, these aspiring martyrs must have unshakeable faith in order to believe that their bargain for heavenly rewards will be fulfilled. But true believers, by definition, are not motivated by material gains. Second, a proportion of those ready to give their lives in order to kill their enemies are non-believers.

All the research carried out to date has highlighted that most of those who have killed themselves on suicide missions had in common a strong desire for revenge against an enemy country, its government, army and population.[70] Sometimes this stems from general political convictions, for example the suffering, abuse, humiliations and violence undergone by a martyr's own people at the hands of Israel, the United States or other Western countries. In other cases it is triggered by personal reasons, namely by the everyday painful experiences suffered by his or her closest family, relatives, friends, particularly if any have been beaten, wounded, raped or killed. This sentiment is especially widespread among Chechen women. Many of them have lived through air raids, bombardments, landmine explosions and many other military operations carried out by the Russian armed forces, and they have seen neighbours or close family members die. This was why many of these women who lost a husband or other close relative were called the 'black widows' by the Russians and the international media. The strong emotions they felt – anguish, anger, despair, and guilt because they had been unable to save others – aroused a strong desire for revenge, which was reinforced within their culture by the norms that encourage vendetta and retaliation. However, the desire for revenge is also quite prominent among Palestinian suicide bombers. A survey of 180 attackers showed that close to half of them embarked on their suicide missions shortly after they had lost a person very close to them.[71]

All those who have sacrificed their lives in suicide missions share another, even more important characteristic: the conviction of dying for a noble cause, of performing a heroic act not for personal reasons but for the community, for the interests of a group to which they belong and with which they identify.

7.8   For a noble cause

Even though the thesis that suicide missions are solely linked to Islamic fundamentalism has no bearing on reality, there is no question that religious and ideological preferences can impede or encourage their use. Terrorist or guerrilla organizations that are inspired by Marxism or those that seek to represent the demands and interests of populations from the Christian or Buddhist tradition do not usually resort to suicide attacks.

To give just one example: IRA militants did sometimes die for their cause through hunger strikes and they killed both civilians and British soldiers, but they never used suicide attacks. The same can be said of ETA in Spain, the Red Brigade in Italy and other rebel and revolutionary groups operating in Latin America.[72]

Suicide missions were a cultural innovation, devised by small pioneering groups that also elaborated an ideology to legitimate their use in particular circumstances. But the principles, beliefs, myths and interpretative categories of this ideology are drawn from the cultural repertoire of the peoples whom, both in the Middle East and in Asia, these small groups were trying to represent and defend.

For example, in the case of the Tamil Tigers (LTTE), the organization that first adopted the innovation introduced by Hezbollah and used it by adapting it to its own circumstances, enormous importance has always been given to the self-sacrifice of militants. Already in 1974, thirteen years before launching the first suicide mission, they made their members carry a small leather strip round their neck containing a phial of cyanide, called *kuppi*, and they would be instructed to bite the phial in the event of capture so that the poison would enter the bloodstream immediately through cuts made by the splintered glass. The numerous virtues of *kuppi* were the subject of endless eulogies in song and poetry. The use of these phials served a dual function: to prevent members revealing valuable information if tortured by the enemy, and as proof of the strength of an individual's commitment and loyalty to the organization because they had overcome all fear of death.[73] Indeed, the Tamils did not consider cyanide poisoning as suicide in the strict sense of the term, but as an anticipation of the death that would have been caused by the enemy and for which only the latter was ultimately responsible.

When the LTTE eventually launched their first suicide mission, they made the point – as we have already seen – that this was not a form of *thatkolai*, self-killing, but of *thatkodai*, namely self-immolation and a gift of the self. In its political and ideological manifestos, the group declared that, those who chose this path and sacrificed their life for the Tamil cause would be declared martyrs and honoured and celebrated as such. Their bodies would not be buried but 'planted' in the earth, like a seed that would be reborn. Today, the northern and most densely populated Tamil region of Sri Lanka is full of temples built for those who donated their lives and who deserve the title of *mavirar* or 'great hero'. They are commemorated and honoured with the same rites reserved for the gods and the saints, and the temples are decorated with gifts of flowers and oil. There are ten days of commemoration and celebrations in the Tamil calendar. The most important of these is 27 November, when the leader of the movement, Velupillai Prabhakaran, was expected to give a speech in honour of the 'great heroes'. Another day, 5 July, is dedicated entirely to 'Captain Miller', who drove a bomb-filled truck into a group of Sinhalese soldiers on that day in 1987.[74] Two other militants are commemorated on 19 April and 26 September, when they respectively died of hunger strike in protest against the presence of Indian military units in their country.[75]

These ideas, beliefs and ways of understanding life and death, as well as these values and rites can in part be attributed to the creative abilities of the LTTE leaders. But their reception would have been much more problematic in the West or in many Latin American or African countries. Instead in Sri Lanka they have been seen as both credible and convincing because they are closely linked to a very long tradition, that of Hinduism, that has always attributed enormous importance to self-sacrifice, not only in a passive sense but also aggressively, in other words not only for but also against someone, not only as *sati* but also as *traga* and *dharna*, that is suicide committed as protest and as vendetta.[76]

Arab organizations have followed a similar path. As a matter of fact, there have been lively debates between theologians and scholars of Islamic law on the significance of suicide missions, something that is not surprising given that the Koran (like the Bible) does not give an unequivocal judgement and interpretation of voluntary death. The Koran touches on the question in four passages, but it does so in a way that the interpretations of their meaning are very discordant. Yet, there is no question that, from the eighth century at the latest, the authorities of the *hadith*, or literature based on the oral tradition that brings together the sayings of the Prophet Muhammad, had come to condemn suicide as a grave sin.

In one of the most frequently cited passages, which tells of a wounded man who killed himself, there is a statement ascribed to God himself who was present and said: 'My servant anticipated my action by taking his soul [life] in his own hand; therefore, he will not be admitted into Paradise.'[77] Suicide was therefore considered an act against God and those who committed it ran the risk of provoking his anger and being punished with fire.[78] A person who commits suicide must continually repeat in Hell the action by which he killed himself.[79] The judgement of Islamic law on suicide was so severe that an early eighteenth-century *fatwa* (a legal opinion expressed by a qualified jurist or scholar) concluded that suicide was to be judged more severely than homicide (as was the case, moreover, in the Christian religion for many centuries).[80] In practice, the only suicides that were treated with greater leniency were those committed by military leaders after defeat, to avoid torture and humiliation.[81]

In some cases prayers for those who had taken their life were prohibited. According to tradition, it was also said that Muhammad had refused burial to a person who killed himself. However, in Islamic societies, it is customary to perform the funeral rites also for suicides.[82]

These ethical principles have been underlined on various occasions over the past decades and they are still firmly held today throughout the Islamic world. Research results show that almost all Algerians, Saudis, Egyptians, Iranians, Moroccans and Turks think suicide is never justified, while the percentage of Westerners expressing this opinion varies between 28 and 57 per cent, depending on the country (Table 7.1). Even Muslims

Table 7.1 Percentage of persons who think suicide is never justifiable in some Western and non-Western countries (1999–2001).

Western countries		Non-Western countries	
Canada	52	Algeria	94
Denmark	51	Saudi Arabia	88
France	26	Egypt	95
Germany	54	India	72
United Kingdom	39	Iran	95
Italy	62	Morocco	98
Netherlands	28	Turkey	90
Spain	47		
United States	57		
Sweden	29		
Switzerland	38		

Source: Elaborated using data from World Values Survey (http://www. worldvaluessurvey. org/).

Table 7.2 Percentage of persons who think suicide is morally acceptable in France, Germany, United Kingdom and in the Muslim population in Paris, Berlin and London, in 2008.

		Muslims in	
France	40	Paris	4
Germany	33	Berlin	6
United Kingdom	38	London	4

Source: Gallup, 23 May 2008.

living in the major European capitals – London, Paris and Berlin – are in full accord with the ethical principles of their fellow countrymen in their countries of origin and they condemn voluntary death on moral grounds (Table 7.2). Moreover, both the population in traditionally Muslim countries and those minority Muslim populations in other countries have always had extremely low suicide rates.[83] Muslims living in Ceylon in the mid twentieth century committed suicide far less often than the Tamils did. The Arab population now living in Israel have far fewer suicides than the Jews (Table 7.3). The two Indian states with Muslim majorities – the Lakshadweep archipelago, and Jammu and Kashmir – had suicide rates close to zero in 2001, levels that were much lower than the rest of the country.

However, this has not prevented Islamic religious authorities from arriving at a completely different conclusion regarding suicide missions. Some theologians and jurists have denied their lawfulness, both because they cause massacres of unarmed civilians, including women and children, and because they are carefully prepared and therefore 'premeditated'.[84]

Table 7.3 Suicide rates per 100,000 inhabitants in Ceylon (1946) and Sri Lanka (1996), and in other countries with Islamic, Hindu, Buddhist and Jewish religious traditions (1995–2002).

Iran	6.0
Syria	0.1
Egypt	0.1
Kuwait	2.0
Turkey	3.9
Israel	
Arab population	2.0
Jewish population	7.0
Ceylon (1946)	
Sinhalese	4.9
Tamil from Ceylon	10.6
Tamil from India	7.9
Muslims	2.1
Sri Lanka (1996)	21.6
India (2001)	10.6
Jammu and Kashmir	1.5
Laccadive	0.0

Source: Elaborated using data from Straus and Straus (1953); Turkey's Statistical Yearbook, 2005; Central Bureau of Statistics, Israel, 2002; Aliverdinia and Pridemore (2008) (my estimate of global rate); WHO, Establet (2012).

Yet the prevailing position among theologians and scholars of Islamic law is based on the contrast between suicide and an individual's act of blowing himself up in order to kill his enemies. The first is an expression of weakness, cowardice, a desire to desert and escape, while the second is a form of noble sacrifice undertaken by a courageous person with an inflexible sense of purpose. The first puts an end to a period of despair, the second marks the start of a new phase of hope and serenity. The first is therefore to be condemned and discouraged, the second exalted and emulated.[85]

This position was supported by a very high proportion of the population in several Muslim countries.[86] In 2002, three-quarters of Muslims living in Lebanon and almost half those living in Jordan, Bangladesh and Nigeria thought that suicide missions were always or sometimes justified. In 2007 the same opinion was expressed by 70 per cent of the population in the Palestinian territory (Plate 51, Table 7.4). But in many of these countries the last decade has seen a steep drop in the percentage of the population that approves of suicide missions.

This led to the culture of martyrdom referring to those suicide bombers who detonated themselves to kill the enemy. A complex Arabic vocabulary has been developed with the addition of new terms referring to the various forms of self-sacrifice. The word for martyr (*shahid*) has been joined by 'martyr operation', 'someone who gives themselves over to martyrdom',

Table 7.4 Levels of support among Muslims for suicide bombing (2002–13).

	% Saying often/sometimes justified									
	2002 %	2004 %	2005 %	2006 %	2007 %	2008 %	2009 %	2010 %	2011 %	2013 %
Pakistan	33	41	25	14	9	5	5	8	5	3
Indonesia	–	–	15	10	10	11	13	15	10	6
Nigeria	–	–	–	–	–	–	–	34	–	8
Jordan	43	–	57	29	23	25	12	20	13	12
Tunisia	–	–	–	–	–	–	–	–	–	12
Turkey	13	15	14	17	16	3	4	6	7	16
Senegal	–	–	–	–	–	–	–	–	–	18
Egypt	–	–	–	28	8	13	15	20	28	25
Malaysia	–	–	–	–	26	–	–	–	–	27
Lebanon	74	–	39	–	34	32	38	39	35	33
Palestinian teritories	–	–	–	–	70	–	68	–	68	62

Asked of Muslims only

Source: Pew Research Center.
http://www. pewglobal. org/2013/09/10/muslim-publics-share-concerns-about-extremist-groups/

a 'martyr who dies in battle', a 'happy martyr' (*shahid as-said*) and even an 'unintentional martyr' (*shahid al-mazlum*). This last expression was coined by Hezbollah to describe the passenger sitting beside the driver of a truck-load of explosives, when Israel, on the erroneous assumption that suicide bombers always acted alone, ordered that only trucks carrying a minimum of two people – a driver and a passenger – could circulate in the occupied territories. Therefore, when describing a suicide attack, the term 'happy martyr' was used to refer to the driver and 'unintentional martyr' to his companion.[87]

This culture of martyrdom found different forms of expression. Many of the Palestinians who became suicide bombers left a video recording as their spiritual testament. Standing upright, and holding a Koran and a Kalashnikov rifle with the flag of their particular group in the background, they address their viewers asking them to join them in paradise. Their actions have been magnified by the media and in mosques. Their deaths are usually described not as an end, but as a new beginning; their funeral is seen as a wedding because in paradise they will wed a large number of black-eyed women. Numerous streets in towns and even small villages are named after these heroes and their photos are displayed as part of politi-cal and religious processions, or shown in calendars to commemorate the 'martyr of the month'. Their families and relatives receive recognition and repayment, both symbolic and financial. To give an example, in 2001 Hamas presented them with a sum of between 500 and 5,000 dollars as well as a monthly payment of some 100 dollars.[88] To commemorate their role, 11 November was proclaimed as 'the day of the martyr' in memory of the first suicide mission organized by Hezbollah in 1982.

Somewhat different is the Salafi–Jihadist movement, a religious ideology that has acquired great importance since the start of the globalization of suicide missions. Among the total number of groups conducting suicide missions, those professing this ideology have risen from 17 per cent in 1998 to 25 per cent the following year, reaching 67 per cent in 2000 and 70 per cent in 2006.[89] Salafism (from *salaf*, which in Arabic means predecessors, forebears) is a radical Islamic doctrine that teaches a return to the purity of the fundamentals of the religion, the Koran, uncontaminated by the political compromises and influences of the Western world. By nature it is internationalist, because it holds that the teachings of Islam are valid for all countries and all people.[90] They believe that Islam is in decline from a religious, political, economic and military point of view, for which they blame the West, and they aim to redefine and strengthen the identity of disoriented Muslims, uniting them in a global Islamic community, the *umma*, and presenting a programme of war, also based on suicide actions, to reverse the decline and return the faith to its ancient glory. By reaffirming the legitimacy and need for *tafkir* (the equivalent of excommunication in the catholic world), they believe that the battle must be fought not only against the 'infidels' (Westerners) but also against 'apostate' Islamic regimes.

Here, too, the leaders of these groups have introduced a number of innovations, designed to encourage and support those militants willing to sacrifice their lives for the cause, which are nonetheless linked to the cultural traditions of each country. The concept of *jihad* has always been enormously important in the history of these people. In Arabic it means 'striving' or 'exerting oneself', committing oneself 'with regard to one's religion'. But for some time, it has usually been translated as 'holy war', or 'military action with the object of the expansion of Islam and, if need be, of its defense'.[91]

In the Islamic religion, a martyr who dies fighting for this cause against the infidels is rewarded in a number of ways. First and foremost is the assurance of life after death and entry into Paradise. The often quoted verse from the Koran reads: 'And do not think those who have been killed in the way of Allah are dead; they are rather living with their Lord, well-provided for.'[92] Here the martyr would have many of the desirable things that were forbidden on earth: refined and exquisite food and wine, gold and silk clothing, beautiful dark-eyed women (*hur'ni*). Even before the blood of his wounds has dried, two of these will pick him up. Then, as soon as he arrives in Paradise, each martyr will have seventy-two virgins who will give him great pleasure. In the ranks of Paradise, the martyrs will achieve the highest levels, immediately below God and the prophets, and this gives them the privilege of interceding on behalf of a certain number of Muslims at the Day of Judgement. According to some interpretations, each martyr can intercede for seventy members of his family.

Of course, this should not make us overlook the fact that, as the political scientist Gaetano Mosca noted in the late nineteenth century, 'if every believer were to guide his conduct by that assurance in the Koran, every time a Mohammedan army found itself faced by unbelievers it ought either to conquer or to fall to the last man. It cannot be denied that a certain number of individuals do live up to the letter of the Prophet's word, but as between defeat and death followed by eternal bliss, the majority of Mohammedans normally elect defeat.'[93]

In addition to a system of norms, beliefs and symbols, the ideologies and modern practice of suicide missions link back to a repertoire of actions experimented over time. A case in point was the Shiite Muslim sect known as the Assassins, based in the mountains of Syria and Lebanon between the eleventh and thirteenth century. On their own and armed with daggers, the appointed Assassin sect would attack and kill a governor of Islam, a minister, a general or major religious functionary, paying for this heroic action with their lives, because it was deemed a disgrace to survive a mission of this sort.[94]

The suicide attacks carried out in Asia several centuries later more closely resemble those of the past thirty years. These were undertaken by some Islamic societies to defend themselves against the expanding hegemony and colonization of the Western powers. The first of these attacks started in Malabar, in southwest India, in the first half of the eighteenth century and they were followed by others in Atjeh on the island of Sumatra, and in the southern Philippines in the nineteenth century.[95] Known as moors by the English, and *moros* by the Spanish, these Muslims usually launched their attacks against the European overlords but occasionally also against Hindu landowners.

The suicide mission was seen as a form of *jihad* against the infidels and heavily ritualized.[96] The young man who aspired to be chosen had to obtain permission first from his parents and then from a higher religious authority before taking a solemn oath (hence the Spanish term *juramentado*, which indicated both the action and the agent). Next he underwent a series of ritual preparations: shaving his head, purifying himself in river water, burning incense and offering prayers. If he changed his mind after all these operations, he was derided by all and known as a 'half martyr'.

Armed with just a *kris*, a dagger with a sinuous blade, the aspiring *juramentado* sought out a place where there was a large number of Christians and then rushed in among them, shouting 'There is no God but Allah' and trying to kill as many as possible in the full knowledge that he too would not survive the attack. Yet he firmly believed that the dead *juramentado* would mount to Paradise riding a white horse, where forty wives awaited him and he would be served with the finest food he could desire. From then on, he would be regarded as a martyr and venerated by all.

Fulfilling *juramentado* was also permitted to those prompted by other motives. In the first place, a man who had committed a serious crime might prefer to die by killing Christians rather than await execution, or secondly a man who was tired of life because he had lost honour, or undergone serious family or economic problems, might chose *juramentado* as a way of avoiding the Islamic prohibition against suicide.[97] In this case, *juramentado* was a form of indirect suicide that to some extent resembled the solutions used in some European countries to avoid eternal damnation in the seventeenth and eighteenth centuries.[98]

This practice survived at least until the early twentieth century when the US army took control of the province of the *moros* in the Philippines. Rather than resorting to the forced disarmament of these *moros*, General John Pershing, who was in command, tried to eliminate *juramentado* using a stratagem that used Islamic beliefs to the Americans' advantage. He publicly announced that a pig would be buried with the body of any *moro* who died while attacking American soldiers, because in the eyes of the would-be martyr this meant going to hell rather than going to paradise.[99]

7.9   An army of roses

'When an 18-year-old Palestinian girl is induced to blow herself up and in the process kills a 17-year-old Israeli girl, the future itself is dying.'[100] These words, pronounced by President George W. Bush in April 2002 after the suicide bombing by Ayat al-Akhras, accurately summed up the feelings and opinions of most Westerners who found acts of this kind even harder to understand than those committed by men, because they went against all traditional expectations and gender relation norms.

Profound changes have occurred in this respect as well during the last twenty years in the Middle and Far East. Traditionally, in wars and in terrorist and guerrilla operations, women were almost always assigned support rather than combat roles. The first, unexpected change took place in secular organizations in the late 1960s, many years before the first suicide attacks. A woman, Leila Khaled, was one of the militants of the Popular Front for the Liberation of Palestine (PFLP) who hijacked a plane flying from Rome to Athens on 29 August 1969. Two more women were also involved three years later in the Sabena hijack at Brussels. A second and even less predictable change occurred in 1985, when the Syrian Social Nationalist Party sent San'a Mehaydali, a seventeen-year-old Lebanese woman, to blow herself up by driving into an Israeli convoy, killing five soldiers. San'a's sacrifice, who became known as the 'bride of the south', was followed by five further suicide attacks carried out by women and organized by the same party.

In the years that followed, all the main groups that had resorted to suicide operations decided to enrol female suicide bombers. The LTTE was the first. Already in 1984 this organization had allowed women members and they soon accounted for 15 per cent of its ten thousand armed militants. Seven years later, a young woman was asked to carry out a suicide mission: the attack on the Indian Prime Minister, Rajiv Gandhi, which was discussed earlier. The PKK did the same in 1996. Islamic organizations found it harder to come to the same decision, because their religion did not allow women to engage in *jihad*. In June 2000 a Chechen woman, Hawa Barayev, became the first female suicide bomber from this organization.

Other groups belonging to the Islamic tradition had to overcome doubts and considerable resistance before reaching this decision. In 1987, during the first Intifada (literally 'revolt') against Israel's military occupation of Palestine, the PLO leaders asserted that women too should play an active role in the struggle, becoming 'mothers of the nation'. A Hamas document produced the following year states, that 'The Muslim woman has a role no less important than that of the Muslim man in the battle for liberation. She is the maker of men.' Elsewhere, it was claimed that 'the woman who rocks the baby's cradle with one hand, rocks the nation with the other'.[101] Therefore, it followed that women's contribution was principally to bear and rear children and the woman who refused to do so harmed the nation.

As well as nationalizing women's bodies and militarizing their wombs, the Palestinian leaders took all possible steps to limit the ways that women could take part in the first Intifada. Resolute in their defence of tradition, firmly holding to the principle that public space was reserved to men, and humiliated by the daily sight of Israeli soldiers who 'handled' the bodies of their sisters, wives and mothers as they carried out searches, the Hamas leaders banned Palestinian women from appearing in public without covering their heads (*hijab*) and bodies (*jilbah*).[102]

The turning point came on 27 January 2002 in a speech made by Yasser Arafat, leader of Fatah. 'Women and men are equal', he said to thousands of Palestinian women who had gathered to listen to him. 'You are my army of roses that will crush Israeli tanks.' He added, 'You are the hope of Palestine. You will liberate your husbands, your fathers, your sons from oppression. You will sacrifice the way you, women, have always sacrificed for your family.'[103] To underline the importance of this moment, the PLO leader coined a new term for the occasion, *shahida*, the female version of the word used by Arabs to describe a male martyr, *shahid*. He started to repeat it, over and over again, until the women began to chant along with him: '*Shahida, shahida . . .* until Jerusalem. We will give our blood and soul to you and to Palestine.'[104] That same day, in the afternoon, Wafa Idris, a twenty-six-year-old Palestinian woman, blew herself to pieces in the centre of Jerusalem, killing one Israeli man and wounding 131 bystanders.

This woman's sacrifice resonated strongly around the world and was greeted by the Arab population as the sign of a far-reaching change in gender relations. At the memorial held for Wafa Idris, Rabeeha Thiab, head of the Fatah women's committees, shouted: 'She's the mother of the martyr, sister of the martyr, daughter of the martyr – and now she's the martyr herself.'[105] An editorial in Egypt's weekly *Al-sha'ab* on 1 February 2002 exclaimed: 'It's a woman! It is a woman who teaches you today a lesson in heroism, who teaches you the meaning of Jihad, and the way to die a martyr's death . . . It is a woman who has shocked the enemy with her thin, meagre, and weak body . . . It is a woman who blew herself up, and with her exploded all myths about women's weakness, submissiveness and enslavement.'[106] On 18 February 2002, the al-Aqsa martyrs' brigade, a group very close to Fatah, officially opened a women's suicide unit in honour of Wafa Idris.[107]

Yet this woman's action also prompted much criticism and debate. A few days after her death, the spiritual head of Hamas, Ahmad Yassin, expressed a number of value judgements, reiterating the traditional principles. He said that the female body was maternal, sheltering, grieving and suffering, and that women should be at home to shelter fugitives and prepare for the loss of her sons, brothers and husband. He stated that a man who recruited a woman for a suicide mission broke Islamic law, because he acted without the permission of her male relatives. He asserted that if she goes out to *jihad* and is absent from home for more than a day and a night, she must be accompanied by a *mahram* (a male relative she is forbidden by consanguinity to marry).[108] But he also noted views he thought were factually true. He cautioned that women were untrustworthy and had a tendency to reveal their plans more than men; they were also psychologically weaker because they were incapable of staying alone 'in the darkness of an orange grove or at the bottom of a garbage dump' until the moment for the attack arrived.[109]

However, even the two most religious Palestinian organizations followed suit. In early 2003, the Islamic *jihad* started to recruit and train women, entrusting the first suicide mission to a nineteen-year-old female student and a second to another young law student. Hamas did the same in January the following year, using a mother of two young children, Reem Saleh al-Riyashi (Plate 52).

All these organizations made every effort to legitimize this change and to bring it into line with traditional customs. In some countries, Islamic religious authorities justified the change by reinterpreting sacred texts and histories. This led to the discovery of a passage in the Koran which states that, if an Islamic country is attacked by the enemy, every Muslim, irrespective of gender, is bound by the duty of *jihad*. Emphasis was also given to the story of A'ishah, Muhammad's wife, who courageously led thousands of the faithful in the Battle of Bassora.[110] At the same time, they exalted the traditional female virtues of Wafa Idris and the other women who had given their lives in the name of the cause: beauty, purity, devotion, piety.[111]

The LTTE also rediscovered the figure of Satyabhama, who was Krishna's wife in Hindu mythology and fought alongside him, and in more recent history the role of women in the Indian National Army who fought for independence from the British Empire.[112] Tamil women who carried out suicide attacks were given the honorific title of *mavirar*, or 'great hero'. Yet they were still praised for their femininity and it was said that they suspended but did not abandon their feminine qualities when they entered combat and then returned to being gentle, kind and passionate creatures when it ended.[113]

Moreover, in response to those who were concerned that the arrival of women in the organizations would 'distract' the men, the LTTE leaders tried to separate militants by gender (during training, for example, or also during regimented everyday life) and to mimic familial relations by obliging recruits to address each other as 'brother' and 'sister' and initially prohibited marriage (although this was later allowed after five years of militancy and combat).[114]

Suicide missions carried out by women have not remained sporadic and isolated. The last twenty years have seen a steady rise in numbers. Overall, between 1985 and 2006, they accounted for 15 per cent of the total.[115] However, this proportion differed from one organization to another. The number of women as a percentage of all suicide bombers has remained very low in those organizations closest to Islamic fundamentalism (less than five per cent in al-Qaeda and Palestinian groups), whereas it nearly reached 20 per cent among the Tamil Tigers, 60 per cent among Chechens and as high as 70 per cent for the PKK.[116]

Once again, in order to understand this major change it is important not to look at 'who fired the shot', but rather 'who paid for the bullet'. The use of women in suicide missions started and spread above all to meet the needs of terrorist and guerrilla groups that until then had used only men. It allowed the organizations to provide a more balanced response to the relationship between the supply and demand for suicide bombers. For example, the admission of women to the LTTE in 1984, resulting in the assassination of Rajiv Gandhi seven years later, became necessary after the organization had lost many men in the armed struggle and needed to replace them.[117]

Furthermore, the use of women suicide bombers gave the organizations two important tactical advantages. The first is linked to the resonance of these operations and their ability to provoke terror in society. Attacks by women receive eight times the media coverage as attacks by men.[118] They strike more fear in the public because they give the impression that there can be no place of safety, no protection even from those who have traditionally cared for and supported others. On this aspect, a document from the Chechen rebels in July 2000 reads as follows: 'The young woman who was martyred, Hawa Barayev, is one of the few women whose name will be recorded in history. Undoubtedly, she has set the most marvellous example by her sacrifice. The Russians may well await death from every quarter now, and their hearts may appropriately be filled with terror on account of women like her [. . .] She has done what few men have done.'[119]

The second tactical advantage is that women raise fewer suspicions than men and can reach places and targets inaccessible to the latter. They can hide explosives under their robes more easily, pretending to be pregnant or simply because, until a few years ago, no one suspected that they would blow themselves up. The fact that even the most traditional Palestinian organizations started to use women as suicide bombers, even though this went against their moral principles, was also motivated by the fact that by the mid 1990s it was impossible for unmarried Arab men, under the age of forty, to get through Israeli checkpoints.[120] Similarly, the fact that the LTTE followed the same path was also because it was more difficult for a man to approach an Indian or Sinhalese politician and blow himself up than it was for a woman.

The use of women in suicide missions was also fostered by the changes in gender relations in many Arab countries, coupled with the demand for greater equality put forward by the more educated groups of women. In the early years of the new millennium, some Palestinian women rebelled against the concept of 'mother of the nation', stating quite categorically that they did not want to become 'mothers of martyrs'. 'I couldn't sleep during the entire past month', wrote one of them. 'I visited his grave and I called out to him, "Arise, awaken, son; don't remain there buried under the earth." "I don't want a son who is a hero", said another; "I want my son back. He is mine!"'[121] This marked the start of a sort of privatization of motherhood. Other women, moreover, demanded greater civil rights.

Palestinian organizations presented the decision to allow women to undertake suicide missions as a step forward in gender parity, and indeed it is possible that it has reinforced this trend. The announcement by Islamic religious authorities in some countries that women need no longer ask a male relative for permission every time they wish to do anything outside the home will certainly contribute to their increased autonomy. However, inside those organizations that use them to carry out suicide attacks women count for little or nothing. They rarely form part of the leadership group and are not usually consulted before a decision is taken.

They also know that if they decide to sacrifice their lives they will receive smaller rewards than men, both in this world and the next. In terms of this world, all the Palestinian organizations (Hamas, Islamic *jihad* and the PLO) pay out a monetary reward to the families of those who carry out a suicide mission, and this amounts to 400 dollars for a male suicide bomber and 200 dollars for a woman.[122] As for the heavenly rewards that are promised, women do not receive any of the sexual gratification waiting for men. Even in the afterlife they will have a single husband to whom they must remain faithful. When they arrive in Paradise, as Ahmad Yassin said, they will 'become even more beautiful than the seventy-two virgins [. . .] If they are not married, they will be guaranteed a pure husband in Paradise, and of course they are entitled to bring seventy of their relatives to join them, without suffering the anguish of the grave.'[123] But Hamas gave an even clearer answer to the question of whether a female martyr would have seventy-two husbands as a reward: 'she will gain the same reward as does the male, with the exception of this one aspect, so that the female martyr will be with the same husband with whom she dies. [. . .] The one who is martyred and has no husband will be married to one of the people of Paradise.'[124]

All this helps us to understand why many women who choose to carry out suicide missions do so because they have broken (often involuntarily or through no fault of their own) the strict laws governing their society and have therefore lost their dignity and honour, and they try to regain it through martyrdom, sacrificing themselves for a greater cause. Wafa Idris, for example, had been married to her cousin for seven or eight years, but had divorced because she was barren. Having returned home to live with her parents, she had no chances of building a new life and starting a family. Hanadi Garedat, another Palestinian woman who carried out a suicide attack, found herself in the untenable position (in her society) of being twenty-seven and unmarried. Faiza Iuma, a third Palestinian woman who followed the same path, was a transsexual and had reached the age of thirty-five and was still a spinster.[125] Likewise, many Chechen or Tamil women who decided to choose self-sacrifice did so because they had been raped.[126]

Conclusions

A few Western travellers in the early nineteenth century reported having visited countries where suicide was unknown. In 1815, the German voyager, Otto von Kotzebue, wrote that when Kadu, an inhabitant of the Caroline Islands, heard that a European had taken his own life, he thought he had misunderstood and announced that this was the most ridiculous thing he had ever heard.[1] Twenty years later, Sir George Grey, writing of the countless Aborigines he had met on his expeditions, observed: 'whenever I have interrogated them on this point, they have invariably laughed at me, and treated my question as a joke'.[2] Evidence of this nature, together with a wealth of statistics on European countries, helped to convince sociologists and demographers that voluntary death was an inevitable consequence of civilization and that 'savages' would not kill themselves 'except for hunger'.[3] This conviction was overthrown in 1894 when the results of the first systematic study on 'primitive' societies was published,[4] and the authors put forward new interpretations. It was probably then that Durkheim reached the conclusion that, while egoistic suicide was unknown 'among lower societies', altruistic suicide 'exists among them in an endemic state'.[5]

But this thesis too is not borne out by the findings and facts presented in this book nor by those available from other sources including archeological digs, anthropological research carried out over the past century, and travel journals written by European explorers, merchants and missionaries who, from the sixteenth century onwards, came into contact with all manner of different peoples. From this huge body of documentation, relating to over four hundred hunter-gatherer, nomadic or agricultural societies,[6] four key conclusions can be drawn, which reveal the inadequacy of the theory put forward by the illustrious French sociologist and of the 'aetiological types' of suicide – egoistic, altruistic, and anomic – on which it is based.

Firstly, some archeological studies in Asiatic countries have revealed that the hundreds of bodies found in imperial tombs do not belong to suicides who took their own lives to follow their sovereign, but rather to slaves or prisoners who were killed.[7] Moreover, anthropological research and travellers' accounts show that, in the main, the inhabitants of hunter-gatherer, nomadic and agricultural societies took their lives not for altruism but for the same motives that usually underlie this choice in modern Western countries: disappointment in love, jealousy, illness, unbearable physical pain, the death of a loved one, loss of honour, fear of punishment, or poverty.[8]

Secondly, even in hunter-gatherer, nomadic and agricultural societies with a laxer attitude to voluntary death, there were groups who opposed it. While studying the population of the small island of Tikopia, in the Pacific Ocean, in the mid twentieth century, the anthropologist Raymond Firth noted that the 'potential suicide situation' was one of 'much greater flexibility and even uncertainty' than Durkheimian theory supposed, because suicides were at the centre of conflicting obligations and social expectations from groups with opposing interests and attitudes.[9] As we have seen, this is exactly what often happened to the 'faithful maidens' in seventeenth- and eighteenth-century China.

Third, in some hunter-gatherer, nomadic and agricultural societies, far from being regarded as obligatory, let alone praised and rewarded in some way, voluntary death was considered a crime or at least morally reprehensible. For example, the Ashanti, who lived on the Gold Coast of West Africa, decapitated anyone who took their own life and their property was confiscated.[10] In other societies, it was widely believed that the spirits of suicides ceased to exist or at least did not join all the other spirits, and instead were condemned to remain poor and unhappy, and to feed off leaves, roots or what little they could find in the forest.[11] On the other hand, the Sioux believed that the Father of Life would punish those who hanged themselves from a tree to drag its trunk for all eternity, and for this reason suicides always chose as small a tree as possible.[12] As in medieval Europe, in some of these societies a suicide's corpse was also regarded as contaminated and consequently had to be buried separately.[13]

Lastly, in these societies self-murder, or the threat of it, was sometimes used to express a complaint or claim, to put pressure on another person in order to obtain something, or to attack another and cause severe harm as a means of revenge: all motives that are hardly 'altruistic'. The anthropologist Bronislaw Kaspar Malinowski happened on these practices, almost by chance, in the early 1920s, while carrying out field research in the Trobriand Islands (modern Papua New Guinea). An eighteen-year-old youth called Kima'i, 'put on festive attire and ornamentation, climbed a coconut palm and addressed the community', who had gathered in an open space below, as he bid them farewell. 'He explained the reasons for his desperate deed and also launched forth a veiled accusation against the man who had driven him to his death [. . .]. Then he wailed aloud, as is the custom, jumped from a palm some sixty feet high and was killed on the spot.'[14] By talking to some members of the community and observing the events that followed, Malinowski managed to understand what had happened. The suicide had had an affair with the daughter of his

24. Handprints (made with the right hand) of widows who had decided to burn themselves on the funeral pyres of their husbands. On the gates of the ancient city of Jodhpur, Rajasthan.

25. 'The Widow's Gate', Deopatan, Nepal; once a widow left the city through this gate, having declared her intention to self-immolate, she could not re-enter it.

26. Procession of the Indian widow towards the funeral pyre. Miniature, late 17th cent.

27. Drawings of funeral stele erected to commemorate widows who had burned on their husband's pyre.

28. Sati stele at Waldhwan showing marriage bracelets, swastika, lemon, sun and moon.

29. Jasvanat Kanvar on the pyre, on 12 March 1985, with her head covered by a red veil, a symbol of marriage, and her right hand raised in blessing. The police forced the woman down from the pyre and the rite did not take place.

30–33. Four etchings (based on real life sketches) made in Calcutta, in 1796, by the Flemish artist Balthazar Solvyns. 30. *Sati* in the form of *sahagamana* (going with). After bathing in the river (in the background) to purify herself, the widow wears a white garment and is accompanied by two Brahmins as she walks around the pyre onto which she then ascends to be burned with her husband's corpse. 31. *Sati* in the form of *sahagamana*. The widow, assisted by two Brahmins, throws

herself into the flames where her husband's corpse is burning. 32. *Sati* in the form of *anumarana* (dying after). A widow self-immolates some time after her husband's death, holding objects that belonged to him. 33. *Sati* with interment. The widow of a man from the *jugi* or weaver caste is buried alive with her husband's corpse. The pit, into which the woman descends by way of a ladder, is immediately filled with earth by the relatives. *Les Hindous* 4 vols. Paris: Chez L'Auteur, 1808–1812. Reproduced with permission from the collection of Robert L. Hardgrave, Jr.

34. Thomas Rowlandson, *The Burning System Illustrated* (1815). In this engraving the caricaturist criticizes the British government's attitude to *sati*. In one of the cartoons, these words have been put in the mouth of a British official, who holds a large bag of rupees: 'This custom, tho' shocking to humanity, is still allowed in consequence of the revenue it brings in which is of importance! I have also private reasons for not suppressing the burning System immediately.'

35. After weeping copiously for her husband's death, an Indian widow who has decided not to burn with her husband, is undressed by two women: her red robe and numerous bracelets are removed. She is washed for purification and then her head is shaved. Miniature, late 17th cent.

36. Commemorative arches in honour of chaste Chinese widows who committed suicide rather than remarry.

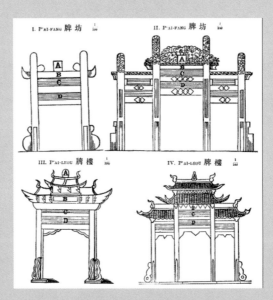

37. Chinese models of commemorative arches in honour of women who took their own life after the death of their husband, fiancé or to avoid rape.

38. A young Chinese woman disfigures her face by cutting her hair, ears and nose in order to remain faithful to her dead fiancé.

39. A young woman cuts her finger to draw blood to add to a healing soup (shown in the foreground being heated) for her sick mother-in-law.

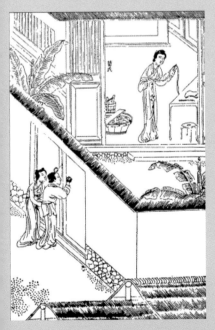

40. A Chinese woman prepares to commit suicide.

41. Having mourned for ten days, a widow jumps into a river to drown herself.

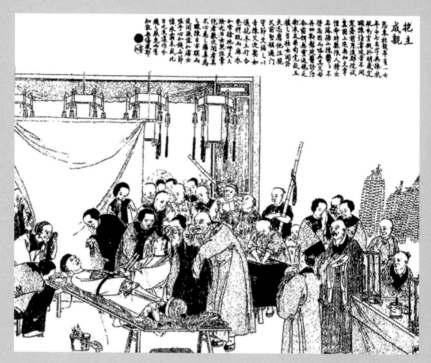

42. Marriage of a 'faithful maiden' to her dead fiancé (1880).

43. The chaste Mrs Wang as she writes her testament on the rock, in her own blood, before taking her own life.

44. Print by Utagawa Kuniyoshi, showing the Samurai Taira Tomomori, defeated in the naval battle of Dannoura (1185), as he throws himself into the sea tied to a heavy anchor (detail).

45. General Nogi Maresuke on 11 September 1912, a few hours before committing *junshi* before a photo of the emperor.

46. Nogi Shizuko, his wife, who committed suicide with him.

47.   Saigon, 11 June 1963. The Buddhist monk, Quang Duc, set himself alight
after being covered with petrol by other monks. He is shown completely calm
during this act of protest against the Vietnam regime, Ngo Dinh Diem. (c)AP/PA

48. Sriperumbudur, 21 May 1991. Dhanu exploded the belt of grenades worn under her robe, killing herself, Rajiv Gandhi and a further sixteen people.

49. Karbala, Iraq, October 2007: a failed suicide bomber, photographed with explosives after the incident.

50. A Taleban training camp for aspiring suicide attackers, in a tribal area on the border between Afghanistan and Pakistan, 9 June 2007.

51. A Palestinian boy wearing a belt of explosives during a protest.

52. January 2004. Reem Saleh al-Riyashi, the first female Hamas suicide bomber, who died on the border of Erez. She was the mother of two sons.

53. The Egyptian Mohamed Atta, head of the suicide unit that hijacked an American Airways plane on 11 September 2001 and flew it into the North Tower of the World Trade Center.

54. December 2007. A truck bomb driven by a suicide terrorist exploded in Kabul while a Nato convoy was passing, causing injuries to about a dozen civilians. © AP/PA

55. 7 July 2005. Ambulances at Russell Square tube station, London, after suicide attacks by four young Islamic terrorists caused the death of 52 people and injured 700 others.

mother's sister, breaking the society's rules on exogamy and causing disapproval and criticism. One day, the girl's former fiancé had insulted him in public, accusing him of incest. It was at this point that Kima'i, having been insulted and dishonoured, realized there was only one remedy and decided to kill himself in atonement for his crime but at the same time to avenge himself by identifying the man responsible for his act and ensuring that he would be made to pay for it. Indeed, both before and after the youth's funeral there were quarrels and fights in which the rival was wounded.

This custom has been found in many other societies and on every continent.[15] In Alaska, among the Thlinkets the person offended could only avenge himself by committing suicide and prompting his relatives and friends to take vengeance on his behalf.[16] In Argentina, among the Matako Indians of the Gran Chaco, it was frequent for people to commit suicide by eating the poisonous fruit of a particular plant in order to punish their offender.[17] In some islands of New Caledonia, an insulted or betrayed woman took her own life in the belief that, after death, she would 'be able to torment her husband as a punishment and keep him terrified. She kills herself to become one of the Furies.'[18] On the African Gold Coast, among some populations in the second half of the nineteenth century, custom dictated that should a person commit suicide for revenge, and before doing so attribute his or her act to another person, then the latter was required to do the same unless his or her relatives paid a sum of money as compensation.[19] Even in the last two decades of the twentieth century, the women of the Lurs tribe in southwestern Iran occasionally took their life to reopen the issue of strong gender inequalities.[20]

In these cases suicide was not an impulsive act carried out in secret, but was carefully planned, and involved making others party to the intention. For example, the women of Kaliai, in Papua New Guinea, informed others of their intention by destroying a number of personal objects, like their canoe or cooking pots. The woman committing suicide then put on her finest clothes and killed herself in the presence of others, preferably the person whom she held responsible for her act, shouting her intention before acting and drinking a poisonous substance or hanging herself from a tree.[21] But also in other societies, revenge suicide was always committed in public and the person deemed responsible was clearly indicated. These cases were referred to using the expression, 'killing oneself to take someone's head', because the suicide called out the name of the person who had prompted the act or singled them out in some other way.[22]

Similar forms of suicide existed for a long time in India and China (as we have seen) and in Japan. In the mid eighteenth century, the Jesuit Pierre-François-Xavier de Charlevoix wrote that, in the Land of the Rising Sun, 'every warrior who receives an insult feels he must wash the stain in his own blood', killing himself in front of the house of the person who offended him, who must then choose whether to renounce life or honour.[23]

Similar forms of suicide also occurred in pre-Christian Europe. Certainly in Ireland, where the custom of *troscad* (literally: 'fast against a person' or 'attain justice through death by starvation') was current for a long time. In order to ensure payment of a debt, the creditor fasted in front of the debtor's house. If this led to his death, the person who had refused to repay the sum owed was then obliged to pay the family a two-part compensation: the price of the body, which was quantified as seven slaves, and the price of honour which varied (from one to twenty slaves) depending on the social status of the dead man.[24]

But suicide was also sometimes practised in ancient Greek and Roman rural societies as a form of revenge against an enemy, if this could not be satisfied in any other way. The works of classical Greek and Roman historians, philosophers, playwrights and poets are filled with examples of revenge suicide.[25] At Delphi, Charila, an orphan girl, hanged herself as revenge on the king who had chased her away, striking her with a sandal, when she had asked for food at a time of dearth. Likewise, Ajax, enraged and shamed by the two Atreidae, Agamemnon and Menelaus, who had refused to give him the arms of the dead hero Achilles, resolved to impale himself on his sword in order to take revenge on his enemies and restore his honour (Plate 1). But before doing so, he turned to the gods and asked Hermes to send him painlessly to sleep, and Zeus to defend his body from the ravages of dogs and ravens. Then he called on:

> . . . the immortal virgins
> Who feed on the sufferings of man.
> You far-treading Furies,
> Mark how I am being destroyed
> By the sons of Atreus.
> Overtake that foul pair with some horrific fate
> As they see me brought down by suicide;
> So might it be suicide for them when they
> Are destroyed by their nearest and dearest.
> Come, Furies, to a feast of vengeance –
> Feed on the whole army; devour them all![26]

Dido's suicide was also for revenge, committed not for Aeneas but against him.[27] Having no other means of stopping him, Dido issued this terrible last threat:

> Yet if the virtuous gods have power, I hope that you
> will drain the cup of suffering among the reefs, and call out Dido's
> name again and again. Absent, I'll follow you with dark fires,
> and when icy death has divided my soul and body, my ghost
> will be present everywhere.[28]

As well as in epic poems, voluntary deaths for revenge were also part and parcel of everyday life in ancient Rome.[29]

Notable differences can undoubtedly be found between these suicides carried out with aggressive intent in the hunter-gatherer, nomadic or agricultural societies of Asia, Africa, America and Europe. Yet they have a number of important features in common. Firstly, those who take their own lives for these reasons always belong to the weakest social groups, including women and orphans, those who have no other way of influencing the actions of others.[30] This probably explains why in the vast majority of those (non-Western) pre-industrial societies on which information exists, women killed themselves more frequently than men.[31]

Secondly, these forms of suicide are only possible in the context of particular beliefs or particular social customs, or both. Taking one's life to spite someone because there was no other way of getting revenge in life meant delegating this task to a supernatural being, if one believed in the 'swift-footed Erinyes', or in the possibility of becoming a ghost who would haunt the person who had deceived and deluded one (as Dido said). But revenge suicide was also possible in a society in which the law inflicted penalties against those held responsible for maltreating and humiliating the victim while they had been alive.

Both these conditions were present in some societies. As late as the second half of the twentieth century, for example, Gainij women (in Papua New Guinea) who took their own lives in revenge for their husbands' violence thought they could harm these men in two ways. Above all, a woman believed that after death she would have a greater effect on her husband's life, causing him the same trials and tribulations that he had inflicted on her. Secondly, she knew that her death would result in both economic and social damage. The husband would forfeit the money and goods given to his in-laws at the time of marriage (the so-called 'bride price') and he would also have to pay a further sum in compensation for their daughter's death. His social standing would also be threatened, because everyone would realize that he had been trumped by his wife and deprived of the productive and reproductive power he had purchased from his in-laws, sometimes in exchange for a considerable sum of money. Therefore, when a woman took her own life as a form of revenge against her husband, the latter was often derided by friends and neighbours because he had not managed to assert control over her.[32]

Far from being a manifestation of the absolute subordination of the individual to the group, all of these suicides, whether committed for revenge or with vindicative or aggressive aims, were instead acts of disobedience, rebellion, protest and challenge. They have always represented the potent act of the impotent, the forceful act of the powerless, the hopeful act of the despairing. Moreover they represented an attack on the community, to the extent that – as has been seen – individuals, families, tribes and cities felt so threatened by the avenging ghost of the suicide that they responded by mutilating the corpse, casting it into a river or burying it as far as possible from the other dead.[33]

That there is no 'close link' between the absolute subordination of the individual to the group and altruistic suicide (as proposed by those scholars who follow Durkheim) is also demonstrated by many of the findings and facts presented in this book. For some centuries in China, the widows and 'faithful maidens' who killed themselves after their husband's or fiancé's death were not docile, passive women, subordinated to the higher needs of society to which they belonged. While it is true that their gesture was often rewarded with honorificences by the court and emperor, it is equally true that to pursue their ideal, and to remain faithful to the man to whom they were bound, even if they had had no part in choosing him, the women often came into conflict with family and relatives, kith and kin, and indeed on occasions it was precisely to overcome this resistance that they committed suicide. On the other hand, the suicide bombings carried out in many countries since 1983 show that altruistic motives can prompt suicide, for one's own people or for one's ethnic group, even if those committing the attacks form part of a modern society, have a high educational level and a cosmopolitan outlook, and have lived in different countries and speak their language.

Therefore, while social integration and regulation are neither the sole nor the most important factors affecting the variations in the suicide phenomenon over time and space, the famous 'aetiological' distinction, which is based on these alone, can no longer help us to understand what is happening in this field. Given the state of current knowledge, in order to explain these variations, it is much more useful to classify suicide types according to intention and the significance attributed to the act by the person carrying it out. This can be set out by intersecting two dichotomous variables (Figure C.1). The first concerns the people for the benefit of whom suicide is committed. One can only bid farewell to the world for oneself or for others. The second variable concerns the people against whom the suicide acts. Again one can only act against oneself or against others.

The first type of suicide is called egoistic and includes those who kill themselves thinking only of themselves, to put an end to unbearable pain caused by a variety of reasons (loss of a loved one, loss of honour, severe illness, bankruptcy, etc.). The second is defined as altruistic suicide and includes those who renounce life also for the good of someone else. Key historical examples of this type are Indian and Chinese widows or the 'faithful maidens' who took their lives following their husbands' or fiancés' death. But equally one could cite the early Christian martyrs who died rather than abjure their faith. Yet there are those who claim that even these widows, the faithful maidens or martyrs (just to limit ourselves to these examples) commit suicide for personal advantages, for glory or for otherworldly rewards. Even if we accept this view, there is no question that these individuals also act for the good of others, be it their husbands, relatives or the church to which they belong. The third type is defined as aggressive suicide and refers to those who, as well as wishing to leave a life of suffering, desire to punish the person whom they see as being responsible. Eighteen-year-old Kima'i from the Trobriand Islands or Dido from

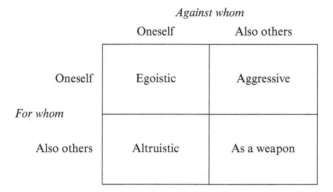

Figure C.1 Types of suicide according to the intentions of the person carrying it out.

classical mythology are good examples of these intentions. Lastly, the fourth form, suicide as a weapon, indicates those who, by dying for a noble cause, whether political or religious, aim to strike at, damage or even kill their enemies. Among this group we find the Buddhist monk, Thich Quang Duc, who set fire to himself in Saigon on 11 June 1963 in protest against the Diem regime of South Vietnam; the Irish prisoners who died on hunger strike in 1923 against the British government; the *juramentados* of the eighteenth, nineteenth or early twentieth century; or those who have carried out suicide attacks in the last thirty or so years.

The first two types (egoistic and altruistic) copy the labels coined by Durkheim but here they are used in their original sense, namely as proposed by George Henry Savage, a psychiatrist from London. In other words, they refer to the intentions of the person carrying out suicide and to the significance given by the latter to this act, not to the social causes that produce the suicides. Therefore, like the other two types (aggressive suicide and suicide as a weapon), they not only depend on social integration and regulation but also on other factors of which the following are the most important.

In the first place come factors of a psychiatric nature. These lack any importance when the voluntary death is regarded as part of an armed struggle. Those who carry out suicide missions do not usually suffer from mental disorders, largely because the organizations that recruit them have a vested interest in using completely normal people who will not raise suspicion or make mistakes. It is also possible that voluntary death for altruistic reasons largely depends on moral education rather than on an individual's mental health. But in the absence of rigorous studies, we do not know (nor shall we ever know with certainty) if the tiny minority of widows, faithful maidens, soldiers, generals or monks in Eastern countries, who self-immolated when faced with particular events, did not differ in some respect, from a mental health point of view, from the vast majority who preferred to carry on living. Without reliable data, we cannot even make any hypothetical assumptions regarding Kima'i's mental health, the youth recalled by Malinowski, or the women in hunter-gatherer, nomadic or agricultural societies who left the world to spite someone else. Some studies have indeed shown that in these societies other forms of aggressive suicide were often chosen by people affected by manic depression or other mental illnesses.[34] Lastly, we know for certain that those who suffer from major depression, schizophrenia, bipolar disorder or any personality disorder have a much greater risk of killing themselves for egoistical reasons, not only in Western but also in Eastern societies.[35]

Secondly, there are those factors related to the structure of society, its level of integration and its regulation. Although these are neither the sole factors nor the most important, they help us to explain chronological and geographical variations in the rate of egoistic suicide. Anyone belonging to a wide network of strong relationships and enjoying its support in various ways (cognitive, emotive, material) is better able to deal with adversity and runs fewer risks of voluntary death. Consequently, if these bonds are undermined, for whatever reason, there will be a greater probability that the individuals will take their own lives. It is this reason, a diminished level of social integration, that led to an increased frequency of egoistic suicide in some areas of Europe during the nineteenth and early twentieth centuries. Conversely, if this frequency diminished in some countries during the two World Wars, it was also because individuals formed more closely knit communities faced with a common threat, and they attributed their misfortunes to the latter. On the other hand, in the West during the last two centuries, the fact that suicide rates are lower among married couples or those living together, compared to those who are single, unmarried, divorcees or widows,[36] can be attributed to marriage as an element of integration and regulation. Marriage builds social networks that can be both solid and flexible, providing various forms of support. It disciplines, moderates, contains. It sets rules of conduct for everyday life, for work and leisure, diet and rest. It imposes a daily schedule, a healthy way of eating, caring for one's health, taking heed of symptoms of illness, and avoiding dangerous forms of behaviour. Lastly, the huge rise in voluntary deaths that occurred in Russia after 1991 can be attributed, not only to the severe crisis of the health system, but also to the anomie and disorientation many felt as a result of the collapse of the Soviet regime.

The importance of regulation can also be seen from all those events that, as we have seen, increase the likelihood that an individual may kill herself or himself when unforeseen and unforeseeable incidents suddenly happen, overturning future plans and seriously undermining expectations from others and from life.[37] The African slaves who were taken to America by force committed suicide more often either during the crossing or in the first two months after landing; immigrants generally have higher suicide rates than natives due to the cultural shock and difficulties of integrating in the new society; detainees kill themselves more frequently in the first few days after starting their prison sentence.

Then, in third place, there are the cultural factors, those cognitive schemata and classification frameworks, and the belief systems, norms, meanings and symbols available to men and women. They play a primary role in helping us to understand the long periods of continuity, the watersheds and radical changes, and to explain why in some societies and at some periods people killed themselves not only because of the loss of honour, disappointment in love, grave illness or the death of a loved one, but also as a way of benefiting or attacking others. The most intricate and complex systems structured around these cultural elements, namely religions, and in particular the universal religions, have had an enormous influence on the history of these four categories of voluntary death.

Early Christianity adopted the pagan glorification of altruistic suicide and, during the first two centuries, martyrs preferred to die rather than renounce their faith, taking the lead from those Romans who had sacrificed their life for a noble cause.[38] This continuity between pagan and Christian culture came to an end in the fifth century when Augustine condemned all forms of voluntary death. From that moment, Europe slowly began to witness a shrinking repertoire of the different forms of suicide, and the numbers of people taking their own lives for altruistic and aggressive reasons fell and subsequently remained very low.

The thesis, backed by psychologists and psychoanalysts, that there is sometimes a tendency to commit suicide to spite or punish someone, as a form of vendetta,[39] should not prevent us from noting the huge differences between West and East over the past two thousand years. Indeed, this idea was first proposed back in 1637 by the Anglican minister John Sym, who argued that human beings were occasionally constrained to take their own life by the desire for revenge against themselves ('either for what he hath done; or else, for what he presently is')[40] or against others. This latter instance could occur when someone was 'implacably offended by others, from whom he can neither have satisfaction, nor reformation of his grievances' and 'when his death by his owne hands may redound to the hurt, or disgrace, as he thinks, of those that have wronged him'.[41] This form of suicide, as John Sym noted, was most practised by those who had no other means of enforcing their claim, 'persons of the weakest sexe, and worst disposition and conditions; such as be women, and servants, and men sympathizing with them in qualities'.[42]

Indeed, in Western countries, the idea of using death, whether involuntary or voluntary, as a way of punishing someone appears most frequently in those, including children, who lack any other direct means of aggression. For example, Tom Sawyer, Mark Twain's famous hero, imagined taking revenge on Aunt Polly for having unjustly slapped him because she thought, wrongly, he had broken the sugar bowl:

'He pictured himself lying sick unto death and his aunt bending over him beseeching one little forgiving word, but he would turn his face to the wall, and die with that word unsaid. Ah, how would she feel then?'[43]

This thought was followed by another that was even more moving. He fancied throwing himself into the Mississippi and being carried back home from the river, 'dead, with his curls all wet, and his sore heart at rest. How she would throw herself upon him, and how her tears would fall like rain, and her lips pray God to give her back her boy and she would never, never abuse him any more! But he would lie there cold and white and make no sign–a poor little sufferer, whose griefs were at an end.'[44]

By drowning himself in the river Tom Sawyer wanted to make his aunt feel remorse and regret. Instead the revenge suicide described by John Sym served to discredit and damage the offending person. But, unlike ancient Greek and Roman societies or those in many Eastern countries, for the past two thousand years Christian Europe has never had the beliefs or social customs that would allow suicides to achieve these ends. To use the apt words written by Albert Camus: 'How do I know that I don't have any friends? Very simple: I found out on the day when I considered killing myself in order to play a trick on them – to punish them in a way. But to punish whom? Some people would be surprised, but no one would feel punished.'[45] But even if this does not happen, the most that can be achieved by a person committing suicide for revenge in a Western country is that someone will be made to feel a slight sense of guilt. Camus knew that neither the Furies nor spirits, neither family members nor magistrates could punish the person who made him suffer.

Christianity has had an enormous influence also on egoistic suicide, the only (or almost the only) form that persisted in Europe after its arrival. After the fifth century, the birth of a coherent and complex system of beliefs, values, laws, punishments, symbols, meanings and interpretative categories that discouraged men and women from taking their own lives, using a myriad of internal and external controls, had the effect of limiting the number of these deaths. But the gradual erosion and final collapse of this ethical and symbolic system instead resulted, between the end of the seventeenth and early eighteenth century, in a rapid and apparently unstoppable growth in the rates of egoistic suicide, which started in central and northern Europe before spreading later to the southern and Eastern countries.

On the other hand, in those areas where other religions and other systems of beliefs, laws, symbols and meanings (Hinduism, Confucianism, Buddhism and Shintoism) took hold and spread, such as Asia and the Middle East, men and women continued to take their lives also for revenge or altruistic reasons. Whereas in Europe the model of the Roman Empire was no longer followed, in Asia the customs whereby generals, soldiers and sometimes even bureaucrats committed suicide after a military defeat became increasingly important. This was the case not only in India and China, as we have seen. In twelfth-century Japan if Samurai warriors were defeated they resorted to *seppuku* (which took the form of slicing open one's belly from left to right) in order not to lose honour and fall into enemy hands. Occasionally, while carrying out the same act, they committed *junshi*, or in other words they killed themselves at the death of their leader, a gesture that reinforced the clan to which they belonged by bringing it greater prestige. Exact the opposite was true in Europe during the same historical period, since a suicide risked bringing ruin and disgrace to his family.[46]

This cultural divergence helps us to understand why a number of independent variables have had such a different influence, in Europe and in Asia, on the frequency with which people bid farewell to the world. The first of these is certainly gender. In Western countries, suicide rates have always been much higher in men than in women. Indeed this is one aspect that was not reversed by the affirmation of Christian morality after the fifth century. All the available information points to the fact that, even in ancient Greece and Rome, the male population killed themselves more frequently.[47] At the time the main reason for this difference was cultural, in the sense that suicide was regarded as a particularly virile act. In order to explain why Lucretia took her own life, Valerius Maximus wrote in the first century that, 'by an evil turn of fate', she had been given a male soul in a female body. Where this culture became established, as was the case in northern and southern America, the suicide rate today, and probably also during the nineteenth and twentieth centuries, was higher among men than women.

Outside this universe of meanings and symbols, things were very different. In hunter-gatherer or agricultural societies, which permitted aggressive suicide, it was the female population that most frequently chose this option in response to everyday conflicts and problems. But the same was true in many Asiatic societies. In India women took their lives more often than men, even in the early twentieth century. In China this was the case for centuries.

The second variable that has had a different influence in Europe and in Asia on the frequency with which people commit suicide is civil status. As mentioned earlier, in Europe during the past two centuries, marriage has always protected both men and women from voluntary death, although the former more so than the latter because husbands generally receive more understanding, more care, more attention and more affection than they are capable of giving. On the other hand, the data available seem to point to the fact that today, in Asiatic countries, marriage is not a protection from suicide. Spouses kill themselves more frequently than bachelors or spinsters in China,[48] and more than divorcees in Japan.[49] In India, married persons take their own life more than bachelors, among the male population, and more than widows, among the female population.[50] No statistical figures are available for the past, but it seems probable that the situation was different in the seventeenth and eighteenth centuries. Perhaps in India, then, married women took their own lives less frequently than widows, and therefore marriage offered women greater protection compared to men.

The third variable is social background. In Europe, over the past three centuries, the relationship between social background and suicide rates has undergone a complete reversal. Having spearheaded the change, the bourgeoisie, aristocracy and intellectual classes initially showed higher suicide rates than other social groups. Yet over time, these differences diminished, only to reappear much later in a completely different guise. For many decades now, in Western countries, it is the most disadvantaged classes who, having the greatest problems and the fewest resources with which to deal with them, most frequently take their own lives. This is now also the case in Asiatic countries.[51] However, the surviving documentation leads us to suppose that in the past, in India, China and Japan, some kinds of suicide were more commonplace in particular groups, while different ones were more widespread in others. Those belonging to the most powerless sectors of society were more likely to kill themselves with aggressive intent, for revenge, and 'to harm others'. *Sati* and *seppuku*, on the other hand, were for centuries the prerogative of families in the warrior castes or classes.

We still know relatively little about the influence of a fourth variable: sexual orientation. However, men and women who feel attracted by persons of the same sex and who fall in love with them probably run a greater risk than others of committing suicide, in both Europe and Asia. Among the homoerotic populations of both continents there were also other similarities. In the first half of the twentieth century, both in some European countries and in Japan, gay and lesbian couples often carried out double suicides, holding hands or embracing the person they loved.[52] Yet there are also differences in the significance given to suicide. In twentieth-century China, for example, men who had fallen in love with a partner of the same sex then killed themselves in revenge against those who had prevented their union with their beloved, in the conviction that they would be able to torment them from the afterlife.[53]

The distance between Europe and Asia widened over time. Both in India and in China, the importance of some forms of altruistic suicide grew over the centuries, reaching a high point in the eighteenth century or early decades of the nineteenth. Having first appeared in the third century BCE, the use of *sati* remained socially and geographically limited for centuries. It started to spread in the eleventh century, but this was very slow at first. Only in the fourteenth century did the spread become more rapid, reaching a peak around the late eighteenth century, just before the custom was banned by the Governor General of India, Lord William Bentinck. In China, the practice whereby widows killed themselves instead of remarrying after their husband's death probably started later than that of *sati*, in around the third century CE. It too remained quite contained for over a millennium and only became a significant trend after the fourteenth century, reaching an apex during the eighteenth century. Lastly, the frequency of *junshi* in Japan increased above all after the fourteenth century and reached its maximum spread in the seventeenth.[54]

However, the differences in this respect between Europe and Asia have dwindled steadily since the nineteenth century. In part this was an effect of colonialism. The Muslims who governed India for long periods made numerous attempts to discourage the use of *sati*, without success. Instead the English, who started to rule areas of the country in the eighteenth century, finally – after much debate, and many doubts and uncertainties – approved a law in 1829 that forbade widows from self-immolating on their husband's pyre, and over time this certainly had the effect of discouraging this custom and bringing about its decline.

In part, however, the crisis in the cultural repertoires of Asiatic countries was hastened by other social transformations. In 1912, in Japan, after the death of the Meiji emperor, General Nogi Maresuke removed his military uniform and, having put on his traditional garments, committed *junshi* in front of his master's photo; his wife committed suicide with him (Plates 45 and 46). This act produced enormous shockwaves worldwide, but it was one of the last instances of a custom that had continued for centuries and which already for several decades had entered an irreversible decline. On 12 August 1900, in China, 570 women hanged or drowned themselves to escape the sexual assaults of the Japanese, Russian, American, British, French, German and Italian troops who formed part of the expeditionary force sent to Peking to quash the Boxer uprising.[55] On the other hand, even after the fall of the empire in 1911, there were still remnants of the age-old practice of rewarding the virtuous. The first president of the republic, Yuan Shikai, approved a decree in 1914 on the honorificences to be given to those acting in an exemplary fashion, including also chaste women and the 'faithful maidens'. But five years later, the May Fourth movement targeted this practice with ferocious criticism and marked its end.[56] In India, the cases of *sati* in the last decade of the twentieth century can be counted in single figures.

That the differences between Europe and Asia have been diminishing for at least the past one hundred years also emerges from an analysis of the relationship between gender and the risk of voluntary death. In most of India it is no longer the female but rather the male population that has the higher risk of suicide. More recently, the same change has occurred in China, where suicide rates for women are now slightly lower than for men. Moreover, in many European countries the gap between men and women in this respect has shrunk in the last century.

Yet, the differences that once existed between Europe and Asia have not yet altogether disappeared. In China, some people still take their own lives 'to make the strong tremble', for revenge, even though the task of seeing justice done is no longer delegated to a spirit. Moreover, today women there still kill themselves more frequently than in Europe, as was the case in the seventeenth and eighteenth centuries. From this point of view, India is more similar to China than to Western countries because female suicides are only slightly less frequent than male suicides. Furthermore, even nowadays, 15 per cent of women commit suicide by self-immolation, even if they no longer do so to follow their husband into the tomb.[57]

In Japan the residual influence of past customs has hindered and still hinders the medicalization of voluntary death, a process that started centuries ago in the West and is now almost complete. Psychiatrists sometimes struggle to convince Japanese patients with a history of attempted suicide due to serious mental illnesses to undergo treatment, because the patients interpret their behaviour quite differently and refuse to view their condition as pathological. These difficulties are amply illustrated in the public reactions to the suicide in 1999 of the literary critic Etō Jun. Many doctors and psychiatrists attributed it to the severe depression suffered by the famous publicist, caused by his wife's death and a recent apoplectic attack that had robbed him of the pleasure of writing. But this interpretation failed to convince Japanese intellectuals who, drawing on historic models, described the death in heroic and aesthetic terms.[58]

Lastly, there are political factors, power struggles, the conflicts they provoke between the strongest and the weakest groups, and the actions that each carries out in order to change or preserve the status quo. In those societies where these relationships are deeply asymmetrical, and where there is absolute dependency of the weakest groups (slavery and feudal societies), suicide aquired a completely different role and meaning in West and East. For centuries, in Europe, it was prohibited and punished for two different reasons. The first was that, in a situation in which 'the act of killing is claimed as a monopoly and privilege of the power holder', anyone taking their own life violated this rule and 'avoided any form of surrender'.[59] The second is that, having decided to take leave of the world, the subordinate deprives his master of his manual labour; he robs him, thereby damaging him. Instead, in medieval China, a vassal could threaten his lord and influence his decisions by swearing to kill himself for revenge, and sons could do the same to their fathers.

For a long time the weakest groups or populations in Asia and the Middle East used suicide as a weapon. In what was an authentic cultural innovation devised by a small number of creative leaders in response to the urgent demands of the particular political or military situation in which they found themselves, this tactic was accepted by the vast majority of their followers and soon proved effective. The ideators of these new customs always drew inspiration from their own cultural repertoire, for the most part from aggressive or altruistic forms of suicide, yet they transformed them from acts with individual consequences into methods of confrontation used for collective purposes.

With regard to the adoption of suicide as a weapon wielded in the name of one's own people I know of five key examples. The first started in India, almost two centuries ago. In this country the practice of 'sitting *dhurna*', namely fasting in order to force a creditor to repay a debt, can be dated back at least to the fourth century CE, and it continued for as long as the victim, the debtor, had greater faith in the threat of revenge through death than in the justice of the state. In the late eighteenth century, at Benares, an armed Brahmin could still approach his creditor's door and threaten to kill himself if his debt was not settled. But a few decades later when courts were set up to resolve these private disputes differently, the practice of sitting *dhurna* began to lose its efficacy.[60] Moreover, by 1861, it was banned by a governmental decree all over India. But before this happened, it was rediscovered, transformed and reutilized not for individual purposes but rather for collective ones.

This change, which happened in the early nineteenth century, was clearly described by Reginald Heber, who was Anglican bishop of Calcutta from 1823. In his diary, he recounts how the introduction of a tax on housing by the British administration created profound resentment among the Indian population. When a petition from the inhabitants of Benares was turned down, and fearing further taxation, the locals decided to 'sit *dhurna*', in other words they chose to remain motionless and refuse food until their requests were met. They were led by some Brahmins who circulated hand-written notes throughout the city and the neighbouring villages in which they explained their reasons and invited 'all lovers of their country' to join with them. Just three days later, a large and wholly unexpected movement had started: 'three hundred thousand persons, as it is said, deserted their houses, shut up their shops, suspended the labour of their farms, forbore to light fires, dress victuals, many of them even to eat, and sate down with folded arms and drooping heads, like so many sheep, on the plain which surrounds Benares'.[61] Concern spread among the British government that some of the protesters might die and a few days later the unpopular tax was repealed. A century later, the use of hunger striking as a means of political redress was reappropriated by Mahatma Gandhi, prompting a deeply emotional response not only in India but in many countries around the world, and since then it has gained a permanent place among the forms of protest used by the weakest groups, albeit losing some of its original characteristics.

The second example, in some sense quite similar to the first, occurred in twentieth-century Ireland. There the *troscad* had been in use since ancient times, although it did not continue as long as the Indian practice of 'sitting *dhurna*' since some experts affirm that from the ninth century the custom altered completely after changing social norms meant that the severe punishments on anyone causing a debtor to die of starvation fell into disuse.[62] Yet this custom too was rediscovered and reappropriated for wholly different aims. This happened in 1913, during a period of explosive tension between the Irish republicans and the British government. Over the following decade at least fifteen hunger strikes were recorded, involving over nine thousand prisoners and leading to seven deaths.[63] A further two hunger strikes, organized by IRA militants, took place in 1980 and 1981 at Long Kesh prison in Northern Ireland, during which ten prisoners lost their lives.

Differences in the history of *troscad* compared to Indian 'sitting *dhurna*' and the inclusion of suicide in the arsenal of militant struggle are, at least in part, due to Christianity. It only arrived in Ireland in the fifth century and for some time it involved the use of liturgical practices that differed from the rest of Europe. In spite of this, it seems likely that it hastened the declining use of *troscad*. Furthermore, there is no doubt that the reinstatement and revival of the custom as a means of political protest in the early decades of the twentieth century was opposed by some of the Catholic clergy. In 1923 a Catholic prison chaplain refused to administer extreme unction to Denis Barry, an Irishman dying from hunger strike, and the bishop would not allow the corpse to be carried into any Catholic church in his diocese or allow 'religious exercises which constitute Christian burial to take place'.[64]

The third example took place in Japan in the closing phase of the Second World War, from October 1944 to August the following year,[65] when the country found itself in an extremely difficult military situation. On 15 June 1944 the US Marines landed on the island of Saipan, and for three weeks fought against the Japanese army, decimating it. At the end, hundreds of civilians, men, women and often children in arms, killed themselves by throwing themselves into the sea to avoid the dishonour of capture.

Having lost most of their ships and airplanes, and fearing that US forces would conquer the Philippines, the Japanese supreme political and military authorities decided, prior to launching the final attack, to resort to a new form of combat, suicide attacks, which were regarded as the best way of using the scarce available resources to effect the greatest damage. In October 1944 the special attack corps was set up with the name *Shinpū*. The characters were also read as 'kamikaze' by Western translators but *Shinpū* means 'heavenly wind', an allusion to the ferocious typhoons that had saved Japan, in 1274 and 1281, from the Mongol invasions.

This corps operated with a sort of glider, called an *oka*, whose warhead was packed with high-grade explosive. It was towed by a mother plane to within forty kilometres of the target vessel, a huge US aircraft carrier. At this point the kamikaze, who had been seated beside the pilot of the mother plane, climbed into the *oka* and, after releasing the tow rope, glided an appropriate distance before dive bombing the target. The kamikaze had to keep his eyes open as he hurtled towards the target in order to correct the trajectory. In this way, and in other forms of suicide attack, over three thousand Japanese soldiers lost their lives.

This too was an innovation, a reinterpretation of the Japanese cultural repertoire that was inspired by Samurai traditions, also based on vanquished heroes (Plate 44), capable of appreciating the nobility of defeat because it was viewed in the light of an idea, repeated in an age-old Japanese proverb, that 'Life is as the weight of a feather compared to one's duty'. Indeed, the symbolic power of this repertoire was endlessly recalled in that difficult period of the war, starting with the names chosen for the first four suicide units, which recalled the verses of a famous eighteenth-century nationalist writer about the 'wild cherry blossom radiant in the rising sun'. As one of the Kamikaze pilots wrote, these flowers 'spread their radiance and then scatter without any regret; just so we must be prepared to die, without regret'.[66]

The fourth example occurred twenty years later, in South Vietnam, in a case of public self-immolation. This had been practised in China for centuries, also because the concept of self-immolation has always been very fluid and has been reinterpreted numerous times. In the closing decades of the twentieth century, when it was regarded as being in decline, it reappeared in South Vietnam, in a situation with very different aims, and with a very different impact. This unexpected development took place, as we have already mentioned, on 11 June 1963 when, during a Buddhist procession in Saigon, a sixty-six-year-old monk, Quang Duc, sat down in a lotus position, the most suitable for meditation according to yoga teachings, and after being drenched with petrol by a fellow monk, he set himself on fire and died in the flames, in an attitude of the utmost calm, while all around him people were shouting.

This event happened at the peak of a period of extreme tension between Buddhists and the regime of Ngo Dinh Diem, a politician from a Catholic background who, as soon as he came to power in the late 1950s, passed a series of measures intended to discriminate against the Buddhists who made up over 80 per cent of his country's population. On 8 May 1963, Buddha's birthday, the regime banned Buddhists from flying their flags. A mass demonstration was organized and the police killed eight protesters. It was then that the monk Quang Duc suggested to the movement's leaders that he was willing to make the ultimate sacrifice in public, watched by thousands of onlookers, as 'a donation to the struggle'.

His death by fire on 11 June 1963 was, as has been written, 'an unexpected combination of modern technology and religious tradition'[67] and it constituted a notable cultural innovation. For the first time, an act of self-immolation was accomplished using petrol and it was also immortalized by a professional photographer, Malcolm Browne (Plate 47), whose shocking images became headline news across the world, winning the Pulitzer prize. Quang Duc's act had been performed for centuries in many Asiatic countries. Before dying, he expressed a plea: 'I pray to Buddha to give light to President Ngo Dinh Diem, so that he will accept the five minimum requests of the Vietnamese Buddhists. Before closing my eyes to go to Buddha, I have the honour to present my words to President Diem, asking him to be kind and tolerant towards his people and enforce a policy of religious equality.'[68] His act had an enormous impact with repercussions both in South Vietnam and around the world. It definitively discredited the Diem regime and led to its downfall.

In this way, from altruistic form of suicide, self-immolation became a means of collective protest against political or religious adversaries. This is how it continues to be used today: in 1964 it was used by the Tamil militants, who had not yet discovered the power of suicide missions, and

then by many others, by the Kurds and by persons from countries were
death by burning had been practised for centuries, like India, Vietnam
and Korea.[69]

The fifth and last example started in October 1983 when Hezbollah
militants launched the first suicide missions in Lebanon against American,
French and Israeli soldiers. This was a different form of combat to that
used by Japan in the closing phase of the Second World War, because this
latest method was not used by a state and it could also be used against the
civilian population. The results obtained by Hezbollah were so successful
that this innovation was reused and adopted by many other organizations
(of different religious faiths), in the conviction that this was the only means
of achieving their stated ends given the limited resources available to them.
But here too they drew inspiration from the cultural traditions of their
own people.

As a matter of fact, the oldest suicide attack was caried out in Gaza
by Samson who, according to the Old Testament, killed many more
through his death, by making the temple collapse, than during his life.
Yet Westerners have never followed his example. Above all because, after
Augustine's denunciation, it did not form part of their repertoire of ways
of thinking and acting. But partly also because, after this cultural tradition
weakened, they were never prompted to revive it in a situation of *force
majeure*. With a sophisticated array of armaments at its disposal, for centuries the West has had no need to use the body as a bomb.

Appendix

Statistics on suicide

Part of the research carried out for this book took the form of finding, processing and analysing statistical data on suicide in order to identify the trends and changes of suicide rates over time and to make comparisons between countries, as well as to make a detailed study of the situation in Italy over the past 150 years.

On the first two points, Graph 1.1 shows the suicide rate (number of deaths) in London between 1686 and 1750; Graph 3.1 compares the number of suicides and homicides in Zurich between 1500 and 1798; Graph 4.1 shows the suicide rate of East and West Germany from 1898 to 2007; Graph 4.2 those for Vienna and Austria from 1980 to 2004; Graph 4.6 the rates in Sweden, Denmark, Germany, Austria and Russia between 1960 and 2003; Graph 4.7 the suicide rates for men and women in Russia from 1956 to 2002. Tables 1.1, 4.1, 5.1 and 6.1 show the ratio between male and female suicides, or where possible the suicide rates for men and women, in a number of Eastern and Western countries during various historical periods.

Tables A.1–A.4 show the historical data series of suicide rates per 100,000 inhabitants from 1841 to 2011, which I have reconstructed for nineteen Western European states, six Eastern European ones, and twelve from other continents. As readers will immediately note it is the former that predominate.

The first European countries that started, in the mid eighteenth century, to collect statistical data on the number of deaths per category, and hence to identify the number of suicides and victims of homicide, was Sweden.[1] Norway, Austria, Prussia and Mecklenburg followed its example some seventy years later, between 1815 and 1820. Over the following fifteen years, statistics on suicide were also collected and published by France, Belgium, Denmark and Britain. As for Italy, data exist for the kingdom of Lombardy-Venetia from 1819 to 1854,[2] and for the kingdom of Sardinia from 1824 to 1838.[3] The first statistics relating to the entire country date from 1864.[4]

To start with, these figures (and those concerning violent deaths in general) were collected by very different official bodies, depending on the country: in some it was the church, in others the courts, the health authorities, or the registrars.[5] In Sweden and Norway, for example, details of violent deaths were initially collected and transmitted by pastors. In Austria, too, responsibility for collecting these data lay with the church until 1871 when it passed to the health authorities. From 1864, in Italy the statistics on violent deaths were collected by the municipal registrars based on the declarations of doctors carrying out post-mortem examinations. Gradually, however, in all European countries (and subsequently in non-European ones, too) the task of certifying and transmitting information on violent deaths passed to the health authorities. For years now, these data have been collected and published by the World Health Organization.[6]

In Italy, since 1955, there have been two sources of data on suicides: cases certified by a judicial officer (GPs and pathologists), and those cases certified by the police (*polizia di stato*) and carabinieri and then transmitted to a judicial officer. The latter source strongly underestimates the number of suicides occurring each year. For example, in 2000 there were 4,108 cases of suicide in Italy according to the first source, and only 3,093 according to the second.

The volume of statistics on suicides in countries on other continents is considerably smaller. It is striking that in 1991, only 56 of the 166 UN member-states collected or transmitted suicide figures to the World Health Organization. On a similar note, there are not many countries for which long historical data series are available. This is true, in particular, of the Asiatic countries: the earliest figures for Japan date from 1878,[7] those for India start in 1965,[8] and the first statistics for China appeared in the early 1990s. However, as I said earlier in the book, there are statistical data on suicides for British India in 1907, for Taiwan in 1905, and for some Chinese cities in 1929.

In order to make a more detailed analysis of what has happened in Italy over the past 150 years, I carried out three different studies. Firstly, I created a data set for the number of suicides (and the rates as a percentage of the resident population) in each province, provincial capital and lesser provincial cities, from 1881 to 2002, using the data from the volumes of *Causes of Death* (published annually, from 1881 to 1965, first by the Directorate General for Statistics and subsequently by Istat) or from the digitized Istat files. This information was used to compile Graphs 4.3, 4.4 and 4.5.

Secondly, I calculated the suicide rate by age, schooling level and geographical area in 1981, 1991 and 2001 (Table A.5), using the data on causes of death given in the digitized Istat files and combining this with national census details in each of these three years.

Thirdly, I calculated the frequency of the different methods used by those committing suicide in Italy in 2001 and 2002, subdivided by schooling level and gender (Table A.6), again working on the digitized Istat files for causes of death.

Table A.1 Suicide rate per 100,000 inhabitants in Western European countries, from 1841 to 1991.

	1841–50	1881–85	1901	1910	1920	1930	1940	1950	1960	1970	1980	1990	1991
Austria	4.5	16.2	17.3	–	22.4	38.3	–	23.8	23.1	24.2	25.7	23.6	22.6
Belgium	9.1	10.7	12.7	14.2	13.2	16.8	18.1	12.9	14.6	16.5	22.1	19.0	18.0
Denmark	23.8	24.8	22.7	–	13.9	17.6	17.8	23.3	20.3	21.5	31.6	23.9	–
Finland	4.0	3.9	6.1	8.7	10.6	23.1	20.9	15.6	20.4	21.3	25.7	30.3	29.8
France	9.1	19.4	22.8	21.8	17.5	19.0	18.7	15.2	15.8	15.4	19.4	20.0	20.2
Germany	11.5	21.1	20.8	21.6	21.7	27.8	–	22.0	22.7	23.5	23.6	17.8	17.5
West Germany	–	–	17.3	–	–	–	–	19.2	20.3	21.5	20.9	15.6	15.6
East Germany	–	–	30.8	–	–	–	–	29.4	30.1	30.5	33.6	24.6	25.1
Great Britain	6.7	–	–	–	–	–	–	–	–	–	–	–	–
England and Wales	–	7.5	9.6	10.0	9.0	12.7	11.3	9.5	10.7	7.9	8.8	8.1	7.9
Scotland	–	5.3	5.3	6.1	4.9	10.3	7.9	10.2	11.1	8.0	8.8	7.8	7.6
Greece	–	–	–	–	–	4.7	–	5.2	3.8	3.2	3.3	3.6	3.7
Ireland	–	–	2.9	3.6	2.1	2.8	3.3	2.6	2.9	1.8	6.3	9.5	9.8
Italy	3.1	4.9	6.2	8.4	7.3	9.6	5.9	6.5	6.1	5.8	7.3	7.6	7.8
Luxembourg	–	–	–	–	–	16.8	14.5	14.5	–	14.2	12.9	17.8	19.9
Norway	–	6.7	5.5	5.5	4.8	7.2	6.9	7.4	6.4	8.4	12.4	15.5	15.8
Netherlands	–	5.3	5.8	6.2	7.3	8.1	10.8	5.5	6.6	8.1	10.1	9.7	10.7
Portugal	–	–	–	6.0	6.2	6.9	11.6	10.1	8.7	7.5	7.4	8.8	9.5
Spain	–	2.5	2.0	4.5	5.1	5.7	6.1	5.4	5.5	4.2	4.4	7.5	7.5
Sweden	6.7	9.7	13.1	17.8	14.7	15.8	17.1	14.9	17.4	22.3	19.4	17.2	17.2
Switzerland	–	23.3	22.4	22.7	22.6	26.1	23.6	23.5	19.0	18.6	25.7	21.9	–

Table A.2 Suicide rate per 100,000 inhabitants in Western European countries, from 2001 to 2011.

	2001	2002	2003	2004	2005	2006	2007	2008	2009	2010	2011
Austria	18.5	19.2	17.9	17.4	17.0	15.7	15.5	15.2	15.3	15.0	15.3
Belgium			20.3	19.1	19.3	18.3	17.5	18.7	18.6		
Denmark	13.6	12.8	11.7	12.2	11.6	11.9	10.6	11.0	11.3	10.1	10.6
Finland	23.2	21.0	20.5	20.3	18.9	20.1	18.8	19.4	19.3	17.7	16.8
France	17.4	17.8	18.0	17.8	17.5	16.9	16.3	16.6	16.7		
Germany	13.6	13.5	13.5	12.4	12.4	11.9	11.4	11.5	11.7	12.3	12.4
West	13.0	13.1	13.0	12.6	12.3	11.6	11.1	11.2			
East	15.7	15.5	15.6	14.7	13.0	12.8	12.6	12.5			
Greece	3.0	2.9	3.4	3.2	3.6	3.5	2.9	3.3	3.5	3.4	
England/Wales	9.3	9.0	9.1	9.1	8.8	8.3	7.9	8.4	9.5	8.1	8.7
Scotland	12.0	12.6	11.1	11.9	10.7	10.0	10.0	10.0	10.9	10.9	10.0
Northern Ireland	9.3	10.8	8.5	8.5	12.3	16.7	13.7	15.6	14.5	17.3	15.9
Ireland	12.6	11.4	11.4	11.4	10.9	10.6	10.4	11.4	11.8	10.8	
Italy	7.1	7.1	7.1			6.3	6.3	6.5	6.6	6.6	
Luxembourg	16.6	19.1	10.6	13.5	10.5	13.7	16.2	8.8	9.6	10.8	10.6
Norway	12.1	10.9	11.0	11.5	11.5	11.3	10.3	10.6	11.9	11.2	12.0
Netherlands	9.2	9.7	9.2	9.3	9.6	9.3	8.2	8.7	9.2	9.9	9.8
Portugal	7.3	11.6	10.9				9.7	9.8	9.7	10.4	9.6
Spain	7.8	8.2	8.3	8.2	7.8	7.4	7.3	7.6	7.5	6.9	6.9
Sweden	13.4	13.2	12.3	12.8	13.5	13.2	12.3	12.7	13.3	12.1	
Switzerland	18.5	19.8	17.2	17.3	17.4	17.5	18.0	17.1	14.2	12.8	

Table A.3 Suicide rate per 100,000 inhabitants in other countries, from 1841 to 1991.

	1841–50	1881–85	1901	1910	1920	1930	1940	1950	1960	1970	1980	1990	1991
Eastern Europe													
Bulgaria	–	–	–	–	–	–	–	–	–	11.9	13.6	14.6	15.4
Poland	–	–	–	–	–	–	–	–	8.2	11.2	11.2	13.0	13.9
Czech Rep.	–	–	–	–	–	–	–	–	–	–	–	19.3	18.5
Romania	–	–	–	–	–	–	–	–	–	–	–	9.0	9.3
Russia	2.6	4.0	4.8	–	–	–	–	–	15.2	30.2	34.8	26.9	27.1
Hungary	–	8.4	17.6	–	–	–	–	–	24.8	34.8	44.9	39.9	38.5
Other countries													
Argentina	–	–	–	–	–	–	–	–	–	–	–	–	–
Australia	–	11.1	11.3	11.8	11.9	14.6	10.6	9.3	10.6	12.4	11.0	12.9	13.2
Brazil	–	–	–	–	–	–	–	–	–	–	3.3	3.2	3.4
Canada	–	–	–	–	6.7	9.9	8.3	7.7	7.6	11.3	14.0	12.7	13.2
Chile	–	–	–	–	3.1	5.8	4.6	4.2	7.5	6.0	4.9	5.6	5.9
Cuba	29.7	–	14.9	–	–	–	–	18.2	10.3	11.8	–	20.2	–
Japan	–	14.4	17.6	18.9	19.1	21.8	13.8	19.6	21.5	15.2	17.6	16.3	16.1
India	–	–	–	–	–	–	–	–	–	8.0	6.3	8.9	–
Mexico	–	–	–	–	–	–	–	1.8	1.9	1.1	1.7	2.2	2.4
New Zealand	–	–	10.2	10.1	11.2	13.6	10.9	9.2	9.6	9.6	10.8	12.4	13.6
Sri Lanka	–	1.5	3.8	–	–	5.2	6.3	6.5	9.9	–	29.0	31.0	31.3
United States	–	–	10.4	15.4	10.2	15.6	14.4	11.4	10.6	11.5	11.8	12.4	12.2

Table A.4 Suicide rate per 100,000 inhabitants in other countries from 2001 to 2011.

	2001	2002	2003	2004	2005	2006	2007	2008	2009	2010	2011
Eastern Europe											
Bulgaria	16.4	16.7	13.9	13.0	12.7	12.7	11.9	12.5	11.7	11.6	
Poland	15.3	15.4	15.3	15.9	15.8	15.2	15.3	14.9	16.9	16.6	15.9
Czech Rep.	15.9	15.4	16.9	15.5	15.3	13.7	13.3	13.2	14.0	14.3	
Romania	12.3	14.1	13.5	12.7	12.2	12.8	11.6	12.0	12.7	13.7	
Russia	39.2	38.1	35.8	34.3	32.2	30.0	29.1	27.0	26.5		
Hungary	29.2	28.0	27.6	27.1	26.0	24.4	24.3	23.8	24.6	24.9	
Other countries											
Argentina	8.4	8.4	8.7	8.2	7.9	8.0	7.5	7.7			
Australia	12.7	11.8	10.8	10.6		8.1	10.7	11.0	10.8	11.0	10.2
Brazil	4.3	4.3	4.3	4.3	4.6	4.6	4.7	4.8			
Canada	11.9	11.6	11.9	11.3	11.6	10.8	11.0	11.1	11.6		
Chile	10.4	10.1	10.3	10.7	10.3	10.9	11.1	12.4	12.6		
Cuba	14.8	14.3	12.8	13.4	12.4	12.2	11.6	12.2			
Japan	23.1	23.5	25.1	23.7	23.9	23.4	24.1	23.7	24.1	23.2	22.6
India		10.5	10.4	10.5	10.3	10.5	10.8	10.8	10.9	11.4	11.2
Mexico	3.6	3.6	3.8	3.7	3.9	3.8	3.8	4.1	4.3	4.2	
New Zealand	13.1	11.8	12.8	12.1	12.4	12.5	11.7	12.2	11.9		
Sri Lanka	23.3	23.6				20.2			19.6		
USA	10.7	11.0	10.8	11.0	11.0	11.1	11.5	11.8	11.9	12.3	

Sources: Tables A.1–A.4: Krose (1906), Von Mayr (1917), Halbwachs (1930), Bunle (1954), Chesnais (1976), Venkoba Rao (1983), WHO (1951; 1956), Ministry of Home Affairs (2013), http://stats.oecd.org/index.aspx?DataSetCode=HEALTH_STAT; also data from Werner Felber (www.suizidprophelaxe.de, see statistics)

Table A.5 Suicide rate per 100,000 inhabitants in Italy, from 1981 to 2001, subdivided by schooling level, age and geographical area.

Year	Age	Central-northern Italy					Southern Italy and islands					Italy				
		Degree	High-school	Middle school	Primary school or none	Total	Degree	High-school	Middle school	Primary school or none	Total	Degree	High-school	Middle school	Primary school or none	Total
1981	0–44 years old	4.4	3.8	4.2	2.9	3.9	4.5	3.5	2.6	2.1	2.6	4.4	3.7	3.7	2.6	3.4
	≥45 years old	11.6	9.2	11.1	14.1	14.9	9.2	6.4	6.9	9.4	9.9	10.9	8.5	10.1	12.6	13.3
	Total	6.9	4.9	5.6	8.4	8.1	6.0	3.9	3.2	4.9	4.9	6.7	4.6	4.8	7.1	6.9
1991	0–44 years old	4.4	4.1	6.4	3.1	4.9	4.4	3.5	3.9	2.1	3.2	4.4	3.9	5.5	2.6	4.2
	≥45 years old	7.5	8.8	8.4	16.3	14.3	8.0	6.8	8.9	10.6	10.5	7.7	8.3	8.5	14.4	13.1
	Total	5.6	5.2	6.9	11.0	8.9	5.7	4.1	4.7	5.9	5.6	5.6	4.8	6.2	9.0	7.7
2001	0–44 years old	3.0	3.1	7.1	2.5	4.9	2.4	3.2	4.2	1.6	3.6	2.8	3.2	5.9	2.1	4.4
	≥45 years old	5.9	6.1	8.5	13.4	11.5	5.2	2.7	8.1	8.0	8.0	5.6	5.1	8.4	11.5	10.3
	Total	4.3	4.0	7.6	9.9	8.0	3.7	3.1	5.2	5.3	5.4	4.1	3.7	6.8	8.2	7.1

Table A.6 Methods used by people to commit suicide in Italy between 2001 and 2002, subdivided by gender and schooling level (%).

	Men				Women			
	Degree	High-school	Middle school	Primary school or none	Degree	High-school	Middle school	Primary school or none
Hanging	32.1	41.9	50.3	52.8	17.2	30.1	33.6	32.6
Poisoning	8.6	11.1	9.3	5.8	8.6	13.3	9.0	9.3
Drowning	3.6	2.5	3.1	5.4	3.4	4.3	6.2	14.6
Gun or explosive	21.7	21.7	17.7	16.3	3.4	6.6	5.0	1.6
Knife	2.7	1.8	1.2	1.8	3.4	1.2	0.7	1.9
Jumping	29.0	16.4	13.6	15.4	56.9	36.3	39.3	37.1
Other	2.3	4.7	4.8	2.5	6.9	8.2	6.2	2.9
Total percentage	100.0	100.0	100.0	100.0	100.0	100.0	100.0	100.0
No. of suicides	221	794	1,832	2,576	58	256	420	874

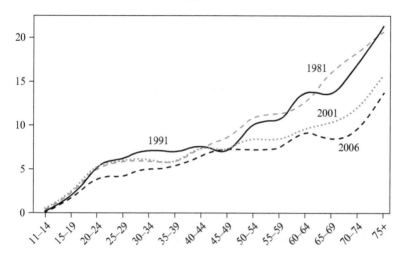

Graph A.1 Suicide rates in Italy in 1981, 1991, 2001 and 2006 divided by age cohorts.

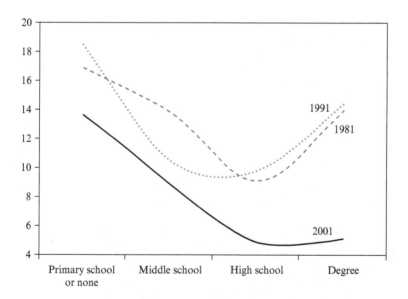

Graph A.2 Suicide rates of over-65-year-olds living in Italy in 1981, 1991 and 2001, divided by schooling level.

Notes

Introduction

1 Durkheim (1897; English trans., 1951, 281).
2 Ibid., 214–15.
3 Ibid., 363.
4 Ibid., 221.
5 Ibid., 219.
6 Ibid., 247.
7 Ibid., 253.
8 Ibid., 276.
9 On this, and on the reception and success of Durkheim's book, see the important essay by Besnard (2000).
10 For a review of the criticism and debate surrounding Durkheim's book, see: Pope (1976); Pickering and Walford (2000); Besnard (2000); Berk (2006). For the statistics and printed sources used by Durkheim, see the extensive study by Borlandi (2000).
11 Johnson (1965) was one of the first scholars to put forward this thesis. But Halbwachs (1930, 7 and 312) had already proposed that only one of the two factors supporting Durkheim's theory – social integration – was important. Doubts regarding Durkheim's distinction between 'egoistic' and 'anomic' suicide were voiced by Giddens in 1968 (Giddens 1971, 98). Johnson's thesis was supported, in their early works, also by the two most renowned experts on the French sociologist: Lukes (1967, 139) and Poggi (1972, 200), although both changed opinion later (Lukes 1973, 206; Poggi 2000).
12 Pope (1976, 30–1).
13 For Douglas (1967, 54) the concept of social integration is open to three different interpretations, for Berk (2006, 62–9) as many as five.
14 Douglas (1967, 163–231). On this question see also Timmermans (2005).
15 This aspect was first discussed over a century ago by Krose (1906a, 7–10) and then by Halbwachs (1930, 19–40). 'Suicide statistics are extensively debated and with good reason' (ibid., 19), he wrote before showing how the reform of the Prussian registration system in 1883 produced an increase in the number of suicides (ibid., 23–4). This did not prevent these scholars from using the official statistics for the various countries.
16 Besnard (1976); Pescosolido and Mendelsohn (1986); Diekstra (1995). That these figures are reliable, also when used in international comparative studies,

was an aspect that emerged from a number of studies carried out on migration processes in the United States, Canada and Australia (Sainsbury and Barraclough 1968; Whitlock 1971; Burvill 1998), which highlighted that even when the registration system is the same (that of the country of arrival), national differences in the suicide rates among immigrants remain similar to those found in populations in the country of origin. Sainsbury and Barraclough state that the suicide figures are the 'most accurate' of the statistics on the cause of death because they are subject to controls by several independent bodies (police, courts, medical authorities). For further information on the statistics and the sources, see the Appendix.

17 Biggs (2005).

18 Durkheim (1897; English trans 1951, 146).

19 George Henry Savage (1842–1921) was a prominent psychiatrist or 'alienist'; he was co-editor of the *Journal of Mental Science* and enjoyed a certain degree of notoriety in his lifetime. For his studies on suicide, see Gates (1980).

20 It is likely that Durkheim adapted his distinction between egoistic and altruistic suicide from George Henry Savage, although the latter had used the terms in a different context. See Goldney and Schioldann (2004).

21 Douglas (1967, 26–32); Lukes (1973, 200–2); Poggi (2000, 63–6). Lukes adds that an aetiological classification, like the one proposed by Durkheim, precluded the consideration of the possibilities that '(i) there might be other typologies of suicide that fit the suicide data better, and (ii) that there might be other causal factors at work'.

22 Lukes (1973, 202).

23 In 1951, in an important study of the use of revenge suicide in some African populations (republished in a new version in 1971), Jeffreys proposed adding it as a fourth category to the three main forms outlined by Durkheim (Jeffreys 1971, 185–6). On the other hand, Bohannan (1960, 12) argues against Jeffreys 'because the criterion of vengeance suicide is not to be found in the degree and sort of integration of the social group, the primary criterion in the Durkheim classification'. Both were right in part. The former because revenge suicide was more widespread and important than he thought at the time (see below). The latter because he was aware that Durkheim's classification was aetiological and did not concern the suicides' intentions but rather the social causes of their act. At the time Jeffreys could not have known that Gabriel Tarde, in a study of 1897 that was only published in 2000, had also criticized the inadequacy of Durkheim's classification as a means of studying revenge suicide (Tarde 1897) (see below, note 25).

24 From the outset of his book, Durkheim affirmed that the actors' motives had little importance: 'the diversity of motives capable of actuating these resolves can give rise only to secondary differences' (Durkheim 1897; English trans., 1951, 44). This choice was criticized by numerous scholars (Halbwachs 1930; Douglas 1967; Lukes 1973, 199–201).

25 Durkheim never mentions revenge suicide. He only recalls (1897; English trans., 1951, 284) that some suicides are 'threats and accusations against a particular person to whom the responsibility for the suicide's unhappiness is imputed'. Halbwachs discusses revenge suicide only in the conclusions to his work (1930, 465–9). The importance of revenge suicide did not however escape Gabriel Tarde (1897). Having recently read Matignon's article (1897) on China, which was published in the magazine he edited, he observed that

this type of suicide found no place in Durkheim's classification. 'Suicide for revenge, which is a characteristic of Chinese suicide' was certainly not altruistic, he wrote. 'It is egoistic and evil to the greatest degree. The *end* is the same as our *homicides*, only the *means* used by the suicide differs, owing to Chinese prejudices. Could we perhaps say that our revenge murders are *altruistic*?' (Tarde 1897, 250). Instead, Jean Baechler dedicated many pages to revenge suicide (1975).

26 Ricci (1942, no. 159/9).

27 Sumner Maine (1875) and Tamassia (1897) studied *dharna* (see Chapter 6); Steinmetz (1898) and Lasch (1898) also studied revenge suicides in Africa, China and South America.

28 Wisse (1933, 49, 62, 77, 115, 142, 311, 315, 436, 493); Metraux (1943); Jeffreys (1971); Strathern (1972); Panoff (1977); Baechler (1975, 534–42); Counts (1980; 1984; 1990); Bonnemère (1992); Ropp et al. (2001); Theiss (2004b).

29 As Giddens wrote (1965, 10), the analysis of suicide became a critical issue in the struggle to establish sociology as a recognized academic discipline in France. This was, of course, largely due to Durkheim's own stage-management; as Levi-Strauss remarks, 'the clash occurred on the ground Durkheim had himself chosen: the problem of suicide.' The *thèse psychiatrique* concerning the causes of suicide was countered by the *thèse sociologique*. Of course, psychologists and psychiatrists ignored or attacked Durkheim's book (Giddens 1965; Besnard 2000). It is worth remembering that one psychological study of suicide, which was long regarded as the most authoritative (Menninger 1938), never once mentioned Durkheim's book. In their recent reconstruction of the suicide theories proposed by nineteenth-century French psychiatrists, Berrios and Mohanna (1990) argue that Durkheim only considered a handful of these and offered a distorted version of their views so that he could criticize them more readily.

30 It is worth recalling, however, that Durkheim (1897; English trans. 1951) sought to construct not just a sociology but also a psychology of suicide. In Chapter 6 of his book, he tried to infer 'morphological traits' from the 'aetiological' ones, to classify 'acts and agents . . . in a certain number of species; these species also correspond in essential traits with the types of suicide we have established previously in accordance with the nature of the social causes on which they rest. They are like prolongations of these causes inside of individuals' (ibid., 287). The egoistic suicide is therefore characterized by 'a condition of melancholic languor which relaxes all the springs of action (. . .) The moment the individual becomes so enamoured of himself, inevitably he increasingly detaches himself from everything external' (ibid., 278–9). Anomic suicide is the result of 'anger and all the emotions customarily associated with disappointment' (ibid., 284). Poggi (2000, 95) suggests 'there is something rather cavalier about this way of proceeding'. Baudelot and Establet (2008, 184) state that Durkheim wrote 'the curious chapter on individual forms of suicide (. . .) inspired by an unashamed imperialism'.

31 Readers will find numerous pointers in the footnotes to the chapters of this book to these studies. Much information on the history of law is available in Marra (1987). For an initial review of historical studies of suicide, see Healy (2006) and Lederer (2006) for Europe, Ropp (2001) for China, Andriolo (1993), Weiberger-Thomas (1996) and Major (2007) for India. Both Seaver and Mcguire (2011) and Merrick and Lee (2012) offer a wealth of documentation

on the history of suicide in England from 1650 to 1850. On suicide missions: Gambetta (2005); Pedahzur (2005); Moghadam (2008). There is no good recent overview of anthropological research. The study with the most information in this regard continues to be Wisse (1933), which should of course be updated. On psychological and psychiatric factors: Cavanagh et al. (2003); Joiner et al. (2005).

32 Instead, as observed by Thomas Scheff (2006, 205) referring to two of these disciplines, 'another example of premature specialization is the way both sociological and psychological studies of suicide are mesmerized into disciplinary rather than interdisciplinary approaches. Each of the disciplines is justifiably proud of the advances that mono-disciplinary approaches have made, so they keep repeating them with virtually no further advances. It appears that the need for integration in the approaches to understanding suicide is a bitter pill, but it must be swallowed.'

33 Poggi (2000; Italian trans. 2003, 114). This idea was expressed, using different words, by one of Durkheim's pupils, Albert Bayet (1922), in a book that continues to be essential for the documentation it includes, in which he wrote that, 'after dedicating over three hundred pages to suicide as a social phenomenon', the master had then dedicated 'just ten to an assessment of suicide as a moral phenomenon'. Moreover, he only considered the law, and had relied too heavily on Garrison's work, which 'contained grave errors' that he too had repeated (ibid., 7–9). See also Marra (1987). To avoid any risk of misunderstanding, I would like to add that Durkheim made important contributions to the study of culture in his other works. His book, *Les formes élémentaires de la vie religieuse*, published in 1912, is now regarded by some scholars as the classic founding text of cultural analysis in sociology. This was not the case of his book on suicide, in which he was preoccupied with the social disintegration of Western Europe.

34 Berk (2006, 67).

35 This is how the concept of culture is now defined by a growing and increasingly influential group of experts. In addition to the classic work by Geertz (1973), see Swidler (1986); Di Maggio (1997); Santoro and Sassatelli (2009).

36 Seneca, *Of Anger*, 3, 15, 4.

37 Elster (1993, 1999).

38 In a nutshell, this is the main thesis of appraisal theory. For a useful introduction to the study of emotions, see Anolli (2002).

39 There are important exceptions however. Giddens (1971) put forward a new classification that takes these factors into account. Baechler devoted considerable space to these factors (1975). Baudelot and Establet (2006, 248–50) adopted the thesis of the epidemiologist Jean-Pierre Kahn that the prime risk factors for suicide are psychiatric disorders (as well as family precedents), while secondary factors include negative life events (early death of a parent, widowhood); they also state that the variables usually considered by sociologists (gender, age, social background) are tertiary risk factors that have no predictive value in the absence of other risk factors.

40 Harris and Barraclough (1997); Cavanagh et al. (2003); Joiner et al. (2005).

41 Palmer et al. (2005).

42 Harris and Barraclough (1997); Joiner et al. (2005); Kapur (2006).

43 Dumais et al. (2005); Swann et al. (2005); Zouk et al. (2006).

44 Moeller et al. (2001, 1784).

45 Woolf (1988; Italian trans. 1989, 41).
46 Woolf (1999, 1375). The English translation is from Woolf (1980, 3: 110–11).
47 Durkheim (1897; English trans. 1951, 96).
48 Martin (2006).
49 Roy (1987); Joiner et al. (2005); Voraceck and Loibl (2007).
50 Courtet et al. (2005).
51 Joiner et al. (2005); Courtet et al. (2005).
52 For the research on suicide statistics carried out for this book, consult the Appendix.
53 The awareness of social and legal norms on suicide in Europe between the thirteenth and nineteenth centuries varies considerably between countries and was higher in England, Holland, Germany, Switzerland, France, Sweden and Russia than in Spain and Italy. When working on this aspect in Italy, using printed sources, my results were inconclusive. For a preliminary overview, see Pertile (1876, vol. V); Motta (1888); Massetto (2004).

1 The Worst Sin and the Gravest Crime

1 Morselli (English trans. 1882, 15).
2 Durkheim (1897; English trans. 1951, 370).
3 Plaut and Anderson (1999, 47).
4 Engels (1845; English ed. 1993, 127).
5 Morselli (English trans. 1882, 23).
6 Durkheim (1893; English edition 2014, 10).
7 See the tables reproduced in the Appendix.
8 Morselli (1879, 92); this passage is absent from the abridged 1882 English translation.
9 Fedden (1938, 146–50).
10 Krose (1906a, 25–6); Murray (1998, 356–62). R. and M. Wittkower (1963; trad. it. 1968, 160) point out that only eight suicides are mentioned in the Florentine diary started in 1450 by Luca Landucci and continued anonymously until 1542. However, see also their comments on suicides by European artists between 1350 and 1800 (ibid., 163–4).
11 Midelfort (1996).
12 Minois (1995, 75).
13 Murray (1998, 368–378) and Lederer (2005, 61–69), who reports a historical series of the number of suicides in Augsburg, Baviera, from 1555 to 1694.
14 Robbins (1986); Robson (1995).
15 Hopes (2011, 109).
16 Bartel (1959–60, 147).
17 Ibid.
18 Miller (1937, 371).
19 Wade (1931, 30); Peyre (1950, 110).
20 Cited by Gidal (2003, 23–4).
21 Cheyne (1733, i-iii).
22 Montesquieu (1749; English trans. 1973, 253).
23 Hopes (2011, 171).
24 Voltaire (1759; English trans. 2006, 28).
25 Madame de Staël (1813, 189; English trans. 1813, 74–5).

26 Cited by Bernardini (1999, 267).
27 These figures come from the first (now forgotten) statistical table on suicides published in Europe. It was included in a book by Johann Peter Süßmilch (1761), a German Protestant pastor, now regarded as one of the founding fathers of demography. During the period from 1686 to 1750 he kept a historical series of annual data for London on the number of suicides, corpses found with no known cause of death, murders and the total number of deaths. To give an example, in the English capital in 1686, there were 22,609 deaths, of which 11 were suicides, 14 were killed and 11 were found dead for unknown reasons. It is possible that the latter group may have also included suicides (a suggestion made by Krose (1906a, 24)). Over the 64 years in question, the number of suicides and those found dead for unknown reasons followed the same rising trend, while the number of people killed fell for reasons that are considered in Chapter 3.
28 Montagu (1837, 303).
29 Minois (1995, 217; English trans. 1999, 184).
30 Longino Farrell (1992).
31 De Sévigné (1972; English trans. 1811, 185, 187–8).
32 McManners (1981, 430).
33 Mercier (1781, 60–1).
34 Ibid.
35 Stendhal (1829, 425).
36 Merrick (1989, 1–2). For other contemporary views, see Godineau (2012, 32–4).
37 All the nineteenth-century scholars affirmed that Paris had a much higher suicide rate than London, based on statistical data. According to Quételet (1835, 147), in around 1820, the suicide rate in Paris was 49 per 100,000 inhabitants, Hamburg 45, Berlin 34, and London 20. The French capital continued to hold this unenviable record for many years. Publishing their results fifteen years apart and based on statistical figures from different sources for the main European cities, both Brierre de Boismont (1865, 492) and Morselli (1879, 282) announced that Paris was the capital in which suicide claimed most victims. Not long after, Oettingen (1881, 49) reported these rates for the period 1875–9: London 8.5; St Petersburg 16; Berlin 28; Paris 40; Leipzig 45. But see also Morselli (1885, 31–33).
38 Krose (1906a, 26); Watt (2001, 66).
39 Krose (1906a, 26).
40 Outram (1989, 90–1).
41 Jansson (1998, 25–6 and 138).
42 Morselli (1879, 58–69).
43 Verkko (1951, 122).
44 Schär (1985, 31–5, 261–5).
45 Watt (2001, 24) and personal communication from this author.
46 Watt (2001, 322).
47 Bell (2012, 1–10).
48 Wagner (1864, 197–207); Brierre de Boismont (1865, 491–493); Morselli (1879, 270–87).
49 In Chapter 3 I will return to the question of the classes in which this change first started.
50 Morselli (1879, 270–87); Halbwachs (1930, 169–96).
51 For more statistical data on the differences between male and female suicides

for many European countries during the nineteenth century, see Krose (1906b, 15–24).
52 Watt (2001, 34–5).
53 Here too I have used the results of Watt's research (2001, 273–6). We know nothing (and probably never will) on the relationship between age and the frequency of suicide in the Middle Ages, in spite of the extraordinary documentation collected by Murray (1998, 395–9).
54 Quételet (1835, 156); Lisle (1856, 42–51); Morselli (1879, 308–31).
55 Durkheim (1897; English trans. 1951, 333).
56 Ibid.
57 Ibid., 333–4.
58 Beccaria (1965, 79); English translation in Bellamy (1995, 83).
59 Geiger (1889b, 389–90; 1891, 5–6); Murray (2000, 23–4). According to Dieselhorst (1953, 63), in Nuremberg the custom of carrying the suicide's corpse out of the window lasted until the mid seventeenth century.
60 Joblin (1994).
61 Giansante (1993).
62 Porteau-Bitker (1999).
63 Murray (2000, 188–91).
64 Manara (1668, 699); Le Brun de la Rochette (1661), cited by Joblin (1994, 118–19).
65 Iodocus Damhouderius (1601), cited by Massetto (2004, 142).
66 Burton (1932, vol. III, 408).
67 'A caveat against suicide; wherein the heinious sin of that unnatural crime is clearly pointed out', cited by Houston (2010, 27).
68 Murray (1998, 132–3).
69 Pertile (1876, vol. V, 171); Carbasse (2006, 305–6).
70 Montesquieu (1721; English trans. Letter 74, 103).
71 Cited by Vandekerckhove (2000, 54).
72 Ibid.
73 Bayet (1922, 440).
74 Murray (2000, 34–5).
75 Pertile (1876, 510).
76 Ibid. For other sanctions against suicides in Italy, from the thirteenth to the fifteenth century, see Murray (2000, 29–30, 35–7).
77 Kohler et al. (1909, 88–9 and 203).
78 Watt (2001, 85).
79 Mäkinen (1997, paper III, 6 and 11).
80 Kushner (1991, 22).
81 Paperno (1997, 55–6); Morrisey (2005, 130).
82 Silving (1957, 83).
83 *Codice penale* (Anon.1839, 175).
84 Westermarck (1912, vol. II, 254–7).
85 Wacke (1980, 33).
86 Joblin (1994, 111).
87 Van der Made (1948, 37).
88 Fedden (1938, 140).
89 Watt (2001, 82–3).
90 Massetto (2004, 148).
91 Murray (2000, 37–41).

92 Massetto (2004, 162–3).
93 Cited by Vandekerckhove (2000, 60).
94 Bayet (1922, 438).
95 Carbasse (2006, 277).
96 Bayet (1922, 437).
97 Cited by Vandekerckhove (2000, 97).
98 Groot (2000).
99 Geiger (1889b, 391–2; 1891, 15).
100 Eleonora of Arborea (1805, 23). In the original document 'appensatamente', a word of Catalan origin, means 'deliberately' or 'with premeditation'. I owe this information to Anna Oppo and Giovanni Lupiu.
101 On the differences between England, Scotland and other European countries, see Houston (2010, 27–9).
102 Watt (2001, 83).
103 Signori (1994, 29).
104 Motta (1888). Clashes in this sense between the spiritual and temporal powers also happened in other parts of Europe, for example in some German states (Koslofsky 2004).
105 Guiance (1998, 367–9).
106 Vivanco (2004, 88).
107 Plato, *Laws* (Book IX, 268–9).
108 Murray (2000, 42).
109 Ariés (1977); Brown (1981).
110 Alvis (2004).
111 On the Lutherans, see Dieselhorst (1953, 78–9).
112 Besta (1908–09, vol. II, 219).
113 Vandekerckhove (2000, 63–4).
114 MacDonald and Murphy (1990, 47).
115 Westermarck (1912, vol. II, 255).
116 Vandekerckhove (2000).
117 Massetto (2004, 159); Koslofsky (2001, 51); Vandekerckhove (2000, 21).
118 Geremia 22, 19.
119 Koslofsky (2001, 51). According to Schmidt-Kohlberg's study (2003) in seventeenth-century Württemberg, the corpse was interred under the gallows if the suicide had a bad reputation, otherwise the body would be taken to a deserted place, far from the town.
120 Jansson (1998, 29).
121 Massetto (2004, 159).
122 Joblin (1994, 109).
123 Massetto (2004, 159); Lederer (2006, 251).
124 Kushner (1991, 14).
125 Bayet (1922, 441).
126 Lederer (2005, 51–55).
127 Murray (2000, 38).
128 Lederer (2005, 51–3; 2006, 251–2).
129 Koslofsky (2001, 51).
130 Joblin (1994, 109).
131 Jansson (1998, 29); Koslofsky (2001, 51).
132 Vidor (2008). On practices in Saxony in the seventeenth and eighteenth century, see Kästner (2012, 192–224).

133 Morrisey (2006, 25, 29).
134 Geiger (1891, 11).
135 Dieselhorst (1953, 139–43).
136 Vandekerckhove (2000, 67).
137 De l'Arbre (1921, 25–7).
138 Vandekerckhove (2000, 68).
139 Tognina (2003).
140 For slaves and soldiers, see 1.13 below.
141 In ancient Rome, suicide by hanging was regarded as a shameful act and it provoked a strong sense of moral outrage (Voisin 1979).
142 Grisé (1982, passim); Van Hooff (1990, 79–133).
143 To quote Pliny the Elder (1991, 14) 'The chief consolation for Nature's shortcomings in regard to man is that not even God can do all things. For he cannot, even if he should so wish, commit suicide, which is the greatest advantage he has given man among all the great drawbacks of life.'
144 Griffin (1986).
145 Macrobius (1952, 140).
146 Volterra (1933); Grisé (1982, 263–79); Murray (2000, 165–77).
147 Bels (1975).
148 Amundsen (1999).
149 Augustine (1998, Book 1, Ch. 20, 25).
150 As Van der Horst (1971, 288) has observed, the difference between Augustine and Macrobius is that for the former suicide was a sin against God.
151 Augustine (1887, 531).
152 Augustine (1998, Book 1, Ch. 26, pp. 39–40).
153 Ibid. (Judges, 16:30).
154 Ibid., 39.
155 Ibid., 34.
156 Bels (1975, 173).
157 Augustine (1998, 34).
158 Livy (1960, 101–102).
159 Amundsen (1999, 99–102).
160 Eusebius of Cesarea (2007, 277).
161 Augustine (1998, 29).
162 Ibid.
163 Ibid., 31.
164 Ibid., 35.
165 Durkheim (1897; English trans. 1951, 327).
166 Bayet (1922, 377–8).
167 Ibid., 387.
168 Vandekerckhove (2000, 21).
169 Midelfort (1996).
170 Paperno (1997, 49–53); Morrisey (2006, 20–9).
171 Donaldson (1982, 23–5).
172 Senault (1644; English trans. 1650, 148).
173 Tibbetts Schulenberg (1986).
174 Ibid., 37–8.
175 Müller (1989, 19–21).
176 Ibid., 22.
177 Ibid.

178 Ibid., 23–32.
179 Hitchcock (2008, x).
180 Drees (1990, 70).
181 Safran (2001). Arabs were also influenced by the cultured of the defeated peoples, not least because many Muslim men married Christian women.
182 Wolf (1988, 23); Hitchcock (2008, 29–30).
183 Wolf (1988, 30).
184 Ibid., 35.
185 Drees (1990, 74).
186 Safran (2013, 96).
187 Drees (1990, 83–9).
188 Sorabji (2000).
189 Evagrius Ponticus (2003, 104).
190 Casagrande and Del Vecchio (2000, 182–3).
191 Schmitt (1976).
192 Bunge (1999; English trans. 2009, 87).
193 Ibid., 30 and 55.
194 Cassian (1563, 58; English trans. 2000, 196).
195 Cutter (1983, 135–137).
196 Katzenellenbogen (1939, 8, note 1).
197 John Chrysostom (2002, 25).
198 Cited by Bunge (1995; English trans. 2009, 89).
199 St John Chrysostom (1880, 83).
200 Evagrius Ponticus, cited by Bunge (1995; English trans. 2009, 89).
201 Cassian (1563, 63; English trans. 2000, 211).
202 *Second Letter of Paul to the Corinthians*, 7: 10.
203 Cassian (1563, 65; English trans. 2000, 213).
204 *Second Letter of Paul to the Corinthians*, 2: 6–7.
205 Evagrius Ponticus (2003, 81).
206 Cassian (1563, 64; English trans. 2000, 212).
207 Evagrius Ponticus, cited by Bunge (1995; English trans. 2009, 58).
208 Wenzel (1960).
209 Murray (2000, 376).
210 Sachs (1964).
211 Porteau-Bitker (1999, 306–7); Murray (2000, 382).
212 Augustine (1998, 27).
213 Murray (2000, 323–30); Robson (2002).
214 Bourquelot (1841–2); Sachs (1964).
215 Cutter (1983, 156–62).
216 Schnitzler (1996; 2000).
217 Marro (1925); Plesch (2006).
218 Plesch (2006, 206).
219 Snyder (1965); Harris and Newhauser (2005).
220 Midelfort (1996).
221 Cited by MacDonald and Murphy (1990, 34).
222 MacDonald (1988, xviii).
223 Sym (1637, 246–7); cited by MacDonald and Murphy (1990, 34).
224 Spenser (2007, 119).
225 Spenser (2007, 120).
226 Frank (1994, 169–75).

227 This thesis is backed by many who study folk beliefs (see Lederer 2005), but not by Murray (2000, 38).
228 Westermarck (1912, vol. II, 255–6).
229 Ivanits (1992).
230 Joblin (1994, 110).
231 Murray (1998, 111–13).
232 Bayet (1922, 93).
233 Lederer (1998, 361–4).
234 Watt (2001, 86).
235 Burckhardt (1860; English trans. 1955, 321).
236 Lederer (1998, 360–1).
237 Morrisey (2005, 117 and 142).
238 Plato, *Phaedo*, 62C. (1993, 6–7).
239 Hirzel (1908, 273).
240 Cicero (1923, 20–73).
241 Macrobius (1952, 139).
242 Bayet (1922, 303); Grisé (1982, 270–6).
243 Grisé (1982, 277–8).
244 Bayet (1922, 503).
245 Cited by Van der Made (1948, 47–8).
246 Timbal (1943–44, 78).
247 Cited by Vandekerckhove (2000, 96–97).
248 Gomez (1998, 119–120).
249 Walker (2004, 23–26).
250 Piersen (1977, 152–4).
251 Steinmetz (1894, 51); Lasch (1898, 38).
252 Jeffreys (1971, 193–4).
253 Courcelle (1958, 229).
254 Petrarch (1993, 927). *Epistolae familiares*, Book XVII: 3.
255 Dumont (1948, 557).
256 As he wrote in his memoirs, published at Amsterdam in 1718: 'facinus novum, nec admodum credibile'. A long passage is cited by Stuart (2008, 422).
257 Ibid.
258 Paul Wulff left a long holograph confession. It has been summarized by Jansson (1998, 51–2; 2004).
259 Jansson (1998; 2004); Lind (1999, 61–2, 175–7, 180–1); Martschukat (2000); Koslofsky and Rabin (2005); Stuart (2008).
260 Jansson (1998, 59).
261 Stuart (2008), 415). Krogh (2012).
262 Koslofsky and Rabin (2005, 53).
263 Ibid.
264 Krogh (2012, 36–45).
265 Schreiner (2003, 61). The exact expression used by Hommel is 'mittelbarer Selbstmord'.
266 Lind (1999, 61–3, 189–92, 335–8) called it 'concealed suicide', Stuart (2008) 'suicide by proxy'.
267 Lind (1999, 335); Stuart (2008, 429–30).
268 Dieselhorst (1953, 126–9); Lind (1999, 325–34).
269 Stuart (2008, 431).
270 Jansson (2004, 97).

271 Ibid., 81–2.
272 Stuart (2008, 440).
273 Krogh (2012, 146–61).
274 Jansson (2004, 98–9).
275 Lind (1999, 62–3).
276 Quoted from a law passed in Prussia (Stuart 2008, 443).
277 Fedden (1938, 152).
278 Morillo (2001).
279 Robson (2002, 34).
280 MacDonald and Murphy (1990, 50).
281 Villon (1971, 76–7; English trans. 1965, 52–3).
282 Cellini (1973, 261–2; English trans. 1983, 106–7).
283 Cited by Vandekerckhove (2000, 128).

2 The Key to our Prison

1 Sprott (1961, 15).
2 Bernardini (2001, 348).
3 Trevor (2000).
4 Roberts (1947).
5 Beauchamp (1976).
6 Bourquelot (1841–2, 475).
7 Patrick (1984); Garavini (1991); Bernardini (2001).
8 Montaigne (1966, 449; English trans. 2004, 392).
9 More (1981, 97; English edition, 2002, 78).
10 Cahn (1998, 95–122).
11 More (1981, 98; English edition, 2002, 79).
12 Montaigne (1966, 466; English trans. 2004, 406).
13 Donne (1624; Meditation XII).
14 Siemens (2001); Kitzes (2006, 105–22).
15 Donne (1608; 1984, 49).
16 Ibid., 129.
17 Cited by Trevor (2000, 93).
18 Collmer (1969).
19 Borges (1974; English trans. 1964, 92).
20 Montesquieu (1721; English trans. 2008, 103).
21 Radicati di Passerano (1732, 94).
22 Beccaria (1965, 79–82; English trans. 1778, ch. 32 Of Suicide).
23 Cahn (1998, 104–8).
24 Montaigne (1966, vol. I, 450–1; English trans. 2004, 393).
25 Ibid., 394.
26 Hume (1799, 3).
27 Donne (1608; 1984, 39).
28 Ibid., 171.
29 Roberts (1947); Allison (1991).
30 Cited by Roberts (1947, 958).
31 Montesquieu (1721; English trans. 2008, 213).
32 Radicati di Passerano (1732, 86–7).
33 Beccaria (1965, 79).

34 Montesquieu (1721; 2008, 103–4).
35 Hume (1799, 12).
36 Montesquieu (1721; 2008, 104).
37 Ibid.
38 Radicati di Passerano (1732, 14); Cavallo (2003).
39 Hume (1799, 11).
40 Ibid., 7.
41 Cahn (1998, 110).
42 Bayet (1922, 455–60).
43 Ibid., 481–93.
44 Rolfs (1981, 33–4).
45 Boccaccio (1963, 371; English trans. 1993, 364).
46 Day Four, first novella.
47 Rolfs (1981); Iventosch (1974).
48 Bayet (1922, 524). The title of the *roman* is *Le lict d'honneur de Chariclée.*
49 Paulin (1977, 264–9, 310, 462–76); Wymer (1982).
50 Paulin (1977, 462–79).
51 Wymer (1982, 156). Albeit open to a wide range of interpretations
    (Donaldson 1982; Hults 1991; Bousquet 2002), the huge artistic and literary
    output, above all in the sixteenth and seventeenth centuries, that focused on
    the story of Lucretia raises the likelihood that Augustine's moral condemna-
    tion of her suicide prompted growing doubts and concerns among painters,
    writers and their audiences. Some showed an increasingly eroticized image
    of this Roman wife, others showed her as an exemplary woman worthy of
    the greatest admiration for her virtues, courage and chastity. Her suicide
    was more often seen as a comprehensible, not to say an acceptable act.
    Moreover, the illustrious group described in Baldassarre Castiglione's
    Book of the Courtier, who gathered at the court of Urbino in the early
    sixteenth century to engage in pleasant conversation, were far removed from
    Augustine's teaching when they praised the women who, in those same years
    after Capua had been sacked by the French, or on other similar occasions,
    had 'chosen to die rather than to lose their chastity' and had drowned
    themselves out of 'grief for (her) lost virginity' (Castiglione 1998, 316–19;
    English trans. 2002, 184).
52 Grisé (1982, 23).
53 Porteau-Bitker (1999, 307).
54 Daube (1972).
55 Bayet (1922, 678).
56 Dumas (1773).
57 Barraclough and Shepherd (1994); Shepherd and Barraclough (1997).
58 Bähr (2013).
59 Dolev (1999, 134) recalls that, in fifteenth-century monastic life, there were
    three classes and the *conversi* were in the middle rank.
60 Wittkower and Wittkower (1963, 108 et seq.); Midelfort (1999, 26–32); Dolev
    (1999).
61 Gowland (2006a, 2006b).
62 Lederer (2006a, 19).
63 Bright (1586, 111).
64 Burton (1932, vol. III, 431–2).
65 Ibid., 439.

66 Klibansky et al. (1964).
67 This is the anonymous author of *De mundi constitutione*, attributed by some to Bede.
68 Cited by Klibansky et al. (1964; Italian trans. 2002, 7).
69 Brann (1979).
70 Burton (1932, vol. I, 66–7).
71 Guaccio (1626, 186; English trans. 1929, 106).
72 Perkins (1606, 46).
73 Simonazzi (2004, 155–61).
74 Shakespeare (*Hamlet*, Act 2, Scene 2, ll. 600–5).
75 Gowland (2006b, 86).
76 Bright (1586, 233).
77 Ibid., 237.
78 Simonazzi (2004, 125–9, 134–8). See also Jorden, (1603, 2v).
79 Babb (1951, 26–30).
80 Schmidt (2007, 152).
81 Cheyne (1733, ii).
82 Simonazzi (2004, 185–252).
83 Durkheim (1897; English trans. 1951, 327).
84 Bayet (1922, 666–78); Minois (1995, 326–8).
85 Voltaire (1777, 15 February, Art. V).
86 Cited by Bayet (1922, 675).
87 Merrick (1989, 29–30).
88 Mercier (1781, 60).
89 Bayet (1922, 674–6).
90 Ibid., 677. Findings for other regions of France presented by Godineau point to the same conclusion (2012, 46–8).
91 Burgess-Jackson (1982, 75).
92 Seabourne and Seabourne (2000).
93 Groot (2000); Seabourne and Seabourne (2000); Butler (2006a).
94 MacDonald and Murphy (1990).
95 Ibid., 29.
96 Seaver (2004, 25).
97 Seaver (2004).
98 Bosman (2004).
99 Ibid.
100 Deschrjiver (2011).
101 Porret (2007, 173).
102 Watt (2001).
103 Porret (2007, 174).
104 Watt (2001, 81 and 123).
105 Lind (1999); Lederer (2006a).
106 Dieselhorst (1953, 122–3).
107 Lederer (2006a, 251).
108 Ibid., 242–56.
109 Lind (1999, 347–62).
110 Minois (1995, 327–8).
111 Alvis (2004, 244–6).
112 Kselman (1988, 320–1).
113 Morrisey (2006, 235).

114 Kushner (1991, 30).
115 Lind (1999, 56).
116 Bernardini (1994, 94–6); Lind (1999, 57–8).
117 Bernstein (1907, 33–4).
118 Bayet (1922, 698).
119 Bernstein (1907, 44–5).
120 Bosman (2004).
121 Geiger (1891, 30).
122 MacDonald and Murphy (1990, 346–7).
123 Anderson (1987, 266–9).
124 Anon. (1839, 174).
125 Morrisey (2006, 93–105).
126 Catechism of the Catholic Church, available online http://www. vatican.va/archive/ENG0015/_INDEX.HTM. The articles cited can be found in Part 3, section 2: the Fifth Commandment; I. Respect for human life.
127 Kästner (2011, 378–9).
128 Kästner (2013, 636–7).
129 Manni (1826, 112–20); Kästner (2011, 378–9), Bell (2012, 81–114).
130 Vicentini (1769, a.2).
131 Manni (1826, 116).
132 Vicentini (1769, 63–4).
133 Manni (1826, 157).
134 Manni (1826, 155).
135 As defined by MacDonald (1989).
136 Bernardini (1994, 94–5).
137 Cited by Wymer (1982, 20–1).
138 Trevor (2004, 108).
139 MacDonald and Murphy (1990, 157–9, 273–4, 319–21).
140 Lind (2004, 68–9).
141 Ibid., 70.
142 Donne (1611; 2000, 212).
143 Thomas (1971); Macfarlane (2000).
144 The proposal was put forward by Lazare Carnot. Article 5 of his draft stated that 'each citizen shall hold the right to his own life and death; each shall have the right to talk, write, print and publish his thoughts; the right to practise the religion that suits him; and lastly the right to do all that he deems appropriate, provided it does not disrupt the social order' (Saitta 1975, 300). His proposal was not approved and did not form part of the Constitution of 24 June 1793, which in any case was never implemented. During this period in France, many others also claimed that citizens had the right to take their own lives. See Godineau (2012, 239–40).

3 Killing God, Oneself and Others

1 Goethe (1816–17; 1970, 129, 145, 347).
2 Ibid., 144.
3 Ibid., 145.
4 According to Eisner's estimates (2003, 99), the homicide rate in Italy was at

least 10 per 100,000 inhabitants, while, according to my estimates, the suicide rate was probably less than 2 per 100,000 inhabitants.

5 Murray (1998, 359–62).
6 Schär (1985, 263); Spierenburg (1996, 80); Watt (2001, 24 and 56); Jansson (1998, 16 and 26).
7 According to figures published by Süßmilch (1761, 541–52), over the five-year period, 1686–90, there were 89 suicides and 101 persons were killed (ermordete). However, the latter also included those who received death sentences from the courts. Therefore, if we exclude these, it is probable that there were actually fewer murders than suicides. In any case, in 1691–95, suicides rose to 93 and those 'killed' diminished to 86. Since then, the number of suicides continued to rise (as has already been seen), growing to 235 by 1721–5, and those 'killed' were ever fewer, amounting to 42 in that same five-year period.
8 Schär (1985, 263); Watt (2001, 24 and 56); Jansson (1998, 16 and 26).
9 In Prussia, the number of suicides in 1876 was almost ten times higher than the number of murder victims (Direzione generale della statistica 1879, 261).
10 Shoemaker (2001, 191). But Süßmilch (1761, 551) had already observed that in London, in the late seventeenth century, there were few murders, and that thefts and kidnappings led to fewer deaths than in Paris.
11 These figures come from a data set I created during the course of my research for this book. See Appendix, p. 402.
12 Eisner (2003, 101).
13 Spierenburg (1996, 94).
14 See the data presented by Eisner (2003, 99).
15 According to Eisner's data (ibid.), this happened in Italy around the mid nineteenth century.
16 Eisner (ibid., 99–101).
17 There are no estimates for the trend of homicide and suicide rates in nineteenth-century Russia. However, judging from the results of Herrmann's pioneering research (1833–4), in 1821–2 there were three times as many suicides in Russia as murders.
18 Unnithan et al. (1994); He et al. (2003).
19 Guerry (1833, 65).
20 Morselli (1886).
21 Ferri (1925, 729).
22 Durkheim (1897; English trans. 1951, 340).
23 Ferri (1925, 722).
24 Henry and Short (1954); He et al. (2003).
25 Augustine (1887, 530).
26 Mauss (1896).
27 Gauvard (1991, 798–813); Carbasse (2006, 300–10).
28 Leveleux (2001, 125, 128–32, 166).
29 Flynn (1995); Nash (2007).
30 Kantorowicz (1957, 13).
31 Ibid., 15.
32 Jousse (1771, 709–710).
33 Carbasse (2006, 306).
34 Muyart de Vouglans (1757, 537).
35 Eisner (2003).
36 Zorzi (2002, 140).

37 Zorzi (2002).
38 Hanawalt (1979, 59–61).
39 Eisner (2003, 129).
40 De Beaumanoir (1899, vol. I, 430); cited by Eisner (2003, 93).
41 Gauvard (1991, vol. I, 281); Smail (2003, 167).
42 Zorzi (2002, 140).
43 Onori (2009).
44 Some scholars use the term 'infrajustice'.
45 Zorzi (2007).
46 Petkov (2003); Niccoli (2007, 76–85); Spierenburg (2008, 43–57).
47 Niccoli (2007, 81).
48 Pertile (1876, 194–211); Carbasse (2006, 91–3 and 117–18).
49 Rousseaux (1999b, 254).
50 Waardt (1996).
51 Gauvard (2001, 378–379).
52 Gauvard (1991).
53 Ibid., 798–806 and Gauvard (2005, 60–5).
54 Leveleux (2001, passim).
55 Gauvard (1991, 808).
56 Rousseaux (1999a).
57 Angelozzi and Casanova (2003, 19).
58 Ruff (2001, 45–9).
59 Ibid.
60 Eisner (2003, 127–8).
61 About (1861a, 140–2); Nivette and Eisner (2013).
62 Shoemaker (2000).
63 Spierenburg (2006).
64 Ibid., 20.
65 Larner (1972, 66–8).
66 Delumeau (1983; English trans. 1990, 214).
67 Niccoli (2007, 172).
68 Ibid., 183.
69 Ibid., 190.
70 Lisle (1856, 59–64).
71 Durkheim (1897; English trans. 1951, 207).
72 Morselli (1879, 361; English trans. 1882, 248).
73 Krose (1906b, 109). But see also Morselli (1885, 52–5); Von Mayr (1917, 330–336); Rice Miner (1922, 47–59). The results of these studies – as Krose observed (1906b, 109) – 'contradict the widely held prejudice that the cause of suicide is usually material need or unfavourable financial circumstances'. Rice Miner (1922, 50) commented that, to judge from data for Italy and England, even domestic servants had a relatively high suicide rate.
74 Morselli, 248.
75 Durkheim (1897; English trans. 1951, 168–9).
76 Watt (2001, 147–91).
77 Chesnais (1981; Italian trans. 1982, 261–2).
78 Lorant et al. (2005). For Italy see also below (pp. 123–4) and Table A.5 in the Appendix.
79 Zorzi (2002, 156).
80 Smail (2001, 93–4).

81 Blanshei (1982, 123–4).
82 Ruggiero (1980; Italian trans. 1982, 144).
83 Ibid., 150–1.
84 Eisner (2003, 117).
85 Romei (1586, 131).
86 Eisner (2003, 117).
87 Angelozzi and Casanova (2003, 19–20).
88 Ibid., 63–71.
89 Doneddu (1991, 600–2).
90 Shoemaker (2001, 196–7).
91 Spierenburg (1998a; 1998b).
92 Boschi (1998); Gallant (2000).
93 About (1861b, 132).
94 Huizinga (1919; English trans. 1968, 9).
95 Ibid., 11,13.
96 Ibid., 15.
97 Elias (1968; English trans. 1994, 164).
98 Ibid., 319.
99 Ibid., 164.
100 Ibid., 443.
101 Ibid., 453.
102 Rosenwein (2002) and Pollock (2004) mention some.
103 Reddy (2000).
104 Speaking of this hydraulic understanding of human action, Rosenwein (2002, 834–7; 2006, 10–14) rightly observed that Elias was influenced by Freud, as well as by Weber.
105 On these studies, see Rosenwein (1998; 2002; 2006); Reddy (2000); Smail (2001); Petkov (2003, 137–87); Pollock (2004), McNamara and Ruys (2014).

4 When Poverty Does not Protect

1 Halbwachs (1930, 91*et seq.*, cited on 99).
2 Eight years earlier, Rice Miner had noted the tendency of the suicide rate in Europe to stabilize (1922, 7–8).
3 Ibid., 107.
4 Durkheim (1951, 258).
5 The term 'medicalization' has often been used by social scientists in a negative and critical way (Conrad 1992). Instead, I use it here in a neutral sense.
6 See, below, the figures in Table 7.1.
7 'Active euthanasia' is used to describe actions taken by doctors to accelerate or cause the death of an individual, when the latter considers that his or her suffering has become unbearable. Instead 'passive euthanasia' is used to refer to the doctor's abstention from carrying out any actions that might prolong a patient's life. Lastly, 'assisted suicide' refers to the act of a sick person who is aided by a doctor (who may, for example, prescribe the necessary drugs).
8 Midelfort (1996).
9 Wagner (1864, 179–89).
10 Ibid., 188.

11 Morselli (1879, 210; English trans. 1882, 120–1).
12 Ibid., 127. However, Morselli did not present statistical data (even more difficult to obtain then than now) on what he called 'the followers of Mahommet'.
13 Ferracuti (1957).
14 Merton (1949; Italian trans. 1966, 154–6).
15 Pope and Danigelis (1981).
16 Halbwachs (1930, 256–9), but see also Lederer (2013).
17 Ibid., 244–6.
18 This refers to the territories that corresponded, from 7 October 1949 to 3 October 1990, to West Germany (the Federal Republic of Germany) and East Germany (Democratic Republic of Germany).
19 See the figures in Tables A.1 and A.2 in the Appendix.
20 Helliwell (2006).
21 Arendt (1943; 1994, 113).
22 Durkheim (1897; English trans. 1951, 155).
23 Durkheim (1906).
24 Halbwachs (1930, 244).
25 Ruppin (1930, 247–8).
26 Kwiet (1984, 142–4). It may have been because they prompted these concerns that, from 1927, suicide statistical figures were no longer identified by religion.
27 Ruppin (1930, 247–8); Kwiet (1984, 144–6).
28 Goeschel (2009, 97).
29 Kwiet (1984, 148).
30 Dawidowicz (1975, 232).
31 Lester (2005b, 83–4).
32 Hartig (2007, 261).
33 Kwiet (1984, 155).
34 Goeschel (2009, 135).
35 Maurer (2005, 367).
36 Goeschel (2007, 33).
37 Guthmann Opfermann (1999, 44–6).
38 Baumann (2001, 373–375). Cited in English by Goeschel (2007: 29).
39 Arendt (1943: 112–13).
40 Kaplan (1998, 182).
41 Cited by Maurer (2005, 367).
42 Cited by Kwiet (1984, 160).
43 Goeschel (2007, 24).
44 De Felice (1988, 336).
45 Arendt (1943; Italian trans. 2001, 38).
46 Goeschel (2009, 100–1).
47 Lester (2005b, 92).
48 Sonneck et al. (2012).
49 Levi (2003, 46–52; English trans. 2013, 61–4).
50 Lester and Krysinka (2000–1).
51 Rossi (1963, 454).
52 Matard-Bonucci (2007).
53 Sarfatti (2000, 207–11).
54 Milano (1987, 100–17).
55 Segre (1995, 221).
56 Lombroso (1945, 63–4).

57 Goffman (1961).
58 Viktor Frankl (1995, 121; English trans. 2004, 78).
59 I refer to these concentration camps alone.
60 Ibid., 86.
61 Minois (1995, 235–6).
62 Morselli (1879, 376–80; English trans. 1882, 261); Liebling (1992, 17–67).
63 Fruehwald et al. (2000a; 2000b).
64 Bernheim (1987); Liebling (1992; 1999); Fruehwald et al. (2000a; 2000b); Duthé et al. (2009).
65 Langbein (2003, 122).
66 Arendt (1951; Italian trans. 1996, 623).
67 Viktor Frankl (1995, 46–7; 2004, 31).
68 Arendt (1951; English trans. 1958, 455).
69 Solzhenitsyn (1975, IV, 601).
70 Levi (2003); Bettelheim (1963); Améry (1966); Cohen (1953); Mandel'štam (1970); Bronisch (1996); Stark (2001).
71 Bettelheim (1963, 151–58); Sofsky (1993).
72 Bronisch (1996).
73 Levi (2003, 43; English trans. 2013, 48–9).
74 Kogon (1947, 219–20).
75 Solzhenitsyn (1975, IV, 599).
76 Levi (2003, 8; English trans. 2013, 8–9).
77 Cited by Appelbaum (2003, 312).
78 Arendt (1951; Italian trans. 1996, 623).
79 Dachau was the first concentration camp to be opened in March 1933.
80 Bettelheim (1963, 151).
81 F. Kral, cited by Bronisch (1996, 135).
82 Cited by Stark (2001, 97).
83 Conquest (1968, 267).
84 Bronisch (1996).
85 Levi (1976, 110; English trans. 2013, 98); Frankl (1995, 27).
86 Cited by Levi (2003, 60: English trans. 1989, 59).
87 The words said by Adelsberger are cited by Cohen (1953, 159).
88 Cohen (ibid., 162).
89 Améry (1966; English trans. 1977 reissue, 1980, 17).
90 See on this aspect, Gambetta (1999).
91 Levi (2003, 120; English trans. 2013, 167).
92 Ibid., 79–80.
93 Ibid.
94 Solzhenitsyn (1975, IV, 599).
95 Langbein (2003, 121).
96 Ibid.
97 Bland et al. (1998); Rasmussen et al. (1999); Fazel and Danesh (2002).
98 Sattar (2001); Sattar and Killias (2005).
99 Durkheim (1897; English trans. 1951, 253–4).
100 Chesnais (1976, 53–5).
101 Ibid., 58–60.
102 Ibid.
103 Durkheim (1897; English trans. 1951, 208).
104 Baechler (1975, 449).

105 Ibid., 450–1.
106 Skog (1993).
107 Who (1956); Rojcewicz (1971); Noomen (1975); Van Tubergen and Ultee (2006).
108 Who (1956, 245).
109 Elsner (1983).
110 Bessel (2005, 199).
111 Goeschel (2006, 160–1).
112 Baumann (2001, 376–7); Bessel (2005, 200).
113 Heyer (2007, 440).
114 Woolf (1979–85, vol. V, 166).
115 Ibid., 215.
116 Ibid.
117 Ibid., 284.
118 Ibid., 288.
119 Ibid., 292–3.
120 Van Tubergen and Ultee (2006).
121 Noomen (1975, 176).
122 Van Tubergen and Ultee (2006).
123 Baumann (2001, 358).
124 Malaparte (1979, 328).
125 Ibid., 350–68.
126 Arendt (1945, 154).
127 Andreas-Friedrich (1986, 22; English trans.1990, 16).
128 Mark (2005).
129 Pasteur (2000).
130 Naimark (1995); Grossmann (2007, 48–86).
131 Grossmann (1995, 52).
132 Grossmann (2007, 291); English trans. Anon., (2005, 75).
133 Anon. (2003; English trans. 2005, 75).
134 Ibid., 147.
135 Ibid., 63.
136 Grossmann (1995, 53).
137 Beevor (2002, 107).
138 Anon (2003; English trans. 2005, 110).
139 Naimark (1995, 81).
140 Ibid., 82.
141 Beevor (2002; Italian trans. 2002, 437); Epp (1997, 73–4).
142 Andreas-Friedrich (1986, 23; English trans.1990, 16–17).
143 Beevor (2002; Italian trans. 2002, 410).
144 Pasteur (2000).
145 Lilly (2003).
146 Gribuadi (2005, 510–74); Baris (2004, 93–112).
147 Who (1956).
148 Goeschel (2009, 150–1).
149 Weinberg (1998, 378–9).
150 Goeschel (2006, 160). On suicide in Germany under Nazism see Goeschel (2009).
151 Brahimi (1980); Khlat and Courbage (1995); Singh and Siahpush (2002b).
152 Bhugra (2004).

153 Bhugra (2004); Fung et al. (2006).
154 Cited by Kushner (1991, 151–2).
155 Cavan (1928); Dublin (1963).
156 Sainsbury and Barraclough (1968). This had already been highlighted by Rice Miner (1922, 16) by studying the suicide rate between 1906 and 1914 among immigrants to New York depending on their country of origin.
157 Kliewer and Ward (1988); Burvill (1998); Kliewer (1991); Wadsworth and Kubrin (2007).
158 Wadsworth and Kubrin (2007).
159 Morselli (1879, 449; English trans. 1882, 328).
160 Burvill et al. (1973, 1983).
161 Luca da Caltanissetta (1973, 171).
162 Zucchelli da Gradisca (1712, 356).
163 Eltis (2000, 157).
164 Walker (2004, 25); Snyder (2007).
165 Piersen (1977, 147).
166 Piersen (1993, 6–7).
167 Piersen (1977, 149–50).
168 Thornton (2003).
169 Chapter 1.
170 Pérez (2005, 36).
171 Edwards (1794, vol. II, 89).
172 Rawley and Behrendt (2005, 42).
173 Baechler (1975, 379–81).
174 Lester (1998).
175 Oquendo et al. (2001).
176 Early (1992, 10–12).
177 Hendin (1969).
178 Early (1992); http://webappa.cdc.gov/sasweb/ncipc/mortrate10_ sy.html.
179 Burrow and Laflamme (2006).
180 Early (1992, 31).
181 Mattis (2002).
182 Kendal (2007).
183 Early (1992).
184 Holland Barnes (2006).
185 Higonnet (1985).
186 Esquirol (1838, 584; English trans. 1845, 278).
187 Culbertson (1997).
188 Hopcroft and Bradley (2007).
189 In order to examine this, I used two different indices: the *gender related development index* (http://hdrstats.undp.org/indicators/269.html) and the *global gender gap index* (http://www.weforum.org/pdf/gendergap/report2007. pdf). The coefficient of correlation between the ratio of male and female suicide rates, on the one hand, and the first index, on the other, is −0, 17, and −0, 10 for the second index.
190 Canetto and Sakinofsky (1998).
191 Murphy (1998).
192 Kerkhof (2000).
193 http://www.giovannidallorto.com/testi/gaylib/ormando/ormando.html#1a.
194 For example, this was the stance taken by an authoritative representa-

tive of the gay movement like Giovanni Dall'Orto. See also: http://www. giovannidallorto.com/testi/gaylib/ormando/ormando.html#1a.
195 Russell (2003); Fitzpatrick et al. (2005); Lhomond and Saurel-Cubizolles (2006).
196 http://www.gaynews.it/view.php?ID=71736.
197 Tamagne (2000, 261–4 and 296–7).
198 Hirschfeld (1914; English trans. 2000, 1010–11).
199 Ibid., 1024.
200 Ibid., 1022 and 1024.
201 Ibid., 1011–18. The work by Hirschfeld (1914; English trans. 2000, 1010–24) is still the best study of suicide among homosexuals between the late nineteenth and early twentieth century. Bray (1995, 91 and 94–5) has documented, also using early eighteenth-century woodcuts (see Fig.1), how some English homosexuals, known as mollies, took their lives after being discovered by the police in molly houses.
202 http://www.geocities.com/kruppcapri/krupp.html; Tamagne (2000, 430).
203 Tamagne (2000, 317).
204 Ibid., 124.
205 Durkheim (1897; English trans. 1951, 254).
206 Ibid., 246.
207 Halbwachs (1930, 355–74).
208 Chesnais (1976, 64–7).
209 Ibid., 66. In the United States, Spain and Austria the suicide rate rose from 25 to 29% compared to 1928, reaching a peak in 1932. In Germany and Britain, it increased by 15%.
210 Baudelot and Establet (2006, 85–107).
211 See the data in the Appendix (Tables A.1 and A.2).
212 Chesnais (1981; Italian trans. 1982, 193–4); Baudelot and Establet (2006, 133–61).
213 Clarke and Lester (1989).
214 This is affirmed by some experts interviewed by Anderson (2008).
215 Lester (1990).
216 Clarke and Lester (1989, 87–8).
217 Halbwachs (1930, 177).
218 Kapusta et al. (2008).
219 Chesnais (1976, 86).
220 Saunderson et al. (1998); Singh and Siahpush (2002a).
221 Baudelot and Establet (2006, 169–71).
222 McKeown et al. (2006).
223 Morell et al. (2007); Biddle et al. (2008).
224 Jervis (2002).
225 MacKenzie et al. (2014). Although it has increased, this percentage is still low, but it varies according to the illness, its severity and the country. See: ESEMED/MHEDEA 2000 Investigators (2004); Wang et al. (2007).
226 Nordentoft et al. (2004).
227 Meltzer (2005). In the second half of the twentieth century, there was a clear decline in the number of schizophrenia cases in Western countries. However unsatisfactory, the figures published by researchers in different areas point to the fact that the number of people affected by this mental disorder seem to have fallen. This decline has been attributed to major changes in diet and

care during pregnancy and immediately after birth: a rational approach to nutrition, the use of vitamins, immunizetion against infectious diseases (including rubella and polio), breastfeeding. See Bresnahan et al. (2003).
228 Baldessarini et al. (2006a, 2006b); Yerevanian et al. (2007).
229 Ludwig et al. (2007); Erlangsen et al. (2008); Castelpietra et al. (2008) on Italy.
230 Harris and Barraclough (1994).
231 Twombly (2006); Schraier et al. (2006).
232 Lorant et al. (2005).
233 Hem and Loge (2004); Björkenstam et al. (2005); Kendal (2007).
234 Harris and Barraclough (1994).
235 Björkenstam et al. (2005).
236 Hem and Loge (2004); Björkenstam et al. (2005); Lorant et al. (2005).
237 Pliny the Elder (1956, Book 25, 7).
238 Penttinen (1995, 236).
239 Fishbain (1996); Fisher et al. (2001).
240 Paperno (1997, 76).
241 Mäkinen (2006, 312).
242 Grashoff (2006, 276–7).
243 Pinnow (2007).
244 Pinnow (2003, 661); Pinnow (2010).
245 Pinnow (2003); Pinnow (2010).
246 Pinnow (2007, 139); Pinnow (2010).
247 Serge (1951; Italian trans. 1999, 219–20).
248 Fitzpatrick (1999, 175).
249 Pinnow (2003, 670–5).
250 Pridemore and Spivak (2003); Pridemore and Chamlin (2006).
251 Solzhenitsyn (1975, IV, 600).
252 Mandel'štam (1970, 57).
253 Ibid.
254 Pridemore and Chamlin (2006).
255 Pridemore and Spivak (2003).
256 More recently, the suicide rate in Russia has continued to fall: from 34 per 100,000 inhabitants in 2004 to 25 in 2009.
257 Pridemore and Spivak (2003).
258 The suicide rate of Lithuania was 25 per 100,000 inhabitants in 1970, peaking at 46 per 100,000 in 1996. Estonia and Latvia reached a peak the previous year with a rate of 41 per 100,000 inhabitants (Värnik et al. 2000).
259 Grashoff (2006).
260 Fitzpatrick (1999, 172–5).
261 Biggs (2005).
262 Grashoff (2006, 340–71).
263 Skog (1991). On the explanatory hypotheses put forward by various scholars concerning the link between alcohol and suicide risk, see Andreeva (2005, 68–9).
264 Pridemore (2006).
265 Ibid., 413.
266 Pridemore et al. (2013).
267 Andreeva (2005); Leon et al. (1997).
268 Durkheim (1897; English trans. 1951, 252–3).
269 Alexievich (1993; Italian trans. 2005, 253).

270 Ibid., 254.
271 Ibid., 55–67.

5 Before Becoming a Widow

1 Narasimhan (1998); Sen (2001).
2 Chen (2000, 51–2); Vijayakumar (2004).
3 Thompson (1928); Stratton Hawley (1994); Weinberger-Thomas (1996).
4 Chen (2000, 44).
5 The first engravings of *sati* date from 1598 and are the work of the Dutch traveller Jan Huygen van Linschoten who lived in India from 1583 to 1588. For engravings from the next three centuries, see Hardgrave (1998) and Schürer (2008). Among the most famous are those made in 1796 by the Flemish artist Baltazard Solvyns, who lived in Calcutta from 1791 to 1804 (Plates 30, 31, 32 and 33) or by Thomas Rowlandson in 1815 (Plate 34). Particularly evocative are the numerous miniatures commissioned in the late seventeenth century from various Indian artists by the Venetian Nicolò Manuzzi (or Manucci) to illustrate his *Storia del Mogol*, six of which show widows and the *sati* (Plates 26 and 35). For an account of Manuzzi's extraordinary life – he emigrated to India in around 1652 and remained there until his death – his work and the miniatures he commissioned from local artists, see Falchetta (1986), Bussagli (1986) and Subrahmanyam (2008).
6 On the attitudes of European travellers to *sati* see Rubies (2001) and Major (2006). On the different way they depicted it, Schürer (2008).
7 Vincenzo Maria di Santa Caterina da Siena (1678, 345).
8 Hardgrave (1998).
9 Weinberger-Thomas (1996, 15–18).
10 On this and other aspects of celebrating the ritual, see Colebrooke (1795) who gives details of the rules and instructions taken from many renowned Sanskrit authors.
11 Michaels (1998, 150).
12 Dubois (1825, 30).
13 Ibid.
14 Kennedy (1843, 242). Richard Hartley Kennedy's account is one of the most detailed we have.
15 Della Valle (1667, 241).
16 Ibn Battuta (2006, 453; English trans. 1971, 615).
17 Fedrici (1587, 1031).
18 Balbi (1590, 83).
19 Della Valle (1667, 241; English trans. 1892, 266).
20 Ibid., 267.
21 Dubois (1825, 29–30).
22 Fedrici (1587, 1031).
23 Ibid.
24 Zachariae (1904, 204 and 398).
25 Manucci (1964, 268).
26 Pigafetta (1524–5, 941).
27 Barbosa (1554, 609).
28 Manucci (1964, 269–70).

29 Tavernier (1676, 388).
30 Diodorus Siculus (1988; English trans. 1947, 321–3).
31 Conti (1492, 791).
32 Ibid., 790.
33 Colebrooke (1795).
34 Fisch (1998; English trans. 2006, 241–2).
35 Fedrici (1587, 1031).
36 The information that follows on the rites and symbols were taken from the studies by Zachariae (1904; 1905); Van den Bosch (1995); Weinberger-Thomas (1996).
37 Zachariae (1904; 1905); Weinberger-Thomas (1996).
38 Zachariae (1904, 309–10 and 395–400) gives a critical overview of the meaning attributed by various authors to this use of the lemon. For some, it was a symbol of purity. According to Angelo de Gubernatis, it signified 'a life grown bitter after the husband's death'. Using convincing documentation, Zachariae instead affirms that the lemon brought good luck.
39 Van den Bosch (1995).
40 Zachariae (1904, 209).
41 Zachariae (1904; 1905); Weinberger-Thomas (1996).
42 Weinberger-Thomas (1996, 215–16).
43 Ibn Battuta (2006, 454).
44 Barbosa (1554, 609).
45 Varthema (1535, 60).
46 Bernier (1670; English trans. 1916, 312).
47 Cited by Weinberger-Thomas (1999, 98–9).
48 Hodges (1794, 82).
49 Major (2006, 167).
50 Tavernier (1676, 391); cited by Weinberger-Thomas (1999, 38–39).
51 Major (2006, 166).
52 Weinberger-Thomas (1996, passim).
53 Della Valle (1667, 241; English trans. 1892, 263).
54 Ibid., 273–5.
55 Rubies (2001, 399–400).
56 Ibid., 399.
57 Altekar (1959, 134–8).
58 Mazumdar (1978).
59 Della Valle (1667, 249).
60 Thompson (1928); Mani (1998, 171).
61 Conti (1492, 811).
62 Varthema (1535, 60).
63 Conti (1492, 811).
64 Thompson (1928); Altekar (1959).
65 Filliozat (1967); Caillat (1977); Olivelle (1978); Andriolo (1993); Keith (2003).
66 Andriolo (1993, 60).
67 Thakur (1963, 39).
68 Ibid., 54.
69 Ibid., 58.
70 Murray (2000, 544–5).
71 Olivelle (1978, 20).
72 Justice (2005).

73 Andriolo (1993, 32).
74 Polo (2001, 258).
75 Filliozat (1967).
76 Thakur (1963, 96–101).
77 Ibid., 161–169.
78 Andriolo (1993, 44–7).
79 Ibid., 48–49.
80 Thakur (1963, 77–111).
81 Ibid., 63–64.
82 Whitehead (1921, 124).
83 Steinmetz (1898); Hopkins (1900).
84 Steinmetz (1898, 43).
85 Ibid., 52.
86 Winternitz (1915, 57–9); Garzilli (1997, 209–12).
87 Yang (1989, 15).
88 Garzilli (1997, 212).
89 Ibid., 215–25 and 339–49
90 Cited by Piretti Santangelo (1991, 25). English trans. Diodorus Siculus (1947, 321).
91 Banerjee (2003, 137–73).
92 Fedrici (1587, 1032).
93 This thesis has been backed by all the main experts: Thompson (1928, 21–3); Altekar (1959, 122–5); Thakur (1963, 133, 139–41).
94 Thompson (1928, 30–5).
95 Harlan (2003, 99).
96 Altekar (1959, 129); Thakur (1963, 141).
97 Sharma (1988, 29).
98 Ibid., 30.
99 The widow described by Hodges (1794, 81) belonged to the merchant caste.
100 Roy (1987); Yang (1989, 23–4).
101 Thompson (1928, 38).
102 Piretti Santangelo (1991, 128).
103 Thompson (1928, 30–35).
104 On the meaning of the swastika, see Zachariae (1905, 77).
105 Cited by Altekar (1959, 124).
106 Dutt (1938, 677–8). 'Manu's laws' are a sacred text traditionally attributed to Manu, the mythical son of Brahma, the founder of the human race.
107 Vijayakumar (2004, 77).
108 Yang (1989, 18–20).
109 Altekar (1959); Thakur (1963).
110 Thompson (1928, 60).
111 Roy (1987); Yang (1989).
112 Fisch (1998; English trans. 2006, 237).
113 Altekar (1959, 132–8); Yang (1989, 22–3).
114 Yang (1989, 25).
115 These data, which were published by a formerly well-known German statistician, Von Mayr (1917, 266–7 and 299–300), did not prompt any interest in those studying suicide at the time, probably because they were only interested in European countries. Even though they have been forgotten since then, they are nonetheless very important as the first statistical proof

that women took their own lives more frequently than men in some Asian populations.

116 See Table A.1 in the Appendix.
117 Women continued to kill themselves more frequently than men in some Indian states even in the latter half of the twentieth century (Venkoba Rao 1983, 220).
118 Tafur (2004, 90).
119 Cited by Fisch (1998; English trans. 2006, 225).
120 Marco Polo (2001, 258–9; English trans. 1958, 264–5).
121 Barbosa (1554, 610; English trans. 1918, 216).
122 Sharma (1988, 77–8).
123 Bernier (1670; English trans. 1916, 123).
124 Sharma (1988); Harlan (1994); Van den Bosch (1995); Chakravarti (1998); Sogani (2002).
125 Thapar (1988, ora 2007, 456–7).
126 Harlan (2002, 122).
127 Leslie (1989, 293–4).
128 Ibid., 292.
129 Major (2007, xxvii).
130 Chen (2000, 25).
131 Ibid., 28.
132 Sogani (2002, 7).
133 Dubois (1825, 12).
134 Ibid., 15.
135 Chakravarti (1998, 77).
136 Leslie (1989, 303).
137 Dubois (1825, 14).
138 Leach (1958); Hershman (1974).
139 Dutt (1938, 671–2); Leslie (1989, 299).
140 Colebrooke (1795, 211–13).
141 Thompson (1928, 71–2).
142 Winternitz (1915, 34–41).
143 Altekar (1959, 83–4).
144 Winternitz (1915, 47–8).
145 Altekar (1959); Piretti Santangelo (1991).
146 Dutt (1938, 663).
147 Altekar (1959, passim).
148 Bernier (1670; English trans. 1916, 308).
149 Ibid.
150 Grandpré (1801, 71–3; English trans. 1789–90, 70–4).
151 Kennedy (1843, 243–4).
152 Thompson (1928); Cassels (1965); Mani (1998); Banerjee (2003).
153 Bernier (1670; English trans. 1916, 306–7).
154 Fisch (1998; English trans. 2006, 350).
155 Voltaire (2006, 139).
156 Hardgrave (1998).
157 On this aspect, see the 1827 pamphlet by the missionary J. Peggs, which contains interesting information even if it is biased.
158 Thompson (1928, 69). On the attitudes and actions of the British political authorities, see Buckingham (2005).

159 Peggs (1830, 15).
160 Bentinck (1922).
161 Cited by Stein (1988, 470).
162 Hardgrove (1999).

6 Making the Strong and Powerful Tremble

1 Phillips et al. (1999; 2002a).
2 Meijer (1971, 103–5); Diamant (2000, 111–17, 165–6).
3 Chang (2005, 328–9).
4 Ibid., 329.
5 Diamant (2001).
6 Lester (2005a).
7 Lau (1989).
8 Ricci (1942, no. 159/9).
9 Huc (1879; English trans. 1855, vol. I, 290).
10 Gray (1878, vol. I, 329).
11 Pumpelly (1918, 386).
12 Ball (1893, 434).
13 Matignon (1897, 367).
14 Morrison (1902, 111).
15 Pim (1863, 205).
16 Cohen (1971, 315).
17 Ibid., 316.
18 Cited by Pérez (2005, 59).
19 Pérez (2005, 55).
20 Matignon (1897, 369).
21 Gamble (1921, 116–17 and 418–19).
22 Wolf (1975).
23 Liu and Yip (2008) and Zhang et al. (2009).
24 Zhang *et al.* (2014).
25 In Iran the overall suicide rate is very low. 80% of those women who take their own lives do so through self-immolation: Ahmadi (2007); Aliverdinia and Pridemore (2008);
26 On these regions of Turkey, see Altindag et al. (2005).
27 In the Aguarana tribe, in northern Peru, the numerical ratio between male and female suicides is 0.46 (Brown 1986). Women kill themselves more than men also in Papua New Guinea (Lyons Johnson 1981). In 1871, some scholars found that women committed suicide more often than men in the Caucasus and they regarded female suicides as a form of protest. See Morrisey (2013, 7–8).
28 Pritchard (1996).
29 Phillips et al. (1999).
30 Zhang et al. (2014).
31 Reardon (2002).
32 Phillips et al. (2002a).
33 Giles (1876, 143). Murray also asserted this (1836, 298–9).
34 Fielde (1887, 139).
35 Ross (1912, 198).
36 Johnston (1910, 224).

37 Wolf (1975).
38 Levy (1949, 117 and 306).
39 Wolf (1975).
40 In 1905–10, the population of Taiwan had a suicide rate of 57 per 100,000 residents of the same age, from 20 to 24 years old, and just over 15 per 100,000 among the over-60 year olds (Wolf 1975, 122).
41 This fact is arrived at by comparing the figures presented by Wolf (ibid., 122 and 130) and those, for 1901–5, published by Von Mayr (1917, 312–15). In the early twentieth century, Switzerland, France and Denmark were among the European countries with the highest suicide rate.
42 Hu (1995); Ikels (2004).
43 Ikels (1983).
44 Doolittle (1865, vol. I, 140).
45 Zhang (2004, 78).
46 Yan (2003); Ikels (2004); Whyte (2004); Miller (2004); Jing (2004); Zhang (2004).
47 Eberhard (1967, 94–116); T'ien Ju-K'ang (1988); Ropp (2001); Zamperini (2001); Theiss (2004a; 2004b).
48 Amiot et al. (1779, 437–8).
49 Tao Yi (1919, 84).
50 Witke (1967).
51 Mao Zedong (1919, 86).
52 Witke (1967, 141).
53 Durkheim (1897; English trans. 1951, p. 276, note 25).
54 Tao Yi (1919, 84).
55 Ebrey (2003).
56 Ko (1994); Ropp (2001).
57 Zamperini (2001); Fong (2001); Ropp (2001); Theiss (2004a; 2004b).
58 Matignon (1936, 193).
59 Cited by Bisetto (2000, 23). This translation is from *The Analects of Confucius*, Bk IV: X.
60 Hsieh and Spence (1980); Lee and Kleinman (2000).
61 Lau (1989, 722).
62 Bisetto (2004, 13).
63 Martin (1988, 177); Whyte (1988, 306).
64 Matignon (1936, 180–1).
65 Zhao et al. (2006, 1295).
66 Filliozat (1963); Benn (2007).
67 Elvin (1984, 115).
68 On the celebratory stone arches commemorating different virtuous actions, see Hoang (1898, 243–53).
69 Lu (2008, 82–86).
70 Elvin (1984); Mann (1987); T'ien Ju-K'ang (1988); Carlitz (1997); Elliott (1999); Theiss (2001); Du and Mann (2003); Theiss (2004b).
71 Elvin (1984, 118–22).
72 Hoang (1898, 251).
73 Lu (2008, 69).
74 Elvin (1984, 151–2).
75 Carlitz (1997, 614).
76 Bisetto (2000, 25).

77　Theiss (2001).
78　Elvin (1984, 128–9); Theiss (2004b, 33–4).
79　Ibid., 129.
80　Du and Mann (2003, 229). Some widows in Korea also took their own lives in the eighteenth and nineteenth century in order to remain 'chaste': Kim (2014).
81　Elvin (1984, 140); Lu (2008, 156–7).
82　Zamperini (2001, 80, 100).
83　Bisetto (2004, 28).
84　Zamperini (2001, 80).
85　Spence (1978, 100; Italian trans. 2002, 146).
86　Lu (2008, 30).
87　Liu (2001, 1059).
88　Raphals (1998, 240–1); Fong (2001, 106).
89　T'ien Ju-K'ang (1988, 1).
90　Du and Mann (2003, 231).
91　Wolf and Huang (1980).
92　Du and Mann (2003, 236).
93　Conversation with Weijing Lu (10 March 2008).
94　Matignon (1897, 404–8).
95　Ross (1912, 196).
96　Ibid., 150.
97　T'ien Ju-K'ang (1988).
98　Ibid., 51.
99　Doolittle (1865, vol. I, 108–10); Medhurst (1873, 112–14); Gray (1878, vol. I, 338–40). According to Medhurst (1873, 114), the Chinese widows performed 'a completely voluntary act'.
100　T'ien Ju-K'ang (1988, 54).
101　Lu (2008).
102　Ibid., 142.
103　T'ien Ju-K'ang (1988, 61–2).
104　Lu (2008, 106–7),
105　Hoang (1898, 250).
106　Ibid., 89–96.
107　Lu (2008, 185–90).
108　Ebrey (1993, 62–4).
109　Personal communication of Weijing Lu (14 March 2008).
110　Diamant (2000, 106).
111　Davis (1996, 4).
112　Ibid., 112.
113　Smith (1998).
114　Backhouse and Bland (1914, 102).
115　According to Weijing Lu (personal communication of 16 September 2008), in other versions, the emperor's feet were both bare. Writing on the lapel of robe had no symbolic meaning.
116　Ibid., 103.
117　Davis (1996, 78).
118　Wakeman (1985, 568–9).
119　Fong (2001).
120　Davis (1996, 116).
121　Fong (2001).

122 Du and Mann (2003, 230).
123 T'ien Ju-K'ang (1988, 42).
124 Du and Mann (2003, 230).
125 Lu (2008, 40–8).
126 Davis (1996, 117).
127 Paderni (1991, 135–6).
128 Ibid., 143–144.
129 Du and Mann (2003, 226).
130 Theiss (2004a; 2004b).
131 Theiss (2004b, 189).
132 Paderni (1991); Zamperini (2001); Fong (2001); Theiss (2001; 2004a; 2004b).
133 Theiss (2004b, 179).
134 Paderni (1991, 153–4).
135 Theiss (2004b, 198–9).
136 Ibid., 177–8.
137 MacCormack (1991, 43–4); Paderni (2005); MacCormack (2010).
138 Paderni (1991, 150).
139 Theiss (2004a, 521).
140 Zamperini (2001).
141 Huntington (2005, 20–1).
142 Yu (1987).
143 Stockard (1989).
144 Ibid., 108–9.
145 Gray (1878, vol. I, 185–6); Smith (1899, 287).
146 Holmgren (1985); Ebrey (1993); Birge (1995; 2002).
147 Elvin (1984, 123–4).
148 Du and Mann (2003).
149 T'ien Ju-K'ang (1988, 17).
150 Theiss (2004b, 26–30).
151 Elvin (1984, 137–8).
152 Theiss (2004a, 513).
153 Wolf (1975, 112).
154 Ibid., 112.
155 Cited by Wolf (1975, 113).
156 Dalby (1982); Bianco (2001).
157 Ricci (1942, n. 159/9).
158 Granet (1929; English trans. 1996, 315).
159 Ibid., 341.
160 Morrison (1902, 112).
161 Giles (1911, 219).
162 Ibid., 219–20.
163 Huc (1879, 304–5; English trans. 1855, 290).
164 Amiot et al. (1779, 439).
165 Ibid., 440.
166 Huc (1879, 306; English trans. 1855, 291).
167 Danton (1938, 162).
168 Bianco (1978, 280).
169 Matignon (1897, 374).
170 Simon (1885, 227).
171 Matignon (1897, 373).

172 Reclus and Reclus (1902, 604–5). The French expression is: 'le mort saisit le vif'.
173 Baker (1979, 115).
174 Meijer (1991, 66).
175 Alabaster (1899, 311–12).
176 Ibid., 313–314.
177 Matignon (1936, 124–5).
178 Meijer (1991, 21).
179 MacCormack (1991, 38–9).
180 Pérez (2005, 53–64).
181 Cited by Pérez (2005, 58).
182 Smith (1899, 286).
183 Zhang et al. (2014).
184 Xiaojing (2001); Liu (2002); Pearson and Liu (2002).
185 Liu (2002, 307–8).
186 Pearson and Liu (2002).
187 Lee and Kleinman (2000, 230).

7 The Body as a Bomb

1 Hoffman (2006, 143).
2 Crenshaw (2007, 135–40).
3 Bloom (2005, 76); Ricolfi (2005, 78–80); Hafez (2006, 4); Moghadam (2006b).
4 Hafez (2006, 72).
5 Alonso and Reinares (2006).
6 Hoffman (2006, 160).
7 Strenski (2003, 22).
8 Pape (2005, 65).
9 Pedahzur (2005, 54–5).
10 Unama (2007).
11 Merari (2007; 2009).
12 Gambetta (2005).
13 Pape (2005, 220).
14 Pedahzur (2005, 13); Pape (2005, 38).
15 Pape (ibid., 15 and 39).
16 Hoffman and McCormick (2004, 248).
17 Pedahzur and Perliger (2006, 2).
18 Lewis (2007, 224).
19 Sprinzak (2000, 66).
20 Pedahzur and Perliger (2006).
21 Hoffman (2006, 134).
22 Ibid., 173–4.
23 Benmelech and Berrebi (2007).
24 Stack-O'Connor (2007, 53).
25 Hafez (2006, 26).
26 Pape (2005, 100).
27 Moghadam (2006a, 713).
28 Abrahms (2006).
29 Pape (2005, 74).
30 Gunaratna (2000), cited by Hoffman (2006, 141).

31 Bloom (2005).
32 Pape (2005, 130).
33 Ibid., 33–4; Gambetta (2005, 262).
34 Pedahzur (2005, 18).
35 Ibid., 18–19.
36 Tosini (2007, 94).
37 Pape (2005, 77).
38 Moghadam (2006a, 716).
39 Berman and Laitin (2006, 39).
40 Gambetta (2005, 288–91).
41 Ibid., 298.
42 Merari (2007, 29).
43 Hafez (2007).
44 Pedahzur and Perliger (2006, 2–4).
45 Gerges (2005).
46 Hafez (2006; 2007).
47 Unama (2007).
48 Hafez (2007, 165–211).
49 Zanini and Edwards (2002).
50 Hoffman (2006, 282–9); Sageman (2008, passim).
51 Sageman (2008, 136).
52 Moghadam (2006a, 523).
53 Hoffman (2006, 226).
54 Ibid., 205–206.
55 Weimann (2006, 82–7).
56 Hoffman (2006, 214–16).
57 Roy (2004); Moghadam (2006a).
58 Weimann (2006, 123).
59 Hoffman (2006, 219).
60 Sageman (2008, 113–23).
61 Pape (2005, 207–8). These figures refer to the period 1980–2003.
62 Krueger and Malecková (2003); Sageman (2004, 73–9); Pape (2005, 214–16); Bergman and Pandey (2006).
63 Gambetta and Hertog (2007).
64 Unama (2007).
65 Lester et al. (2004).
66 Sageman (2004, 80–91).
67 Ricolfi (2005, 106–7).
68 Wintrobe (2006).
69 Hoffman and McCormick (2004, 252).
70 Bloom (2005, 86–7); Elster (2005, 241); Kalyvas and Sanchez-Cuenca (2005, 230); Pedahzur (2005, 142–51); Ricolfi (2005, 106, 111–12); Berko (2007, passim).
71 Pedahzur (2005, 147).
72 Gambetta (2005, 292–3); Kalyvas and Sanchez-Cuenca (2005, 209 and 213–15).
73 Hopgood (2005, 68); Roberts (2005, 494–6).
74 Hoffman and McCormick (2004).
75 Roberts (2005, 497).
76 Weinberger-Thomas (1996, 64–71).

77 Rosenthal (1946, 244).
78 Patton (2003).
79 Rosenthal (1946, 245).
80 Ibid.
81 Ibid., 251–5.
82 Patton (2003).
83 The suicide rates in Iraq are extremely low according to figures for the period 1934–74 published by Al-Kassir (1983, 291–2); so are those for Jordan, to judge by figures for the period 1968–81 published by Barhoum (1983, 325–6). See also the documentation published by Lester (2006).
84 Reuter (2002, 120–5).
85 Cook (2005a; Italian trans. 2007, 213–21).
86 Merari (2007, 30).
87 Reuter (2002, 65).
88 Levitt (2005, 59).
89 Moghadam (2008).
90 Hafez (2007, 64–83); Moghadam (2008).
91 Cook (2005a; Italian trans. 2007, xvii–xviii).
92 Ibid., 37.
93 Mosca (1953, vol. I, 267; English trans. 1939, 181–2).
94 Lewis (1967).
95 Dale (1988).
96 Ewing (1955); Kiefer (1972, 132–4); Andriolo (2002).
97 Ewing (1955, 149); Andriolo (2002, 739).
98 Similarities to *juramentado* can also be found in *amok*, which used to be practised in Malaysia by the Muslim population. *Amok*, which some believe derives its name from the pirates' battlecry, is a state of homicidal frenzy (often affecting persons suffering from bipolar disorder) in which the subject runs towards others, brandishing a knife and killing as many as possible, before he too is killed in turn (Baechler 1975, 527–8).
99 Smythe (1962, 243–4).
100 Ness (2005, 354).
101 Tzoreff (2006, 14).
102 Victor (2003, 12–13).
103 Ibid., 19–20.
104 Ibid., 20.
105 Hasso (2005, 34).
106 Cunningham (2003, 183).
107 Victor (2003, 30–1).
108 Hasso (2005, 31); Victor (2003, 30–1).
109 Victor (2003, 197–8 and 208).
110 Yadlin (2006, 53).
111 Ness (2005, 366).
112 Ibid., 363.
113 Ibid., 364.
114 Ibid.; Stack-O'Connor (2007, 50).
115 Schweitzer (2006, 8).
116 Pape (2005, 208–9). These data refer to the period 1980–2003.
117 Stack-O'Connor (2007, 47).
118 Bloom (2007, 100); Schweitzer (2006, 28–9).

119 Ness (2005, 360–1).
120 Bloom (2005, 143).
121 Tzoreff (2006, 19).
122 Victor (2003, 35).
123 Ibid., 112.
124 Cook (2005a; Italian trans. 2007, 220).
125 Tzoreff (2006, 18–20).
126 Van Knopf (2007, 400).

Conclusions

1 Kotzebue et al. (1821, 195).
2 Grey (1841, vol. 2, 248).
3 Morselli (1879, 205).
4 Steinmetz (1894).
5 Durkheim (1897; English trans. 1951, 217).
6 Arbois de Joubainville (1886); Steinmetz (1894; 1898); Lasch (1898; 1899); Hopkins (1900); Glotz (1904); Westermarck (1912, vol. II, 229–64); Malinowski (1926); Wisse (1933); Delcourt (1939); Metraux (1943); Bohannan (1960); Firth (1961); Berndt (1962); Hoskin et al. (1969); Jeffreys (1971); Strathern (1972); Panoff (1977); Healey (1979); Johnson (1981); Counts (1980; 1984; 1990); Grisé (1982); Brown (1986); Marra (1987); Van Hooff (1990); Bonnemère (1992); Hill (2004); Wardlow (2006); Bargen (2006); Hamlin and Brym (2006).
7 Lewis (1990, 26–7); Bargen (2006, 18–19); Sanadjian (2008).
8 Westermarck (1912, vol. II, 233); Wisse (1933, 460–94); Van Hooff (1990, 126).
9 Firth (1961).
10 Hoebel (1954; Italian trans. 1973, 335–6).
11 Westermarck (1912, vol. II, 236–40); Wisse (1933, 80, 132, 149, 189, 255–6, 481–2).
12 Bradbury (1817, 89).
13 Wisse (1933, 132, 189–90, 256–9); La Fontaine (1960, 110–11).
14 Malinowski (1926, 78 (77–96)).
15 Steinmetz (1894); Wisse (1933, 49, 62, 77, 115, 142, 311, 315, 436, 493); Jeffreys (1971); Strathern (1972); Panoff (1977); Baechler (1975, 534–42); Counts (1980, 1984, 1990); Bonnemère (1992).
16 Westermarck (1912, vol. II, 234).
17 Metraux (1943).
18 Counts (1984, 87).
19 Westermarck (1912, vol. II, 233).
20 Sanadjian (2008).
21 Counts (1984, 87).
22 Steinmetz (1898, 49); Jeffreys (1971, 191).
23 Cited by Duchac (1964, 413).
24 Arbois de Jubainville (1886, 246–7).
25 Glotz (1904, 63–9); Delcourt (1939); Grisé (1982).
26 Sophocles (2007, 55; English trans. 2007, 37).
27 Delcourt (1939, 170).
28 Virgil, *Aeneid*, IV, 382–6.

29 Grisé (1982, 135).
30 Panoff (1977, 55).
31 Wisse (1933, 524).
32 Johnson (1981).
33 Glotz (1904, 66).
34 Andriolo (1998).
35 Phillips et al. (2004).
36 Besnard (1997).
37 Collins (2009).
38 Droge and Tabor (1992); Bowersock (1995, 72–3).
39 Zilboorg (1936); Maltsberger and Buie (1980).
40 Sym (1637, 232).
41 Ibid., 236.
42 Ibid. For the recent case of a protest suicide in Italy, see Santoro (2010).
43 Twain (1876; Italian trans. 2003, 27).
44 Ibid., 27–8.
45 Camus (1987; English trans. 2006, 46).
46 Morillo (2001, 254–5). Several experts sustain that some Asiatic countries (China and Japan, in particular) give greater importance to shame than Western cultures (Creighton 1988; Inki Ha 1995). On the other hand, a number of studies (Mokros 1995; Lester 1997) show that a strong sense of shame creates a desire to hide, to disappear or to commit suicide.
47 Van Hooff (1990, 21–2).
48 Phillips et al. (2002c). In a study on Taiwan for the years 1997–2003, Yeh et al. (2008) show that unmarried women under thirty-five and widows aged over sixty-five kill themselves less than married women.
49 Stack (1992).
50 Mayer and Ziaian (2002). Unfortunately, however, the two authors do not take account of age when presenting statistical data on the correlation between married status and suicide rate.
51 Phillips et al. (2002c); Vijayakumar et al. (2005a).
52 Robertson (1999).
53 Hinsch (1990, 123).
54 Bargen (2006, 26–8).
55 Judge (2008, 179–82).
56 Lu (2008, 253–4).
57 In 2006, in India, out of 42,410 female suicides, 6,809 used this method (National Crime Records Bureau, 2008: http://ncrb.nic.in/accdeaths.htm).
58 Kitanaka (2008a; 2008b).
59 Popitz (1992; Italian trans. 2002, 44–5).
60 Steinmetz (1898).
61 Heber (1856, 185).
62 Binchy (1973).
63 Sweeney (1993b).
64 Ibid., 430.
65 Morris (1975); Hill (2005).
66 Morris (1975, 274).
67 Biggs (2005, 178).
68 Joiner (1964, 918).
69 Biggs (2005, 180–8).

Appendix

1 Verkko (1951, 13–15).
2 These were presented by Wagner (1864, 110–13).
3 Also published by Morselli (1879, 90).
4 Somogyi and Somogyi (1995).
5 Direzione generale della statistica (1879, 261–70); Morselli (1879, 509–10).
6 Who (1951, 1956). For the most recent figures: http://www.who.int/mental_health/prevention/suicide/country_reports/en/index.html.
7 Von Mayr (1917, 279).
8 Venkoba Rao (1983).

References

About, E. 1861a *La question romaine*, Paris, Michel Lévy.
— 1861b *Rome contemporaine*, Paris, Michel Lévy.
Abrahms, M. 2006 Why terrorism does not work, *International Security*: 42–79.
Ahmadi, A. 2007 Suicide by self-immolation. Comprehensive overview, experiences and suggestions, *Journal of Burn Care and Research*: 30–41.
Alabaster, E. 1899 *Notes and Commentaries on Chinese Criminal Law and Cognate Topics with Special Relation to Ruling Cases*, London, Luzac and Co.
Alexievich, S. 1993 *Zacarovannye smert'ju*, Moscow, Slovo; Italian trans., *Incantati dalla morte*, Rome, edizioni e/o, 2005.
Al-Hakim, K. 1983 Syria, in L. A. Headley (ed.), *Suicide in Asia and the Near East*, Berkeley, University of California Press, pp. 296–320.
Al-Kassir, M. A. 1983 Iraq, in L. A. Headley (ed.), *Suicide in Asia and the Near East*, Berkeley, University of California Press, pp. 284–95.
Aliverdinia, A. and Pridemore, W. A. 2008 Women's fatalistic suicide in Iran: A partial test of Durkheim in an Islamic Republic, in *Violence Against Women*.
Allison, M. 1991 Re-visioning the death wish: Donne and suicide, *Mosaic*, Inverno, pp. 31–46.
Alonso, R. and Reinares, F. 2006 Maghreb immigrants becoming suicide terrorist: A case study on religious radicalization processes in Spain, in A. Pedahzur (ed.), *Root Causes of Suicide Terrorism*, London, Routledge, pp. 179–97.
Altekar, A. S. 1959 *The Position of Women in Hindu Civilization*, Delhi, Motilal Banardsidass.
Altindag, A. et al. 2005 Suicide in Batman, Southeastern Turkey, *Suicide and Life-Threatening Behavior*: 478–92.
Alvis, R. E. 2004 Hallowed ground, contagious corpses, and the moral economy of the graveyard in early nineteenth-century Prussia, *Journal of Religion*: 234–55.
Améry, J. 1966 *Jenseits von Schuld and Sühne*, Stuttgart, Klett-Cotta; Italian trans., *Intellettuale a Auschwitz*, Turin, Boringhieri, 1987. English trans. *At the Mind's Limits*, trans. Sidney Rosenfeld and Stella P. Rosenfeld, Indiana University Press, 1977 reissue, 1980.
Amiot, J.-M. et al. 1779 *Mémoires concernant l'histoire, les sciences, les arts, les moeurs, les usages, & c. des Chinois*, Paris, Nyon, vol. IV.
Amundsen, D. W. 1999 *Medicine, Society, and Faith in the Ancient and Medieval Worlds*, Baltimore, MD, Johns Hopkins University Press.
Anderson, O. 1987 *Suicide in Victorian and Edwardian England*, Oxford, Clarendon Press.

Anderson, S. 2008 The urge to end it all, *New York Times*, 6 July.

Andreas-Friedrich, R. 1986 *Schauplatz Berlin. Tagebuchaufzeichnungen 1945 bis 1948*, Frankfurt a. M., Suhrkamp. English trans. *Battleground Berlin: Diaries, 1945–1948*, trans. Anna Boerresen, Paragon House, 1990.

Andreeva, E. 2005 *Mortality due to External Causes of Death in the Russian Federation: Spatial Aspects and Explanatory Models*, Berlin, Ph.D. Thesis.

Andriolo, K. 1993 Solemn departures and blundering escapes: Traditional attitudes toward suicide in India, *International Journal of Indian Studies*: 1–8.

— 1998 Gender and the cultural construction of good and bad suicides, *Suicide and Life-Threatening Behavior*: 37–49.

— 2002 Murder by suicide: Episodes from Muslim history, *American Anthropologist*: 736–42.

Angelozzi, G. and Casanova, C. 2003 *La nobiltà disciplinata. Violenza nobiliare, procedure di giustizia e scienza cavalleresca a Bologna nel XVII secolo*, Bologna, Clueb.

Anolli, L. 2002 *Le emozioni*, Milan, Unicopli.

Anon. 1839 *Codice penale per gli Stati di S. M. il Re di Sardegna*, Turin, Stamperia Reale.

Anon. (M. Hillers) 2003 *Eine Frau in Berlin*, Frankfurt a. M., Eichborn; English trans. *A Woman in Berlin: Eight Weeks in the Conquered City*, trans. Philip Boehm. New York: Metropolitan Books, 2005.

Appelbaum, A. 2003 *Gulag. A History of the Soviet Camps*, London, Allen Lane.

Arbois de Joubainville, H. 1886 La procedure du jeune en Irland, *Revue Celtique*: 245–9.

Arendt, H. 1943 We refugees, *The Menorah Journal*, January: 69–77; cited in Marc Robinson (ed.) *Altogether Elsewhere: Writers on Exile*, Faber and Faber, 1994.

— 1945 Organized guilt and universal responsibility, *Jewish Frontier*: 19–23; Italian trans., *Colpa organizzata e responsabilità universale*, in *Ebraismo e modernità*, Milan, Feltrinelli, 2001, pp. 63–76.

— 1951 *The Origins of Totalitarianism*, New York, Harcourt; Italian trans., *Le origini del totalitarismo*, Milan, Comunità, 1996.

Ariés, P. 1977 *L'homme devant la mort*, Paris, Seuil; Italian trans., *L'uomo e la morte dal Medioevo a oggi*, Roma-Bari, Laterza, 1979.

Augustine 1887 'On Patience', trans. Rev. H. Browne, in *A Select Library of the Nicene and Post-Nicene Fathers of the Christian Church*. vol. 3, ed. Philip Schaff. Buffalo: The Christian Literature Co., pp. 525–37.

— 1998 *The City of God Against the Pagans*, ed. and trans. R. W. Dyson. Cambridge, Cambridge University Press.

Babb, L. 1951 *The English Malady. A Study of Melancholia in English Literature from 1580 to 1642*, East Lansing, Michigan State College Press.

Backhouse, E. and Bland, J. O. P. 1914 *Annals and Memoirs of the Court of Peking*, London, Heinemann.

Baechler, J. 1975 *Les suicides*, Paris, Calmann-Lévy. English trans. *Suicides*, trans. Barry Cooper, New York: Basic Books, 1979.

Bähr, A. 2013 Between 'self-murder' and 'suicide': The modern etymology of self-killing, *Journal of Social History*: 620–32.

Baker, C. 1969 *Ernest Hemingway: A Life Story*, New York, Charles Scribner's Sons; Italian trans., *Ernest Hemingway*, Milan, Mondadori, 1970.

Baker, H. D. R. 1979 *Chinese Family and Kinship*, London, Macmillan.

Balbi, G. 1590 *Viaggio dell'Indie Orientali*, Venice, Appresso Borgominieri.

Baldessarini, R. J. et al. 2006a Decreased risk of suicides and attempted suicides during long-term lithium treatment: A meta-analytic review, *Bipolar Disorder*: 625–39.

— 2006b Suicide in bipolar disorder: Risks and management, *Spectrum*: 465–71.

Ball, J. D. 1893 *Things Chinese: Or Notes Connected with China*, New York, Charles Scribner's Sons.

Banerjee, P. 2003 *Burning Women*, London, Palgrave Macmillan.

Barbosa, O. 1554 *Libro di Odoardo Barbosa*, in G. B. Ramusio (ed.), *Navigazioni e viaggi*, Turin, Einaudi, 1979, vol. 2, pp. 543–709. English trans. *The Book of Duarte Barbosa*, trans. Mansel Longworth Dames, vol. I, London: Hakluyt Society, 1918.

Bargen, D. G. 2006 *Suicidal Honor*, Honolulu, University of Hawaii Press.

Barhoum, M. I. 1983 Jordan, in L. A. Headley (ed.), *Suicide in Asia and the Near East*, Berkeley, University of California Press, pp. 321–32.

Baris, T. 2004 *Tra due fuochi*, Roma-Bari, Laterza.

Barraclough, B. and Shepherd, D. 1994 A necessary neologism: The origin and uses of suicide, *Suicide and Life-Threatening Behavior*: 113–26.

Barry, R. L. 1994 *Breaking the Thread of Life*, New Brunswick, NJ, Transaction Publishers.

Bartel, R. 1959–60 Suicide in eighteenth-century England: The myth of a reputation, *Huntington Library Quarterly*: 145–58.

Baudelot, C. and Establet, R. 2006 *Suicide. L'envers de notre monde*, Paris, Seuil. English trans. *Suicide. The Hidden Side of Modernity*, trans. David Macey, Polity, 2008.

Baumann, U. 2001 *Vom Recht auf den eigenen Tod*, Weimar, Herman Boehlaus.

Bayet, A. 1922 *Le suicide et la morale*, Paris, Librairie Félix Alcan.

Beauchamp, T. L. 1976 An analysis of Hume's essay 'On Suicide', *Review of Metaphysics*: 73–95.

Beccaria, C. 1965 *Dei delitti e delle pene* (1764), Turin, Einaudi. English trans. *An essay on crimes and punishments. Written by the Marquis Beccaria, of Milan. With a commentary attributed to Monsieur de Voltaire*. Philadelphia: Printed and sold by R. Bell, next door to St Paul's Church, in Third-Street (1778).

Beevor, A. 2002 *Berlin: The Downfall, 1945*, London, Viking; Italian trans., *Berlino 1945*, Milan, Rizzoli, 2002.

Bell, R. 2012 *We Shall Be No More: Suicide and Self-Government in the Newly United States*, Cambridge, Harvard University Press.

Bellamy, Richard (ed.) 1995 *Beccaria: 'On Crimes and Punishments' and Other Writings*, trans. Richard Davies, Cambridge University Press.

Bels, J. 1975 La mort volontaire dans l'oeuvre de saint Augustin, *Revue de l'histoire des religions*: 147–80.

Benmelech, E. and Berrebi, C. 2007 *Attack assignments in terror organizations and the productivity of suicide bombers*, Cambridge, MA, National Bureau of Economic Research, Nber Working Paper n. 12910.

Benn, J. A. 2007 *Burning for the Buddha*, Honolulu, University of Hawaii Press.

Bentinck, W. 1922 *Minute on Sati*, in A. B. Keith (ed.), *Speeches and Documents on Indian Policy (1750–1921)*, London, Oxford University Press; in A. Major (ed.), *Sati. A Historical Anthology*, Oxford, Oxford University Press, 2007, pp. 102–15.

Bergman, P. and Pandey, S. 2006 The Madrassa scapegoat, *Washington Quarterly*: 117–25.

Berk, B. B. 2006 Macro-micro relationships in Durkheim's analysis of egoistic suicide, *Sociological Theory*: 58–80.

Berko, A. 2007 *The Path to Paradise*, Westport, CT, Praeger Security International.

Berman, E. and Laitin, D. D. 2006 Hard target. Theory and evidence on suicide attacks, unpublished paper.

Bernardini, P. 1994 Dal suicidio come crimine al suicidio come malattia, *Materiali per una storia della cultura giuridica*: 1, 81–101.

— 1999 'Melancholia gravis' o della relazione fra suicidio e malinconia, *Intersezioni*: 257–68.

— 2001 Le rive fatali di Keos. Montaigne o il cauto inizio del modern trattamento morale del suicidio, *Materiali per una storia della cultura giuridica*: December, 335–51.

— 2004 I have the keys of my prison in myne own hand. Prime note sul 'Biathanatos' di John Donne, *Materiali per una storia della cultura giuridica*: June, 3–17.

Berndt, R. M. 1962 *Excess and Restraint: Social Control among a New Guinea Mountain People*, Chicago, IL, University of Chicago Press.

Bernheim, J. C. 1987 *Les suicides en prison*, Montreal, Editions du Meridien.

Bernier, P. 1670 *Histoire de la dernière révolution des Etats du Grand-Mogol*, Paris, Barbin; English trans. *Travels in the Mogul Empire, AD 1656–1668*, trans. Archibald Constable on the basis of Irving Brock's version. Ed. Vincent A. Smith. Oxford University Press, 1916.

Bernstein, O. 1907 *Die Bestrafung des Selbstmords und ihr Ende*, Breslau, Schletter'sche Buchhandlung.

Berrios, G. E. and Mohanna, M. 1990 Durkheim and French psychiatric views on suicide during the 19th century. A conceptual history, *British Journal of Psychiatry*: 1–9.

Besnard, P. 1976 Anti- ou ante-durkheimisme? Contribution au débat sur les statistiques officiels, *Revue française de sociologie*: 313–41.

— 1997 Mariage et suicide: la théorie durkheimienne de la régulation conjugale a l'épreuve d'un siècle, *Revue française de sociologie*: 735–58.

— 2000 *La destinée du 'Suicide'. Réception, diffusion et postérité*, in Borlandi and Cherkaoui (2000, pp. 185–218).

Bessel, R. 2005 Hatred after war. Emotion and the postwar history of East Germany, *History and Memory*: 195–216.

Besta, E. 1908–09 *La Sardegna medievale*, Palermo, Reber, 2 vols.

Bettelheim, B. 1963 *The Informed Heart*, Glencoe, IL, The Free Press; Italian trans., *Il prezzo della vita*, Milan, Adelphi, 1965.

Bhugra, D. 2004 Migration and mental health, *Acta Psychiatrica Scandinavica*: 243–58.

Bianco, L. 1978 Peasant movements, in *The Cambridge History of China*, vol. 13, *Republican China 1912–1949*, Cambridge, Cambridge University Press, pp. 270–328.

— 2001 *Xiedou et équité*, in I. Thireau and W. Hansheng (eds.), *Disputes au village chinois*, Paris, Editions de la Maison des sciences de l'homme, pp. 287–327.

Biddle, L. et al. 2008 Suicide rates in young men in England and Wales in the 21st century: Time trend study, *BMJ. British Medical Journal*: 539–42.

Biggs, M. 2005 Dying without killing: Self-immolations, 1963–2002, in D. Gambetta (ed.), *Making Sense of Suicide Missions*, Oxford, Oxford University Press, pp. 173–208.

Binchy, D. A. 1973 *Distraint in Irish law*, Celtica: 22–71.

Birge, B. 1995 Levirate marriage and the revival of widow chastity in Yuan China, *Asia Major*: 107–46.

— 2002 *Women, Property and Confucian Reaction in Sung and Yuan China (960–1368)*, Cambridge, Cambridge University Press.

Bisetto, B. 2000 La retorica del suicidio femminile nella letteratura cinese, *Asiatica veneziana*: 21–34.

— 2004 *La morte le si addice. Etica ed estetica del suicidio femminile nella Cina imperiale*, tesi di dottorato di ricerca in Civiltà dell'India e dell'Asia orientale.

Björkenstam, C. et al. 2005 Are cancer patients at higher suicide risk than the general population? A nationwide register study in Sweden from 1965 to 1999, *Scandinavian Journal of Public Health*: 208–14.

Bland, R. C. et al. 1998 Psychiatric disorders in the population and in prisoners, *International Journal of Law and Psychiatry*: 273–9.

Blanshei, S. R. 1982 Crime and law enforcement in medieval Bologna, *Journal of Social History*: 121–38.

Bloom, M. 2005 *Dying to Kill. The Allure of Suicide Terror*, New York, Columbia University Press.

— 2007 Female suicide bombers: A global trend, *Daedalus*: 94–102.

Boccaccio, G. 1963 *Il Decameron* (1348–53), Turin, Einaudi. English trans. *The Decameron*, trans. Guido Waldman and introduced by Jonathan Usher, Oxford University Press 1993.

Bohannan, P. 1960 Theories of homicide and suicide, in Bohannan (ed.), *African Homicide and Suicide*, Princeton, NJ, Princeton University Press, pp. 3–29.

Bonnemère, P. 1992 Suicide et homicide: deux modalités vindicatoires en Nouvelle-Gui- née, *Stanford French Review*: 19–43.

Borges, J. L. 1974 *Obras completas*, Buenos Aires, Emecé; Italian trans., *Tutte le opere*, Milan, Mondadori, 1984. English trans. *Other Inquisitions, 1937–52*, trans. and ed. Ruth L. C. Simms, University of Texas Press 1964.

Borlandi, M. 2000 Lire ce que Durkheim a lu. Enquête sur les sources statistiques et médicales du 'Suicide', in Borlandi and Cherkaoui (2000, pp. 9–46).

Borlandi, M. and Cherkaoui, M. 2000 '*Le suicide*' *un siècle après Durkheim*, Paris, Puf.

Boschi, D. 1998 Homicide and knife fighting in Rome, 1845–1914, in P. Spierenburg (ed.), *Men and Violence*, Columbus, Ohio State University Press, pp. 128–58.

Bosman, M. 2004 The judicial treatment of suicide in Amsterdam, in J. R. Watt (ed.), *From Sin to Insanity*, Ithaca, NY, Cornell University Press, pp. 9–24.

Bourquelot, F. 1841–42 *Recherches sur les opinions et la legislation en matière de mort volontaire*, Bibliothèque de l'école des Chartes, III (pp. 539–60) and IV (pp. 242–66, 457–75).

Bousquet, P. 2002 *Le suicide féminin au XVIIe siècle: un acte héroïque?*, in R. G. Hogdson (ed.), *La femme au XVIIe siècle*, Tübingen, Gunter Narr Verlag, pp. 183–200.

Bowersock, G. W. 1995 *Martyrdom and Rome*, Cambridge, Cambridge University Press.

Bradbury, J. 1817 *Travels in the Interior of America, in the Years 1809, 1810, and 1811*, London, Sherwood, Neely and Jones.

Brahimi, M. 1980 La mortalité des étrangères en France, *Population*: 603–22.

Brainerd, E. 2001 Economic reform and mortality in the former Soviet Union: A study of the suicide epidemic in the 1990s, *European Economic Review*: 1007–19.

Brann, N. L. 1979 Is acedia melancholy? A re-examination of this question in the light of fra Battista da Crema's Della cognitione et vittoria di se stesso (1531), *Journal for the History of Medicine and Allied Sciences*: 80–99.

Bray, A. 1995 *Homosexuality in Renaissance England*, New York, Columbia University Press.

Bresnahan, M. et al. 2003 Temporal variation in the incidence, course and outcome of schizophrenia, in R. M. Murray et al. (eds.), *The Epidemiology of Schizophrenia*, Cambridge, Cambridge University Press, pp. 34–48.

Brierre de Boismont, A. 1865 *Du suicide et de la folie suicide*, Paris, Librairie Germer Bailliere.

Bright, T. 1586 *A Treatise of Melancholy*, London, Vantrollier; Italian trans., *Della melancholia*, Milan, Giuffrè, 1990.

Bronisch, T. 1996 Suicidality in German concentration camps, *Archives of Suicide Research*: 129–44.

Brown, M. F. 1986 Power, gender and the social meaning of Agaruna suicide, *Man*: 311–28.

Brown, P. 1981 *The Cult of the Saints: Its Rise and Function in Latin Christianity*, Chicago, IL, University of Chicago Press; Italian trans., *Il culto dei santi*, Turin, Einaudi, 1983.

Brown, R. M. 2001 *The Art of Suicide*, London, Reaktion Books.

Buckingham, J. 2005 'To make the precedent fit the crime': British legal responses to sati in early nineteenth-century north India, in *Crime Empire 1840–1940*, B. Godfrey and G. Dunstall (eds.), Willan Pub., pp. 189–201.

Bunge, G. 1995 *Akedia*, Würzburg, Der Christliche Osten; Italian trans., *Akedia*, Magnano, Qiqajon, 1999.

— 1999 *Drachenwein und Engelsbrot*, Würzburg, Der Christliche Osten; English trans. *Dragon's Wine and Angel's Bread. The Teachings of Evagrius Ponticus on Anger and Meekness*, trans. Anthony P. Gythiel, New York: St Vladimir's Seminary Press, 2009.

Bunle, H. 1954 *Le mouvement naturel de la population dans le monde de 1906 à 1936*, Paris, Ined.

Burckhardt, J. 1860 *Die Kultur der Renaissance in Italien*, Basle, Schweighauser; English trans. *The Civilization of the Renaissance in Italy*, trans. S. G. C. Middlemore, Phaidon, London 1955.

Burgess-Jackson, K. 1982 The legal status of suicide in early America: A comparison with the English experience, *Wayne Law Review*: 57–87.

Burrow, S. and Laflamme, L. 2006 Suicide mortality in South Africa, *Social Psychiatry and Psychiatric Epidemiology*: 108–14.

Burton, R. 1932 *The Anatomy of Melancholy* (1621), London, J. M. Dent and Sons, 3 vols.

Burvill, P. W. 1998 Migrant suicide rates in Australia and in country of birth, *Psychological Medicine*: 201–8.

Burvill, P. W. et al. 1973 Methods of suicide of English and Welsh immigrants in Australia, *British Journal of Psychiatry*: 285–94.

— 1983 Comparison of suicide rates and methods in English, Scots and Irish migrants in Australia, *Social Science and Medicine*: 705–8.

Bussagli, M. 1986 *Figurae Mogoricae: nota all'iconografia*, in P. Falchetta (ed.), *Storia del Mogol di Nicolò Manuzzi veneziano*, Milan, Franco Maria Ricci Editore, vol. 1.

Butler, S. M. 2006a Degrees of culpability: Suicide verdicts, mercy and the jury in medieval England, *Journal of Medieval and Early Modern Studies*: 263–90.

— 2006b Women, suicide and the jury in later medieval England, *Signs*: 141–66.

Cahn, Z. G. 1998 *Suicide in French Thought from Montesquieu to Cioran*, New York, Peter Lang.

Caillat, C. 1977 Fasting unto death according to the Jaina tradition, *Acta Orientalia*: 43–66.

Camus, A. 1987 *Oeuvres complètes*, Paris, Gallimard; English trans. *The Fall*, trans. Robin Buss, Penguin Modern Classics 2006.

Canetto, S. S. and Sakinofsky, I. 1998 The gender paradox in suicide, *Suicide and Life-Threatening Behavior*: 1–23.

Carbasse, J.-M. 2006 *Histoire du droit pénal et de la justice criminelle*, Paris, Puf.

Carlitz, K. 1994 Desire, danger and the body: Stories of woman's virtue in late Ming China, in C. K. Gilmartin et al. (eds.), *Engendering China. Women, Culture and the State*, Cambridge, MA, Harvard University Press, pp. 101–24.

— 1997 Shrines, governing-class identity, and the cult of widow fidelity in mid-Ming Jiangnan, *Journal of Asian Studies*: 612–40.

— 2001 The daughter, the singing-girl, and the seduction of suicide, in Ropp et al. (2001, pp. 22–46).

Casagrande, C. and Vecchio, S. 2000 *I sette vizi capitali*, Turin, Einaudi.

Cassels, N. G. 1965 Bentinck: Humanitarian and imperialist – The abolition of Suttee, *Journal of British Studies*: 78–87.

Cassian, J. 1563 *Delle costitutioni et origine de monachi, et de remedij & cause de tutti li vitij*, Venice, Michele Tramezzino. English trans. in John Cassian, *The Institutes*, trans. and annotated Boniface Ramsey, The Newman Press, 2000.

Castelpietra, G. et al. 2008 Antidepressant use and suicide prevention: A prescription database study in the region Friuli Venezia Giulia, Italy, *Acta Psychiatrica Scandinavica*: 382–8.

Castiglione, B. 1998 *Il libro del cortegiano* (1528), Turin, Einaudi. English trans. *The Book of the Courtier. The Singleton Translation*, Daniel Javitch (ed.), New York: Norton and Company, 2002.

Cavallo, T. 2003 Introduzione, in A. Radicati di Passerano, *Dissertazione filosofica sulla morte*, Pisa, Ets, pp. 9–64.

Cavan, R. S. 1928 *Suicide*, Chicago, IL, University of Chicago Press.

Cavanagh, J. T. O. et al. 2003 Psychological autopsy studies of suicide: A systematic review, *Psychological Medicine*: 395–405.

Cellini, B. 1973 *La vita*, Turin, Einaudi. English trans. *Cellini*, ed. and abridged by Charles Hope and Alessandro Nova, from the trans. by John Addington Symonds, Phaidon Oxford, 1983

Chakravarti, U. 1998 Gender, caste and labour: The ideological and material structure of widowhood, in M. A. Chen (ed.), *Widow in India. Social Neglect and Public Action*, London, Sage, pp. 63–92.

Chandler, C. R. and Tsai, Y. M. 1993 Suicide in Japan and in the West, *International Journal of Comparative Sociology*: 244–59.

Chang, J. 2005 *Mao*, New York, Knopf.

Chen, M. A. 2000 *Perpetual Mourning. Widowhood in Rural India*, Oxford, Oxford University Press.

Cheng, A. 1997 *Histoire de la pensée chinoise*, Paris, Seuil; Italian trans., *Storia del pensiero cinese*, Turin, Einaudi, 2000, 2 vols.

Cheng, A. T. and Lee, C. S. 2000 Suicide in Asia and the Far East, in K. Hawton and K. van Heeringen (eds.), *The International Handbook of Suicide and Attempted Suicide*, New York, Wiley, pp. 29–48.

Chesnais, J.-C. 1976 *Les morts violentes en France depuis 1826. Comparaison internationales*, Paris, Puf.

— 1981 *Histoire de la violence en Occident de 1880 à nos jours*, Paris, Laffont; Italian trans., *Storia della violenza in Occidente*, Milan, Longanesi, 1982.

Cheyne, G. 1733 *The English Malady or a Treatise of Nervous Diseases of all Kinds*, London, Printed for G. Strahan in Cornhill.

Chyrsostom, St John. 2002 *A Stagirio tormentato da un demone*, Rome, Città Nuova.

— 1880 *Saint John Chrysostom, His Life and Times*, Stephens, W. R. W. (ed.), London.

Cicero. 1923 *On Old Age*, trans. by W. A. Falconer, vol. 20, Loeb Classical Library, Harvard University Press.

Clarke, R. V. and Lester, D. 1989 *Suicide: Closing the Exits*, New York, Springer Verlag.

Cobb, R. 1978 *Death in Paris*, Oxford, Oxford University Press.

Cohen, E. A. 1953 *Human Behavior in the Concentration Camp*, New York, The Universal Library.

Cohen, L. M. 1971 The Chinese of the Panama railroad: Preliminary notes on the migrants of 1854 who 'failed', *Ethnohistory*: 309–20.

Colebrooke, H. T. 1795 On the duties of a faithful Hindu widow, *Asiatic Researches*: 4, 209–19; in Colebrooke, *Miscellaneous Essays*, London, W. H. Allen, 1837, pp. 114–22.

Collins, R. 2009 One hundred years advance on Durkheim, *Sociologica*: 2/3.

Collmer, R. G. 1969 Donne and Borges, *Revue de literature comparée*: 219–32.

Conquest, R. 1968 *The Great Terror: A Reassessment*, London, Macmillan; Italian trans., *Il grande terrore*, Milan, Bur, 2002.

Conrad, P. 1992 Medicalization and social control, *Annual Review of Sociology*: 209–32.

Conti, N. de 1492 *Viaggio di Nicolò di Conti*, in G. B. Ramusio (ed.), *Navigazioni e viaggi*, Turin, Einaudi, 1979, vol. II, pp. 789–820.

Cook, D. 2005a *Understanding Jihad?*, Berkeley, University of California Press; Italian trans., *Storia del Jihad*, Turin, Einaudi, 2007.

— 2005b Women fighting in Jihad?, *Studies in Conflict and Terrorism*: 375–84.

Coope, J. A. 1995 *The Martyrs of Cordoba: Community and Family Conflict in an Age of Mass Conversion*, Lincoln, University of Nebraska Press.

Counts, D. 1980 Fighting back is not the way: Suicide and the women of Kaliai, *American Ethnologist*: 332–51.

— 1984 Revenge suicide by Lusi women: An expression of power, in D. O'Brien and S. Tiffany (eds.), *Rethinking Women's Roles: Perspectives from the Pacific*, Berkeley, University of California Press, pp. 71–93.

— 1990 Suicide in different ages from cross-cultural perspective, in A. A. Leenaars (ed.), *Life Span Perspectives of Suicide*, New York, Plenum, pp. 215–30.

Courcelle, P. 1958 La posterité chrétienne du songe de Scipion, *Revue des etudes religieuses*: 205–34.

Courtet, P. et al. 2005 Suicidal behavior: Relationship between phenotype and serotonergic genotype, *American Journal of Medical Genetics*: 133C, 25–33.

Courtright, P. B. 1994 The iconographies of Sati, in J. Stratton Hawley (ed.), *Sati. The Blessing and the Curse*, Oxford, Oxford University Press, pp. 27–49.

— 1995 Sati, sacrifice and marriage, in L. Harlan and P. B. Courtright (eds.), *From the Margins of Hindu Marriage: Essays on Gender, Religion and Culture*, pp. 184–203.

Creighton, M. R. 1988 Revisiting shame and guilt cultures: A forty year pilgrimage, *Ethos*: 279–307.

Crenshaw, M. 2007 Explaining suicide terrorism: A review essay, *Security Studies*: 133–62.

Culbertson, F. M. 1997 Depression and gender. An international review, *American Psychologist*: 25–31.

Cunningham, K. J. 2003 Cross-regional trends in female terrorism, *Studies in Conflict and Terrorism*: 171–95.

Cutter, F. 1983 *Art and the Wish to Die*, Chicago, IL, Nelson-Hall.

Dalby, M. 1982 Revenge and the law in traditional China, *American Journal of Legal History*: 267–307.

Dale, S. F. 1988 Religious suicide in islamic Asia: Anticolonial terrorism in India, Indonesia, and the Philippines, *Journal of Conflict Resolution*: 37–59.

Danton, G. H. 1938 *The Chinese People*, Boston, MA, Marshall Jones Company.

Darbagh, N. T. 2005 *Suicide in Palestine*, London, Hurst and Company.

Daube, D. 1972 The linguistic of suicide, *Philosophy and Public Affairs*: 387–437.

Davis, R. L. 1996 *Wind against the Mountain. The Crisis of Politics and Culture in Thirteenth-Century China*, Cambridge, MA, Harvard University Press.

Dawidowicz, I. S. 1975 *The War against the Jews, 1933–1945*, New York, Holt, Rinehart and Winston.

De Beaumanoir, P. 1899–1900 *Coutumes de Beauvaisis*, Paris, A. Picard et fils, 2 vols.

De Felice, R. 1988 *Storia degli ebrei Italiani sotto il fascismo*, Turin, Einaudi.

De l'Arbre, A. 1921 *De la confiscation des biens des suicides*, Bulletin de la Commission Royale des Anciennes Lois et Ordonnances de Belgique: 9–44.

Delcourt, M. 1939 Le suicide par vengeance dans la Grèce ancienne, *Revue de l'histoire des religions*: 154–71.

Della Valle, P. 1667 *Viaggi di Pietro della Valle, il Pellegrino descritti da lui medesimo in 54 lettere familiari*, Venice, Paolo Baglioni. English trans. *The Travels of Pietro della Valle in India*, from the old English trans. of 1664 by G. Havers, ed. Edward Grey, 2 vols. London: Hakluyt Society 1892.

Delumeau, J. 1983 *Le peché et la peur*, Paris, Fayard; English trans. *Sin and Fear. The Emergence of a Western Guilt Culture (13th – 18th centuries)*, trans. Eric Nicholson, New York: St Martin's Press, 1990.

Deschrijver, S. 2011 From sin to insanity? Suicide trials in the Spanish Netherlands, sixteenth and seventeenth centuries, *Sixteenth Century Journal*: 981–1002.

De Sévigné, M. 1972 *Correspondance*, Paris, Pleiade; English trans. *Letters of Madame de Sevigne to her daughter and her friends*, London: Printed for J. Walker et al. 1811, vol. 1.

Desjarlais, R. et al. 1995 *World Mental Health*, Oxford, Oxford University Press; Italian trans., *La salute mentale nel mondo*, Bologna, Il Mulino, 1998.

Diamant, N. J. 2000 *Revolutionizing the Family. Politics, Love, and Divorce in Urban and Rural China, 1949–1968*, Berkeley, University of California Press.

— 2001 Between martyrdom and mischief: The political and social predicament of Ccp war widows and veterans, 1949–66, in D. Lary (ed.), *Scars of Wars*, Vancouver, Ubc Press, pp. 162–87.

Diekstra, R. F. W. 1995 The epidemiology of suicide and parasuicide, in Diekstra (ed.), *Preventive Strategies on Suicide*, Leiden, Brill, pp. 1–34.

Dieselhorst, J. 1953 *Die Bestrafung der Selbstmörder im Territorium der Reichstadt Nürnberg*, Mitteilungen des Vereins für Geschichte der Stadt Nürnberg: 58–230.

Di Maggio, P. 1997 Culture and cognition, *Annual Review of Sociology*: 263–87.

Diodorus Siculus 1988 *Biblioteca storica. Libri 18–20*, Milan, Rusconi. English trans. *Library of History*, trans. Russel M Geer, Loeb, 1947, Bk XIX: 33–4.

Direzione generale della statistica 1879 *Movimento dello stato civile. Anni dal 1862 al 1877. Introduzione con raffronti di statistica internazionale*, Rome.

Dolev, N. 1999 Gaspar Ofhuys' Chronicle and Hugo van der Goes, *Assaph*: 4, 125–37.

Doolittle, J. 1865 *Social Life of the Chinese*, New York, Harper and Row.

Donaldson, I. 1982 *The Rapes of Lucretia. A Myth and its Transformations*, Oxford, Clarendon Press.

Doneddu, G. 1991 Criminalità e società nella Sardegna del secondo Settecento, in L. Berlinguer and F. Colao (eds.), *Criminalità e società in età moderna*, Milan, Giuffrè, pp. 581–632.

Donne, J. 1608 *Biathanatos. A Declaration of that Paradox or Thesis, that Self-Homicide is not so naturally Sin that it may never be otherwise*, ed. Ernest W. Sullivan II, University of Delaware Press, 1984.

— 1611 *An Anatomy of the World*; Italian trans., *Il primo anniversario. Una anatomia del mondo*, in *Poesie*, Milan, Bur, 2007.

— 1624 *Devotions upon Emergent Occasions and Severall Steps in my Sicknes*; Italian trans., *Devozioni per occasioni di emergenza*, Rome, Editori Riuniti, 1994.

— 2000 An Anatomy of the World, in John Donne, *The Major Works*, ed. John Carey, Oxford University Press.

Douglas, J. D. 1967 *The Social Meanings of Suicide*, Princeton, NJ, Princeton University Press.

Drees, C. J. 1990 Sainthood and suicide: The motives of the martyrs of Cordoba, *Journal of Medieval and Renaissance Studies*: 59–89.

Droge, A. J. and Tabor, J. D. 1992 *A Noble Death. Suicide and Martyrdom among Christians and Jews in Antiquity*, San Francisco, CA, Harper.

Du, F. and Mann, S. 2003 Competing claims on womanly virtue in late imperial China, in D. Ko et al. (eds.), *Women and Confucian Cultures in Premodern China, Korea, and Japan*, Berkeley, University of California Press, pp. 219–47.

Dublin, L. 1963 *Suicide: A Sociological and Statistical Study*, New York, The Ronald Press.

Dubois, Abbé J. A. 1825 *Moeurs, institutions et cérémonies des peuples de l'Inde*, Paris, Imprimerie Royale.

Duchac, R. 1964 Suicide au Japan, suicide à la japonaise, *Revue française de sociologie*: 402–15.

Dumais, A. et al. 2005 Risk factors for suicide completion in major depression: A case-control study of impulsive and aggressive behaviors in men, *American Journal of Psychiatry*: 2116–24.

Dumas, J. 1773 *Traité du suicide, ou du meurtre volontaire de soi-même*, Amsterdam, Chez D. J. Changuion.

Dumont, E. 1948 La repression du suicide, *Revue de droit penal et de criminologie*: 547–70.

Durkheim, É. 1893 *De la division du travail social*, Paris, Puf; English edn. *The Division of Labor in Society*, trans. W. D. Halls, New York, The Free Press 2014.

— 1897 *Le suicide: étude de sociologie*, Paris, Puf; English trans. *Suicide. A Study in Sociology*, trans. John A. Spaulding and George Simpson, Free Press, Glencoe, IL, 1951.

— 1906 Compte rendu: Krose, Die Ursachen der Selbstmordhäufigkeit, *L'Année sociologique*: 511–14.

Duthé, G. et al. 2009 Suicide en prison: la France comparée à ses voisins européens, *Population et sociétés*: 462, 1–4.

Dutt, N. K. 1938 Widow in ancient India, *The Indian Historical Quarterly*: 661–97.

Early, K. E. 1992 *Religion and Suicide in the African-American Community*, Westport, CT, Greenwood Press.

Eberhard, W. 1967 *Guilt and Sin in Traditional China*, Berkeley, University of California Press.

Ebrey, P. B. 1993 *The Inner Quarters*, Berkeley, University of California Press.

— 2003 *Women and the Family in Chinese History*, London, Routledge.

Edwards, B. 1801 *The History, Civil and Commercial, of the British Colonies in the West Indies*, London, John Stockdale, 3rd edn, 3 vols.

Eisner, M. 2003 Long-term historical trends in violent crime, *Crime and Justice: A Review of Research*: 83–142.

Eleonora of Arborea 1805 *Le costituzioni di Eleonora, giudicessa d'Arborea, intitolate Carta de Logu*, Rome, Antonio Fulgoni.

Elias, N. 1968 *Über den Prozess der Zivilisation*, Frankfurt a. M., Suhrkamp; English trans. *The Civilizing Process*, trans. Edmund Jephcott, Blackwell 1994.

Elliott, M. 1999 Manchu widows and ethnicity in Qing China, *Comparative Studies in Society and History*: 33–71.

Elsner, E. 1983 *Der Selbstmord in Berlin*, Berliner Statistik: 218–39.

Elster, J. 1993 Sadder but wiser? Rationality and the emotions, *Social Science Information*; Italian trans., *Più tristi ma più saggi*, Milan, Anabasi, 1994.

1999 *Alchemies of the Mind*, Cambridge, Cambridge University Press.

2005 Motivations and beliefs in suicide missions, in D. Gambetta (ed.), *Making Sense of Suicide Missions*, Oxford, Oxford University Press, pp. 233–58.

Eltis, D. 2000 *The Rise of American Slavery in the Americas*, Cambridge, Cambridge University Press.

Elvin, M. 1984 Female virtue and the state in China, *Past and Present*: 111–52.

Engels, F. 1845 *Die Lage der arbeitenden Klasse in England*, Leipzig, Verlag Otto Wigand; English edn. David McLellan (ed.) *The Condition of the Working-Class in England in 1844*, Oxford University Press, 1993, p. 127.

Epp, M. 1997 The memory of violence. Soviet and East European Mennonite refugees and rape in the Second World War, *Journal of Women's History*: 58–87.

Erlangsen, A. et al. 2008 Increased use of anti depressants and decreasing suicide rates: A population-based study using Danish register data, *Journal of Epidemiology and Community Health*: 448–54.

ESEMED/MHEDEA 2000 Investigators

— 2004 Use of mental health services in Europe: results from the European Study of the Epidemiology of Mental Disorders (ESEMeD) project, *Acta Psychiatrica Scandinavica*: 47–54.

Esquirol, J.-E. D. 1838 *Des maladies mentales: considerées sous les rapports médical, hi- giénique et médico-légal*, Paris, J.-B. Baillière, vol. 1. English trans. *Mental Maladies*, trans. E. K. Hunt, Philadelphia 1845.

Establet, R. 2012 *Le suicide en Inde au début du XXIe siècle*, in 'Sociologie', pp. 117–43.

Eusebius of Cesarea. 2007 *The Church History*, trans. Paul Maier, Kregel Academic.

Evagrius Ponticus. 1990 *Gli otto spiriti malvagi*, Parma, Pratiche Editrice. English trans. in *Evagrius of Pontus. The Corpus of Greek Ascetic Texts*, trans. Robert E. Sinekewicz, Oxford University Press, 2003, pp. 66–90.

— 1992 *Trattato pratico sulla vita monastica*, Rome, Città Nuova. English trans. in *Evagrius of Pontus. The Corpus of Greek Ascetic Texts*, trans. Robert E. Sinekewicz, Oxford University Press, 2003, pp. 91–114.

Ewing, J. F. 1955 Juramentado: Institutionalized suicide among the Moros of Philippines, *Anthropological Quarterly*: 148–55.

Ezzat, D. H. 1983 *Kuwait*, in L. A. Headley (ed.), *Suicide in Asia and the Near East*, Berkeley, University of California Press, pp. 272–83.

Falchetta, P. 1986 Venezia, madre lontana. Vita e opere di Niccolò Mannuzi (1638–1717), in P. Falchetta (ed.), *Storia del Mogol di Nicolò Manuzzi veneziano*, Milan, Franco Maria Ricci Editore, vol. 1, pp. 15–63.

Fazel, S. and Danesh, J. 2002 Serious mental disorders in 23,000 prisoners: A systematic review of 62 surveys, *Lancet*: 545–50.

Fedden, H. R. 1938 *Suicide. A Social and Historical Study*, London, Peter Davies Limited.

Fedrici, C. de. 1587 *Viaggio de M. Cesare de Fedrici nell'India Orientale, e oltra l'India: nel quale si contengono cose dilettevoli dei riti, di costumi di questi paesi, Venezia, Andrea Muschio*; in G. B. Ramusio (ed.), *Navigazioni e viaggi*, Turin, Einaudi, 1979, vol. 6, pp. 1017–82; English trans. *The voyage and trauaile of M. Cæsar Frederick, merchant of Venice, into the East India, the Indies, and beyond the Indies* [. . .] *Out of Italian, by Thomas Hickock*, At London: Printed by Richard Jones and Edward White, 1588.

Ferracuti, F. 1957 Suicide in a catholic country, in E. S. Shneidman and N. L. Farberow (eds.), *Clues to Suicide*, New York, McGraw-Hill, pp. 70–7.

Ferri, E. 1925 *L'omicida nella psicologia e nella psicopatologia criminale. L'omicidio-suicidio. Responsabilità giuridica*, Turin, Utet.

Fielde, A. M. 1887 *Pagoda Shadow. Studies from Life in China*, London, T. Ogilvie Smith.

Filliozat, J. 1963 La mort volontaire par le feu et la tradition bouddhique indienne, *Journal Asiatique*: 21–51.

— 1967 L'abandon de la vie par le sage et les suicides du criminal et du héros dans la tradition indienne, *Arts Asiatiques*: 65–88.

Firth, R. 1961 Suicide and risk-taking in Tikopia society, *Psychiatry*: 1–17.

Fisch, J. 1998 *Tödliche Rituale. Die indische Witwenverbrennung und andere Formen der Totenfolge*, Frankfurt a. M., Campus; English trans. *Burning Women. A Global History of Widow-sacrifice from Ancient Times to the Present*, London, Seagull Books, 2006.

Fishbain, D. A. 1996 Current research on chronic pain and suicide, *American Journal of Public Health*: 1320–1.

Fisher, B. J. et al. 2001 Suicidal intent in patients with chronic pain, *Pain*: 199–206.

Fitzpatrick, K. K. et al. 2005 Gender role, sexual orientation and suicide risk, *Journal of Affective Disorders*: 35–42.

Fitzpatrick, S. 1999 *Everyday Stalinism: Ordinary Life in Extraordinary Times: Soviet Russia in the 1930*, Oxford, Oxford University Press.

Flynn, M. 1995 Blasphemy and the play of anger in sixteenth-century Spain, *Past and Present*: 149, 29–56.

Fong, G. S. 2001 Signifying bodies: The cultural significance of suicide writings by women in Ming-Quing China, in Ropp et al. (2001, pp. 105–42).

Frank, M. 1994 Die fehlende Geduld Hiobs. Suizid und Gesellschaft in der Grafschaft Lippe (1600–1800), in G. Signori (ed.), *Trauer, Verzweiflung und Anfechtung*, Tübingen, Diskord, pp. 152–88.

Frankl, V. E. 1995 *Uno psicologo nei lager*, Milan, Ares. English trans. *Man's Search for Meaning*, trans. Isle Lasch, Rider 2004.

Fruehwald, S. et al. 2000a Fifty years of prison suicide in Austria – Does legislation have an impact?, *Suicide and Life-Threatening Behavior*: 272–81.
— 2000b Prison suicide in Austria, 1975–1997, *Suicide and Life-Threatening Behavior*: 360–9.
Fung, W. L. A. et al. 2006 Ethnicity and mental health: The example of schizophrenia in migrant populations across Europe, *Psychiatry*: 396–401.
Gallant, T. W. 2000 Honor, masculinity and ritual knife fighting in nineteenth-century Greece, *American Historical Review*: 359–82.
Gambetta, D. 1999 Primo Levi's last moments, *Boston Review*: Summer.
— 2005 Can we make sense of suicide missions?, in Gallant (ed.), *Making Sense of Suicide Missions*, Oxford, Oxford University Press, pp. 259–99.
Gambetta, D. and Hertog, S. 2007 *Engineers of Jihad*, University of Oxford, Department of Sociology, Sociology Working Papers.
Gamble, S. D. 1921 *Peking, a Social Survey*, New York, G. H. Doran Company.
Garavini, F. 1991 *Mostri e chimere. Montaigne, il testo, il fantasma*, Bologna, Il Mulino.
Garzilli, E. 1997 First Greek and Latin documents on Sahagamana and some connected problems, *Indo-Iranian Journal*: 205–43 and 339–65.
Gates, B. T. 1980 Suicide and the Victorian physicians, *Journal of the History of the Behavioral Sciences*: 164–74.
Gauvard, C. 1991 *'De grace especial'. Crime, Etat et societé en France à la fin du Moyen Âge*, Paris, Publications de la Sorbonne, 2 vols.
— 1997 *La justice penale du roi de France à la fin du Moyen Age*, in X. Rousseaux and R. Levy (eds.), *Le pénal dans tous ses Etats*, Bruxelles, Publications des Facultés universitaires Saint-Louis, pp. 81–112.
— 2001 *Conclusion*, in *Le règlement des conflits au Moyen Âge*, Atti del Convegno, Paris, Publications de la Sorbonne, pp. 369–91.
— 2005 *Violence et ordre public au Moyen Age*, Paris, Picard.
Geertz, C. 1973 *The Interpretation of Cultures: Selected Essays*, New York, Basic Books; Italian trans., *Interpretazione di culture*, Bologna, Il Mulino, 1998.
Geiger, A. 1889a Der Selbstmord im Kirchenrecht, *Archiv für Kirchenrecht*: 61, 225–32.
— 1889b Der Selbstmord im französischen Recht, *Archiv für Kirchenrecht*: 62, 385–99.
— 1891 Der Selbstmord im deutschen Recht, *Archiv für Kirchenrecht*: 65, 3–36.
Gerges, F. A. 2005 *The Far Enemy: Why Jihad Went Global*, Cambridge, Cambridge University Press.
Giansante, M. 1993 *Il caso di Lucia da Varignana. Psicopatologia della vita quotidiana in un processo per infanticidio del 1672*, Atti e memorie della Deputazione di storia patria per le province di Romagna: 303–12.
Gibbs, J. T. 1997 African-American suicide: A cultural paradox, *Suicide and Life-Threatening Behavior*: 68–79.
Gidal, E. 2003 Civic melancholy: English gloom and French enlightenment, *Eighteenth-Century Studies*: 1, 23–45.
Giddens, A. 1965 The suicide problem in French sociology, *British Journal of Sociology*: 3–18.
— 1971 A typology of suicide (1968), in Giddens (ed.), *The Sociology of Suicide. A Selection of Readings*, London, Frank Cass, pp. 97–120.
Giles, H. A. 1876 *Chinese Sketches*, London, Truebner and Co.
— 1911 *The Civilization of China*, London, Holt.

Glotz, G. 1904 *La solidarité de la famille dans le droit criminel en Grèce*, Paris, Albert Fontemoing.

Godineau, D. 2012 *S'abréger les jours. Le suicide en France au XVIIIe siècle*, Paris, Colin.

Goeschel, C. 2005 Suicide in Weimar and Nazi Germany, Cambridge, Darwin College, Ph.D. Thesis.

— 2006 Suicide at the end of the Third Reich, *Journal of Contemporary History*: 151–71.

— 2007 Suicide of German Jews in the Third Reich, *German History*: 22–45.

— 2009 *Suicide in Nazi Germany*, Oxford, Oxford University Press.

Goethe, J. W. 1816–17 *Italienische Reise*, Stuttgart-Tübingen, Cotta; English trans. *Goethe's Italian Journey 1886–88*, Elizabeth Mayer, Penguin Classics 1970.

Goffman, E. 1961 *Asylums*, New York, Doubleday; Italian trans., *Asylums*, Turin, Einaudi, 1968.

Goldney, R. D. and Schioldann, S. 2004 Evolution of the concept of altruistic suicide in pre-Durkheim suicidology, *Archives of Suicide Research*: 23–27.

Gomez, M. A. 1998 *Exchanging Our Country Marks: The Transformation of African Identities in the Colonial and Antebellum South*, Chapel Hill, University of North Carolina Press.

Goodman, B. 2005 The new woman commits suicide: The press, cultural memory and the new republic, *Journal of Asian Studies*: 67–101.

Gowland, A. 2006a The problem of early modern melancholy, *Past and Present*: 77–120.

— 2006b *The Worlds of Renaissance Melancholy*, Cambridge, Cambridge University Press.

Graham, M. 1814 *Letters on India*, London, Longman, Green and Co.

Grandpré, L.-M.-J. O'Hier de. 1801 *Voyage dans l'Inde et au Bengale fait dans les années 1789 et 1790*, Paris, Dentu, 2 vols. English trans. *Voyage in the Indian Ocean and to Bengal, 1789–90*.

Granet, M. 1929 *La civilisation chinoise*, Paris, La Renaissance du livre; English trans. *Chinese Civilisation*, trans. Kathleen Innes and Mabel Brailsford, London, Routledge, 1996.

Grashoff, U. 2006 *'In einem Anfall von Depression': Selbsttötungen in der DDR*, Berlin, Links Verlag.

Gray, J. H. 1878 *China. A History of the Laws, Manners and Customs of the People*, London, Macmillan.

Grey, G. 1841 *Journals of Two Expeditions of Discovery in Northwest and Western Australia*, London, 2 vols.

Gribaudi, G. 2005 *Guerra totale*, Turin, Bollati Boringhieri.

Griffin, M. 1986 Philosophy, Cato, and Roman suicide, *Greece and Rome*: April (64–77) and October (192–202).

Grisé, Y. 1982 *Le suicide dans la Rome antique*, Paris, Les Belles Lettres.

Groot, R. 2000 When suicide became felony, *Journal of Legal History*: 1–20.

Grossmann, A. 1995 A question of silence: The rape of German women by occupation soldiers, *October*: 43–63.

— 2007 *Jews, Germans, and Allies: Close Encounters in Occupied Germany*, Princeton, NJ, Princeton University Press.

Guaccio, F. M. 1626 *Compendium maleficarum*, Milan, Ex. Collegii ambrosiani typofraphia. English trans. *Compendium maleficarum*, ed. Montague Summers and trans. E. A. Ashwin, London: John Rodker, 1929.

Guerry, A.-M. 1833 *Essai sur la statistique morale de la France*, Paris, Chez Cro- chard.

Guiance, A. 1998 *Los discursos sobre la muerte en la Castilla medieval: siglos VII-XV*, Valladolid, Junta de Castilla y León.

Gunaratna, R. 2000 Suicide terrorism: A global threat, *Jane's Security News*.

Guthmann Opfermann, C.1999 Suicides or murders, in H. J. Cargas (ed.), *Problems Unique to the Holocaust*, Lexington, University Press of Kentucky, pp. 43–50.

Hafez, M. M. 2006 *Manufacturing Human Bombs. The Making of Palestinian Suicide Bombers*, Washington, DC, United States Institute of Peace.

— 2007 *Suicide Bombers in Iraq*, Washington, DC, United States Institute of Peace.

Halbwachs, M. 1930 *Les causes du suicide*, Paris, Alcan. English trans. *The Causes of Suicide*, trans. Harold Goldblatt, London: Routledge and Kegan Paul, 1978.

Hamlin, C. L. and Brym, R. J. 2006 The return of the native: A cultural and social-psychological critique of Durkheim's Suicide based in the Guarani-Kaiowà of Southwestern Brazil, *Sociological Theory*: 42–57.

Hanawalt, B. 1979 *Crime and conflict in English communities, 1300–1348*, Cambridge, MA, Harvard University Press.

Hardgrave, R. L. 1998 The representation of Sati: Four eighteenth century etchings by Baltazard Solvyns, *Bengal Past and Present*: 57–80.

Hardgrove, A. 1999 Sati worship and Marwari public identity in India, *Journal of Asian Studies*: 723–52.

Harlan, L. 1994 Perfection and devotion: Sati tradition in Rajasthan, in J. Stratton Hawley (ed.), *Sati. The Blessing and the Curse*, Oxford, Oxford University Press, pp. 3–26.

— 2002 Truth and sacrifice: Sati immolations in India, in M. Cormack (ed.), *Sacrificing the Self. Perspectives on Martyrdom and Religion*, Oxford, Oxford University Press, pp. 118–31.

— 2003 *The Goddesses' Henchmen: Gender in Indian Hero Worship*, Oxford, Oxford University Press.

Harris, E. C. and Barraclough, B. M. 1994 Suicide as an outcome for medical disorders, *Medicine*: 281–96.

— 1997 Suicide as an outcome for mental disorders, *British Journal of Psychiatry*: 205–28.

Harris, N. and Newhauser, R. 2005 Visuality and moral culture in the late middle ages, in R. Newhauser (ed.), *In the Garden of Evil*, Toronto, Pontifical Institute of Mediaeval Studies, pp. 234–76.

Hartig, C. 2007 'Conversations about taking our own lives – Oh, a poor expression for a forced deed in hopeless circumstances!' Suicide among German Jews 1933–1943, *Leo Baeck Institute Yearbook*: 247–65.

Hassan, R. 1995 *Suicide Explained. The Australian Experience*, Melbourne, Melbourne University Press.

Hasso, F. S. 2005 Discursive and political deployments by/of the 2002 Palestinian women suicide bombers/martyrs, *Feminist Review*: 24–51.

He, L. et al. 2003 Forces of production and direction, *Homicide Studies*: 36–57.

Healey, C. 1979 Women and suicide in New Guinea, *Social Analysis*: 89–106.

Healy, R. 2006 Suicide in early modern and modern Europe, *The Historical Journal*: 903–12.

Heber, R. 1856 *Narrative of a Journey through the Upper Provinces of India*, London, John Murray, 2 vols.

Heilä, H. and Lönnqvist, J. 2003 The clinical epidemiology of suicide in schizophrenia, in R. M. Murray et al. (eds.), *The Epidemiology of Schizophrenia*, Cambridge, Cambridge University Press, pp. 288–316.

Helliwell, J. F. 2006 Well-being and social capital: Does suicide pose a puzzle?, *Social Indicators Research*: 455–96.

Hem, E. and Loge, J. H. 2004 Suicide risk in cancer patients from 1960 to 1999, *Journal of Clinical Oncology*: 4209–16.

Hendin, H. 1969 *Black Suicide*, New York, Allen Lane.

Henry, A. F. and Short, J. F. 1954 *Suicide and Homicide*, Glencoe, IL, The Free Press.

Herrmann, C. T. 1833–34 *Recherches sur le nombre des suicides et des homicides*, Memoires de l'Académie Impériale des Sciences de St -Pétersbourg, II, pp. 263–295.

Hershman, P. 1974 Hair, sex and dirt, *Man*: 274–98.

Heyer, A. 2007 Suicide in the fiction of Georges Bernanos and Stefan Zweig: The death of two female adolescents, *Christianity and Culture*: 437–56.

Higonnet, M. 1985 Suicide: Representations of the feminine in the nineteenth century, *Poetics Today*: 103–17.

Hill, P. 2005 Kamikaze, 1943–45, in D. Gambetta (ed.), *Making Sense of Suicide Missions*, Oxford, Oxford University Press, pp. 1–42.

Hill, T. 2004 *Ambitiosa mors. Suicide and Self in Roman Thought and Literature*. London, Routledge.

Hinsch, B. 1990 *Passions in the Cut Sleeve*, Berkeley, University of California Press.

— 2002 *Women in Early Imperial China*, Lanham, MD, Rowman and Littlefield.

Hirschfeld, M. 1914 *Die Homosexualität des Mannes und des Weibes*, Berlin, Marcus; English trans. *The Homosexuality of Men and Women*, Amherst, Prometheus Books, 2000.

Hirzel, R. 1908 *Der Selbstmord*, Archiv für Religionswissenschaft: 75–104, 243–89, 417–76.

Hitchcock, R. 2008 *Mozarabs in Medieval and Early Modern Spain: Identities and Influences*, Aldershot, Ashgate.

Hoang, P. 1898 *Le mariage chinois*, Shanghai, Imprimerie de la mission catholique.

Hodges, W. R. A. 1794 *Travels in India during the years 1780, 1781, 1782 and 1783*, London, J. Edwards.

Hoebel, E. A. 1954 *The Law of Primitive Man. A Study in Comparative Legal Dynamics*, Cambridge, MA, Harvard University Press; Italian trans., *Il diritto nelle società primitive*, Bologna, Il Mulino, 1973.

Hoffman, B. 2006 *Inside Terrorism*, New York, Columbia University Press.

Hoffman, B. and McCormick, G. H. 2004 Terrorism, signaling, and suicide attack, *Studies in Conflict and Terrorism*: 243–81.

Holland Barnes, D. 2006 The aftermath of suicide among African Americans, *Journal of Black Psychology*: 335–48.

Holmgren, J. 1985 The economic foundations of virtue: Widow-remarriage in early modern China, *Australian Journal of Chinese Affairs*: 1–27.

Hopcroft, R. L. and Bradley, D. B. 2007 The sex differences in depression across 29 countries, *Social Forces*: 1483–507.

Hopes, J. 2011 'La maladie anglaise' in French eighteenth-century writing: From stereotype to individuation, *Studies in Literary Imagination*: 109–32.

Hopgood, S. 2005 Tamil tigers, 1987–2002, in D. Gambetta (ed.), *Making Sense of Suicide Missions*, Oxford, Oxford University Press, pp. 43–76.

Hopkins, W. 1900 On the Hindu custom of dying to redress a grievance, *Journal of the American Oriental Society*: 146–59.

Hoskin, J. O. et al. 1969 A high incidence of suicide in a preliterate-primitive society, *Psychiatry*: 200–10.

Hotchner, A. E. 2005 *Papa Hemingway: A Personal Memoir*, New York, Da Capo Press.

Houston, R. A. 2010 *Punishing the Dead? Suicide, Lordship and Community in Britain, 1500–1830*, Oxford University Press.

Hsieh, A. C. V. and Spence, J. D. 1980 Suicide and the family in pre-modern Chinese society, in A. Kleinman and T. Y. Lin (eds.), *Normal and Abnormal Behavior in Chinese Cultures*, Dordrecht, Reidel, pp. 29–47.

Hu, Y. H. 1995 Elderly suicide risk in family contexts: A critique of the Asian family care model, *Journal of Cross-Cultural Gerontology*: 199–217.

Huc, E. R. 1854 *L'empire chinois*, Paris, Gaume. English trans. *A Journey through the Chinese Empire*, 2 vols. New York. Harper and Brothers Publishers, 1855.

Huizinga, J. 1919 *Herfsttij der iddeleeuwen*, Haarlem, H. D. Tjeenk Willink; Italian trans., *L'autunno del Medio Evo*, Florence, Sansoni, 1966. English trans. *The Waning of the Middle Ages*, trans. F. Hopman, 1924 (Penguin Books, 1968).

Hults, L. C. 1991 Dürer's Lucretia: Speaking the silence of woman, *Signs*: 205–37.

Hume, D. 1799 *Essays on Suicide and the Immortality of the Soul*, Basil. Sold by James Decker, printer and bookseller.

Huntington, R. 2005 Ghost seeking substitutes: Female suicide and repetition, *Late Imperial China*: 1–40.

Ibn Battuta 2006 *I viaggi*, Turin, Einaudi. English trans. *The Travels of Ibn Battuta, A.D. 1325–1354*, Hakluyt Society 1971, vol. 3, 1971.

Ikels, C. 1983 *Aging and Adaptation. Chinese in Hong Kong and the United States*, Hamden, CT, Archon Books.

— 2004 (ed.), *Filial Piety. Practice and Discourse in Contemporary East Asia*, Stanford, CA, Stanford University Press.

Inki Ha, F. 1995 Shame in Asian and Western cultures, *American Behavioral Scientist*: 1114–31.

Ivanits, L. 1992 *Suicide and Volk beliefs in Dostoevsky's Crime and Punishment*, in D. Offord (ed.), *The Golden Age of Russian Literature and Thought*, London, St Martin's Press, pp. 138–48.

Iventosch, H. 1974 Cervantes and courtly love: The Grisostomo-Marcela episode of Don Quixote, *PMLA*: 1, 64–76.

Jacques, K. and Taylor, P. J. 2008 Male and female suicide bombers: Different sexes, different reasons?, *Studies in Conflict and Terrorism*: 304–26.

Jansson, A. 1998 *From Sword to Sorrow. Homicide and Suicide in Early Modern Stockholm*, Stockholm, Almquist and Wiksell.

— 2004 Suicide murders in Stockholm, in J. R. Watt (ed.), *From Sin to Insanity*, Ithaca, NY, Cornell University Press, pp. 81–99.

Jeffreys, M. D. W. 1971 Samsonic suicide: Or suicide of revenge among Africans, in A. Giddens (ed.), *The Sociology of Suicide. A Selection of Readings*, London, Frank Cass, pp. 185–96.

Jervis, G. 2002 *La depressione*, Bologna, Il Mulino.

Jing, J. 2004 *Meal rotation and filial piety*, in Ikels (2004, pp. 53–62).

Joblin, A. 1994 Le suicide à l'époque moderne. Un exemple dans la France du Nord-Ouest: à Boulogne-sur-Mer, *Revue historique*: 85–119.

Johnson, B. D. 1965 Durkheim's one cause of suicide, *American Sociological Review*: 875–86.

Johnson, P. L. 1981 When dying is better than living: Female suicide among the Gainj of Papua New Guinea, *Ethnology*: 325–34.

Johnston, R. F. 1910 *Lion and Dragon in Northern China*, New York, Dutton and Co.

Joiner, C. A. 1964 South Vietnam's Buddhist crisis, *Asian Survey*: 915–28.

Joiner, T. E. et al. 2005 The psychology and neurobiology of suicidal behavior, *Annual Review of Psychology*: 287–314.

Jorden, E. 1603 *A briefe discourse of a disease called the Suffocation of the Mother*. London. Printed by John Windet, dwelling at the Signe of the Crosse Keyes at Powles Wharfe.

Jousse, D. 1771 *Traité de la justice criminelle en France*, Paris, Debure père, vol. II.

Judge, J. 2008 *The Precious Raft of History*, Stanford, CA, Stanford University Press.

Justice, C. 2005 Drowning oneself in the river Ganges: Problems of religious suicide in India, in A. Bahr and H. Medick (eds.), *Sterben von eigener Hand. Selbsttötung als kulturelle Praxis*, Köln, Böhlau, pp. 291–307.

Kalyvas, S. N. and Sanchez-Cuenca, I. 2005 Killing without dying: The absence of suicide missions, in D. Gambetta (ed.), *Making Sense of Suicide Missions*, Oxford, Oxford University Press, pp. 208–32.

Kantorowicz, E. H. 1957 *The King's Two Bodies*, Princeton, NJ, Princeton University Press; Italian trans., *I due del Re*, Turin, Einaudi, 1989.

Kaplan, M. 1998 *Between Dignity and Despair*, Oxford, Oxford University Press.

Kapur, N. 2006 Suicide in the mentally ill, *Psychiatry*: 279–82.

Kapusta, N. D. et al. 2008 Rural-urban differences in Austrian suicides, *Social Psychiatry and Psychiatric Epidemiology*: 311–18.

Kästner, A. 2011 *Tödliche Geschichte(n). Selbsttötungen in Kursachsen im Spannungsfeld von Normen und Praktiken (1547–1815)*, Uvk Verlags.

— 2013 Saving self-murderers: Lifesaving programs and the treatment of suicides in late eighteenth-century Europe, *Journal of Social History*: 46, 633–50.

Katzenellenbogen, A. 1939 *Allegories of the Virtues and Vices in Medieval Art*, London, The Warburg Institute.

Keith, A. B. 2003 Suicide (Hindu), in J. Hastings (ed.), *Encyclopedia of Religion and Ethics*, New York, Charles Scribner's Sons, vol. 23, pp. 33–5.

Kendal, W. S. 2007 Suicide and cancer: A gender-comparative study, *Annals of Oncology*: 381–7.

Kennedy, R. H. 1843 The Suttee: The narrative of an eye-witness, in *Bentley's Miscellany*, London, Bentley, vol. 13, pp. 241–56.

Kerkhof, J. F. M. 2000 Attempted suicide: Patterns and trends, in K. Hawton and K. van Heeringen (eds.), *The International Handbook of Suicide and Attempted Suicide*, New York, Wiley, pp. 49–64.

Khlat, M. and Courbage, Y. 1995 La mortalité et les causes de décès des Marocains en France 1979 à 1991, *Population*: 447–72.

Kiefer, T. M. 1972 *The Tausug. Violence and Law in a Philippine Moslem Society*, New York, Holt, Rinehart and Winston.

Kim, J. 2014 'You must avenge on my behalf': Widow chastity and honour in nineteenth-century Korea, *Gender and History*: 128–46.

Kitanaka, J. 2008a Diagnosing suicides of resolve: Psychiatric practice in contemporary Japan, *Culture, Medicine and Psychiatry*: 152–76.

— 2008b Questioning the suicide of resolve: Medico-legal disputes regarding 'overwork suicide' in twentieth century Japan, in J. Weaver and D. Wright (eds.), *Histories of Suicide: International Perspectives on Self-Destruction in the Modern World*, Toronto, University of Toronto Press, pp. 257–80.

Kitzes, A. 2006 *The Politics of Melancholy from Spenser to Milton*, London, Routledge.

Klibansky, R., Panofsky, E. and Saxl, F. 1964 *Saturn and Melancholy*, London, Nelson; Italian trans., *Saturno e la malinconia*, Turin, Einaudi, 2002.

Kliewer, E. 1991 Immigrant suicide in Australia, Canada, England and Wales, and the United States, *Journal of Australian Population Association*: 111–28.

Kliewer, E. and Ward, R. H. 1988 Convergence of immigrants suicide rates to those in the destination country, *American Journal of Epidemiology*: 640–53.

Ko, D. 1994 *Teachers of the Inner Chambers: Women and Culture in Seventeenth-century China*, Stanford, CA, Stanford University Press.

Kogon, E. 1947 *Der SS-Staat*, Stockholm, Bermann-Fischer.

Kohler, J. et al. 1909 *Das Florentiner Strafrecht des 14. Jahrhunderts*, Mannheim, Verlag von Bensheimer.

Koslofsky, C. 2001 Suicide and the secularization of the body in early modern Saxony, *Continuity and Change*: 45–70.

— 2004 Controlling the body and the suicide in Saxony, in J. R. Watt (ed.), *From Sin to Insanity*, Ithaca, NY, Cornell University Press, pp. 48–63.

Koslofsky, C. and Rabin, D. 2005 The limits of the state: Suicide, assassination, and execution in early modern Europe, in A. Bahr and H. Medick (eds.), *Sterben von eigener Hand. Selbsttötung als kulturelle Praxis*, Köln, Böhlau, pp. 45–63.

Kotzebue, O. von et al. 1821 *A Voyage of Discovery: Into the South Sea and Beering's Straits*, London, Longman, vol. III.

Krogh, T. 2012 *A Lutheran Plague. Murdering to Die in the Eighteenth Century*, Leiden, Brill.

Krose, H. A. 1906a *Der Selbstmord im 19. Jahrhundert nach seiner Verteilung auf Staaten und der Verwaltungsbezirke*, Freiburg, Herdersche Ver- lagshandlung.

— 1906b *Die Ursachen der Selbstmordhäufigkeit*, Freiburg, Herdersche Verlagshandlung.

Krueger, A. B. and Malecková, J. 2003 Education, poverty and terrorism: Is there a causal connection?, *Journal of Economic Perspectives*: 119–44.

Kselman, T. 1988 Funeral conflicts in nineteenth-century France, *Comparative Studies in Society and History*: 312–32.

Kushner, H. I. 1991 *American Suicide*, New Brunswick, NJ, Rutgers University Press.

Kwiet, K. 1984 The ultimate refuge. Suicide in the Jewish community under Nazis, *Leo Baeck Institute Yearbook*: 29, 135–67.

La Fontaine, J. 1960 Homicide and suicide among the Gisu, in P. Bohannan (ed.), *African Homicide and Suicide*, Princeton, NJ, Princeton University Press, pp. 94–129.

Lan, H. R. and Fong, V. L. (eds.) 1999 *Women in Republican China*, London, Sharpe.

Langbein, H. 2003 *People in Auschwitz*, Chapel Hill, University of North Carolina Press.

Larner, J. 1972 *Order and disorder in Romagna, 1450–1500*, in L. Martines (ed.), *Violence and Civil Disorder in Italian Cities, 1200–1500*, Berkeley, University of California Press, pp. 38–71.

Lasch, R. 1898 Rache als Selbstmordmotiv, *Globus*: 16 July, 36–9.

— 1899 Der Selbstmord aus erotischen Motiven bei den primitive Völkern, *Zeitschrift für Socialwissenschaft*: 578–85.

Lau, J. S. M. 1989 The courage to be: Suicide as self-fulfilment in Chinese history and literature, *Tamkang Review*: 715–34.

Leach, E. R. 1958 Magical hair, *Journal of the Royal Anthropological Institute of Great Britain and Ireland*: 147–64.

Lederer, D. 1994 *Aufruhr auf dem Friedhof. Pfarrer, Gemeinde und Selbstmord in frühneuzeitlichen Bayern*, in G. Signori (ed.), *Trauer, Verzweiflung und Anfechtung*, Tübingen, Diskord, pp. 189–209.

— 1998 *The dishonorable dead: Perceptions of suicide in early modern Germany*, in S. Backmann et al. (eds.), *Ehrkonzept in der Frühen Neuzeit*, Berlin, Akademie Verlag, pp. 349–65.

— 2005 '*Wieder ein Fass aus Augsburg . . . ': Suizid in der frühneuzeitlichen Lechmetropole*, Mitteilungen des Instituts für Europäische Kulturgeschichte: 47–72.

— 2006a *Madness, Religion and the State in Early Modern Europe*, Cambridge, Cambridge University Press.

— 2006b Suicide in early modern Central Europe: A historiographical review, *German Historical Institute Bulletin*: 33–46.

— 2013 Sociology's 'one law': Moral statistics, modernity, religion, and German nationalism in the *Suicide Studies* of Adolf Wager and Alexander von Oettingen, *Journal of Social History*: 684–99.

Lee, S. and Kleinman, A. 2000 Suicide as resistance in Chinese society, in E. J. Perry and M. Selden (eds.), *Chinese Society: Change, Conflict and Resistance*, London, Routledge, pp. 221–40.

Legoyt, A. 1881 *Le suicide ancien et moderne*, Paris, A. Drouin.

Leon, D. et al. 1997 Huge variation in Russian mortality rates 1984–1994: Artefact, alcohol, or what?, *Lancet*: 350, 383–8.

Leslie, I. J. 1989 *The Perfect Wife. The Ortodox Hindu Women according to the Stridharmapaddhati of Tryambakayajvan*, Delhi, Oxford University Press.

— 1991 A problem of choice: The heroic Sati or the widow-ascetic, in Leslie (ed.), *Rules and Remedies in Classic Indian Law*, Leiden, Brill, pp. 46–59.

Lester, D. 1990 The effect of the detoxification of domestic gas in Switzerland on the suicide rate, *Acta Psychiatrica Scandinavica*: 383–4.

— 1997 The role of shame in suicide, *Suicide and Life-Threatening Behavior*: 352–61.

— 1998 Suicidal behavior in African-American slaves, *Omega*: 1–12.

— 2005a Suicide and the Chinese cultural revolution, *Archives of Suicide Research*: 99–104.

— 2005b *Suicide and the Holocaust*, New York, Nova Science.

— 2006 Suicide and Islam, *Archives of Suicide Research*: 77–97.

Lester, D. and Krysinka, K. E. 2000–1 Suicide in the Lodz Ghetto during world war two, *Omega*: 209–17.

Lester, D. and Yang, B. 1998 *Suicide and Homicide in the 20th Century: Changes over Time*, Commack, NY, Nova Science.

Lester, D. et al. 2004 Suicide bombers: Are psychological profiles possible?, *Studies in Conflict and Terrorism*: 283–95.

Leveleux, C. 2001 *La parole interdite. La blaspheme dans la France médiévale*, Paris, De Boccard.

Levi, P. 1976 *Se questo è un uomo*, Turin, Einaudi. English trans. *If this is a Man/ The Truce*, trans. Stuart Woolf, London: Abacus, 2013.

— 2003 *I sommersi e i salvati*, Turin, Einaudi. English trans. *The Drowned and the Saved*, trans. Raymond Rosenthal, Abacus 2013.

Levitt, M. 2005 *Hamas: Politics, Charity, and Terrorism in the Service of Jihad*, New Haven, CT, Yale University Press.

Levy, M. J. 1949 *The Family Revolution in Modern China*, Cambridge, MA, Harvard University Press (new edn London, Octagon Books, 1971).

Lewis, B. 1967 *The Assassins: A Radical Sect in Islam*, London, Weidenfeld and Nicolson; Italian trans., *Gli assassini*, Milan, Mondadori, 2002.

Lewis, J. 2007 Precision terror: Suicide bombing as control technology, *Terrorism and Political Violence*: 2, 223–45.

Lewis, M. E. 1990 *Sanctioned Violence in Early China*, Albany, State University of New York Press.

Lhomond, B. and Saurel-Cubizolles, M.-J. 2006 Violence against women and suicide risk: The neglected impact of same-sex sexual behavior, *Social Science and Medicine*: 2002–13.

Liebling, A. 1992 *Suicides in Prisons*, London, Routledge.

— 1999 Prison suicide and prisoner coping, in M. Tonry and J. Petersilia (eds.), *Prisons*, Chicago, IL, University of Chicago Press, pp. 283–360.

Lilly, J. R. 2003 *Taken by Force*, London, Palgrave Macmillan; Italian trans., *Stupri di guerra: le violenze commesse dai soldati americani in Gran Bretagna, Francia e Germania, 1942–1945*, Milan, Mursia, 2004.

Lind, V. 1999 *Selbstmord in der frühen Neuzeit*, Göttingen, Vandehoeck and Ruprecht.

— 2004 *Suicidal mind and body. Example from Northern Germany*, in J. R. Watt (ed.), *From Sin to Insanity*, Ithaca, NY, Cornell University Press, pp. 64–80.

Lisle, E. 1856 *Du suicide. Statistique, médecine, histoire et legislation*, Paris, J. B. Bailliere.

Liu, Fei-Wen 2001 The confrontation between fidelity and fertility, *Journal of Asian Studies*: 1051–84.

Liu, K. Y. and Yip, P. S. F. 2008 *Mainland China*, in P. S. F. Yip (ed.), *Suicide in Asia. Causes and Prevention*, Hong Kong, Hong Kong University Press, pp. 31–48.

Liu, M. 2002 Rebellion and revenge: The meaning of suicide of women in rural China, *International Journal of Social Welfare*: 300–9.

Livy (Titus Livius) 1960 *The Early History of Rome*, Books I–IV, trans. Aubrey de Selincourt, London: Penguin.

Llorente, M. D. et al. 2005 Prostate cancer. A significant risk factor for late-life suicide, *American Journal of Geriatric Psychiatry*: 195–201.

Lombroso, S. 1945 *Si può stampare*, Rome, Dalmatia.

Longino Farrell, M. 1992 Writing letters, telling tales, making history: Vatel's death told and retold, *French Review*: 229–42.

Lorant, V. et al. 2005 Socio-economic inequalities in suicide: A European comparative study, *British Journal of Psychiatry*: 49–54.

Lotrakul, M. 2006 Suicide in Thailand during the period 1998–2003, *Psychiatry and Clinical Neurosciences*: 90–5.

Lu, W. 2008 *True to Her Word. The Faithful Maiden Cult in Late Imperial China*, Stanford, CA, Stanford University Press.

Luca da Caltanissetta 1973 *Il Congo agli inizi del Settecento nella relazione di P. Luca da Caltanissetta*, Florence, La Nuova Italia.

Ludwig, J. et al. 2007 *Anti-depressants and suicide*, National Bureau of Economic Research, Cambridge, MA.

Lukes, S. 1967 Alienation and anomie, in P. Laslett and W. G. Runciman (eds.), *Philosophy, Politics and Society*, Oxford, Blackwell, pp. 134–56.

— 1973 *Emile Durkheim. His Life and Work*, London, Allen Lane.

Lyons Johnson, P. 1981 When dying is better than living: Female suicide among the Gainj of Papua New Guinea, *Ethnology*: 325–34.

MacCormack, G. 1991 Suicide in traditional Chinese law, *Chinese Culture: A Quarterly Review*: 33–47.

— 2010 Liability for suicide in Qing law on account of filthy words, in *Nan Nü*: 103–41.

MacDonald, M. 1988 *Introduction*, in J. Sym, *Life Preservative against Self-killing*, London, Routledge, pp. vii–liii.

— 1989 The medicalization of suicide in England: Laymen, physicians, and cultural change, 1500–1870, *Mildbank Quarterly*: 69–91.

MacDonald, M. and Murphy, T. R. 1990 *Sleepless Souls. Suicide in Early Modern England*, Oxford, Clarendon Press.

Macfarlane, A. 2000 Civility and the decline of magic, in P. Burke et al. (eds.), *Civil Histories*, Oxford, Oxford University Press, pp. 145–59.

MacKenzie C. et al. 2014 Changes in attitudes toward seeking mental health services. A 40–years cross-temporal meta-analysis, *Clinical Psychology Review*: 99–106.

Macrobius 1952 *Macrobius: Commentary on the Dream of Scipio*, trans. with introduction and notes, William Harris Stahl, New York: Columbia University Press.

Maier, P. and Ziaian, T. 2002 Indian suicide and marriage, *Journal of Comparative Family Studies*: 297–305.

Major, A. 2006 *Pious Flames: European Encounters with Sati*, Oxford, Oxford University Press.

— 2007 *Introduction*, in Major, *Sati. A Historical Anthology*, Oxford, Oxford University Press, pp. xv–lv.

Mäkinen, I. H. 1997 *On Suicide in European Countries*, Stockholm, Almquist and Wiksell.

— 2000 Eastern European transition and suicide mortality, *Social Science and Medicine*: 1405–20.

— 2006 Suicide mortality in Eastern European regions before and after the communist period, *Social Science and Medicine*: 307–19.

Malaparte, C. 1979 *Kaputt*, Milan, Mondadori.

Malinowski, B. 1926 *Crime and Custom in Savage Society*, London, K. Paul, Trench, Trubner and Co.

Maltsberger, J. T. and Buie, D. H. 1980 The devices of suicide: Revenge, riddance, and rebirth, *International Review of Psychoanalysis*: 61–72.

Manara, G. 1668 *Notti malinconiche nelle quali con occasione di assister a' condannati a morte, si propongono varie difficoltà spettanti a simile materia*, Bologna, G. B. Ferroni.

Mandelstam, N. 1970 *Hope against Hope*, trans. Max Hayward, New York, Atheneum.

Mani, L. 1998 *Contentious Traditions. The Debate on Sati in Colonial India*, Berkeley, University of California Press.

Maning, F. E. 1863 *Old New Zealand: Being Incidents of Native Customs and Character in the Old Times*, London, Smith, Elder and Co. (http://www.nzetc. org/tm/scholarly/tei-ManPake-_N65602.html).

Mann, S. 1987 Widows in the kinship, class, and community structures of Qing dynasty China, *Journal of Asian Studies*: 37–56.

Manni, P. 1826 *Del trattamento degli annegati. Istruzione alla medica gioventù*, Pesaro, coi tipi di Annesio Nobili.

Manucci, N. 1964 Usi e costumi dell'India dalla 'Storia del Mogol': *Dalmine*. Mao Zedong, Milan.

— 1919 'The evil of society' and miss Zhao, 21 November, in Lan and Fong (1999, pp. 85–8).

Mark, J. 2005 Remembering rape: Divided social memory and the Red Army in Hungary 1944–1945, *Past and Present*: 133–61.

Marra, R. 1987 Suicidio, diritto e anomia, *Edizioni Scientifiche Italiane*, Naples.

Marro, G. 1925 Il Giuda impiccato del Canavesio (sec. XV) Nostra Signora del Fontano, *Archivio di antropologia criminale, psichiatria e medicina legale*: 39–60.

Martin, C. D. 2006 Ernest Hemingway: A psychological autopsy of a suicide, *Psychiatry*: 351–61.

Martin, E. 1988 Gender and ideological differences in representations of life and death, in J. L. Watson and E. S. Rawski (eds.), *Death Ritual in Late Imperial and Modern China*, Berkeley, University of California Press, pp. 164–79.

Martschukat, J. 2000 Ein Freitod durch die Hand des Henkers, *Zeitschrift für historische Forschung*: 53–74.

Massetto, G. P. 2004 Il suicidio nella dottrina dell'età di mezzo, *Acta Histriae*: 139–76.

Matard-Bonucci, A.-M. 2007 *L'Italie fasciste et la persécution des juifs*, Paris, Perrin.

Matignon, J.-J. 1897 Le suicide en Chine, *Archives d'Anthropologie criminelle, de criminologie et de psychologie normale et pathologique*: 365–417.

— 1936 *La Cine hérmetique. Superstitions, crime et misère*, Paris, Librairie orientaliste Paul Geuthner.

Mattis, J. S. 2002 Religion and spirituality in the meaning-making and coping experiences of African American women: A qualitative analysis, *Psychology of Women Quarterly*: 309–21.

Maurer, T. 2005 From everyday life to a state of emergency: Jews in Weimar and Nazi Germany, in M. A. Kaplan (ed.), *Jewish Daily Life in Germany, 1618–1945*, Oxford, Oxford University Press, pp. 271–374.

Mauss, M. 1896 La religion et les origines du droit pénale d'après un livre récente, *Revue d'histoire des religions*: 269–95.

Mayer, P. and Ziaian, T. 2002 Indian suicide and marriage: A research note, *Journal of Comparative Family Studies*: 297–305.

Mazumdar, V. 1978 Comment on Suttee, *Signs*: 99, 269–73.

McKeown, R. et al. 2006 US suicide rates by age groups, 1970–2002: An examination of recent trends, *American Journal of Public Health*: 1744–51.

McManners, J. 1981 *Death and the Enlightenment*, Oxford, Oxford University Press.

McNamara, R. and Ruys, J. 2014 Unlocking the silences of the self-murdered: textual approaches to suicidal emotions in the Middle Ages. *Exemplaria*, 26(1): 58–80.

Medhurst, W. H. 1873 *The Foreigner in Cathay*, New York, Charles Scribner's Sons.

Meijer, M. J. 1971 *Marriage Law and Policy in the Chinese People's Republic*, Hong Kong, Hong Kong University Press.

— 1991 *Murder and Adultery in Late Imperial China. A Study of Law and Morality*, Leiden, Brill.

Mellow, J. R. 1993 *Hemingway: A Life without Consequences*, New York, Addison Wesley.

Meltzer, H. Y. 2005 Suicidality in schizophrenia: Pharmacological treatment, *Clinical Neuropsychiatry*: 76–83.

Meng, L. 2002 Rebellion and revenge: The meaning of suicide of women in rural China, *International Journal of Social Welfare*: 300–9.

Menninger, K. 1938 *Man against Himself*, New York, Harcourt Brace.

Merari, A. 2007 Suicide attacks as a terrorist tactic: Characteristics and counter-measures, *Strategic Review for Southern Africa*: 23–38.

— 2010 *Driven to Death. Psychological and Social Aspects of Suicide Terrorism*, Oxford, Oxford University Press.

Mercier, L.-S. 1781 Tableau de Paris, *Virchaux*, vol. II, Hamburg.

Merrick, J. 1989 Patterns and prosecution of suicide in eighteenth-century Paris, *Historical Reflections*: 1, 1–53.

Merrick, J., D. Lee (eds.) 2012 *The History of Suicide in England, 1650–1850*, London, Pickering and Chatto Ltd, vols. 5–8.

Merton, R. K. 1949 *Social Theory and Social Structure*, Glencoe, IL, The Free Press; Italian trans., *Teoria e struttura sociale*, Bologna, Il Mulino, 1966.

Metraux, A. 1943 Suicide among the Matako of the Argentine Gran Chaco, *American Indigena*: 199–209.

Michaels, A. 1998 *Hinduism. Past and Present*, Princeton, NJ, Princeton University Press.

Midelfort, H. C. E. 1995 Selbstmord im Urteil von Reformation und Gegenreformation, in W. Reinhard and H. Schilling (eds.), *Die katolische Konfessionalisierung*, Münster, Aschendorff, pp. 296–310.

— 1996 Religious melancholy and suicide: On the reformation origins of a sociological stereotype, in A. D. Weiner and L. V. Kaplan (eds.), *Madness, Melancholy and the Limits of the Self*, Madison, WI, Graven Images, pp. 41–56.

— 1999 *A History of Madness in Sixteenth-Century Germany*, Stanford, CA, Stanford University Press.

Milano, E. 1987 *Angelo Fortunato Formiggini*, Rimini, Misè.

Miller, E. T. 2004 Filial daughters, filial sons: Comparison from rural North China, in Ikels (2004, pp. 34–52).

Miller, M. M. 1937 The English people as portrayed in certain French journals, 1700–1760, *Modern Philology*: 365–76.

Ministry of Home Affairs 2013 *Accidental Deaths and Suicides in India*, New Delhi.

Minois, G. 1995 *Histoire du suicide*, Paris, Fayard. English trans. *History of Suicide: Voluntary Death in Western Culture*, trans. Lydia Cochrane, Johns Hopkins University Press, 1999.

Moeller, F. G. et al. 2001 Psychiatric aspects of impulsivity, *American Journal of Psychiatry*: 1783–93.

Moghadam, A. 2006a 'Suicide terrorism, occupation, and the globalization of martyrdom: A critique of dying to win', *Studies in Conflict and Terrorism*: 707–29.

— 2006b Defining suicide terrorism, in A. Pedahzur (ed.), *Root Causes of Suicide Terrorism*, London, Routledge, pp. 13–24.

— 2006c The roots of suicide terrorism: A multi-causal approach, in A. Pedahzur (ed.), *Root Causes of Suicide Terrorism*, London, Routledge, pp. 81–107.

— 2008 *The Globalization of Martyrdom: Al Qaeda, Salafi Jihad, and the Diffusion of Suicide Attacks*, Baltimore, MD, Johns Hopkins University Press.

Mokros, H. B. 1995 'Suicide and shame', *American Behavioral Scientist*: 1091–103.

Montagu, Mary Wortley 1837 *Letters and Works*, Philadelphia, PA, Carey, Lea and Blanchard, vol. II.

Montaigne, M. de. 1966 *Saggi*, Milan, Adelphi, 2 vols.

— 2004 *The Complete Essays*, trans. and ed. M. A. Screech, Penguin 2004, ch. 3 'A Custom of the Isle of Cea'.

Montesquieu, C. L. 1721 *Lettres persanes*; English trans. *Persian Letters*, trans. Margaret Mauldon, Oxford University Press, 2008.

— 1749 *L'esprit des lois*; English edn. *The Spirit of Laws*, trans. Thomas Nugent, University of California Press, 1977.

Morell, S. et al. 2007 The decline in Australian young male suicide, *Social Science and Medicine*: 747–57.

Morillo, S. 2001 Cultures of death: Warrior suicide in medieval Europe and Japan, *Medieval History Journal*: 241–57.

More, T. 1981 *Utopia* (1516), Roma-Bari, Laterza.

— 2002 *Utopia*, ed. George M. Logan, Robert M. Adams and Clarence H. Miller, Cambridge, Cambridge University Press.

Morrell, S. 1999 Urban and rural suicide differentials in migrants and the Australian-born, *Social Science and Medicine*: 81–91.

Morris, I. 1975 *The Nobility of Failure*, London, Martin Secker.

Morrisey, S. K. 2005 Drinking to death: Suicide, vodka and religious burial, *Past and Present*: 186, pp. 117–46.

— 2006 *Suicide and the Body Politics in Imperial Russia*, Cambridge, Cambridge University Press.

— 2013 Mapping civilization: The cultural geography of suicide statistics in Russia, *Journal of Social History*: 651–67.

Morrison, G. E. 1902 *An Australian in China: Being the Narrative of a Quiet Journey across China*, London, Horace Cox.

Morselli, E. 1879 *Il suicidio*, Milan, Fratelli Dumolard. English trans. Henry Morselli, *Suicide. An Essay on Comparative Moral Statistics*. New York: D. Appleton and Co., 1882.

— 1885 *Le leggi statistiche del suicidio secondo gli ultimi documenti (1879–1885)*, Milan, Civelli.

— 1886 Si le nombre des suicides augmente en rapport inverse de celui des homicides, in *Actes du premier congrès international d'anthropologie criminelle*, Turin, Fratelli Bocca, pp. 202–5.

Mosca, G. 1953 *Elementi di scienza politica*, Bari, Laterza, 2 vols.; English trans. *The Ruling Class*, trans. Hannah D. Kahn, New York and London: McGraw-Hill Book Company, 1939.

Motta, E. 1888 Suicidi nel Quattrocento e nel Cinquecento, *Archivio storico lombardo*: 96–100.

Müller, W. P. 1989 Lucretia and the Medieval canonists, *Bulletin of Medieval Canon Law*: 13–23.

Murphy, G. E. 1998 Why women are less likely than men to commit suicide, *Comprehensive Psychiatry*: 4, 165–75.

Murray, A. 1998 *Suicide in the Middle Ages*, vol. I, *The Violent against Themselves*, Oxford, Oxford University Press.

— 2000 *Suicide in the Middle Ages*, vol. II, *The Curse of Self-Murder*, Oxford, Oxford University Press.

Murray, H. et al. 1836 *An Historical and Descriptive Account of China*, Edinburgh, Oliver and Boyd, vol. II.

Muyart de Vouglans, P. F. 1757 *Institutes au droit criminel, ou principes generaux sur ces matières, suivant le droit civil, canonique et la jurisprudence du Royaume*, Paris, Chez Le Breton.

Naimark, N. M. 1995 *The Russian in Germany: A History of the Soviet Zone of Occupation, 1945–49*, Cambridge, MA, Belknap Press of Harvard University Press.

Narasimhan, S. 1998 *Sati. A Study of Widow Burning in India*, New Delhi, HarperCollins India.

Nash, D. 2007 Analyzing the history of religious crime, *Journal of Social History*: Autumn, 5–29.

Ness, C. D. 2005 In the name of the cause: Women's work in secular and religious terrorism, *Studies in Conflict and Terrorism*: 353–73.

Niccoli, O. 2007 *Perdonare. Idee, pratiche, rituali in Italia fra Cinque e Seicento*, Roma-Bari, Laterza.

Nivette, A. E., M. Eisner 2013 Do legitimate polities have fewer homicides? A Cross national analysis, *Homicide studies*: 3–26.

Noomen, P. 1975 *Suicide in the Netherland*, in N. L. Farberow (ed.), *Suicide in Different Cultures*, Baltimore, MD, University Park Press, pp. 165–72.

Nordentoft, M. et al. 2004 Change in suicide rates for patients with schizophrenia in Denmark, 1981–1997: Nested case-control study, *British Medical Journal*: 261–4.

O'Dea, J. J. 1882 *Suicide. Studies on its Philosophy, Causes and Prevention*, New York, G. P. Putnam's Sons.

Oettingen, A. von 1881 *Über akuten und chronischen Selbstmord*, Karow, Dorpat und Fellin.

Olivelle, P. 1978 Ritual suicide and the rite of renunciation, *Wiener Zeitschrift für die Kunde Südasiens*: 19–44.

Onori, A. M. 2009 'Va' fa' le vendette tue!'. Qualche esempio della documentazione sulla pace privata e la regolamentazione della vendetta nella Val- dinievole del Trecento, in A. Zorzi (ed.), *Conflitti, paci e vendette nell'Italia comunale*, Seminario di studi dell'Università di Firenze.

Oquendo, M. A. et al. 2001 Ethnic and sex differences in suicide rates relative to major depression in the United States, *American Journal of Psychiatry*: 1652–8.

Outram, D. 1989 *The Body and the French Revolution*, New Haven, CT, Yale University Press.

Paderni, P. 1991 Le rachat de l'honneur perdu. Le suicide des femmes dans la Chine du XVIII siècle, *Etudes chinoises*: 135–60.

— 2005 The crime of seduction and women's suicide in eighteenth century China, in A. Bähr and H. Medick (eds.), *Sterben von eigener Hand*, Wien, Böhlau, pp. 241–53.

Palmer, B. A. et al. 2005 The lifetime risk of suicide in schizophrenia, *Archives of General Psychiatry*: 247–53.

Panoff, M. 1977 Suicide and social control in new Britain, *Bijdragen: Tot de Taalland-en Volkenkunde*: 44–62.

Pape, R. 2005 *Dying to Win. The Strategic Logic of Suicide Terrorism*, New York, Random House.

Paperno, I. 1997 *Suicide as a Cultural Institution in Dostoevsky's Russia*, Ithaca, NY, Cornell University Press.

Pasteur, P. 2000 Violences et viols des vainqueurs. Les femmes à Vienne et en Basse-Autriche, avril-août 1945, *Guerres mondiales et conflits contemporains*: 123–36.

Patkin, T. T. 2004 Explosive baggage: Female Palestinian suicide bombers and the rhetoric of emotion, *Women and Language*: 79–88.

Patrick, H. 1984 The dialectic of suicide in Montaigne's 'Coutume de l'Isle de Cea', *Modern Language Review*: 278–89.

Patton, W. M. 2003 Suicide (Muhammadan), in J. Hastings (ed.), *Encyclopedia of Religion and Ethics*, New York, Charles Scribner's Sons, vol. 23, p. 38.

Paulin, B. 1977 *Du couteau à la plume. Le suicide dans la litterature anglaise de la Renaissance (1580–1625)*, Lyon, L'Hermes.

Pearson, V. and Liu, M. 2002 Ling's death: An ethnography of a Chinese women's suicide, *Suicide and Life-Threatening Behavior*: 347–58.

Pedahzur, A. 2005 *Suicide Terrorism*, Cambridge, Polity.

Pedahzur, A. and Perliger, A. 2006 Introduction: *Characteristics of suicide attacks*, in A. Pedahzur (ed.), *Root Causes of Suicide Terrorism: The Globalization of Martyrdom*, London, Routledge, pp. 1–12.

Peggs, J. 1830 *India's Cries to British Humanity relative to the Suttee* [. . .], London, Seely and Son, Fleet Street.

Penttinen, J. 1995 Back pain and risk of suicide among Finnish farmers, *American Journal of Public Health*: 1452–3.

Pérez, L. A. 2005 *To Die in Cuba*, Chapel Hill, University of North Carolina Press.

Perkins, W. 1606 *A Whole Treatise of the Cases of Conscience*, (Cambridge): Printed by Iohn Legat, Printer to the University of Cambridge, 1606 to be sold [in London] in Pauls Church-yard at the signe of the Crowne by Simon Waterson.

Pertile, A. 1876 *Storia del diritto Italiano*, vol. V, *Storia del diritto penale*, Padova, Stabilimento Tipografico alla Minerva.

Pescosolido, B. A. and Mendelsohn, R. 1986 Social causation or social construction of suicide? An investigation into the social organization of official rates, *American Sociological Review*: 80–100.

Petkov, K. 2003 *The Kiss of Peace. Ritual, Self and Society in the High and Low Medieval West*, Leiden, Brill.

Petrarch, F. 1993 *Opere*, Florence, Sansoni. English trans.

Peyre, H. M. 1950 English literature seen through French eyes, *Yale French Studies*: 109–19.

Phillips, M. R. et al. 1999 Suicide and social change in China, *Culture, Medicine and Psychiatry*: 25–50.

— 2002a Suicide rates in China, 1995–1999, *Lancet*: 835–40.

— 2002b Suicide rates in China – Reply, *Lancet*: 2274–5.

— 2002c Risk factors for suicide in China: A national case-control psychological autopsy study, *Lancet*: 360, 1728–36.

— 2004 Suicide and the unique prevalence pattern of schizophrenia in main-land China: A retrospective observational study, *Lancet*: 1062–8.

Pickering, W. S. F. and Walford, G. (eds.) 2000 *Durkheim's Suicide. A Century of Research and Debate*, London, Routledge.

Piersen, W. D. 1977 White cannibals, black martyrs: Fear, depression, and religious faith as causes of suicide among new slaves, *Journal of Negro History*: 147–59.

— 1993 *Black Legacy: America's Hidden Heritage*, Amherst, University of Massachusetts Press.

Pigafetta, A. 1524–5 *Viaggio atorno il mondo fatto e descritto per messer Antonio Pigafetta vicentino, cavalier di Rhodi, e da lui indrizzato al reveren- dissimo gran maestro di Rhodi messer Filippo di Villiers Lisleadam, tradotto di lingua francesa nella Italiana*, in G. B. Ramusio (ed.), *Navigazioni e viaggi*, Turin, Einaudi, 1979, vol. II, pp. 871–948.

Pim, B. 1863 *The Gate of the Pacific*, London, Lovell Reeve and Co.

Pinnow, K. M. 2003 Violence against the collective self and the problem of social integration in early bolschevik Russia, *Kritika: Explorations in Russian and Eurasian History*: 653–77.

— 2007 Lives out of balance: The 'possible world' of Soviet suicide during the 1920s, in A. Brintlinger and I. Vinitsky (eds.), *Madness and the Mad in Russian Cultures*, Toronto, University of Toronto Press, pp. 130–50.

— 2010 *Lost to the Collective: Suicide and the Promise of Soviet Socialism, 1921–1929*, Ithaca, Cornell University Press.

Piretti Santangelo, L. 1991 *Sati. Una tragedia indiana*, Bologna, Clueb.

Plato 1988 *The Laws of Plato*, trans. Thomas L. Pangle, University of Chicago Press.

1993 *Phaedo*, trans. David Gallop, Oxford World Classics, 1993

Plaut, E. A. and Anderson, K. 1999 *Marx on Suicide*, Evanston, IL, Northwestern University Press.

Plesch, V. 2006 *Painter and Priest. Giovanni Canavesio's Visual Rhetoric and the Passion Cycle at la Brigue*, Notre Dame, IN, University of Notre Dame Press.

Pliny the Elder 1956 *Natural History*, vol. 7, Books 24–7, trans. W. H. S. Jones, Loeb Classical Library.

— 1991 *Natural History: A Selection*, trans. John F. Healy. Penguin Classics.

Poggi, G. 1972 *Immagini della società*, Bologna, Il Mulino.

— 2000 *Durkheim*, Oxford, Oxford University Press; Italian trans., *Durkheim*, Bologna, Il Mulino, 2003.

Pollock, L. 2004 Anger and the negotiation of relationships in early modern England, *Historical Journal*: 567–90.

Polo, M. 2001 *Milione*, Milan, Adelphi. English trans. *The Travels*, trans. and introduction, Ronald Latham. Harmondsworth, Middlesex: Penguin, 1958.

Pope, W. 1976 *Durkheim's Suicide. A Classic Analyzed*, Chicago, IL, University of Chicago Press.

Pope, W. and Danigelis, N. 1981 Sociology 'one law', *Social Forces*: 495–516.

Popitz, H. 1992 *Phänomene der Macht*, Tübingen, Mohr; Italian trans., *Fenomenologia del potere*, Bologna, Il Mulino, 2002.

Porret, M. 2007 *Sul luogo del delitto. Pratica penale, inchiesta e perizia giudiziaria a Ginevra nei secoli XVIII-XIX*, Bellinzona, Casagrande.

Porteau-Bitker, A. 1999 Une reflexion sur le suicide dans le droit penal laïque des XIIIe et XIVe siècles, in C. Bontems (ed.), *Nonagesimo anno*, Paris, Puf, pp. 305–323.

Pridemore, W. A. 2006 *Heavy drinking and suicide in Russia*, Social Forces: 413–430.

Pridemore, W. A. and Chamlin, M. B. 2006 A time-series analysis of the impact of heavy drinking on homicide and suicide mortality in Russia, 1956–2002, *Addiction*: 1719–29.

Pridemore, W. A. and Spivak, A. L. 2003 Patterns of suicide mortality in Russia, *Suicide and Life-Threatening Behavior*: 132–150.

Pridemore, W. A. et al. 2013 Reduction in Male Suicide Mortality Following the 2006 Russian Alcohol Policy: An Interrupted Time Series Analysis, *American Journal of Public Health*: 103 (11), 2021–5.

Pritchard, C. 1996 *Suicide in the People's Republic of China categorized by age and gender: Evidence of the influence of culture on suicide*, Acta Psychiatrica Scandinavica: 1–6.

Pumpelly, R. 1918 *My Reminiscences*, New York, Henry Holt and Co., vol. I.

Quételet, A. 1835 *Sur l'homme et le développement de ses facultés ou essai de physique sociale*, Paris, Bachelier, vol. II.

Radicati di Passerano, A. 1732 *A Philosophical Dissertation upon Death Composed for the Consolation of the Unhappy. By a Friend to Truth*, London, Mears.

Raphals, L. 1998 *Sharing the Light. Representation of Women and Virtue in Early China*, Albany, State University of New York.

Rasmussen, K. et al. 1999 Personality disorders, psychopathy, and crime in a Norwegian prison population, *International Journal of Law and Psychiatry*: 91–7.

Rawley, J. A. and Behrendt, S. D. 2005 *The Transatlantic Slave Trade: A History*, Lincoln, University of Nebraska Press.

Reardon, D. C. 2002 Suicide rates in China, *Lancet*: 29, June, 22–74.

Reclus, E. and Reclus, O. 1902 *L'empire du milieu*, Paris, Hachette.

Reddy, W. M. 2000 Sentimentalism and its erasure: The role of emotions in the era of the French revolution, *Journal of Modern History*: 109–52.

Reuter, C. 2002 *My Life as a Weapon*, Princeton, NJ, Princeton University Press.

Ricci, M. 1942 *Storia dell'introduzione del Cristianesimo in Cina. Scritta da Matteo Ricci S. I., nuovamente edita e ampiamente commentata col sussidio di molte fonti inedite da Pasquale M. D'Elia S. I., Professore di sino- logia nella Pontificia Università Gregoriana e nella Regia Università di Roma*, vol. I, parte I, libri I-III, *Da Macao a Nanciam*, Rome, La Libreria dello Stato, 1942.

Rice Miner, J. 1922 Suicide and Its Relation to Climatic and Other Factors, *American Journal of Hygiene Monographic Series*, 2.

Ricolfi, L. 2005 *Palestinians, 1981–2003*, in D. Gambetta (ed.), *Making Sense of Suicide Missions*, Oxford, Oxford University Press, pp. 77–129.

Robbins, T. 1986 Religious mass suicide before Jonestown: The Russian old believers, *Sociological Analysis*: 1–20.

Roberts, D. R. 1947 The death wish of John Donne, *PMLA*: 958–76.

Roberts, M. 2005 Tamil tiger 'martyrs': Regenerating divine potency?, *Studies in Conflict and Terrorism*: 493–514.

Robertson, J. 1999 Dying to tell: Sexuality and suicide in imperial Japan, *Signs*: 1–35.

Robson, J. 2002 Fear of falling: Depicting the death of Judas in late medieval Italy, in A. Scott and C. Kosso (eds.), *Fear and its Representations in the Middle Ages and Renaissance*, Turnhout, Brepols, pp. 33–65.

Robson, R. 1995 *Old Believers in Modern Russia*, De Kalb, North Illinois University Press.

Rogan, A. 2006 *Jihadism Online. A Study of How al-Quaida and Radical Islamist Groups Use the Internet for Terrorist Purposes*, Kjeller, Norwegian Defence Research Establishment.

Rojcewicz, S. J. 1971 War and suicide, *Suicide and Life-Threatening Behavior*: 46–54.

Rolfs, D. 1981 *The Last Cross: A History of the Suicide Theme in Italian Literature*, Ravenna, Longo.

Romei, A. 1586 Discorsi di Annibale Romei, in A. Solerti, *Ferrara e la corte estense nella seconda metà del secolo decimosesto*, Città di Castello, Lapi Tipografo, 1891.

Ropp, P. S. 2001 Introduction, in Ropp et al. (2001, pp. 47–76).

Ropp, P. S. et al. 2001 *Passionate Women. Female Suicide in Late Imperial China*, Leiden, Brill.

Rosenthal, F. 1946 On suicide in Islam, *Journal of American Oriental Society*: 239–59.

Rosenwein, B. H. 1998 *Anger's Past. The Social Uses of an Emotion in the Middle Ages*, Ithaca, NY, Cornell University Press.

2002 Worrying about emotions in history, *American Historical Review*: 821–45.

2006 *Emotional Communities in Early Middle Ages*, Ithaca, NY, Cornell University Press.

Ross, E. A. 1912 *The Changing Chinese. The Conflict of Oriental and Western Cultures in China*, New York, The Century Co.

Rossi, E. 1963 *Elogio della galera. Lettere 1930–43*, Bari, Laterza.

Rousseaux, X. 1994 Ordre moral, justices et violence: l'homicide dans les sociétés européennes (XIIIe-XVIIIe s.), in B. Garnot (ed.), *Ordre moral et délinquances, de l'Antiquité au XXe siècle*, Dijon, Eud, pp. 65–82.

— 1999a From case to crime. Homicide regulation in medieval and modern Europe, in D. Willoweit (ed.), *Die Entstehung des öffentlichen Strafrechts*, Köln, Böhlau, pp. 143–166.

— 1999b Eléments pour une histoire du contrôle social dans les Pays-Bas méridionaux 1500–1815, in H. Schilling (ed.), *Institutionen, Instrumente und Akteure sozialer Kontrolle und Disziplinierung im frühneuzeitlichen Europa*, Frankfurt a. M., Klostermann, pp. 251–274.

Roy, B. B. 1987 *Socioeconomic Impact of Sati in Bengal and the Role of Raja Rammohun Roy*, Kolkata, Naya Prokash.

Roy, O. 2004 *Globalized Islam: The Search for a New Ummah*, New York, Columbia University Press.

Rubies, J.-P. 2001 *Travel and Ethnology in the Renaissance: South India through European Eyes, 1250–1625*, Cambridge, Cambridge University Press.

Ruff, J. R. 2001 *Violence in Early Modern Europe 1500–1800*, Cambridge, Cambridge University Press.

Ruggiero, G. 1980 *Violence in Early Renaissance Venice*, New Brunswick, NJ, Rutgers University Press; Italian trans., *Patrizi e malfattori. La violenza a Venezia nel primo Rinascimento*, Bologna, Il Mulino, 1982.

Ruppin, A. 1930 *Soziologie der Juden*, Berlin, Jüdischer Verlag.

Russel, S. T. 2003 Sexual minority and suicide risk, *American Behavioral Scientist*: 1241–57.

Ruys, J. 2014 'He who kills himself liberates a wretch': Abelard on Suicide, in B. S. Hellemans (ed.) *Rethinking Abelard: A Collection of Critical Essays*, Leiden, Brill.

Sachs, A. 1964 Religious despair in medieval literature, *Medieval Studies*: 231–56.

Safran, J. M. 2001 Identity and differentiation in ninth-century al-Andalus, *Speculum*: 573–98.

— 2013 *Defining Boundaries in al-Andalus: Muslims, Christians, and Jews in Islamic Iberia*, Ithaca, NY, Cornell University Press.

Sageman, M. 2004 *Understanding Terror Networks*, Philadelphia, University of Pennsylvania Press.

— 2008 *Leaderless Jihad. Terror Networks in the Twenty-First Century*, Philadelphia, University of Pennsylvania Press.

Sainsbury, P. and Barraclough, B. 1968 *Differences between suicide rates*, Nature», p. 1252.

Saitta, A. 1975 *Costituenti e costituzioni della Francia rivoluzionaria e liberale (1789–1875)*, Milan, Giuffrè.

Santoro, M. 2010 *Effetto Tenco*, Bologna, Il Mulino.

Santoro, M. and Sassatelli, R. (eds.) 2009 *Studiare la cultura. Nuove prospettive sociologiche*, Bologna, Il Mulino.

Sarfatti, M. 2000 *Gli ebrei nell'Italia fascista*, Turin, Einaudi.

Sattar, G. 2001 *Rates and Causes of Death among Prisoners and Offenders under Community Supervision*, London, Home Office Research Study, no. 231.

Sattar, G. and Killias, M. 2005 The death of offenders in Swizerland, *European Journal of Criminology*: 317–40.

Saunderson, T. et al. 1998 Urban-rural variations in suicides and undetermined deaths in England and Wales, *Journal of Public Health Medicine*: 261–7.

Schär, M. 1985 *Seelennöte der Untertanen. Selbstmord, Melancholie und Religion in Alten Zürich*, Zürich, Chronos.

Scheff, T. 2006 *Goffman Unbound: A New Paradigm for Social Science*, Boulder, CO, Paradigm Publisher.

Schmidt, J. 2007 *Melancholy and the Care of the Soul. Religion, Moral Philosophy and Madness in Early Modern England*, London, Ashgate.

Schmidt-Kohlberg, K. 2003 'Und hat sich selbsten an einem Strikhalter hinge-henckt . . . ' Selbst-mord im Herzogtum Württemberg im 17. und 18. Jahrhundert, in J. Dillinger (ed.), *Zauberer-Selbstmörder-Schatzsucher*, Trier, Kliomedia, pp. 113–30.

Schmitt, J.-C. 1976 Le suicide au moyen âge, *Annales*: 3–28.

Schnitzler, N. 1996 Der Tod des Judas. Ein Beitrag zur Ikonographie des Selbstmordes im Mittelalter, in A. Löther et al. (eds.), *Mundus in imagine. Bildersprache und Lebenswelten im Mittelalter. Festgabe für Klaus Schreiner*, München, Fink, pp. 219–45.

— 2000 Judas' death: Some remarks concerning the iconography of suicide in the middle ages, *Medieval History Journal*: 103–18.

Schraier, C. et al. 2006 Suicide after breast cancer: An international popula-tion based study of 723.810 women, *Journal of the National Cancer Institute*: 1416–19.

Schreiner, J. 2003 *Jenseits vom Glück. Suizid, Melancholie und Hypochondrie in deutschsprachingen Texten des 18. Jahrhunderts*, München, Oldenburg.

Schürer, N. 2008 The impartial spectator of sati, 1757–84, *Eighteenth-Century Studies*: 19–44.

Schweitzer, Y. (ed.) 2006 *Female Suicide Bombers: Dying for Equality?*, Tel Aviv, Jaffee Center for Strategic Studies.

Seabourne, G. and Seabourne, A. 2000 The law on suicide in medieval England, *Journal of Legal History*: 21–48.

Seaver, P. S. 2004 *Suicide and the Vicar General in London: A mystery solved?*, in J. R. Watt (ed.), *From Sin to Insanity*, Ithaca, NY, Cornell University Press, pp. 25–47.

Seaver, P and K. Mcguire (eds.) 2011 *The History of Suicide in England, 1650–1850*, London, Pickering and Chatto Ltd, vols. 1–4.

Segre, R. (ed.) 1995 *Gli ebrei a Venezia. 1938–1945*, Venice, Il Cardo.

Sen, M. 2001 *Death by Fire*, London, Phoenix.

Senault, J.-F. 1644 *L'homme criminel, ou la corruption de la nature par le peché. Selon les sentimens de Saint Augustin*, Paris, Jean Camusat; English trans. *Man become guilty, or, The corruption of nature by sinne, according* to *St Augustine's sense*, Henry Carey, Earl of Monmouth, trans. London: William Leake, 1650.

Seneca 1900 *Of Anger*, trans. Aubrey Stewart, Bohn's Classical Library Edition; London, George Bell and Sons

Serge, V. 1951 *Mémoires d'un révolutionnaire*, Paris, Seuil; Italian trans., *Memorie di un rivoluzionario*, Rome, edizioni e/o, 1999.

Shakespeare, W. 1981 *Amleto*, in *Teatro*, Turin, Einaudi, vol. III, pp. 644–771.

Sharma, A. 1988 *Sati: Historical and Phenomenological Essays*, Delhi, Motilal Banarsidass.

Shepherd, D. M. and Barraclough, B. M. 1997 Suicide – A traveller's tale, *History of Psychiatry*: 395–406.

Shoemaker, R. 2000 The decline of public insult in London, 1660–1800, *Past and Present*: 97–131.

— 2001 Male honour and the decline of public violence in eighteenth-century London, *Social History*: 190–208.

Siemens, R. G. 2001 'I have often such a sickly inclination': Biography and the critical interpretation of Donne's suicide tract, 'Biathanatos', *Early Modern Literary Studies*: n.s. 1, May, 1–26.

Signori, G. 1994 Rechtskonstruktionen und religiöse Fiktionen. Bemerkungen zum Selbstmordfrage im Mittelalter, in Signori (ed.), *Trauer, Verzweiflung und Anfechtung*, Tübingen, Diskord, pp. 9–54.

Silving, H. 1957 Suicide and the law, in E. S. Shneidman and N. L. Farberow (eds.), *Clues to Suicide*, New York, McGraw-Hill, pp. 79–95.

Simon, G. E. 1885 La cité chinoise, *La Nouvelle Revue*, Paris.

Simonazzi, M. 2004 La malattia inglese, *Il Mulino*, Bologna.

Singh, G. K. and Siahpush, M. 2002a Increasing rural-urban gradients in US suicide mortality, 1970–1997, *American Journal of Public Health*: 7, 1161–7.

— 2002b Ethnic-immigrant differentials in health behaviors, morbidity, and cause-specific mortality in the United States: An analysis of two national data bases, *Human Biology*: 83–109.

Skog, O.-J. 1991 Alcohol and suicide. Durkheim revisited, *Acta sociologica*: 193–206.

— 1993 Alcohol and suicide in Denmark 1911–24 – Experiences from a 'natural experiment', *Addiction*: 1189–93.

Smail, D. L. 2001 Hatred as a social institution in late-medieval society, *Speculum*: 90–126.

— 2003 *The Consumption of Justice. Emotions, Publicity, and Legal Culture in Marseille, 1264–1423*, Ithaca, NY, Cornell University Press.

Smith, A. H. 1899 *Village Life in China. A Study in Sociology*, Edinburgh, Oliphant, Anderson and Ferrier.

Smith, R. L. 1998 Review: 'Wind against the Mountain', *Harvard Journal of Asian Studies*: 603–14.

Smythe, D. 1962 Pershing and the disarmament of the Moros, *Pacific Historical Review*: 241–56.

Snyder, S. 1965 The left hand of God: Despair in medieval and renaissance tradition, *Studies in the Renaissance*: 18–59.

Snyder, T. L. 2007 What historians talk about when they talk about suicide: The view from early modern British North America, *History Compass*: 658–74.

Sophocles 2007 *Le tragedie*, Milan, Mondadori. English trans. from *Four Tragedies: Ajax, Women of Trachis, Electra, Philoctetes*, trans. Peter Meineck, Paul Woodruff, Hackett Publishing 2007.

Sofsky, W. 1993 *Die Ordnung des Terrors*, Frankfurt a. M., Fischer; Italian trans., *L'ordine del terrore*, Roma-Bari, Laterza, 1995.

Sogani, R. 2002 *The Hindu Widow in Indian Literature*, New Delhi, Oxford University Press.

Solzhenitsyn, A. 1974 *The Gulag Archipelago*, trans. from Russian, Thomas P. Whitney, London: Collins and Harvill Press, 3 vols. 1974–8.

Somogyi, S. and Somogyi, R. A. 1995 Il suicidio in Italia dal 1864 ad oggi, *Edizioni Kappa*, Rome.

Sonneck, G. et al. 2012 Suizid und Suizidprävention 1938–1945 in Wien, *Neuropsychiatrie*: 111–20.

Sorabji, R. 2000 *Emotion and Peace of Mind. From Stoic Agitation to Christian Temptation*, Oxford, Oxford University Press.

Spence, J. D. 1978 *The Death of Woman Wang*, New York, Viking Press; Italian trans., *La morte della donna Wang*, Milan, Adelphi, 2002.

Spenser, E. 2007 *The Faerie Queene*, ed. A. C. Hamilton. Edinburgh: Pearson Longman.

Spierenburg, P. 1996 Long-term trends in homicide: Theoretical reflections and Dutch evidence, fifteenth to twentieth centuries, in E. A. Johnson and E. K. Monkkonen (eds.), *The Civilization of Crime*, Urbana-Chicago, University of Illinois Press, pp. 63–105.

— 1998a Masculinity, violence, and honor: An introduction, in Spierenburg (ed.), *Men and Violence*, Columbus, Ohio State University Press, pp. 1–29.

— 1998b Knife fighting and popular codes of honor in early modern Amsterdam, in Spierenburg (ed.), *Men and Violence*, Columbus, Ohio State University Press, pp. 103–27.

— 2006 Protestant attitudes to violence: The early Dutch republic, *Crime, Histoire et Sociétés*: 5–31.

— 2008 *A History of Murder*, London, Polity.

Sprinzak, E. 2000 Rational fanatics, *Foreign Policy*: 66–74.

Sprott, S. E. 1961 *The English Debate on Suicide from Donne to Hume*, London, Open Court.

Stack, S. 1992 The effect of divorce on suicide in Japan: A time series analysis, *Journal of Marriage and the Family*: 327–34.

Stack-O'Connor, A. 2007 Lions, tigers, and freedom birds: How and why the Liberation Tigers of Tamil Eelam employs women, *Terrorism and Political Violence*: 43–63.

Staël, Madame de. 1813 Réflexions sur le suicide, in *Oeuvres complètes*, Genève, Slatkine Reprints, 1967, vol. I, pp. 176–96; English trans. *Reflections upon Suicide*, trans. from French, London: Longman, Hurst, Rees, Orme, and Brown, 1813.

Stark, J. 2001 Suicide after Auschwitz, *Yale Journal of Criticism*: 93–114.

Steen, D. M. and Mayer, P. 2004 Modernization and the male–female suicide ratio in India, 1967–1997: Divergence and convergence, *Suicide and Life-Threatening Behavior*: 147–59.

Stein, D. K. 1978 Women to burn: Suttee as a normative institution, *Signs*: 253–73.

— 1988 Burning widows, burning brides: The perils of daughterhood in India, *Public Affairs*: 465–85.

Steinmetz, S. R. 1894 Suicide among primitive people, *American Anthropologist*: 53–60.

— 1898 Gli antichi scongiuri giuridici contro i creditori, *Rivista Italiana di Sociologia*: 36–65.

Stendhal 1829 *Promenades dans Rome*, Paris, Dalauney.
Stockard, J. E. 1989 *Daughters of the Canton Delta. Marriage Patterns and Economic Strategies in South China, 1860–1930*, Stanford, CA, Stanford University Press.
Strathern, M. 1972 *Women in Between. Female Roles in a Male World: Mount Hagen, New Guinea*, London, Seminar Press.
Stratton Hawley, J. 1994 Introduction, in Stratton (ed.), *Sati. The Blessing and the Curse*, Oxford, Oxford University Press, pp. 3–26.
Straus, J. and Straus, M. 1953 Suicide and social structure in Ceylon, *American Journal of Sociology*: 461–9.
Strenski, I. 2003 Sacrifice, gift and the social logic of Muslim 'human bombers', *Terrorism and Political Violence*: 1–34.
Stuart, K. 1999 *Defiled Trades and Social Outcasts: Honor and Ritual Pollution in Early Modern Germany*, Cambridge, Cambridge University Press.
— 2008 Suicide by proxy: The unintended consequences of public executions in eighteenth-century Germany, *Central European History*: 413–45.
Subrahmanyam, S. 2008 Further thoughts on an enigma: The tortuous life of Nicolò Manucci, *Indian Economic and Social History Review*: 35–76.
Sumner Maine, H. 1875 *Lectures on the Early History of Institutions*, London, Murray.
Süßmilch, J. P. 1761 *Die göttliche Ordnung in den Veränderungen des menschlichen Geschlechts aus der Geburt, Tod und Fortpflantzung desselben*, Berlin, Im Verlag des Buchladens der Realschule, vol. I.
Swann, A. C. et al. 2005 Increased impulsivity associated with severity of suicide attempt history in patients with bipolar disorder, *American Journal of Psychiatry*: 1680–7.
Sweeney, G. 1993a Self-immolation in Ireland, *Anthropology Today*: 10–14.
— 1993b Irish hunger strikes and the cult of self-sacrifice, *Journal of Contemporary History*: 421–37.
Swidler, A. 1986 Culture in action: Symbols and strategies, *American Sociological Review*: 273–86.
Sym, J. 1637 *Lifes Preservative against Self-killing or an Useful Treatise Concerning Life and Self-murder*, London, M. Flesher.
Tafur, P. 2004 *Travels and Adventures 1435–1439*, London, Routledge.
Tamagne, F. 2000 *Histoire de l'homosexualité en Europe. Berlin, Londres, Paris, 1919–1939*, Paris, Seuil.
Tamassia, N. 1897 Il 'Dharna' in Germania e in Grecia?, Rivista scientifica del diritto, in *Scritti di storia giuridica*, Milan, Giuffrè, 1964, vol. I, pp. 143–50.
Tao Yi 1919 *Commentary on Miss Zhao's Suicide*, 21 November, in Lan and Fong (1999, pp. 83–5).
Tarde, G. 1897 *Contre Dukheim à propos de son Suicide*, saggio inedito, in Borlandi and Cherkaoui (2000, pp. 219–55).
Tatai, K. 1983 Japan, in L. A. Headley (ed.), *Suicide in Asia and the Near East*, Berkeley, University of California Press, pp. 12–58.
Tavernier, J.-B. 1676 *Les six voyages de Jean-Baptiste Tavernier ecuyer baron d'Aubonne, qu'il a fait en Turquie, en Perse, et aux Indes*, Paris, Gervais Clouzier, part I, book III.
Thakur, U. 1963 *The History of Suicide in India. An Introduction*, Delhi, Munshiram.
Manoharlal, Thapar, R. 1988 In history, Seminar, in A. Major (ed.), *Sati. A Historical Anthology*, Oxford, Oxford University Press, 2007, pp. 452–65.
Theiss, J. M. 2001 Managing martyrdom: Female suicide and statecraft in mid-Quing China, in Ropp et al. (2001, pp. 47–76).

— 2002 Femininity in flux: Gendered virtue and social conflict in the mid-Qing courtroom, in S. Brownell and J. N. Wasserstrom (eds.), *Chinese Femininities/ Chinese Masculinities*, Berkeley, University of California Press, pp. 47–66.

— 2004a Female suicide, subjectivity and the state in eighteenth-century China, *Gender and History*: 513–37.

— 2004b *Disgraceful Matters. The Politics of Chastity in Eighteenth Century China*, Berkeley, University of California Press.

Thomas, K. 1971 *Religion and the Decline of Magic*, London, Weidenfeld and Nicolson; Italian trans., *La religione e il declino del magico*, Milan, Mondadori, 1985.

Thompson, E. 1928 *Suttee*, London, George and Unwin.

Thornton, J. 2003 Cannibals, witches, and slave traders in the Atlantic world, *William and Mary Quarterly*: 273–94.

Tibbets Schulenburg, J. 1986 The eroics of virginity: Brides of Christ and sacrificial mutilation, in M. Beth Rose (ed.), *Women in the Middle Ages and the Renaissance*, New York, Syracuse University Press, pp. 29–72.

T'ien Ju-K'ang 1988 *Male Anxiety and Female Chastity. A Comparative Study of Chinese Ethical Values in Ming-Ch'ing Times*, Leiden, Brill.

Timbal, P. 1943–44 La confiscation dans le droit français des XIIIe et XIVe siècles, *Revue historique de droit français et étranger*: 44–79 (1943) and 35–62 (1944).

Timmermans, S. 2005 Suicide determination and the professional authority of medical examiners, *American Sociological Review*: 311–33.

Titelman, D. et al. 2013 Suicide mortality trends in the Nordic countries 1980–2009, *Nordic Journal of Psychiatry*: 1–10.

Tognina, A. 2003 '*Gran peccato e scandalo'. Tre casi di suicidio a Brusio e il problema della sepoltura nel XVIII secolo*, available online at www. ssvp. ch.

Tosini, D. 2007 *Terrorismo e antiterrorismo nel XXI secolo*, Roma-Bari, Laterza.

Trevor, D. 2000 John Donne and scholarly melancholy, *Studies in English Literature*: 81–102.

— 2004 *The Poetics of Melancholy in Early Modern England*, Cambridge, Cambridge University Press.

Twain, M. 1876 *The Adventures of Tom Sawyer*, London, Chatto and Windus; Italian trans., *Le avventure di Tom Sawyer*, Milan, Mondadori, 2003.

Twombly, R. 2006 Decades after cancer, suicide risk remains high, *Journal of the National Cancer Institute*: 135–8.

Tzoreff, M. 2006 The Palestinian shahida: National patriotism, islamic feminism or social crisis, in Schweitzer (2006, pp. 13–24).

Unama (United Nations Assistance Mission in Afghanistan) 2007 *Suicide Attacks in Afghanistan*, available online at http://www.unama-afg.org/docs/_UN-Docs/ UNAMA%20-%20SUICIDE%20ATTACKS%20STUDY%20-%20SEPT%20 9th%202007.pdf.

Unnithan, N. P. et al. 1994 *The Currents of Lethal Violence: An Integrated Model of Suicide and Homicide*, New York, State University of New York.

Vallerani, M. 2005 *La giustizia pubblica medievale*, Bologna, Il Mulino.

Vandekerckhove, L. 2000 *On Punishment. The Confrontation of Suicide in Old-Europe*, Leuven, Leuven University Press.

Van den Bosch, L. P. 1995 The ultimate journey. Sati and widowhood in India, in J. Bremmer (ed.), *Between Poverty and the Pyre: Movements in the History of Widowhood*, London, Routledge, pp. 171–203.

Van der Horst, P. W. 1971 A pagan platonist and a Christian platonist on suicide, *Vigiliae Christianae*: 282–8.
Van der Made, R. 1948 Une page de l'histoire du droit criminal. La repression du suicide, *Revue du droit pénale et de criminologie*: 1, 22–51.
Van Hooff, A. J. L. 1990 *From Autothanasia to Suicide. Self-Killing in Classical Antiquity*, London, Routledge.
— 1992 Female suicide between ancient fiction and fact, *Laverna*: 3, 142–72.
Van Knopf, K. 2007 The female Jihad: Al Qaeda's women, *Studies in Conflict and Terrorism*: 397–414.
Van Tubergen, F. et al. 2006 Denomination, religion context, and suicide: Neo-durkheimian multilevel explanations tested with individual and contextual data, *American Journal of Sociology*: 797–823.
Van Tubergen, F. and Ultee, W. 2006 Political integration, war and suicide. The Dutch paradox?, *International Sociology*: 221–36.
Värnik, A. et al. 2000 Suicide trends in the Baltic states, 1970–1997, *Trames*: 79–90.
Varthema, L. 1535 *Itinerario de Lodovico de Varthema Bolognese nello Egitto, nella Surria, nella Arabia deserta et infelice, nella Persia, nella India e nella Etiopia*, Venice, Francesco di Alessandro Bindone.
Venkoba Rao, A. 1983 India, in L. A. Headley (ed.), *Suicide in Asia and the Near East*, Berkeley, University of California Press, pp. 210–37.
Verkko, V. 1951 *Homicides and Suicides in Finland and Their Dependence on National Character*, København, Gads Forlag.
Vicentini, F. 1769 *Memoria intorno al metodo di soccorrere i sommersi*, Milan, Giuseppe Galeazzi Regio Stampatore.
Victor, B. 2003 *Army of Roses. Inside the World of Palestinian Women Suicide Bombers*, Emmaus, PA, Rodale Books.
Vidor, G. M. 2008 *Biografia di una necropoli Italiana del XIX secolo: il Cimitero della Certosa di Bologna*, Thèse de Doctorat en Histoire et Civilisations, Modena, Fondazione Collegio San Carlo.
Vijayakumar, L. 2004 Altruistic suicide in India, *Archives of Suicide Research*: 73–80.
Vijayakumar, L. et al. 2005a Suicide in developing countries (1) – Frequency, distribution, and association with socioeconomic indicators, *Crisis*: 104–11.
— 2005b Suicide in developing countries (2) – Risk factors, *Crisis*: 112–19.
Villon, F. 1965 *The Poems of Francois Villon, New Edition*, trans. with introduction and notes, Galway Kinnell, Hanover, London: University Press of New England.
— 1971 *Opere*, Milan, Mondadori.
Vincenzo Maria di Santa Caterina da Siena 1678 *Il viaggio all'Indie orientali*, Venice, Giacomo Zattoni.
Vivanco, L. 2004 *Death in Fifteenth-century Castile: Ideologies of the Elites*, Woodbridge, Tamesis.
Voisin, J. L. 1979 Pendus, crucifiés, oscilla dans la Rome païenne, *Latomus*: 423–50.
Voltaire. 1759 *Candide ou l'optimisme*; English trans. *Candide and Other Stories*, trans. Roger Pearson, Oxford, Oxford University Press, 2006.
— 1777 *Prix de la justice et de l'humanité*, Gazette de Berne», XIV, 15 February, available online at http://www.jura.uni-osnabrueck.de/institut/ivr/Voltaire/PrixJustice.htm.
Volterra, E. 1933 Sulla confisca dei beni dei suicidi, *Rivista di storia del diritto Italiano*: 393–416.

Von Mayr, G. 1917 *Statistik und Gesellschaftslehre*, Tübingen, vol. 3.

Voracek, M. and Loibl, L. M. 2007 Genetics of suicide: A systematic review of twin studies, *Wiener klinische Wochenschrift*: 463.

Waardt, H. de 1996 Feud and atonement in Holland and Zeeland. From private vengeance to reconciliation under state supervision, in A. Schuurman and P. Spierenburg (eds.), *Private Domain, Public Inquiry: Families and Life-styles in the Netherlands and Europe, 1550 to the Present*, Hilversum, Verloren, pp. 15–38.

Wacke, A. 1980 Der Selbstmord im römischen Recht und in der Rechtsentwicklung, *Zeitschrift der Savigny Stiftung für Rechtsgeschichte Abteilung*: 26–72.

Wade, I. O. 1931 Destouches in England, *Modern Philology*: 27–47.

Wadsworth, T. and Kubrin, C. E. 2007 Hispanic suicide in US metropolitan areas: Examining the effects of immigration, assimilation, affluence, and disadvantage, *American Journal of Sociology*: 1848–85.

Wagner, A. 1864 *Die Gesetzmässigkeit in den scheinbar willkührlichen menschlichen Handlungen vom Standpunkte der Statistik*, Hamburg, Boyes and Geisler.

Wahl, C. W. 1957 Suicide as a magical act, in F. S. Shneidman and N. L. Farberow (eds.), *Clues to Suicide*, New York, McGraw-Hill, pp. 22–30.

Wakeman, F. 1985 *The Great Enterprise. The Manchu Reconstruction of Imperial Order in Seventeenth-Century China*, Berkeley, University of California Press.

Walker, D. E. 2004 *No More, No More. Slavery and Cultural Resistance in Havana and New Orleans*, Minneapolis, University of Minnesota Press.

Wang et al. 2007 Use of mental health services for anxiety, mood, and substance disorders in 17 countries in the WHO world mental health surveys, *Lancet* no. 9590, 841–50.

Wardlow, H. 2006 *Wayward Women. Sexuality and Agency in a New Guinea Society*, Berkeley, University of California Press.

Watt, J. R. 2001 *Choosing Death. Suicide and Calvinism in Early Modern Geneva*, Kirksville, Mo., Truman State University Press.

Weimann, G. 2006 *Terror on the Internet: The New Arena, the New Challenges*, Washington, DC, United States Institute for Peace Press.

Weinberg, G. L. 1998 Unexplored questions about the German military during World War II, *Journal of Military History*: 371–80.

Weinberger-Thomas, C. 1996 *Cendres d'immortalité. La crémation des veuves en Inde*, Paris, Seuil; English trans. *Ashes of Immortality: Widow-Burning in India*, trans. Jeffrey Mehlman and David Gordon White, University of Chicago Press, 1999.

Wenzel, S. 1960 *The Sin of Sloth: Acedia*, Chapel Hill, University of North Carolina Press.

Westermarck, E. 1912 *The Origin and Development of the Moral Ideas*, London, Macmillan, 2 vols.

Whitehead, H. 1921 *The Village Gods of South India*, Kolkata, Oxford University Press.

WHO (World Health Organization) 1951 *Annual Epidemiological and Vital Statistics 1939–1946*, Genève, parte I.

— 1956 Mortality from suicide, *Epidemiological and Vital Statistics Report*: 9, 4, pp. 243–87.

Whitlock, F. A. 1971 Migration and suicide, *Medical Journal of Australia*: 840–8.

Whyte, M. K. 1988 Death in the People's Republic of China, in J. L. Watson and E. S. Rawski (eds.), *Death Ritual in Late Imperial and Modern China*, pp. 289–316.

— 2004 *Filial obligations in Chinese families: Paradoxes of modernization*, in Ikels (2004, pp. 106–27).

Winternitz, M. 1915 *Die Frau in den indischen Religionen*, Würzburg, Verlag von Curt Kabitzsch.

Wintrobe, R. 2006 *Rational Extremism. The Political Economy of Radicalism*, Cambridge, Cambridge University Press.

Wisse, J. 1933 *Selbstmord und Todesfurcht bei den Naturvölkern*, Zutphen, W. J. Thieme.

Witke, R. 1967 Mao Tse-tung, women and suicide in the May Fourth era, *China Quarterly*: 128–47.

Wittkower, R. and Wittkower, M. 1963 *Born under Saturn*, London, Weidenfeld and Nicolson; Italian trans., *Nati sotto Saturno*, Turin, Einaudi, 1968.

Wolf, A. P. and Huang, C. 1980 *Marriage and Adoption in China, 1845–1945*, Stanford, CA, Stanford University Press.

Wolf, K. B. 1988 *Christian Martyrs in Muslim Spain*, Cambridge, Cambridge University Press.

Wolf, M. 1975 Women and suicide in China, in M. Wolf and R. Witke (eds.), *Women in Chinese Society*, Stanford, CA, Stanford University Press, pp. 111–141.

Woolf, B. K. 1987 *Christian Martyrs in Muslim Spain*, Cambridge, Cambridge University Press.

Woolf, L. 1988 *Mein Leben mit Virginia*, Frankfurt a. M., Fischer; Italian trans., *La mia vita con Virginia*, Milan, Serra e Riva Editori, 1989.

Woolf, V. 1976–84 *The Diary of Virginia Woolf*, Anne Olivier Bell and Andrew McNeillie (eds.), 5 vols. New York: Harcourt.

— 1998 *Romanzi*, Milan, Mondadori.

Wymer, R. 1982 *Suicide and Despair in the Jacobean Drama*, Essex, The Harvester Press.

Xiaojing, L. 2001 L'art de desserrer les noeuds, in I. Thireau and W. Hansheng (eds.), *Disputes au village chinois*, Paris, Editions de la Maison des sciences de l'homme, pp. 125–66.

Yadlin, R. 2006 Female martyrdom: The ultimate embodiment of Islamic existence?, in Schweitzer (2006).

Yan, Y. 2003 *Private Life under Socialism*, Stanford, CA, Stanford University Press.

Yang, A. A. 1989 Whose Sati? Widow burning in early 19th-century India, *Journal of Women's History*: 8–33.

Yang, C. K. 1959 *Chinese Communist Society: The Family and the Village*, Cambridge, MA, MIT Press.

Yeh, J.-Y. et al. 2008 Does marital status predict the odds of suicidal death in Taiwan? A seven-year population based study, *Suicide and Life-Threatening Behavior*: 302–12.

Yerevanian, B. I. et al. 2007 Bipolar pharmacotherapy and suicide behavior, *Journal of Affective Disorders*: 5–11.

Yu, A. C. 1987 'Rest, rest, perturbed spirit!' Ghosts in traditional Chinese prose fiction, *Harvard Journal of Asiatic Studies*: 397–434.

Zachariae, T. 1904 Zur indischen Witwenverbrennung, *Zeitschrift des Vereins für Volkskunde*: 198–211, 302–13 and 395–407.

— 1905 Zur indischen Witwenverbrennung, *Zeitschrift des Vereins für Volkskunde*: 74–90.

Zamperini, P. 2001 *Untamed hearth: Eros and suicide in late imperial Chinese fiction*, in Ropp et al. (2001, pp. 77–104).

Zanini, M. and Edwards, S. J. A. 2002 The networking of terror in the information age, in J. Arquilla (ed.), *Network and Netwars*, Santa Monica, CA, Rand Corporation, pp. 29–60.

Zhang, H. 2004 'Living alone' and the rural elderly: Strategy and agency in post-Mao rural China, in Ikels (2004, pp. 63–87).

Zhang, J. et al. 2009 Economic growth and suicide rate changes: A case in China from 1982 to 2005, *European Psychiatry*: 159–63.

— 2014 The change in suicide rates between 2002 and 2011 in China, *Suicide and Life-Threatening Behavior*: 1–9.

Zhao, H. L. et al. 2006 The short-lived Chinese emperors, *Journal of American Geriatric Society*: 1295.

Zilboorg, G. 1936 Differential diagnostic types of suicide, *Archives of General Psychiatry*: 270–91.

Zouk, H. et al. 2006 Characterization of impulsivity in suicide completers: Clinical, behavioral and psychosocial dimensions, *Journal of Affective Disorders*: 195–204.

Zorzi, A. 2002 La cultura della vendetta nel conflitto politico in età comunale, in *Le storie e la memoria*, R. Delle Donne and A. Zorzi (eds.), Florence, Florence University Press, pp. 135–70.

— 2007 *La legittimazione delle pratiche della vendetta nell'Italia comunale*, e-Spania, available online at http://e-spania.revues.org/document2043.html.

Zucchelli da Gradisca, A. 1712 *Relazioni del viaggio e missione di Congo nell'Etiopia inferior occidentale*, Venice, per Bartolomeo Giavarina, al ponte del Lovo, all'insegna della Speranza.

Index